WONDER WOMAN
STEVE TREVOR

**WONDER WOMAN created by
WILLIAM MOULTON MARSTON**

Collection cover art by Paul Renaud

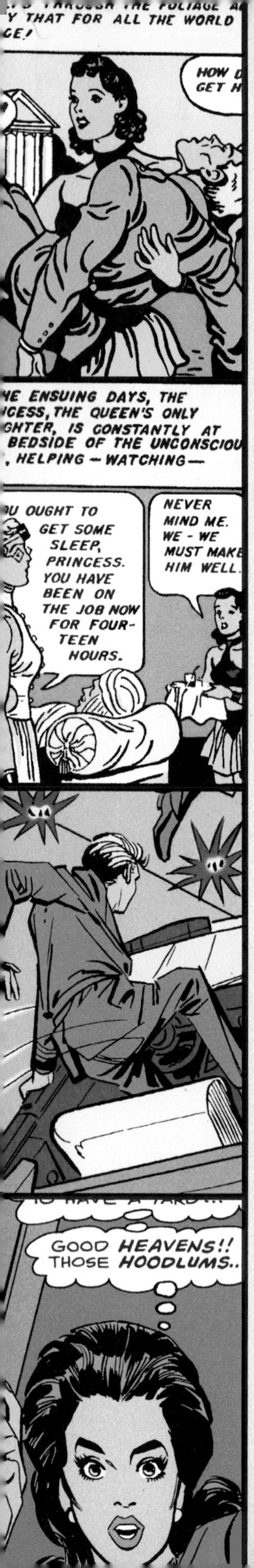
Y THAT FOR ALL THE WORLD
HE ENSUING DAYS, THE ICESS, THE QUEEN'S ONLY GHTER, IS CONSTANTLY AT BEDSIDE OF THE UNCONSCIOU , HELPING — WATCHING—
GET SOME SLEEP, PRINCESS. YOU HAVE BEEN ON THE JOB NOW FOR FOUR-TEEN HOURS.
NEVER MIND ME. WE - WE MUST MAKE HIM WELL.
GOOD HEAVENS!! THOSE HOODLUMS..

TABLE OF CONTENTS

DC strives to be as thorough as possible in its efforts to determine creators' identities from all available sources. This process is not perfect, and as a result, some attributions may be incomplete or wrongly assigned.

The comics reprinted in this volume were produced in a time when racism played a larger role in society and popular culture both consciously and unconsciously. They are presented here without alteration for historical reference.

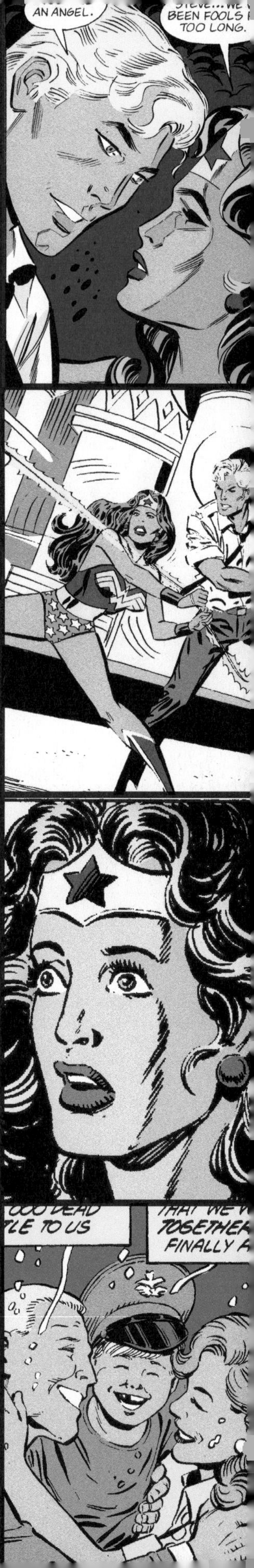

AN ANGEL.
BEEN FOOLS
TOO LONG.

MAXWELL CHARLES GAINES
ROBERT KANIGHER
JACK MILLER
LEN WEIN
ALAN GOLD
KAREN BERGER
CHRIS CONROY
MARK DOYLE
Editors - Original Series

REBECCA TAYLOR
Associate Editor - Original Series

DAVE WIELGOSZ
Assistant Editor - Original Series

JEB WOODARD
Group Editor - Collected Editions

REZA LOKMAN
Editor - Collected Edition

STEVE COOK
Design Director - Books

GABRIEL MALDONADO
Publication Design

SUZANNAH ROWNTREE
Publication Production

BOB HARRAS
Senior VP - Editor-in-Chief, DC Comics

DAN DiDIO
Publisher

JIM LEE
Publisher & Chief Creative Officer

BOBBIE CHASE
VP - New Publishing Initiatives

DON FALLETTI
VP - Manufacturing Operations & Workflow Management

LAWRENCE GANEM
VP - Talent Services

ALISON GILL
Senior VP - Manufacturing & Operations

HANK KANALZ
Senior VP - Publishing Strategy & Support Services

DAN MIRON
VP - Publishing Operations

NICK J. NAPOLITANO
VP - Manufacturing Administration & Design

NANCY SPEARS
VP - Sales

JONAH WEILAND
VP - Marketing & Creative Services

MICHELE R. WELLS
VP & Executive Editor, Young Reader

WONDER WOMAN: STEVE TREVOR

DC Comics, 2900 West Alameda Ave., Burbank, CA 91505
Printed by LSC Communications, Owensville, MO, USA. 4/17/20. First Printing.
ISBN: 978-1-77950-198-1

Library of Congress Cataloging-in-Publication Data is available.

PEFC Certified

This product is from sustainably managed forests and controlled sources

PEFC/29-31-337   www.pefc.org

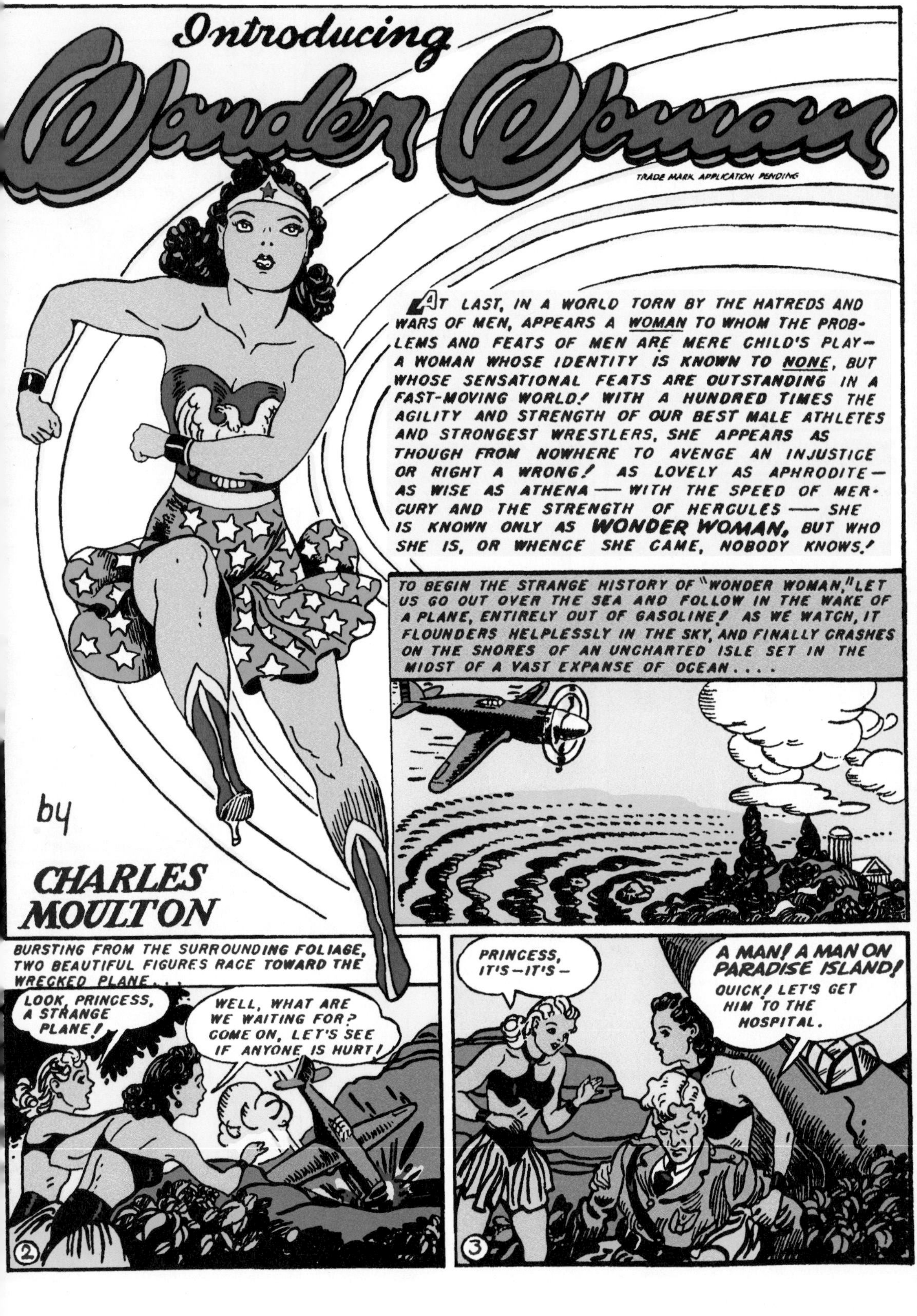

Introducing
Wonder Woman
TRADE MARK APPLICATION PENDING
AT LAST, IN A WORLD TORN BY THE HATREDS AND WARS OF MEN, APPEARS A WOMAN TO WHOM THE PROBLEMS AND FEATS OF MEN ARE MERE CHILD'S PLAY— A WOMAN WHOSE IDENTITY IS KNOWN TO NONE, BUT WHOSE SENSATIONAL FEATS ARE OUTSTANDING IN A FAST-MOVING WORLD! WITH A HUNDRED TIMES THE AGILITY AND STRENGTH OF OUR BEST MALE ATHLETES AND STRONGEST WRESTLERS, SHE APPEARS AS THOUGH FROM NOWHERE TO AVENGE AN INJUSTICE OR RIGHT A WRONG! AS LOVELY AS APHRODITE— AS WISE AS ATHENA — WITH THE SPEED OF MERCURY AND THE STRENGTH OF HERCULES — SHE IS KNOWN ONLY AS WONDER WOMAN, BUT WHO SHE IS, OR WHENCE SHE CAME, NOBODY KNOWS!
TO BEGIN THE STRANGE HISTORY OF "WONDER WOMAN," LET US GO OUT OVER THE SEA AND FOLLOW IN THE WAKE OF A PLANE, ENTIRELY OUT OF GASOLINE! AS WE WATCH, IT FLOUNDERS HELPLESSLY IN THE SKY, AND FINALLY CRASHES ON THE SHORES OF AN UNCHARTED ISLE SET IN THE MIDST OF A VAST EXPANSE OF OCEAN....
by
CHARLES MOULTON
BURSTING FROM THE SURROUNDING FOLIAGE, TWO BEAUTIFUL FIGURES RACE TOWARD THE WRECKED PLANE...
LOOK, PRINCESS, A STRANGE PLANE!
WELL, WHAT ARE WE WAITING FOR? COME ON, LET'S SEE IF ANYONE IS HURT!
2
PRINCESS, IT'S—IT'S—
A MAN! A MAN ON PARADISE ISLAND!
QUICK! LET'S GET HIM TO THE HOSPITAL.
3

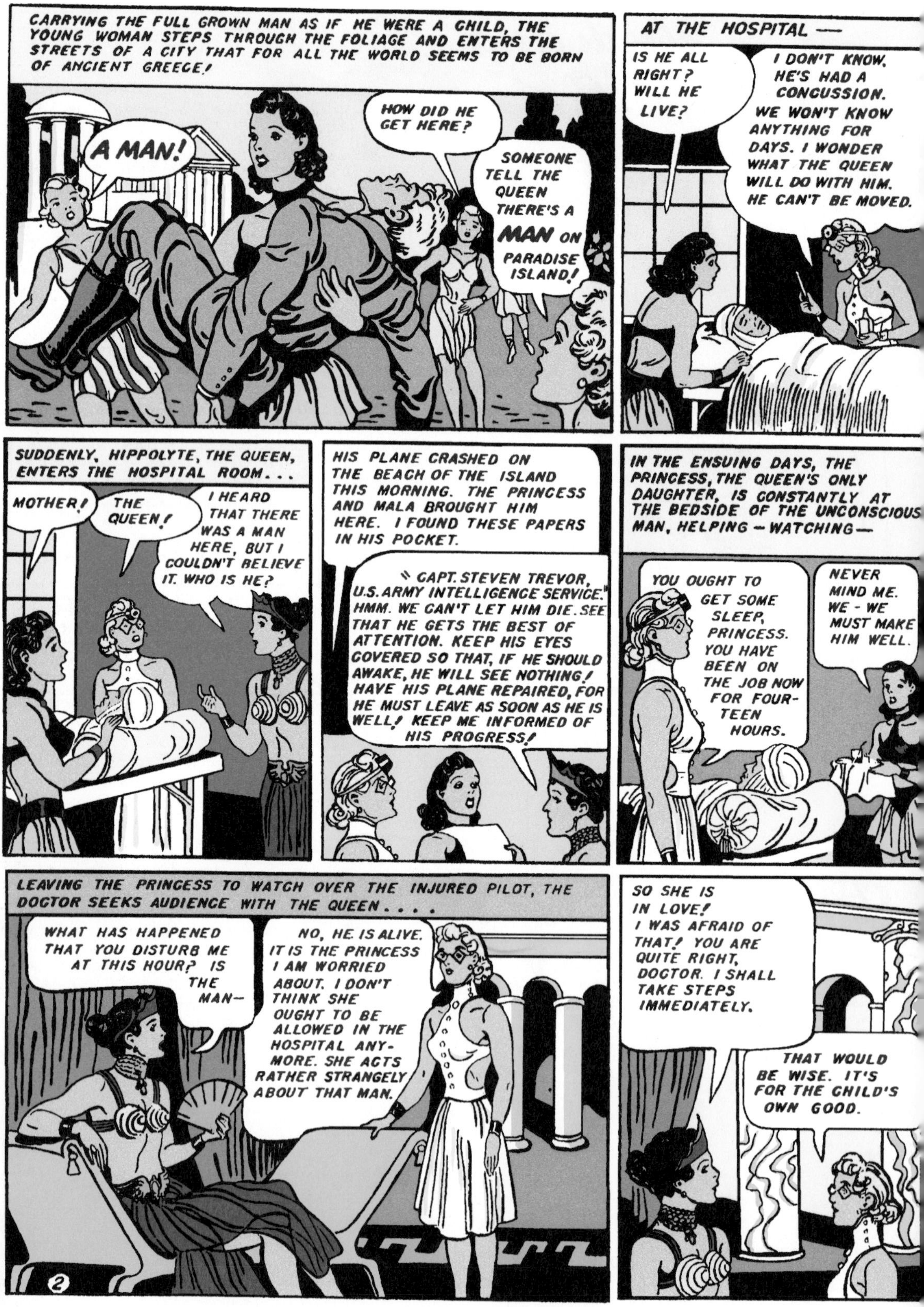
CARRYING THE FULL GROWN MAN AS IF HE WERE A CHILD, THE YOUNG WOMAN STEPS THROUGH THE FOLIAGE AND ENTERS THE STREETS OF A CITY THAT FOR ALL THE WORLD SEEMS TO BE BORN OF ANCIENT GREECE!
A MAN!
HOW DID HE GET HERE?
SOMEONE TELL THE QUEEN THERE'S A MAN ON PARADISE ISLAND!
AT THE HOSPITAL —
IS HE ALL RIGHT? WILL HE LIVE?
I DON'T KNOW. HE'S HAD A CONCUSSION. WE WON'T KNOW ANYTHING FOR DAYS. I WONDER WHAT THE QUEEN WILL DO WITH HIM. HE CAN'T BE MOVED.
SUDDENLY, HIPPOLYTE, THE QUEEN, ENTERS THE HOSPITAL ROOM...
MOTHER!
THE QUEEN!
I HEARD THAT THERE WAS A MAN HERE, BUT I COULDN'T BELIEVE IT. WHO IS HE?
HIS PLANE CRASHED ON THE BEACH OF THE ISLAND THIS MORNING. THE PRINCESS AND MALA BROUGHT HIM HERE. I FOUND THESE PAPERS IN HIS POCKET.
"CAPT. STEVEN TREVOR, U.S. ARMY INTELLIGENCE SERVICE." HMM. WE CAN'T LET HIM DIE. SEE THAT HE GETS THE BEST OF ATTENTION. KEEP HIS EYES COVERED SO THAT, IF HE SHOULD AWAKE, HE WILL SEE NOTHING! HAVE HIS PLANE REPAIRED, FOR HE MUST LEAVE AS SOON AS HE IS WELL! KEEP ME INFORMED OF HIS PROGRESS!
IN THE ENSUING DAYS, THE PRINCESS, THE QUEEN'S ONLY DAUGHTER, IS CONSTANTLY AT THE BEDSIDE OF THE UNCONSCIOUS MAN, HELPING — WATCHING —
YOU OUGHT TO GET SOME SLEEP, PRINCESS. YOU HAVE BEEN ON THE JOB NOW FOR FOURTEEN HOURS.
NEVER MIND ME. WE - WE MUST MAKE HIM WELL.
LEAVING THE PRINCESS TO WATCH OVER THE INJURED PILOT, THE DOCTOR SEEKS AUDIENCE WITH THE QUEEN....
WHAT HAS HAPPENED THAT YOU DISTURB ME AT THIS HOUR? IS THE MAN—
NO, HE IS ALIVE. IT IS THE PRINCESS I AM WORRIED ABOUT. I DON'T THINK SHE OUGHT TO BE ALLOWED IN THE HOSPITAL ANYMORE. SHE ACTS RATHER STRANGELY ABOUT THAT MAN.
2
SO SHE IS IN LOVE! I WAS AFRAID OF THAT! YOU ARE QUITE RIGHT, DOCTOR. I SHALL TAKE STEPS IMMEDIATELY.
THAT WOULD BE WISE. IT'S FOR THE CHILD'S OWN GOOD.

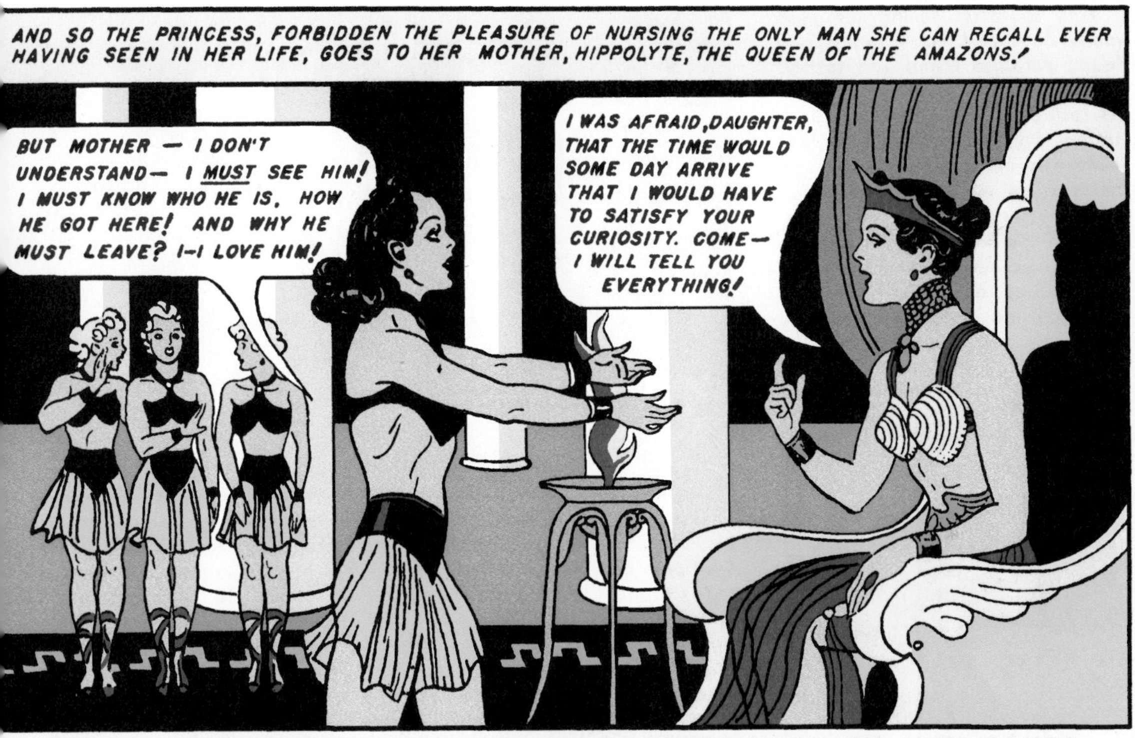
AND SO THE PRINCESS, FORBIDDEN THE PLEASURE OF NURSING THE ONLY MAN SHE CAN RECALL EVER HAVING SEEN IN HER LIFE, GOES TO HER MOTHER, HIPPOLYTE, THE QUEEN OF THE AMAZONS!
BUT MOTHER — I DON'T UNDERSTAND— I MUST SEE HIM! I MUST KNOW WHO HE IS, HOW HE GOT HERE! AND WHY HE MUST LEAVE? I-I LOVE HIM!
I WAS AFRAID, DAUGHTER, THAT THE TIME WOULD SOME DAY ARRIVE THAT I WOULD HAVE TO SATISFY YOUR CURIOSITY. COME— I WILL TELL YOU EVERYTHING!

AND THIS IS THE STARTLING STORY UNFOLDED BY HIPPOLYTE, QUEEN OF THE AMAZONS, TO THE PRINCESS, HER DAUGHTER !

In the days of Ancient Greece, many centuries ago, we Amazons were the foremost nation in the world. In Amazonia, women ruled and all was well. Then one day, Hercules, the strongest man in the world, stung by taunts that he couldn't conquer the Amazon women, selected his strongest and fiercest warriors and landed on our shores. I challenged him to personal combat—because I knew that with my MAGIC GIRDLE, given me by Aphrodite, Goddess of Love, I could not lose.

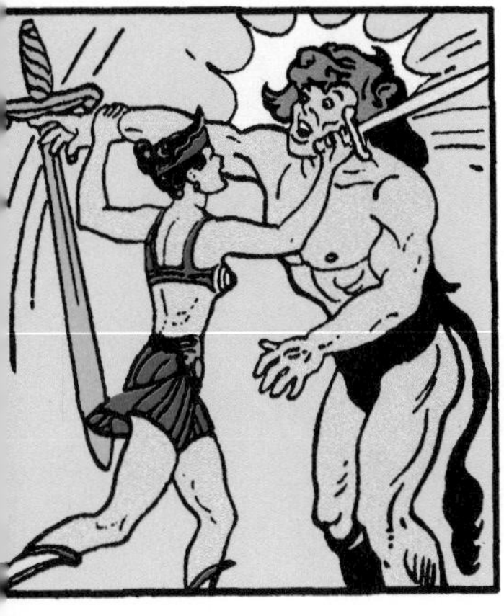

And win I did! But Hercules, by deceit and trickery, managed to secure my MAGIC GIRDLE—and soon we Amazons were taken into slavery. And Aphrodite, angry at me for having succumbed to the wiles of men, would do naught to help us!

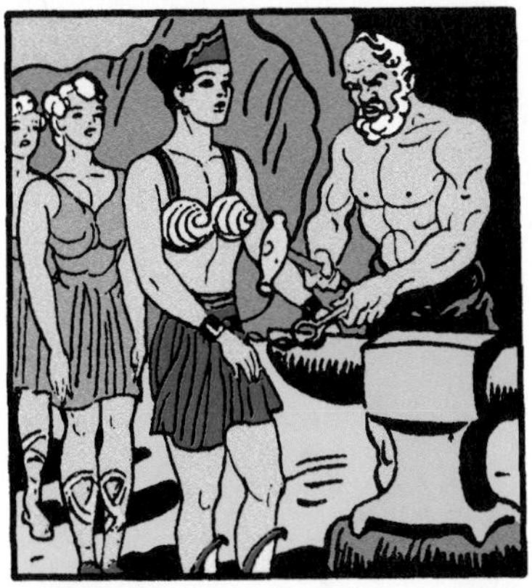

Finally our submission to men became unbearable—we could stand it no longer—and I appealed to the Goddess Aphrodite again. This time not in vain, for she relented and with her help, I secured the MAGIC GIRDLE from Hercules.

With the MAGIC GIRDLE in my possession, it didn't take us long to overcome our masters, the MEN—and taking from them their entire fleet, we set sail for another shore, for it was Aphrodite's condition that we leave the man-made world and establish a new world of our own! Aphrodite also decreed that we must always wear these bracelets fashioned by our captors, as a reminder that we must always keep aloof from men.

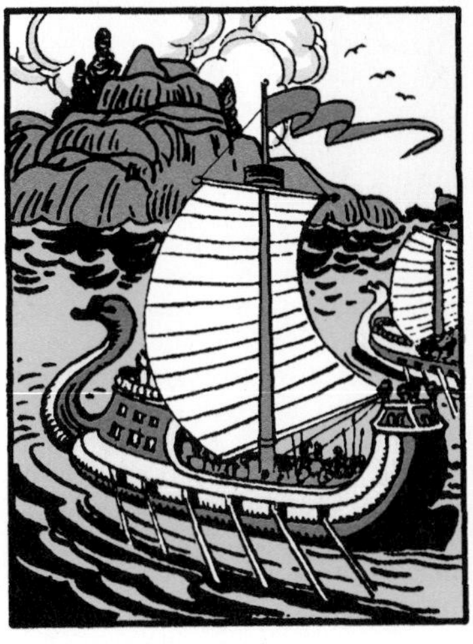

And so, after sailing the seas many days and many nights, we found Paradise Island and settled here to build a new World! With its fertile soil, its marvelous vegetation—its varied natural resources—here is no want, no illness, no hatreds, no wars, and as long as we remain on Paradise Island and I retain the MAGIC GIRDLE, we have the power of Eternal Life—so long as we do not permit ourselves to be again beguiled by men! We are indeed a race of Wonder Women!

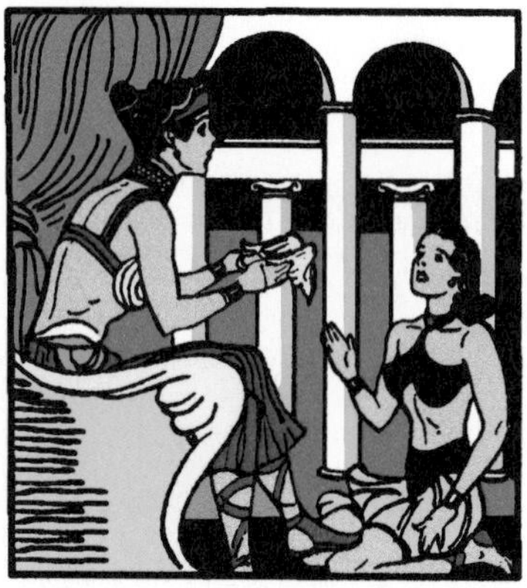

That was the promise of Aphrodite—and we must keep our promise to her if we are to remain here safe and in peace!

That is why this American must go and as soon as possible!

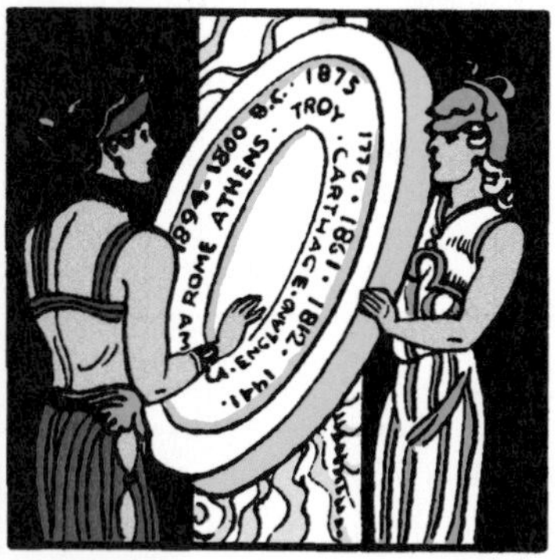
1875
1300 B.C.
TROY
1894
ATHENS
CARTHAGE
1861
1812
1941

Come, let me show you the Magic Sphere you've heard me talk about. It was given to me by Athena, the Goddess of Wisdom, just after we conquered the Herculeans and set sail for Paradise Island! It is through this Magic Sphere that I have been able to know what has gone on and is going on in the other world, and even, at times, forecast the future!

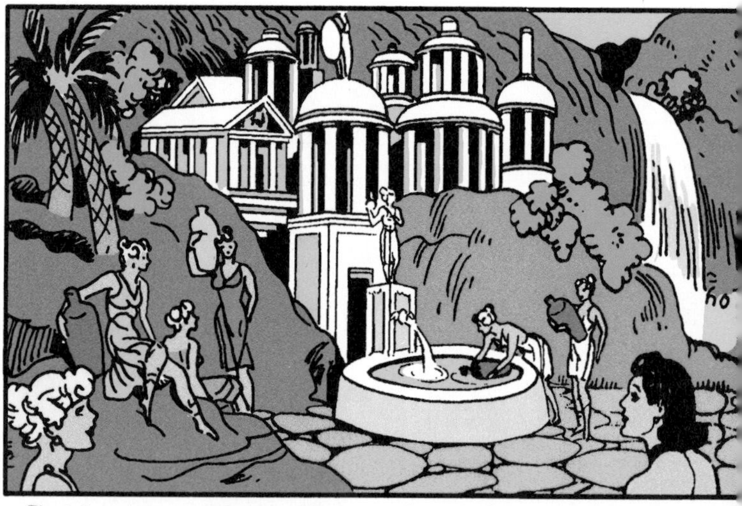

That is why we Amazons have been able to far surpass the inventions of the so-called man-made civilization! We are not only stronger and wiser than men—but our weapons are better—our flying machines are further advanced! And it is through the knowledge that I have gained from the Magic Sphere that I have taught you, my daughter, all the arts and sciences and languages of modern as well as ancient times!

But let us see where your American captain came from and how he got here. Watch closely—

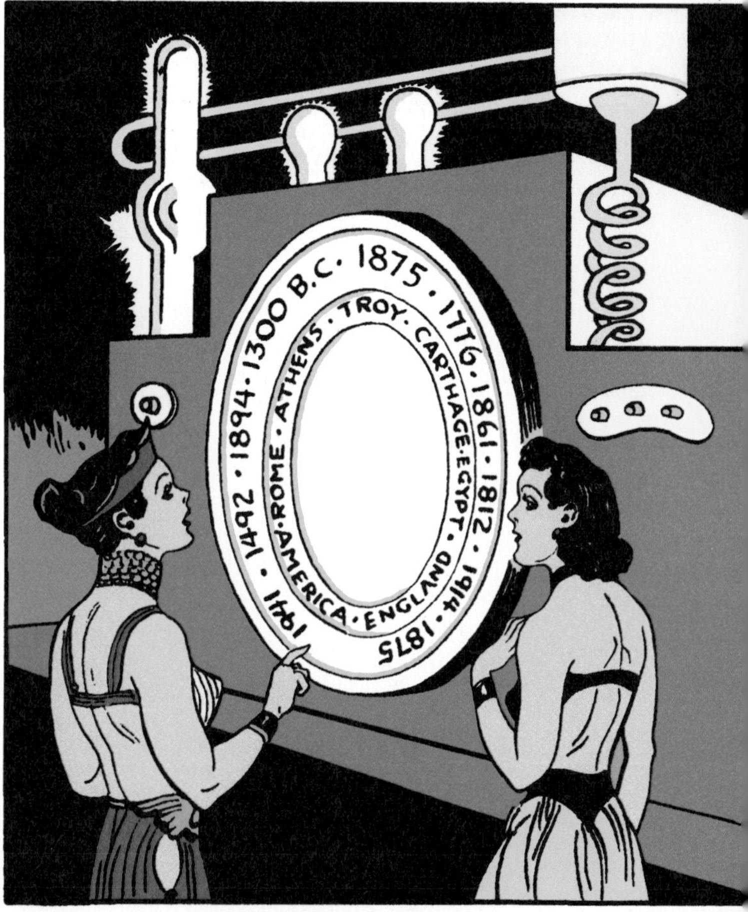
1300 B.C. · 1875 · 1776 · 1861 · 1812 · 1914 · 1875 · ENGLAND · AMERICA · 1941 · 1492 · 1894 · ROME · ATHENS · TROY · CARTHAGE · EGYPT

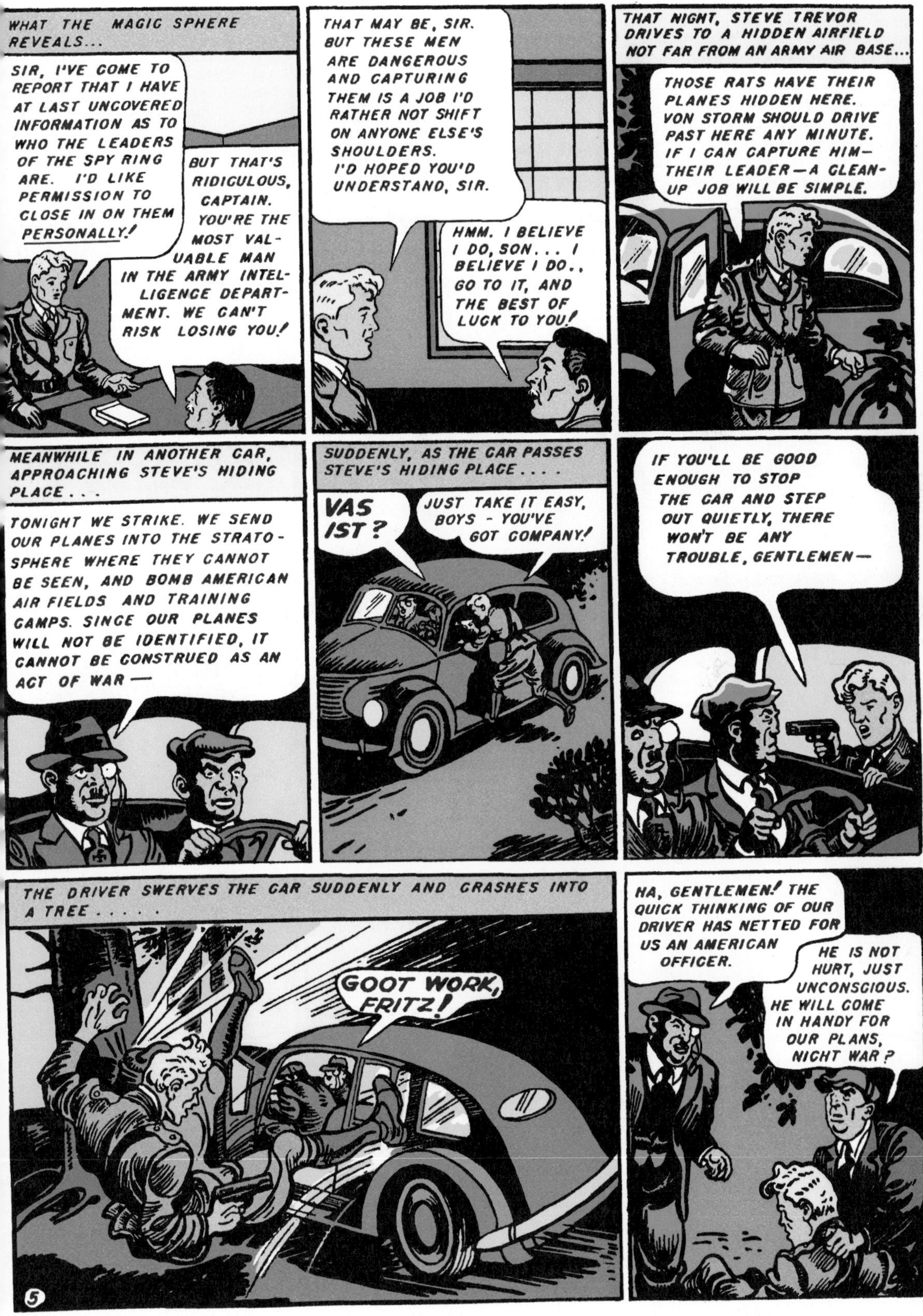

WHAT THE MAGIC SPHERE REVEALS...
SIR, I'VE COME TO REPORT THAT I HAVE AT LAST UNCOVERED INFORMATION AS TO WHO THE LEADERS OF THE SPY RING ARE. I'D LIKE PERMISSION TO CLOSE IN ON THEM PERSONALLY!
BUT THAT'S RIDICULOUS, CAPTAIN. YOU'RE THE MOST VALUABLE MAN IN THE ARMY INTELLIGENCE DEPARTMENT. WE CAN'T RISK LOSING YOU!
THAT MAY BE, SIR. BUT THESE MEN ARE DANGEROUS AND CAPTURING THEM IS A JOB I'D RATHER NOT SHIFT ON ANYONE ELSE'S SHOULDERS. I'D HOPED YOU'D UNDERSTAND, SIR.
HMM. I BELIEVE I DO, SON... I BELIEVE I DO.. GO TO IT, AND THE BEST OF LUCK TO YOU!
THAT NIGHT, STEVE TREVOR DRIVES TO A HIDDEN AIRFIELD NOT FAR FROM AN ARMY AIR BASE...
THOSE RATS HAVE THEIR PLANES HIDDEN HERE. VON STORM SHOULD DRIVE PAST HERE ANY MINUTE. IF I CAN CAPTURE HIM—THEIR LEADER—A CLEAN-UP JOB WILL BE SIMPLE.
MEANWHILE IN ANOTHER CAR, APPROACHING STEVE'S HIDING PLACE...
TONIGHT WE STRIKE. WE SEND OUR PLANES INTO THE STRATOSPHERE WHERE THEY CANNOT BE SEEN, AND BOMB AMERICAN AIR FIELDS AND TRAINING CAMPS. SINCE OUR PLANES WILL NOT BE IDENTIFIED, IT CANNOT BE CONSTRUED AS AN ACT OF WAR —
SUDDENLY, AS THE CAR PASSES STEVE'S HIDING PLACE....
VAS IST?
JUST TAKE IT EASY, BOYS - YOU'VE GOT COMPANY!
IF YOU'LL BE GOOD ENOUGH TO STOP THE CAR AND STEP OUT QUIETLY, THERE WON'T BE ANY TROUBLE, GENTLEMEN—
THE DRIVER SWERVES THE CAR SUDDENLY AND CRASHES INTO A TREE.....
GOOT WORK, FRITZ!
HA, GENTLEMEN! THE QUICK THINKING OF OUR DRIVER HAS NETTED FOR US AN AMERICAN OFFICER.
HE IS NOT HURT, JUST UNCONSCIOUS. HE WILL COME IN HANDY FOR OUR PLANS, NICHT WAR?
5

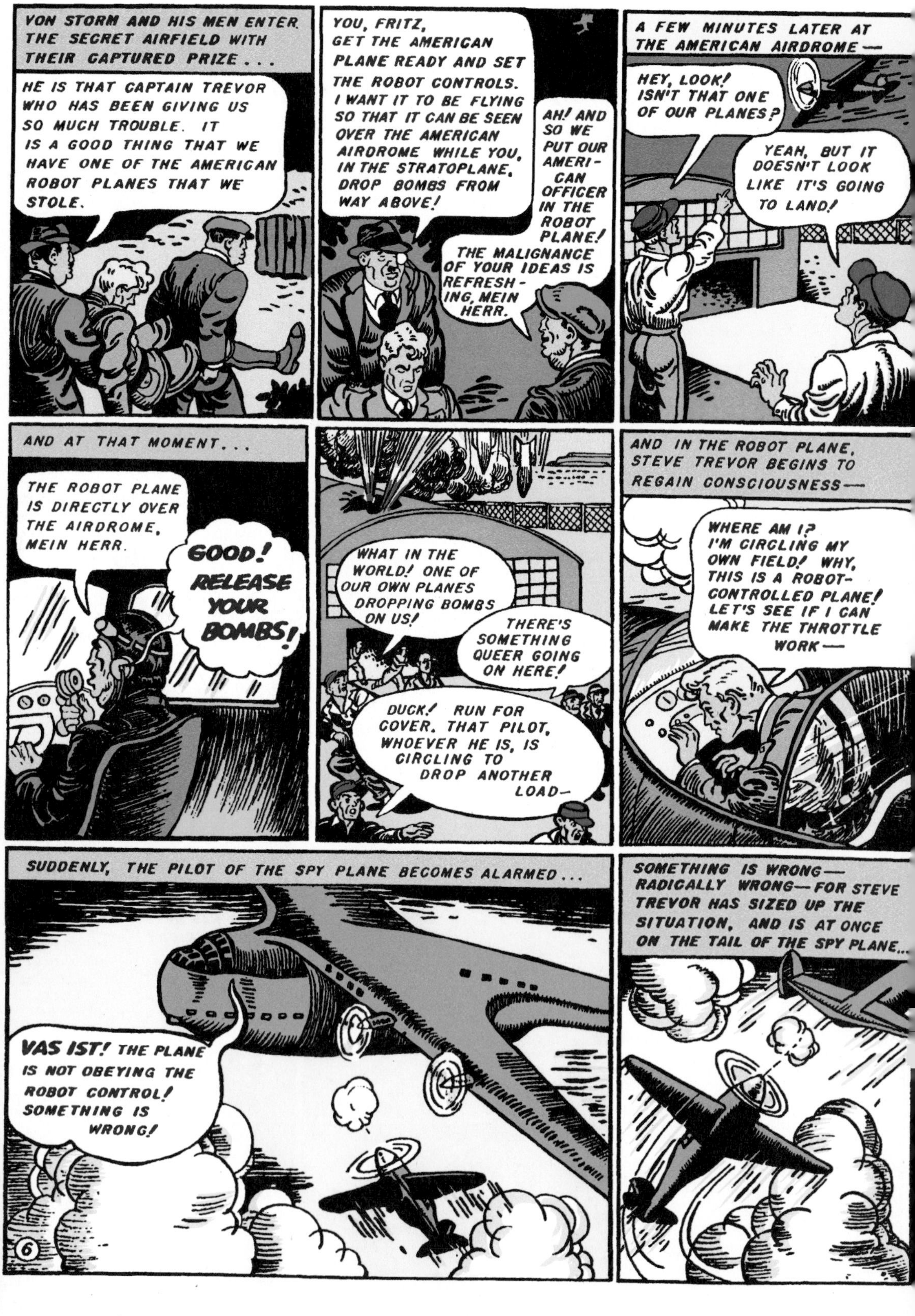
VON STORM AND HIS MEN ENTER THE SECRET AIRFIELD WITH THEIR CAPTURED PRIZE . . .
HE IS THAT CAPTAIN TREVOR WHO HAS BEEN GIVING US SO MUCH TROUBLE. IT IS A GOOD THING THAT WE HAVE ONE OF THE AMERICAN ROBOT PLANES THAT WE STOLE.
YOU, FRITZ, GET THE AMERICAN PLANE READY AND SET THE ROBOT CONTROLS. I WANT IT TO BE FLYING SO THAT IT CAN BE SEEN OVER THE AMERICAN AIRDROME WHILE YOU, IN THE STRATOPLANE, DROP BOMBS FROM WAY ABOVE!
AH! AND SO WE PUT OUR AMERI-CAN OFFICER IN THE ROBOT PLANE!
THE MALIGNANCE OF YOUR IDEAS IS REFRESH-ING, MEIN HERR.
A FEW MINUTES LATER AT THE AMERICAN AIRDROME—
HEY, LOOK! ISN'T THAT ONE OF OUR PLANES?
YEAH, BUT IT DOESN'T LOOK LIKE IT'S GOING TO LAND!
AND AT THAT MOMENT . . .
THE ROBOT PLANE IS DIRECTLY OVER THE AIRDROME, MEIN HERR.
GOOD! RELEASE YOUR BOMBS!
WHAT IN THE WORLD! ONE OF OUR OWN PLANES DROPPING BOMBS ON US!
THERE'S SOMETHING QUEER GOING ON HERE!
DUCK! RUN FOR COVER. THAT PILOT, WHOEVER HE IS, IS CIRCLING TO DROP ANOTHER LOAD—
AND IN THE ROBOT PLANE, STEVE TREVOR BEGINS TO REGAIN CONSCIOUSNESS—
WHERE AM I? I'M CIRCLING MY OWN FIELD! WHY, THIS IS A ROBOT-CONTROLLED PLANE! LET'S SEE IF I CAN MAKE THE THROTTLE WORK—
SUDDENLY, THE PILOT OF THE SPY PLANE BECOMES ALARMED . . .
VAS IST! THE PLANE IS NOT OBEYING THE ROBOT CONTROL! SOMETHING IS WRONG!
6
SOMETHING IS WRONG— RADICALLY WRONG— FOR STEVE TREVOR HAS SIZED UP THE SITUATION, AND IS AT ONCE ON THE TAIL OF THE SPY PLANE . . .

FRITZ, THE PILOT OF THE SPY PLANE, IS PANIC-STRICKEN AS HE REALIZES THAT HE HAS A SKILLED OPPONENT ON HIS TAIL... HE RADIOS FOR INSTRUCTIONS...

VON STORM! THE AMERICAN HAS RECOVERED CONSCIOUSNESS. HE IS TURNING THE ROBOT PLANE AGAINST ME. I CAN'T SHOOT HIM DOWN! WHAT SHALL I DO? HELLO VON STORM, DO YOU HEAR ME?

VON STORM IS FURIOUS AT THE WAY HIS PLANS ARE GOING —

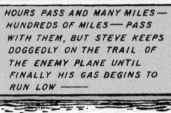

YOU FOOL! DON'T LET HIM SHOOT YOU DOWN! THEY MUST NOT FIND OUT THIS PLAN! THEY MUST NOT KNOW YOU DROPPED THOSE BOMBS! GET HIM AWAY FROM HIS FIELD—

THE STRATOPLANE TURNS TAIL AND RUNS — STEVE FOLLOWS...

HE'S TURNED TAIL, THE SKUNK! I'VE GOT TO SHOOT HIM DOWN, BUT HE KEEPS MOVING TOO HIGH FOR ME. I'LL CATCH HIM IF IT'S THE LAST THING I DO!

ALWAYS OUT OF SHOOTING RANGE, THE BLACK PLANE KEEPS STEVE FOLLOWING UNTIL THEY ARE FAR OUT AT SEA

I WONDER HOW LONG HE'S GOING TO KEEP THIS UP! WELL, AS LONG AS THERE IS GAS LEFT IN THIS CRATE, I'M GOING TO STAY WITH HIM—

HOURS PASS AND MANY MILES— HUNDREDS OF MILES— PASS WITH THEM, BUT STEVE KEEPS DOGGEDLY ON THE TRAIL OF THE ENEMY PLANE UNTIL FINALLY HIS GAS BEGINS TO RUN LOW —

RUNNING SHORT OF GAS! LOOKS LIKE HE HAS ME LICKED! WAIT! WHAT'S THAT BELOW? CAN IT BE AN ISLAND? IT SEEMS SURROUNDED BY CLOUD FORMATIONS!

WELL, DAUGHTER, THERE'S THE HISTORY OF YOUR CAPTAIN UP TO THE VERY MOMENT HIS PLANE CRASHED ON PARADISE ISLAND!

BUT MOTHER, HE MUST BE TAKEN BACK TO AMERICA TO FINISH THE JOB HE STARTED!

GETTING HIM BACK WOULD BE A PROBLEM. LEAVE ME ALONE, MY DAUGHTER. I MUST CONSULT WITH APHRODITE AND ATHENA, OUR GODDESSES. I MUST SEEK THEIR ADVICE!

YES, MOTHER.

IT WOULDN'T BE ANY TRICK AT ALL FOR ME TO FLY HIM BACK MYSELF, BUT MOTHER WOULD NEVER HEAR OF IT.

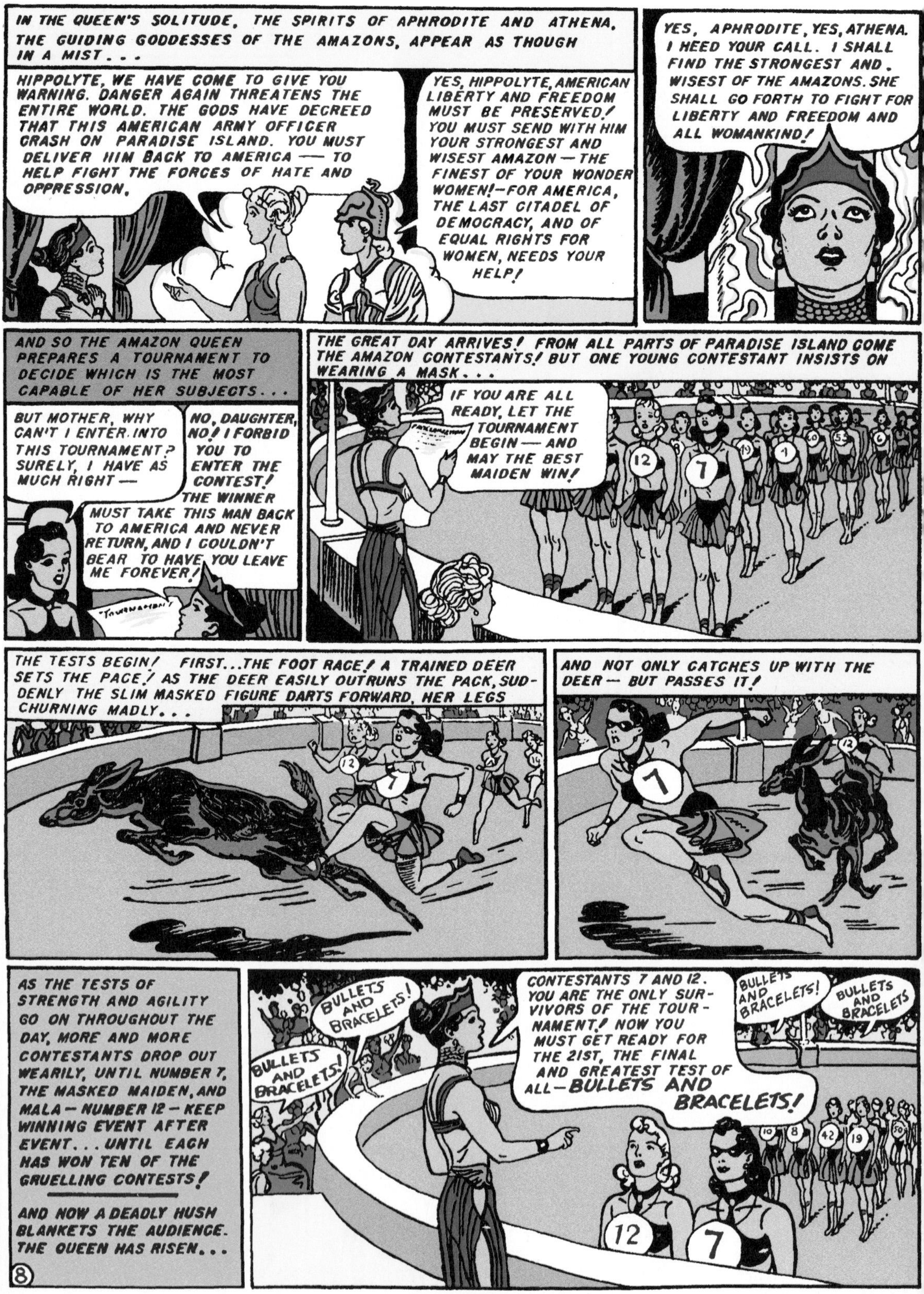

IN THE QUEEN'S SOLITUDE, THE SPIRITS OF APHRODITE AND ATHENA, THE GUIDING GODDESSES OF THE AMAZONS, APPEAR AS THOUGH IN A MIST . . .
HIPPOLYTE, WE HAVE COME TO GIVE YOU WARNING. DANGER AGAIN THREATENS THE ENTIRE WORLD. THE GODS HAVE DECREED THAT THIS AMERICAN ARMY OFFICER CRASH ON PARADISE ISLAND. YOU MUST DELIVER HIM BACK TO AMERICA — TO HELP FIGHT THE FORCES OF HATE AND OPPRESSION.
YES, HIPPOLYTE, AMERICAN LIBERTY AND FREEDOM MUST BE PRESERVED! YOU MUST SEND WITH HIM YOUR STRONGEST AND WISEST AMAZON — THE FINEST OF YOUR WONDER WOMEN! — FOR AMERICA, THE LAST CITADEL OF DEMOCRACY, AND OF EQUAL RIGHTS FOR WOMEN, NEEDS YOUR HELP!
YES, APHRODITE, YES, ATHENA. I HEED YOUR CALL. I SHALL FIND THE STRONGEST AND WISEST OF THE AMAZONS. SHE SHALL GO FORTH TO FIGHT FOR LIBERTY AND FREEDOM AND ALL WOMANKIND!
AND SO THE AMAZON QUEEN PREPARES A TOURNAMENT TO DECIDE WHICH IS THE MOST CAPABLE OF HER SUBJECTS . . .
BUT MOTHER, WHY CAN'T I ENTER INTO THIS TOURNAMENT? SURELY, I HAVE AS MUCH RIGHT —
NO, DAUGHTER, NO! I FORBID YOU TO ENTER THE CONTEST! THE WINNER MUST TAKE THIS MAN BACK TO AMERICA AND NEVER RETURN, AND I COULDN'T BEAR TO HAVE YOU LEAVE ME FOREVER!
"TOURNAMENT"
THE GREAT DAY ARRIVES! FROM ALL PARTS OF PARADISE ISLAND COME THE AMAZON CONTESTANTS! BUT ONE YOUNG CONTESTANT INSISTS ON WEARING A MASK . . .
IF YOU ARE ALL READY, LET THE TOURNAMENT BEGIN — AND MAY THE BEST MAIDEN WIN!
THE TESTS BEGIN! FIRST...THE FOOT RACE! A TRAINED DEER SETS THE PACE! AS THE DEER EASILY OUTRUNS THE PACK, SUDDENLY THE SLIM MASKED FIGURE DARTS FORWARD, HER LEGS CHURNING MADLY . . .
AND NOT ONLY CATCHES UP WITH THE DEER — BUT PASSES IT!
AS THE TESTS OF STRENGTH AND AGILITY GO ON THROUGHOUT THE DAY, MORE AND MORE CONTESTANTS DROP OUT WEARILY, UNTIL NUMBER 7, THE MASKED MAIDEN, AND MALA — NUMBER 12 — KEEP WINNING EVENT AFTER EVENT . . . UNTIL EACH HAS WON TEN OF THE GRUELLING CONTESTS!
AND NOW A DEADLY HUSH BLANKETS THE AUDIENCE. THE QUEEN HAS RISEN . . .
BULLETS AND BRACELETS!
BULLETS AND BRACELETS!
CONTESTANTS 7 AND 12. YOU ARE THE ONLY SURVIVORS OF THE TOURNAMENT! NOW YOU MUST GET READY FOR THE 21ST, THE FINAL AND GREATEST TEST OF ALL — BULLETS AND BRACELETS!
BULLETS AND BRACELETS!
BULLETS AND BRACELETS
8

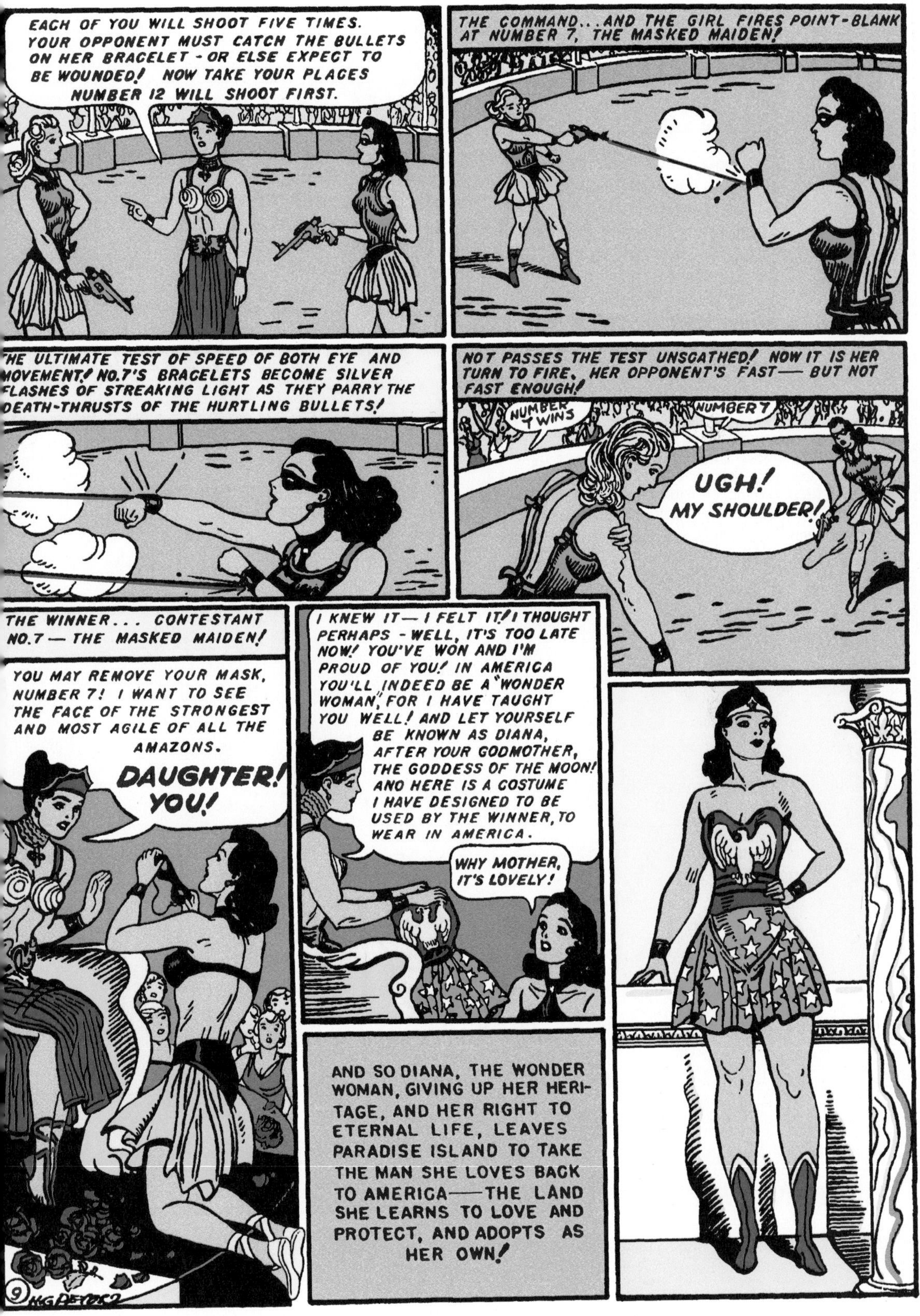

EACH OF YOU WILL SHOOT FIVE TIMES. YOUR OPPONENT MUST CATCH THE BULLETS ON HER BRACELET - OR ELSE EXPECT TO BE WOUNDED! NOW TAKE YOUR PLACES NUMBER 12 WILL SHOOT FIRST.
THE COMMAND... AND THE GIRL FIRES POINT-BLANK AT NUMBER 7, THE MASKED MAIDEN!
THE ULTIMATE TEST OF SPEED OF BOTH EYE AND MOVEMENT! NO.7'S BRACELETS BECOME SILVER FLASHES OF STREAKING LIGHT AS THEY PARRY THE DEATH-THRUSTS OF THE HURTLING BULLETS!
NOT PASSES THE TEST UNSCATHED! NOW IT IS HER TURN TO FIRE. HER OPPONENT'S FAST— BUT NOT FAST ENOUGH!
NUMBER TWINS
NUMBER 7
UGH! MY SHOULDER!
THE WINNER... CONTESTANT NO.7 — THE MASKED MAIDEN!
YOU MAY REMOVE YOUR MASK, NUMBER 7! I WANT TO SEE THE FACE OF THE STRONGEST AND MOST AGILE OF ALL THE AMAZONS.
DAUGHTER! YOU!
I KNEW IT— I FELT IT! I THOUGHT PERHAPS - WELL, IT'S TOO LATE NOW! YOU'VE WON AND I'M PROUD OF YOU! IN AMERICA YOU'LL INDEED BE A "WONDER WOMAN," FOR I HAVE TAUGHT YOU WELL! AND LET YOURSELF BE KNOWN AS DIANA, AFTER YOUR GODMOTHER, THE GODDESS OF THE MOON! AND HERE IS A COSTUME I HAVE DESIGNED TO BE USED BY THE WINNER, TO WEAR IN AMERICA.
WHY MOTHER, IT'S LOVELY!
AND SO DIANA, THE WONDER WOMAN, GIVING UP HER HERITAGE, AND HER RIGHT TO ETERNAL LIFE, LEAVES PARADISE ISLAND TO TAKE THE MAN SHE LOVES BACK TO AMERICA—THE LAND SHE LEARNS TO LOVE AND PROTECT, AND ADOPTS AS HER OWN!
9
H.G.PETER

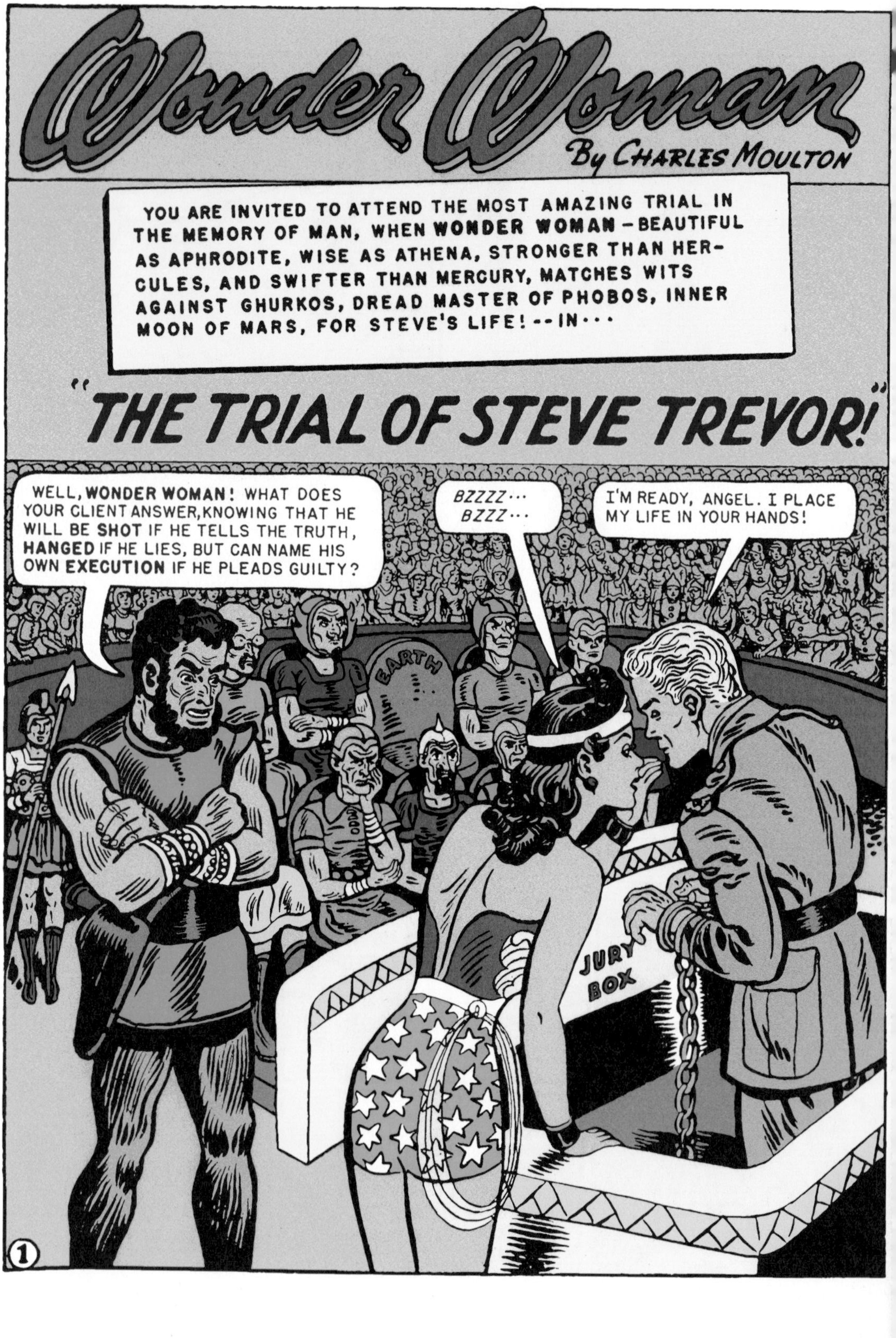
Wonder Woman
By Charles Moulton
YOU ARE INVITED TO ATTEND THE MOST AMAZING TRIAL IN THE MEMORY OF MAN, WHEN WONDER WOMAN – BEAUTIFUL AS APHRODITE, WISE AS ATHENA, STRONGER THAN HERCULES, AND SWIFTER THAN MERCURY, MATCHES WITS AGAINST GHURKOS, DREAD MASTER OF PHOBOS, INNER MOON OF MARS, FOR STEVE'S LIFE! --IN···
"THE TRIAL OF STEVE TREVOR!"
WELL, WONDER WOMAN! WHAT DOES YOUR CLIENT ANSWER, KNOWING THAT HE WILL BE SHOT IF HE TELLS THE TRUTH, HANGED IF HE LIES, BUT CAN NAME HIS OWN EXECUTION IF HE PLEADS GUILTY?
BZZZZ··· BZZZ···
I'M READY, ANGEL. I PLACE MY LIFE IN YOUR HANDS!
EARTH
JURY BOX
1

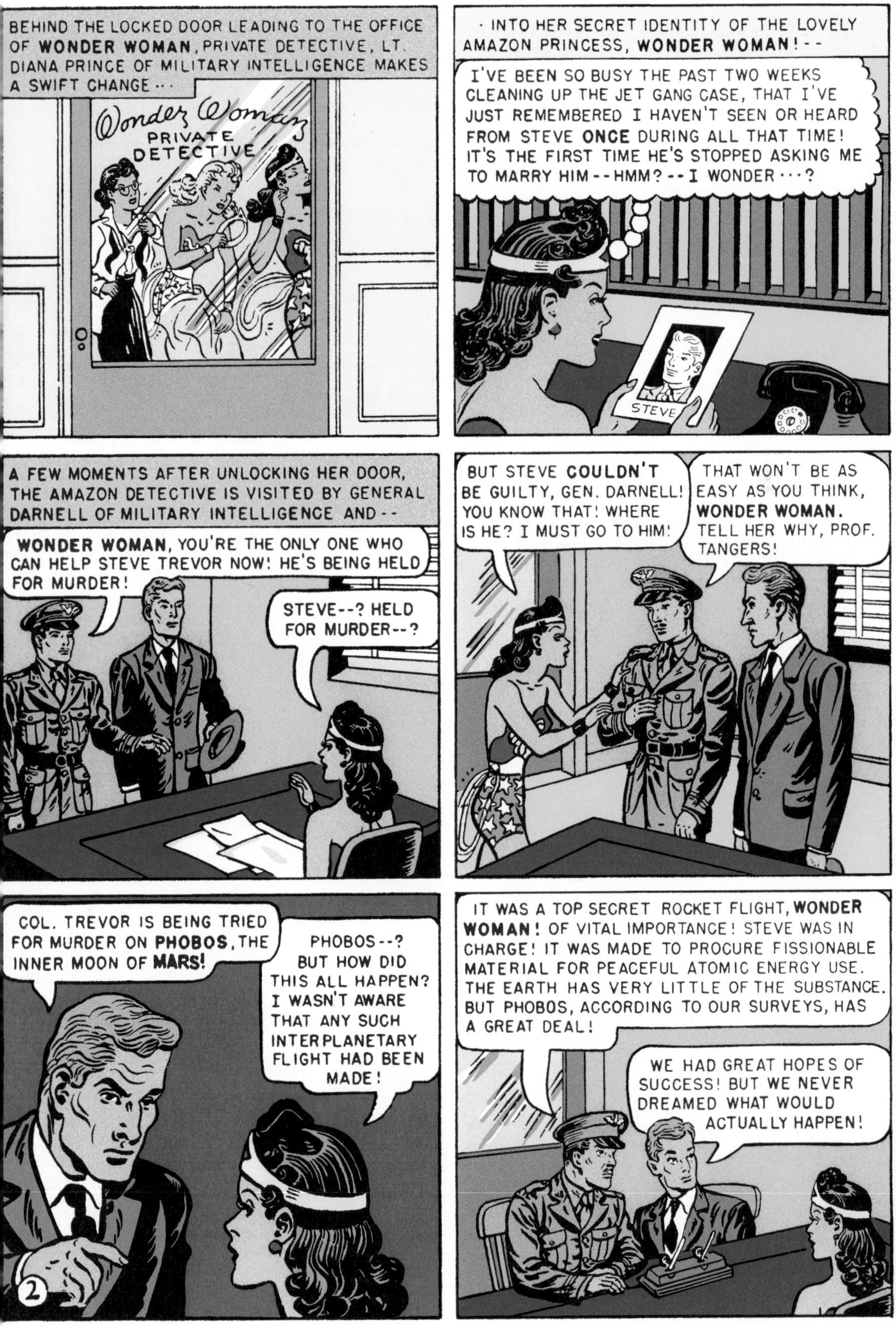
BEHIND THE LOCKED DOOR LEADING TO THE OFFICE OF WONDER WOMAN, PRIVATE DETECTIVE, LT. DIANA PRINCE OF MILITARY INTELLIGENCE MAKES A SWIFT CHANGE···
Wonder Woman PRIVATE DETECTIVE
· INTO HER SECRET IDENTITY OF THE LOVELY AMAZON PRINCESS, WONDER WOMAN!--
I'VE BEEN SO BUSY THE PAST TWO WEEKS CLEANING UP THE JET GANG CASE, THAT I'VE JUST REMEMBERED I HAVEN'T SEEN OR HEARD FROM STEVE ONCE DURING ALL THAT TIME! IT'S THE FIRST TIME HE'S STOPPED ASKING ME TO MARRY HIM--HMM?--I WONDER···?
STEVE
A FEW MOMENTS AFTER UNLOCKING HER DOOR, THE AMAZON DETECTIVE IS VISITED BY GENERAL DARNELL OF MILITARY INTELLIGENCE AND--
WONDER WOMAN, YOU'RE THE ONLY ONE WHO CAN HELP STEVE TREVOR NOW! HE'S BEING HELD FOR MURDER!
STEVE--? HELD FOR MURDER--?
BUT STEVE COULDN'T BE GUILTY, GEN. DARNELL! YOU KNOW THAT! WHERE IS HE? I MUST GO TO HIM!
THAT WON'T BE AS EASY AS YOU THINK, WONDER WOMAN. TELL HER WHY, PROF. TANGERS!
COL. TREVOR IS BEING TRIED FOR MURDER ON PHOBOS, THE INNER MOON OF MARS!
PHOBOS--? BUT HOW DID THIS ALL HAPPEN? I WASN'T AWARE THAT ANY SUCH INTERPLANETARY FLIGHT HAD BEEN MADE!
2
IT WAS A TOP SECRET ROCKET FLIGHT, WONDER WOMAN! OF VITAL IMPORTANCE! STEVE WAS IN CHARGE! IT WAS MADE TO PROCURE FISSIONABLE MATERIAL FOR PEACEFUL ATOMIC ENERGY USE. THE EARTH HAS VERY LITTLE OF THE SUBSTANCE. BUT PHOBOS, ACCORDING TO OUR SURVEYS, HAS A GREAT DEAL!
WE HAD GREAT HOPES OF SUCCESS! BUT WE NEVER DREAMED WHAT WOULD ACTUALLY HAPPEN!

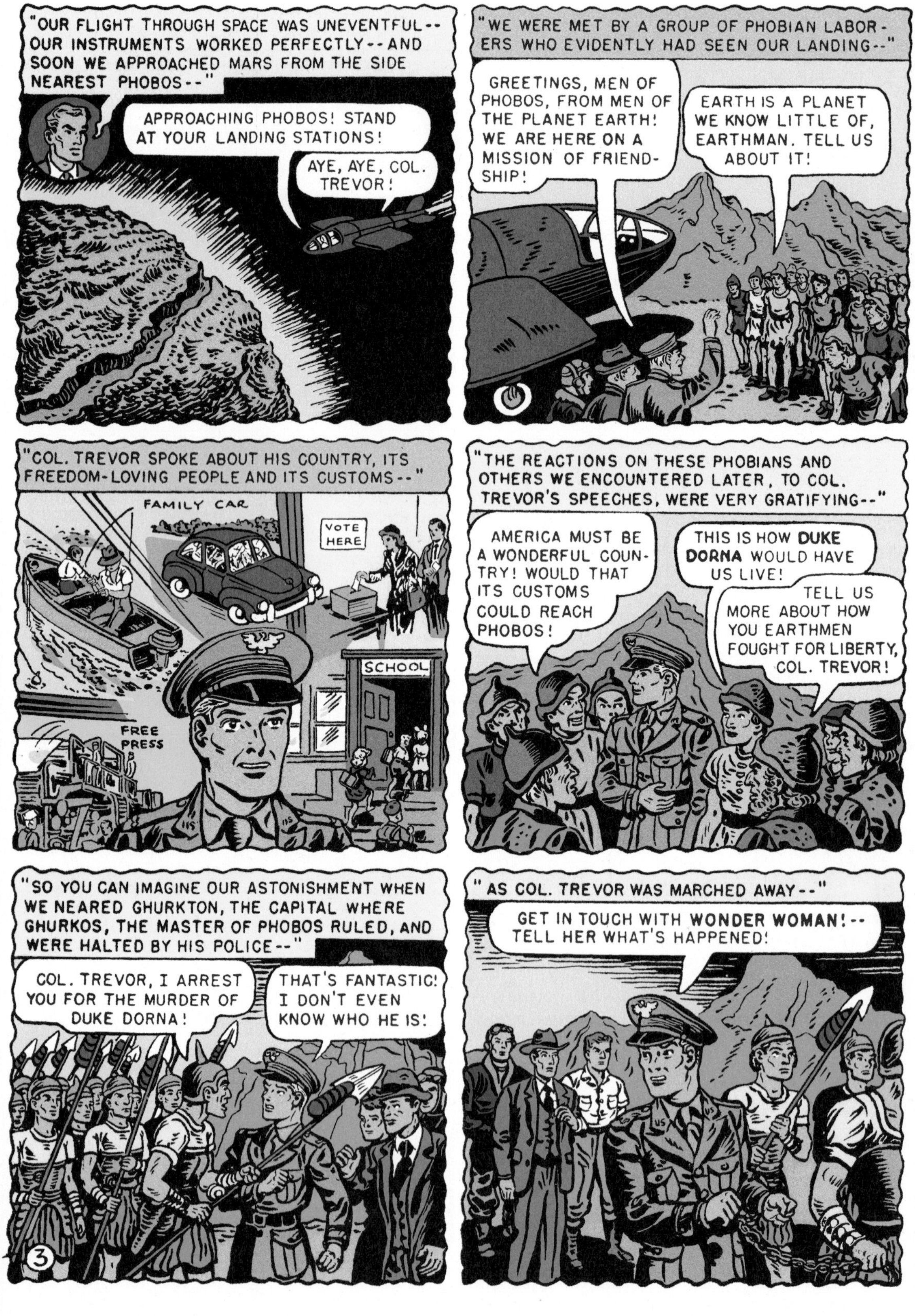
"OUR FLIGHT THROUGH SPACE WAS UNEVENTFUL-- OUR INSTRUMENTS WORKED PERFECTLY--AND SOON WE APPROACHED MARS FROM THE SIDE NEAREST PHOBOS--"
APPROACHING PHOBOS! STAND AT YOUR LANDING STATIONS!
AYE, AYE, COL. TREVOR!
"WE WERE MET BY A GROUP OF PHOBIAN LABOR-ERS WHO EVIDENTLY HAD SEEN OUR LANDING--"
GREETINGS, MEN OF PHOBOS, FROM MEN OF THE PLANET EARTH! WE ARE HERE ON A MISSION OF FRIEND-SHIP!
EARTH IS A PLANET WE KNOW LITTLE OF, EARTHMAN. TELL US ABOUT IT!
"COL. TREVOR SPOKE ABOUT HIS COUNTRY, ITS FREEDOM-LOVING PEOPLE AND ITS CUSTOMS--"
FAMILY CAR
VOTE HERE
SCHOOL
FREE PRESS
"THE REACTIONS ON THESE PHOBIANS AND OTHERS WE ENCOUNTERED LATER, TO COL. TREVOR'S SPEECHES, WERE VERY GRATIFYING--"
AMERICA MUST BE A WONDERFUL COUN-TRY! WOULD THAT ITS CUSTOMS COULD REACH PHOBOS!
THIS IS HOW DUKE DORNA WOULD HAVE US LIVE!
TELL US MORE ABOUT HOW YOU EARTHMEN FOUGHT FOR LIBERTY, COL. TREVOR!
"SO YOU CAN IMAGINE OUR ASTONISHMENT WHEN WE NEARED GHURKTON, THE CAPITAL WHERE GHURKOS, THE MASTER OF PHOBOS RULED, AND WERE HALTED BY HIS POLICE--"
COL. TREVOR, I ARREST YOU FOR THE MURDER OF DUKE DORNA!
THAT'S FANTASTIC! I DON'T EVEN KNOW WHO HE IS!
3
"AS COL. TREVOR WAS MARCHED AWAY--"
GET IN TOUCH WITH WONDER WOMAN!-- TELL HER WHAT'S HAPPENED!

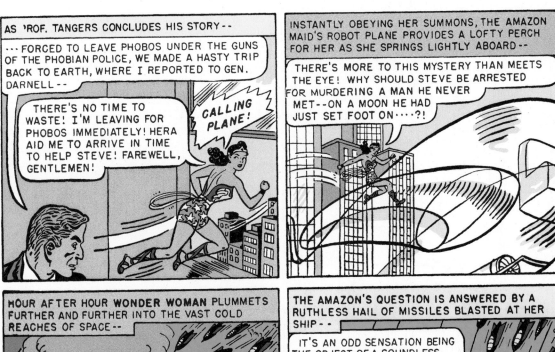

AS 'ROF. TANGERS CONCLUDES HIS STORY--

...FORCED TO LEAVE PHOBOS UNDER THE GUNS OF THE PHOBIAN POLICE, WE MADE A HASTY TRIP BACK TO EARTH, WHERE I REPORTED TO GEN. DARNELL--

THERE'S NO TIME TO WASTE! I'M LEAVING FOR PHOBOS IMMEDIATELY! HERA AID ME TO ARRIVE IN TIME TO HELP STEVE! FAREWELL, GENTLEMEN!

CALLING PLANE!

INSTANTLY OBEYING HER SUMMONS, THE AMAZON MAID'S ROBOT PLANE PROVIDES A LOFTY PERCH FOR HER AS SHE SPRINGS LIGHTLY ABOARD--

THERE'S MORE TO THIS MYSTERY THAN MEETS THE EYE! WHY SHOULD STEVE BE ARRESTED FOR MURDERING A MAN HE NEVER MET--ON A MOON HE HAD JUST SET FOOT ON····?!

HOUR AFTER HOUR WONDER WOMAN PLUMMETS FURTHER AND FURTHER INTO THE VAST COLD REACHES OF SPACE--

STRANGE PATROL SHIPS! I WONDER IF THEY'VE SPOTTED ME?

THE AMAZON'S QUESTION IS ANSWERED BY A RUTHLESS HAIL OF MISSILES BLASTED AT HER SHIP--

IT'S AN ODD SENSATION BEING THE OBJECT OF A SOUNDLESS BOMBARDMENT--BUT THAT'S BE- CAUSE THERE'S NO ATMOSPHERE IN SPACE TO CARRY SOUND! I CAN'T WASTE TIME ANSWERING THIS ATTACK. IT MIGHT MEAN STEVE'S LIFE! WHAT SHALL I DO?

--WHERE IN SPACE CAN I SEEK CONCEALMENT WITHOUT WAST- ING TIME BY GOING OFF MY COURSE?--BY HERA-- THAT COMET COMING THIS WAY GIVES ME AN IDEA!

④

WITHOUT HESITATION THE INGENIOUS AMAZON ROCKETS THROUGH THE DIFFUSED GASEOUS TAIL OF THE APPROACHING COMET!

THEY DON'T SEE ME --THEY'RE SCAT- TERING AWAY FROM THE COMET!

THE PATROL OUTWITTED, **WONDER WOMAN** CONTINUES ON AND ON IN A BLEAK SILENCE IMPOSSIBLE TO DESCRIBE UNTIL--

I'VE JUST FLOWN 47,798,921 MILES FROM THE EARTH. I SHOULD BE SIGHTING MARS SOON--YES--! THERE IT IS! WITH DEIMOS AND PHOBOS, ITS TWIN MOONS, CIRCLING AROUND IT!

AS THE INTREPID AMAZON REACHES HER DESTINATION, THE INNER MOON OF MARS WHICH HAD ENGULFED HER SWEETHEART--

PHOBOS AT LAST! THE **ONLY** BODY IN THE ENTIRE SOLAR SYSTEM WHICH APPEARS TO **RISE** IN THE WEST, AND **SET** IN THE EAST!--BY ARGUS' HUNDRED EYES!--I'M BEING MET BY A WELCOMING COMMITTEE!

ENCIRCLE HER! CAST--!

JOVE'S THUNDER-BOLTS! THEY'RE HURLING LASSOES WITH IRON WEIGHTS AT ME!

THESE PHOBIANS HAVE NEVER SEEN AN AMAZON HIGH-JUMP ROPING CONTEST, OR THEY'D REALIZE THAT AVOIDING THESE LASSOES IS CHILD'S PLAY FOR AN AMAZON!

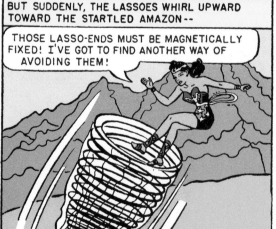

BUT SUDDENLY, THE LASSOES WHIRL UPWARD TOWARD THE STARTLED AMAZON--

THOSE LASSO-ENDS MUST BE MAGNETICALLY FIXED! I'VE GOT TO FIND ANOTHER WAY OF AVOIDING THEM!

⑤

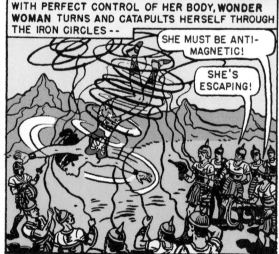

WITH PERFECT CONTROL OF HER BODY, **WONDER WOMAN** TURNS AND CATAPULTS HERSELF THROUGH THE IRON CIRCLES--

SHE MUST BE ANTI-MAGNETIC!

SHE'S ESCAPING!

SWIFTLY HURLING HER GOLDEN LASSO WITH ITS TRUTH-COMPELLING POWERS AT THE STARTLED PHOBIANS --

I COMMAND YOU TO TELL ME WHERE COL. TREVOR, THE EARTHMAN, IS HELD!

I AM...COMPELLED.. TO OBEY -- THE EARTHMAN'S TRIAL IS ON NOW -- IN THE COURT OF INJUSTICE ...AT GHURKTON --

IT TAKES BUT A FEW MINUTES FOR THE FLEET AMAZON MAID TO SPEED TO GHURKTON, THE CAPITAL OF PHOBOS --

STOP! YOU CAN'T ENTER! THIS IS THE COURT OF INJUSTICE!

ITS NAME SHOULD BE CHANGED! BUT -- THANKS FOR THE INFORMATION! THIS IS JUST THE PLACE I'M LOOKING FOR!

AS WONDER WOMAN ALIGHTS GRACEFULLY IN THE COURT YARD --

PHOBOS IS NOT THE EARTH, COL. TREVOR! HERE YOU ARE GUILTY UNTIL YOU PROVE YOURSELF INNOCENT!

WONDER WOMAN! I KNEW YOU WOULDN'T FAIL ME!

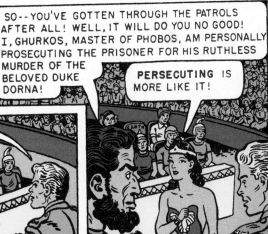

SO -- YOU'VE GOTTEN THROUGH THE PATROLS AFTER ALL! WELL, IT WILL DO YOU NO GOOD! I, GHURKOS, MASTER OF PHOBOS, AM PERSONALLY PROSECUTING THE PRISONER FOR HIS RUTHLESS MURDER OF THE BELOVED DUKE DORNA!

PERSECUTING IS MORE LIKE IT!

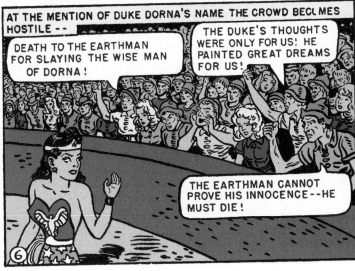

AT THE MENTION OF DUKE DORNA'S NAME THE CROWD BECOMES HOSTILE --

DEATH TO THE EARTHMAN FOR SLAYING THE WISE MAN OF DORNA!

THE DUKE'S THOUGHTS WERE ONLY FOR US! HE PAINTED GREAT DREAMS FOR US!

THE EARTHMAN CANNOT PROVE HIS INNOCENCE -- HE MUST DIE!

SUFFERING SAPPHO! THE MOTIVE FOR THE MURDER HAS JUST OCCURRED TO ME, ALSO THE REASON FOR STEVE'S CAPTURE! BUT BE- FORE I CAN PROVE STEVE'S INNOCENCE, I MUST FIRST CHANGE THE MENACING ATTI- TUDE OF THE CROWD!

WHAT DOES WONDER WOMAN MEAN BY THIS AMAZING STATE- MENT? --- WE SHALL SEE!

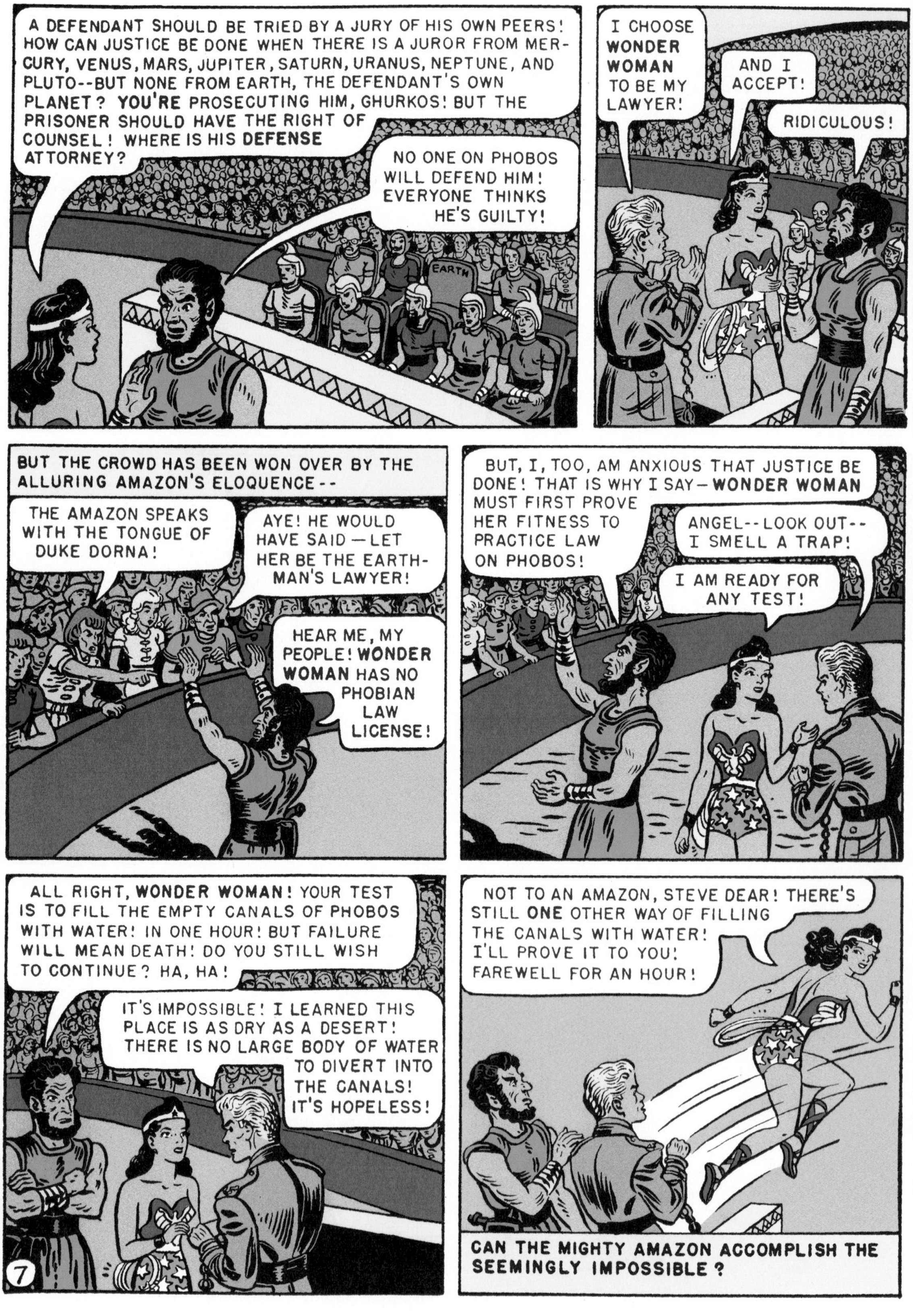
A DEFENDANT SHOULD BE TRIED BY A JURY OF HIS OWN PEERS! HOW CAN JUSTICE BE DONE WHEN THERE IS A JUROR FROM MERCURY, VENUS, MARS, JUPITER, SATURN, URANUS, NEPTUNE, AND PLUTO--BUT NONE FROM EARTH, THE DEFENDANT'S OWN PLANET? YOU'RE PROSECUTING HIM, GHURKOS! BUT THE PRISONER SHOULD HAVE THE RIGHT OF COUNSEL! WHERE IS HIS DEFENSE ATTORNEY?
NO ONE ON PHOBOS WILL DEFEND HIM! EVERYONE THINKS HE'S GUILTY!
EARTH
I CHOOSE WONDER WOMAN TO BE MY LAWYER!
AND I ACCEPT!
RIDICULOUS!
BUT THE CROWD HAS BEEN WON OVER BY THE ALLURING AMAZON'S ELOQUENCE--
THE AMAZON SPEAKS WITH THE TONGUE OF DUKE DORNA!
AYE! HE WOULD HAVE SAID—LET HER BE THE EARTH-MAN'S LAWYER!
HEAR ME, MY PEOPLE! WONDER WOMAN HAS NO PHOBIAN LAW LICENSE!
BUT, I, TOO, AM ANXIOUS THAT JUSTICE BE DONE! THAT IS WHY I SAY—WONDER WOMAN MUST FIRST PROVE HER FITNESS TO PRACTICE LAW ON PHOBOS!
ANGEL--LOOK OUT--I SMELL A TRAP!
I AM READY FOR ANY TEST!
ALL RIGHT, WONDER WOMAN! YOUR TEST IS TO FILL THE EMPTY CANALS OF PHOBOS WITH WATER! IN ONE HOUR! BUT FAILURE WILL MEAN DEATH! DO YOU STILL WISH TO CONTINUE? HA, HA!
IT'S IMPOSSIBLE! I LEARNED THIS PLACE IS AS DRY AS A DESERT! THERE IS NO LARGE BODY OF WATER TO DIVERT INTO THE CANALS! IT'S HOPELESS!
7
NOT TO AN AMAZON, STEVE DEAR! THERE'S STILL ONE OTHER WAY OF FILLING THE CANALS WITH WATER! I'LL PROVE IT TO YOU! FAREWELL FOR AN HOUR!
CAN THE MIGHTY AMAZON ACCOMPLISH THE SEEMINGLY IMPOSSIBLE?

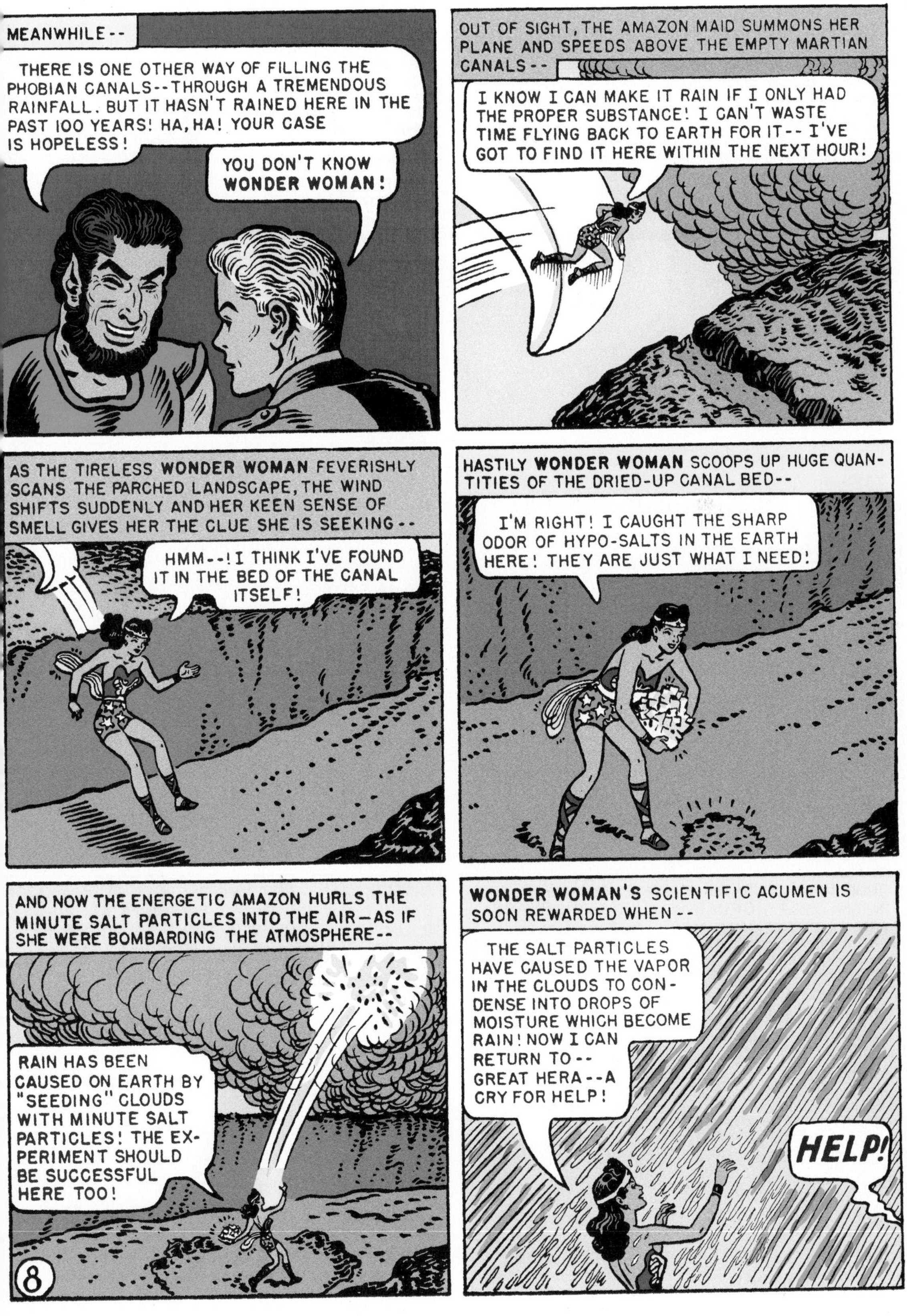

MEANWHILE--
THERE IS ONE OTHER WAY OF FILLING THE PHOBIAN CANALS--THROUGH A TREMENDOUS RAINFALL. BUT IT HASN'T RAINED HERE IN THE PAST 100 YEARS! HA, HA! YOUR CASE IS HOPELESS!
YOU DON'T KNOW WONDER WOMAN!
OUT OF SIGHT, THE AMAZON MAID SUMMONS HER PLANE AND SPEEDS ABOVE THE EMPTY MARTIAN CANALS--
I KNOW I CAN MAKE IT RAIN IF I ONLY HAD THE PROPER SUBSTANCE! I CAN'T WASTE TIME FLYING BACK TO EARTH FOR IT-- I'VE GOT TO FIND IT HERE WITHIN THE NEXT HOUR!
AS THE TIRELESS WONDER WOMAN FEVERISHLY SCANS THE PARCHED LANDSCAPE, THE WIND SHIFTS SUDDENLY AND HER KEEN SENSE OF SMELL GIVES HER THE CLUE SHE IS SEEKING--
HMM--! I THINK I'VE FOUND IT IN THE BED OF THE CANAL ITSELF!
HASTILY WONDER WOMAN SCOOPS UP HUGE QUANTITIES OF THE DRIED-UP CANAL BED--
I'M RIGHT! I CAUGHT THE SHARP ODOR OF HYPO-SALTS IN THE EARTH HERE! THEY ARE JUST WHAT I NEED!
AND NOW THE ENERGETIC AMAZON HURLS THE MINUTE SALT PARTICLES INTO THE AIR—AS IF SHE WERE BOMBARDING THE ATMOSPHERE--
RAIN HAS BEEN CAUSED ON EARTH BY "SEEDING" CLOUDS WITH MINUTE SALT PARTICLES! THE EXPERIMENT SHOULD BE SUCCESSFUL HERE TOO!
8
WONDER WOMAN'S SCIENTIFIC ACUMEN IS SOON REWARDED WHEN--
THE SALT PARTICLES HAVE CAUSED THE VAPOR IN THE CLOUDS TO CONDENSE INTO DROPS OF MOISTURE WHICH BECOME RAIN! NOW I CAN RETURN TO-- GREAT HERA--A CRY FOR HELP!
HELP!

TURNING IN THE DIRECTION OF THE APPEAL FOR HELP, THE AMAZON SEES--

THE HIDEOUT'S FILLING UP! LET'S GET OUT BEFORE WE DROWN!

DUKE DORNA OUGHT TO BE GLAD THAT GHURKOS ORDERED US TO KEEP HIM ALIVE UNTIL HE "REMEMBERS" THE SECRET CHEMICAL FORMULA HE PERFECTED!

MERCIFUL MINERVA! THE MURDERED "VICTIM" AND THE MOTIVE! THE EVIDENCE TO FREE STEVE!

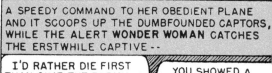

A SPEEDY COMMAND TO HER OBEDIENT PLANE AND IT SCOOPS UP THE DUMBFOUNDED CAPTORS, WHILE THE ALERT WONDER WOMAN CATCHES THE ERSTWHILE CAPTIVE --

I'D RATHER DIE FIRST THAN GIVE THE FORMULA TO GHURKOS! HE'D USE IT FOR DESTRUCTIVE PURPOSES -- WHAT--? AN AMAZON!

YOU SHOWED A TRUE SCIENTIFIC CONSCIENCE, DUKE DORNA!

HELP!

AS WONDER WOMAN RACES BACK TO THE COURT YARD --

BZZ···BZZZ··· UNDERSTAND, DUKE DORNA?

PERFECTLY, WONDER WOMAN!

A FEW MOMENTS LATER, THE CROWD HAILS THE ENERGETIC AMAZON --

THE AMAZON HAS BROUGHT RAIN!

THE CANALS ARE FILLING UP!

SHE HAS EARNED THE RIGHT TO DEFEND THE PRISONER!

ONCE AGAIN GHURKOS IS FORCED TO BOW TO THE INDOMITABLE WONDER WOMAN, AND APPOINT HER AS STEVE'S LAWYER -- BUT ---

ACCORDING TO PHOBIAN LAW, PRISONER, YOU WILL BE SHOT IF YOU TELL THE TRUTH, AND HANGED IF YOU LIE! BUT IF YOU PLEAD GUILTY, YOU CAN NAME YOUR OWN EXECUTION! SPEAK!

WH--WHAT CAN I SAY? ANYTHING I SAY WILL CONDEMN ME!

HMM--?

FASTER THAN LIGHTNING THE INGENIOUS AMAZON EXAMINES EVERY ANGLE OF THE FATAL CONUNDRUM FOR A LOOPHOLE, AND THEN, AFTER RECEIVING PERMISSION TO ADVISE HER CLIENT --

BZZ···BZZZ··· BZZ···

I UNDERSTAND, ANGEL! I'M READY TO PUT MY LIFE IN YOUR HANDS!

WHAT HAS WONDER WOMAN COUNSELED STEVE? HOW CAN HE ESCAPE DEATH?

AS THE RAIN STOPS, AMIDST A HUSHED SILENCE, STEVE ANSWERS--

MY ANSWER IS-- **YOU'RE GOING TO HANG ME!**

CORRECT! HANG HIM, EXECUTIONER! HA, HA! YOU SHOULD HAVE CHOSEN A BETTER LAWYER, PRISONER!

BUT **WONDER WOMAN** SUDDENLY THRUSTS THE NOOSE ASIDE--

WAIT! YOU CAN'T **HANG** THE DEFENDANT! HE TOLD THE **TRUTH!** YOU **ARE** GOING TO **HANG** HIM! **BUT** THE PENALTY FOR TELLING THE **TRUTH** IS **SHOOTING!**

CORRECT! FIRING SQUAD! PREPARE TO **SHOOT** THE PRISONER!

ONCE AGAIN THE INGENIOUS AMAZON INTERRUPTS THE EXECUTION--

STOP! YOU CAN **SHOOT** THE DEFENDANT **ONLY** IF HE **LIES!** BUT HE **HASN'T** LIED EITHER!

H-H-HOW DOES HE PLEAD THEN?

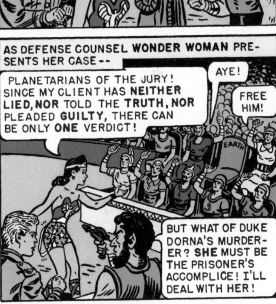

AS DEFENSE COUNSEL **WONDER WOMAN** PRESENTS HER CASE--

PLANETARIANS OF THE JURY! SINCE MY CLIENT HAS **NEITHER** LIED, **NOR** TOLD THE **TRUTH,** NOR PLEADED **GUILTY,** THERE CAN BE ONLY **ONE** VERDICT!

AYE!

FREE HIM!

BUT WHAT OF DUKE DORNA'S MURDERER? **SHE** MUST BE THE PRISONER'S ACCOMPLICE! I'LL DEAL WITH HER!

WHEELING SWIFTLY **WONDER WOMAN** LASSOES GHURKOS AND--

HERE IS DUKE DORNA -- ALIVE! AND YOU, GHURKOS, WILL STAND TRIAL FOR KIDNAPPING WITH INTENT TO KILL!

IT'S···TRUE··· THE EARTHMAN'S TALES OF FREEDOM AND DEMOCRACY WERE MAKING THE PEOPLE DISSATISFIED WITH MY DICTATORSHIP! SO I···ACCUSED **HIM** OF KILLING THE POPULAR DORNA, THUS REMOVING **TWO** THREATS TO ME AT ONCE!

10

LATER--

THANKS TO YOU, **WONDER WOMAN,** WE ON PHOBOS ARE FREE! WE WILL BE HAPPY TO COOPERATE WITH THE EARTH TO HARNESS ATOMIC ENERGY FOR PEACETIME USE!

WHEN PEOPLE EVERYWHERE IN THE SOLAR SYSTEM REALIZE THAT LOVE AND KINDNESS IS THE GREATEST "ATOMIC" FORCE IN THE WORLD, THERE NEED NEVER BE ANY UNHAPPINESS!

END

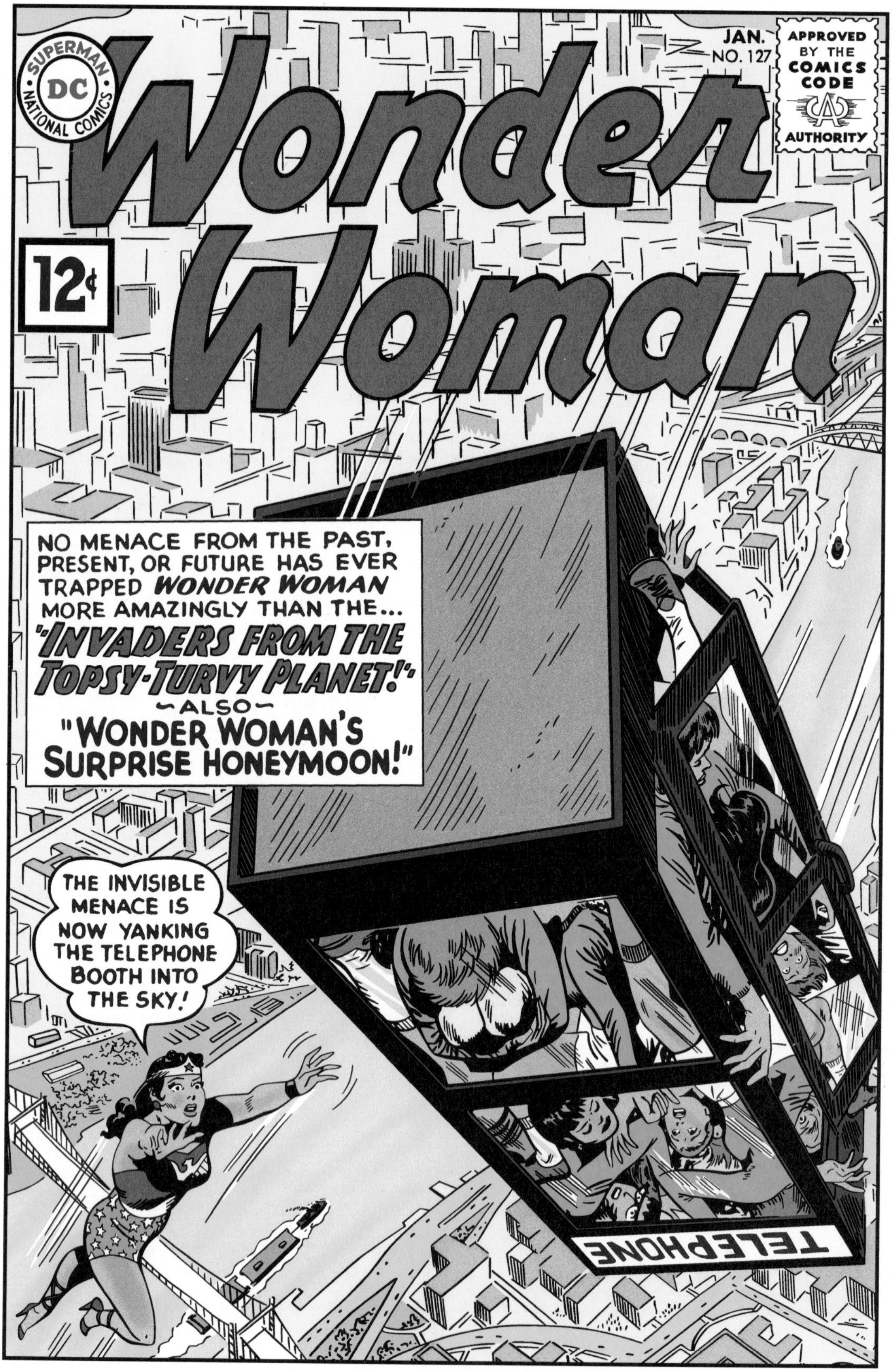

SUPERMAN
DC
NATIONAL COMICS
Wonder Woman
JAN.
NO. 127
APPROVED BY THE COMICS CODE AUTHORITY
12¢
NO MENACE FROM THE PAST, PRESENT, OR FUTURE HAS EVER TRAPPED WONDER WOMAN MORE AMAZINGLY THAN THE... "INVADERS FROM THE TOPSY-TURVY PLANET!" ~ALSO~ "WONDER WOMAN'S SURPRISE HONEYMOON!"
THE INVISIBLE MENACE IS NOW YANKING THE TELEPHONE BOOTH INTO THE SKY!
TELEPHONE

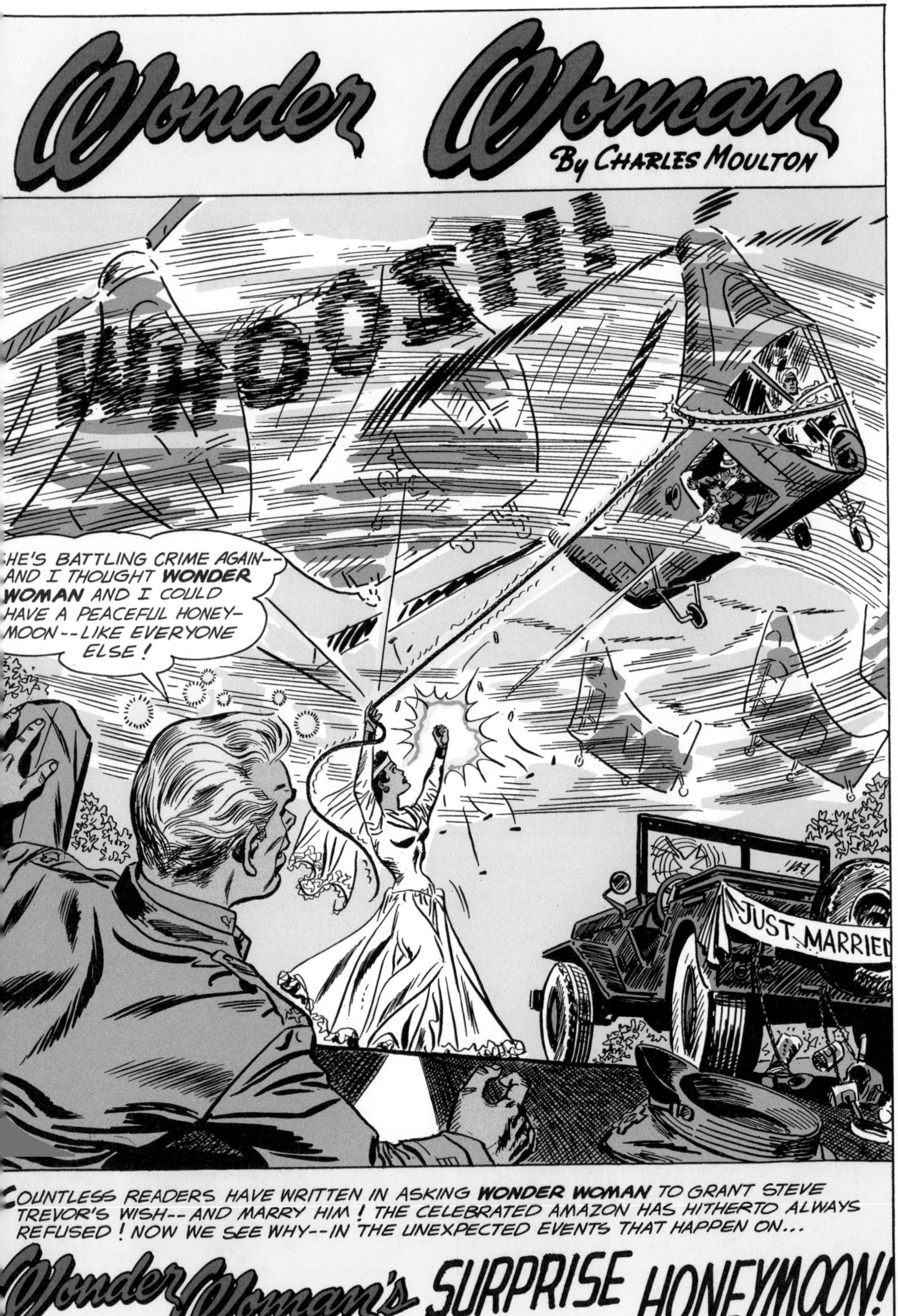

Wonder Woman
By CHARLES MOULTON
WHOOSH!
HE'S BATTLING CRIME AGAIN-- AND I THOUGHT WONDER WOMAN AND I COULD HAVE A PEACEFUL HONEY-MOON--LIKE EVERYONE ELSE!
JUST MARRIED
COUNTLESS READERS HAVE WRITTEN IN ASKING WONDER WOMAN TO GRANT STEVE TREVOR'S WISH-- AND MARRY HIM! THE CELEBRATED AMAZON HAS HITHERTO ALWAYS REFUSED! NOW WE SEE WHY--IN THE UNEXPECTED EVENTS THAT HAPPEN ON...
Wonder Woman's SURPRISE HONEYMOON!
1

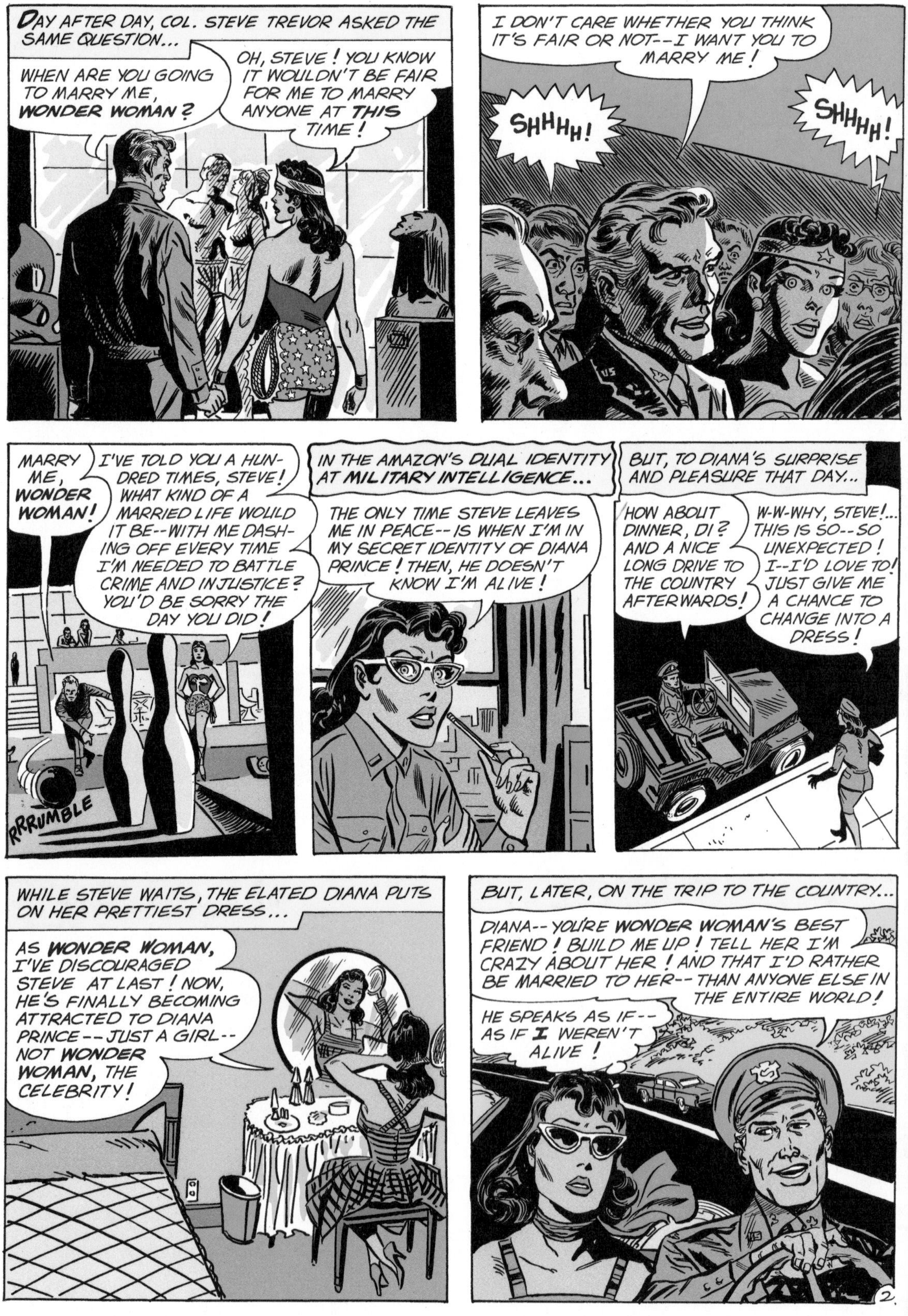
DAY AFTER DAY, COL. STEVE TREVOR ASKED THE SAME QUESTION...
WHEN ARE YOU GOING TO MARRY ME, WONDER WOMAN?
OH, STEVE! YOU KNOW IT WOULDN'T BE FAIR FOR ME TO MARRY ANYONE AT THIS TIME!
I DON'T CARE WHETHER YOU THINK IT'S FAIR OR NOT--I WANT YOU TO MARRY ME!
SHHHH!
SHHHH!
MARRY ME, WONDER WOMAN!
I'VE TOLD YOU A HUNDRED TIMES, STEVE! WHAT KIND OF A MARRIED LIFE WOULD IT BE--WITH ME DASHING OFF EVERY TIME I'M NEEDED TO BATTLE CRIME AND INJUSTICE? YOU'D BE SORRY THE DAY YOU DID!
RRRUMBLE
IN THE AMAZON'S DUAL IDENTITY AT MILITARY INTELLIGENCE...
THE ONLY TIME STEVE LEAVES ME IN PEACE--IS WHEN I'M IN MY SECRET IDENTITY OF DIANA PRINCE! THEN, HE DOESN'T KNOW I'M ALIVE!
BUT, TO DIANA'S SURPRISE AND PLEASURE THAT DAY...
HOW ABOUT DINNER, DI? AND A NICE LONG DRIVE TO THE COUNTRY AFTERWARDS!
W-W-WHY, STEVE!... THIS IS SO--SO UNEXPECTED! I--I'D LOVE TO! JUST GIVE ME A CHANCE TO CHANGE INTO A DRESS!
WHILE STEVE WAITS, THE ELATED DIANA PUTS ON HER PRETTIEST DRESS...
AS WONDER WOMAN, I'VE DISCOURAGED STEVE AT LAST! NOW, HE'S FINALLY BECOMING ATTRACTED TO DIANA PRINCE--JUST A GIRL--NOT WONDER WOMAN, THE CELEBRITY!
BUT, LATER, ON THE TRIP TO THE COUNTRY...
DIANA--YOU'RE WONDER WOMAN'S BEST FRIEND! BUILD ME UP! TELL HER I'M CRAZY ABOUT HER! AND THAT I'D RATHER BE MARRIED TO HER--THAN ANYONE ELSE IN THE ENTIRE WORLD!
HE SPEAKS AS IF--AS IF I WEREN'T ALIVE!
2

SUDDENLY...

THAT TRUCK MUST HAVE SKIDDED INTO THAT ARMORED CAR!

CRAASH!

IT'S NOT AN ACCIDENT! IT'S A HOLDUP!

STAY WHERE YOU ARE, DIANA--I'M GOING TO TACKLE THOSE BANDITS!

IN THAT SAME MOMENT, DIANA MAKES A LIGHTNING CHANGE INTO HER SECRET IDENTITY...

STEVE'S HEAVILY OUT-NUMBERED! HE'LL NEED **WONDER WOMAN'S** HELP!

JUST THEN, A HUGE WINGED SHAPE HOVERS OVER THE ARMORED TRUCK AND...

WHRRRRRRR!

GREAT HERA! THE CROOKS ARE HIJACKING THE ENTIRE TRUCK! IT WILL DISAPPEAR WITHOUT A TRACE INTO THAT GIANT HELICOPTER!

POW! KROW!

3

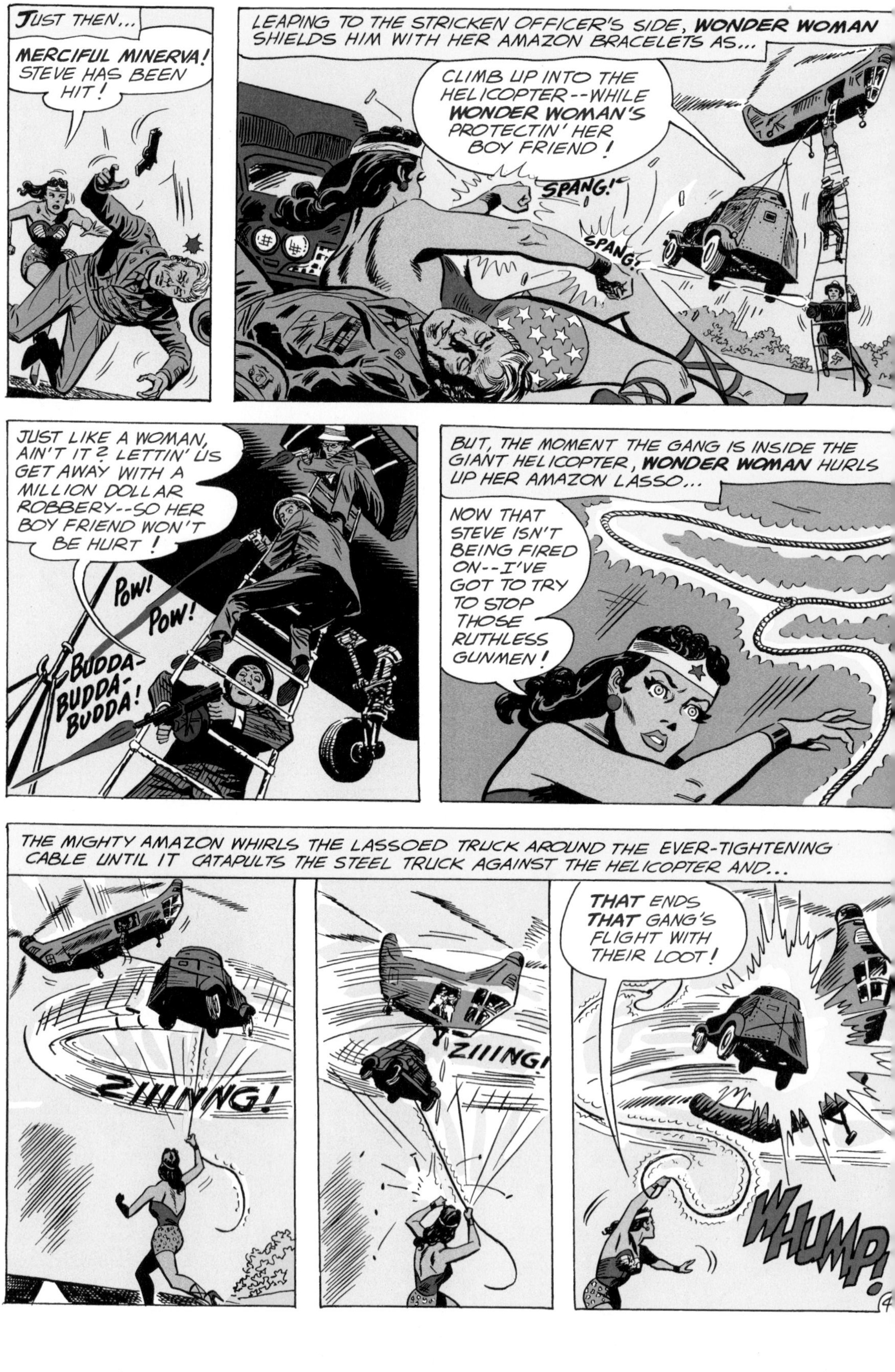

JUST THEN...
MERCIFUL MINERVA! STEVE HAS BEEN HIT!
LEAPING TO THE STRICKEN OFFICER'S SIDE, WONDER WOMAN SHIELDS HIM WITH HER AMAZON BRACELETS AS...
CLIMB UP INTO THE HELICOPTER--WHILE WONDER WOMAN'S PROTECTIN' HER BOY FRIEND!
SPANG!
SPANG!
JUST LIKE A WOMAN, AIN'T IT? LETTIN' US GET AWAY WITH A MILLION DOLLAR ROBBERY--SO HER BOY FRIEND WON'T BE HURT!
POW!
POW!
BUDDA-BUDDA-BUDDA!
BUT, THE MOMENT THE GANG IS INSIDE THE GIANT HELICOPTER, WONDER WOMAN HURLS UP HER AMAZON LASSO...
NOW THAT STEVE ISN'T BEING FIRED ON--I'VE GOT TO TRY TO STOP THOSE RUTHLESS GUNMEN!
THE MIGHTY AMAZON WHIRLS THE LASSOED TRUCK AROUND THE EVER-TIGHTENING CABLE UNTIL IT CATAPULTS THE STEEL TRUCK AGAINST THE HELICOPTER AND...
ZIIINNG!
ZIIING!
THAT ENDS THAT GANG'S FLIGHT WITH THEIR LOOT!
WHUMP!
4

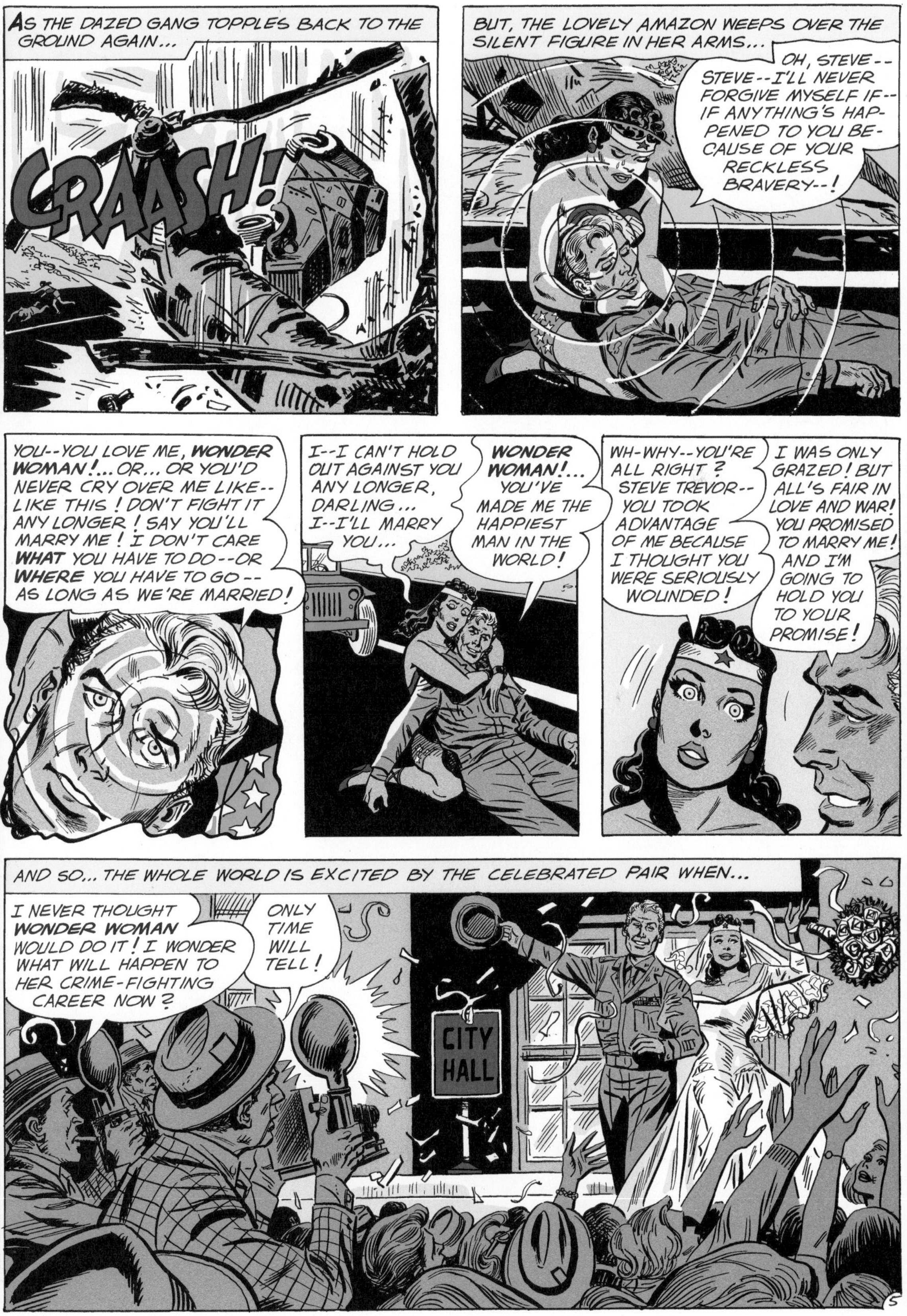

AS THE DAZED GANG TOPPLES BACK TO THE GROUND AGAIN...
CRAASH!
BUT, THE LOVELY AMAZON WEEPS OVER THE SILENT FIGURE IN HER ARMS...
OH, STEVE--STEVE--I'LL NEVER FORGIVE MYSELF IF--IF ANYTHING'S HAPPENED TO YOU BECAUSE OF YOUR RECKLESS BRAVERY--!
YOU--YOU LOVE ME, **WONDER WOMAN!**... OR... OR YOU'D NEVER CRY OVER ME LIKE--LIKE THIS! DON'T FIGHT IT ANY LONGER! SAY YOU'LL MARRY ME! I DON'T CARE **WHAT** YOU HAVE TO DO--OR **WHERE** YOU HAVE TO GO--AS LONG AS WE'RE MARRIED!
I--I CAN'T HOLD OUT AGAINST YOU ANY LONGER, DARLING... I--I'LL MARRY YOU...
WONDER WOMAN!... YOU'VE MADE ME THE HAPPIEST MAN IN THE WORLD!
WH-WHY--YOU'RE ALL RIGHT? STEVE TREVOR--YOU TOOK ADVANTAGE OF ME BECAUSE I THOUGHT YOU WERE SERIOUSLY WOUNDED!
I WAS ONLY GRAZED! BUT ALL'S FAIR IN LOVE AND WAR! YOU PROMISED TO MARRY ME! AND I'M GOING TO HOLD YOU TO YOUR PROMISE!
AND SO... THE WHOLE WORLD IS EXCITED BY THE CELEBRATED PAIR WHEN...
I NEVER THOUGHT **WONDER WOMAN** WOULD DO IT! I WONDER WHAT WILL HAPPEN TO HER CRIME-FIGHTING CAREER NOW?
ONLY TIME WILL TELL!
CITY HALL
5

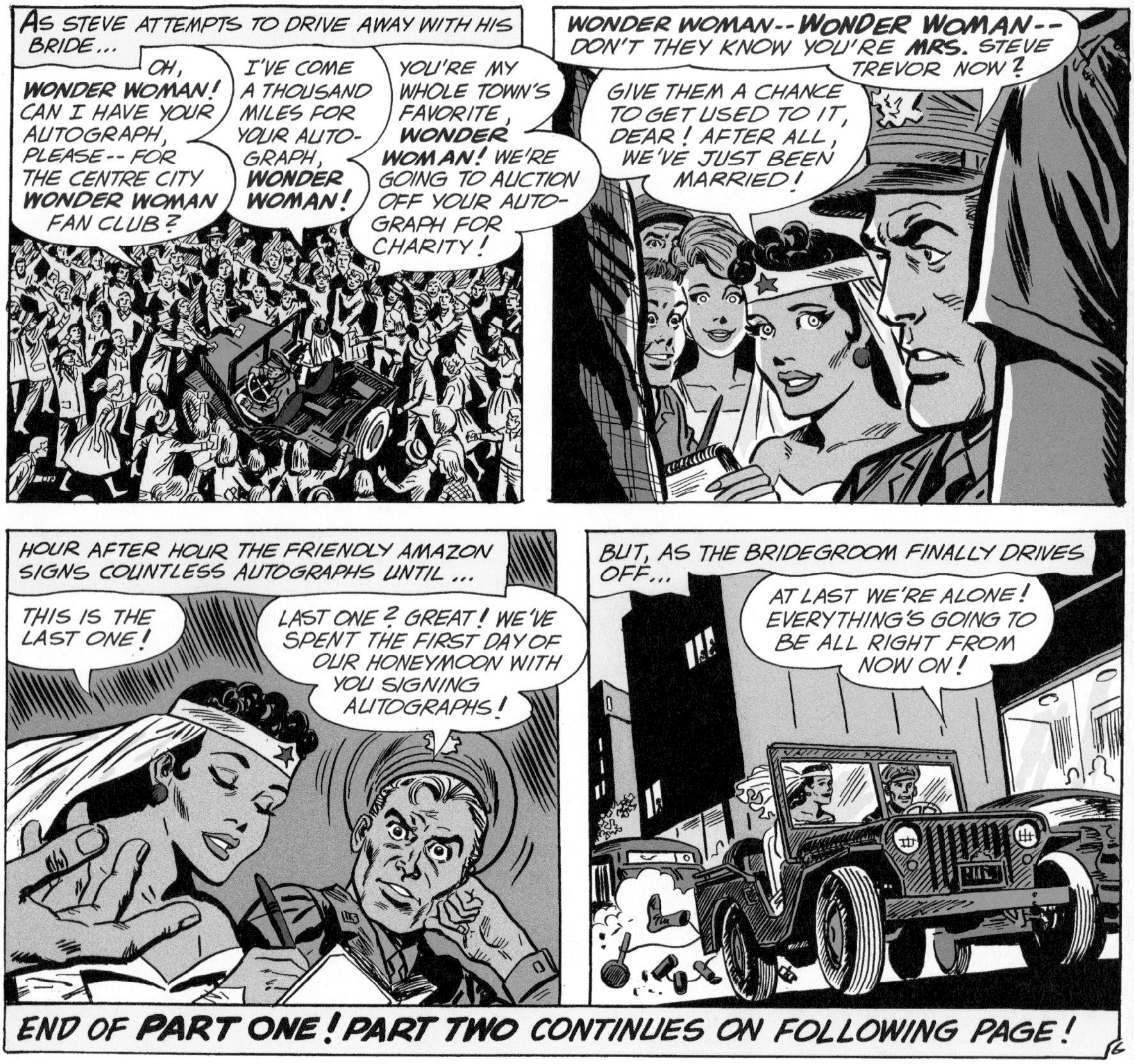
AS STEVE ATTEMPTS TO DRIVE AWAY WITH HIS BRIDE...
OH, WONDER WOMAN! CAN I HAVE YOUR AUTOGRAPH, PLEASE-- FOR THE CENTRE CITY WONDER WOMAN FAN CLUB?
I'VE COME A THOUSAND MILES FOR YOUR AUTOGRAPH, WONDER WOMAN!
YOU'RE MY WHOLE TOWN'S FAVORITE, WONDER WOMAN! WE'RE GOING TO AUCTION OFF YOUR AUTOGRAPH FOR CHARITY!
WONDER WOMAN--WONDER WOMAN-- DON'T THEY KNOW YOU'RE MRS. STEVE TREVOR NOW?
GIVE THEM A CHANCE TO GET USED TO IT, DEAR! AFTER ALL, WE'VE JUST BEEN MARRIED!
HOUR AFTER HOUR THE FRIENDLY AMAZON SIGNS COUNTLESS AUTOGRAPHS UNTIL...
THIS IS THE LAST ONE!
LAST ONE? GREAT! WE'VE SPENT THE FIRST DAY OF OUR HONEYMOON WITH YOU SIGNING AUTOGRAPHS!
BUT, AS THE BRIDEGROOM FINALLY DRIVES OFF...
AT LAST WE'RE ALONE! EVERYTHING'S GOING TO BE ALL RIGHT FROM NOW ON!
END OF PART ONE! PART TWO CONTINUES ON FOLLOWING PAGE!
6

WONDER WOMAN

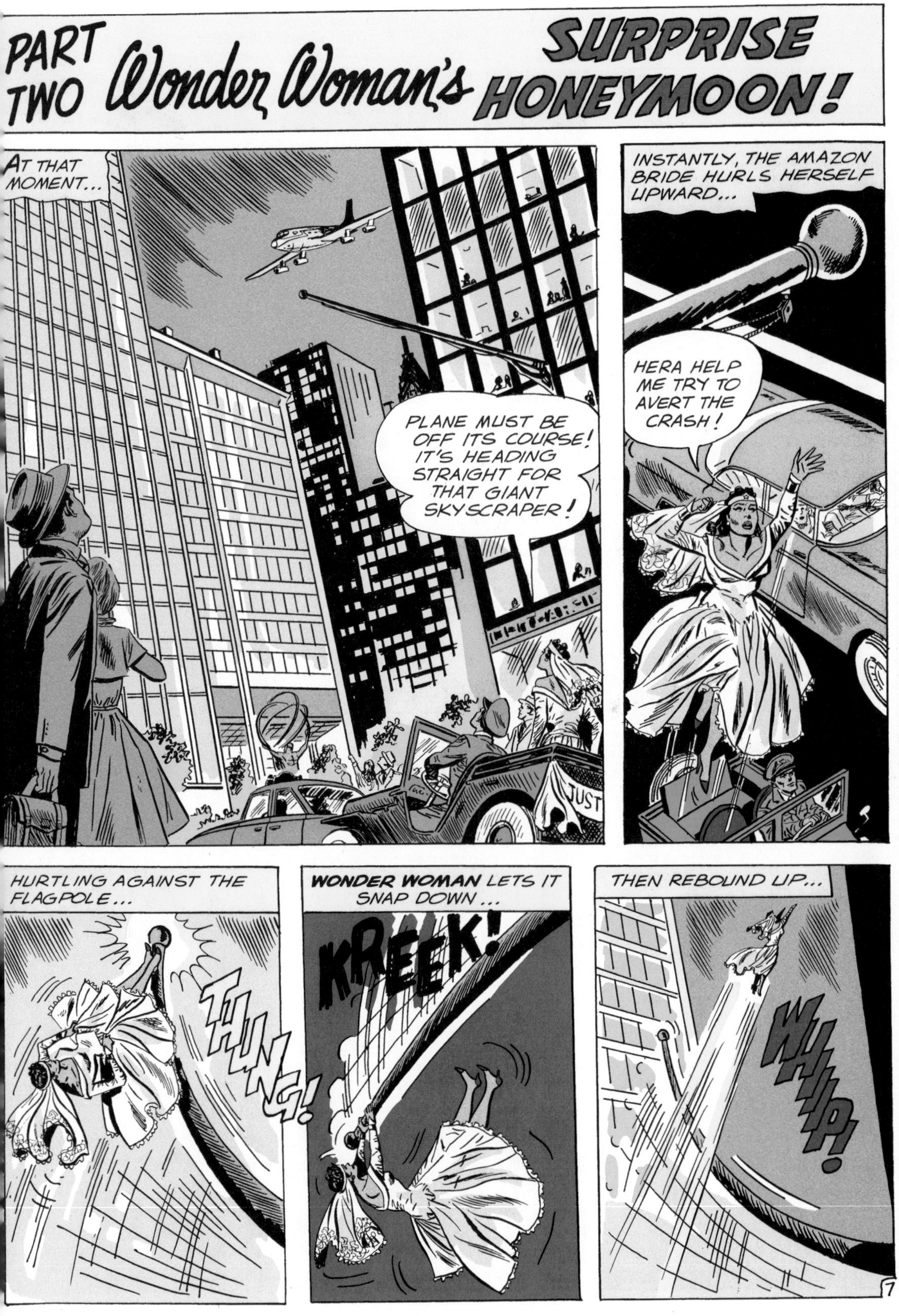
PART TWO Wonder Woman's SURPRISE HONEYMOON!
AT THAT MOMENT...
PLANE MUST BE OFF ITS COURSE! IT'S HEADING STRAIGHT FOR THAT GIANT SKYSCRAPER!
JUST
INSTANTLY, THE AMAZON BRIDE HURLS HERSELF UPWARD...
HERA HELP ME TRY TO AVERT THE CRASH!
HURTLING AGAINST THE FLAGPOLE...
THUNG!
WONDER WOMAN LETS IT SNAP DOWN...
KREEK!
THEN REBOUND UP...
WHIP!
7

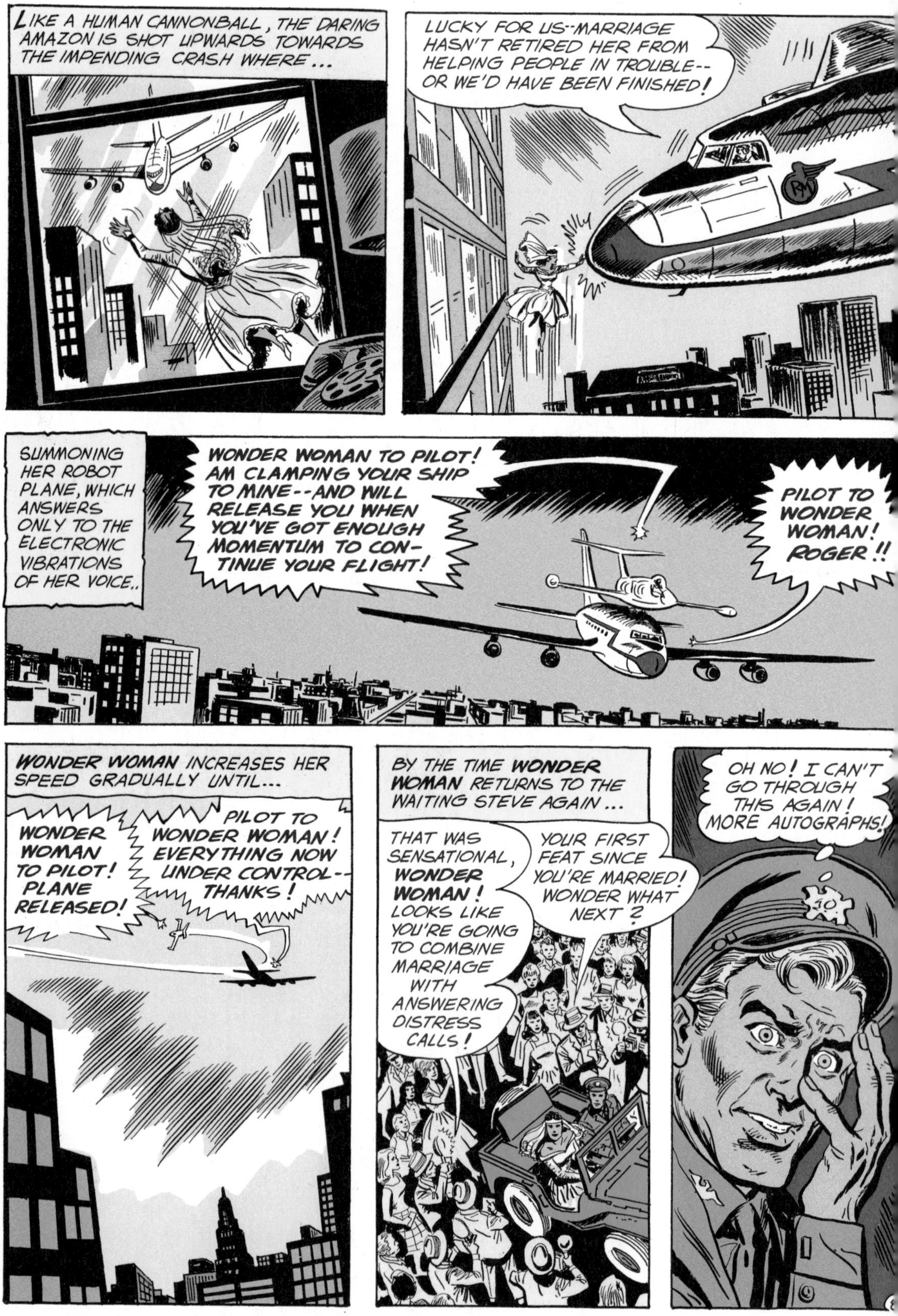
LIKE A HUMAN CANNONBALL, THE DARING AMAZON IS SHOT UPWARDS TOWARDS THE IMPENDING CRASH WHERE...
LUCKY FOR US--MARRIAGE HASN'T RETIRED HER FROM HELPING PEOPLE IN TROUBLE--OR WE'D HAVE BEEN FINISHED!
SUMMONING HER ROBOT PLANE, WHICH ANSWERS ONLY TO THE ELECTRONIC VIBRATIONS OF HER VOICE..
WONDER WOMAN TO PILOT! AM CLAMPING YOUR SHIP TO MINE--AND WILL RELEASE YOU WHEN YOU'VE GOT ENOUGH MOMENTUM TO CONTINUE YOUR FLIGHT!
PILOT TO WONDER WOMAN! ROGER!!
WONDER WOMAN INCREASES HER SPEED GRADUALLY UNTIL...
WONDER WOMAN TO PILOT! PLANE RELEASED!
PILOT TO WONDER WOMAN! EVERYTHING NOW UNDER CONTROL--THANKS!
BY THE TIME WONDER WOMAN RETURNS TO THE WAITING STEVE AGAIN...
THAT WAS SENSATIONAL, WONDER WOMAN! LOOKS LIKE YOU'RE GOING TO COMBINE MARRIAGE WITH ANSWERING DISTRESS CALLS!
YOUR FIRST FEAT SINCE YOU'RE MARRIED! WONDER WHAT NEXT?
OH NO! I CAN'T GO THROUGH THIS AGAIN! MORE AUTOGRAPHS!

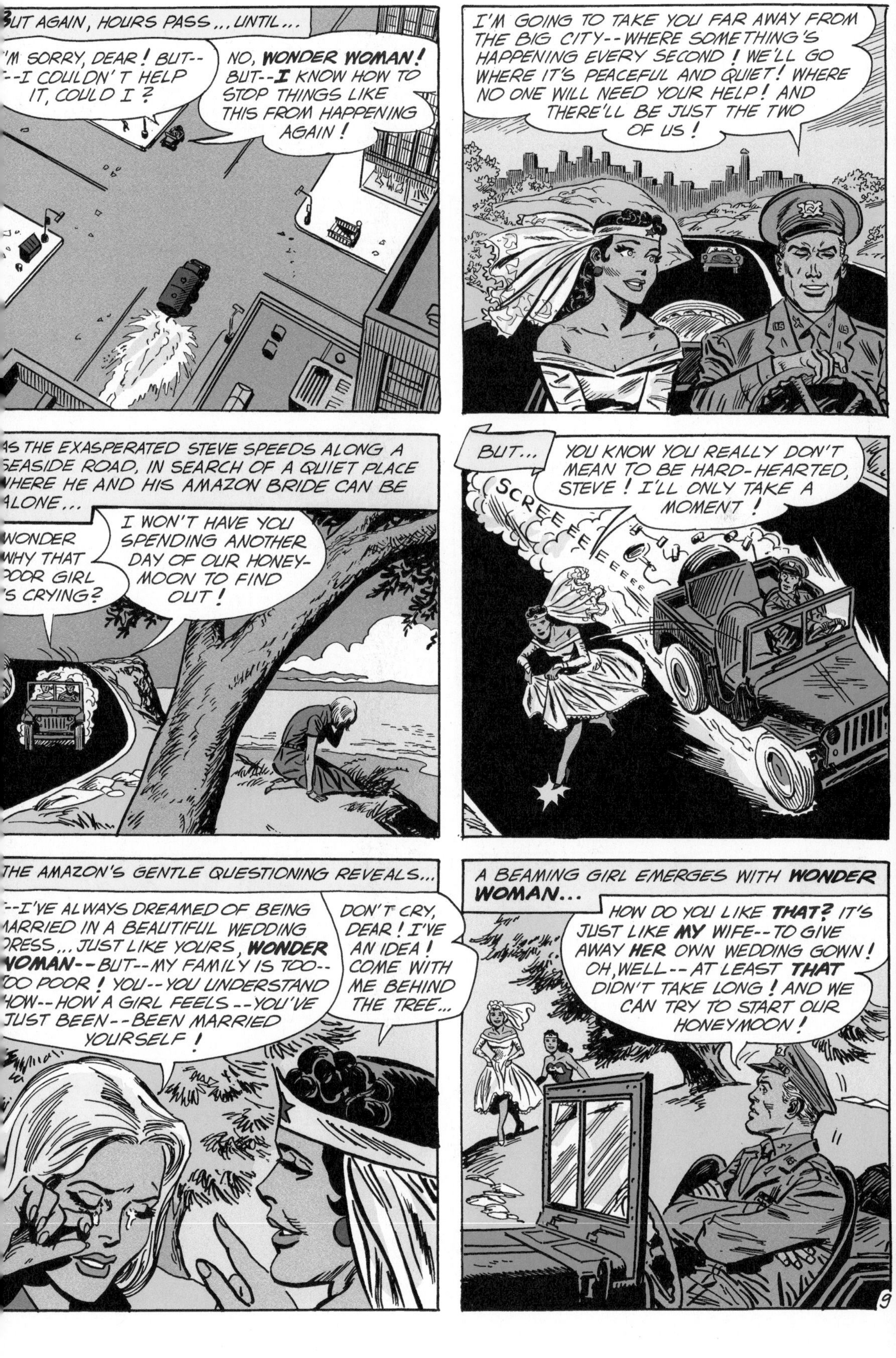

BUT AGAIN, HOURS PASS,.. UNTIL...
'M SORRY, DEAR! BUT-- --I COULDN'T HELP IT, COULD I?
NO, WONDER WOMAN! BUT--I KNOW HOW TO STOP THINGS LIKE THIS FROM HAPPENING AGAIN!
I'M GOING TO TAKE YOU FAR AWAY FROM THE BIG CITY--WHERE SOMETHING'S HAPPENING EVERY SECOND! WE'LL GO WHERE IT'S PEACEFUL AND QUIET! WHERE NO ONE WILL NEED YOUR HELP! AND THERE'LL BE JUST THE TWO OF US!
AS THE EXASPERATED STEVE SPEEDS ALONG A SEASIDE ROAD, IN SEARCH OF A QUIET PLACE WHERE HE AND HIS AMAZON BRIDE CAN BE ALONE...
WONDER WHY THAT POOR GIRL 'S CRYING?
I WON'T HAVE YOU SPENDING ANOTHER DAY OF OUR HONEY-MOON TO FIND OUT!
BUT...
YOU KNOW YOU REALLY DON'T MEAN TO BE HARD-HEARTED, STEVE! I'LL ONLY TAKE A MOMENT!
SCREEEEEEEEEEE
THE AMAZON'S GENTLE QUESTIONING REVEALS...
--I'VE ALWAYS DREAMED OF BEING MARRIED IN A BEAUTIFUL WEDDING DRESS... JUST LIKE YOURS, WONDER WOMAN--BUT--MY FAMILY IS TOO-- TOO POOR! YOU--YOU UNDERSTAND HOW--HOW A GIRL FEELS--YOU'VE JUST BEEN--BEEN MARRIED YOURSELF!
DON'T CRY, DEAR! I'VE AN IDEA! COME WITH ME BEHIND THE TREE...
A BEAMING GIRL EMERGES WITH WONDER WOMAN...
HOW DO YOU LIKE THAT? IT'S JUST LIKE MY WIFE--TO GIVE AWAY HER OWN WEDDING GOWN! OH, WELL--AT LEAST THAT DIDN'T TAKE LONG! AND WE CAN TRY TO START OUR HONEYMOON!
9

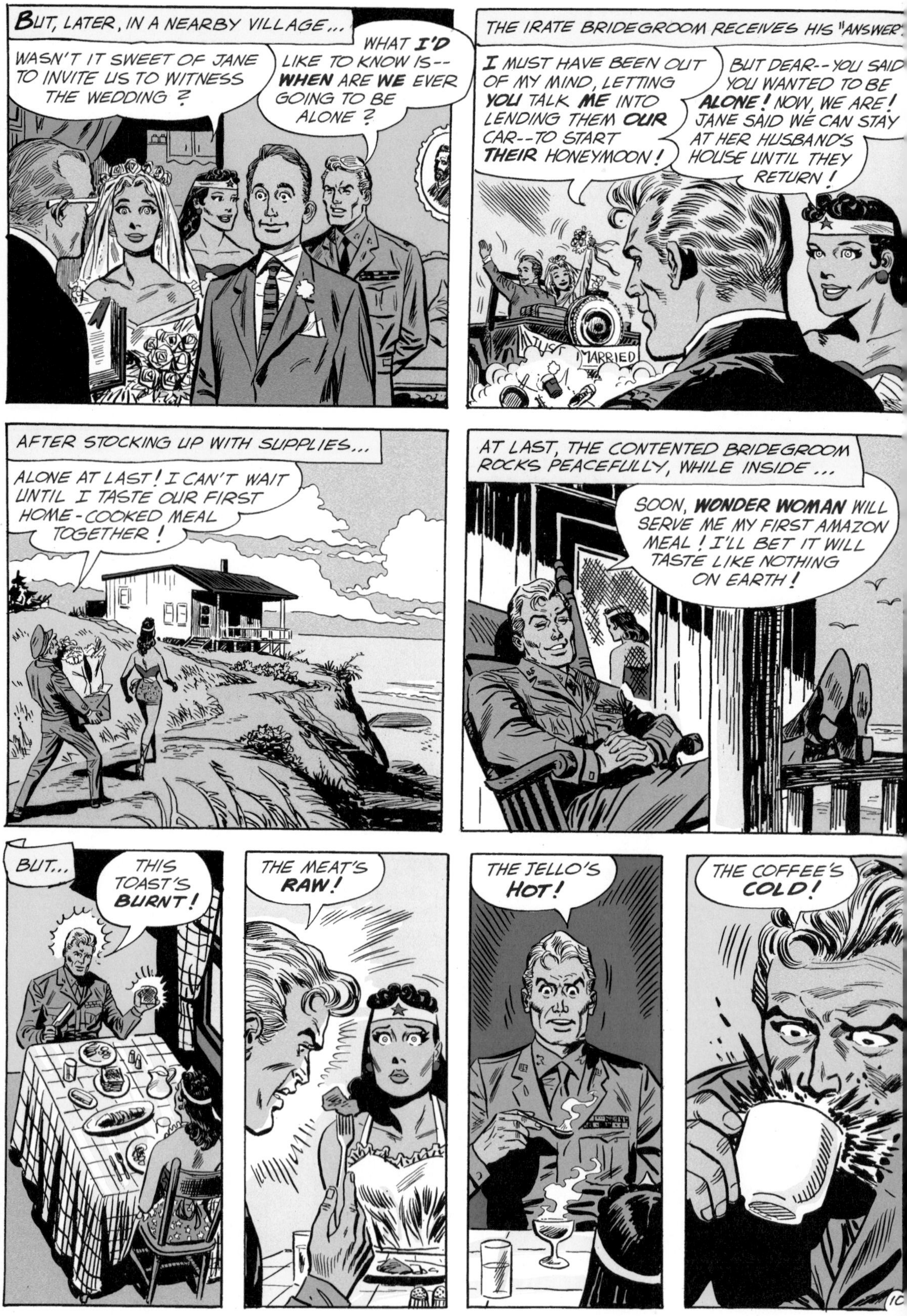
BUT, LATER, IN A NEARBY VILLAGE...
WASN'T IT SWEET OF JANE TO INVITE US TO WITNESS THE WEDDING ?
WHAT I'D LIKE TO KNOW IS-- WHEN ARE WE EVER GOING TO BE ALONE ?
THE IRATE BRIDEGROOM RECEIVES HIS "ANSWER"
I MUST HAVE BEEN OUT OF MY MIND, LETTING YOU TALK ME INTO LENDING THEM OUR CAR--TO START THEIR HONEYMOON !
BUT DEAR--YOU SAID YOU WANTED TO BE ALONE ! NOW, WE ARE ! JANE SAID WE CAN STAY AT HER HUSBAND'S HOUSE UNTIL THEY RETURN !
JUST MARRIED
AFTER STOCKING UP WITH SUPPLIES...
ALONE AT LAST ! I CAN'T WAIT UNTIL I TASTE OUR FIRST HOME-COOKED MEAL TOGETHER !
AT LAST, THE CONTENTED BRIDEGROOM ROCKS PEACEFULLY, WHILE INSIDE ...
SOON, WONDER WOMAN WILL SERVE ME MY FIRST AMAZON MEAL ! I'LL BET IT WILL TASTE LIKE NOTHING ON EARTH !
BUT...
THIS TOAST'S BURNT !
THE MEAT'S RAW !
THE JELLO'S HOT !
THE COFFEE'S COLD !
10

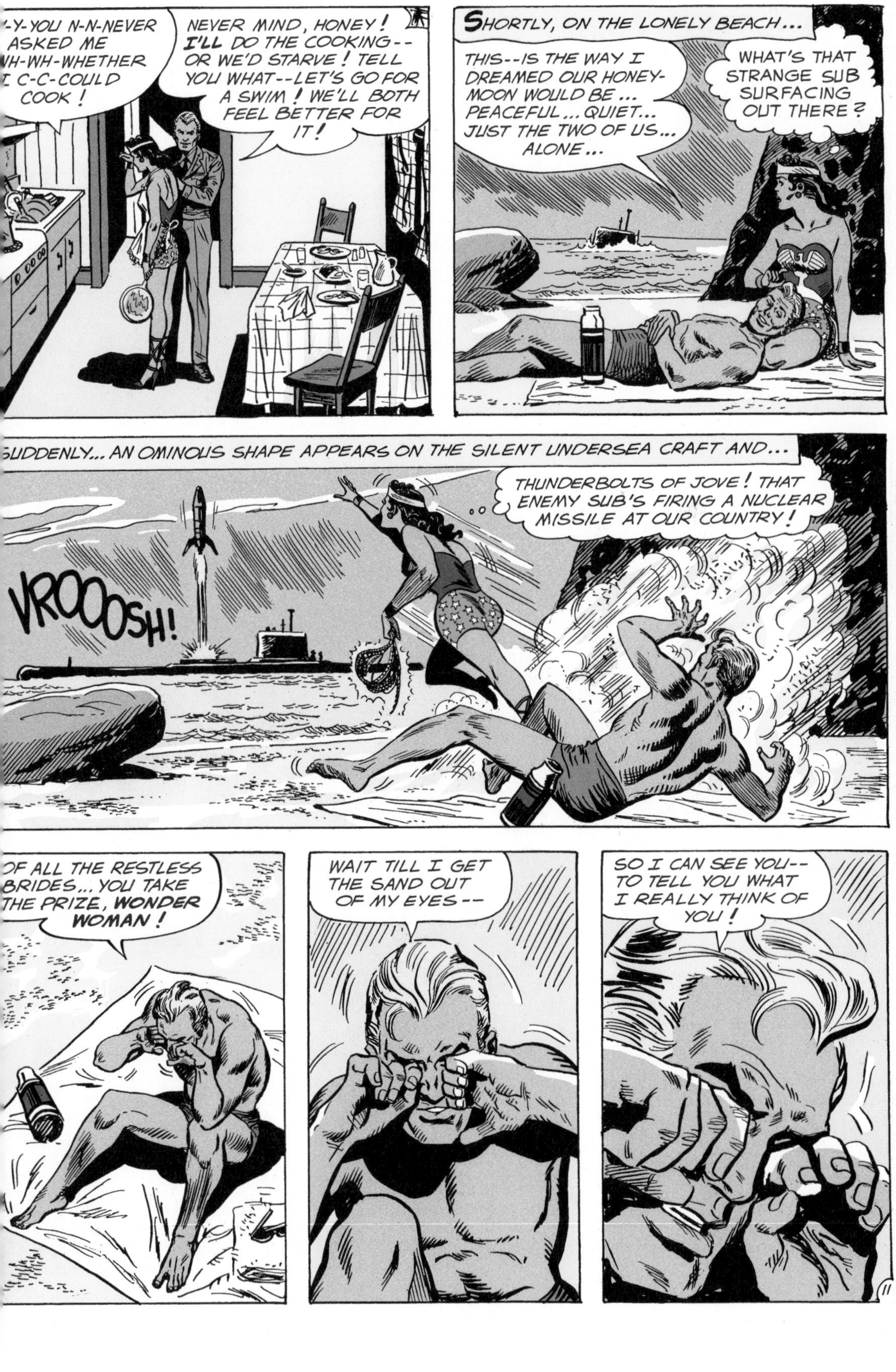
-Y-YOU N-N-NEVER ASKED ME WH-WH-WHETHER I C-C-COULD COOK!
NEVER MIND, HONEY! I'LL DO THE COOKING-- OR WE'D STARVE! TELL YOU WHAT--LET'S GO FOR A SWIM! WE'LL BOTH FEEL BETTER FOR IT!
SHORTLY, ON THE LONELY BEACH...
THIS--IS THE WAY I DREAMED OUR HONEYMOON WOULD BE... PEACEFUL... QUIET... JUST THE TWO OF US... ALONE...
WHAT'S THAT STRANGE SUB SURFACING OUT THERE?
SUDDENLY... AN OMINOUS SHAPE APPEARS ON THE SILENT UNDERSEA CRAFT AND...
THUNDERBOLTS OF JOVE! THAT ENEMY SUB'S FIRING A NUCLEAR MISSILE AT OUR COUNTRY!
VROOOOSH!
OF ALL THE RESTLESS BRIDES... YOU TAKE THE PRIZE, WONDER WOMAN!
WAIT TILL I GET THE SAND OUT OF MY EYES--
SO I CAN SEE YOU-- TO TELL YOU WHAT I REALLY THINK OF YOU!
11

BUT THE MIGHTY AMAZON, WITH A DESPERATE LEAP, AND A WHIP-LIKE CAST OF HER MAGIC LASSO..

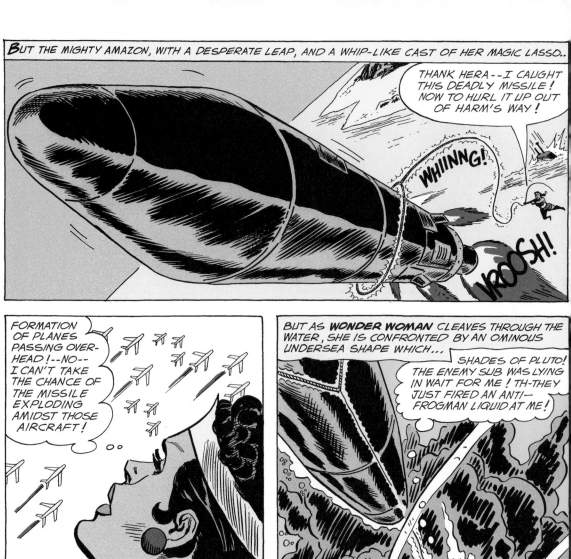

THANK HERA--I CAUGHT THIS DEADLY MISSILE! NOW TO HURL IT UP OUT OF HARM'S WAY!

WHIINNG!

VROOSH!

FORMATION OF PLANES PASSING OVER-HEAD!--NO-- I CAN'T TAKE THE CHANCE OF THE MISSILE EXPLODING AMIDST THOSE AIRCRAFT!

BUT AS **WONDER WOMAN** CLEAVES THROUGH THE WATER, SHE IS CONFRONTED BY AN OMINOUS UNDERSEA SHAPE WHICH...

SHADES OF PLUTO! THE ENEMY SUB WAS LYING IN WAIT FOR ME! TH-THEY JUST FIRED AN ANTI-FROGMAN LIQUID AT ME!

L-L-LOSING... CONSCIOUSNESS...

INSTANTLY...

I'D BETTER DIVE WITH THE MISSILE DEEP UNDER THE SURFACE--WHERE IT WON'T DO ANY HARM WHEN IT EXPLODES! AND THAT MUST BE-- ONLY MOMENTS AWAY!

WHOOSH!

12

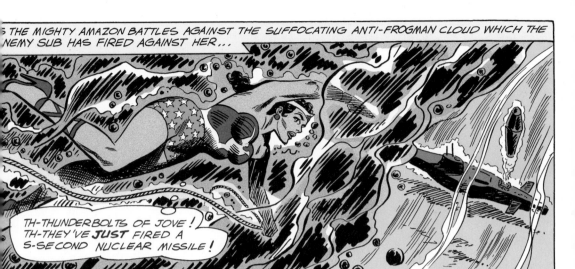

AS THE MIGHTY AMAZON BATTLES AGAINST THE SUFFOCATING ANTI-FROGMAN CLOUD WHICH THE ENEMY SUB HAS FIRED AGAINST HER...

TH-THUNDERBOLTS OF JOVE! TH-THEY'VE **JUST** FIRED A S-SECOND NUCLEAR MISSILE!

FROM DEEP WITHIN HER, **WONDER WOMAN** SUMMONS A LAST SURGE OF STRENGTH AND...

N-NOTHING LEFT TO STOP IT--BUT THE F-F-FIRST MISSILE I CAUGHT--!

KAAANG!

THE FORCE WITH WHICH THE AMAZON HURLED THE FIRST NUCLEAR MISSILE DRIVES IT INTO THE SECOND--AND TOGETHER--THE TWO HURTLE TOWARDS THE ENEMY SUB...

SWISHHH-SHHHH!

DESPERATELY, **WONDER WOMAN** HURLS HERSELF OUT OF THE WATER, AS BEHIND HER...

TH-THANK HERA-- THE PERIL HAS BEEN AVERTED! VIOLENCE HAS TURNED AGAINST ITS CREATOR! THE SUB DESTROYED!

VROOOM!

NOW TO GET BACK TO STEVE!

13

37

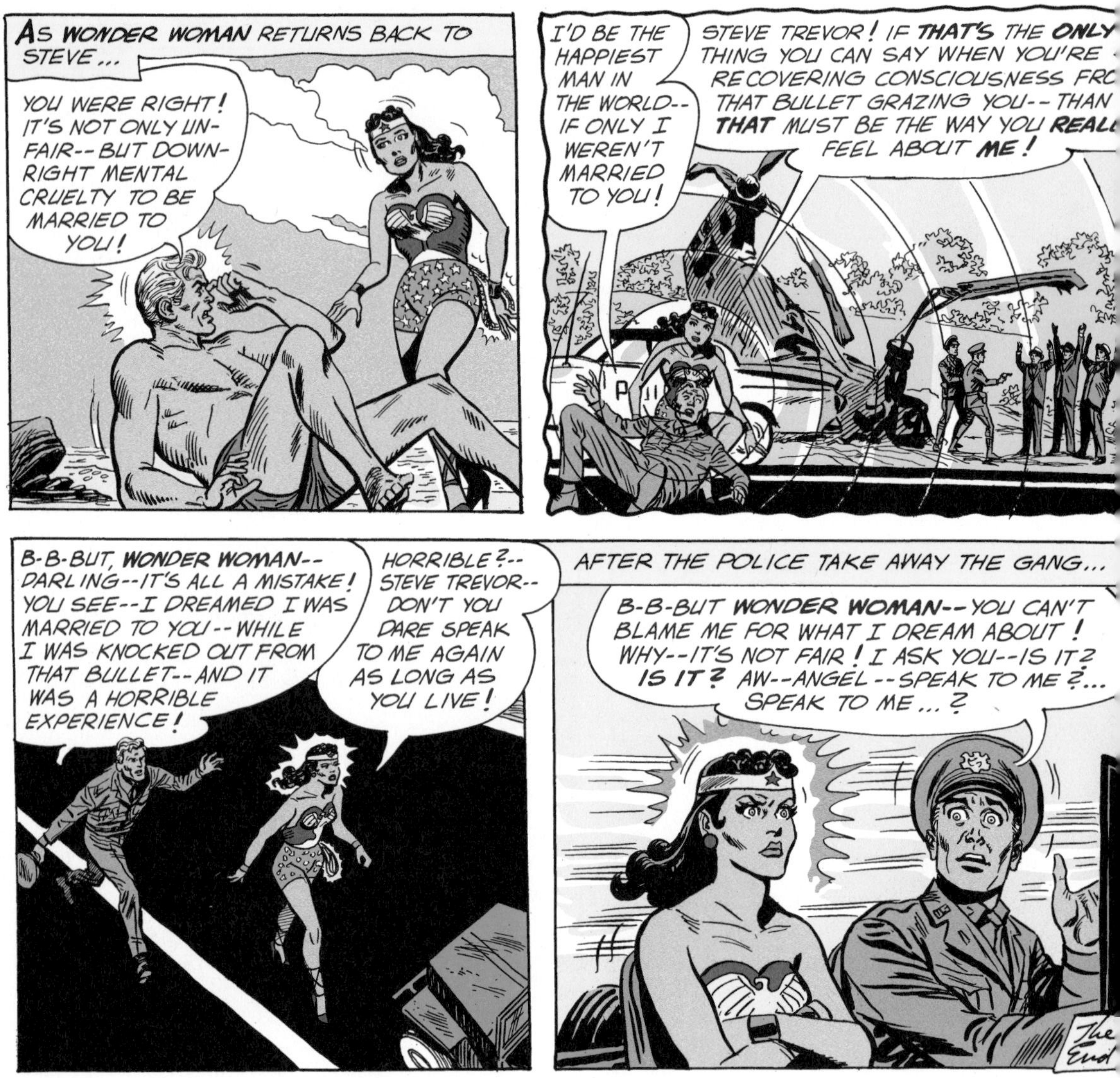
AS WONDER WOMAN RETURNS BACK TO STEVE...
YOU WERE RIGHT! IT'S NOT ONLY UNFAIR--BUT DOWNRIGHT MENTAL CRUELTY TO BE MARRIED TO YOU!
I'D BE THE HAPPIEST MAN IN THE WORLD--IF ONLY I WEREN'T MARRIED TO YOU!
STEVE TREVOR! IF THAT'S THE ONLY THING YOU CAN SAY WHEN YOU'RE RECOVERING CONSCIOUSNESS FRO THAT BULLET GRAZING YOU--THAN THAT MUST BE THE WAY YOU REALL FEEL ABOUT ME!
B-B-BUT, WONDER WOMAN--DARLING--IT'S ALL A MISTAKE! YOU SEE--I DREAMED I WAS MARRIED TO YOU--WHILE I WAS KNOCKED OUT FROM THAT BULLET--AND IT WAS A HORRIBLE EXPERIENCE!
HORRIBLE?--STEVE TREVOR--DON'T YOU DARE SPEAK TO ME AGAIN AS LONG AS YOU LIVE!
AFTER THE POLICE TAKE AWAY THE GANG...
B-B-BUT WONDER WOMAN--YOU CAN'T BLAME ME FOR WHAT I DREAM ABOUT! WHY--IT'S NOT FAIR! I ASK YOU--IS IT? IS IT? AW--ANGEL--SPEAK TO ME?... SPEAK TO ME...?
The End

WONDER WOMAN

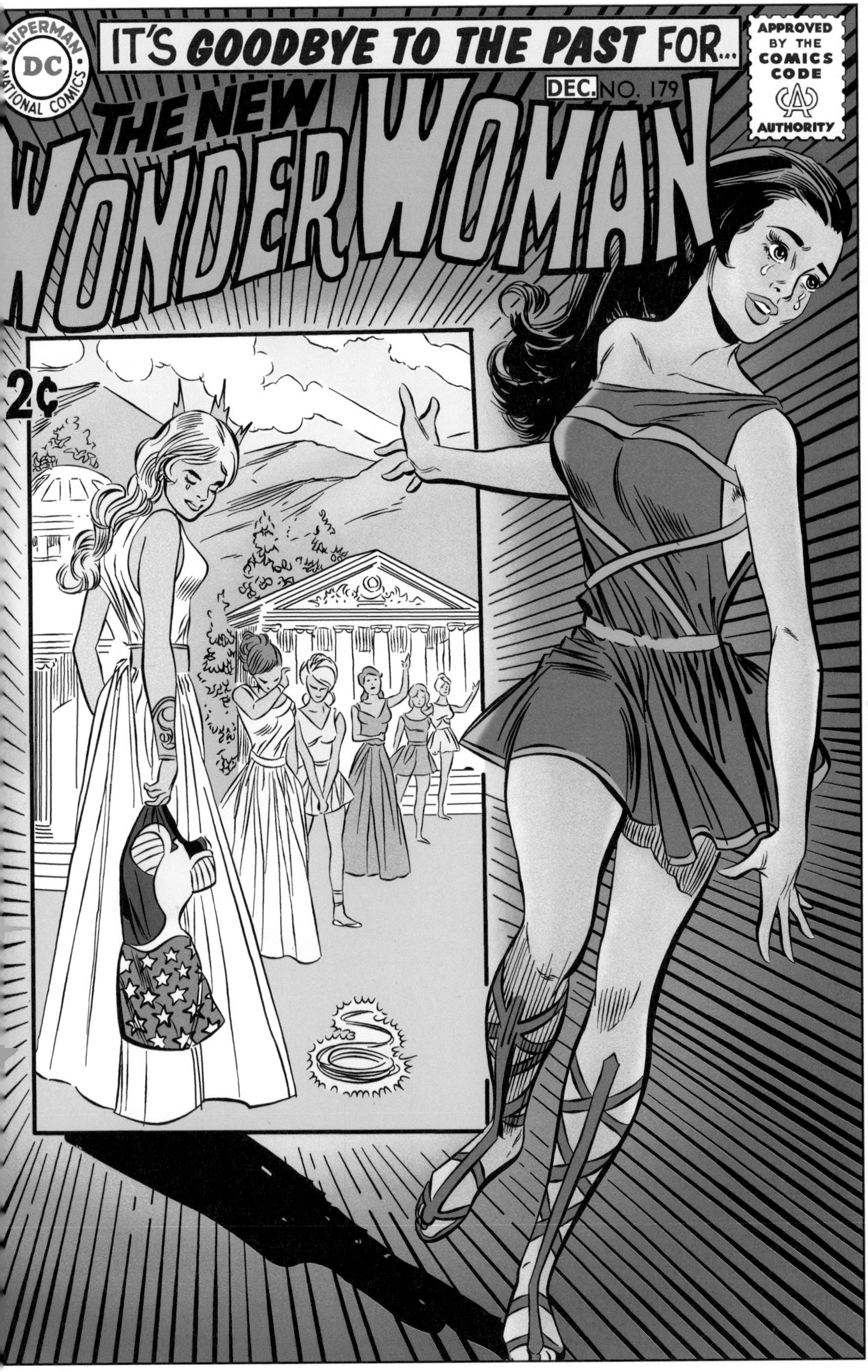
SUPERMAN
DC
NATIONAL COMICS
IT'S GOODBYE TO THE PAST FOR...
APPROVED BY THE COMICS CODE AUTHORITY
DEC. NO. 179
THE NEW
WONDER WOMAN
2¢

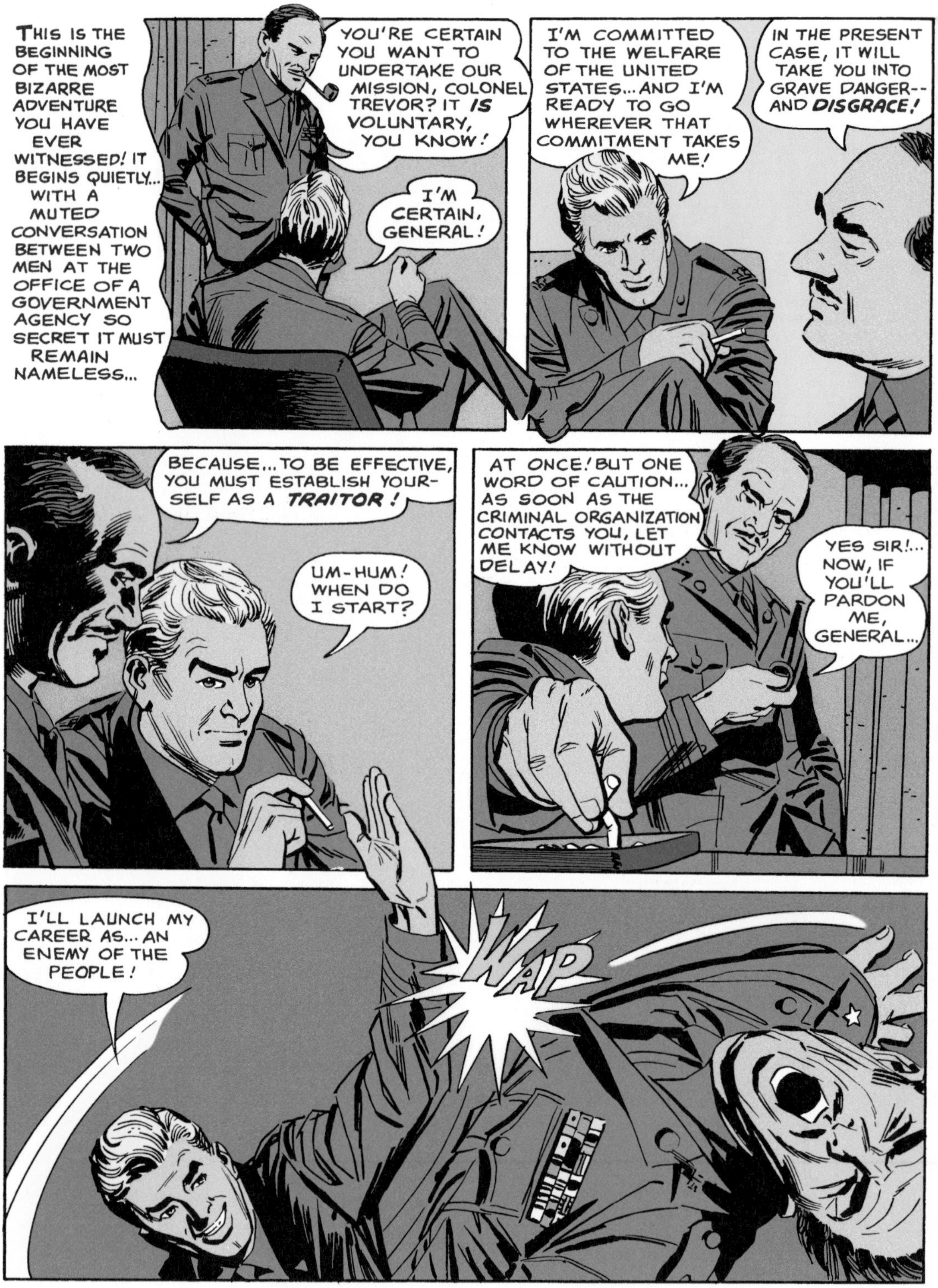
THIS IS THE BEGINNING OF THE MOST BIZARRE ADVENTURE YOU HAVE EVER WITNESSED! IT BEGINS QUIETLY... WITH A MUTED CONVERSATION BETWEEN TWO MEN AT THE OFFICE OF A GOVERNMENT AGENCY SO SECRET IT MUST REMAIN NAMELESS...
YOU'RE CERTAIN YOU WANT TO UNDERTAKE OUR MISSION, COLONEL TREVOR? IT IS VOLUNTARY, YOU KNOW!
I'M CERTAIN, GENERAL!
I'M COMMITTED TO THE WELFARE OF THE UNITED STATES...AND I'M READY TO GO WHEREVER THAT COMMITMENT TAKES ME!
IN THE PRESENT CASE, IT WILL TAKE YOU INTO GRAVE DANGER-- AND DISGRACE!
BECAUSE...TO BE EFFECTIVE, YOU MUST ESTABLISH YOURSELF AS A TRAITOR!
UM-HUM! WHEN DO I START?
AT ONCE! BUT ONE WORD OF CAUTION... AS SOON AS THE CRIMINAL ORGANIZATION CONTACTS YOU, LET ME KNOW WITHOUT DELAY!
YES SIR!... NOW, IF YOU'LL PARDON ME, GENERAL...
I'LL LAUNCH MY CAREER AS... AN ENEMY OF THE PEOPLE!
WAP

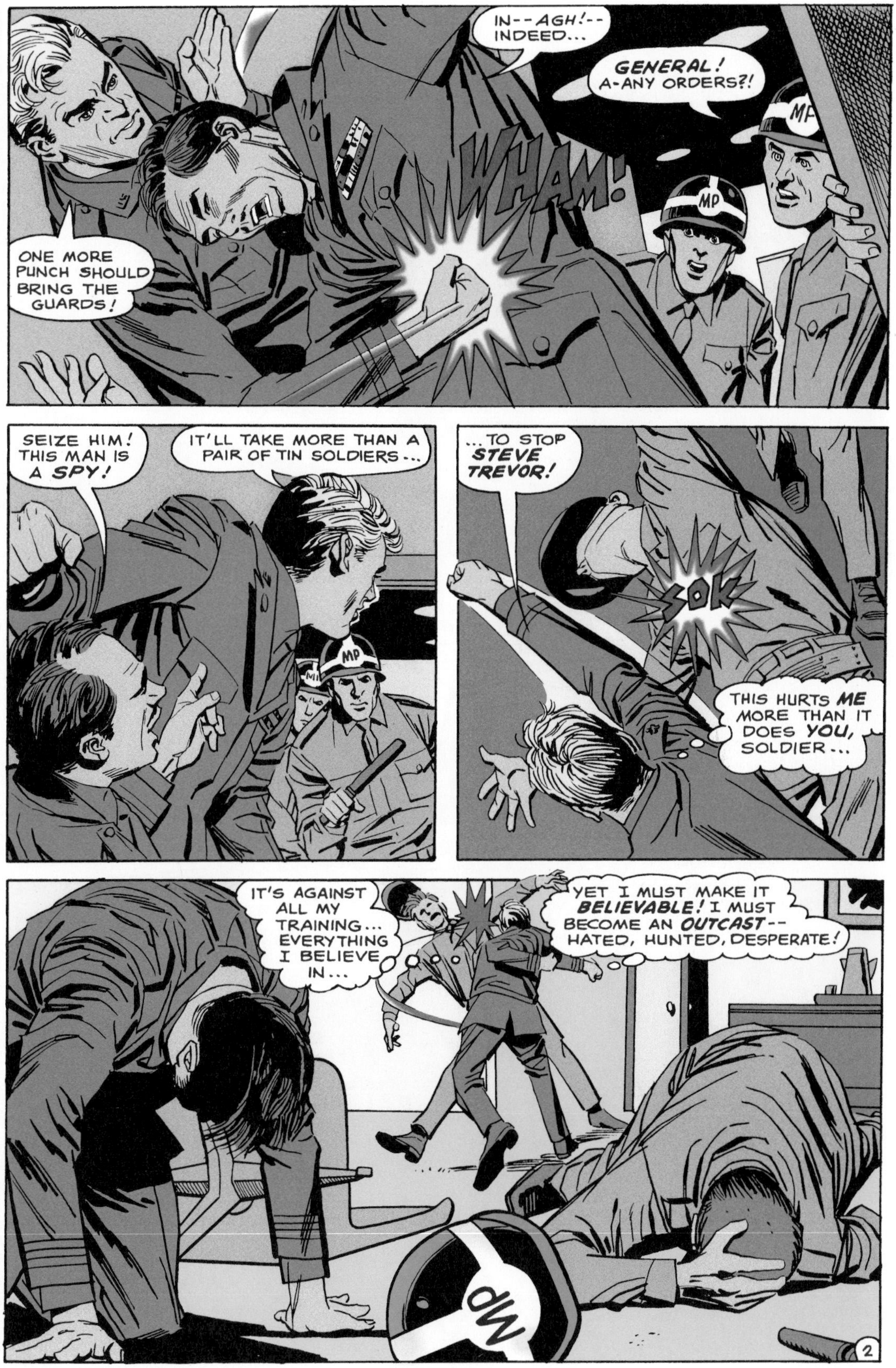

IN--AGH!--
INDEED...
GENERAL!
A-ANY ORDERS?!
WHAM!
ONE MORE PUNCH SHOULD BRING THE GUARDS!
SEIZE HIM! THIS MAN IS A SPY!
IT'LL TAKE MORE THAN A PAIR OF TIN SOLDIERS--...
...TO STOP STEVE TREVOR!
SOK
THIS HURTS ME MORE THAN IT DOES YOU, SOLDIER...
IT'S AGAINST ALL MY TRAINING... EVERYTHING I BELIEVE IN...
YET I MUST MAKE IT BELIEVABLE! I MUST BECOME AN OUTCAST--HATED, HUNTED, DESPERATE!
2

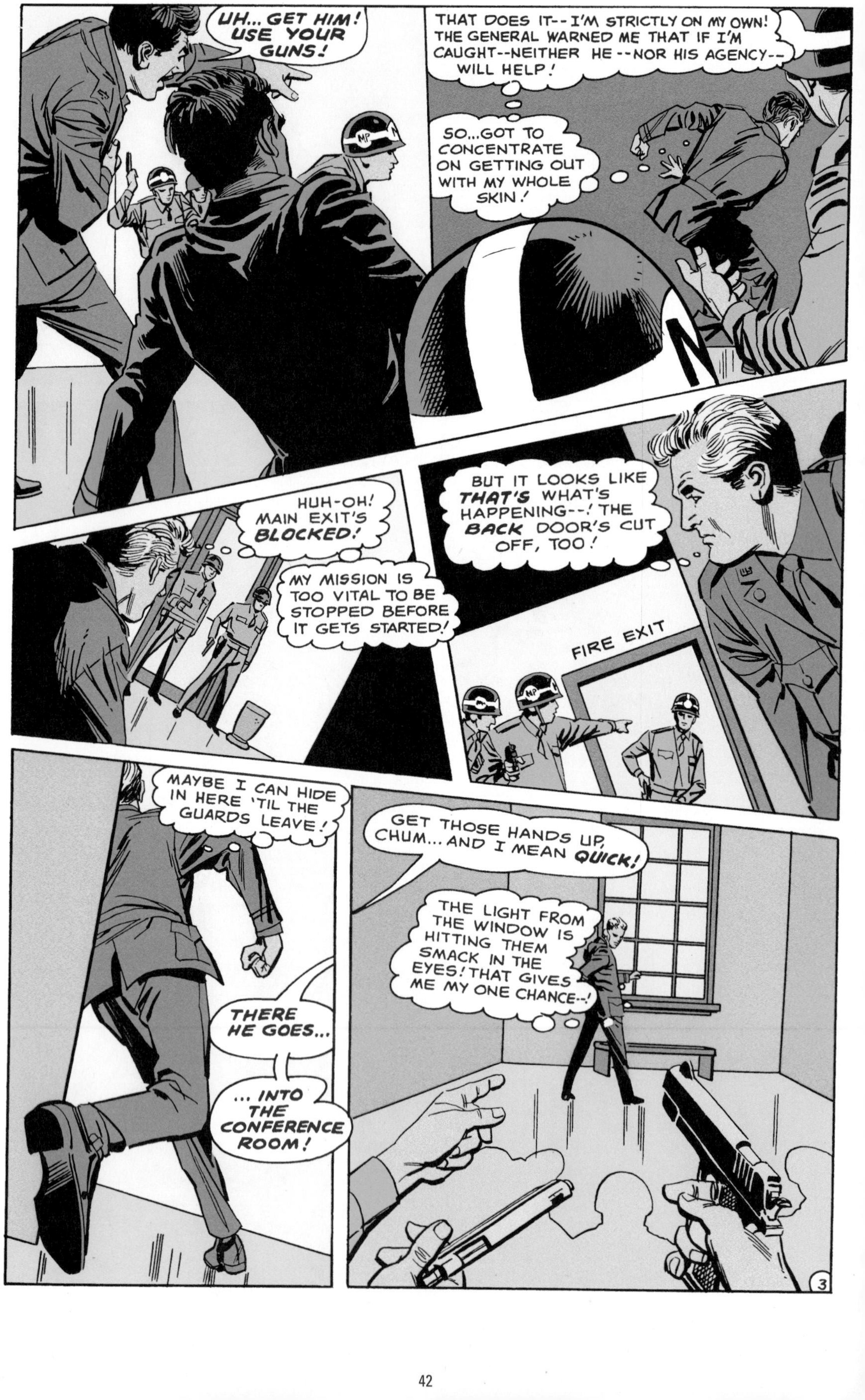
UH... GET HIM! USE YOUR GUNS!
THAT DOES IT-- I'M STRICTLY ON MY OWN! THE GENERAL WARNED ME THAT IF I'M CAUGHT--NEITHER HE --NOR HIS AGENCY-- WILL HELP!
SO...GOT TO CONCENTRATE ON GETTING OUT WITH MY WHOLE SKIN!
HUH-OH! MAIN EXIT'S BLOCKED!
MY MISSION IS TOO VITAL TO BE STOPPED BEFORE IT GETS STARTED!
BUT IT LOOKS LIKE THAT'S WHAT'S HAPPENING--! THE BACK DOOR'S CUT OFF, TOO!
FIRE EXIT
MAYBE I CAN HIDE IN HERE 'TIL THE GUARDS LEAVE!
THERE HE GOES...
... INTO THE CONFERENCE ROOM!
GET THOSE HANDS UP, CHUM... AND I MEAN QUICK!
THE LIGHT FROM THE WINDOW IS HITTING THEM SMACK IN THE EYES! THAT GIVES ME MY ONE CHANCE--!
3

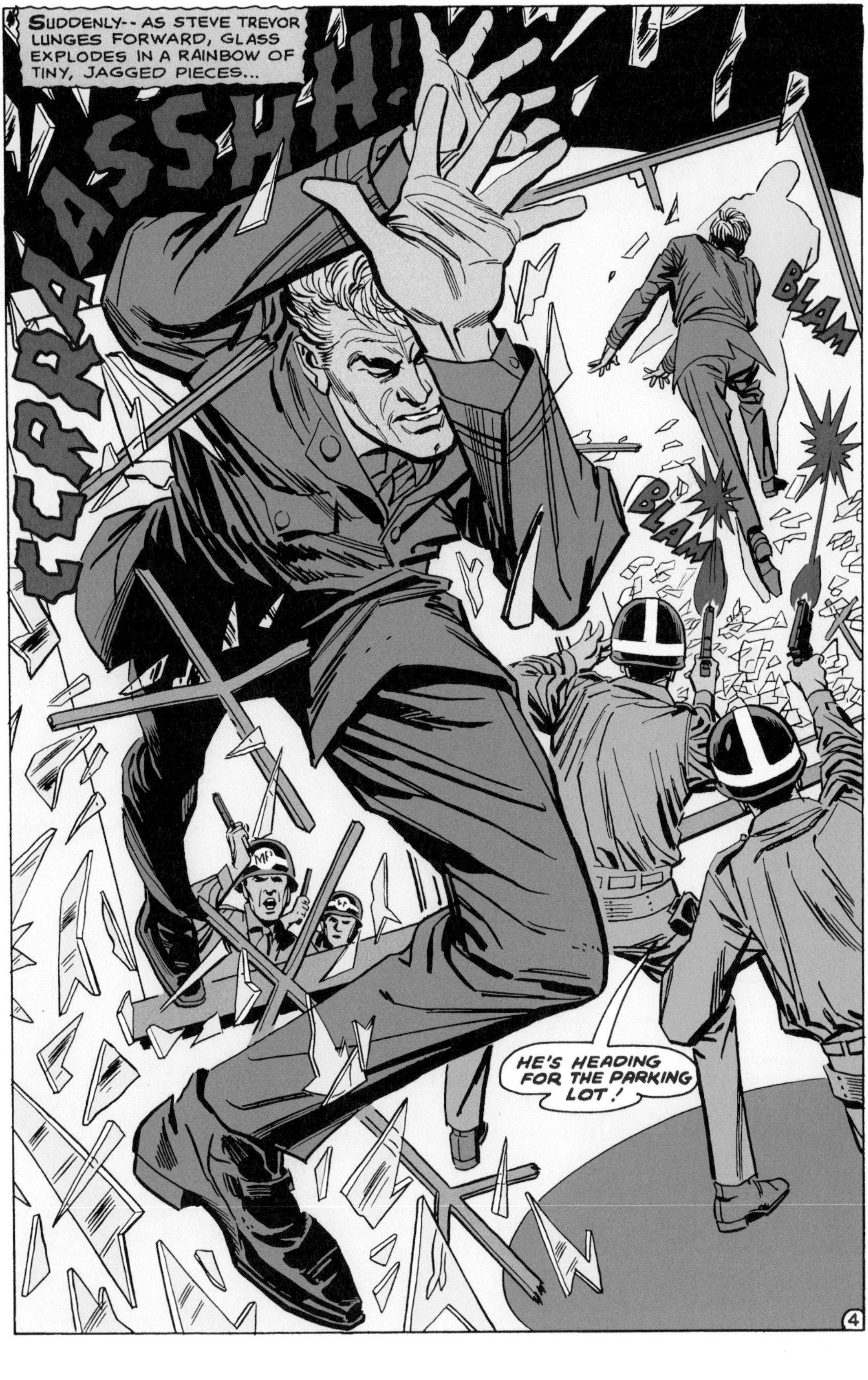
SUDDENLY-- AS STEVE TREVOR LUNGES FORWARD, GLASS EXPLODES IN A RAINBOW OF TINY, JAGGED PIECES...
CCRRAASSHH!
BLAM
BLAM
HE'S HEADING FOR THE PARKING LOT!
4

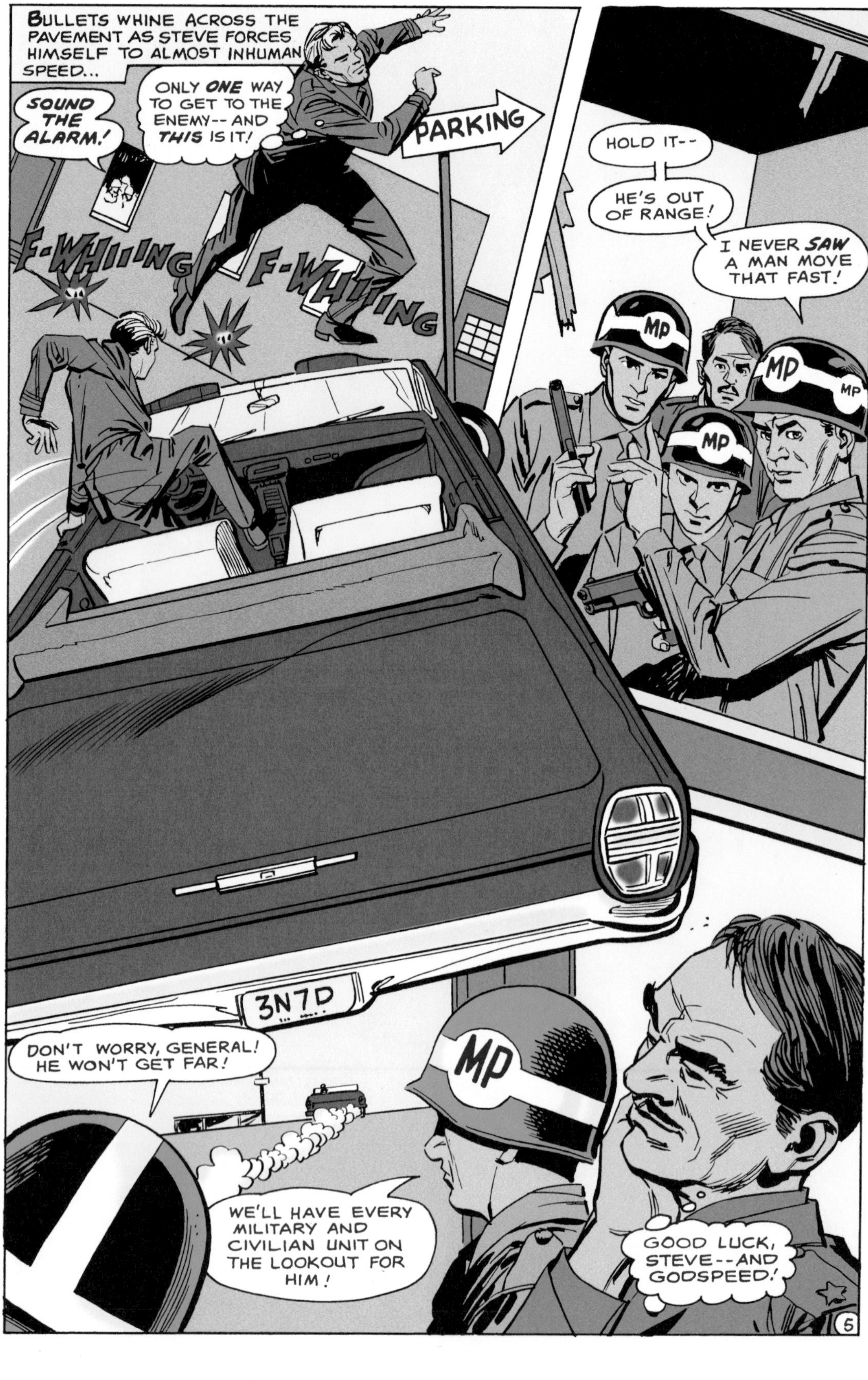
BULLETS WHINE ACROSS THE PAVEMENT AS STEVE FORCES HIMSELF TO ALMOST INHUMAN SPEED...
SOUND THE ALARM!
ONLY ONE WAY TO GET TO THE ENEMY-- AND THIS IS IT!
PARKING
F-WHIIING
F-WHIIING
HOLD IT--
HE'S OUT OF RANGE!
I NEVER SAW A MAN MOVE THAT FAST!
MP
MP
MP
MP
3N7D
DON'T WORRY, GENERAL! HE WON'T GET FAR!
MP
WE'LL HAVE EVERY MILITARY AND CIVILIAN UNIT ON THE LOOKOUT FOR HIM!
GOOD LUCK, STEVE--AND GODSPEED!
5

RETURN TO YOUR POSTS, MEN!

SO FAR, SO GOOD! COLONEL TREVOR, THE MOST LOYAL OFFICER I'VE EVER KNOWN, IS BRANDED A TRAITOR!

MP

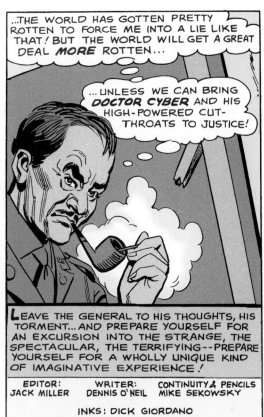

...THE WORLD HAS GOTTEN PRETTY ROTTEN TO FORCE ME INTO A LIE LIKE THAT! BUT THE WORLD WILL GET A GREAT DEAL *MORE* ROTTEN...

...UNLESS WE CAN BRING *DOCTOR CYBER* AND HIS HIGH-POWERED CUT-THROATS TO JUSTICE!

LEAVE THE GENERAL TO HIS THOUGHTS, HIS TORMENT...AND PREPARE YOURSELF FOR AN EXCURSION INTO THE STRANGE, THE SPECTACULAR, THE TERRIFYING--PREPARE YOURSELF FOR A WHOLLY UNIQUE KIND OF IMAGINATIVE EXPERIENCE!

EDITOR: JACK MILLER   WRITER: DENNIS O'NEIL   CONTINUITY & PENCILS MIKE SEKOWSKY

INKS: DICK GIORDANO

WONDER WOMAN

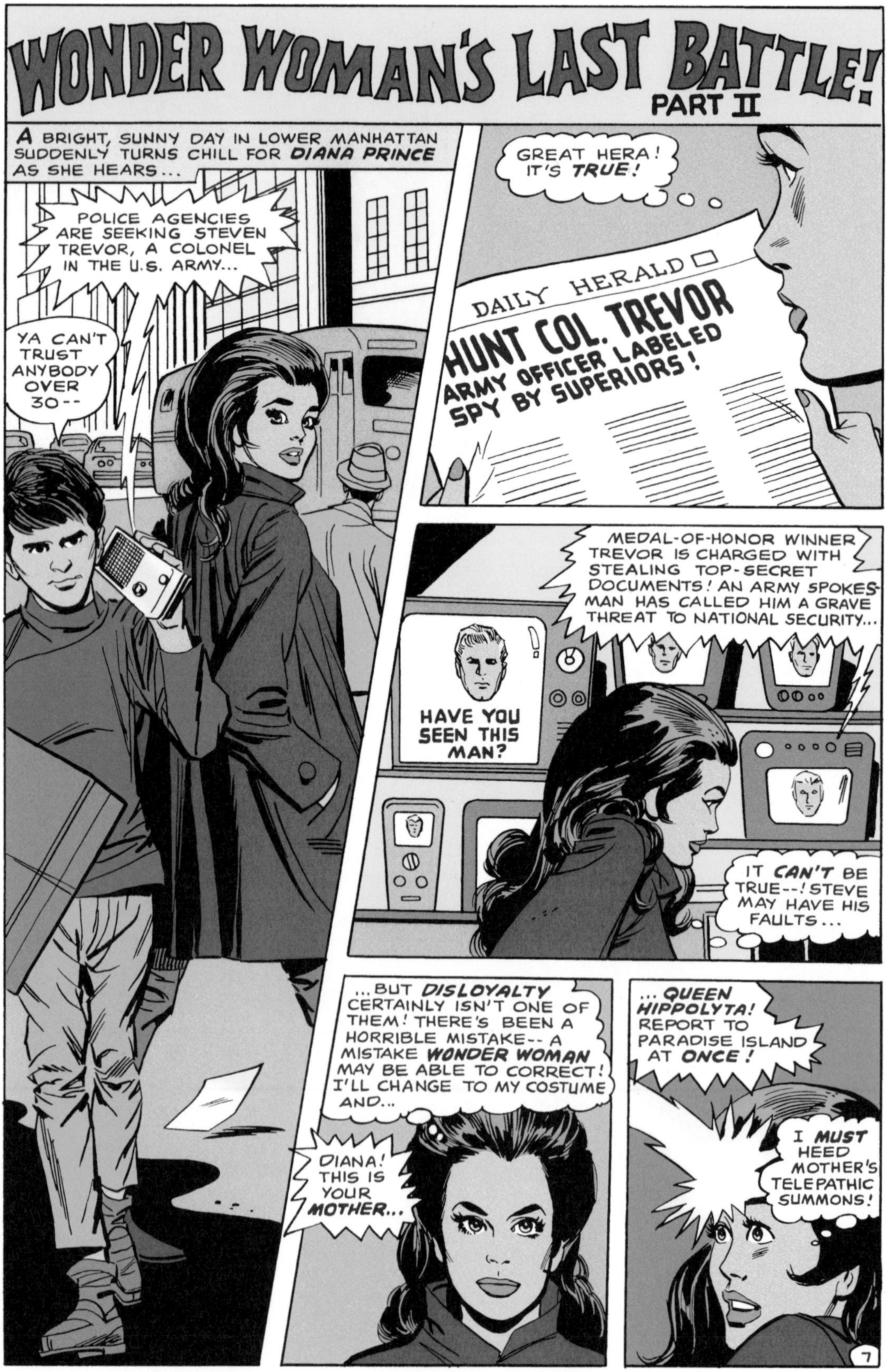
WONDER WOMAN'S LAST BATTLE! PART II
A BRIGHT, SUNNY DAY IN LOWER MANHATTAN SUDDENLY TURNS CHILL FOR DIANA PRINCE AS SHE HEARS...
POLICE AGENCIES ARE SEEKING STEVEN TREVOR, A COLONEL IN THE U.S. ARMY...
YA CAN'T TRUST ANYBODY OVER 30--
GREAT HERA! IT'S TRUE!
DAILY HERALD
HUNT COL. TREVOR
ARMY OFFICER LABELED SPY BY SUPERIORS!
MEDAL-OF-HONOR WINNER TREVOR IS CHARGED WITH STEALING TOP-SECRET DOCUMENTS! AN ARMY SPOKESMAN HAS CALLED HIM A GRAVE THREAT TO NATIONAL SECURITY...
HAVE YOU SEEN THIS MAN?
IT CAN'T BE TRUE--! STEVE MAY HAVE HIS FAULTS...
...BUT DISLOYALTY CERTAINLY ISN'T ONE OF THEM! THERE'S BEEN A HORRIBLE MISTAKE-- A MISTAKE WONDER WOMAN MAY BE ABLE TO CORRECT! I'LL CHANGE TO MY COSTUME AND...
DIANA! THIS IS YOUR MOTHER...
...QUEEN HIPPOLYTA! REPORT TO PARADISE ISLAND AT ONCE!
I MUST HEED MOTHER'S TELEPATHIC SUMMONS!
7

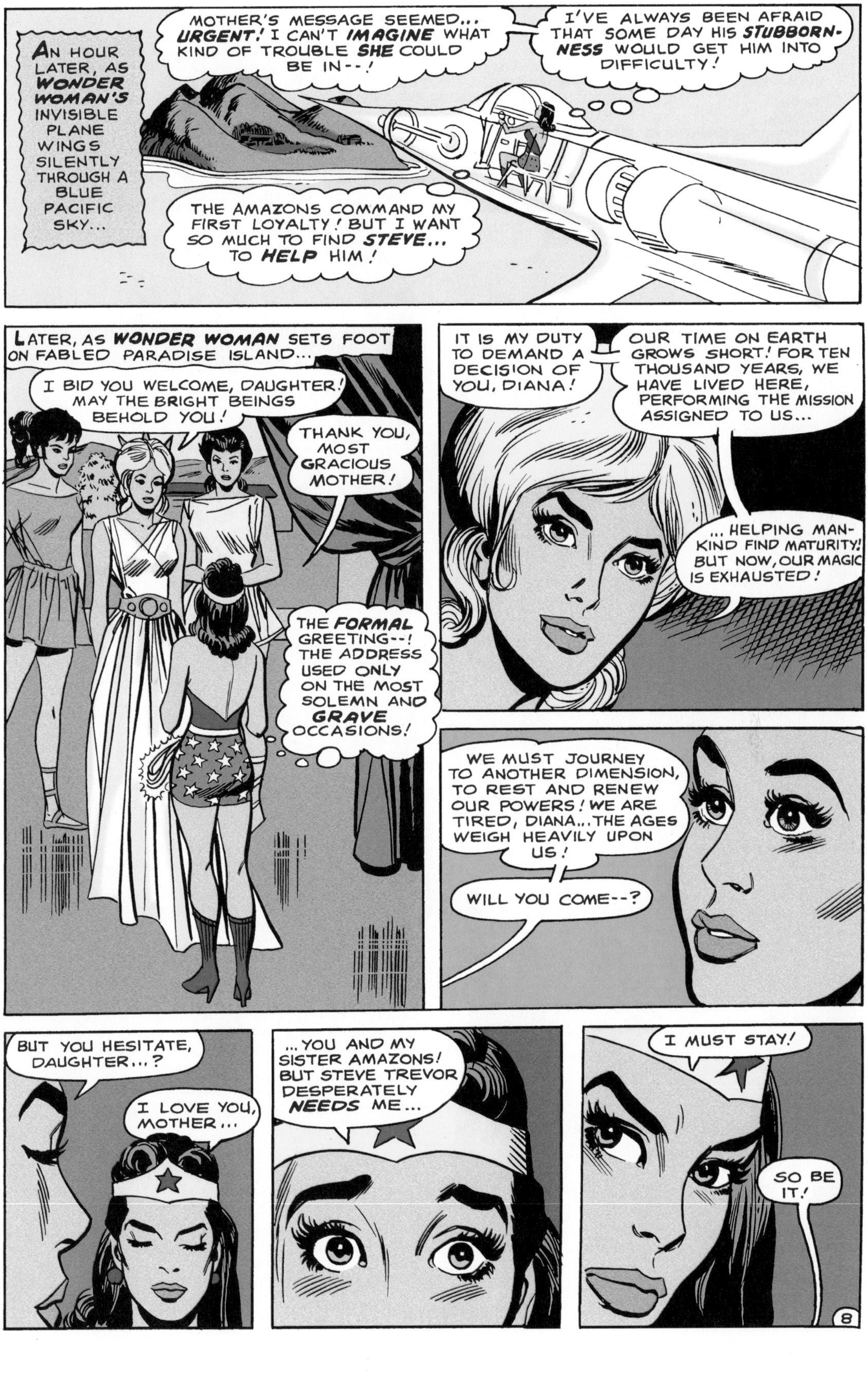

AN HOUR LATER, AS WONDER WOMAN'S INVISIBLE PLANE WINGS SILENTLY THROUGH A BLUE PACIFIC SKY...
MOTHER'S MESSAGE SEEMED... URGENT! I CAN'T IMAGINE WHAT KIND OF TROUBLE SHE COULD BE IN--!
I'VE ALWAYS BEEN AFRAID THAT SOME DAY HIS STUBBORNNESS WOULD GET HIM INTO DIFFICULTY!
THE AMAZONS COMMAND MY FIRST LOYALTY! BUT I WANT SO MUCH TO FIND STEVE... TO HELP HIM!
LATER, AS WONDER WOMAN SETS FOOT ON FABLED PARADISE ISLAND...
I BID YOU WELCOME, DAUGHTER! MAY THE BRIGHT BEINGS BEHOLD YOU!
THANK YOU, MOST GRACIOUS MOTHER!
THE FORMAL GREETING--! THE ADDRESS USED ONLY ON THE MOST SOLEMN AND GRAVE OCCASIONS!
IT IS MY DUTY TO DEMAND A DECISION OF YOU, DIANA!
OUR TIME ON EARTH GROWS SHORT! FOR TEN THOUSAND YEARS, WE HAVE LIVED HERE, PERFORMING THE MISSION ASSIGNED TO US...
... HELPING MANKIND FIND MATURITY! BUT NOW, OUR MAGIC IS EXHAUSTED!
WE MUST JOURNEY TO ANOTHER DIMENSION, TO REST AND RENEW OUR POWERS! WE ARE TIRED, DIANA... THE AGES WEIGH HEAVILY UPON US!
WILL YOU COME--?
BUT YOU HESITATE, DAUGHTER...?
I LOVE YOU, MOTHER...
...YOU AND MY SISTER AMAZONS! BUT STEVE TREVOR DESPERATELY NEEDS ME...
I MUST STAY!
SO BE IT!
8

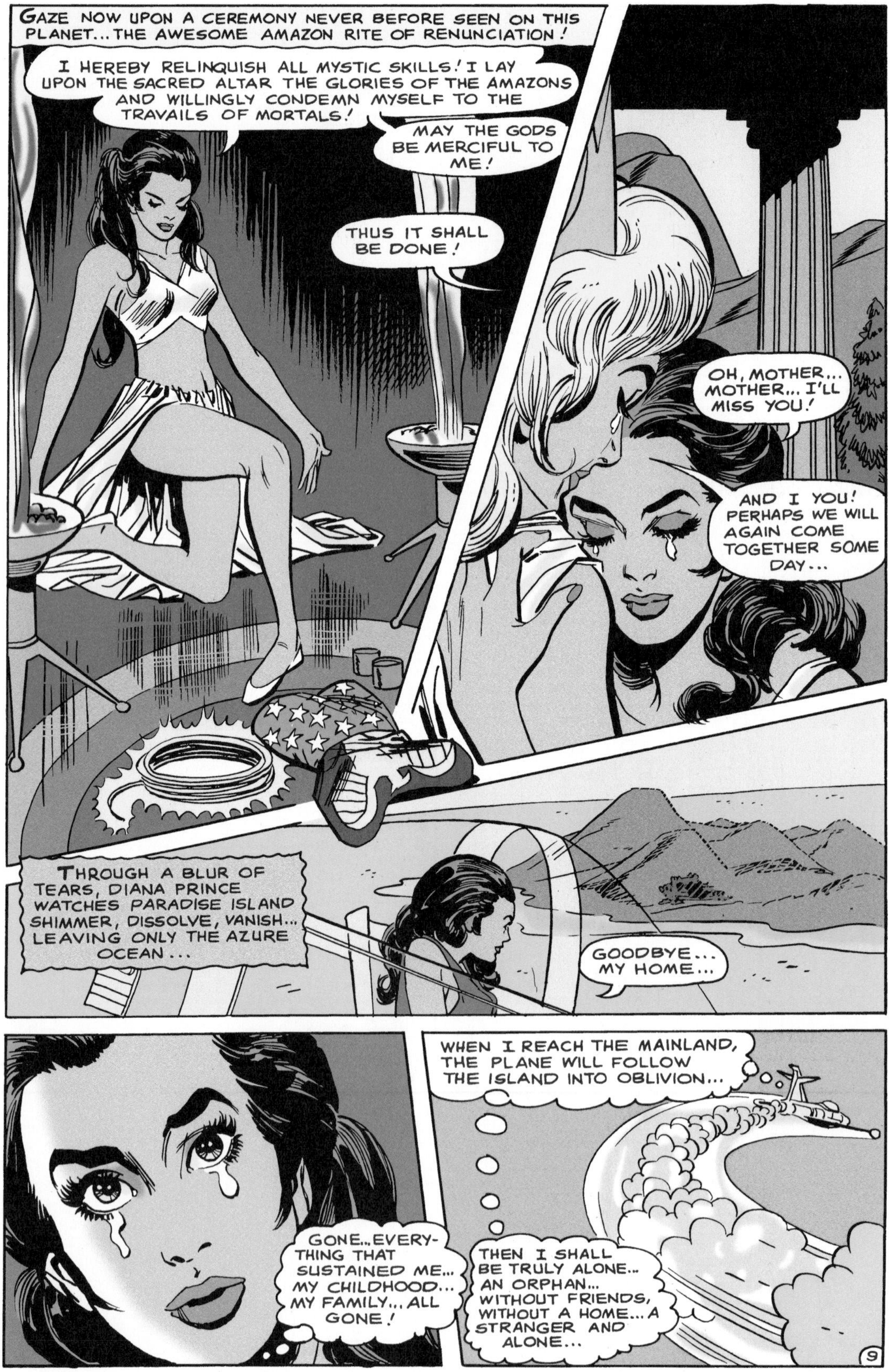
GAZE NOW UPON A CEREMONY NEVER BEFORE SEEN ON THIS PLANET... THE AWESOME AMAZON RITE OF RENUNCIATION!
I HEREBY RELINQUISH ALL MYSTIC SKILLS! I LAY UPON THE SACRED ALTAR THE GLORIES OF THE AMAZONS AND WILLINGLY CONDEMN MYSELF TO THE TRAVAILS OF MORTALS!
MAY THE GODS BE MERCIFUL TO ME!
THUS IT SHALL BE DONE!
OH, MOTHER... MOTHER... I'LL MISS YOU!
AND I YOU! PERHAPS WE WILL AGAIN COME TOGETHER SOME DAY...
THROUGH A BLUR OF TEARS, DIANA PRINCE WATCHES PARADISE ISLAND SHIMMER, DISSOLVE, VANISH... LEAVING ONLY THE AZURE OCEAN...
GOODBYE... MY HOME...
GONE... EVERYTHING THAT SUSTAINED ME... MY CHILDHOOD... MY FAMILY... ALL GONE!
WHEN I REACH THE MAINLAND, THE PLANE WILL FOLLOW THE ISLAND INTO OBLIVION...
THEN I SHALL BE TRULY ALONE... AN ORPHAN... WITHOUT FRIENDS, WITHOUT A HOME... A STRANGER AND ALONE...
9

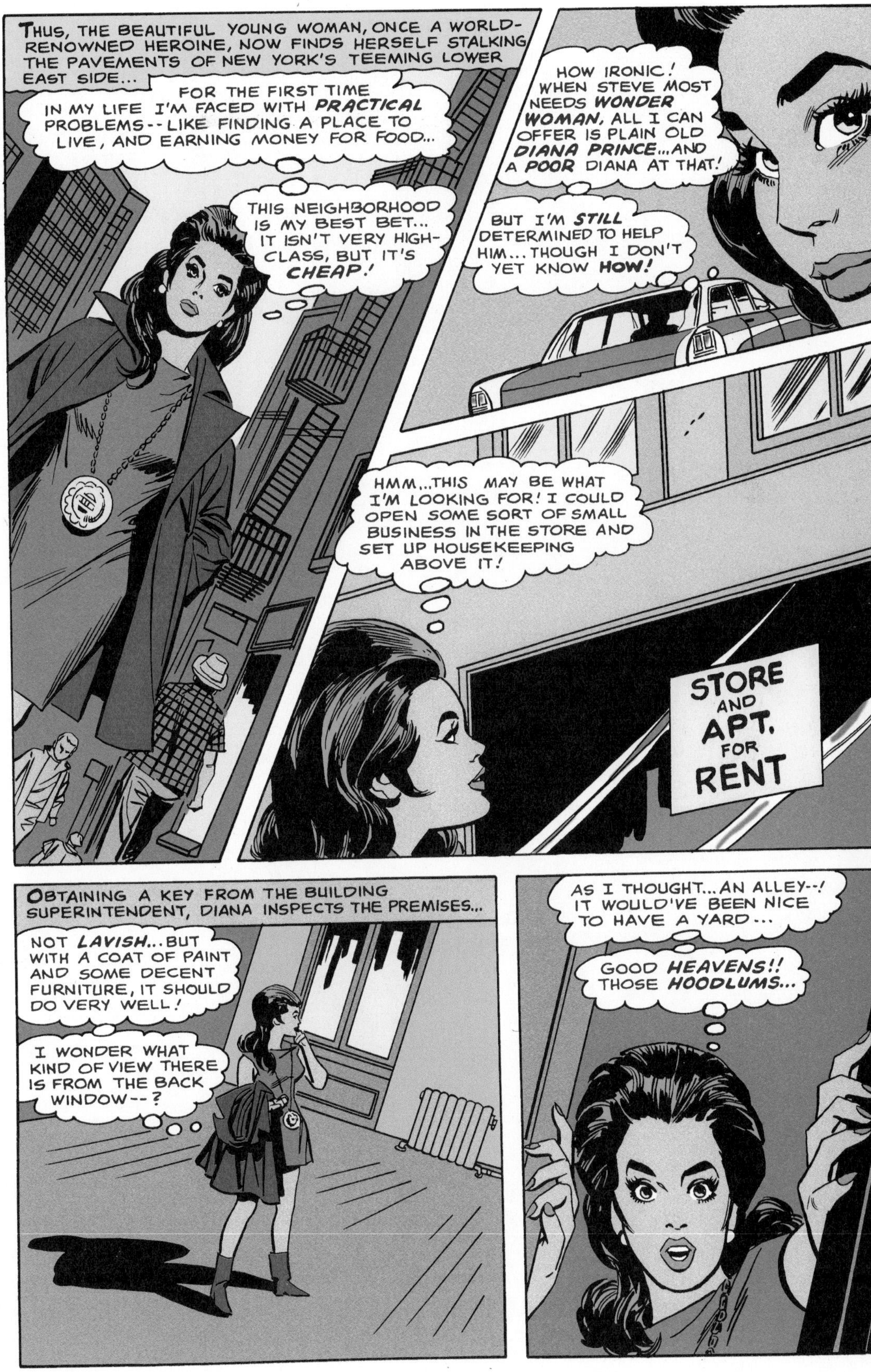
THUS, THE BEAUTIFUL YOUNG WOMAN, ONCE A WORLD-RENOWNED HEROINE, NOW FINDS HERSELF STALKING THE PAVEMENTS OF NEW YORK'S TEEMING LOWER EAST SIDE...
FOR THE FIRST TIME IN MY LIFE I'M FACED WITH PRACTICAL PROBLEMS--LIKE FINDING A PLACE TO LIVE, AND EARNING MONEY FOR FOOD...
THIS NEIGHBORHOOD IS MY BEST BET... IT ISN'T VERY HIGH-CLASS, BUT IT'S CHEAP!
HOW IRONIC! WHEN STEVE MOST NEEDS WONDER WOMAN, ALL I CAN OFFER IS PLAIN OLD DIANA PRINCE...AND A POOR DIANA AT THAT!
BUT I'M STILL DETERMINED TO HELP HIM...THOUGH I DON'T YET KNOW HOW!
HMM...THIS MAY BE WHAT I'M LOOKING FOR! I COULD OPEN SOME SORT OF SMALL BUSINESS IN THE STORE AND SET UP HOUSEKEEPING ABOVE IT!
STORE AND APT. FOR RENT
OBTAINING A KEY FROM THE BUILDING SUPERINTENDENT, DIANA INSPECTS THE PREMISES...
NOT LAVISH...BUT WITH A COAT OF PAINT AND SOME DECENT FURNITURE, IT SHOULD DO VERY WELL!
I WONDER WHAT KIND OF VIEW THERE IS FROM THE BACK WINDOW--?
AS I THOUGHT...AN ALLEY--! IT WOULD'VE BEEN NICE TO HAVE A YARD...
GOOD HEAVENS!! THOSE HOODLUMS...
10

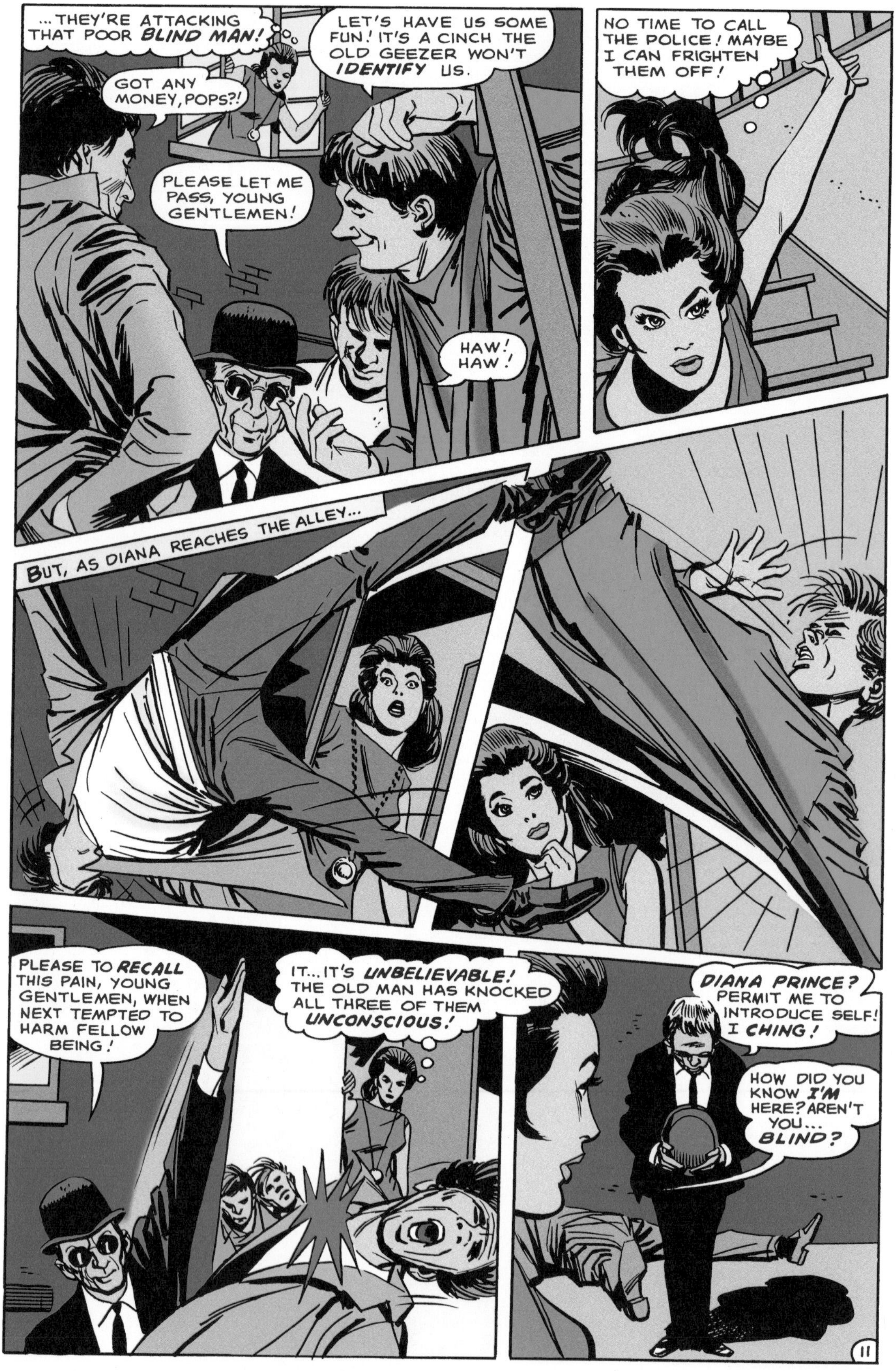
...THEY'RE ATTACKING THAT POOR BLIND MAN!
LET'S HAVE US SOME FUN! IT'S A CINCH THE OLD GEEZER WON'T IDENTIFY US.
GOT ANY MONEY, POPS?!
PLEASE LET ME PASS, YOUNG GENTLEMEN!
HAW! HAW!
NO TIME TO CALL THE POLICE! MAYBE I CAN FRIGHTEN THEM OFF!
BUT, AS DIANA REACHES THE ALLEY...
PLEASE TO RECALL THIS PAIN, YOUNG GENTLEMEN, WHEN NEXT TEMPTED TO HARM FELLOW BEING!
IT...IT'S UNBELIEVABLE! THE OLD MAN HAS KNOCKED ALL THREE OF THEM UNCONSCIOUS!
DIANA PRINCE? PERMIT ME TO INTRODUCE SELF! I CHING!
HOW DID YOU KNOW I'M HERE? AREN'T YOU... BLIND?
11

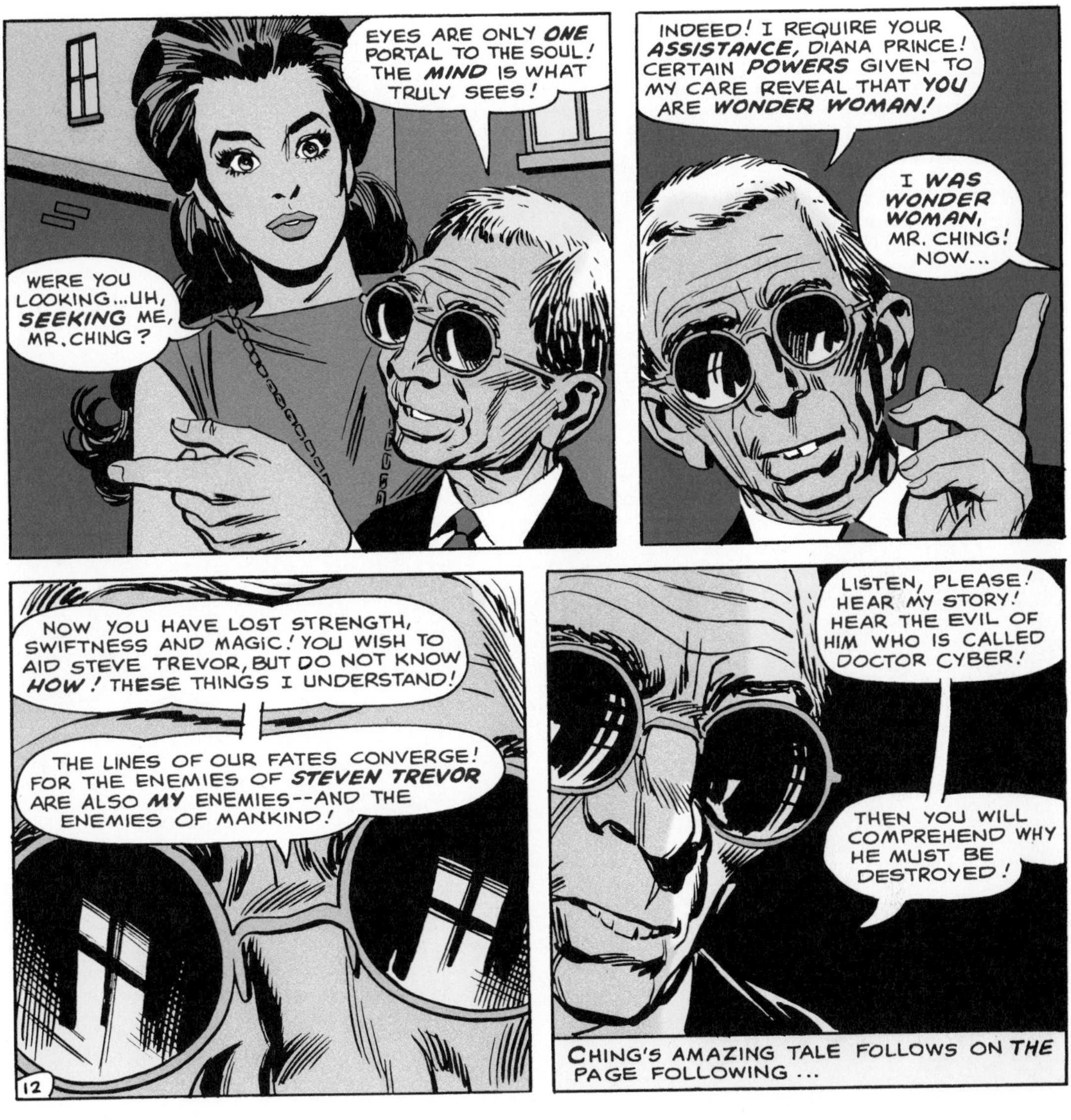

WERE YOU LOOKING...UH, SEEKING ME, MR. CHING?
EYES ARE ONLY ONE PORTAL TO THE SOUL! THE MIND IS WHAT TRULY SEES!
INDEED! I REQUIRE YOUR ASSISTANCE, DIANA PRINCE! CERTAIN POWERS GIVEN TO MY CARE REVEAL THAT YOU ARE WONDER WOMAN!
I WAS WONDER WOMAN, MR. CHING! NOW...
NOW YOU HAVE LOST STRENGTH, SWIFTNESS AND MAGIC! YOU WISH TO AID STEVE TREVOR, BUT DO NOT KNOW HOW! THESE THINGS I UNDERSTAND!
THE LINES OF OUR FATES CONVERGE! FOR THE ENEMIES OF STEVEN TREVOR ARE ALSO MY ENEMIES--AND THE ENEMIES OF MANKIND!
12
LISTEN, PLEASE! HEAR MY STORY! HEAR THE EVIL OF HIM WHO IS CALLED DOCTOR CYBER!
THEN YOU WILL COMPREHEND WHY HE MUST BE DESTROYED!
CHING'S AMAZING TALE FOLLOWS ON THE PAGE FOLLOWING ...

WONDER WOMAN

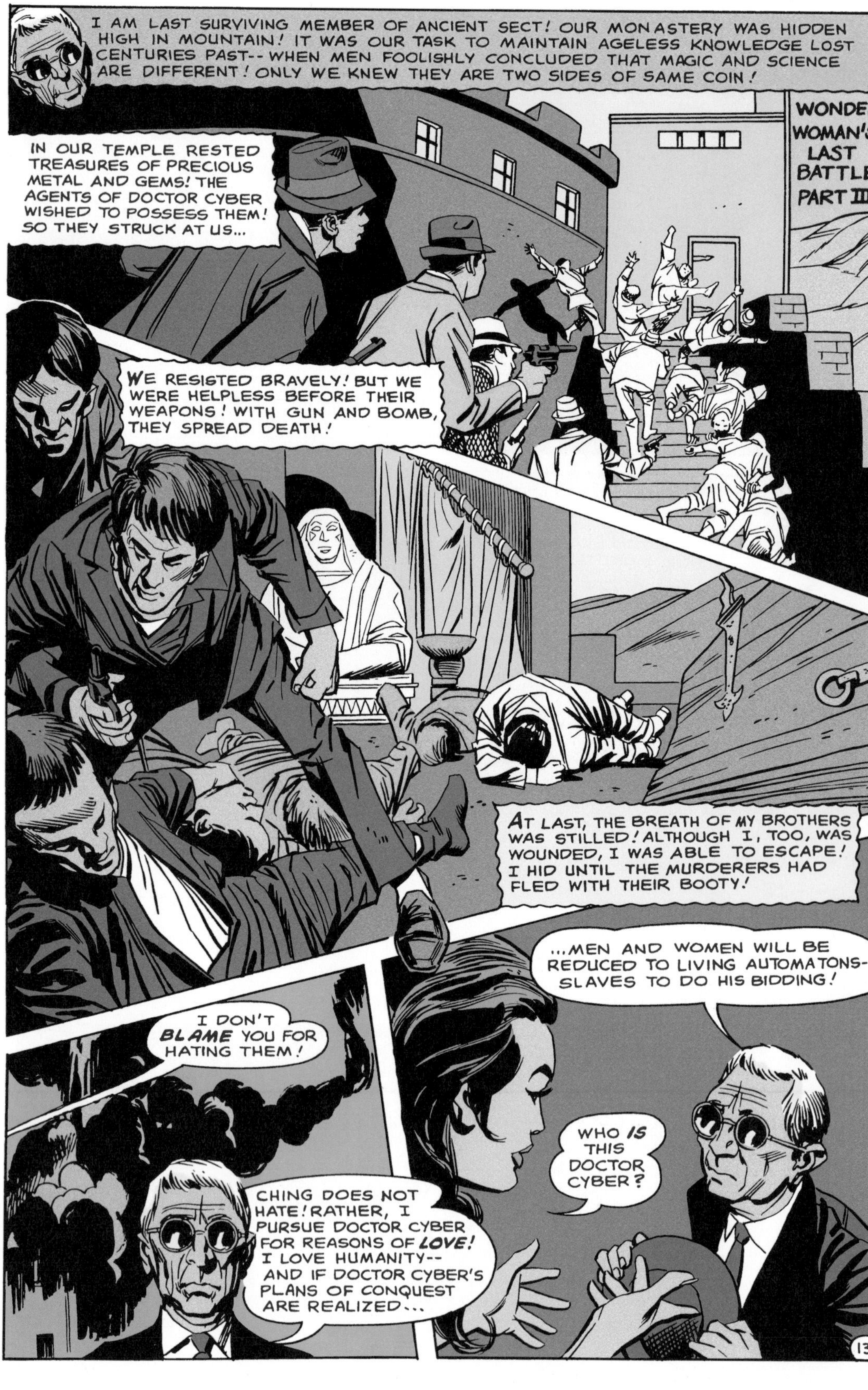

I AM LAST SURVIVING MEMBER OF ANCIENT SECT! OUR MONASTERY WAS HIDDEN HIGH IN MOUNTAIN! IT WAS OUR TASK TO MAINTAIN AGELESS KNOWLEDGE LOST CENTURIES PAST-- WHEN MEN FOOLISHLY CONCLUDED THAT MAGIC AND SCIENCE ARE DIFFERENT! ONLY WE KNEW THEY ARE TWO SIDES OF SAME COIN!
WONDER WOMAN'S LAST BATTLE PART III
IN OUR TEMPLE RESTED TREASURES OF PRECIOUS METAL AND GEMS! THE AGENTS OF DOCTOR CYBER WISHED TO POSSESS THEM! SO THEY STRUCK AT US...
WE RESISTED BRAVELY! BUT WE WERE HELPLESS BEFORE THEIR WEAPONS! WITH GUN AND BOMB, THEY SPREAD DEATH!
AT LAST, THE BREATH OF MY BROTHERS WAS STILLED! ALTHOUGH I, TOO, WAS WOUNDED, I WAS ABLE TO ESCAPE! I HID UNTIL THE MURDERERS HAD FLED WITH THEIR BOOTY!
I DON'T BLAME YOU FOR HATING THEM!
CHING DOES NOT HATE! RATHER, I PURSUE DOCTOR CYBER FOR REASONS OF LOVE! I LOVE HUMANITY-- AND IF DOCTOR CYBER'S PLANS OF CONQUEST ARE REALIZED...
...MEN AND WOMEN WILL BE REDUCED TO LIVING AUTOMATONS-- SLAVES TO DO HIS BIDDING!
WHO IS THIS DOCTOR CYBER?
13

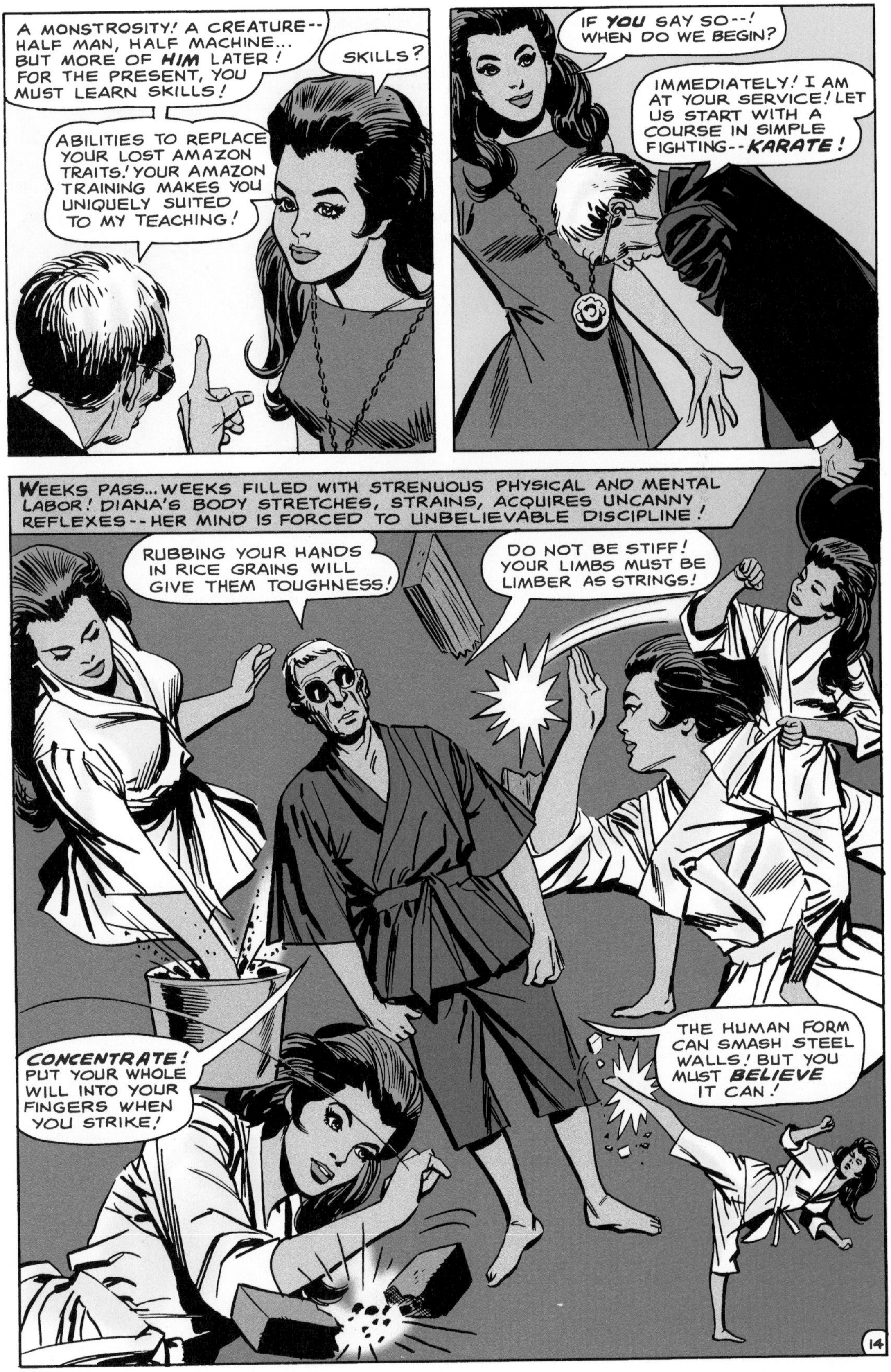
A MONSTROSITY! A CREATURE-- HALF MAN, HALF MACHINE... BUT MORE OF HIM LATER! FOR THE PRESENT, YOU MUST LEARN SKILLS!
SKILLS?
ABILITIES TO REPLACE YOUR LOST AMAZON TRAITS! YOUR AMAZON TRAINING MAKES YOU UNIQUELY SUITED TO MY TEACHING!
IF YOU SAY SO--! WHEN DO WE BEGIN?
IMMEDIATELY! I AM AT YOUR SERVICE! LET US START WITH A COURSE IN SIMPLE FIGHTING--KARATE!
WEEKS PASS...WEEKS FILLED WITH STRENUOUS PHYSICAL AND MENTAL LABOR! DIANA'S BODY STRETCHES, STRAINS, ACQUIRES UNCANNY REFLEXES--HER MIND IS FORCED TO UNBELIEVABLE DISCIPLINE!
RUBBING YOUR HANDS IN RICE GRAINS WILL GIVE THEM TOUGHNESS!
DO NOT BE STIFF! YOUR LIMBS MUST BE LIMBER AS STRINGS!
CONCENTRATE! PUT YOUR WHOLE WILL INTO YOUR FINGERS WHEN YOU STRIKE!
THE HUMAN FORM CAN SMASH STEEL WALLS! BUT YOU MUST BELIEVE IT CAN!
14

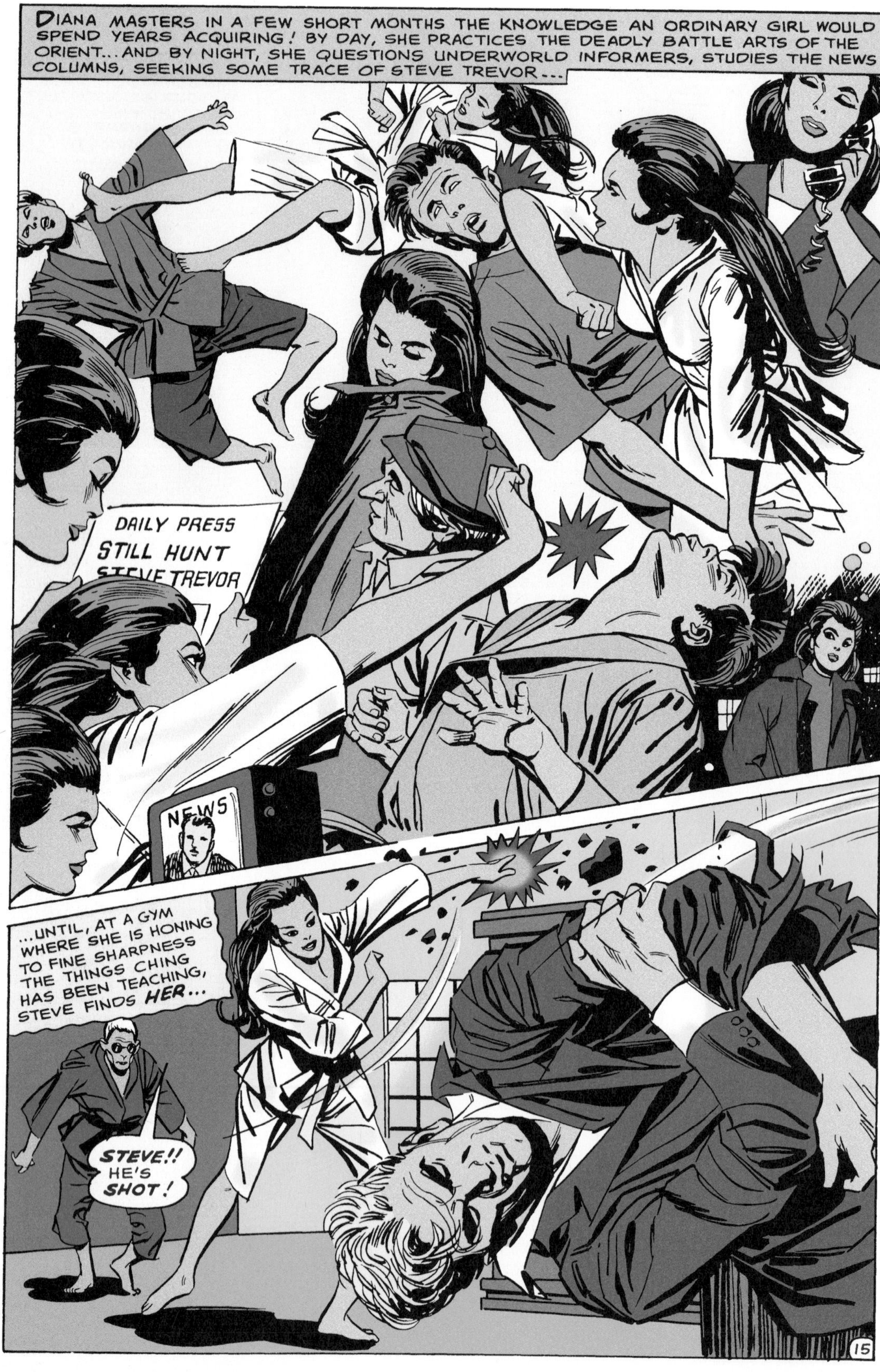

DIANA MASTERS IN A FEW SHORT MONTHS THE KNOWLEDGE AN ORDINARY GIRL WOULD SPEND YEARS ACQUIRING! BY DAY, SHE PRACTICES THE DEADLY BATTLE ARTS OF THE ORIENT... AND BY NIGHT, SHE QUESTIONS UNDERWORLD INFORMERS, STUDIES THE NEWS COLUMNS, SEEKING SOME TRACE OF STEVE TREVOR...
DAILY PRESS
STILL HUNT
NEWS
...UNTIL, AT A GYM WHERE SHE IS HONING TO FINE SHARPNESS THE THINGS CHING HAS BEEN TEACHING, STEVE FINDS HER...
STEVE!! HE'S SHOT!
15

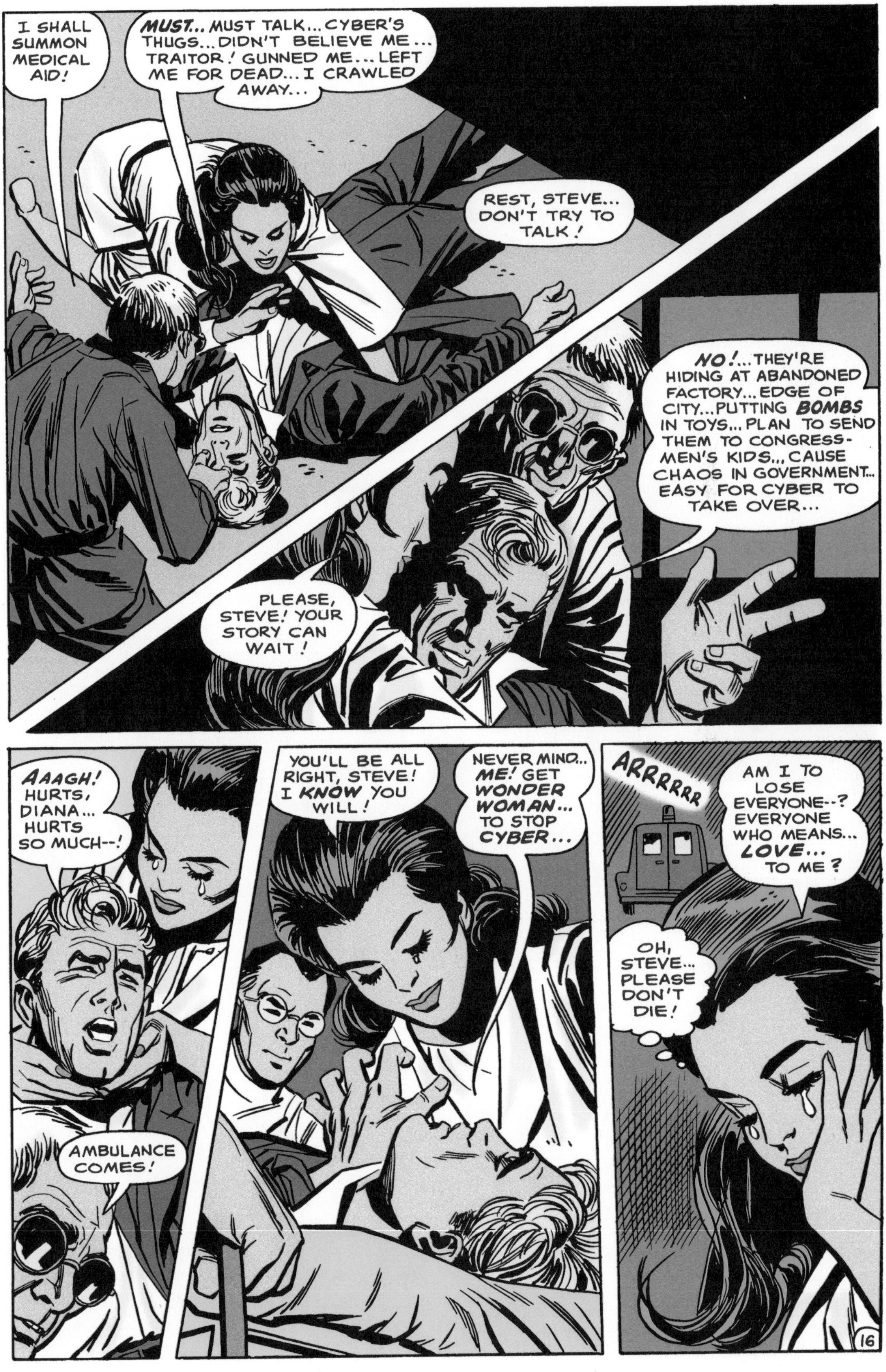

I SHALL SUMMON MEDICAL AID!
MUST... MUST TALK... CYBER'S THUGS... DIDN'T BELIEVE ME... TRAITOR! GUNNED ME... LEFT ME FOR DEAD... I CRAWLED AWAY...
REST, STEVE... DON'T TRY TO TALK!
NO!... THEY'RE HIDING AT ABANDONED FACTORY... EDGE OF CITY... PUTTING BOMBS IN TOYS... PLAN TO SEND THEM TO CONGRESS-MEN'S KIDS... CAUSE CHAOS IN GOVERNMENT... EASY FOR CYBER TO TAKE OVER...
PLEASE, STEVE! YOUR STORY CAN WAIT!
AAAGH! HURTS, DIANA... HURTS SO MUCH--!
AMBULANCE COMES!
YOU'LL BE ALL RIGHT, STEVE! I KNOW YOU WILL!
NEVER MIND... ME! GET WONDER WOMAN... TO STOP CYBER...
ARRRRRR
AM I TO LOSE EVERYONE--? EVERYONE WHO MEANS... LOVE... TO ME?
OH, STEVE... PLEASE DON'T DIE!
16

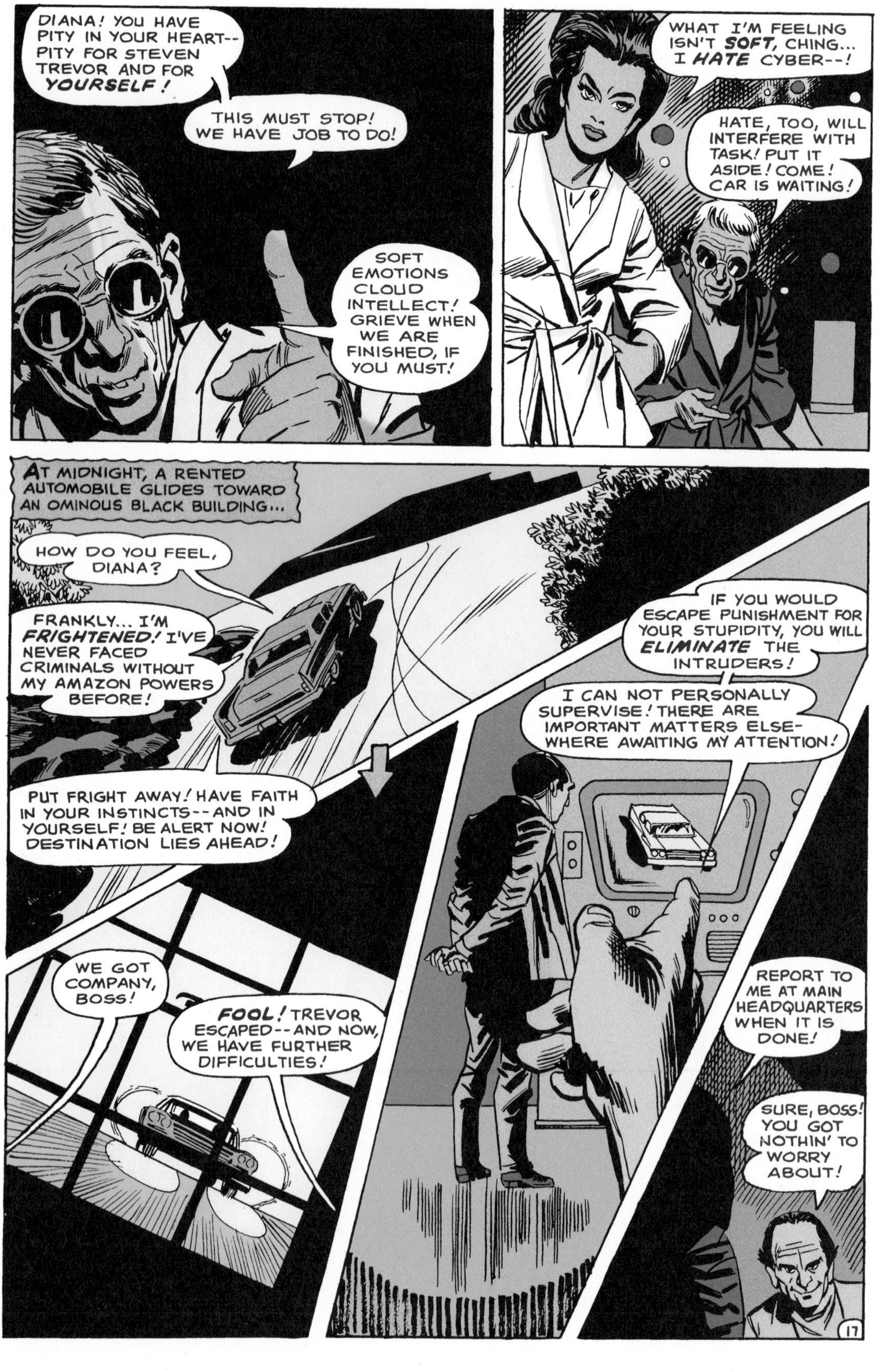

DIANA! YOU HAVE PITY IN YOUR HEART-- PITY FOR STEVEN TREVOR AND FOR YOURSELF!
THIS MUST STOP! WE HAVE JOB TO DO!
SOFT EMOTIONS CLOUD INTELLECT! GRIEVE WHEN WE ARE FINISHED, IF YOU MUST!
WHAT I'M FEELING ISN'T SOFT, CHING... I HATE CYBER--!
HATE, TOO, WILL INTERFERE WITH TASK! PUT IT ASIDE! COME! CAR IS WAITING!
AT MIDNIGHT, A RENTED AUTOMOBILE GLIDES TOWARD AN OMINOUS BLACK BUILDING...
HOW DO YOU FEEL, DIANA?
FRANKLY... I'M FRIGHTENED! I'VE NEVER FACED CRIMINALS WITHOUT MY AMAZON POWERS BEFORE!
PUT FRIGHT AWAY! HAVE FAITH IN YOUR INSTINCTS--AND IN YOURSELF! BE ALERT NOW! DESTINATION LIES AHEAD!
WE GOT COMPANY, BOSS!
FOOL! TREVOR ESCAPED--AND NOW, WE HAVE FURTHER DIFFICULTIES!
IF YOU WOULD ESCAPE PUNISHMENT FOR YOUR STUPIDITY, YOU WILL ELIMINATE THE INTRUDERS!
I CAN NOT PERSONALLY SUPERVISE! THERE ARE IMPORTANT MATTERS ELSEWHERE AWAITING MY ATTENTION!
REPORT TO ME AT MAIN HEADQUARTERS WHEN IT IS DONE!
SURE, BOSS! YOU GOT NOTHIN' TO WORRY ABOUT!
17

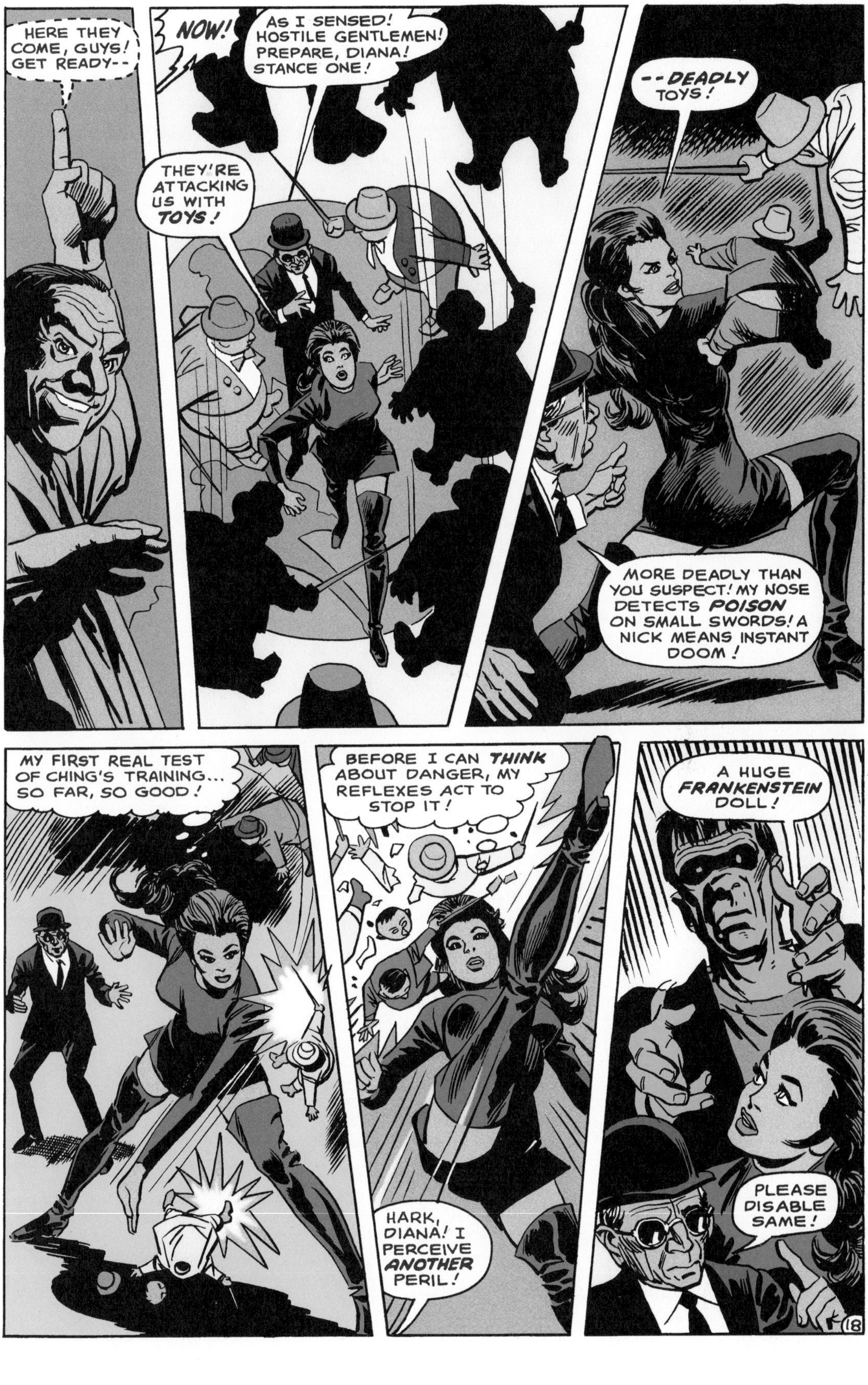
HERE THEY COME, GUYS! GET READY--
NOW!
AS I SENSED! HOSTILE GENTLEMEN! PREPARE, DIANA! STANCE ONE!
THEY'RE ATTACKING US WITH TOYS!
--DEADLY TOYS!
MORE DEADLY THAN YOU SUSPECT! MY NOSE DETECTS POISON ON SMALL SWORDS! A NICK MEANS INSTANT DOOM!
MY FIRST REAL TEST OF CHING'S TRAINING... SO FAR, SO GOOD!
BEFORE I CAN THINK ABOUT DANGER, MY REFLEXES ACT TO STOP IT!
HARK, DIANA! I PERCEIVE ANOTHER PERIL!
A HUGE FRANKENSTEIN DOLL!
PLEASE DISABLE SAME!
18

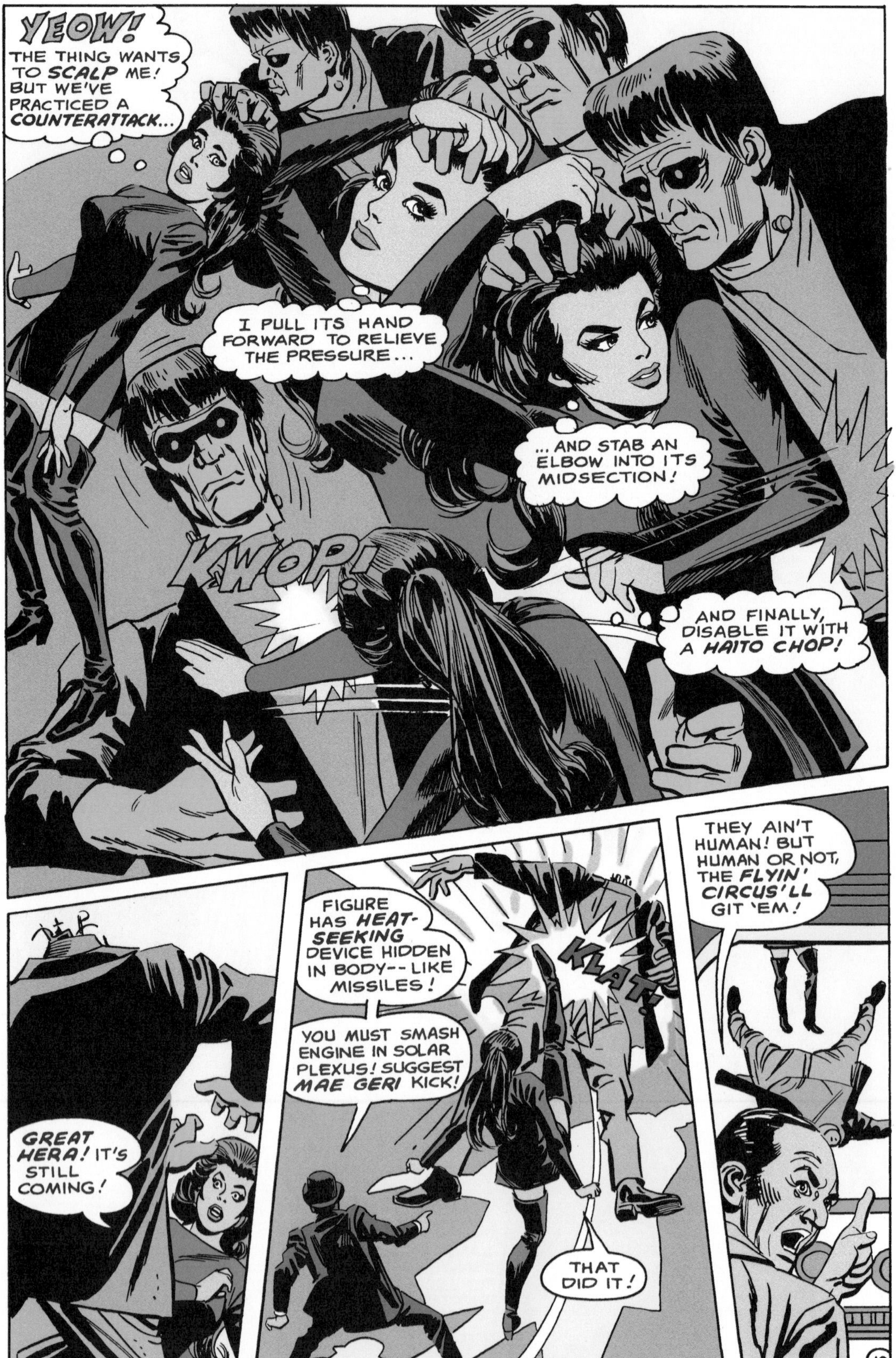
YEOW! THE THING WANTS TO SCALP ME! BUT WE'VE PRACTICED A COUNTERATTACK...
I PULL ITS HAND FORWARD TO RELIEVE THE PRESSURE...
...AND STAB AN ELBOW INTO ITS MIDSECTION!
KWOP!
AND FINALLY, DISABLE IT WITH A HAITO CHOP!
GREAT HERA! IT'S STILL COMING!
FIGURE HAS HEAT-SEEKING DEVICE HIDDEN IN BODY-- LIKE MISSILES!
YOU MUST SMASH ENGINE IN SOLAR PLEXUS! SUGGEST MAE GERI KICK!
KLAT!
THAT DID IT!
THEY AIN'T HUMAN! BUT HUMAN OR NOT, THE FLYIN' CIRCUS'LL GIT 'EM!
19

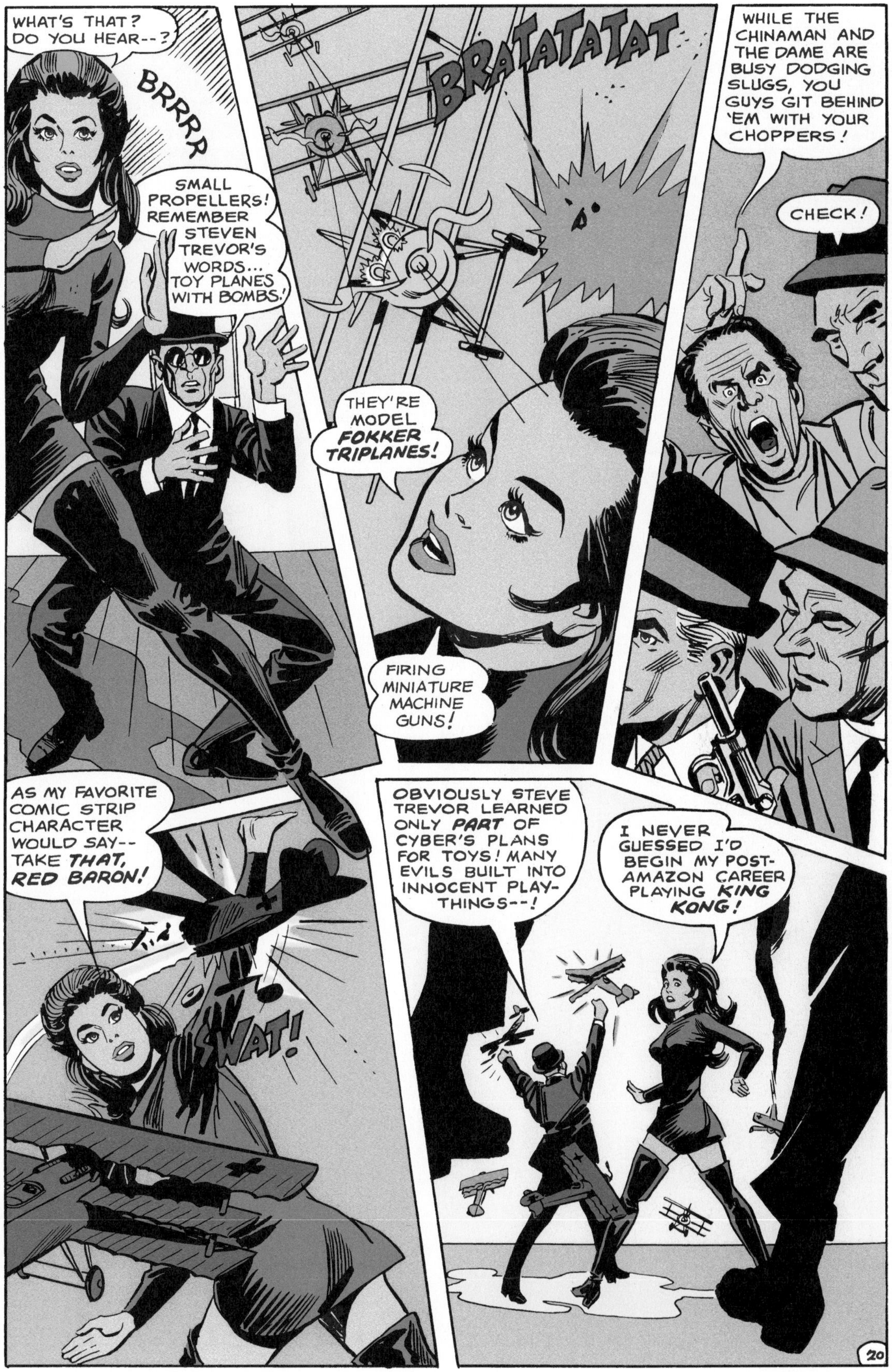
WHAT'S THAT? DO YOU HEAR--?
BRRRR
SMALL PROPELLERS! REMEMBER STEVEN TREVOR'S WORDS... TOY PLANES WITH BOMBS!
BRATATATAT
THEY'RE MODEL FOKKER TRIPLANES!
FIRING MINIATURE MACHINE GUNS!
WHILE THE CHINAMAN AND THE DAME ARE BUSY DODGING SLUGS, YOU GUYS GIT BEHIND 'EM WITH YOUR CHOPPERS!
CHECK!
AS MY FAVORITE COMIC STRIP CHARACTER WOULD SAY-- TAKE THAT, RED BARON!
SWAT!
OBVIOUSLY STEVE TREVOR LEARNED ONLY PART OF CYBER'S PLANS FOR TOYS! MANY EVILS BUILT INTO INNOCENT PLAY-THINGS--!
I NEVER GUESSED I'D BEGIN MY POST-AMAZON CAREER PLAYING KING KONG!
20

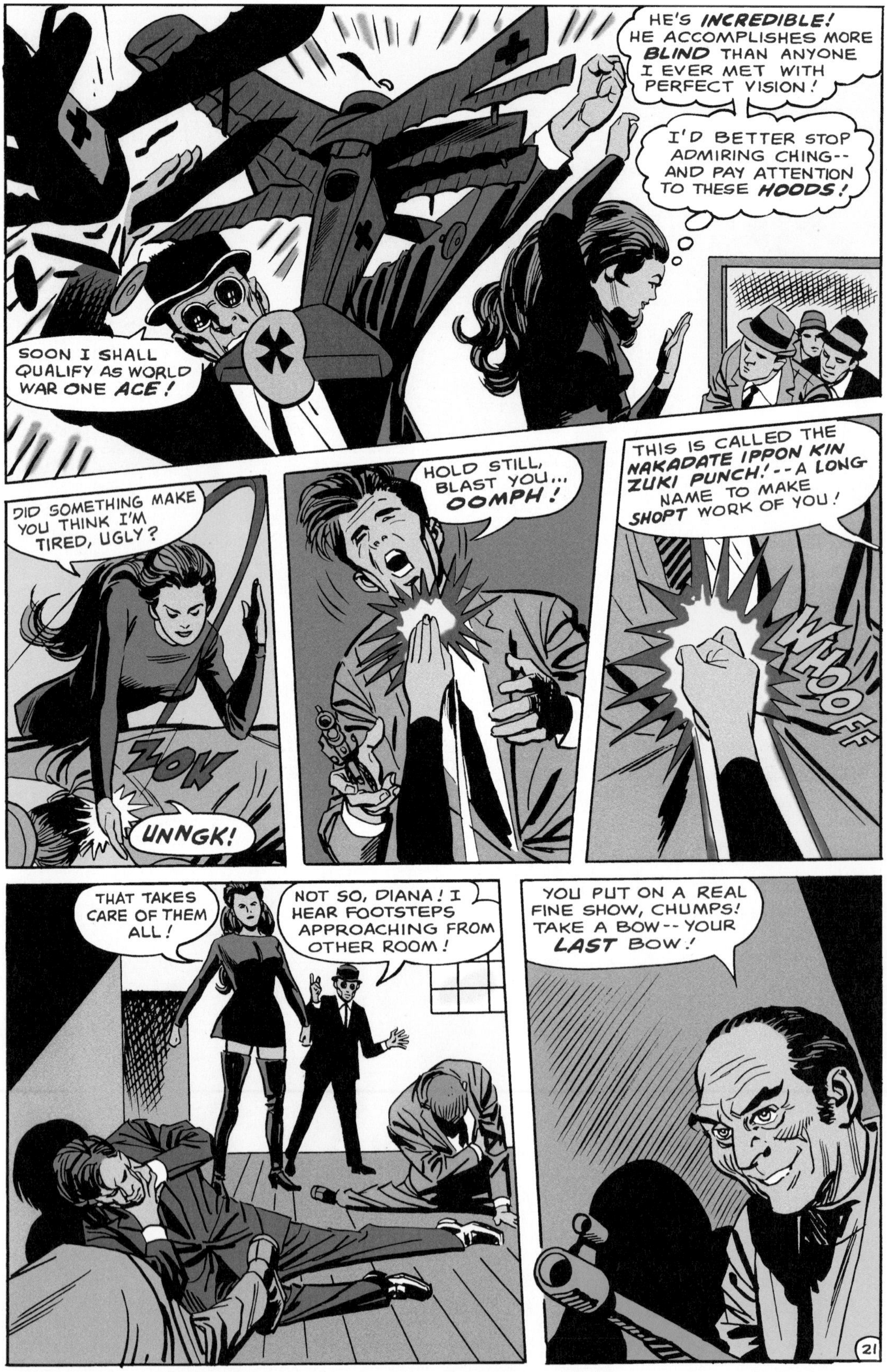

HE'S INCREDIBLE! HE ACCOMPLISHES MORE BLIND THAN ANYONE I EVER MET WITH PERFECT VISION!
I'D BETTER STOP ADMIRING CHING-- AND PAY ATTENTION TO THESE HOODS!
SOON I SHALL QUALIFY AS WORLD WAR ONE ACE!
DID SOMETHING MAKE YOU THINK I'M TIRED, UGLY?
ZOK
UNNGK!
HOLD STILL, BLAST YOU... OOMPH!
THIS IS CALLED THE NAKADATE IPPON KIN ZUKI PUNCH!--A LONG NAME TO MAKE SHOPT WORK OF YOU!
WHOOFF
THAT TAKES CARE OF THEM ALL!
NOT SO, DIANA! I HEAR FOOTSTEPS APPROACHING FROM OTHER ROOM!
YOU PUT ON A REAL FINE SHOW, CHUMPS! TAKE A BOW-- YOUR LAST BOW!
21

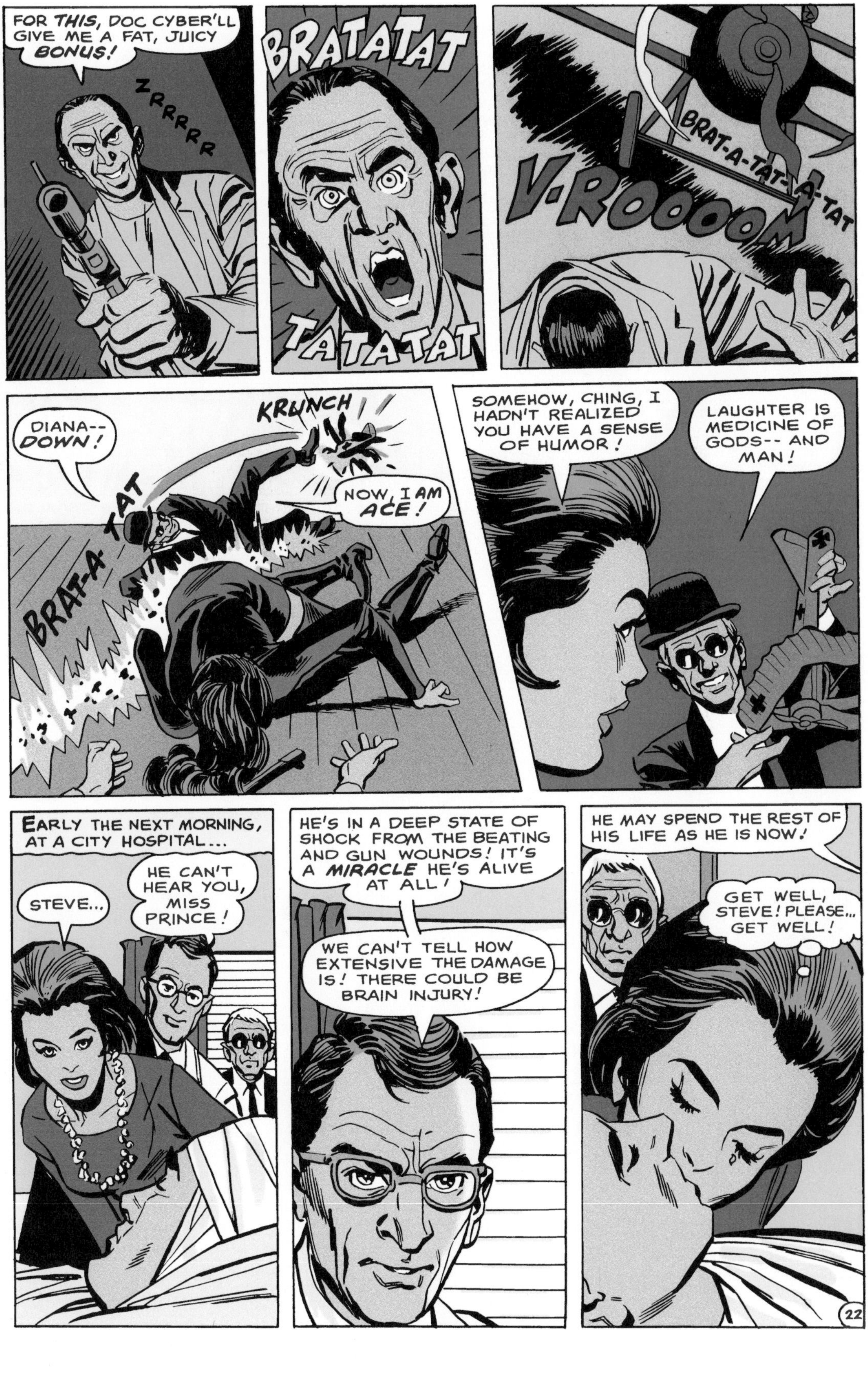
FOR THIS, DOC CYBER'LL GIVE ME A FAT, JUICY BONUS!
ZRRRRRR
BRATATAT
TATATAT
BRAT-A-TAT-A-TAT
V-ROOOOOM
DIANA-- DOWN!
KRUNCH
NOW, I AM ACE!
BRAT-A-TAT
SOMEHOW, CHING, I HADN'T REALIZED YOU HAVE A SENSE OF HUMOR!
LAUGHTER IS MEDICINE OF GODS-- AND MAN!
EARLY THE NEXT MORNING, AT A CITY HOSPITAL...
STEVE...
HE CAN'T HEAR YOU, MISS PRINCE!
HE'S IN A DEEP STATE OF SHOCK FROM THE BEATING AND GUN WOUNDS! IT'S A MIRACLE HE'S ALIVE AT ALL!
WE CAN'T TELL HOW EXTENSIVE THE DAMAGE IS! THERE COULD BE BRAIN INJURY!
HE MAY SPEND THE REST OF HIS LIFE AS HE IS NOW!
GET WELL, STEVE! PLEASE... GET WELL!
22

THEN, OUTSIDE, IN THE COOL DAWN AIR...

I'M EXHAUSTED... AND A BIT *NUMB!* MY LIFE HAS CHANGED SO MUCH...

NO! WE HAVE BARELY *STARTED!* DOCTOR CYBER IS STILL *FREE!* HE IS LIKE AN *INFECTION* IN HUMAN STRAIN! OUR TASK IS TO *CURE* DISEASE--BY CRUSHING HIM!

23

AS FOR *CHANGES--* THEY HAVE JUST BEGUN!

A GOOD-LOOKING DAME AND A BLIND CHINESE... THOSE THE PEOPLE I'M AFTER, ALL RIGHT!

THUS, THE FIRST CHAPTER IN THE SAGA OF THE *NEW WONDER WOMAN* ENDS... WITH DIANA AND HER AGED MENTOR BEING OBSERVED BY A SINISTER FIGURE HIDDEN IN THE SHADOWS! MORE DANGER--MORE HIGH-VOLTAGE EXCITEMENT--MORE HEARTBREAK-- AWAIT DIANA PRINCE AS SHE AND CHING CONTINUE THEIR PURSUIT OF THE SUPREMELY DEPRAVED *DOCTOR CYBER!*

WONDER WOMAN

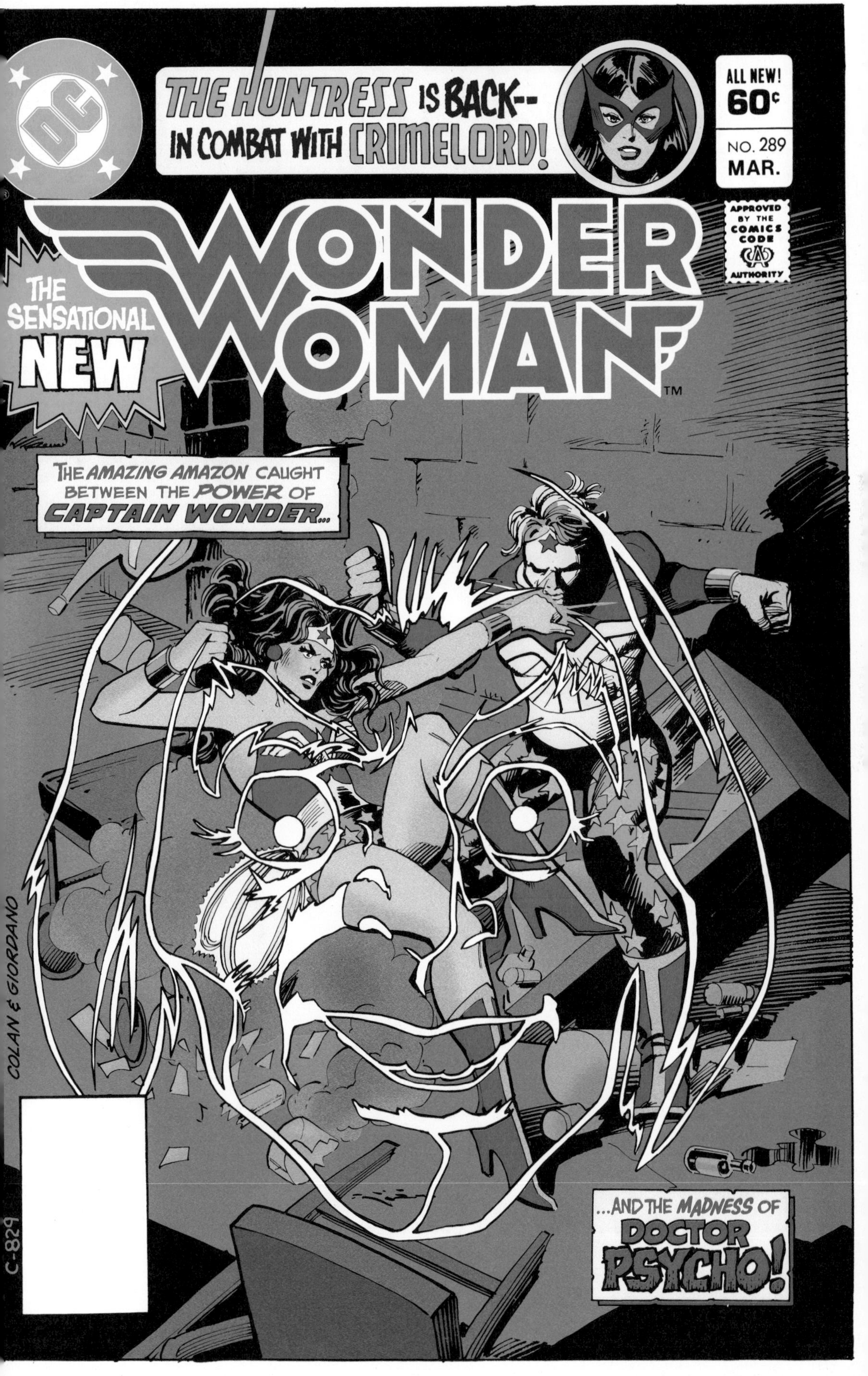
THE HUNTRESS IS BACK-- IN COMBAT WITH CRIMELORD!
ALL NEW! 60¢
NO. 289 MAR.
APPROVED BY THE COMICS CODE AUTHORITY
THE SENSATIONAL NEW
WONDER WOMAN
TM
THE AMAZING AMAZON CAUGHT BETWEEN THE POWER OF CAPTAIN WONDER...
...AND THE MADNESS OF DOCTOR PSYCHO!
COLAN & GIORDANO
C-829

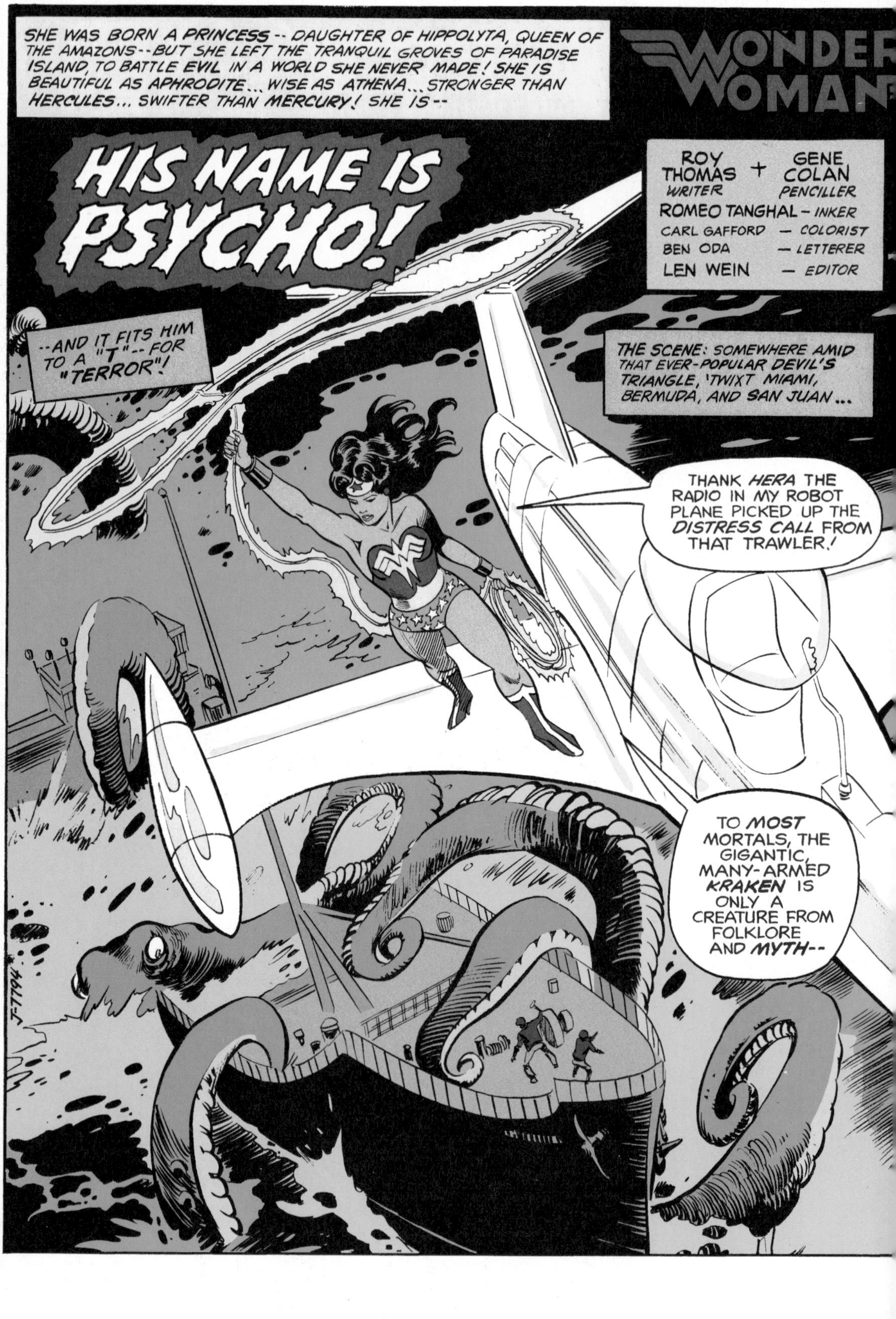

SHE WAS BORN A PRINCESS -- DAUGHTER OF HIPPOLYTA, QUEEN OF THE AMAZONS -- BUT SHE LEFT THE TRANQUIL GROVES OF PARADISE ISLAND, TO BATTLE EVIL IN A WORLD SHE NEVER MADE! SHE IS BEAUTIFUL AS APHRODITE... WISE AS ATHENA... STRONGER THAN HERCULES... SWIFTER THAN MERCURY! SHE IS --
WONDER WOMAN
HIS NAME IS PSYCHO!
ROY THOMAS WRITER + GENE COLAN PENCILLER
ROMEO TANGHAL - INKER
CARL GAFFORD - COLORIST
BEN ODA - LETTERER
LEN WEIN - EDITOR
--AND IT FITS HIM TO A "T"-- FOR "TERROR"!
THE SCENE: SOMEWHERE AMID THAT EVER-POPULAR DEVIL'S TRIANGLE, 'TWIXT MIAMI, BERMUDA, AND SAN JUAN...
THANK HERA THE RADIO IN MY ROBOT PLANE PICKED UP THE DISTRESS CALL FROM THAT TRAWLER!
TO MOST MORTALS, THE GIGANTIC, MANY-ARMED KRAKEN IS ONLY A CREATURE FROM FOLKLORE AND MYTH--
J-7794

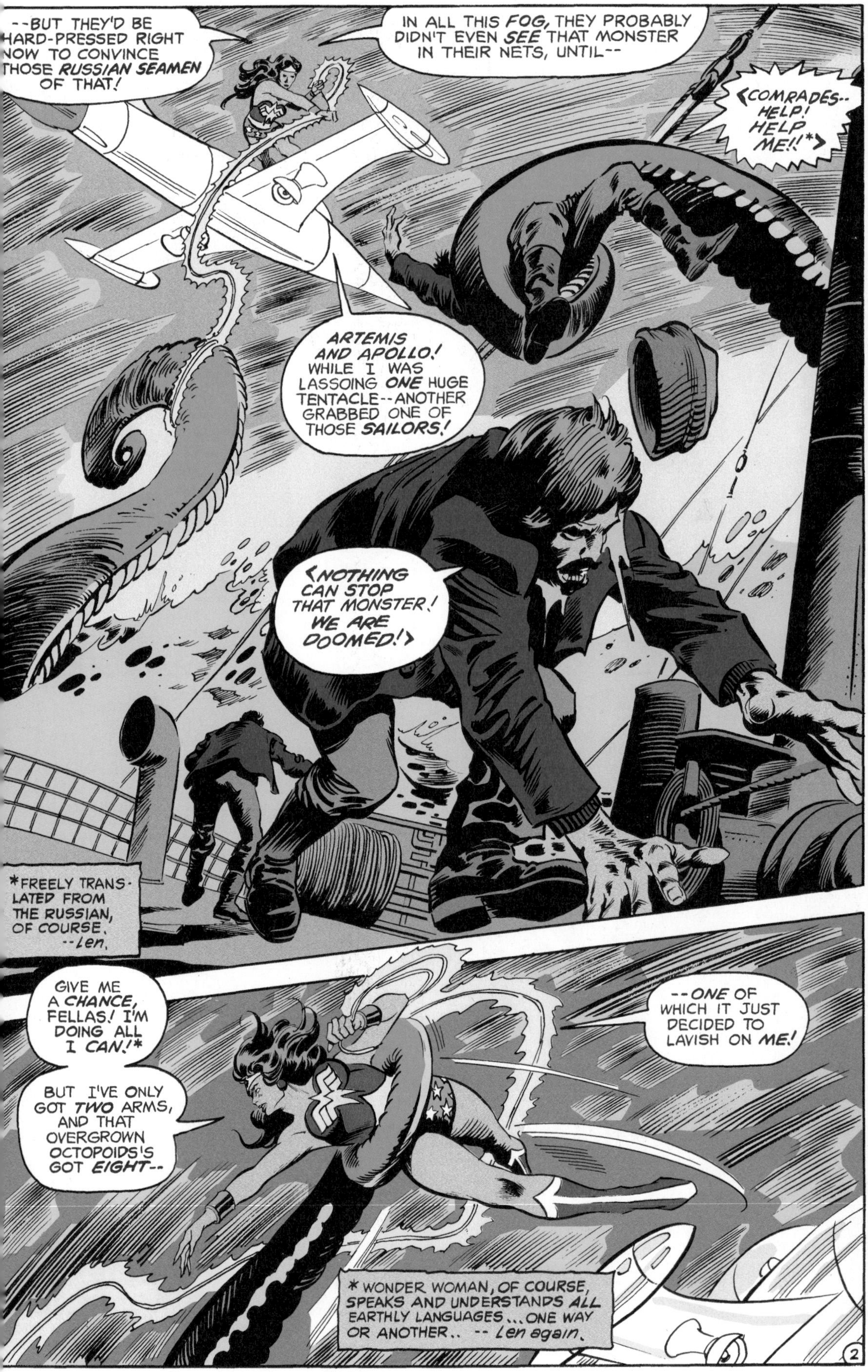
--BUT THEY'D BE HARD-PRESSED RIGHT NOW TO CONVINCE THOSE RUSSIAN SEAMEN OF THAT!
IN ALL THIS FOG, THEY PROBABLY DIDN'T EVEN SEE THAT MONSTER IN THEIR NETS, UNTIL--
<COMRADES-- HELP! HELP ME!!*>
ARTEMIS AND APOLLO! WHILE I WAS LASSOING ONE HUGE TENTACLE--ANOTHER GRABBED ONE OF THOSE SAILORS!
<NOTHING CAN STOP THAT MONSTER! WE ARE DOOMED!>
*FREELY TRANSLATED FROM THE RUSSIAN, OF COURSE. --Len.
GIVE ME A CHANCE, FELLAS! I'M DOING ALL I CAN!*
BUT I'VE ONLY GOT TWO ARMS, AND THAT OVERGROWN OCTOPOIDS'S GOT EIGHT--
--ONE OF WHICH IT JUST DECIDED TO LAVISH ON ME!
* WONDER WOMAN, OF COURSE, SPEAKS AND UNDERSTANDS ALL EARTHLY LANGUAGES... ONE WAY OR ANOTHER.. -- Len again.
2

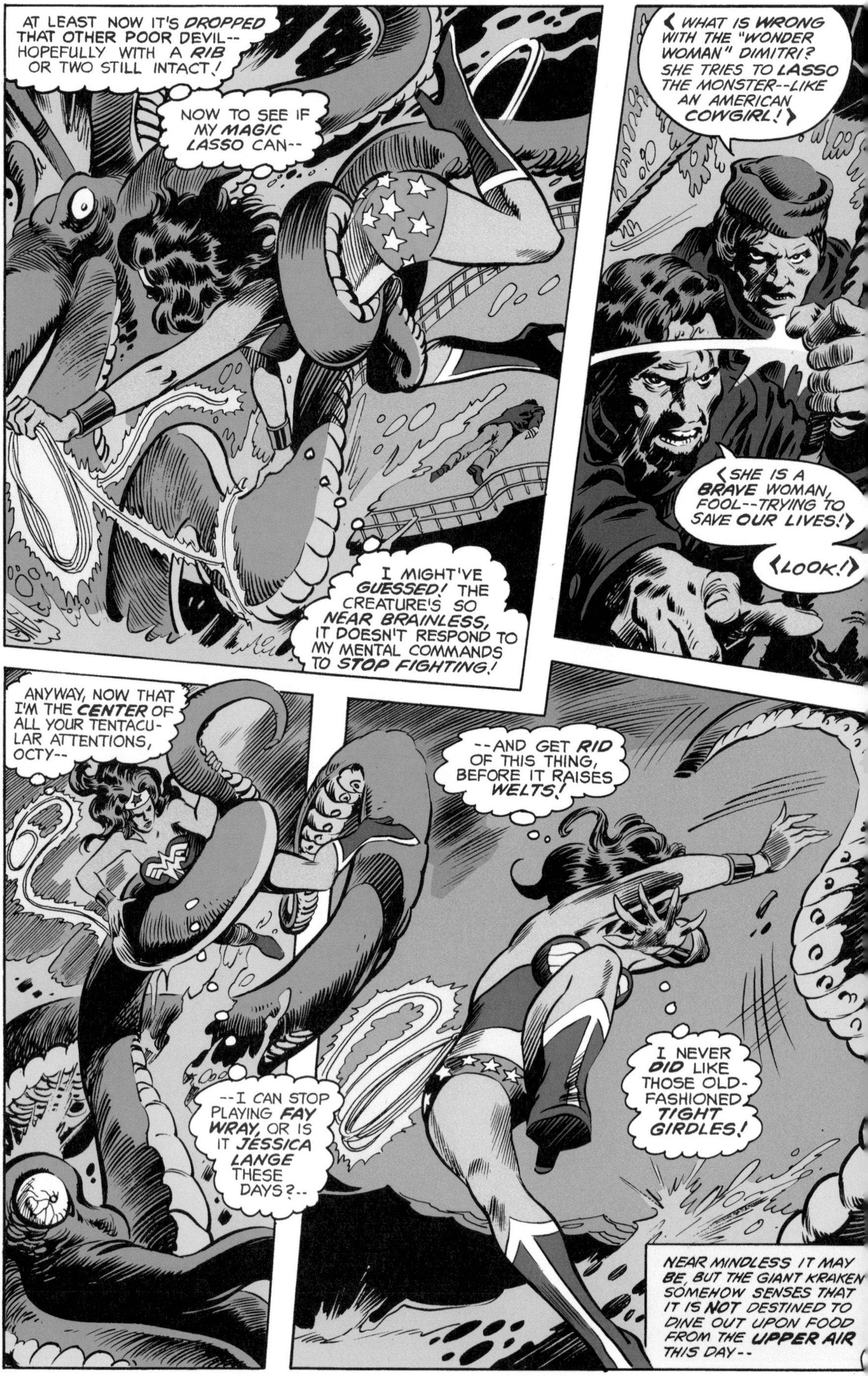
AT LEAST NOW IT'S DROPPED THAT OTHER POOR DEVIL-- HOPEFULLY WITH A RIB OR TWO STILL INTACT!
NOW TO SEE IF MY MAGIC LASSO CAN--
I MIGHT'VE GUESSED! THE CREATURE'S SO NEAR BRAINLESS, IT DOESN'T RESPOND TO MY MENTAL COMMANDS TO STOP FIGHTING!
‹WHAT IS WRONG WITH THE "WONDER WOMAN" DIMITRI? SHE TRIES TO LASSO THE MONSTER--LIKE AN AMERICAN COWGIRL!›
‹SHE IS A BRAVE WOMAN, FOOL--TRYING TO SAVE OUR LIVES!›
‹LOOK!›
ANYWAY, NOW THAT I'M THE CENTER OF ALL YOUR TENTACULAR ATTENTIONS, OCTY--
--I CAN STOP PLAYING FAY WRAY, OR IS IT JESSICA LANGE THESE DAYS?--
--AND GET RID OF THIS THING, BEFORE IT RAISES WELTS!
I NEVER DID LIKE THOSE OLD-FASHIONED TIGHT GIRDLES!
NEAR MINDLESS IT MAY BE, BUT THE GIANT KRAKEN SOMEHOW SENSES THAT IT IS NOT DESTINED TO DINE OUT UPON FOOD FROM THE UPPER AIR THIS DAY--

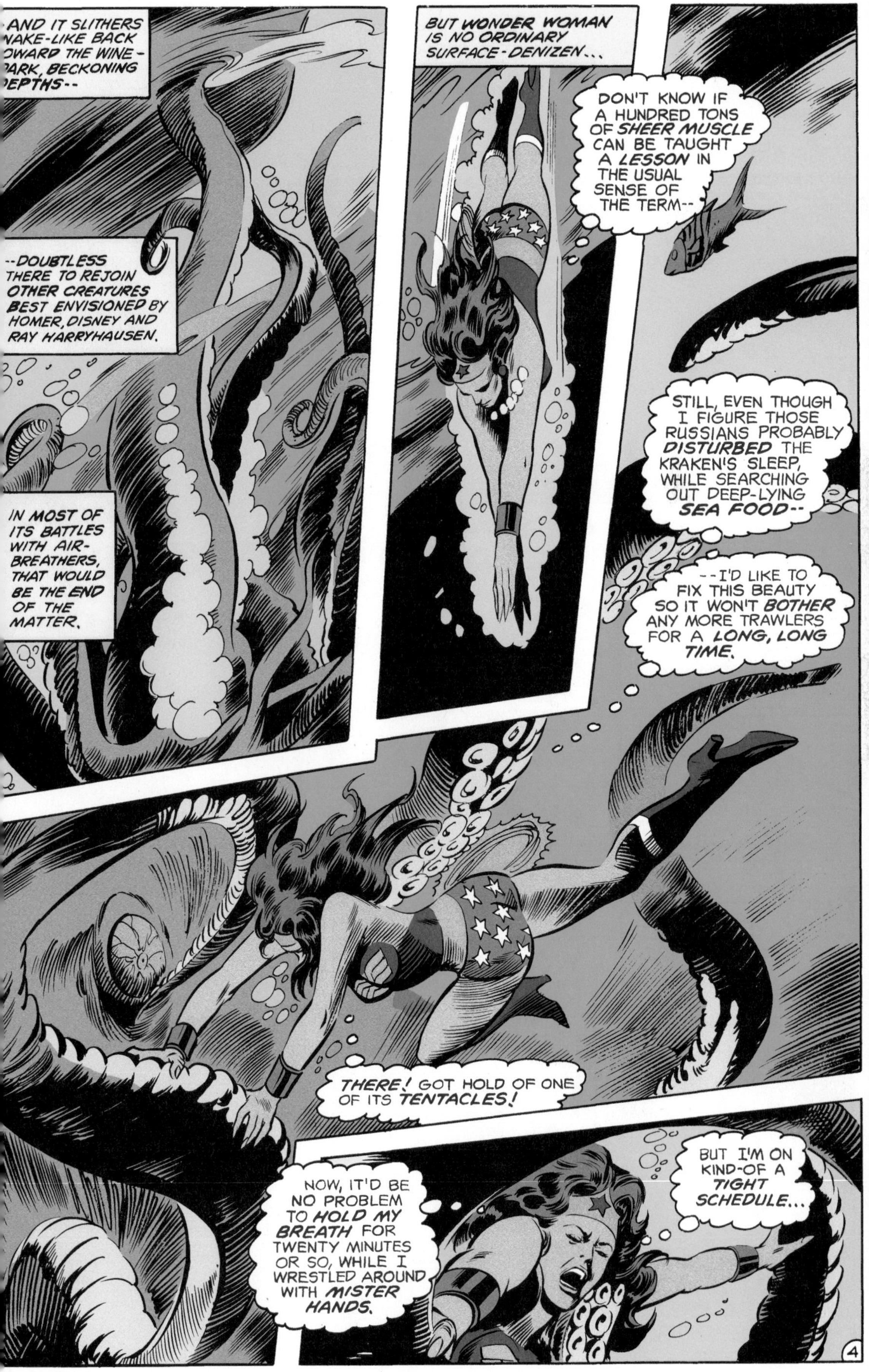
-AND IT SLITHERS NAKE-LIKE BACK OWARD THE WINE-DARK, BECKONING EPTHS--
--DOUBTLESS THERE TO REJOIN OTHER CREATURES BEST ENVISIONED BY HOMER, DISNEY AND RAY HARRYHAUSEN.
IN MOST OF ITS BATTLES WITH AIR-BREATHERS, THAT WOULD BE THE END OF THE MATTER.
BUT WONDER WOMAN IS NO ORDINARY SURFACE-DENIZEN...
DON'T KNOW IF A HUNDRED TONS OF SHEER MUSCLE CAN BE TAUGHT A LESSON IN THE USUAL SENSE OF THE TERM--
STILL, EVEN THOUGH I FIGURE THOSE RUSSIANS PROBABLY DISTURBED THE KRAKEN'S SLEEP, WHILE SEARCHING OUT DEEP-LYING SEA FOOD--
--I'D LIKE TO FIX THIS BEAUTY SO IT WON'T BOTHER ANY MORE TRAWLERS FOR A LONG, LONG TIME.
THERE! GOT HOLD OF ONE OF ITS TENTACLES!
NOW, IT'D BE NO PROBLEM TO HOLD MY BREATH FOR TWENTY MINUTES OR SO, WHILE I WRESTLED AROUND WITH MISTER HANDS.
BUT I'M ON KIND-OF A TIGHT SCHEDULE...
4

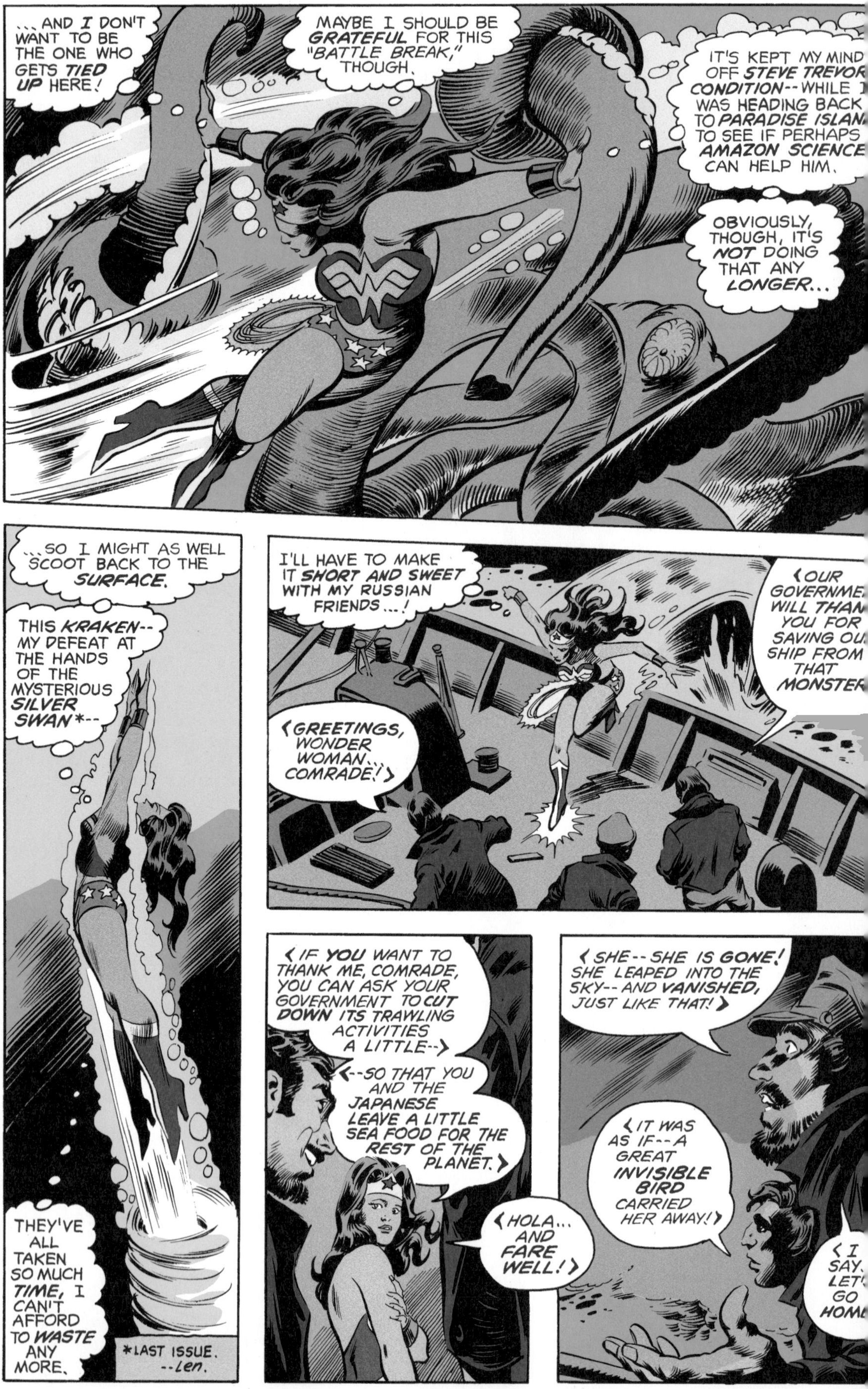

...AND I DON'T WANT TO BE THE ONE WHO GETS TIED UP HERE!
MAYBE I SHOULD BE GRATEFUL FOR THIS "BATTLE BREAK," THOUGH.
IT'S KEPT MY MIND OFF STEVE TREVOR CONDITION--WHILE I WAS HEADING BACK TO PARADISE ISLAN TO SEE IF PERHAPS AMAZON SCIENCE CAN HELP HIM.
OBVIOUSLY, THOUGH, IT'S NOT DOING THAT ANY LONGER...
...SO I MIGHT AS WELL SCOOT BACK TO THE SURFACE.
THIS KRAKEN--MY DEFEAT AT THE HANDS OF THE MYSTERIOUS SILVER SWAN*--
THEY'VE ALL TAKEN SO MUCH TIME, I CAN'T AFFORD TO WASTE ANY MORE.
*LAST ISSUE. --Len.
I'LL HAVE TO MAKE IT SHORT AND SWEET WITH MY RUSSIAN FRIENDS...!
‹OUR GOVERNME WILL THAN YOU FOR SAVING OU SHIP FROM THAT MONSTER
‹GREETINGS, WONDER WOMAN... COMRADE!›
‹IF YOU WANT TO THANK ME, COMRADE, YOU CAN ASK YOUR GOVERNMENT TO CUT DOWN ITS TRAWLING ACTIVITIES A LITTLE--›
‹--SO THAT YOU AND THE JAPANESE LEAVE A LITTLE SEA FOOD FOR THE REST OF THE PLANET.›
‹HOLA... AND FARE WELL!›
‹SHE--SHE IS GONE! SHE LEAPED INTO THE SKY--AND VANISHED, JUST LIKE THAT!›
‹IT WAS AS IF--A GREAT INVISIBLE BIRD CARRIED HER AWAY!›
‹I SAY. LET' GO HOM

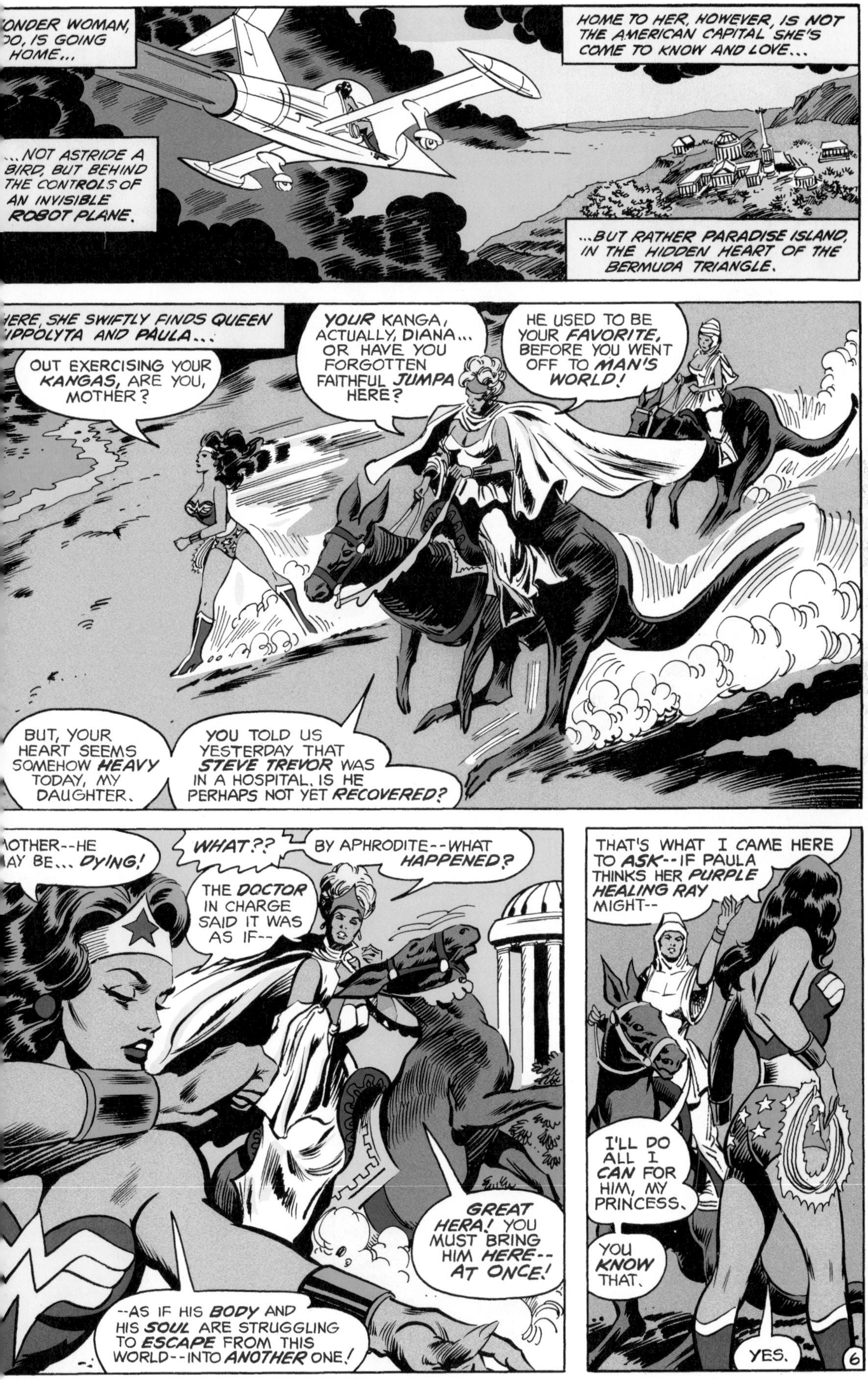
ONDER WOMAN, OO, IS GOING HOME...
HOME TO HER, HOWEVER, IS NOT THE AMERICAN CAPITAL SHE'S COME TO KNOW AND LOVE...
...NOT ASTRIDE A BIRD, BUT BEHIND THE CONTROLS OF AN INVISIBLE ROBOT PLANE.
...BUT RATHER PARADISE ISLAND, IN THE HIDDEN HEART OF THE BERMUDA TRIANGLE.
HERE, SHE SWIFTLY FINDS QUEEN IPPOLYTA AND PAULA...
OUT EXERCISING YOUR KANGAS, ARE YOU, MOTHER?
YOUR KANGA, ACTUALLY, DIANA... OR HAVE YOU FORGOTTEN FAITHFUL JUMPA HERE?
HE USED TO BE YOUR FAVORITE, BEFORE YOU WENT OFF TO MAN'S WORLD!
BUT, YOUR HEART SEEMS SOMEHOW HEAVY TODAY, MY DAUGHTER.
YOU TOLD US YESTERDAY THAT STEVE TREVOR WAS IN A HOSPITAL. IS HE PERHAPS NOT YET RECOVERED?
MOTHER--HE AY BE... DYING!
WHAT??
BY APHRODITE--WHAT HAPPENED?
THE DOCTOR IN CHARGE SAID IT WAS AS IF--
GREAT HERA! YOU MUST BRING HIM HERE--AT ONCE!
--AS IF HIS BODY AND HIS SOUL ARE STRUGGLING TO ESCAPE FROM THIS WORLD--INTO ANOTHER ONE!
THAT'S WHAT I CAME HERE TO ASK--IF PAULA THINKS HER PURPLE HEALING RAY MIGHT--
I'LL DO ALL I CAN FOR HIM, MY PRINCESS.
YOU KNOW THAT.
YES.
6

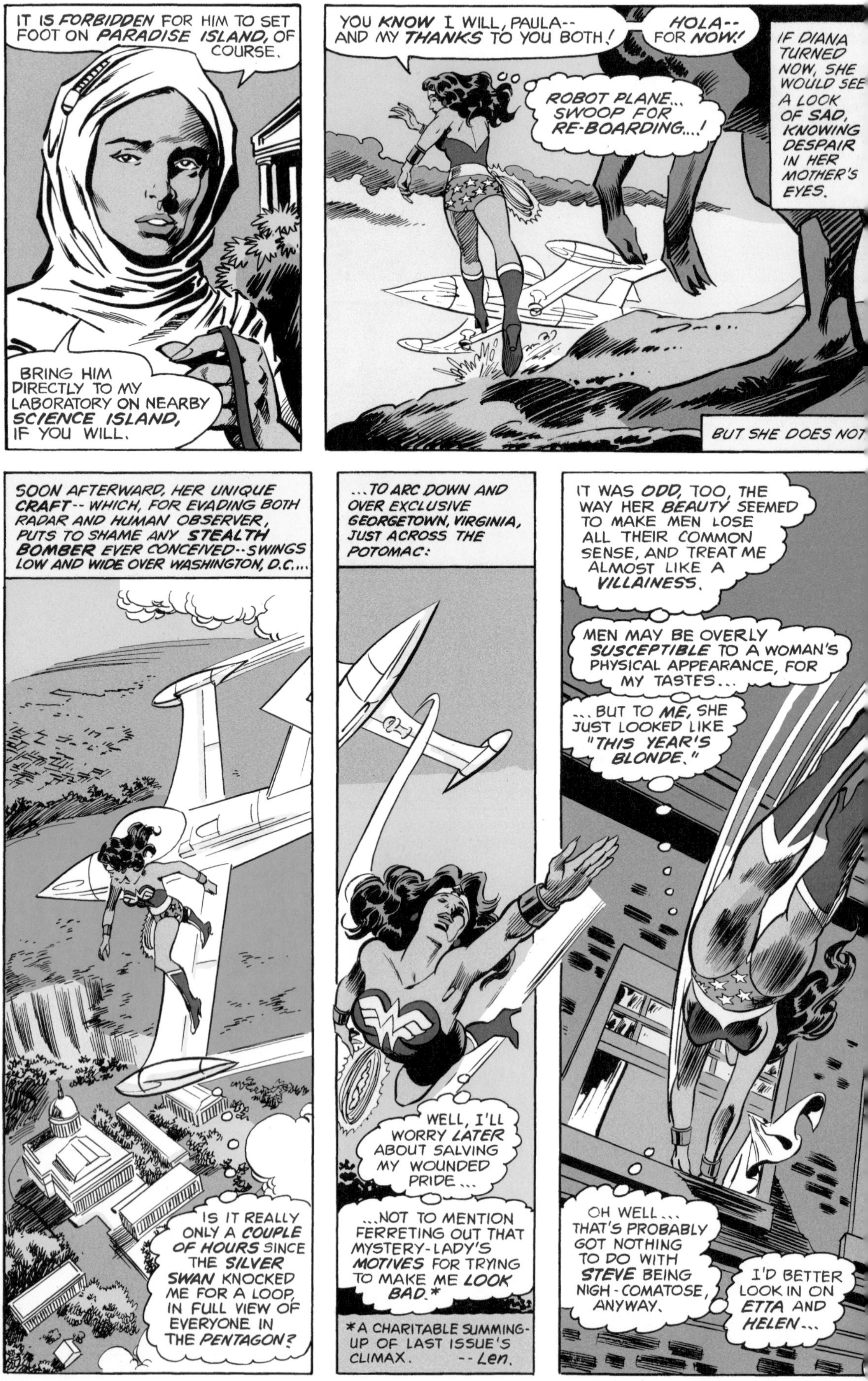
IT IS FORBIDDEN FOR HIM TO SET FOOT ON PARADISE ISLAND, OF COURSE.
BRING HIM DIRECTLY TO MY LABORATORY ON NEARBY SCIENCE ISLAND, IF YOU WILL.
YOU KNOW I WILL, PAULA-- AND MY THANKS TO YOU BOTH!
HOLA-- FOR NOW!
ROBOT PLANE... SWOOP FOR RE-BOARDING...!
IF DIANA TURNED NOW, SHE WOULD SEE A LOOK OF SAD, KNOWING DESPAIR IN HER MOTHER'S EYES.
BUT SHE DOES NOT
SOON AFTERWARD, HER UNIQUE CRAFT-- WHICH, FOR EVADING BOTH RADAR AND HUMAN OBSERVER, PUTS TO SHAME ANY STEALTH BOMBER EVER CONCEIVED--SWINGS LOW AND WIDE OVER WASHINGTON, D.C....
IS IT REALLY ONLY A COUPLE OF HOURS SINCE THE SILVER SWAN KNOCKED ME FOR A LOOP, IN FULL VIEW OF EVERYONE IN THE PENTAGON?
...TO ARC DOWN AND OVER EXCLUSIVE GEORGETOWN, VIRGINIA, JUST ACROSS THE POTOMAC:
WELL, I'LL WORRY LATER ABOUT SALVING MY WOUNDED PRIDE...
...NOT TO MENTION FERRETING OUT THAT MYSTERY-LADY'S MOTIVES FOR TRYING TO MAKE ME LOOK BAD.*
*A CHARITABLE SUMMING-UP OF LAST ISSUE'S CLIMAX. --Len.
IT WAS ODD, TOO, THE WAY HER BEAUTY SEEMED TO MAKE MEN LOSE ALL THEIR COMMON SENSE, AND TREAT ME ALMOST LIKE A VILLAINESS.
MEN MAY BE OVERLY SUSCEPTIBLE TO A WOMAN'S PHYSICAL APPEARANCE, FOR MY TASTES...
...BUT TO ME, SHE JUST LOOKED LIKE "THIS YEAR'S BLONDE."
OH WELL... THAT'S PROBABLY GOT NOTHING TO DO WITH STEVE BEING NIGH-COMATOSE, ANYWAY.
I'D BETTER LOOK IN ON ETTA AND HELEN...

AS CAPT. DIANA PRINCE!

HI, ETTA, CARE TO GO LOOK IN ON *STEVE* WITH ME?

SURE, DI! GUESS WHAT! OUR NEW *ROOMIE'S* A GREAT *COOK*!

JUST WHAT MY WAISTLINE *NEEDS*!

UH... *DIANA*...

...I KNOW I'M *NEW* HERE, BUT WOULD YOU MIND IF *I* WENT ALONG?

UH....OF COURSE NOT, HELEN, IF YOU'RE CERTAIN YOU'RE *UP* TO IT! YOU KNOW HOW *HOSPITALS* ARE.

I'D *LIKE* TO SEE YOUR... *COLONEL TREVOR.*

SOMETHING STRANGE ABOUT HELEN ALEXANDROS-- THE WAY SHE *POPPED* UP THIS MORNING, WITH THAT *IMPORTANT BRIEFCASE* I'D LOST!

NO TIME *NOW* TO LOOK THAT PARTICULAR GIFT HORSE IN THE MOLARS... BUT I'M STILL NOT *SOLD* ON THAT *STORY* OF HERS.

C'MON, HELEN! YOU'LL LEARN YOU'VE REALLY GOTTA *MOVE* IF YOU WANNA KEEP UP WITH *DI* WHEN SHE'S IN A HURRY.

I THINK I ALREADY *KNOW* THAT, ETTA.

BUT I REALLY BELIEVE I CAN *MANAGE*... HONEST!

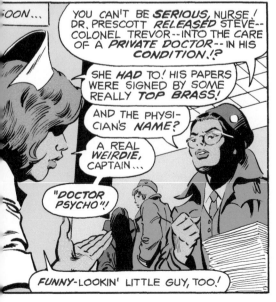

SOON...

YOU CAN'T BE *SERIOUS*, NURSE! DR. PRESCOTT *RELEASED* STEVE-- COLONEL TREVOR--INTO THE *CARE* OF A *PRIVATE DOCTOR*--IN HIS *CONDITION*!?

SHE *HAD* TO! HIS PAPERS WERE SIGNED BY SOME REALLY *TOP BRASS*!

AND THE PHYSI-CIAN'S *NAME*?

A REAL *WEIRDIE*, CAPTAIN...

"*DOCTOR PSYCHO*"!

FUNNY-LOOKIN' LITTLE GUY, TOO!

A COMBINATION OF *THREATS* AND *CAJOLING* SOON NETS AT LEAST THE *ADDRESS* TO WHICH STEVE WAS REMOVED, AND--

SO, DI, YOU WANNA HEAD OUT TO--?

IF YOU DON'T MIND, ETTA, I...I'D REALLY RATHER GO *ALONE* THIS TIME.

TELL HIM "*HI*" FOR US, HUH, DIANA?

8

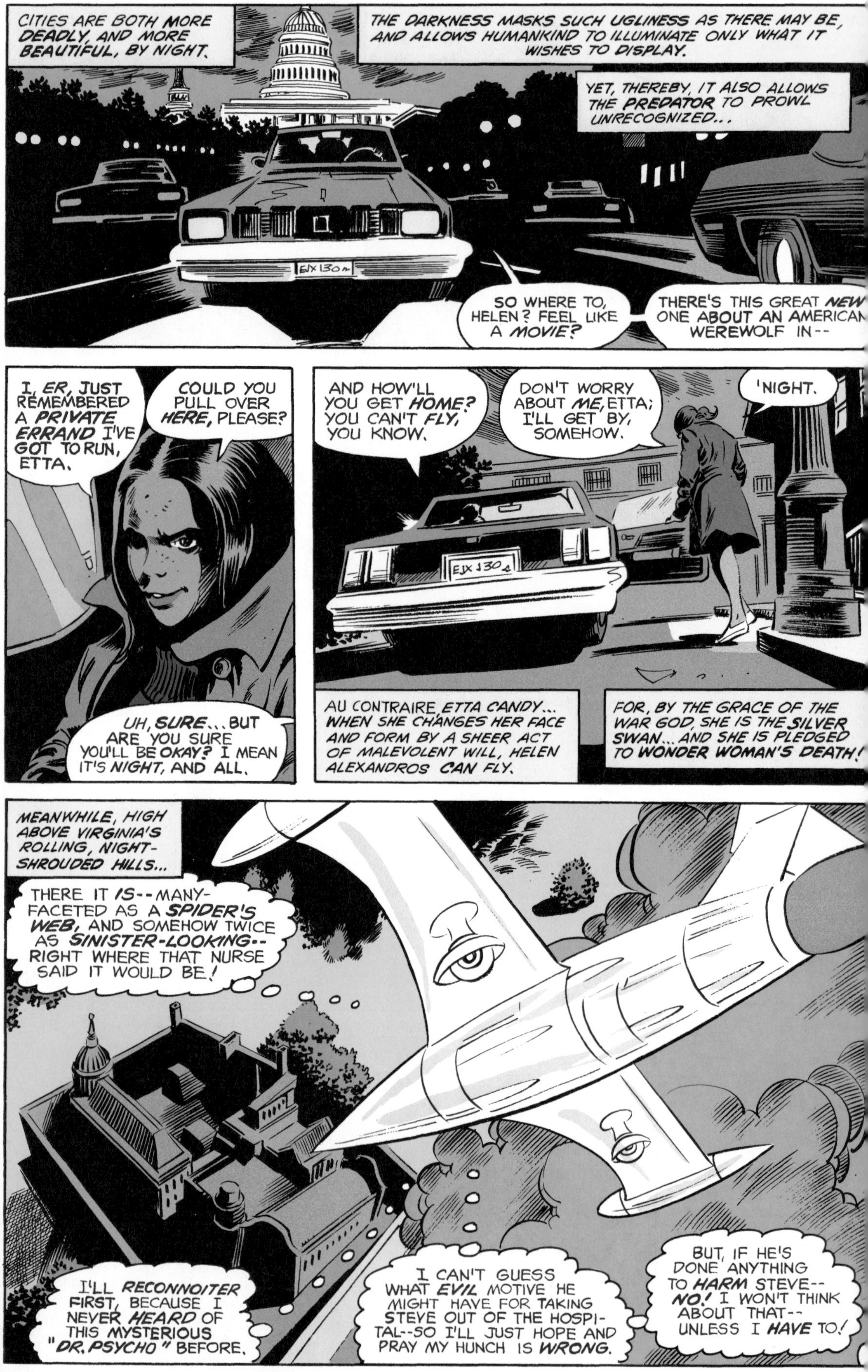

CITIES ARE BOTH MORE DEADLY, AND MORE BEAUTIFUL, BY NIGHT.
THE DARKNESS MASKS SUCH UGLINESS AS THERE MAY BE, AND ALLOWS HUMANKIND TO ILLUMINATE ONLY WHAT IT WISHES TO DISPLAY.
YET, THEREBY, IT ALSO ALLOWS THE PREDATOR TO PROWL UNRECOGNIZED...
EJX 130
SO WHERE TO, HELEN? FEEL LIKE A MOVIE?
THERE'S THIS GREAT NEW ONE ABOUT AN AMERICAN WEREWOLF IN--
I, ER, JUST REMEMBERED A PRIVATE ERRAND I'VE GOT TO RUN, ETTA.
COULD YOU PULL OVER HERE, PLEASE?
UH, SURE... BUT ARE YOU SURE YOU'LL BE OKAY? I MEAN IT'S NIGHT, AND ALL.
AND HOW'LL YOU GET HOME? YOU CAN'T FLY, YOU KNOW.
DON'T WORRY ABOUT ME, ETTA; I'LL GET BY, SOMEHOW.
'NIGHT.
EJX 130
AU CONTRAIRE, ETTA CANDY... WHEN SHE CHANGES HER FACE AND FORM BY A SHEER ACT OF MALEVOLENT WILL, HELEN ALEXANDROS CAN FLY.
FOR, BY THE GRACE OF THE WAR GOD, SHE IS THE SILVER SWAN... AND SHE IS PLEDGED TO WONDER WOMAN'S DEATH!
MEANWHILE, HIGH ABOVE VIRGINIA'S ROLLING, NIGHT-SHROUDED HILLS...
THERE IT IS--MANY-FACETED AS A SPIDER'S WEB, AND SOMEHOW TWICE AS SINISTER-LOOKING--RIGHT WHERE THAT NURSE SAID IT WOULD BE!
I'LL RECONNOITER FIRST, BECAUSE I NEVER HEARD OF THIS MYSTERIOUS "DR. PSYCHO" BEFORE.
I CAN'T GUESS WHAT EVIL MOTIVE HE MIGHT HAVE FOR TAKING STEVE OUT OF THE HOSPITAL--SO I'LL JUST HOPE AND PRAY MY HUNCH IS WRONG.
BUT, IF HE'S DONE ANYTHING TO HARM STEVE--NO! I WON'T THINK ABOUT THAT--UNLESS I HAVE TO!

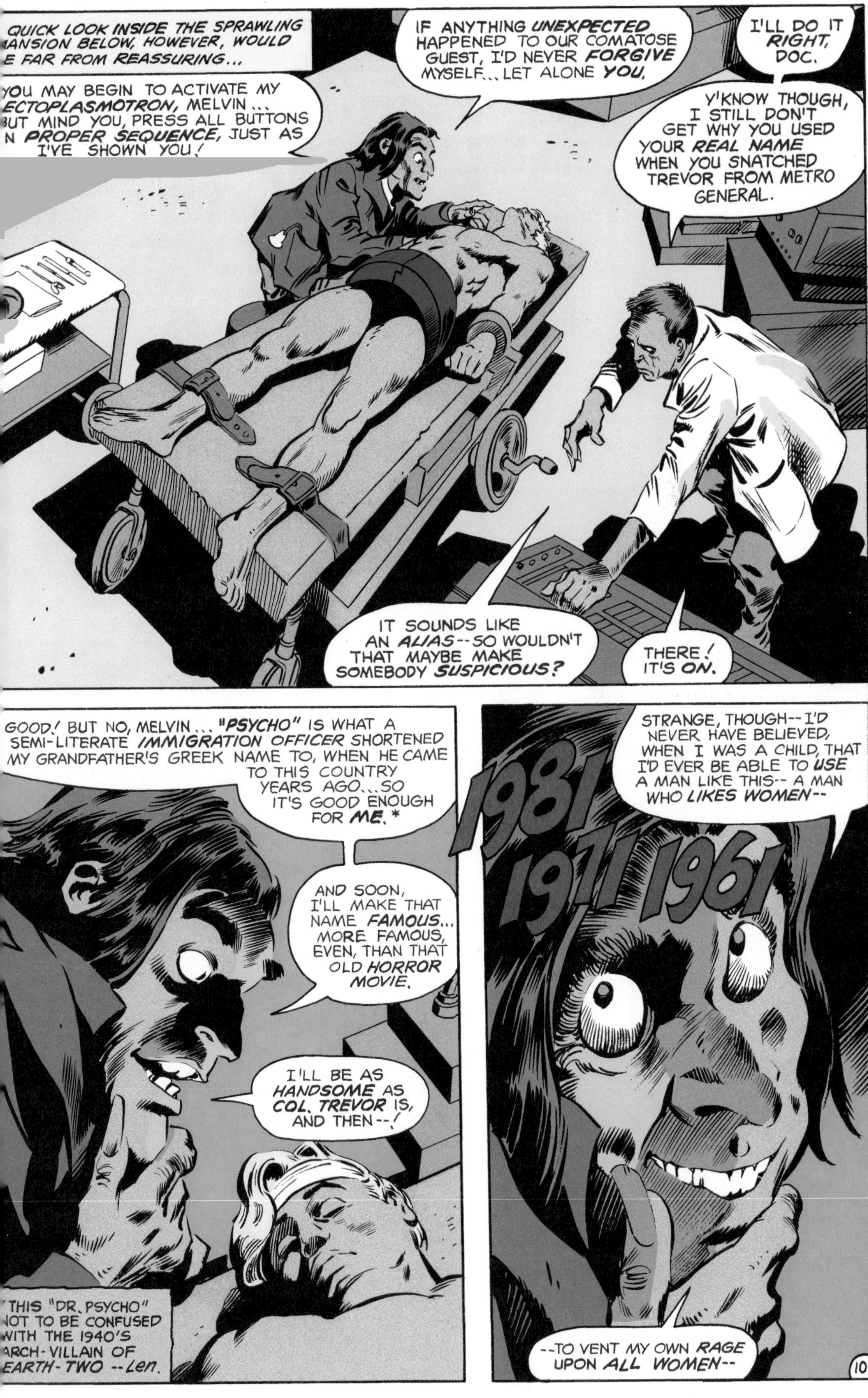
QUICK LOOK INSIDE THE SPRAWLING
MANSION BELOW, HOWEVER, WOULD
E FAR FROM REASSURING...
YOU MAY BEGIN TO ACTIVATE MY ECTOPLASMOTRON, MELVIN... BUT MIND YOU, PRESS ALL BUTTONS IN PROPER SEQUENCE, JUST AS I'VE SHOWN YOU!
IF ANYTHING UNEXPECTED HAPPENED TO OUR COMATOSE GUEST, I'D NEVER FORGIVE MYSELF... LET ALONE YOU.
I'LL DO IT RIGHT, DOC.
Y'KNOW THOUGH, I STILL DON'T GET WHY YOU USED YOUR REAL NAME WHEN YOU SNATCHED TREVOR FROM METRO GENERAL.
IT SOUNDS LIKE AN ALIAS--SO WOULDN'T THAT MAYBE MAKE SOMEBODY SUSPICIOUS?
THERE! IT'S ON.
GOOD! BUT NO, MELVIN... "PSYCHO" IS WHAT A SEMI-LITERATE IMMIGRATION OFFICER SHORTENED MY GRANDFATHER'S GREEK NAME TO, WHEN HE CAME TO THIS COUNTRY YEARS AGO... SO IT'S GOOD ENOUGH FOR ME.*
AND SOON, I'LL MAKE THAT NAME FAMOUS... MORE FAMOUS, EVEN, THAN THAT OLD HORROR MOVIE.
I'LL BE AS HANDSOME AS COL. TREVOR IS, AND THEN--!
*THIS "DR. PSYCHO" NOT TO BE CONFUSED WITH THE 1940'S ARCH-VILLAIN OF EARTH-TWO --Len.
1981
1971 1961
STRANGE, THOUGH--I'D NEVER HAVE BELIEVED, WHEN I WAS A CHILD, THAT I'D EVER BE ABLE TO USE A MAN LIKE THIS-- A MAN WHO LIKES WOMEN--
--TO VENT MY OWN RAGE UPON ALL WOMEN--
10

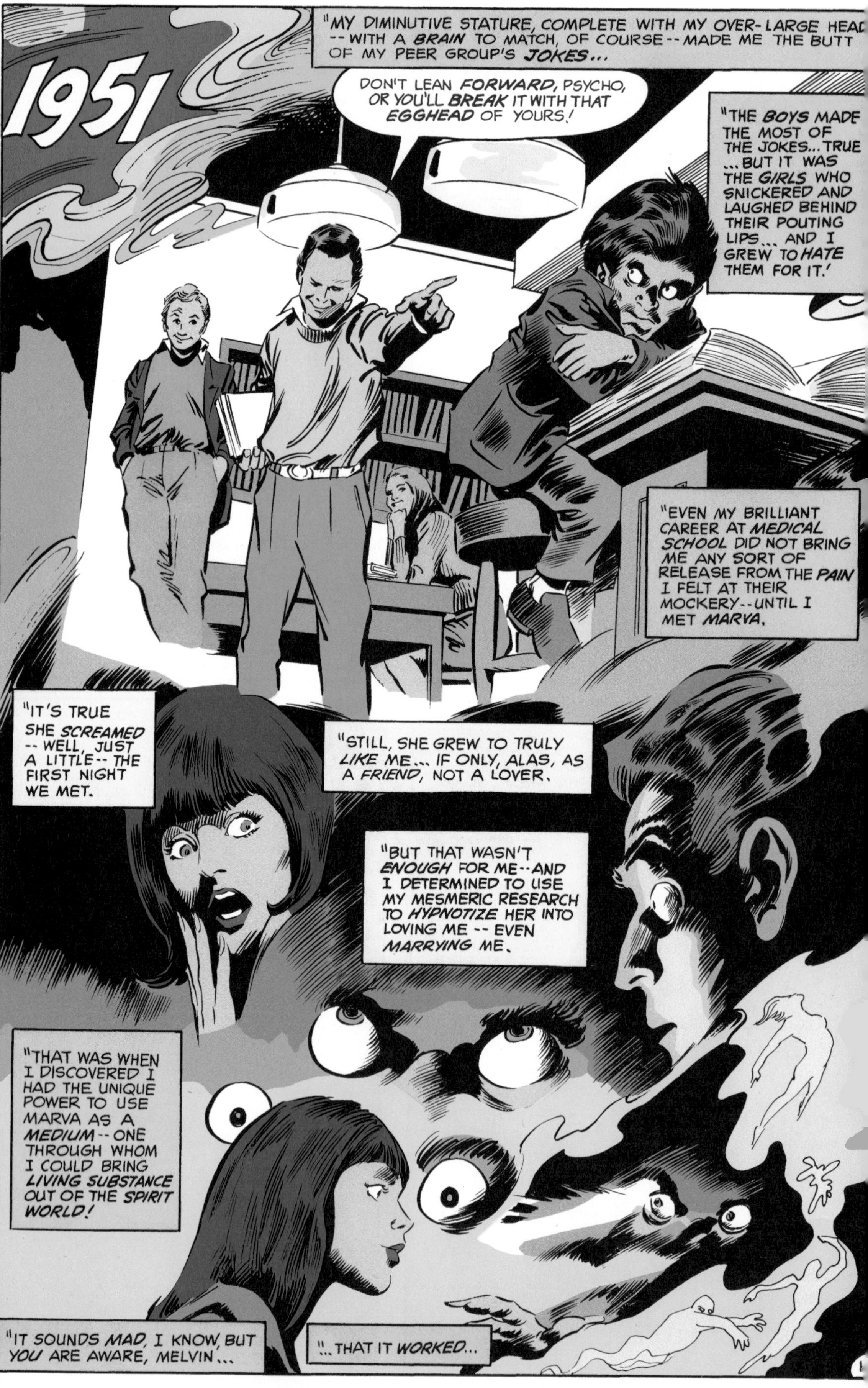
1951
"MY DIMINUTIVE STATURE, COMPLETE WITH MY OVER-LARGE HEAD -- WITH A BRAIN TO MATCH, OF COURSE -- MADE ME THE BUTT OF MY PEER GROUP'S JOKES...
DON'T LEAN FORWARD, PSYCHO, OR YOU'LL BREAK IT WITH THAT EGGHEAD OF YOURS!
"THE BOYS MADE THE MOST OF THE JOKES... TRUE ...BUT IT WAS THE GIRLS WHO SNICKERED AND LAUGHED BEHIND THEIR POUTING LIPS... AND I GREW TO HATE THEM FOR IT.'
"EVEN MY BRILLIANT CAREER AT MEDICAL SCHOOL DID NOT BRING ME ANY SORT OF RELEASE FROM THE PAIN I FELT AT THEIR MOCKERY--UNTIL I MET MARVA.
"IT'S TRUE SHE SCREAMED -- WELL, JUST A LITTLE -- THE FIRST NIGHT WE MET.
"STILL, SHE GREW TO TRULY LIKE ME... IF ONLY, ALAS, AS A FRIEND, NOT A LOVER.
"BUT THAT WASN'T ENOUGH FOR ME -- AND I DETERMINED TO USE MY MESMERIC RESEARCH TO HYPNOTIZE HER INTO LOVING ME -- EVEN MARRYING ME.
"THAT WAS WHEN I DISCOVERED I HAD THE UNIQUE POWER TO USE MARVA AS A MEDIUM -- ONE THROUGH WHOM I COULD BRING LIVING SUBSTANCE OUT OF THE SPIRIT WORLD!
"IT SOUNDS MAD, I KNOW, BUT YOU ARE AWARE, MELVIN...
"...THAT IT WORKED...

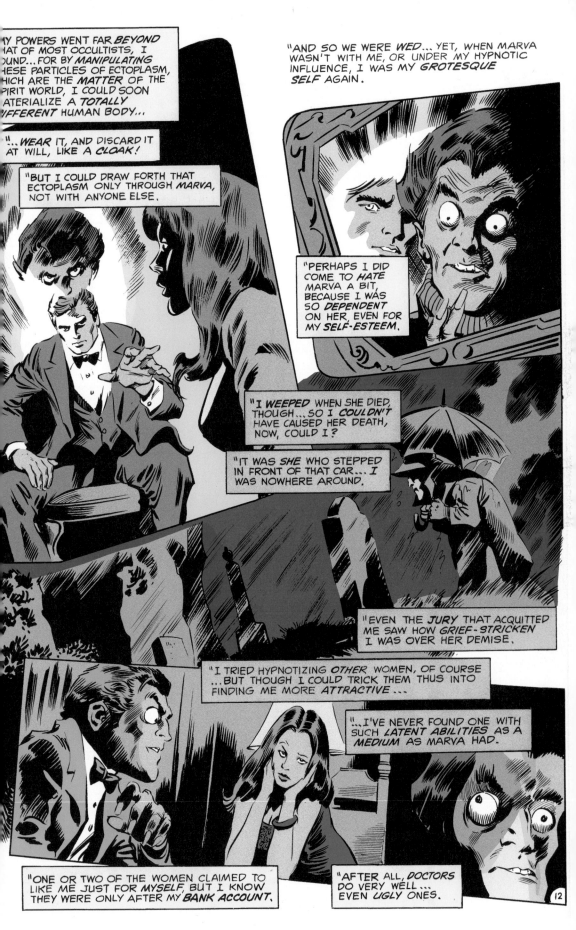

"MY POWERS WENT FAR *BEYOND* THAT OF MOST OCCULTISTS, I FOUND... FOR BY *MANIPULATING* THESE PARTICLES OF ECTOPLASM, WHICH ARE THE *MATTER* OF THE *SPIRIT WORLD*, I COULD SOON MATERIALIZE A *TOTALLY DIFFERENT* HUMAN BODY...

"...*WEAR* IT, AND DISCARD IT AT WILL, LIKE A *CLOAK!*

"BUT I COULD DRAW FORTH THAT ECTOPLASM ONLY THROUGH *MARVA*, NOT WITH ANYONE ELSE.

"AND SO WE WERE *WED*... YET, WHEN MARVA WASN'T WITH ME, OR UNDER MY HYPNOTIC INFLUENCE, I WAS MY *GROTESQUE SELF* AGAIN.

"PERHAPS I DID COME TO *HATE* MARVA A BIT, BECAUSE I WAS SO *DEPENDENT* ON HER, EVEN FOR MY *SELF-ESTEEM*.

"I *WEEPED* WHEN SHE DIED, THOUGH... SO I *COULDN'T* HAVE CAUSED HER DEATH, NOW, COULD I?

"IT WAS *SHE* WHO STEPPED IN FRONT OF THAT CAR... I WAS NOWHERE AROUND.

"EVEN THE *JURY* THAT ACQUITTED ME SAW HOW *GRIEF-STRICKEN* I WAS OVER HER DEMISE.

"I TRIED HYPNOTIZING *OTHER* WOMEN, OF COURSE ...BUT THOUGH I COULD TRICK THEM THUS INTO FINDING ME MORE *ATTRACTIVE* ...

"...I'VE NEVER FOUND ONE WITH SUCH *LATENT ABILITIES* AS A *MEDIUM* AS MARVA HAD.

"ONE OR TWO OF THE WOMEN CLAIMED TO LIKE ME JUST FOR *MYSELF*, BUT I KNOW THEY WERE ONLY AFTER MY *BANK ACCOUNT*.

"AFTER ALL, *DOCTORS* DO VERY WELL... EVEN *UGLY* ONES.

12

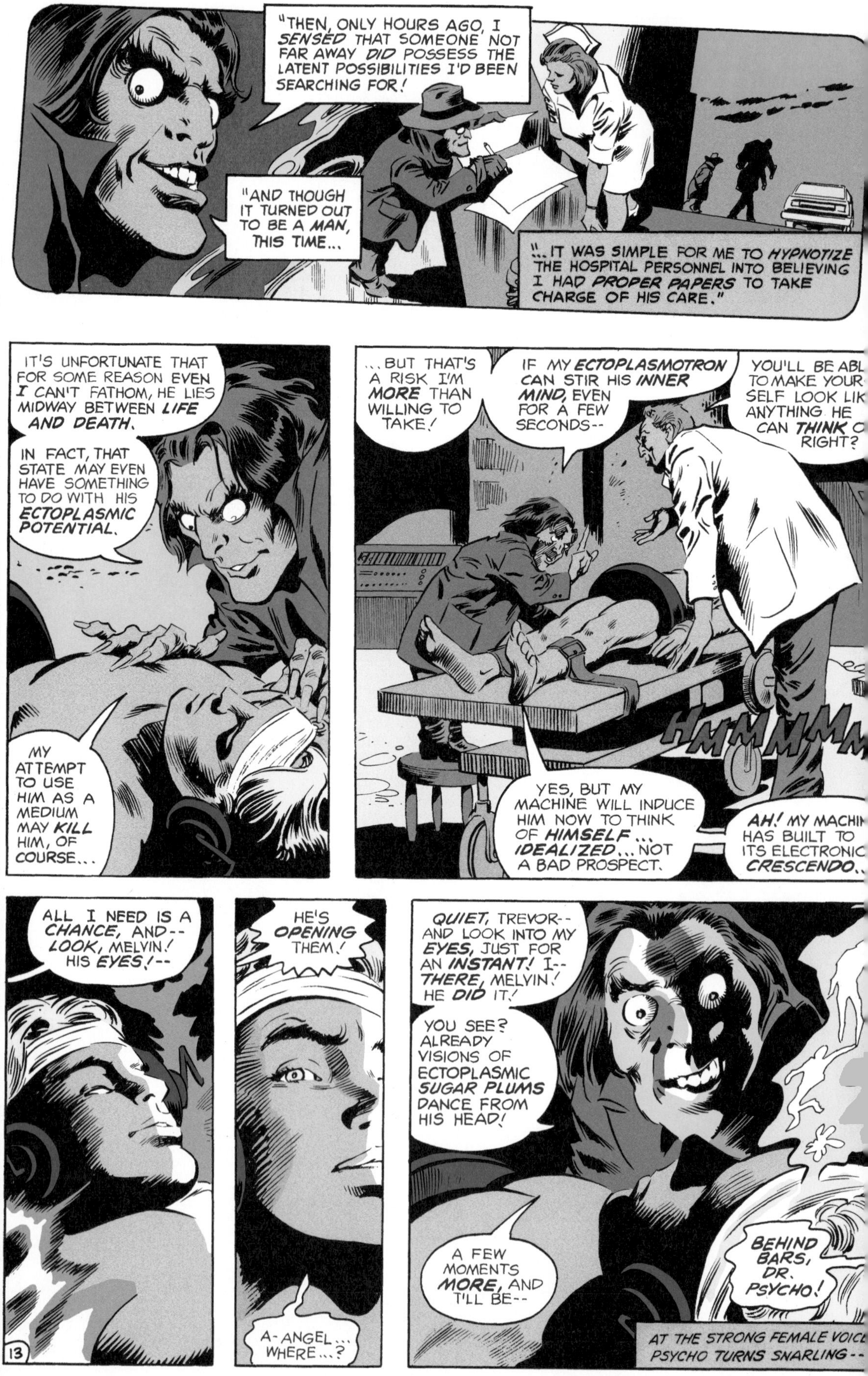
"THEN, ONLY HOURS AGO, I SENSED THAT SOMEONE NOT FAR AWAY DID POSSESS THE LATENT POSSIBILITIES I'D BEEN SEARCHING FOR!
"AND THOUGH IT TURNED OUT TO BE A MAN, THIS TIME...
"...IT WAS SIMPLE FOR ME TO HYPNOTIZE THE HOSPITAL PERSONNEL INTO BELIEVING I HAD PROPER PAPERS TO TAKE CHARGE OF HIS CARE."
IT'S UNFORTUNATE THAT FOR SOME REASON EVEN I CAN'T FATHOM, HE LIES MIDWAY BETWEEN LIFE AND DEATH.
IN FACT, THAT STATE MAY EVEN HAVE SOMETHING TO DO WITH HIS ECTOPLASMIC POTENTIAL.
MY ATTEMPT TO USE HIM AS A MEDIUM MAY KILL HIM, OF COURSE...
...BUT THAT'S A RISK I'M MORE THAN WILLING TO TAKE!
IF MY ECTOPLASMOTRON CAN STIR HIS INNER MIND, EVEN FOR A FEW SECONDS--
YOU'LL BE ABL TO MAKE YOUR SELF LOOK LIK ANYTHING HE CAN THINK O RIGHT?
HMMMMMM
YES, BUT MY MACHINE WILL INDUCE HIM NOW TO THINK OF HIMSELF... IDEALIZED... NOT A BAD PROSPECT.
AH! MY MACHIN HAS BUILT TO ITS ELECTRONIC CRESCENDO..
ALL I NEED IS A CHANCE, AND-- LOOK, MELVIN! HIS EYES!--
13
HE'S OPENING THEM!
A-ANGEL... WHERE...?
QUIET, TREVOR-- AND LOOK INTO MY EYES, JUST FOR AN INSTANT! I-- THERE, MELVIN! HE DID IT!
YOU SEE? ALREADY VISIONS OF ECTOPLASMIC SUGAR PLUMS DANCE FROM HIS HEAD!
A FEW MOMENTS MORE, AND I'LL BE--
BEHIND BARS, DR. PSYCHO!
AT THE STRONG FEMALE VOIC PSYCHO TURNS SNARLING--

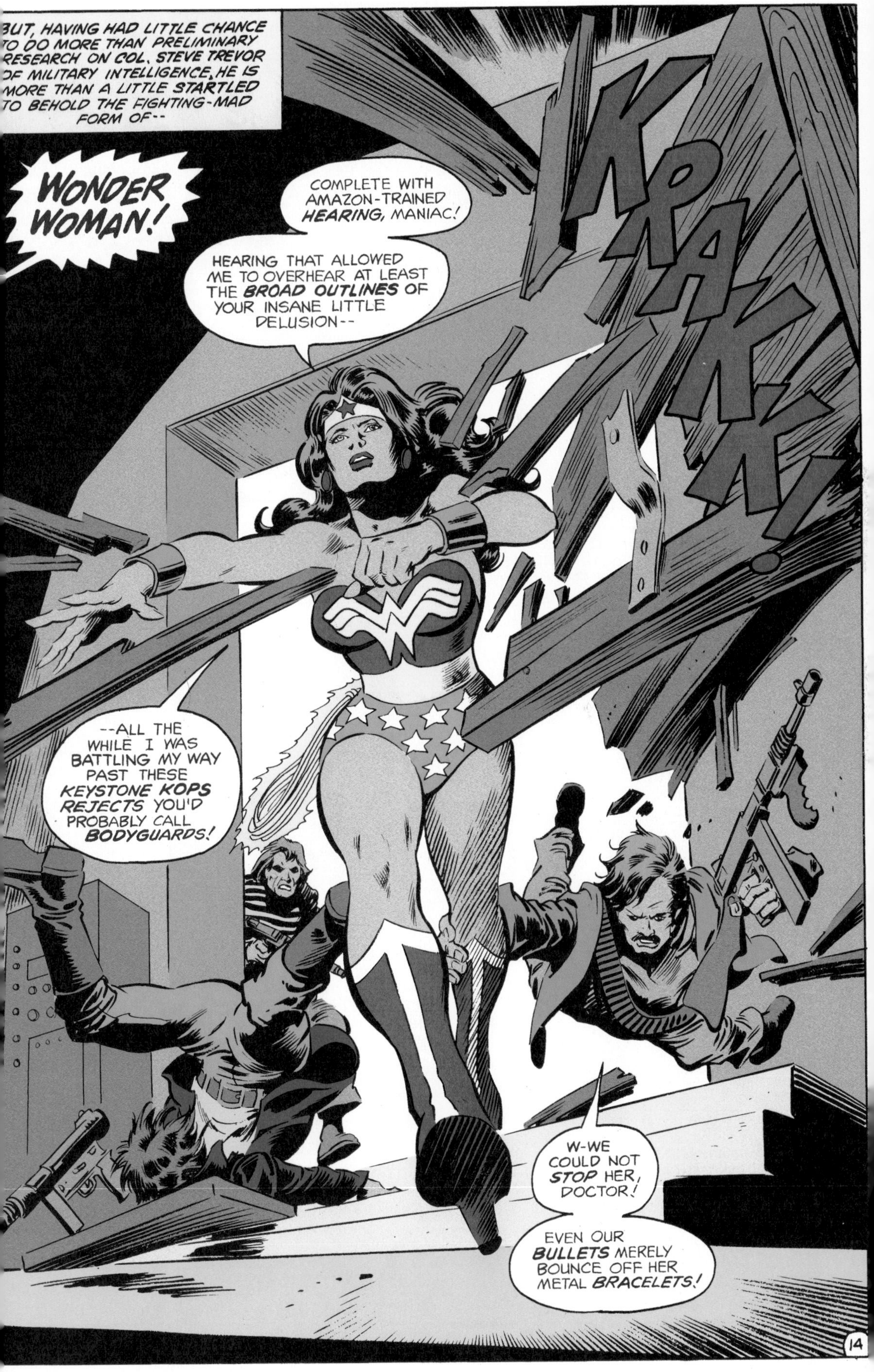

BUT, HAVING HAD LITTLE CHANCE TO DO MORE THAN PRELIMINARY RESEARCH ON COL. STEVE TREVOR OF MILITARY INTELLIGENCE, HE IS MORE THAN A LITTLE STARTLED TO BEHOLD THE FIGHTING-MAD FORM OF--
WONDER WOMAN!
KRAKK!
COMPLETE WITH AMAZON-TRAINED HEARING, MANIAC!
HEARING THAT ALLOWED ME TO OVERHEAR AT LEAST THE BROAD OUTLINES OF YOUR INSANE LITTLE DELUSION--
--ALL THE WHILE I WAS BATTLING MY WAY PAST THESE KEYSTONE KOPS REJECTS YOU'D PROBABLY CALL BODYGUARDS!
W-WE COULD NOT STOP HER, DOCTOR!
EVEN OUR BULLETS MERELY BOUNCE OFF HER METAL BRACELETS!
14

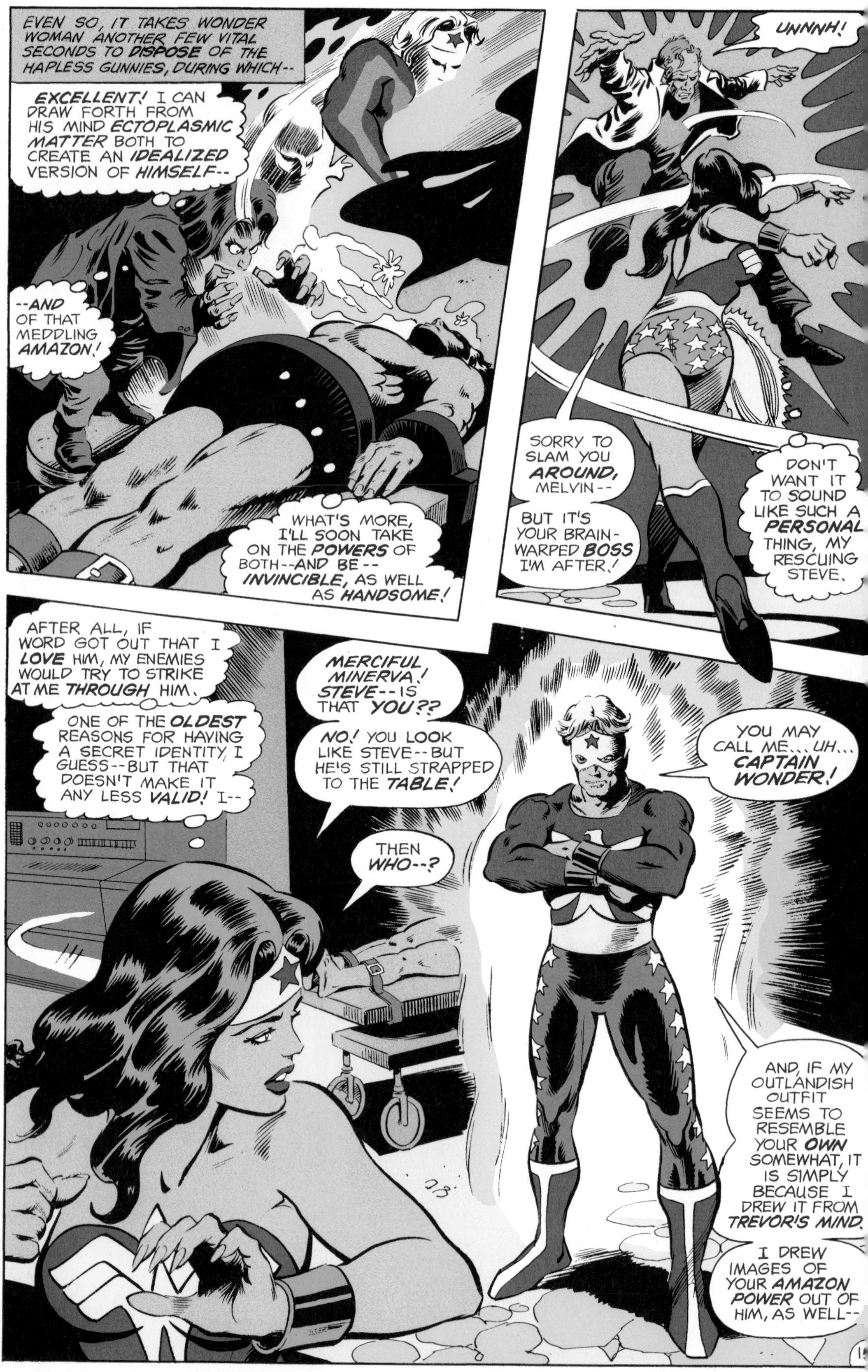
EVEN SO, IT TAKES WONDER WOMAN ANOTHER FEW VITAL SECONDS TO DISPOSE OF THE HAPLESS GUNNIES, DURING WHICH--
EXCELLENT! I CAN DRAW FORTH FROM HIS MIND ECTOPLASMIC MATTER BOTH TO CREATE AN IDEALIZED VERSION OF HIMSELF--
--AND OF THAT MEDDLING AMAZON!
WHAT'S MORE, I'LL SOON TAKE ON THE POWERS OF BOTH--AND BE--INVINCIBLE, AS WELL AS HANDSOME!
UNNNH!
SORRY TO SLAM YOU AROUND, MELVIN--
BUT IT'S YOUR BRAIN-WARPED BOSS I'M AFTER!
DON'T WANT IT TO SOUND LIKE SUCH A PERSONAL THING, MY RESCUING STEVE.
AFTER ALL, IF WORD GOT OUT THAT I LOVE HIM, MY ENEMIES WOULD TRY TO STRIKE AT ME THROUGH HIM.
ONE OF THE OLDEST REASONS FOR HAVING A SECRET IDENTITY, I GUESS--BUT THAT DOESN'T MAKE IT ANY LESS VALID! I--
MERCIFUL MINERVA! STEVE--IS THAT YOU??
NO! YOU LOOK LIKE STEVE--BUT HE'S STILL STRAPPED TO THE TABLE!
THEN WHO--?
YOU MAY CALL ME... UH... CAPTAIN WONDER!
AND, IF MY OUTLANDISH OUTFIT SEEMS TO RESEMBLE YOUR OWN SOMEWHAT, IT IS SIMPLY BECAUSE I DREW IT FROM TREVOR'S MIND.
I DREW IMAGES OF YOUR AMAZON POWER OUT OF HIM, AS WELL--

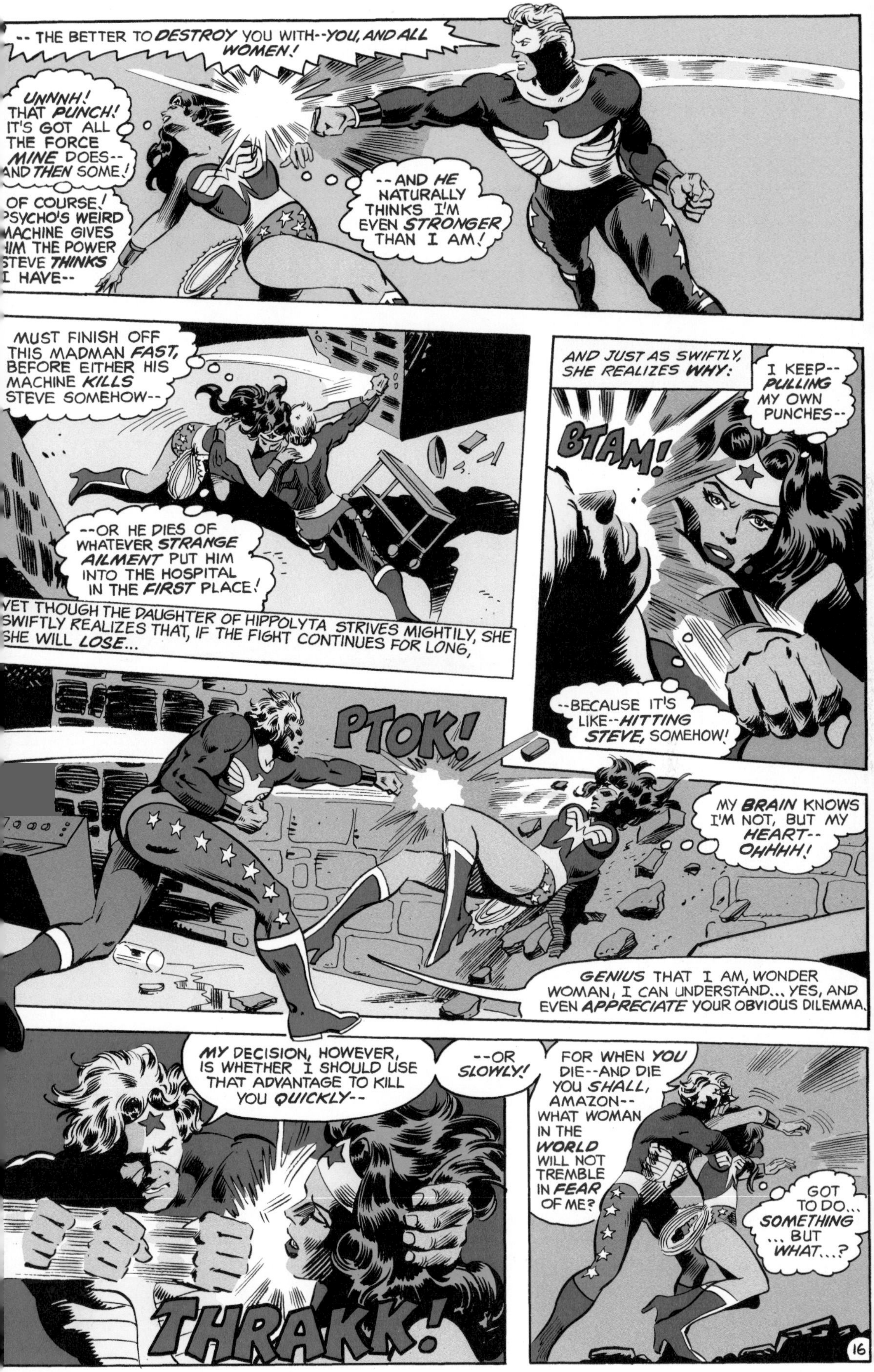
-- THE BETTER TO DESTROY YOU WITH--YOU, AND ALL WOMEN!
UNNNH! THAT PUNCH! IT'S GOT ALL THE FORCE MINE DOES-- AND THEN SOME!
OF COURSE! PSYCHO'S WEIRD MACHINE GIVES HIM THE POWER STEVE THINKS I HAVE--
--AND HE NATURALLY THINKS I'M EVEN STRONGER THAN I AM!
MUST FINISH OFF THIS MADMAN FAST, BEFORE EITHER HIS MACHINE KILLS STEVE SOMEHOW--
--OR HE DIES OF WHATEVER STRANGE AILMENT PUT HIM INTO THE HOSPITAL IN THE FIRST PLACE!
YET THOUGH THE DAUGHTER OF HIPPOLYTA STRIVES MIGHTILY, SHE SWIFTLY REALIZES THAT, IF THE FIGHT CONTINUES FOR LONG, SHE WILL LOSE...
AND JUST AS SWIFTLY, SHE REALIZES WHY:
I KEEP-- PULLING MY OWN PUNCHES--
BTAM!
--BECAUSE IT'S LIKE--HITTING STEVE, SOMEHOW!
PTOK!
MY BRAIN KNOWS I'M NOT, BUT MY HEART-- OHHHH!
GENIUS THAT I AM, WONDER WOMAN, I CAN UNDERSTAND... YES, AND EVEN APPRECIATE YOUR OBVIOUS DILEMMA.
MY DECISION, HOWEVER, IS WHETHER I SHOULD USE THAT ADVANTAGE TO KILL YOU QUICKLY--
--OR SLOWLY!
THRAKK!
FOR WHEN YOU DIE--AND DIE YOU SHALL, AMAZON-- WHAT WOMAN IN THE WORLD WILL NOT TREMBLE IN FEAR OF ME?
GOT TO DO... SOMETHING ... BUT WHAT...?
16

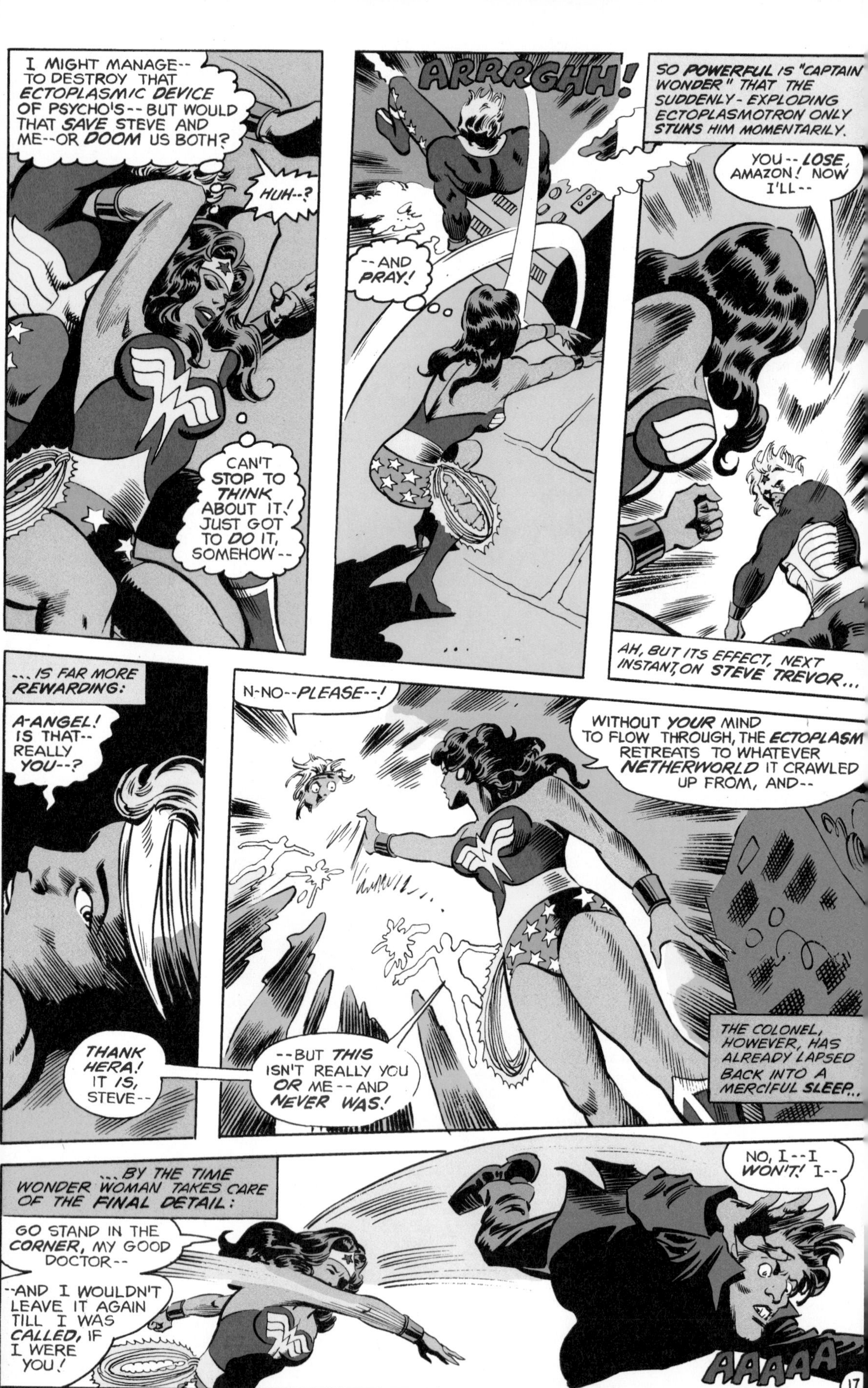
I MIGHT MANAGE-- TO DESTROY THAT ECTOPLASMIC DEVICE OF PSYCHO'S-- BUT WOULD THAT SAVE STEVE AND ME--OR DOOM US BOTH?
HUH--?
CAN'T STOP TO THINK ABOUT IT! JUST GOT TO DO IT, SOMEHOW--
ARRRGHH!
--AND PRAY!
SO POWERFUL IS "CAPTAIN WONDER" THAT THE SUDDENLY-EXPLODING ECTOPLASMOTRON ONLY STUNS HIM MOMENTARILY.
YOU--LOSE, AMAZON! NOW I'LL--
AH, BUT ITS EFFECT, NEXT INSTANT, ON STEVE TREVOR...
...IS FAR MORE REWARDING:
A-ANGEL! IS THAT-- REALLY YOU--?
THANK HERA! IT IS, STEVE--
N-NO--PLEASE--!
WITHOUT YOUR MIND TO FLOW THROUGH, THE ECTOPLASM RETREATS TO WHATEVER NETHERWORLD IT CRAWLED UP FROM, AND--
--BUT THIS ISN'T REALLY YOU OR ME--AND NEVER WAS!
THE COLONEL, HOWEVER, HAS ALREADY LAPSED BACK INTO A MERCIFUL SLEEP...
...BY THE TIME WONDER WOMAN TAKES CARE OF THE FINAL DETAIL:
GO STAND IN THE CORNER, MY GOOD DOCTOR--
--AND I WOULDN'T LEAVE IT AGAIN TILL I WAS CALLED, IF I WERE YOU!
NO, I--I WON'T! I--
AAAAA
17

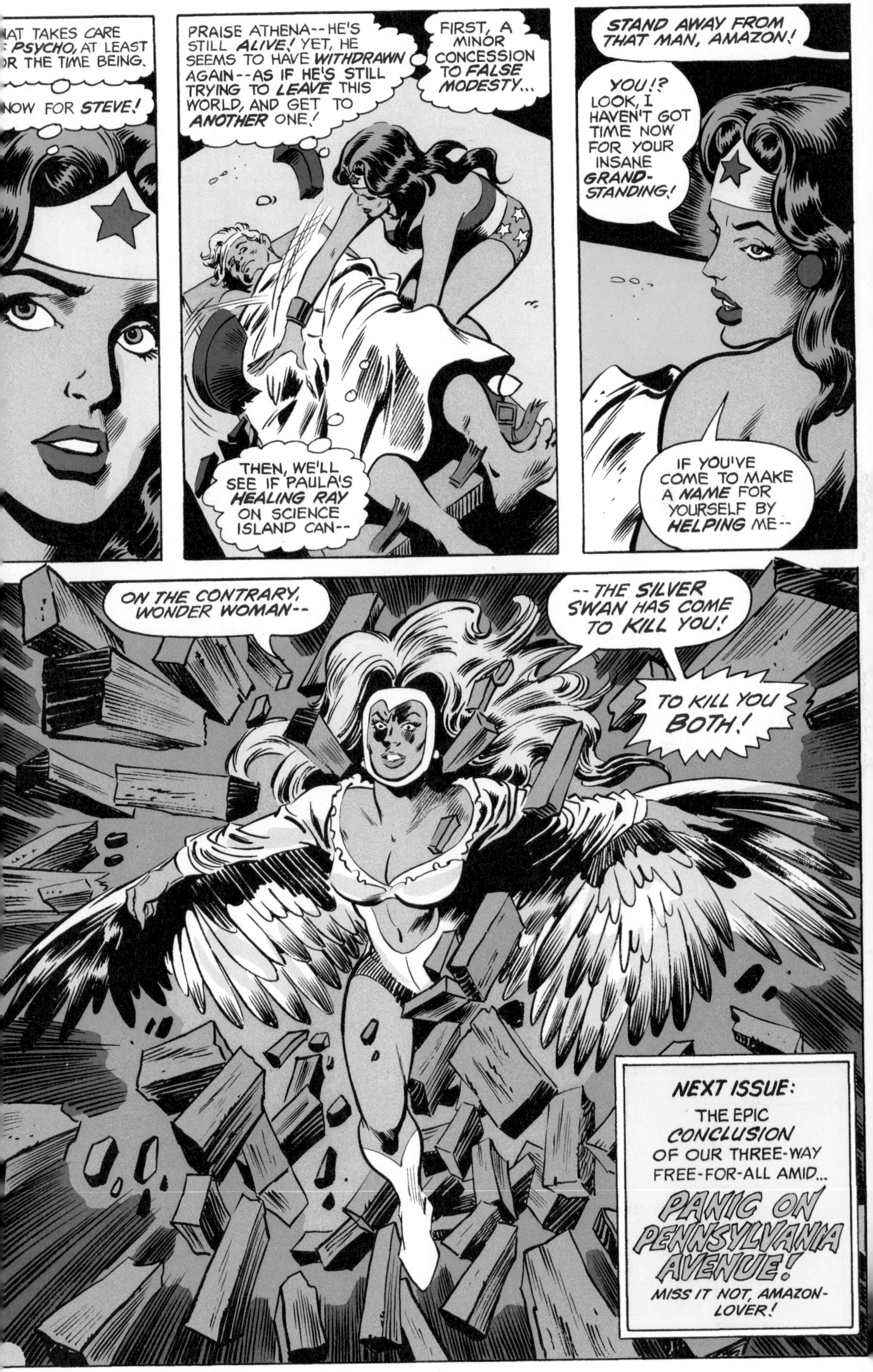

AT TAKES CARE
PSYCHO, AT LEAST
OR THE TIME BEING.
NOW FOR STEVE!
PRAISE ATHENA--HE'S STILL ALIVE! YET, HE SEEMS TO HAVE WITHDRAWN AGAIN--AS IF HE'S STILL TRYING TO LEAVE THIS WORLD, AND GET TO ANOTHER ONE!
FIRST, A MINOR CONCESSION TO FALSE MODESTY...
THEN, WE'LL SEE IF PAULA'S HEALING RAY ON SCIENCE ISLAND CAN--
STAND AWAY FROM THAT MAN, AMAZON!
YOU!? LOOK, I HAVEN'T GOT TIME NOW FOR YOUR INSANE GRAND-STANDING!
IF YOU'VE COME TO MAKE A NAME FOR YOURSELF BY HELPING ME--
ON THE CONTRARY, WONDER WOMAN--
--THE SILVER SWAN HAS COME TO KILL YOU!
TO KILL YOU BOTH!
NEXT ISSUE:
THE EPIC CONCLUSION OF OUR THREE-WAY FREE-FOR-ALL AMID...
PANIC ON PENNSYLVANIA AVENUE!
MISS IT NOT, AMAZON-LOVER!

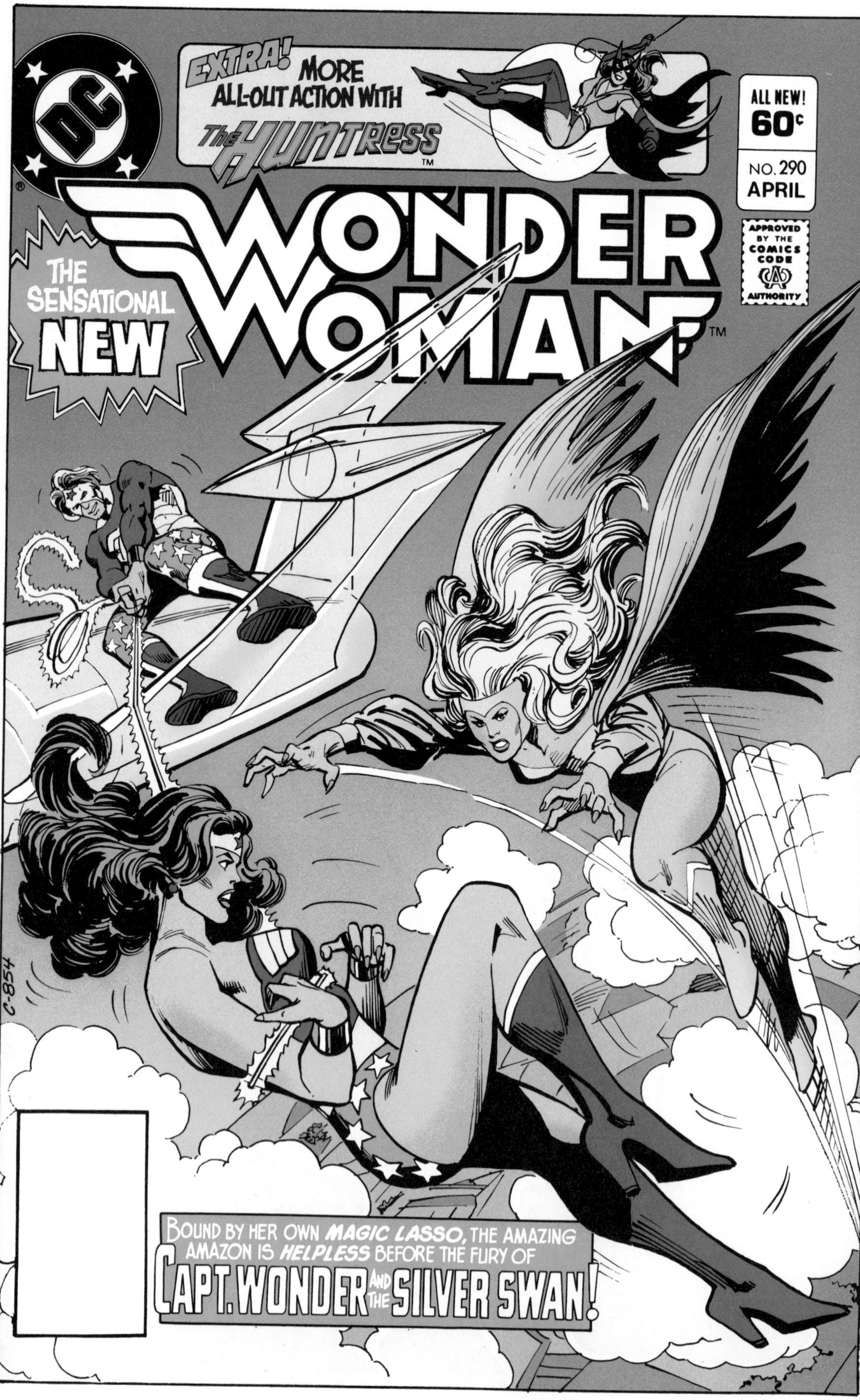

DC
EXTRA! MORE ALL-OUT ACTION WITH
The HUNTRESS ™
ALL NEW! 60¢
NO. 290
APRIL
APPROVED BY THE COMICS CODE AUTHORITY
THE SENSATIONAL NEW
WONDER WOMAN ™
C-854
BOUND BY HER OWN MAGIC LASSO, THE AMAZING AMAZON IS HELPLESS BEFORE THE FURY OF
CAPT. WONDER AND THE SILVER SWAN!

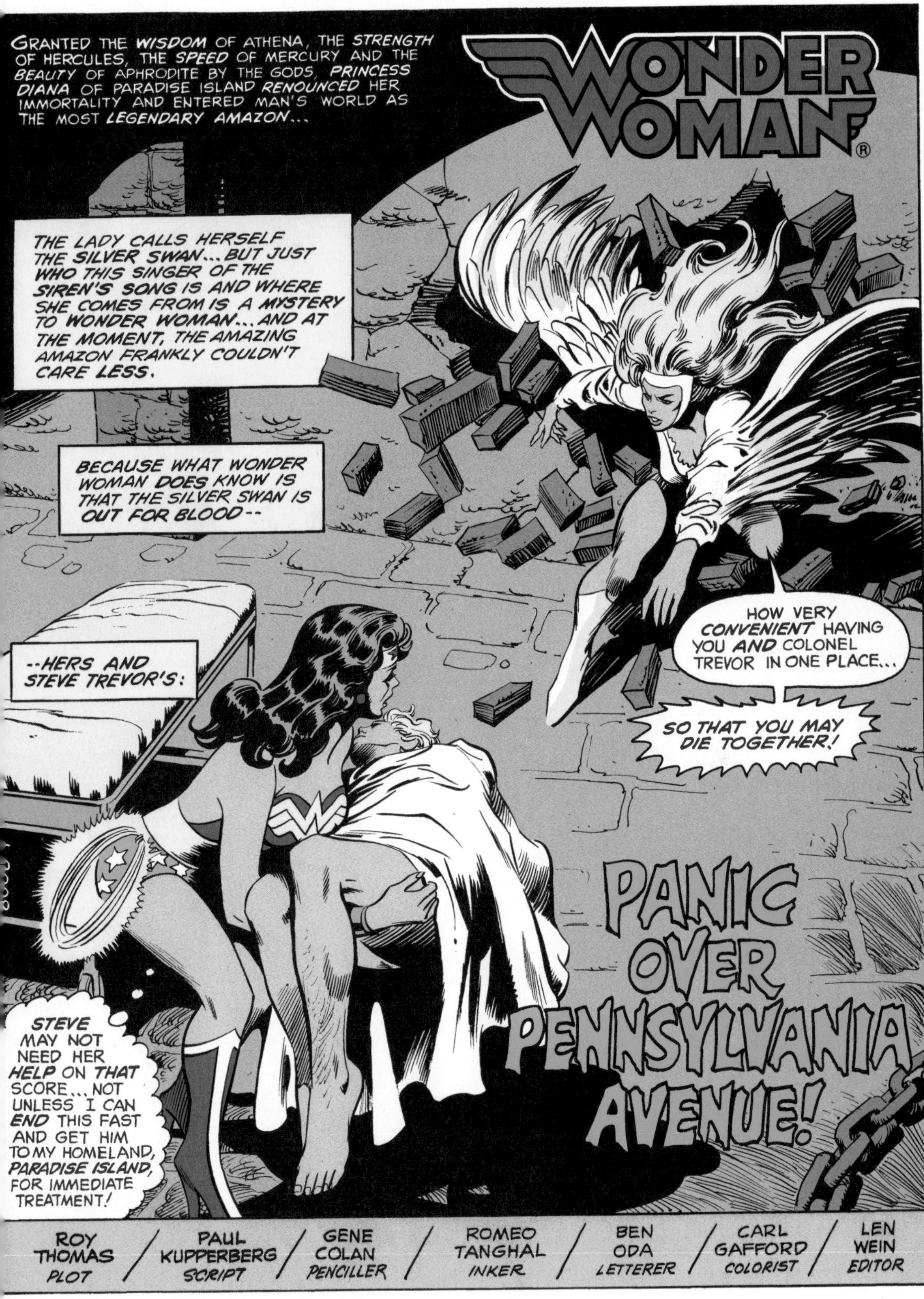
GRANTED THE WISDOM OF ATHENA, THE STRENGTH OF HERCULES, THE SPEED OF MERCURY AND THE BEAUTY OF APHRODITE BY THE GODS, PRINCESS DIANA OF PARADISE ISLAND RENOUNCED HER IMMORTALITY AND ENTERED MAN'S WORLD AS THE MOST LEGENDARY AMAZON...
WONDER WOMAN®
THE LADY CALLS HERSELF THE SILVER SWAN... BUT JUST WHO THIS SINGER OF THE SIREN'S SONG IS AND WHERE SHE COMES FROM IS A MYSTERY TO WONDER WOMAN... AND AT THE MOMENT, THE AMAZING AMAZON FRANKLY COULDN'T CARE LESS.
BECAUSE WHAT WONDER WOMAN DOES KNOW IS THAT THE SILVER SWAN IS OUT FOR BLOOD--
--HERS AND STEVE TREVOR'S:
HOW VERY CONVENIENT HAVING YOU AND COLONEL TREVOR IN ONE PLACE...
SO THAT YOU MAY DIE TOGETHER!
STEVE MAY NOT NEED HER HELP ON THAT SCORE... NOT UNLESS I CAN END THIS FAST AND GET HIM TO MY HOMELAND, PARADISE ISLAND, FOR IMMEDIATE TREATMENT!
PANIC OVER PENNSYLVANIA AVENUE!
ROY THOMAS PLOT / PAUL KUPPERBERG SCRIPT / GENE COLAN PENCILLER / ROMEO TANGHAL INKER / BEN ODA LETTERER / CARL GAFFORD COLORIST / LEN WEIN EDITOR

AND A *FAST BREAK'S* NOT SOMETHING I SHOULD *COUNT* ON... NOT AGAINST *HER.* THE SILVER SWAN MAY NOT BE QUITE AS *STRONG* AS *I* AM, BUT SHE'S *STILL* GOT A FEW THINGS GOING FOR HER.

AFTER ALL, SHE *DID* GIVE ME *MORE* THAN A RUN FOR MY MONEY WITH THAT *SONIC CRY* OF HERS THE FIRST TIME WE FOUGHT...

...NOT TO MENTION *DUPING* GENERAL DARNELL AND HIS STAFF INTO THINKING HER ONE OF THE *GOOD GUYS* WITH HER UNCANNY ABILITY TO *BEGUILE MEN.* *

*AS SEEN IN ISSUE #288 — Len.

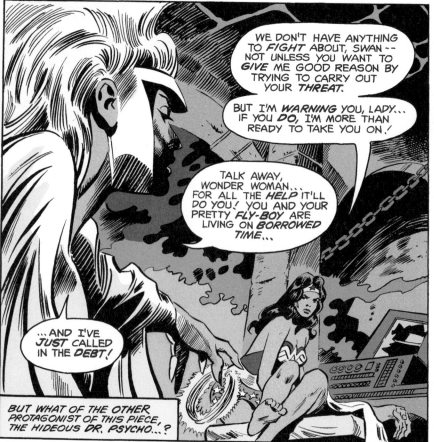

WE DON'T HAVE ANYTHING TO *FIGHT* ABOUT, SWAN -- NOT UNLESS YOU WANT TO *GIVE* ME GOOD REASON BY TRYING TO CARRY OUT YOUR *THREAT.*

BUT I'M *WARNING* YOU, LADY... IF YOU *DO,* I'M MORE THAN READY TO TAKE YOU ON!

TALK AWAY, WONDER WOMAN... FOR ALL THE *HELP* IT'LL DO YOU! YOU AND YOUR PRETTY *FLY-BOY* ARE LIVING ON *BORROWED TIME...*

...AND I'VE *JUST* CALLED IN THE *DEBT!*

BUT WHAT OF THE OTHER PROTAGONIST OF THIS PIECE, THE HIDEOUS *DR. PSYCHO...?*

HE'S ONCE MORE AMONG THE *CONSCIOUS,* AND THOUGH HE IS *TWISTED* OF BODY *AND MIND,* HE'S STILL A MAN, AND LOATHE AS HE IS TO ADMIT IT --

S-SHE'S... *BEAUTIFUL...!*

-- HE IS AS SMITTEN BY THE CHARMS OF THE *SILVER SWAN* AS ANY MAN.

2

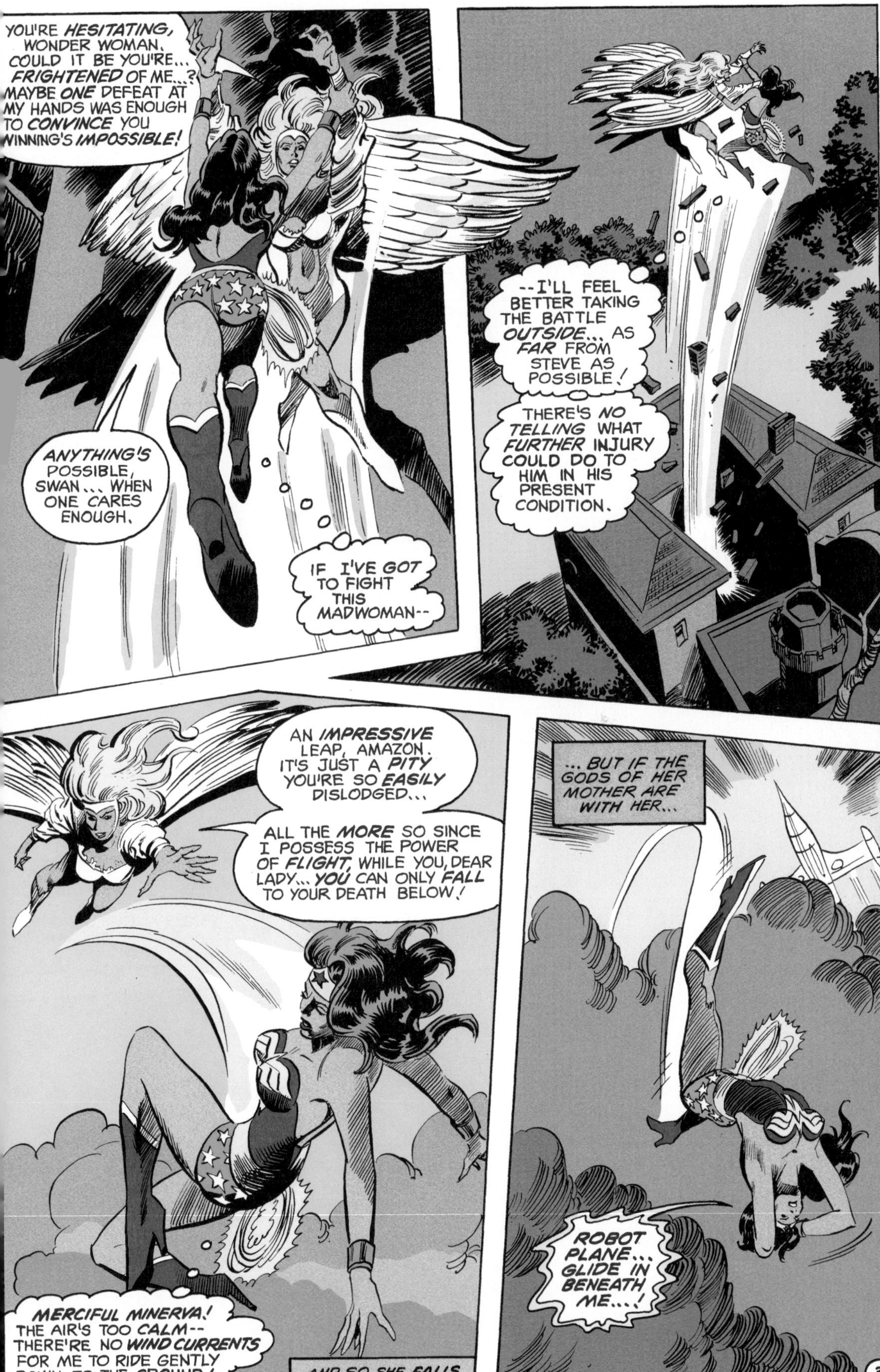
YOU'RE HESITATING, WONDER WOMAN. COULD IT BE YOU'RE... FRIGHTENED OF ME...? MAYBE ONE DEFEAT AT MY HANDS WAS ENOUGH TO CONVINCE YOU WINNING'S IMPOSSIBLE!
ANYTHING'S POSSIBLE, SWAN... WHEN ONE CARES ENOUGH.
IF I'VE GOT TO FIGHT THIS MADWOMAN--
--I'LL FEEL BETTER TAKING THE BATTLE OUTSIDE... AS FAR FROM STEVE AS POSSIBLE!
THERE'S NO TELLING WHAT FURTHER INJURY COULD DO TO HIM IN HIS PRESENT CONDITION.
AN IMPRESSIVE LEAP, AMAZON. IT'S JUST A PITY YOU'RE SO EASILY DISLODGED...
ALL THE MORE SO SINCE I POSSESS THE POWER OF FLIGHT, WHILE YOU, DEAR LADY... YOU CAN ONLY FALL TO YOUR DEATH BELOW!
MERCIFUL MINERVA! THE AIR'S TOO CALM-- THERE'RE NO WIND CURRENTS FOR ME TO RIDE GENTLY DOWN TO THE GROUND!
AND SO SHE FALLS...
...BUT IF THE GODS OF HER MOTHER ARE WITH HER...
ROBOT PLANE... GLIDE IN BENEATH ME...!
3

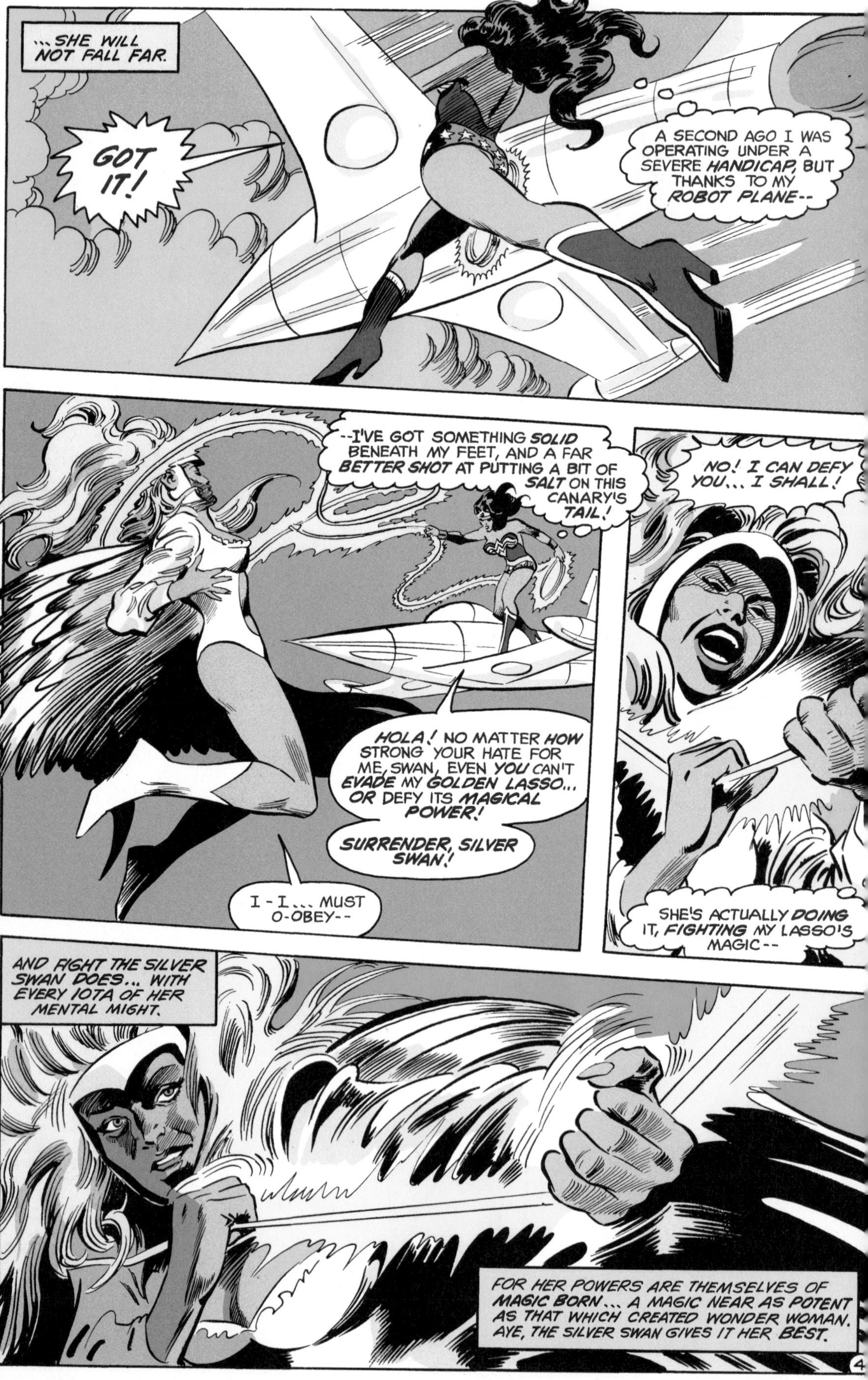
...SHE WILL NOT FALL FAR.
GOT IT!
A SECOND AGO I WAS OPERATING UNDER A SEVERE HANDICAP, BUT THANKS TO MY ROBOT PLANE--
--I'VE GOT SOMETHING SOLID BENEATH MY FEET, AND A FAR BETTER SHOT AT PUTTING A BIT OF SALT ON THIS CANARY'S TAIL!
HOLA! NO MATTER HOW STRONG YOUR HATE FOR ME, SWAN, EVEN YOU CAN'T EVADE MY GOLDEN LASSO... OR DEFY ITS MAGICAL POWER!
SURRENDER, SILVER SWAN!
I-I... MUST O-OBEY--
NO! I CAN DEFY YOU... I SHALL!
SHE'S ACTUALLY DOING IT, FIGHTING MY LASSO'S MAGIC--
AND FIGHT THE SILVER SWAN DOES... WITH EVERY IOTA OF HER MENTAL MIGHT.
FOR HER POWERS ARE THEMSELVES OF MAGIC BORN... A MAGIC NEAR AS POTENT AS THAT WHICH CREATED WONDER WOMAN. AYE, THE SILVER SWAN GIVES IT HER BEST.
4

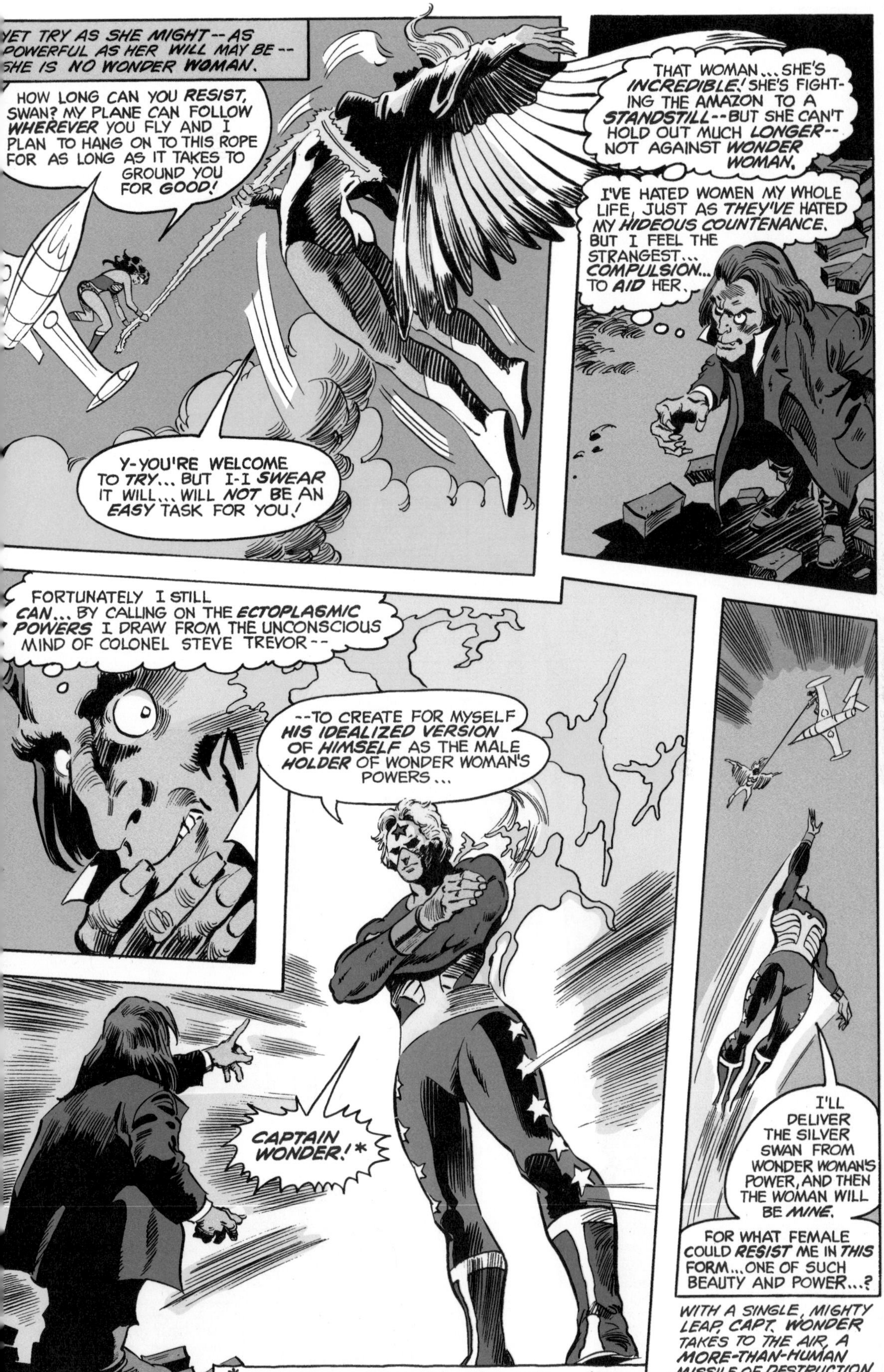
YET TRY AS SHE MIGHT -- AS POWERFUL AS HER WILL MAY BE -- SHE IS NO WONDER WOMAN.
HOW LONG CAN YOU RESIST, SWAN? MY PLANE CAN FOLLOW WHEREVER YOU FLY AND I PLAN TO HANG ON TO THIS ROPE FOR AS LONG AS IT TAKES TO GROUND YOU FOR GOOD!
Y-YOU'RE WELCOME TO TRY... BUT I-I SWEAR IT WILL... WILL NOT BE AN EASY TASK FOR YOU!
THAT WOMAN... SHE'S INCREDIBLE! SHE'S FIGHTING THE AMAZON TO A STANDSTILL -- BUT SHE CAN'T HOLD OUT MUCH LONGER -- NOT AGAINST WONDER WOMAN.
I'VE HATED WOMEN MY WHOLE LIFE, JUST AS THEY'VE HATED MY HIDEOUS COUNTENANCE. BUT I FEEL THE STRANGEST... COMPULSION... TO AID HER.
FORTUNATELY I STILL CAN... BY CALLING ON THE ECTOPLASMIC POWERS I DRAW FROM THE UNCONSCIOUS MIND OF COLONEL STEVE TREVOR --
-- TO CREATE FOR MYSELF HIS IDEALIZED VERSION OF HIMSELF AS THE MALE HOLDER OF WONDER WOMAN'S POWERS...
CAPTAIN WONDER! *
*BY A PROCESS EXPLAINED LAST ISSUE. - Len
I'LL DELIVER THE SILVER SWAN FROM WONDER WOMAN'S POWER, AND THEN THE WOMAN WILL BE MINE.
FOR WHAT FEMALE COULD RESIST ME IN THIS FORM... ONE OF SUCH BEAUTY AND POWER...?
WITH A SINGLE, MIGHTY LEAP, CAPT. WONDER TAKES TO THE AIR, A MORE-THAN-HUMAN MISSILE OF DESTRUCTION AND VENGEANCE.
5

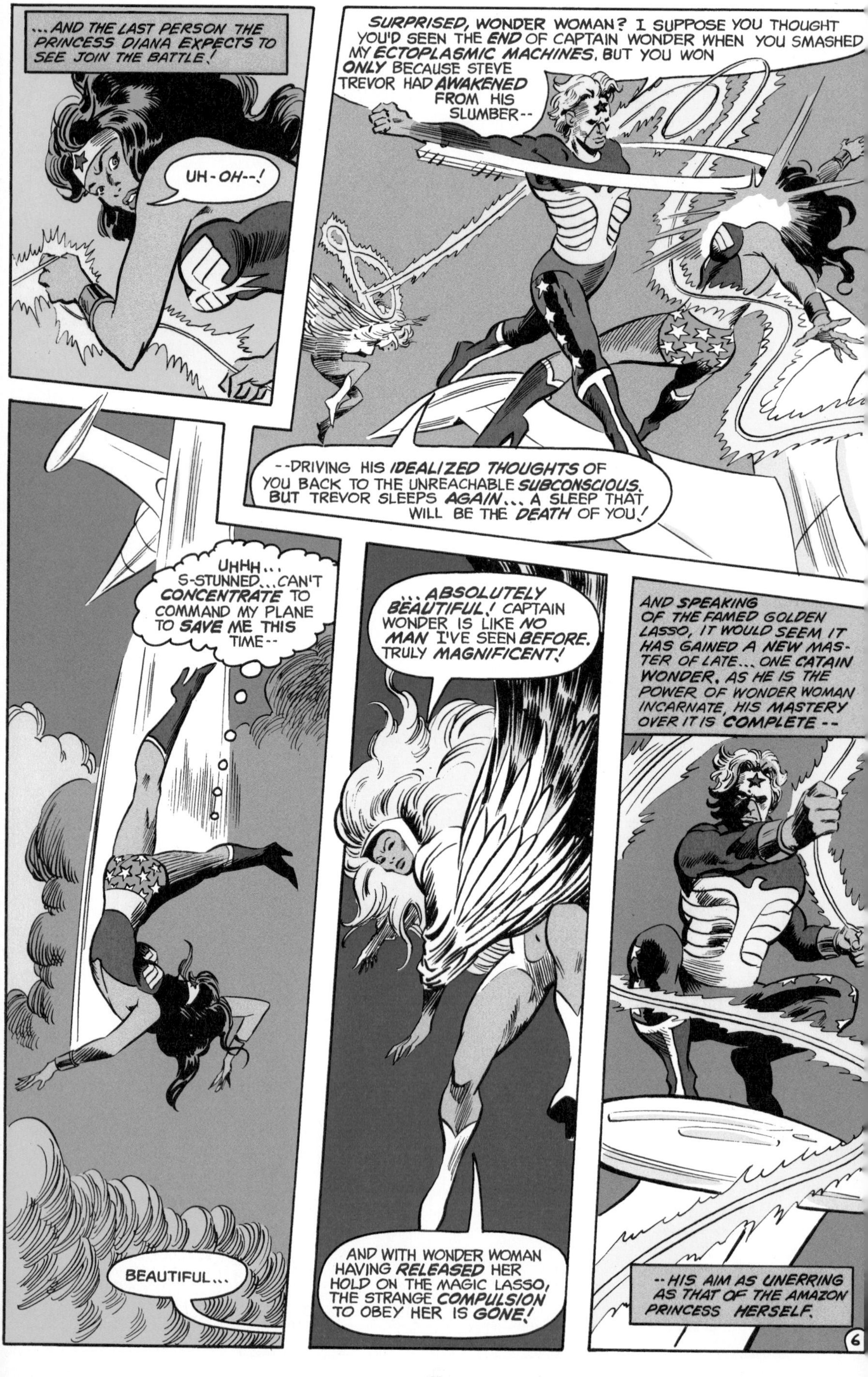
...AND THE LAST PERSON THE PRINCESS DIANA EXPECTS TO SEE JOIN THE BATTLE!
UH-OH--!
SURPRISED, WONDER WOMAN? I SUPPOSE YOU THOUGHT YOU'D SEEN THE END OF CAPTAIN WONDER WHEN YOU SMASHED MY ECTOPLASMIC MACHINES. BUT YOU WON ONLY BECAUSE STEVE TREVOR HAD AWAKENED FROM HIS SLUMBER--
--DRIVING HIS IDEALIZED THOUGHTS OF YOU BACK TO THE UNREACHABLE SUBCONSCIOUS. BUT TREVOR SLEEPS AGAIN... A SLEEP THAT WILL BE THE DEATH OF YOU!
UHHH... S-STUNNED...CAN'T CONCENTRATE TO COMMAND MY PLANE TO SAVE ME THIS TIME--
BEAUTIFUL...
...ABSOLUTELY BEAUTIFUL! CAPTAIN WONDER IS LIKE NO MAN I'VE SEEN BEFORE. TRULY MAGNIFICENT!
AND WITH WONDER WOMAN HAVING RELEASED HER HOLD ON THE MAGIC LASSO, THE STRANGE COMPULSION TO OBEY HER IS GONE!
AND SPEAKING OF THE FAMED GOLDEN LASSO, IT WOULD SEEM IT HAS GAINED A NEW MASTER OF LATE... ONE CATAIN WONDER. AS HE IS THE POWER OF WONDER WOMAN INCARNATE, HIS MASTERY OVER IT IS COMPLETE--
--HIS AIM AS UNERRING AS THAT OF THE AMAZON PRINCESS HERSELF.
6

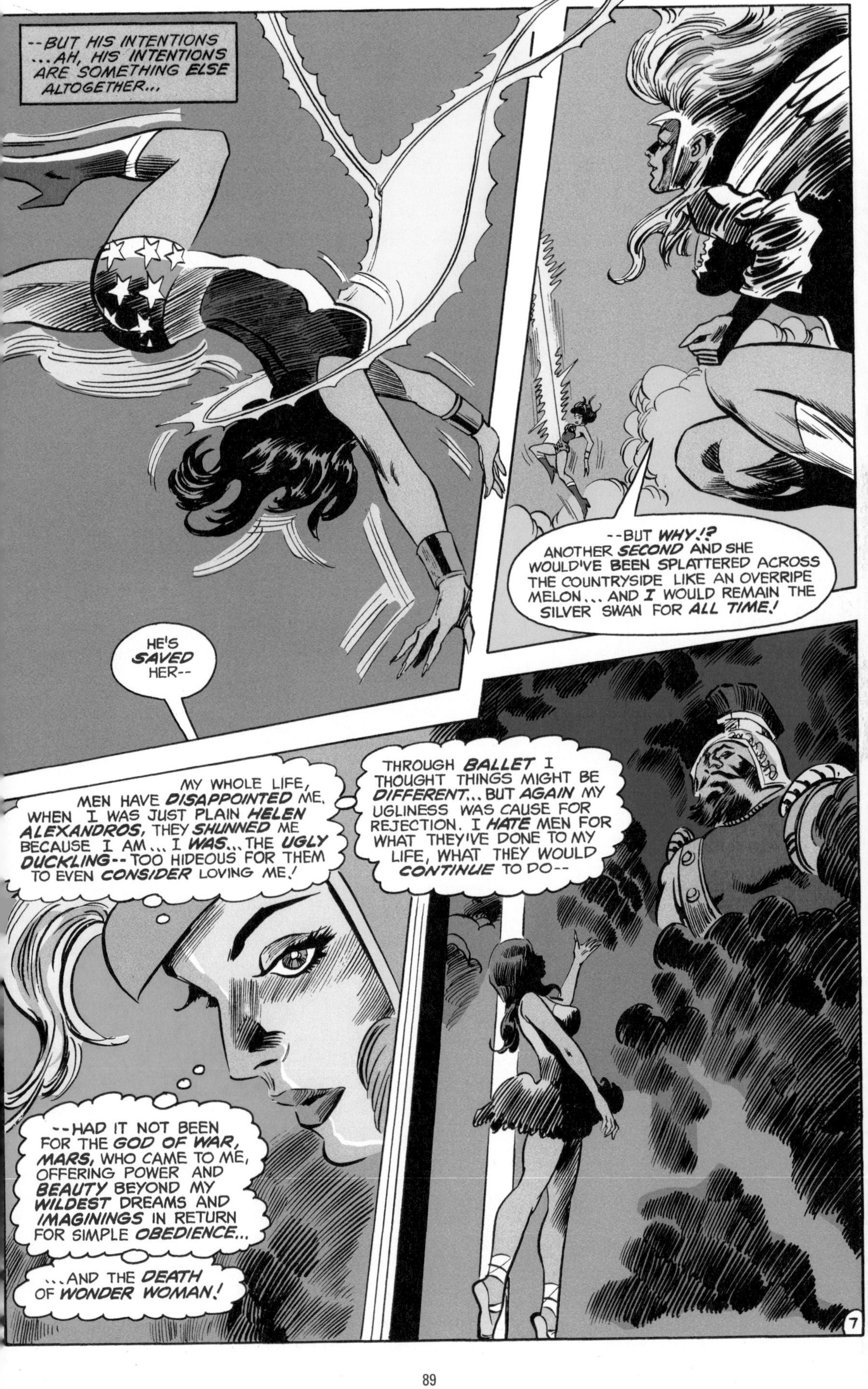
--BUT HIS INTENTIONS ...AH, HIS INTENTIONS ARE SOMETHING ELSE ALTOGETHER...
--BUT WHY!? ANOTHER SECOND AND SHE WOULD'VE BEEN SPLATTERED ACROSS THE COUNTRYSIDE LIKE AN OVERRIPE MELON... AND I WOULD REMAIN THE SILVER SWAN FOR ALL TIME!
HE'S SAVED HER--
MY WHOLE LIFE, MEN HAVE DISAPPOINTED ME. WHEN I WAS JUST PLAIN HELEN ALEXANDROS, THEY SHUNNED ME BECAUSE I AM... I WAS... THE UGLY DUCKLING--TOO HIDEOUS FOR THEM TO EVEN CONSIDER LOVING ME!
THROUGH BALLET I THOUGHT THINGS MIGHT BE DIFFERENT... BUT AGAIN MY UGLINESS WAS CAUSE FOR REJECTION. I HATE MEN FOR WHAT THEY'VE DONE TO MY LIFE, WHAT THEY WOULD CONTINUE TO DO--
--HAD IT NOT BEEN FOR THE GOD OF WAR, MARS, WHO CAME TO ME, OFFERING POWER AND BEAUTY BEYOND MY WILDEST DREAMS AND IMAGININGS IN RETURN FOR SIMPLE OBEDIENCE...
...AND THE DEATH OF WONDER WOMAN!
7

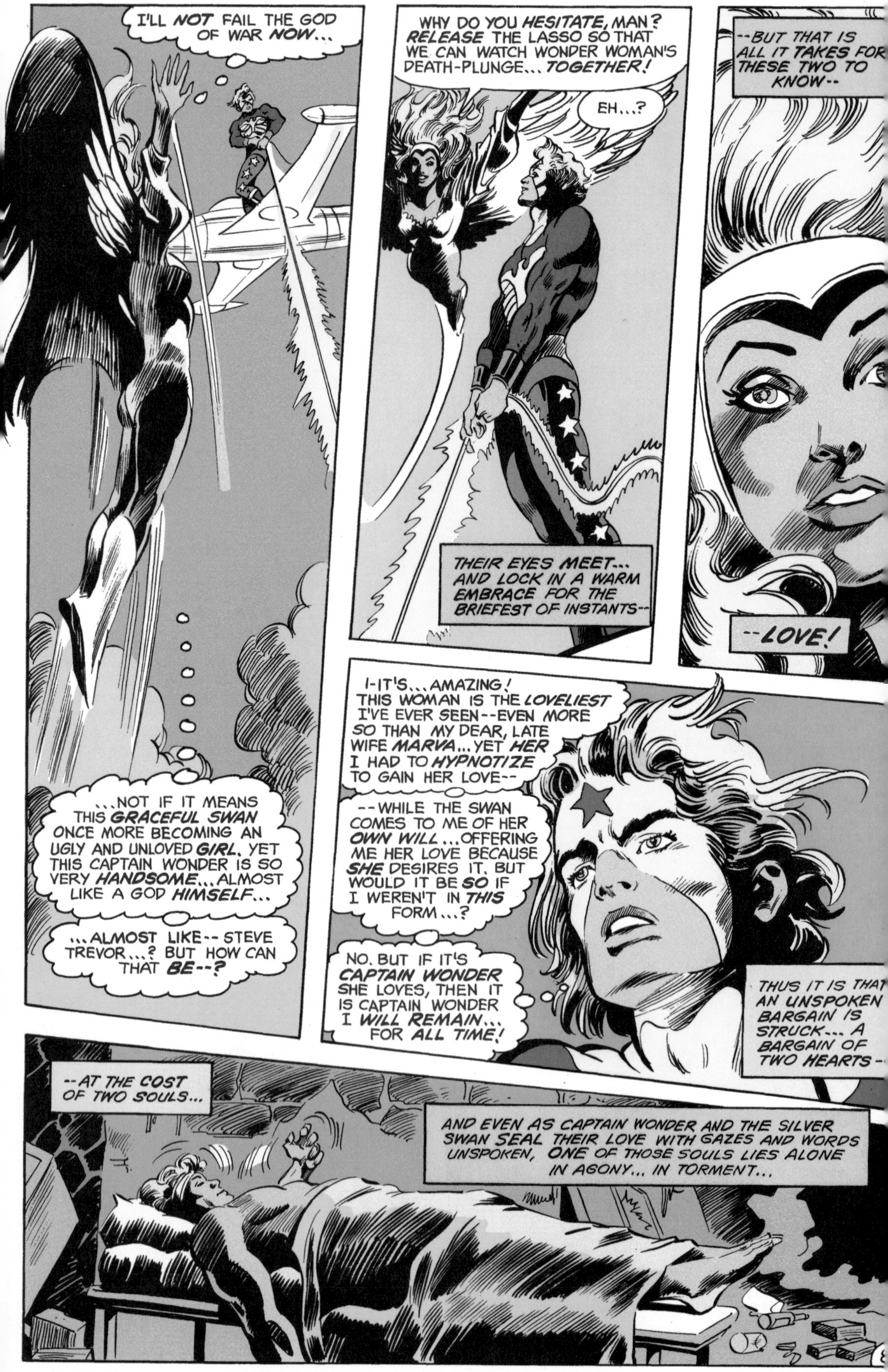

I'LL NOT FAIL THE GOD OF WAR NOW...
...NOT IF IT MEANS THIS GRACEFUL SWAN ONCE MORE BECOMING AN UGLY AND UNLOVED GIRL. YET THIS CAPTAIN WONDER IS SO VERY HANDSOME... ALMOST LIKE A GOD HIMSELF...
...ALMOST LIKE-- STEVE TREVOR...? BUT HOW CAN THAT BE--?
WHY DO YOU HESITATE, MAN? RELEASE THE LASSO SO THAT WE CAN WATCH WONDER WOMAN'S DEATH-PLUNGE... TOGETHER!
EH...?
THEIR EYES MEET... AND LOCK IN A WARM EMBRACE FOR THE BRIEFEST OF INSTANTS--
--BUT THAT IS ALL IT TAKES FOR THESE TWO TO KNOW--
--LOVE!
I-IT'S... AMAZING! THIS WOMAN IS THE LOVELIEST I'VE EVER SEEN--EVEN MORE SO THAN MY DEAR, LATE WIFE MARVA... YET HER I HAD TO HYPNOTIZE TO GAIN HER LOVE--
--WHILE THE SWAN COMES TO ME OF HER OWN WILL... OFFERING ME HER LOVE BECAUSE SHE DESIRES IT. BUT WOULD IT BE SO IF I WEREN'T IN THIS FORM...?
NO. BUT IF IT'S CAPTAIN WONDER SHE LOVES, THEN IT IS CAPTAIN WONDER I WILL REMAIN... FOR ALL TIME!
THUS IT IS THAT AN UNSPOKEN BARGAIN IS STRUCK... A BARGAIN OF TWO HEARTS--
--AT THE COST OF TWO SOULS...
AND EVEN AS CAPTAIN WONDER AND THE SILVER SWAN SEAL THEIR LOVE WITH GAZES AND WORDS UNSPOKEN, ONE OF THOSE SOULS LIES ALONE IN AGONY... IN TORMENT...

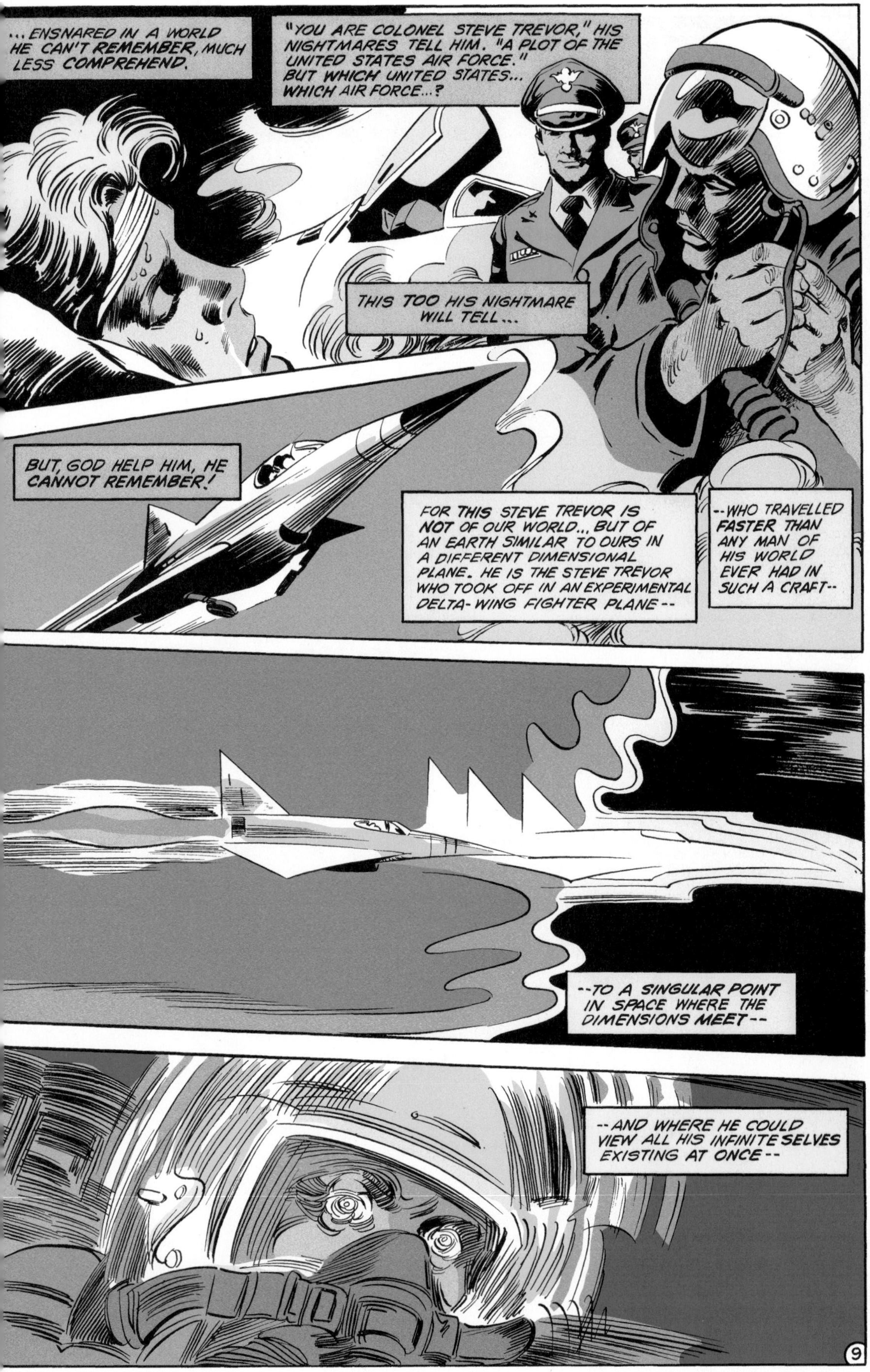

...ENSNARED IN A WORLD HE CAN'T REMEMBER, MUCH LESS COMPREHEND.
"YOU ARE COLONEL STEVE TREVOR," HIS NIGHTMARES TELL HIM. "A PLOT OF THE UNITED STATES AIR FORCE." BUT WHICH UNITED STATES... WHICH AIR FORCE...?
THIS TOO HIS NIGHTMARE WILL TELL...
BUT, GOD HELP HIM, HE CANNOT REMEMBER!
FOR THIS STEVE TREVOR IS NOT OF OUR WORLD..., BUT OF AN EARTH SIMILAR TO OURS IN A DIFFERENT DIMENSIONAL PLANE. HE IS THE STEVE TREVOR WHO TOOK OFF IN AN EXPERIMENTAL DELTA-WING FIGHTER PLANE--
--WHO TRAVELLED FASTER THAN ANY MAN OF HIS WORLD EVER HAD IN SUCH A CRAFT--
--TO A SINGULAR POINT IN SPACE WHERE THE DIMENSIONS MEET--
--AND WHERE HE COULD VIEW ALL HIS INFINITE SELVES EXISTING AT ONCE--
9

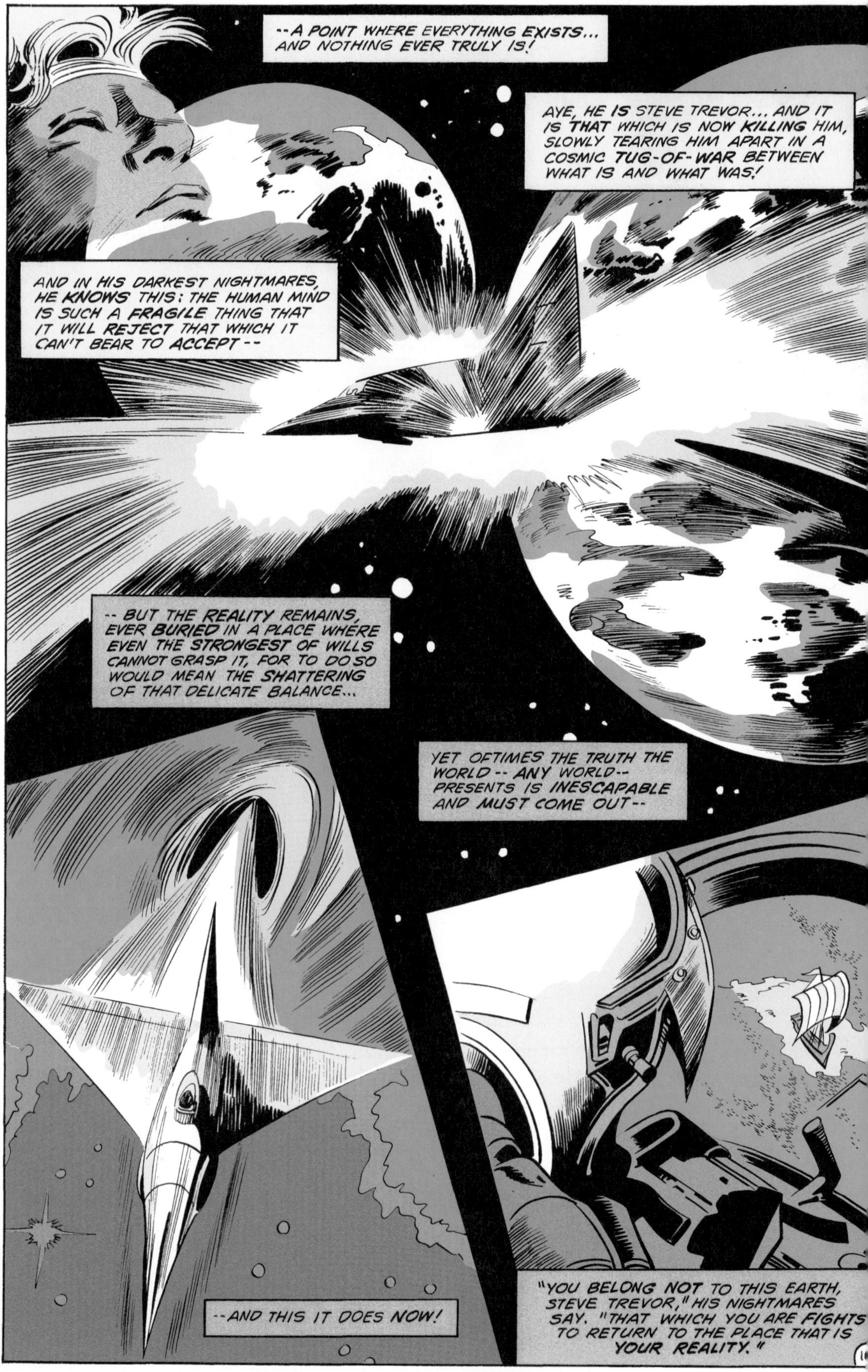
--A POINT WHERE EVERYTHING EXISTS... AND NOTHING EVER TRULY IS!
AYE, HE IS STEVE TREVOR... AND IT IS THAT WHICH IS NOW KILLING HIM, SLOWLY TEARING HIM APART IN A COSMIC TUG-OF-WAR BETWEEN WHAT IS AND WHAT WAS!
AND IN HIS DARKEST NIGHTMARES, HE KNOWS THIS: THE HUMAN MIND IS SUCH A FRAGILE THING THAT IT WILL REJECT THAT WHICH IT CAN'T BEAR TO ACCEPT--
--BUT THE REALITY REMAINS, EVER BURIED IN A PLACE WHERE EVEN THE STRONGEST OF WILLS CANNOT GRASP IT, FOR TO DO SO WOULD MEAN THE SHATTERING OF THAT DELICATE BALANCE...
YET OFTIMES THE TRUTH THE WORLD-- ANY WORLD-- PRESENTS IS INESCAPABLE AND MUST COME OUT--
--AND THIS IT DOES NOW!
"YOU BELONG NOT TO THIS EARTH, STEVE TREVOR," HIS NIGHTMARES SAY. "THAT WHICH YOU ARE FIGHTS TO RETURN TO THE PLACE THAT IS YOUR REALITY."

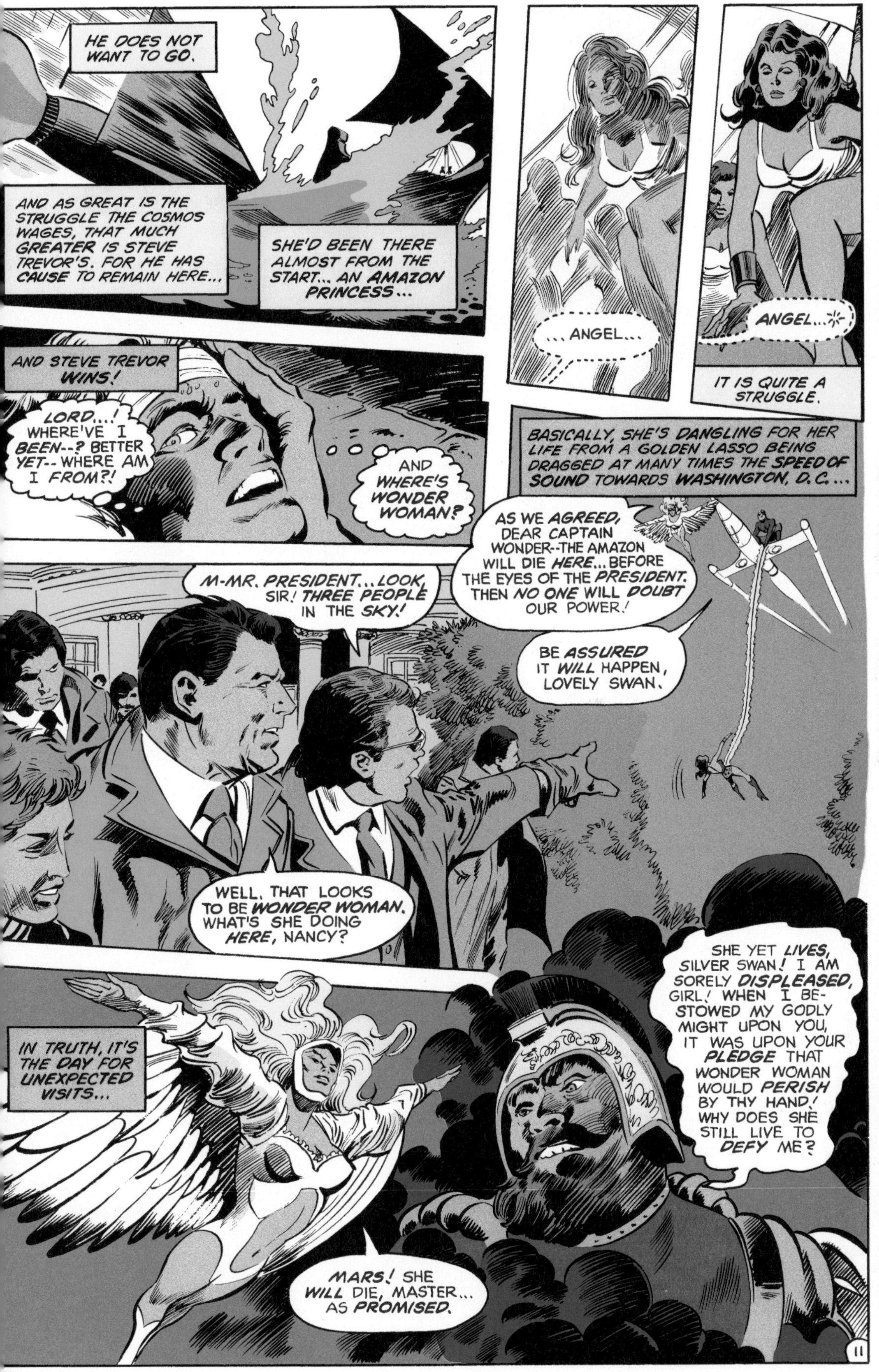
HE DOES NOT WANT TO GO.
AND AS GREAT IS THE STRUGGLE THE COSMOS WAGES, THAT MUCH GREATER IS STEVE TREVOR'S. FOR HE HAS CAUSE TO REMAIN HERE...
SHE'D BEEN THERE ALMOST FROM THE START... AN AMAZON PRINCESS...
...ANGEL...
ANGEL...
IT IS QUITE A STRUGGLE.
AND STEVE TREVOR WINS!
LORD...! WHERE'VE I BEEN--? BETTER YET-- WHERE AM I FROM?!
AND WHERE'S WONDER WOMAN?
BASICALLY, SHE'S DANGLING FOR HER LIFE FROM A GOLDEN LASSO BEING DRAGGED AT MANY TIMES THE SPEED OF SOUND TOWARDS WASHINGTON, D.C. ...
M-MR. PRESIDENT... LOOK, SIR! THREE PEOPLE IN THE SKY!
AS WE AGREED, DEAR CAPTAIN WONDER--THE AMAZON WILL DIE HERE... BEFORE THE EYES OF THE PRESIDENT. THEN NO ONE WILL DOUBT OUR POWER!
BE ASSURED IT WILL HAPPEN, LOVELY SWAN.
WELL, THAT LOOKS TO BE WONDER WOMAN. WHAT'S SHE DOING HERE, NANCY?
IN TRUTH, IT'S THE DAY FOR UNEXPECTED VISITS...
SHE YET LIVES, SILVER SWAN! I AM SORELY DISPLEASED, GIRL! WHEN I BESTOWED MY GODLY MIGHT UPON YOU, IT WAS UPON YOUR PLEDGE THAT WONDER WOMAN WOULD PERISH BY THY HAND! WHY DOES SHE STILL LIVE TO DEFY ME?
MARS! SHE WILL DIE, MASTER... AS PROMISED.
11

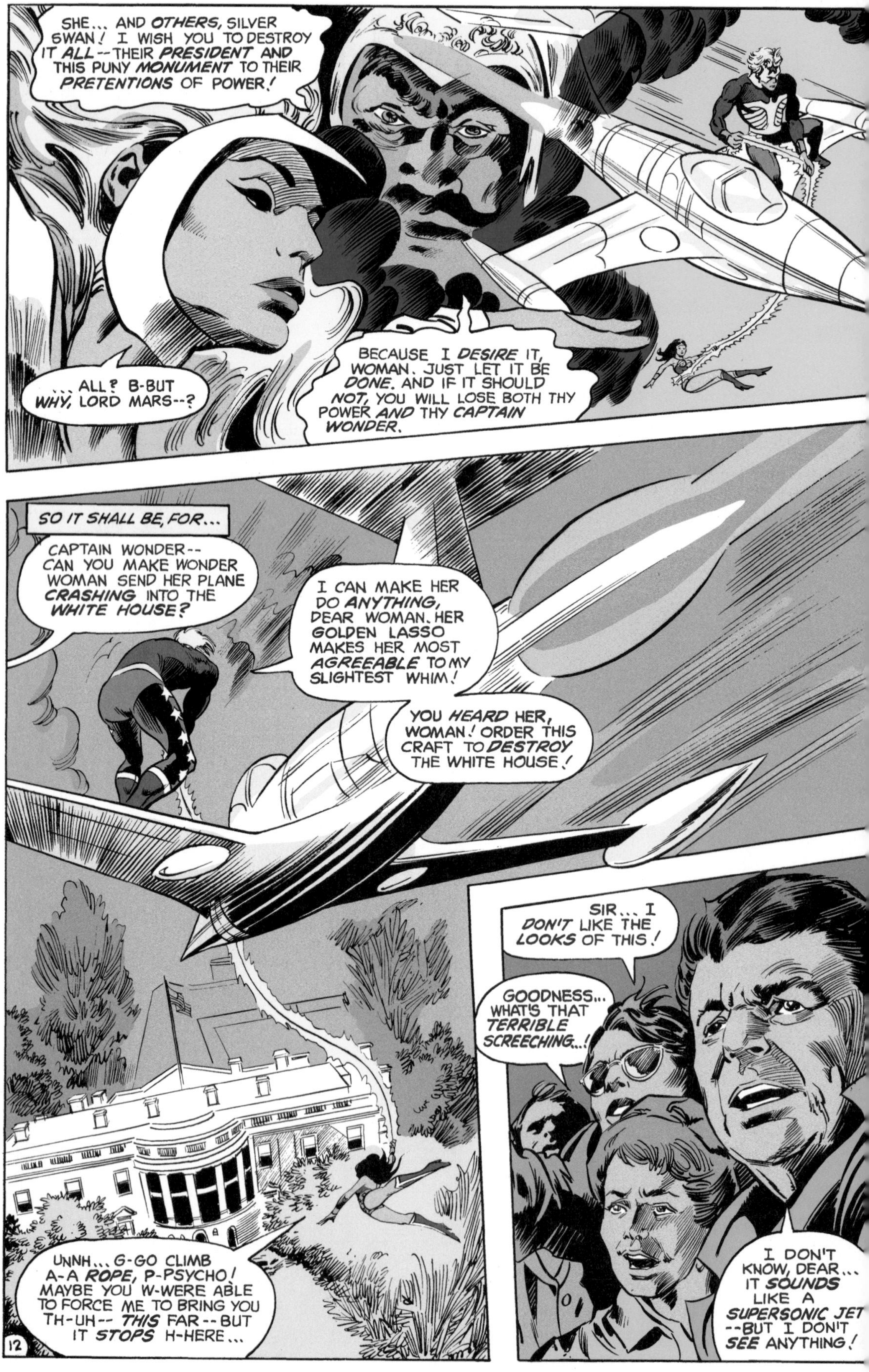
SHE... AND OTHERS, SILVER SWAN! I WISH YOU TO DESTROY IT ALL--THEIR PRESIDENT AND THIS PUNY MONUMENT TO THEIR PRETENTIONS OF POWER!
...ALL? B-BUT WHY, LORD MARS--?
BECAUSE I DESIRE IT, WOMAN. JUST LET IT BE DONE. AND IF IT SHOULD NOT, YOU WILL LOSE BOTH THY POWER AND THY CAPTAIN WONDER.
SO IT SHALL BE, FOR...
CAPTAIN WONDER-- CAN YOU MAKE WONDER WOMAN SEND HER PLANE CRASHING INTO THE WHITE HOUSE?
I CAN MAKE HER DO ANYTHING, DEAR WOMAN. HER GOLDEN LASSO MAKES HER MOST AGREEABLE TO MY SLIGHTEST WHIM!
YOU HEARD HER, WOMAN! ORDER THIS CRAFT TO DESTROY THE WHITE HOUSE!
UNNH... G-GO CLIMB A-A ROPE, P-PSYCHO! MAYBE YOU W-WERE ABLE TO FORCE ME TO BRING YOU TH-UH-- THIS FAR--BUT IT STOPS H-HERE...
12
SIR... I DON'T LIKE THE LOOKS OF THIS!
GOODNESS... WHAT'S THAT TERRIBLE SCREECHING...!
I DON'T KNOW, DEAR... IT SOUNDS LIKE A SUPERSONIC JET --BUT I DON'T SEE ANYTHING!

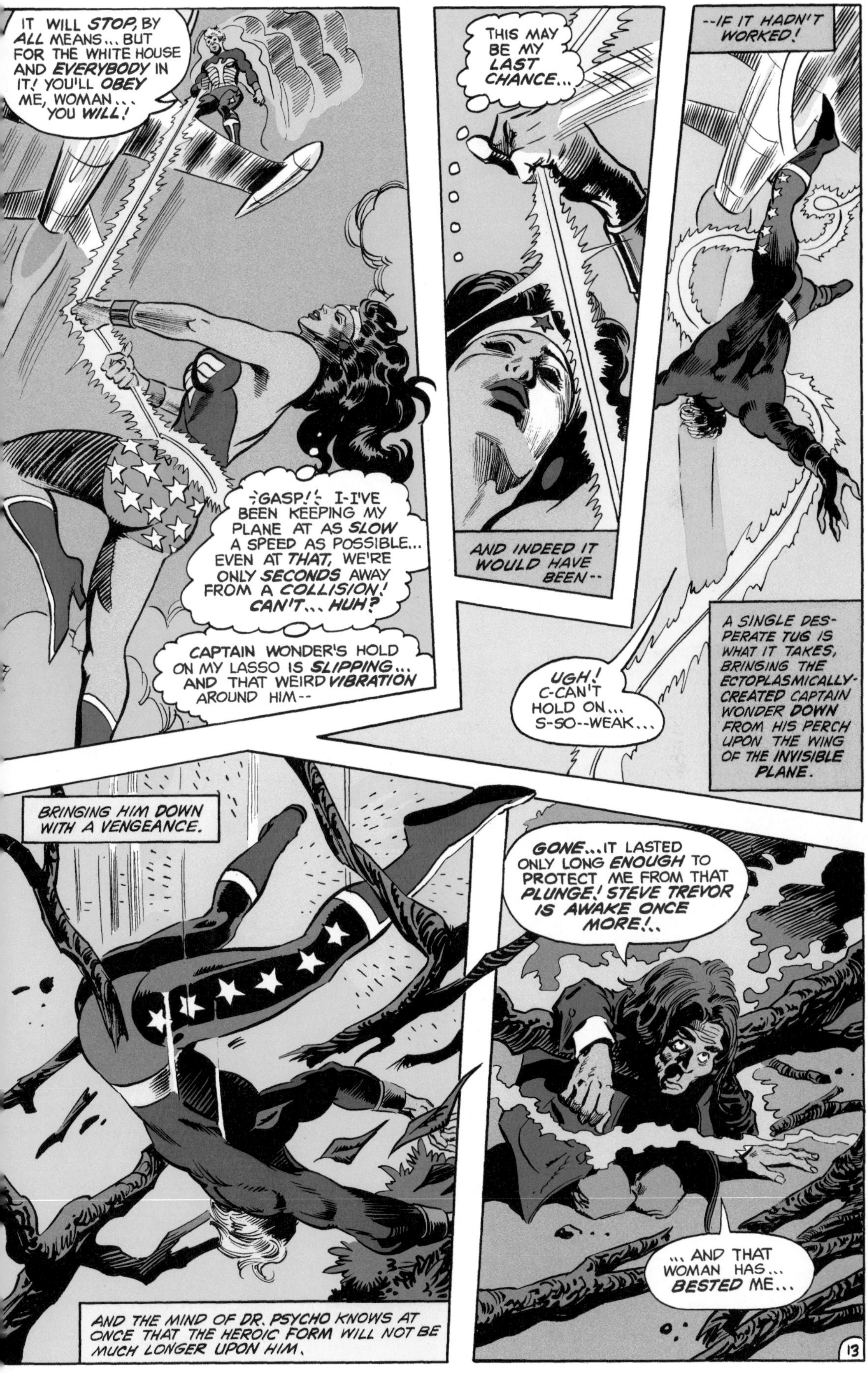
IT WILL STOP, BY ALL MEANS... BUT FOR THE WHITE HOUSE AND EVERYBODY IN IT! YOU'LL OBEY ME, WOMAN... YOU WILL!
-GASP!- I-I'VE BEEN KEEPING MY PLANE AT AS SLOW A SPEED AS POSSIBLE... EVEN AT THAT, WE'RE ONLY SECONDS AWAY FROM A COLLISION! CAN'T... HUH?
CAPTAIN WONDER'S HOLD ON MY LASSO IS SLIPPING... AND THAT WEIRD VIBRATION AROUND HIM--
THIS MAY BE MY LAST CHANCE...
AND INDEED IT WOULD HAVE BEEN--
--IF IT HADN'T WORKED!
UGH! C-CAN'T HOLD ON... S-SO--WEAK...
A SINGLE DESPERATE TUG IS WHAT IT TAKES, BRINGING THE ECTOPLASMICALLY-CREATED CAPTAIN WONDER DOWN FROM HIS PERCH UPON THE WING OF THE INVISIBLE PLANE.
BRINGING HIM DOWN WITH A VENGEANCE.
AND THE MIND OF DR. PSYCHO KNOWS AT ONCE THAT THE HEROIC FORM WILL NOT BE MUCH LONGER UPON HIM.
GONE... IT LASTED ONLY LONG ENOUGH TO PROTECT ME FROM THAT PLUNGE! STEVE TREVOR IS AWAKE ONCE MORE!..
... AND THAT WOMAN HAS... BESTED ME...
13

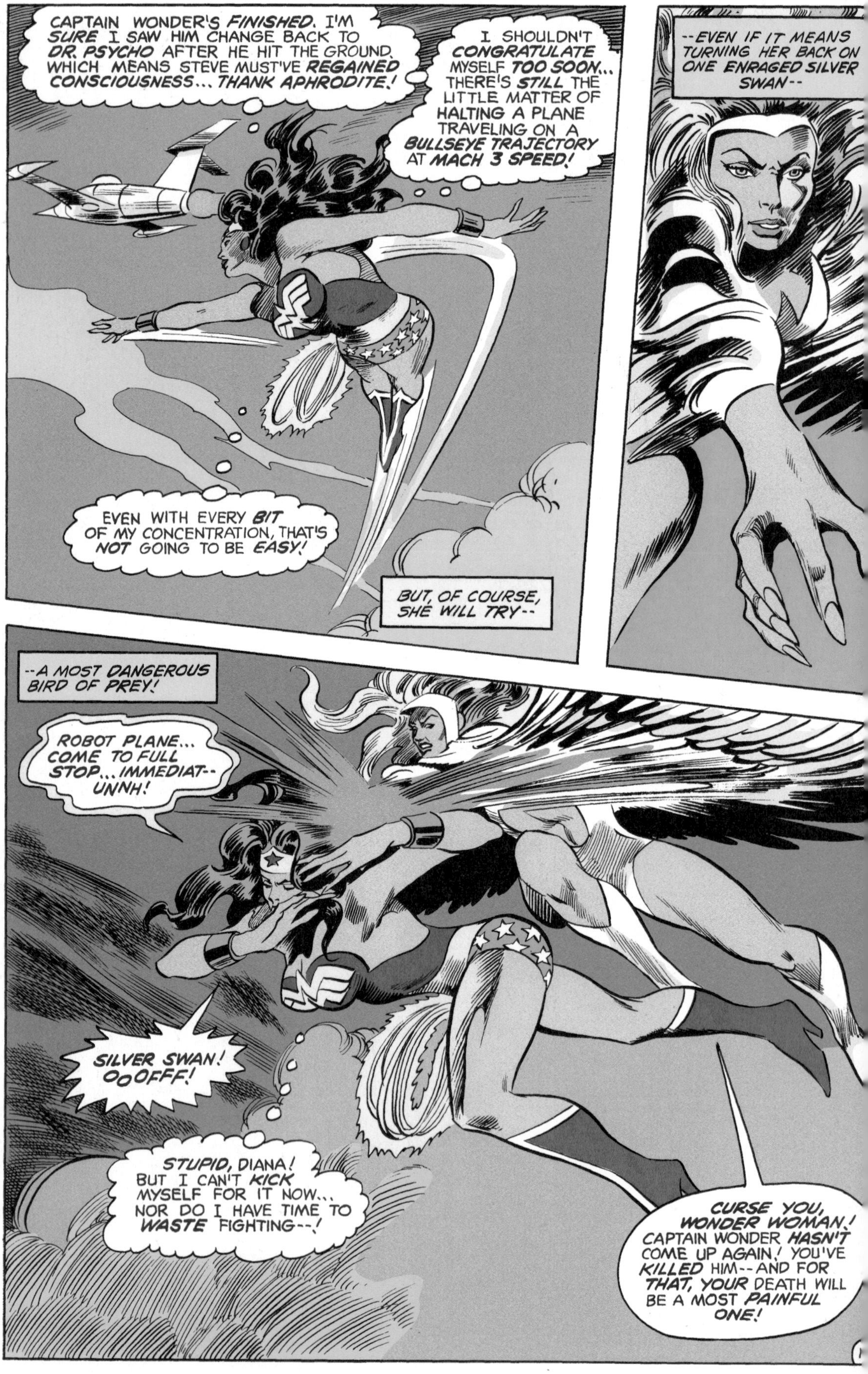
CAPTAIN WONDER'S FINISHED. I'M SURE I SAW HIM CHANGE BACK TO DR. PSYCHO AFTER HE HIT THE GROUND, WHICH MEANS STEVE MUST'VE REGAINED CONSCIOUSNESS... THANK APHRODITE!
I SHOULDN'T CONGRATULATE MYSELF TOO SOON... THERE'S STILL THE LITTLE MATTER OF HALTING A PLANE TRAVELING ON A BULLSEYE TRAJECTORY AT MACH 3 SPEED!
EVEN WITH EVERY BIT OF MY CONCENTRATION, THAT'S NOT GOING TO BE EASY!
BUT, OF COURSE, SHE WILL TRY--
--EVEN IF IT MEANS TURNING HER BACK ON ONE ENRAGED SILVER SWAN--
--A MOST DANGEROUS BIRD OF PREY!
ROBOT PLANE... COME TO FULL STOP... IMMEDIAT-- UNNH!
SILVER SWAN! OOOFFF!
STUPID, DIANA! BUT I CAN'T KICK MYSELF FOR IT NOW... NOR DO I HAVE TIME TO WASTE FIGHTING--!
CURSE YOU, WONDER WOMAN! CAPTAIN WONDER HASN'T COME UP AGAIN! YOU'VE KILLED HIM--AND FOR THAT, YOUR DEATH WILL BE A MOST PAINFUL ONE!

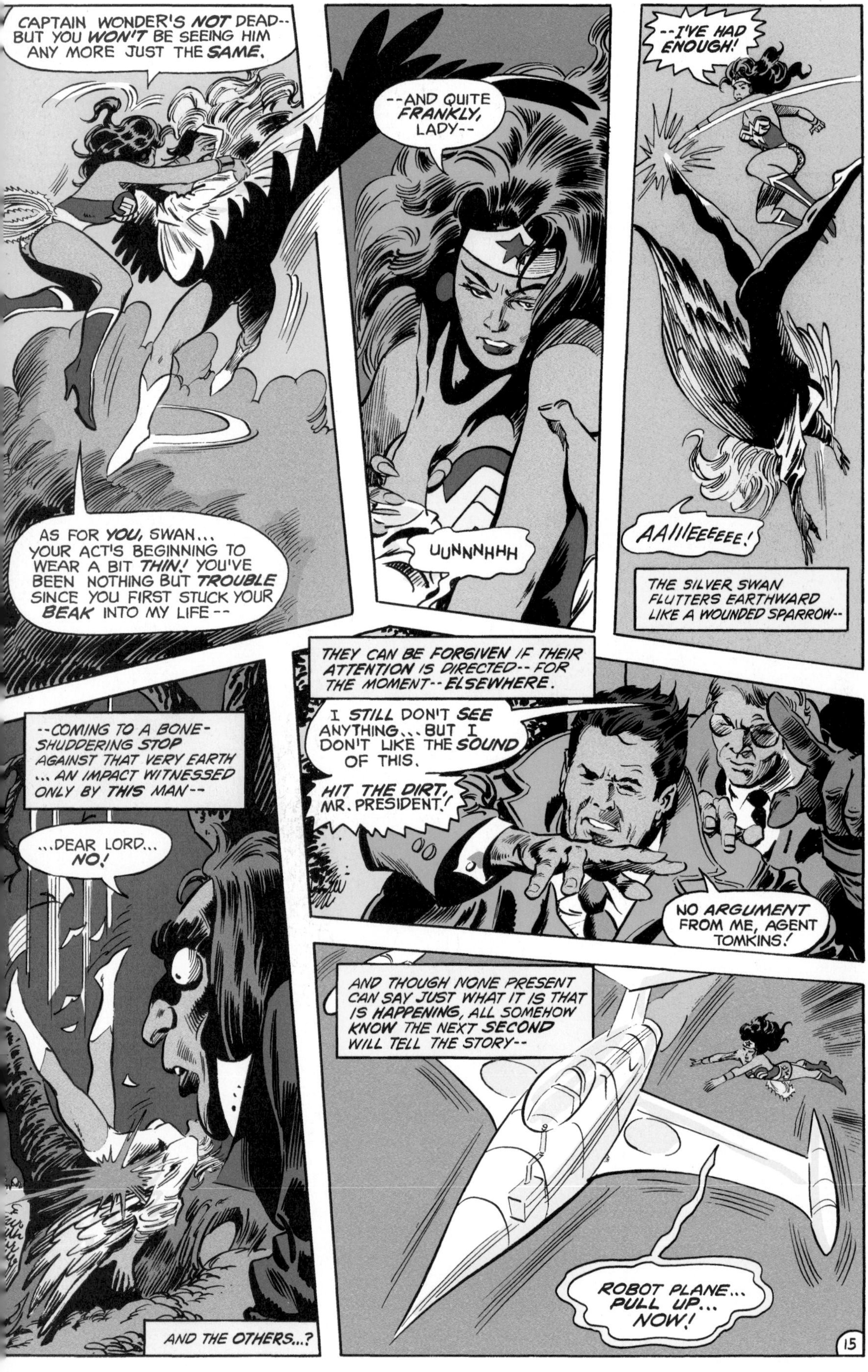
CAPTAIN WONDER'S NOT DEAD-- BUT YOU WON'T BE SEEING HIM ANY MORE JUST THE SAME.
AS FOR YOU, SWAN... YOUR ACT'S BEGINNING TO WEAR A BIT THIN! YOU'VE BEEN NOTHING BUT TROUBLE SINCE YOU FIRST STUCK YOUR BEAK INTO MY LIFE--
--AND QUITE FRANKLY, LADY--
UUNNNHHH
--I'VE HAD ENOUGH!
AAIIIEEEEEE!
THE SILVER SWAN FLUTTERS EARTHWARD LIKE A WOUNDED SPARROW--
--COMING TO A BONE-SHUDDERING STOP AGAINST THAT VERY EARTH ... AN IMPACT WITNESSED ONLY BY THIS MAN--
...DEAR LORD... NO!
AND THE OTHERS...?
THEY CAN BE FORGIVEN IF THEIR ATTENTION IS DIRECTED-- FOR THE MOMENT-- ELSEWHERE.
I STILL DON'T SEE ANYTHING... BUT I DON'T LIKE THE SOUND OF THIS.
HIT THE DIRT, MR. PRESIDENT!
NO ARGUMENT FROM ME, AGENT TOMKINS!
AND THOUGH NONE PRESENT CAN SAY JUST WHAT IT IS THAT IS HAPPENING, ALL SOMEHOW KNOW THE NEXT SECOND WILL TELL THE STORY--
ROBOT PLANE... PULL UP... NOW!
15

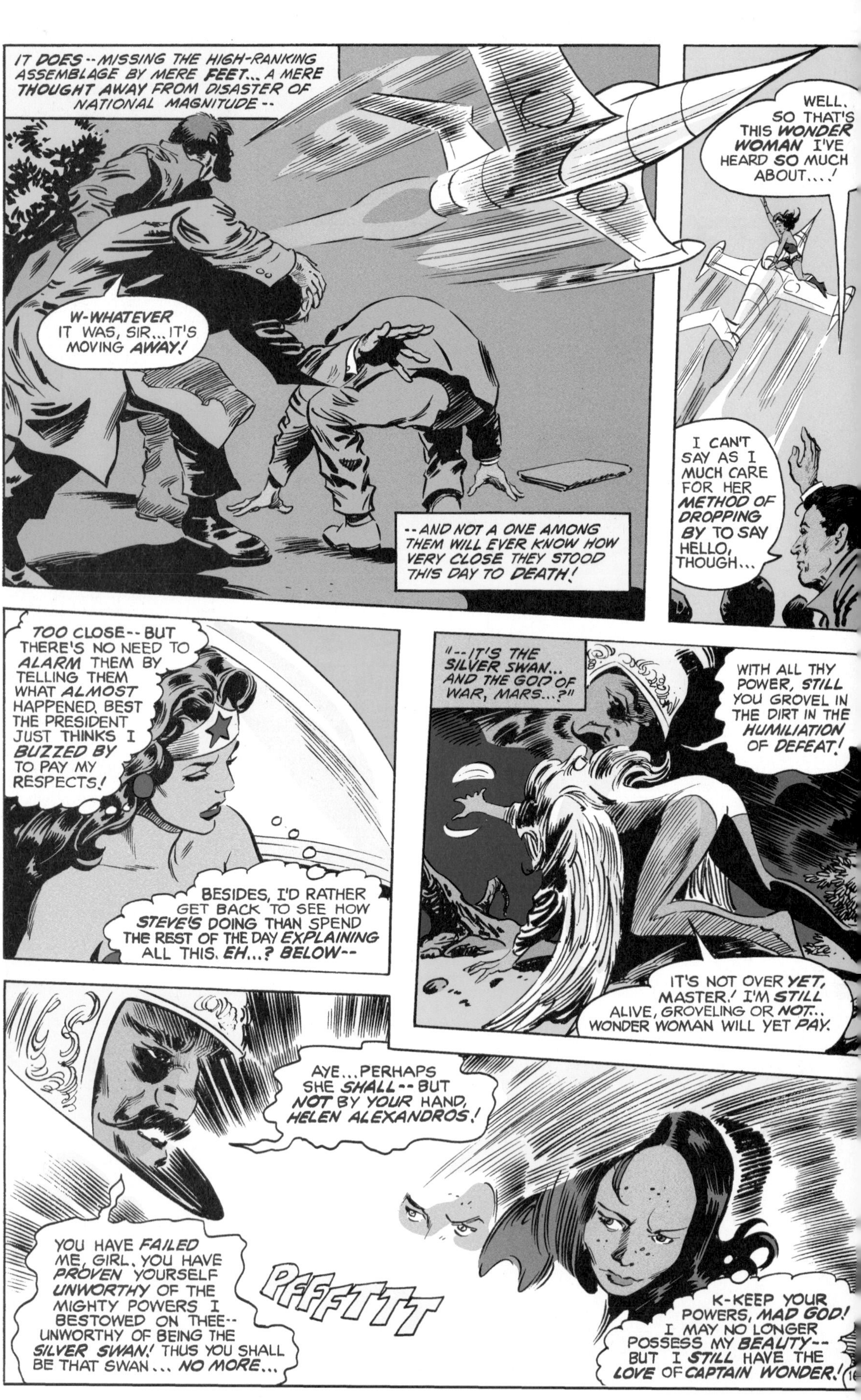

IT DOES -- MISSING THE HIGH-RANKING ASSEMBLAGE BY MERE FEET... A MERE THOUGHT AWAY FROM DISASTER OF NATIONAL MAGNITUDE --
W-WHATEVER IT WAS, SIR... IT'S MOVING AWAY!
-- AND NOT A ONE AMONG THEM WILL EVER KNOW HOW VERY CLOSE THEY STOOD THIS DAY TO DEATH!
WELL, SO THAT'S THIS WONDER WOMAN I'VE HEARD SO MUCH ABOUT....!
I CAN'T SAY AS I MUCH CARE FOR HER METHOD OF DROPPING BY TO SAY HELLO, THOUGH...
TOO CLOSE -- BUT THERE'S NO NEED TO ALARM THEM BY TELLING THEM WHAT ALMOST HAPPENED. BEST THE PRESIDENT JUST THINKS I BUZZED BY TO PAY MY RESPECTS!
BESIDES, I'D RATHER GET BACK TO SEE HOW STEVE'S DOING THAN SPEND THE REST OF THE DAY EXPLAINING ALL THIS. EH...? BELOW --
"-- IT'S THE SILVER SWAN... AND THE GOD OF WAR, MARS...?"
WITH ALL THY POWER, STILL YOU GROVEL IN THE DIRT IN THE HUMILIATION OF DEFEAT!
IT'S NOT OVER YET, MASTER! I'M STILL ALIVE, GROVELING OR NOT... WONDER WOMAN WILL YET PAY.
AYE... PERHAPS SHE SHALL -- BUT NOT BY YOUR HAND, HELEN ALEXANDROS!
YOU HAVE FAILED ME, GIRL. YOU HAVE PROVEN YOURSELF UNWORTHY OF THE MIGHTY POWERS I BESTOWED ON THEE -- UNWORTHY OF BEING THE SILVER SWAN! THUS YOU SHALL BE THAT SWAN... NO MORE...
PFFFTTTT
K-KEEP YOUR POWERS, MAD GOD! I MAY NO LONGER POSSESS MY BEAUTY -- BUT I STILL HAVE THE LOVE OF CAPTAIN WONDER!

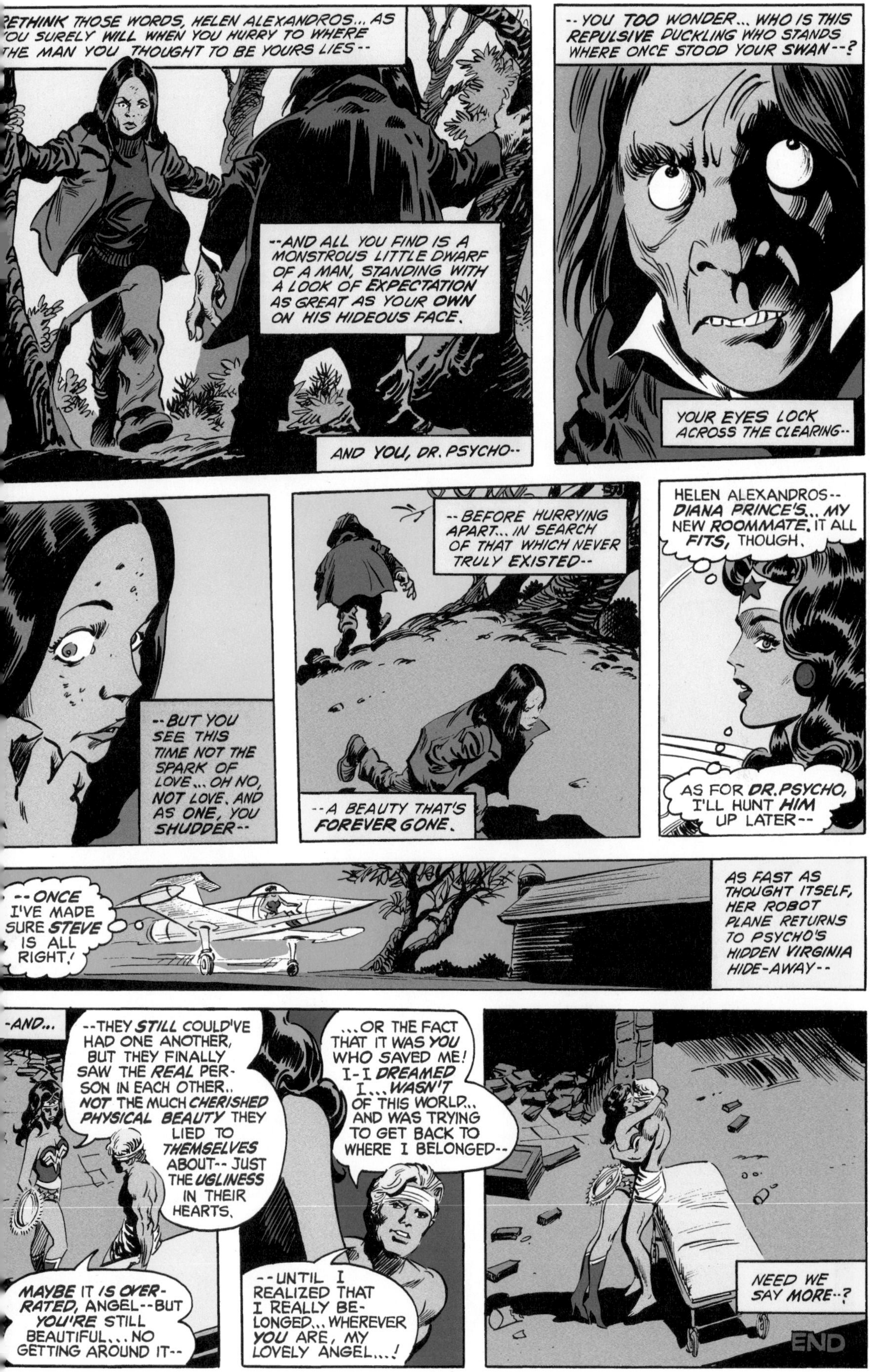
RETHINK THOSE WORDS, HELEN ALEXANDROS... AS YOU SURELY WILL WHEN YOU HURRY TO WHERE THE MAN YOU THOUGHT TO BE YOURS LIES--
--AND ALL YOU FIND IS A MONSTROUS LITTLE DWARF OF A MAN, STANDING WITH A LOOK OF EXPECTATION AS GREAT AS YOUR OWN ON HIS HIDEOUS FACE.
AND YOU, DR. PSYCHO--
--YOU TOO WONDER... WHO IS THIS REPULSIVE DUCKLING WHO STANDS WHERE ONCE STOOD YOUR SWAN--?
YOUR EYES LOCK ACROSS THE CLEARING--
--BUT YOU SEE THIS TIME NOT THE SPARK OF LOVE... OH NO, NOT LOVE. AND AS ONE, YOU SHUDDER--
--BEFORE HURRYING APART... IN SEARCH OF THAT WHICH NEVER TRULY EXISTED--
--A BEAUTY THAT'S FOREVER GONE.
HELEN ALEXANDROS-- DIANA PRINCE'S... MY NEW ROOMMATE. IT ALL FITS, THOUGH.
AS FOR DR. PSYCHO, I'LL HUNT HIM UP LATER--
--ONCE I'VE MADE SURE STEVE IS ALL RIGHT!
AS FAST AS THOUGHT ITSELF, HER ROBOT PLANE RETURNS TO PSYCHO'S HIDDEN VIRGINIA HIDE-AWAY--
-AND...
--THEY STILL COULD'VE HAD ONE ANOTHER, BUT THEY FINALLY SAW THE REAL PERSON IN EACH OTHER.. NOT THE MUCH CHERISHED PHYSICAL BEAUTY THEY LIED TO THEMSELVES ABOUT-- JUST THE UGLINESS IN THEIR HEARTS.
MAYBE IT IS OVER-RATED, ANGEL--BUT YOU'RE STILL BEAUTIFUL... NO GETTING AROUND IT--
...OR THE FACT THAT IT WAS YOU WHO SAVED ME! I-I DREAMED I... WASN'T OF THIS WORLD.. AND WAS TRYING TO GET BACK TO WHERE I BELONGED--
--UNTIL I REALIZED THAT I REALLY BELONGED... WHEREVER YOU ARE, MY LOVELY ANGEL...!
NEED WE SAY MORE..?
END

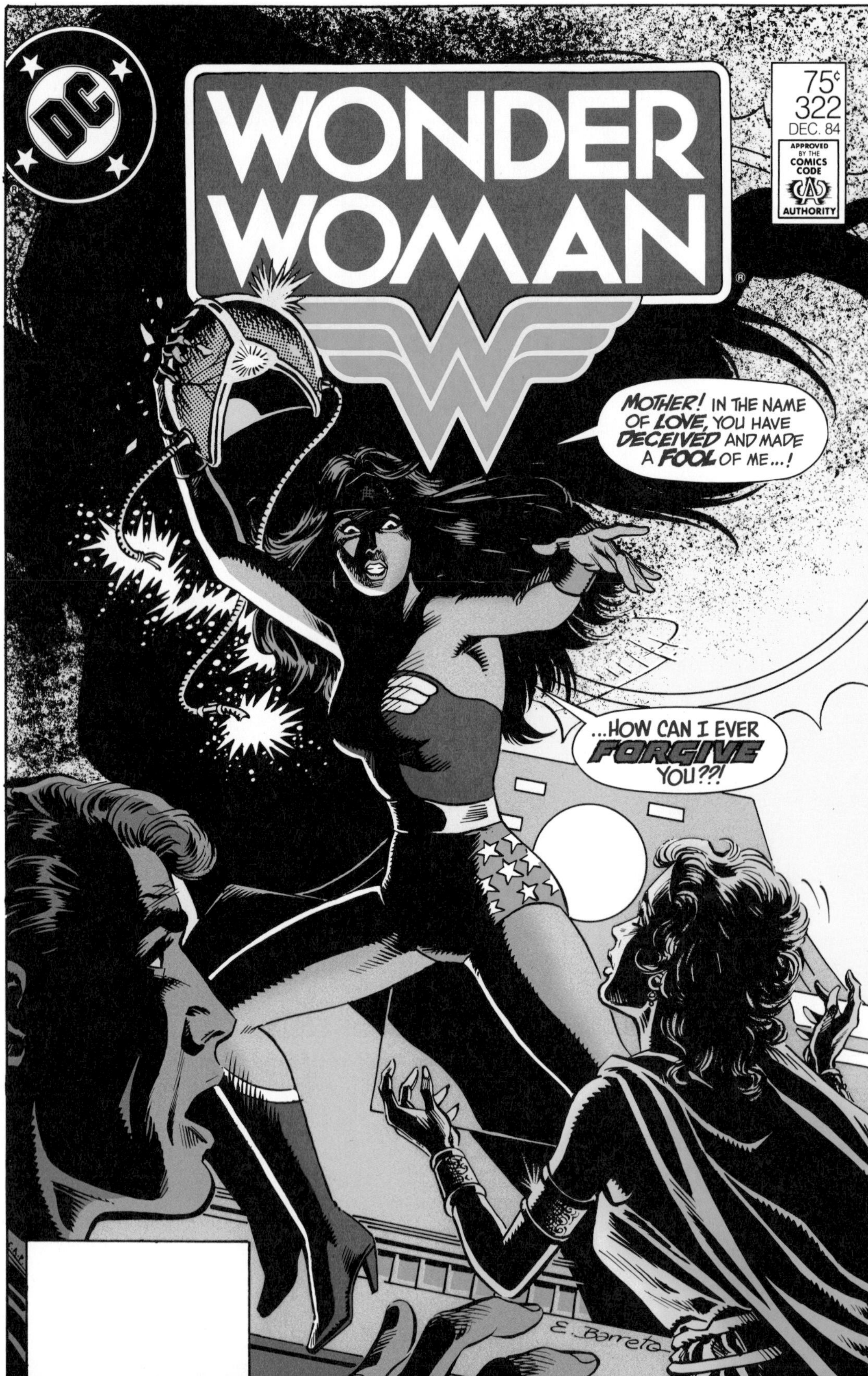
WONDER WOMAN
75¢
322
DEC. 84
APPROVED BY THE COMICS CODE AUTHORITY
MOTHER! IN THE NAME OF LOVE, YOU HAVE DECEIVED AND MADE A FOOL OF ME...!
...HOW CAN I EVER FORGIVE YOU??!
E. Barreto

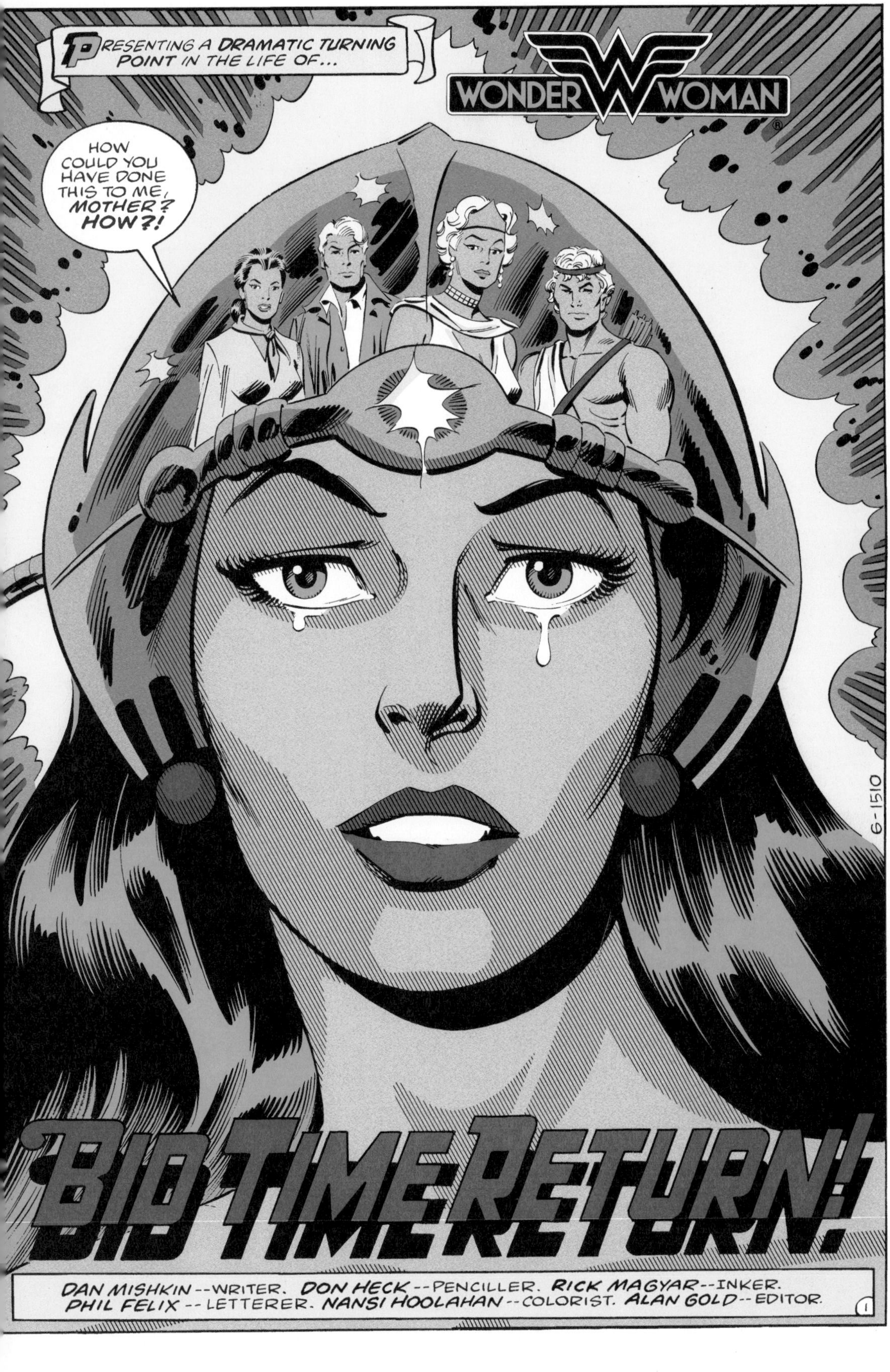

PRESENTING A DRAMATIC TURNING POINT IN THE LIFE OF...
WONDER WOMAN
HOW COULD YOU HAVE DONE THIS TO ME, MOTHER? HOW?!
BID TIME RETURN!
DAN MISHKIN--WRITER. DON HECK--PENCILLER. RICK MAGYAR--INKER. PHIL FELIX--LETTERER. NANSI HOOLAHAN--COLORIST. ALAN GOLD--EDITOR.
G-1510
1

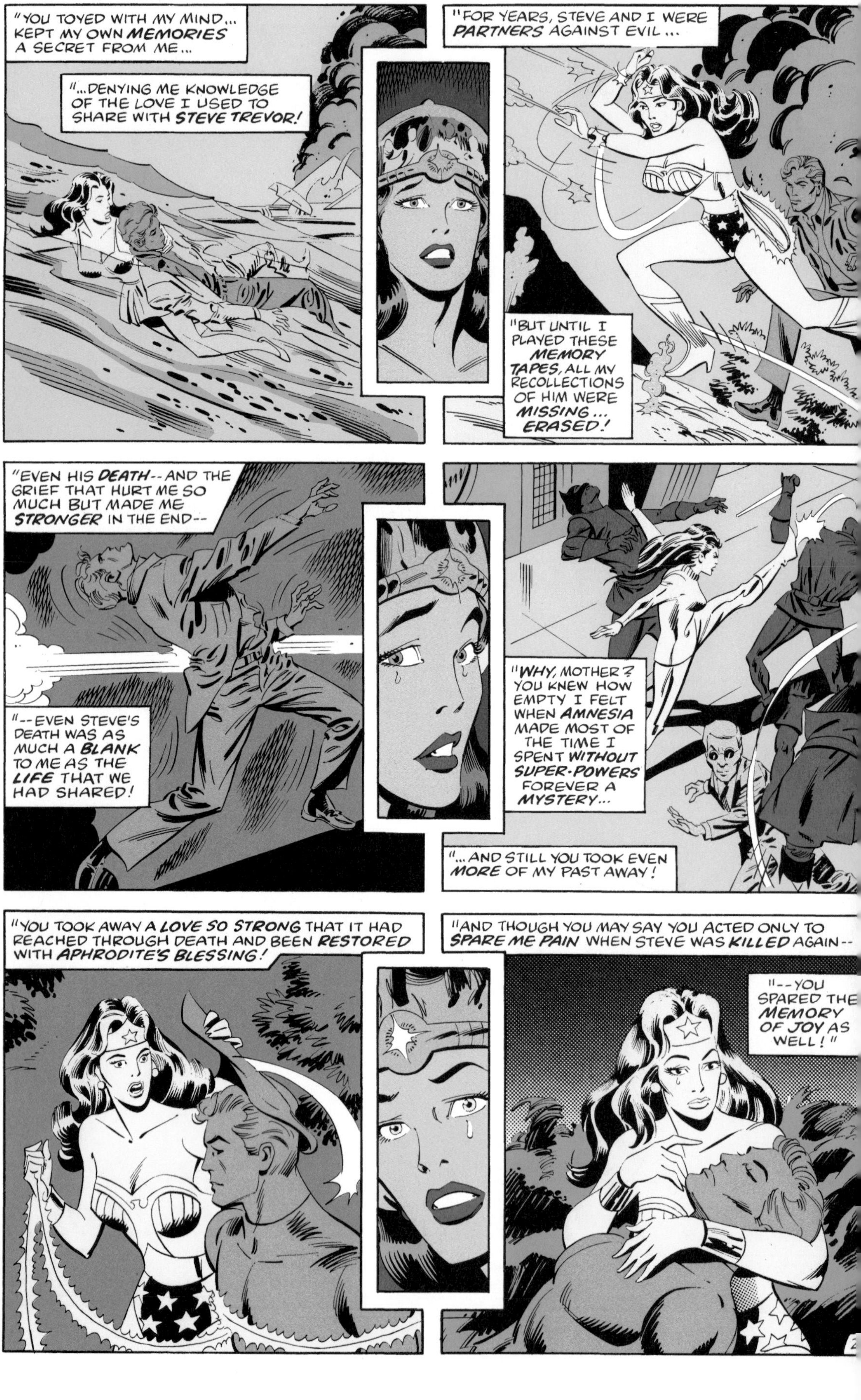
"YOU TOYED WITH MY MIND... KEPT MY OWN MEMORIES A SECRET FROM ME...
"...DENYING ME KNOWLEDGE OF THE LOVE I USED TO SHARE WITH STEVE TREVOR!
"FOR YEARS, STEVE AND I WERE PARTNERS AGAINST EVIL...
"BUT UNTIL I PLAYED THESE MEMORY TAPES, ALL MY RECOLLECTIONS OF HIM WERE MISSING... ERASED!
"EVEN HIS DEATH--AND THE GRIEF THAT HURT ME SO MUCH BUT MADE ME STRONGER IN THE END--
"--EVEN STEVE'S DEATH WAS AS MUCH A BLANK TO ME AS THE LIFE THAT WE HAD SHARED!
"WHY, MOTHER? YOU KNEW HOW EMPTY I FELT WHEN AMNESIA MADE MOST OF THE TIME I SPENT WITHOUT SUPER-POWERS FOREVER A MYSTERY...
"...AND STILL YOU TOOK EVEN MORE OF MY PAST AWAY!
"YOU TOOK AWAY A LOVE SO STRONG THAT IT HAD REACHED THROUGH DEATH AND BEEN RESTORED WITH APHRODITE'S BLESSING!
"AND THOUGH YOU MAY SAY YOU ACTED ONLY TO SPARE ME PAIN WHEN STEVE WAS KILLED AGAIN--
"--YOU SPARED THE MEMORY OF JOY AS WELL!"

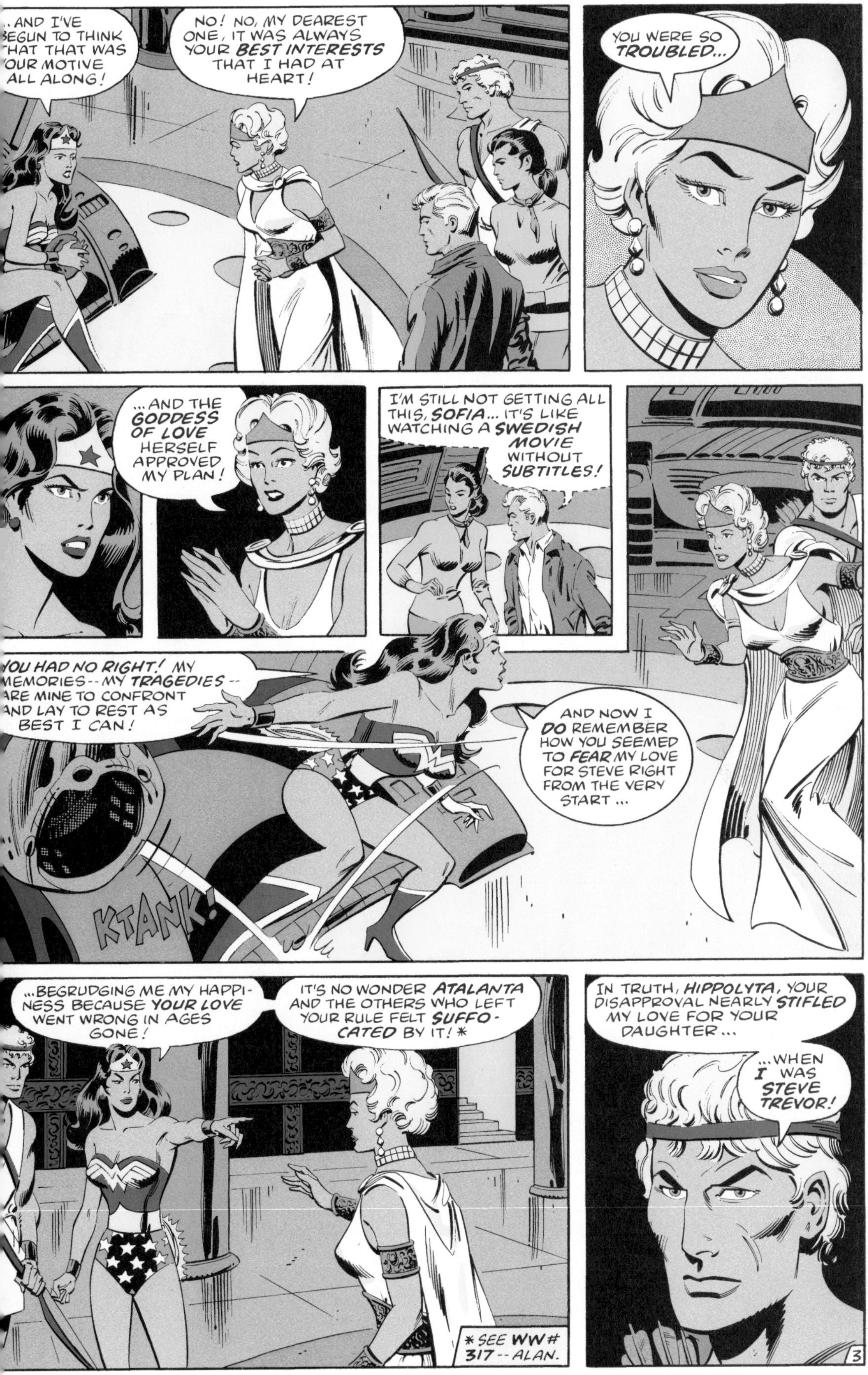
..AND I'VE BEGUN TO THINK THAT THAT WAS YOUR MOTIVE ALL ALONG!
NO! NO, MY DEAREST ONE, IT WAS ALWAYS YOUR BEST INTERESTS THAT I HAD AT HEART!
YOU WERE SO TROUBLED...
...AND THE GODDESS OF LOVE HERSELF APPROVED MY PLAN!
I'M STILL NOT GETTING ALL THIS, SOFIA... IT'S LIKE WATCHING A SWEDISH MOVIE WITHOUT SUBTITLES!
YOU HAD NO RIGHT! MY MEMORIES-- MY TRAGEDIES-- ARE MINE TO CONFRONT AND LAY TO REST AS BEST I CAN!
AND NOW I DO REMEMBER HOW YOU SEEMED TO FEAR MY LOVE FOR STEVE RIGHT FROM THE VERY START...
KTANK!
...BEGRUDGING ME MY HAPPINESS BECAUSE YOUR LOVE WENT WRONG IN AGES GONE!
IT'S NO WONDER ATALANTA AND THE OTHERS WHO LEFT YOUR RULE FELT SUFFOCATED BY IT! *
* SEE WW # 317 -- ALAN.
IN TRUTH, HIPPOLYTA, YOUR DISAPPROVAL NEARLY STIFLED MY LOVE FOR YOUR DAUGHTER...
...WHEN I WAS STEVE TREVOR!
3

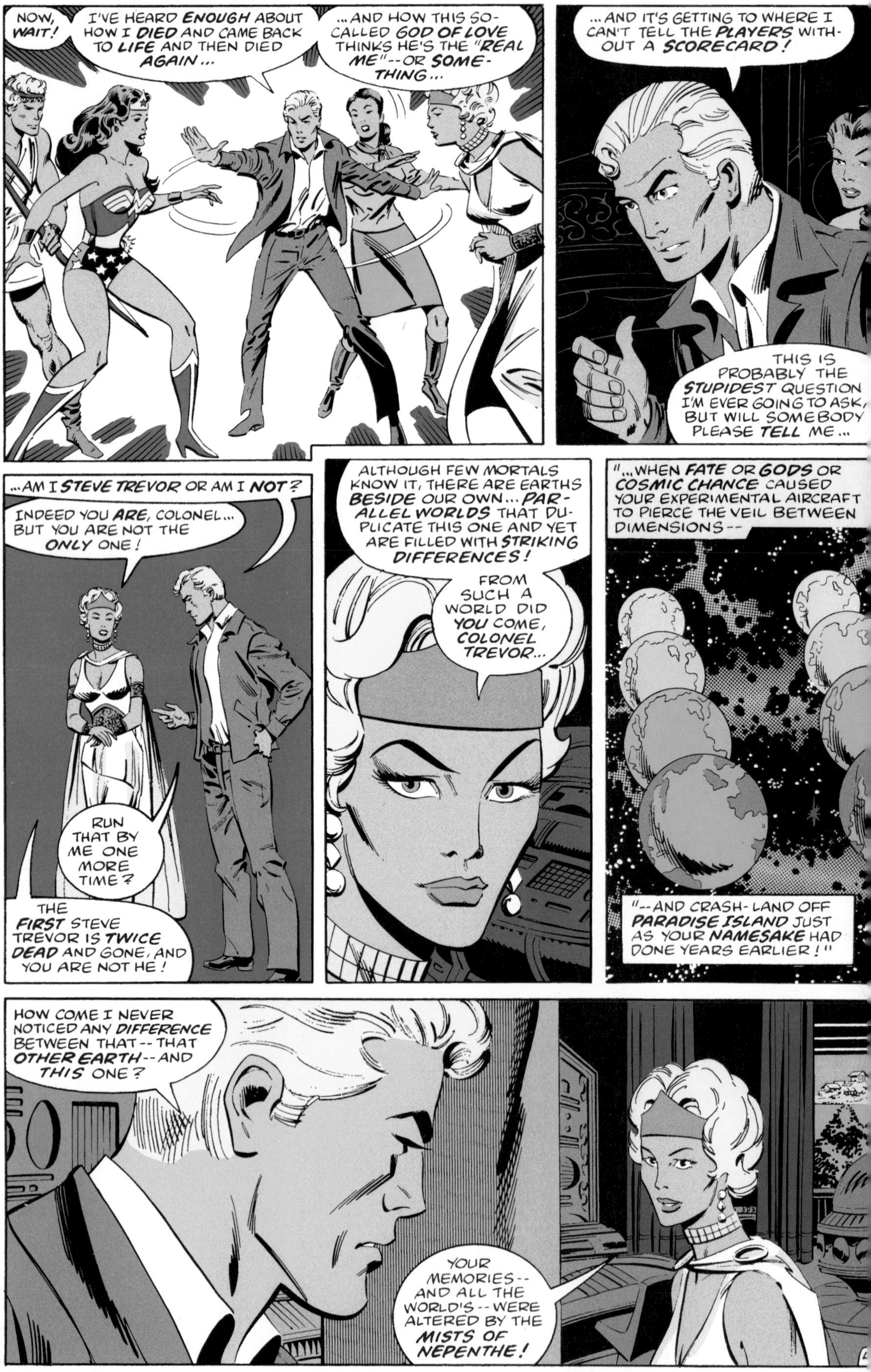
NOW, WAIT!
I'VE HEARD ENOUGH ABOUT HOW I DIED AND CAME BACK TO LIFE AND THEN DIED AGAIN...
...AND HOW THIS SO-CALLED GOD OF LOVE THINKS HE'S THE "REAL ME"--OR SOME-THING...
...AND IT'S GETTING TO WHERE I CAN'T TELL THE PLAYERS WITH-OUT A SCORECARD!
THIS IS PROBABLY THE STUPIDEST QUESTION I'M EVER GOING TO ASK, BUT WILL SOMEBODY PLEASE TELL ME...
...AM I STEVE TREVOR OR AM I NOT?
INDEED YOU ARE, COLONEL... BUT YOU ARE NOT THE ONLY ONE!
RUN THAT BY ME ONE MORE TIME?
THE FIRST STEVE TREVOR IS TWICE DEAD AND GONE, AND YOU ARE NOT HE!
ALTHOUGH FEW MORTALS KNOW IT, THERE ARE EARTHS BESIDE OUR OWN... PAR-ALLEL WORLDS THAT DU-PLICATE THIS ONE AND YET ARE FILLED WITH STRIKING DIFFERENCES!
FROM SUCH A WORLD DID YOU COME, COLONEL TREVOR...
"...WHEN FATE OR GODS OR COSMIC CHANCE CAUSED YOUR EXPERIMENTAL AIRCRAFT TO PIERCE THE VEIL BETWEEN DIMENSIONS--
"--AND CRASH-LAND OFF PARADISE ISLAND JUST AS YOUR NAMESAKE HAD DONE YEARS EARLIER!"
HOW COME I NEVER NOTICED ANY DIFFERENCE BETWEEN THAT--THAT OTHER EARTH--AND THIS ONE?
YOUR MEMORIES--AND ALL THE WORLD'S--WERE ALTERED BY THE MISTS OF NEPENTHE!

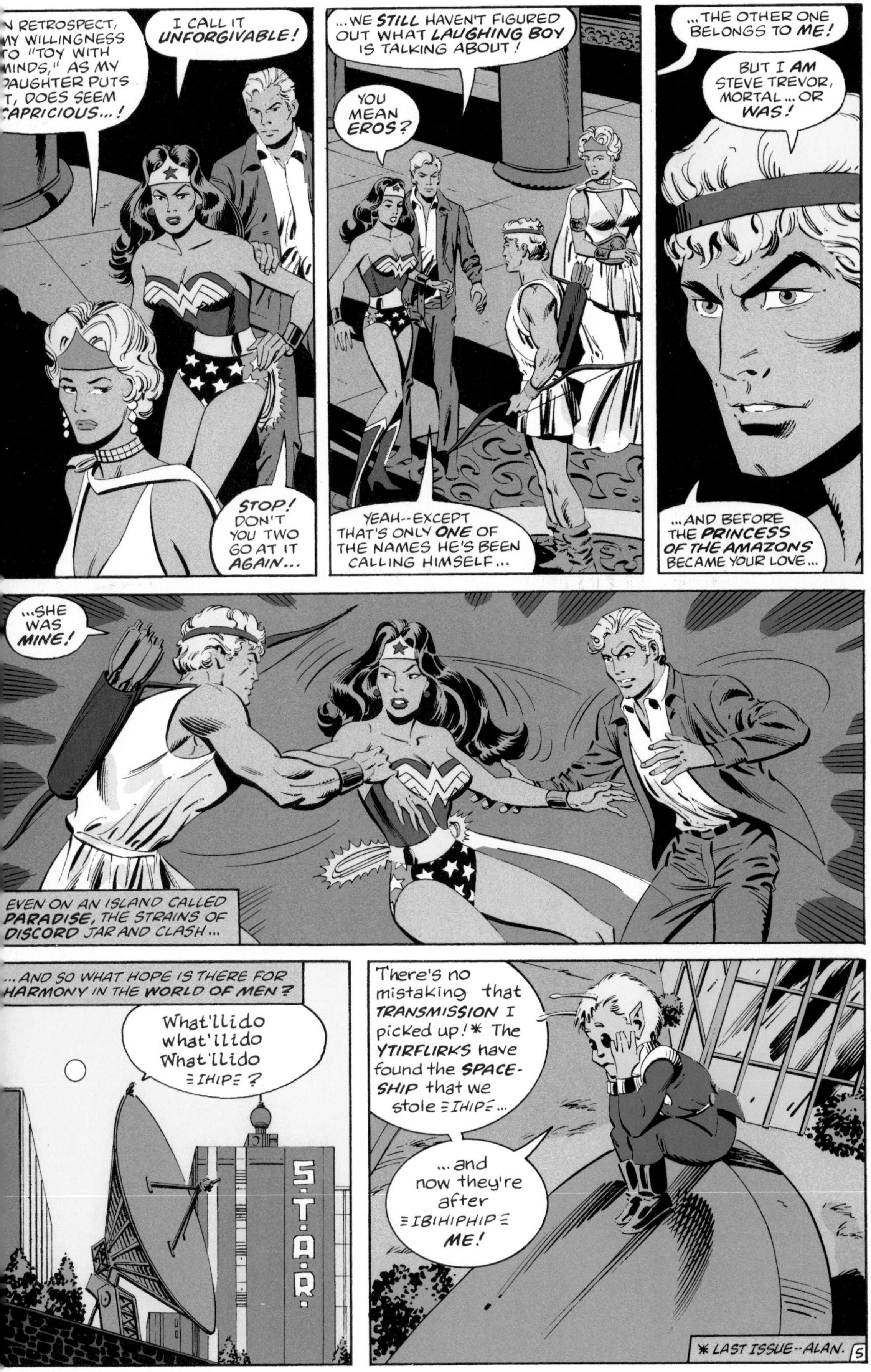

N RETROSPECT, MY WILLINGNESS TO "TOY WITH MINDS," AS MY DAUGHTER PUTS IT, DOES SEEM CAPRICIOUS...!
I CALL IT UNFORGIVABLE!
STOP! DON'T YOU TWO GO AT IT AGAIN...
...WE STILL HAVEN'T FIGURED OUT WHAT LAUGHING BOY IS TALKING ABOUT!
YOU MEAN EROS?
YEAH--EXCEPT THAT'S ONLY ONE OF THE NAMES HE'S BEEN CALLING HIMSELF...
...THE OTHER ONE BELONGS TO ME!
BUT I AM STEVE TREVOR, MORTAL... OR WAS!
...AND BEFORE THE PRINCESS OF THE AMAZONS BECAME YOUR LOVE...
...SHE WAS MINE!
EVEN ON AN ISLAND CALLED PARADISE, THE STRAINS OF DISCORD JAR AND CLASH...
...AND SO WHAT HOPE IS THERE FOR HARMONY IN THE WORLD OF MEN?
What'llido what'llido What'llido ≡IHIP≡?
S.T.A.R.
There's no mistaking that TRANSMISSION I picked up!* The YTIRFLIRKS have found the SPACESHIP that we stole ≡IHIP≡...
...and now they're after ≡IBIHIPHIP≡ ME!
* LAST ISSUE--ALAN.
5

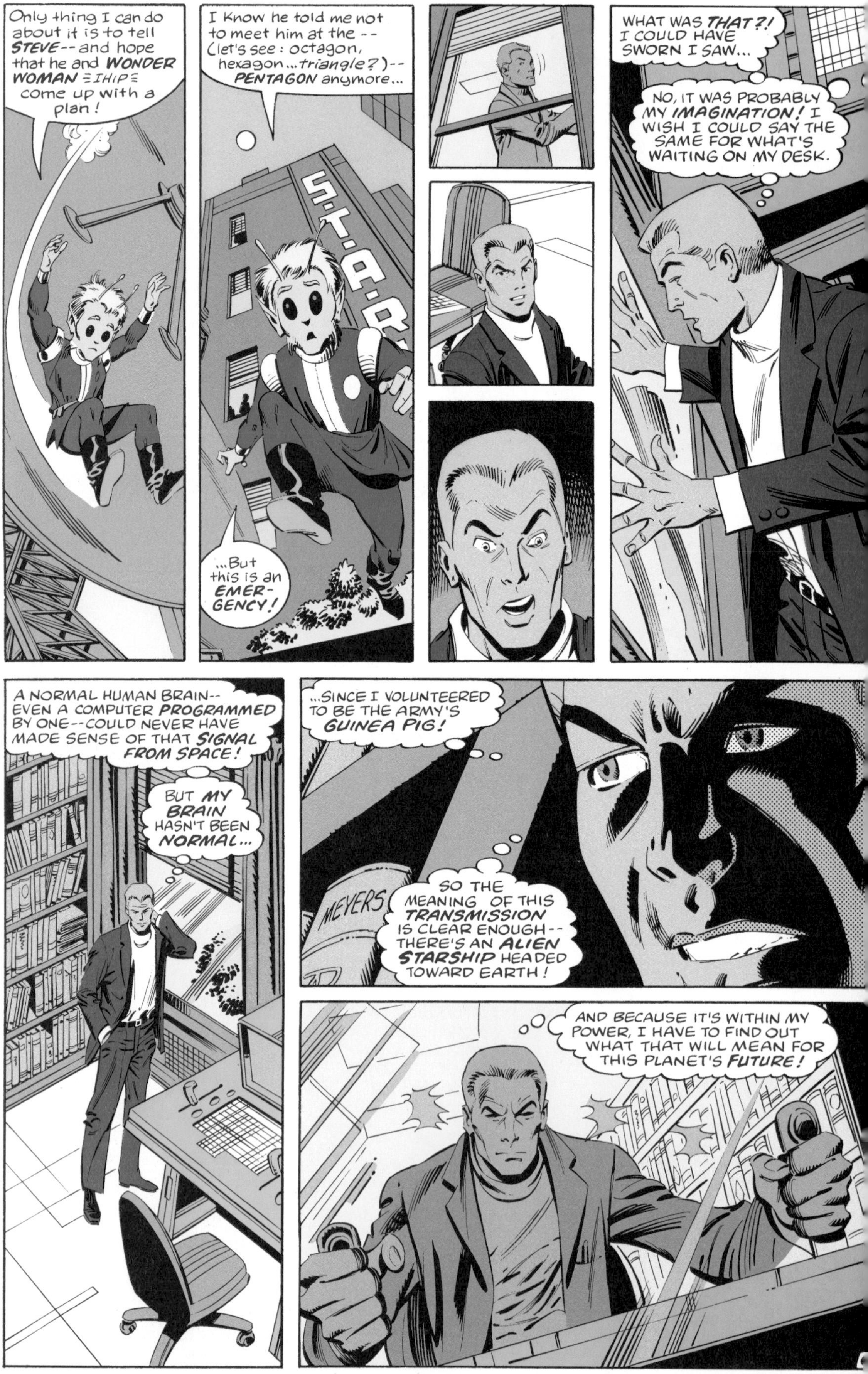

Only thing I can do about it is to tell STEVE-- and hope that he and WONDER WOMAN ΞIHIPΞ come up with a plan!
I know he told me not to meet him at the -- (let's see: octagon, hexagon ...triangle?)-- PENTAGON anymore...
S.T.A.R.
...But this is an EMER-GENCY!
WHAT WAS THAT?! I COULD HAVE SWORN I SAW...
NO, IT WAS PROBABLY MY IMAGINATION! I WISH I COULD SAY THE SAME FOR WHAT'S WAITING ON MY DESK.
A NORMAL HUMAN BRAIN-- EVEN A COMPUTER PROGRAMMED BY ONE--COULD NEVER HAVE MADE SENSE OF THAT SIGNAL FROM SPACE!
BUT MY BRAIN HASN'T BEEN NORMAL...
...SINCE I VOLUNTEERED TO BE THE ARMY'S GUINEA PIG!
MEYERS
SO THE MEANING OF THIS TRANSMISSION IS CLEAR ENOUGH-- THERE'S AN ALIEN STARSHIP HEADED TOWARD EARTH!
AND BECAUSE IT'S WITHIN MY POWER, I HAVE TO FIND OUT WHAT THAT WILL MEAN FOR THIS PLANET'S FUTURE!

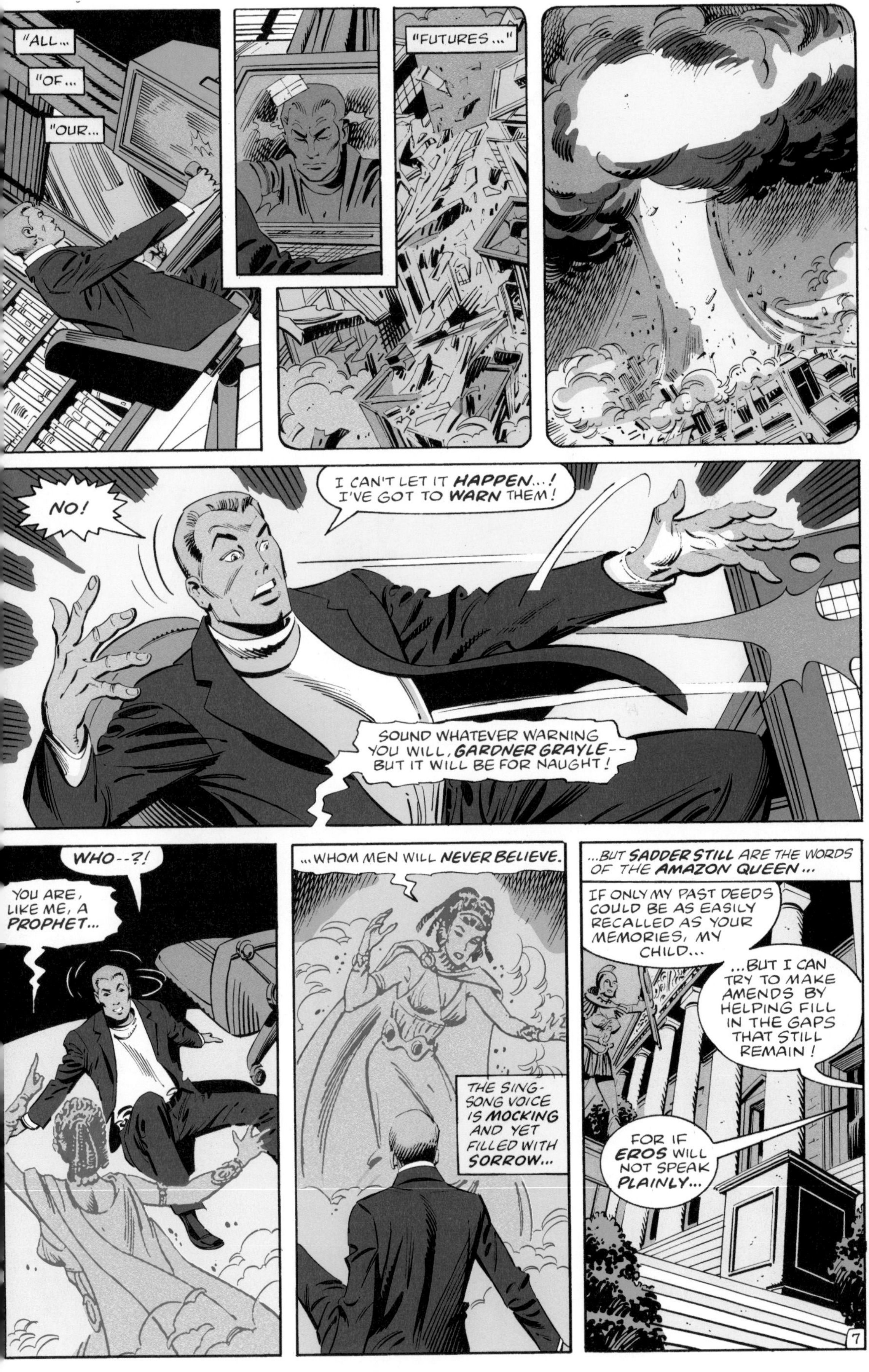
"ALL...
"OF...
"OUR...
"FUTURES..."
NO!
I CAN'T LET IT HAPPEN...! I'VE GOT TO WARN THEM!
SOUND WHATEVER WARNING YOU WILL, GARDNER GRAYLE-- BUT IT WILL BE FOR NAUGHT!
WHO--?!
YOU ARE, LIKE ME, A PROPHET...
...WHOM MEN WILL NEVER BELIEVE.
THE SING-SONG VOICE IS MOCKING AND YET FILLED WITH SORROW...
...BUT SADDER STILL ARE THE WORDS OF THE AMAZON QUEEN...
IF ONLY MY PAST DEEDS COULD BE AS EASILY RECALLED AS YOUR MEMORIES, MY CHILD...
...BUT I CAN TRY TO MAKE AMENDS BY HELPING FILL IN THE GAPS THAT STILL REMAIN!
FOR IF EROS WILL NOT SPEAK PLAINLY...
7

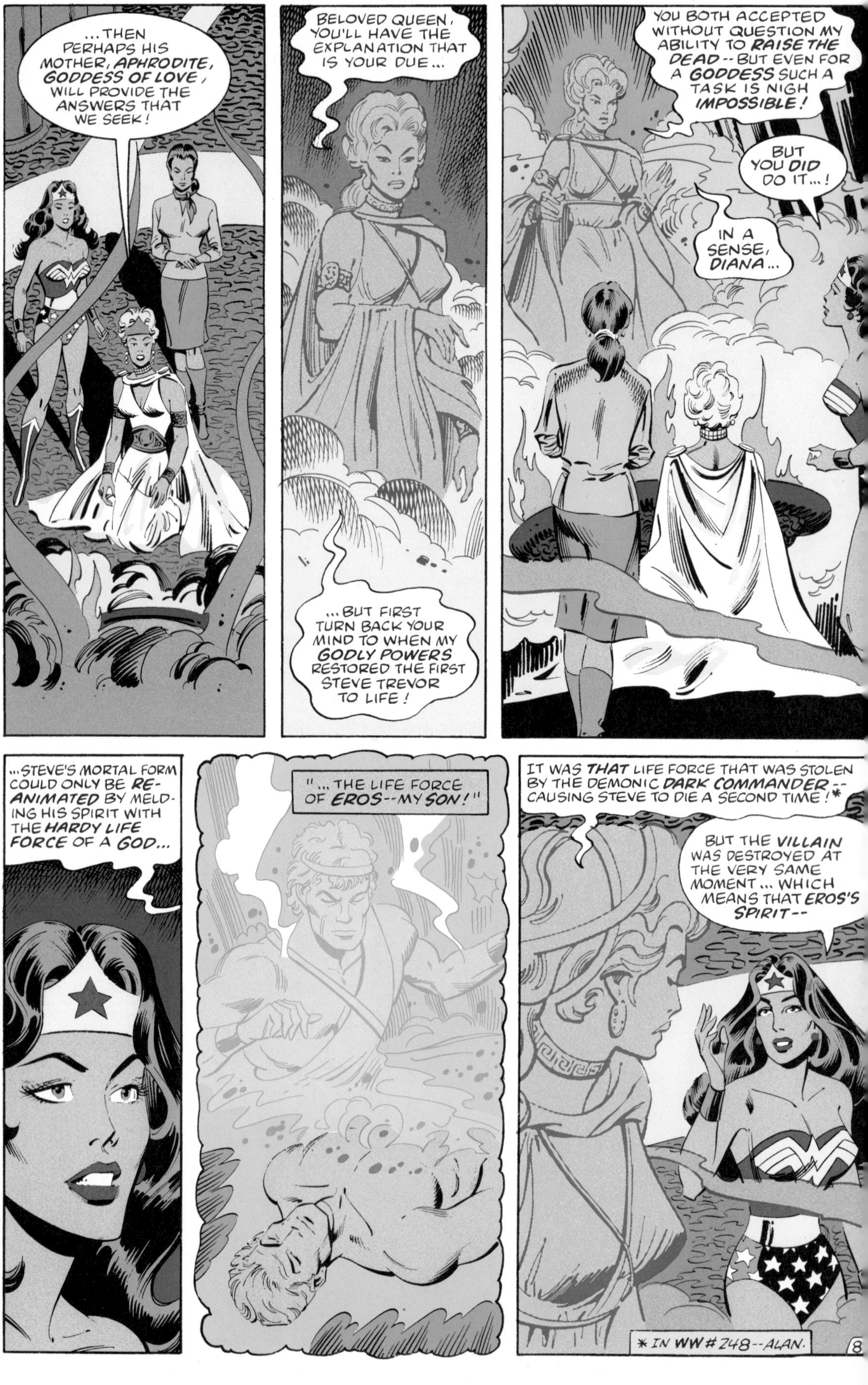

...THEN PERHAPS HIS MOTHER, APHRODITE, GODDESS OF LOVE, WILL PROVIDE THE ANSWERS THAT WE SEEK!
BELOVED QUEEN, YOU'LL HAVE THE EXPLANATION THAT IS YOUR DUE...
...BUT FIRST TURN BACK YOUR MIND TO WHEN MY GODLY POWERS RESTORED THE FIRST STEVE TREVOR TO LIFE!
YOU BOTH ACCEPTED WITHOUT QUESTION MY ABILITY TO RAISE THE DEAD--BUT EVEN FOR A GODDESS SUCH A TASK IS NIGH IMPOSSIBLE!
BUT YOU DID DO IT...!
IN A SENSE, DIANA...
...STEVE'S MORTAL FORM COULD ONLY BE RE-ANIMATED BY MELD-ING HIS SPIRIT WITH THE HARDY LIFE FORCE OF A GOD...
"...THE LIFE FORCE OF EROS--MY SON!"
IT WAS THAT LIFE FORCE THAT WAS STOLEN BY THE DEMONIC DARK COMMANDER--CAUSING STEVE TO DIE A SECOND TIME!*
BUT THE VILLAIN WAS DESTROYED AT THE VERY SAME MOMENT... WHICH MEANS THAT EROS'S SPIRIT--
*IN WW #248--ALAN.
8

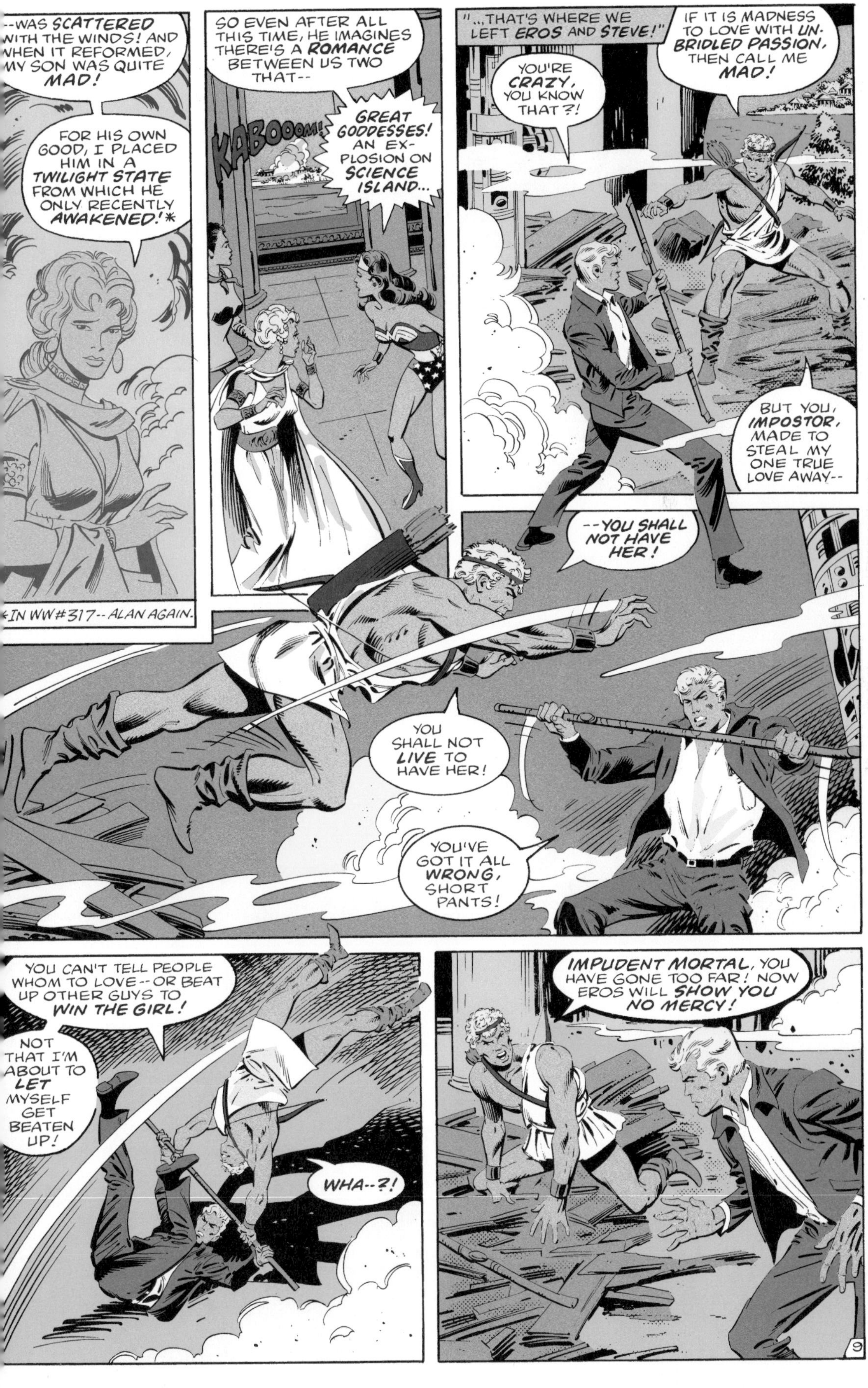
--WAS SCATTERED WITH THE WINDS! AND WHEN IT REFORMED, MY SON WAS QUITE MAD!
FOR HIS OWN GOOD, I PLACED HIM IN A TWILIGHT STATE FROM WHICH HE ONLY RECENTLY AWAKENED!*
*IN WW #317-- ALAN AGAIN.
SO EVEN AFTER ALL THIS TIME, HE IMAGINES THERE'S A ROMANCE BETWEEN US TWO THAT--
KABOOOM!
GREAT GODDESSES! AN EX-PLOSION ON SCIENCE ISLAND...
"...THAT'S WHERE WE LEFT EROS AND STEVE!"
YOU'RE CRAZY, YOU KNOW THAT?!
IF IT IS MADNESS TO LOVE WITH UN-BRIDLED PASSION, THEN CALL ME MAD!
BUT YOU, IMPOSTOR, MADE TO STEAL MY ONE TRUE LOVE AWAY--
--YOU SHALL NOT HAVE HER!
YOU SHALL NOT LIVE TO HAVE HER!
YOU'VE GOT IT ALL WRONG, SHORT PANTS!
YOU CAN'T TELL PEOPLE WHOM TO LOVE--OR BEAT UP OTHER GUYS TO WIN THE GIRL!
NOT THAT I'M ABOUT TO LET MYSELF GET BEATEN UP!
WHA--?!
IMPUDENT MORTAL, YOU HAVE GONE TOO FAR! NOW EROS WILL SHOW YOU NO MERCY!
9

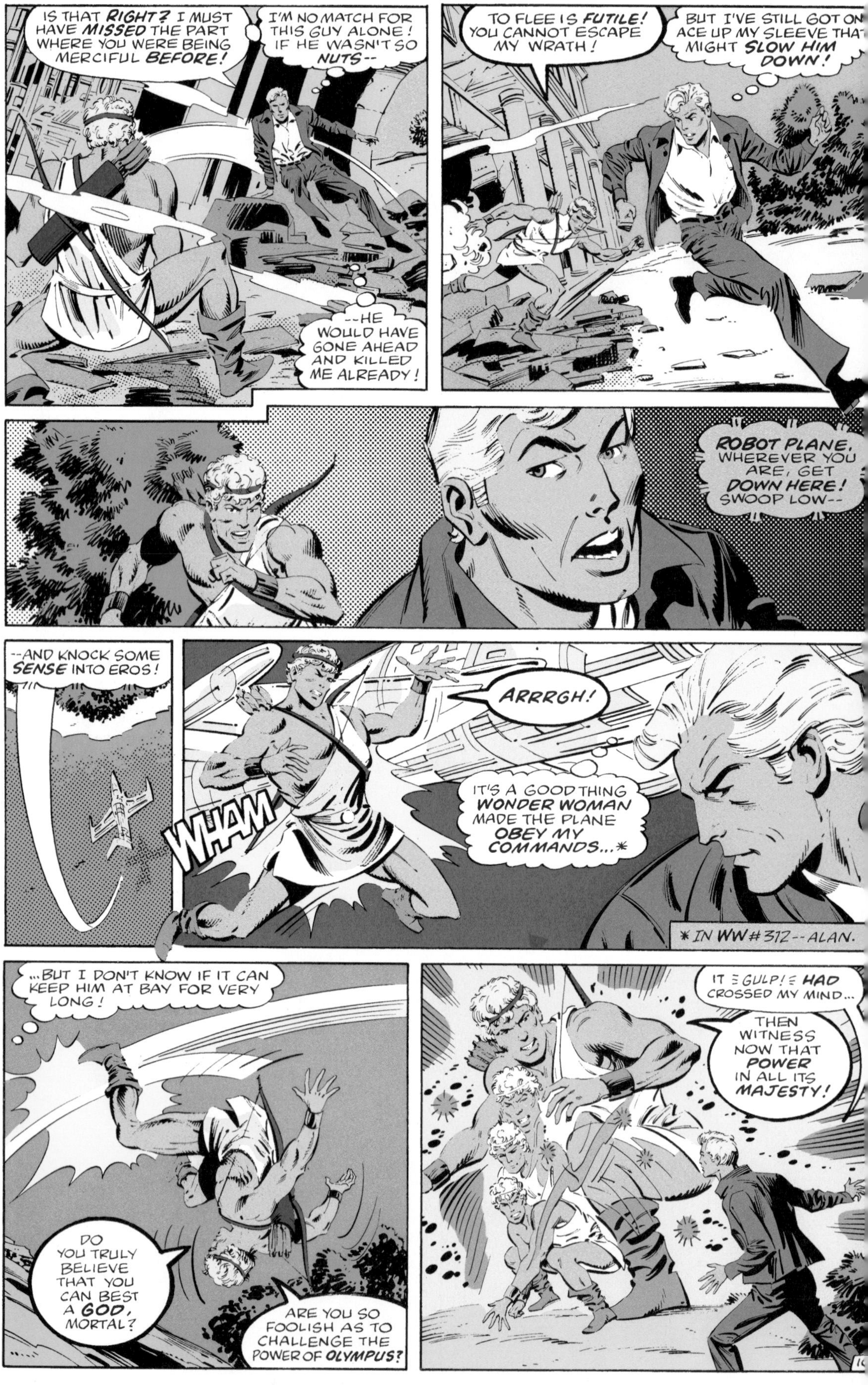
IS THAT RIGHT? I MUST HAVE MISSED THE PART WHERE YOU WERE BEING MERCIFUL BEFORE!
I'M NO MATCH FOR THIS GUY ALONE! IF HE WASN'T SO NUTS--
--HE WOULD HAVE GONE AHEAD AND KILLED ME ALREADY!
TO FLEE IS FUTILE! YOU CANNOT ESCAPE MY WRATH!
BUT I'VE STILL GOT ON ACE UP MY SLEEVE THAT MIGHT SLOW HIM DOWN!
ROBOT PLANE, WHEREVER YOU ARE, GET DOWN HERE! SWOOP LOW--
--AND KNOCK SOME SENSE INTO EROS!
ARRRGH!
WHAM
IT'S A GOOD THING WONDER WOMAN MADE THE PLANE OBEY MY COMMANDS...*
* IN WW #312--ALAN.
...BUT I DON'T KNOW IF IT CAN KEEP HIM AT BAY FOR VERY LONG!
DO YOU TRULY BELIEVE THAT YOU CAN BEST A GOD, MORTAL?
ARE YOU SO FOOLISH AS TO CHALLENGE THE POWER OF OLYMPUS?
IT =GULP!= HAD CROSSED MY MIND...
THEN WITNESS NOW THAT POWER IN ALL ITS MAJESTY!

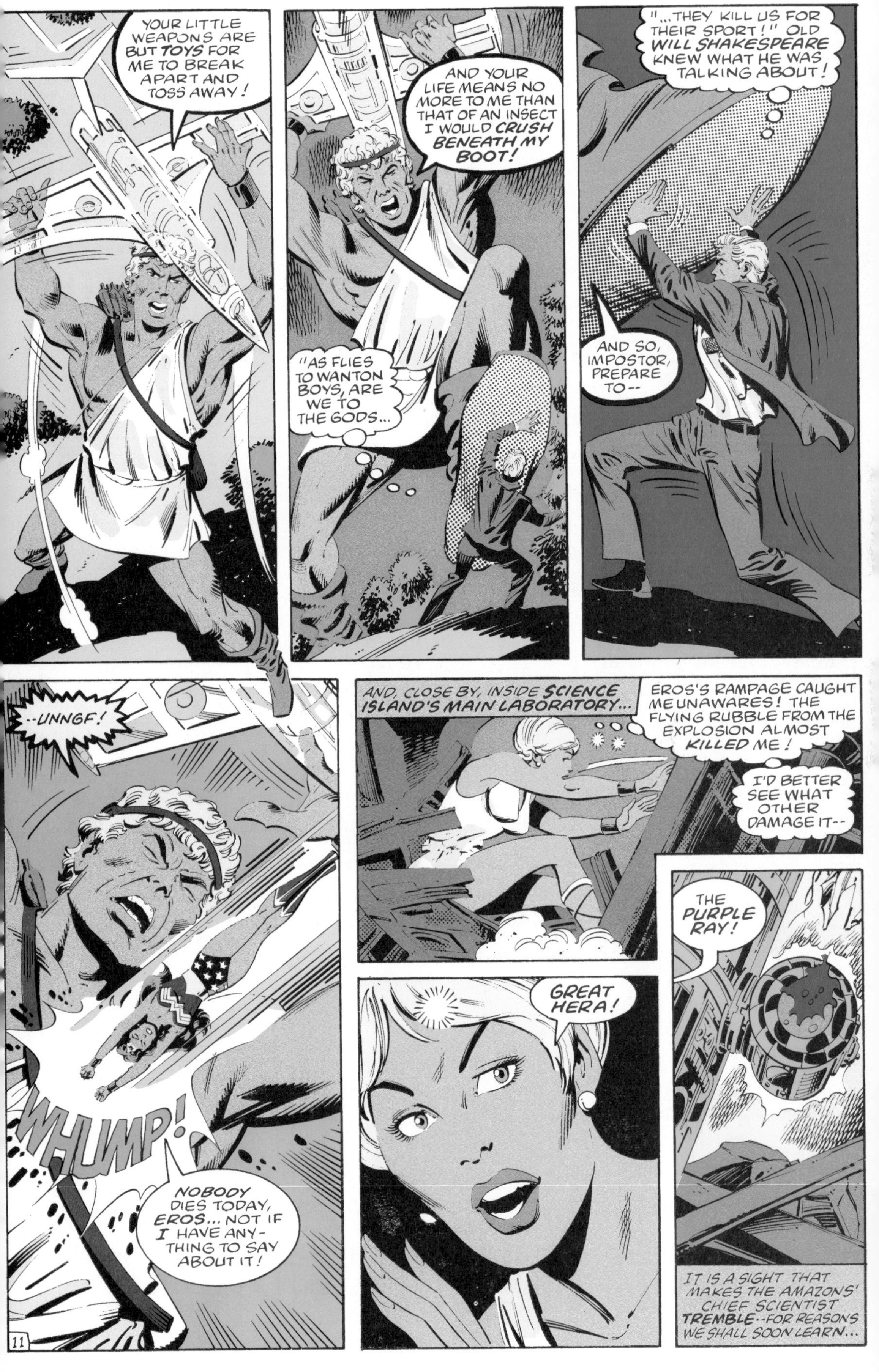
YOUR LITTLE WEAPONS ARE BUT TOYS FOR ME TO BREAK APART AND TOSS AWAY!
AND YOUR LIFE MEANS NO MORE TO ME THAN THAT OF AN INSECT I WOULD CRUSH BENEATH MY BOOT!
"AS FLIES TO WANTON BOYS, ARE WE TO THE GODS...
"...THEY KILL US FOR THEIR SPORT!" OLD WILL SHAKESPEARE KNEW WHAT HE WAS TALKING ABOUT!
AND SO, IMPOSTOR, PREPARE TO--
--UNNGF!
WHUMP!
NOBODY DIES TODAY, EROS... NOT IF I HAVE ANY-THING TO SAY ABOUT IT!
11
AND, CLOSE BY, INSIDE SCIENCE ISLAND'S MAIN LABORATORY...
EROS'S RAMPAGE CAUGHT ME UNAWARES! THE FLYING RUBBLE FROM THE EXPLOSION ALMOST KILLED ME!
I'D BETTER SEE WHAT OTHER DAMAGE IT--
GREAT HERA!
THE PURPLE RAY!
IT IS A SIGHT THAT MAKES THE AMAZONS' CHIEF SCIENTIST TREMBLE--FOR REASONS WE SHALL SOON LEARN...

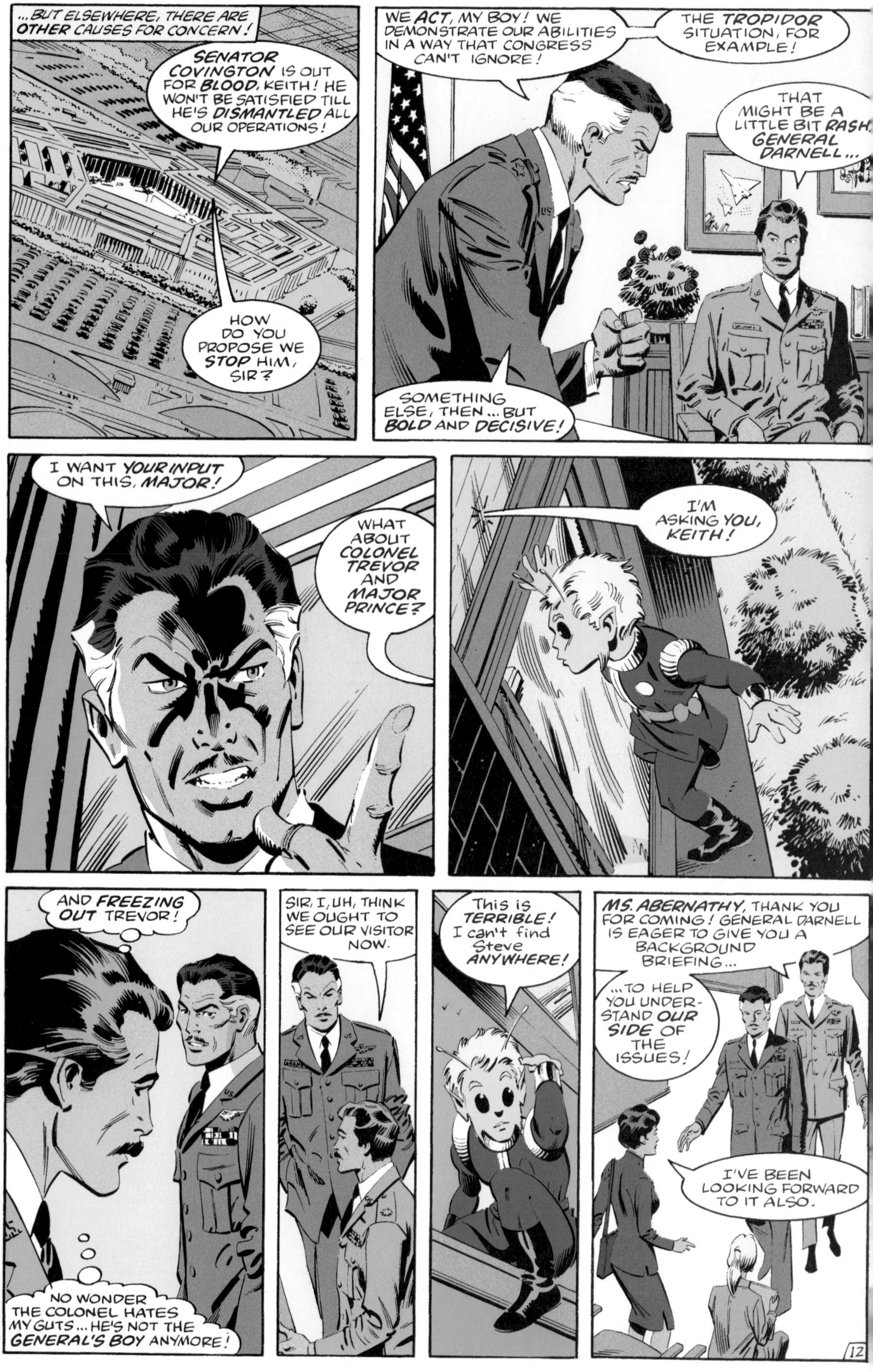
...BUT ELSEWHERE, THERE ARE OTHER CAUSES FOR CONCERN!
SENATOR COVINGTON IS OUT FOR BLOOD, KEITH! HE WON'T BE SATISFIED TILL HE'S DISMANTLED ALL OUR OPERATIONS!
HOW DO YOU PROPOSE WE STOP HIM, SIR?
WE ACT, MY BOY! WE DEMONSTRATE OUR ABILITIES IN A WAY THAT CONGRESS CAN'T IGNORE!
THE TROPIDOR SITUATION, FOR EXAMPLE!
THAT MIGHT BE A LITTLE BIT RASH, GENERAL DARNELL...
SOMETHING ELSE, THEN... BUT BOLD AND DECISIVE!
I WANT YOUR INPUT ON THIS, MAJOR!
WHAT ABOUT COLONEL TREVOR AND MAJOR PRINCE?
I'M ASKING YOU, KEITH!
AND FREEZING OUT TREVOR!
NO WONDER THE COLONEL HATES MY GUTS... HE'S NOT THE GENERAL'S BOY ANYMORE!
SIR, I, UH, THINK WE OUGHT TO SEE OUR VISITOR NOW.
This is TERRIBLE! I can't find Steve ANYWHERE!
MS. ABERNATHY, THANK YOU FOR COMING! GENERAL DARNELL IS EAGER TO GIVE YOU A BACKGROUND BRIEFING...
...TO HELP YOU UNDERSTAND OUR SIDE OF THE ISSUES!
I'VE BEEN LOOKING FORWARD TO IT ALSO.
12

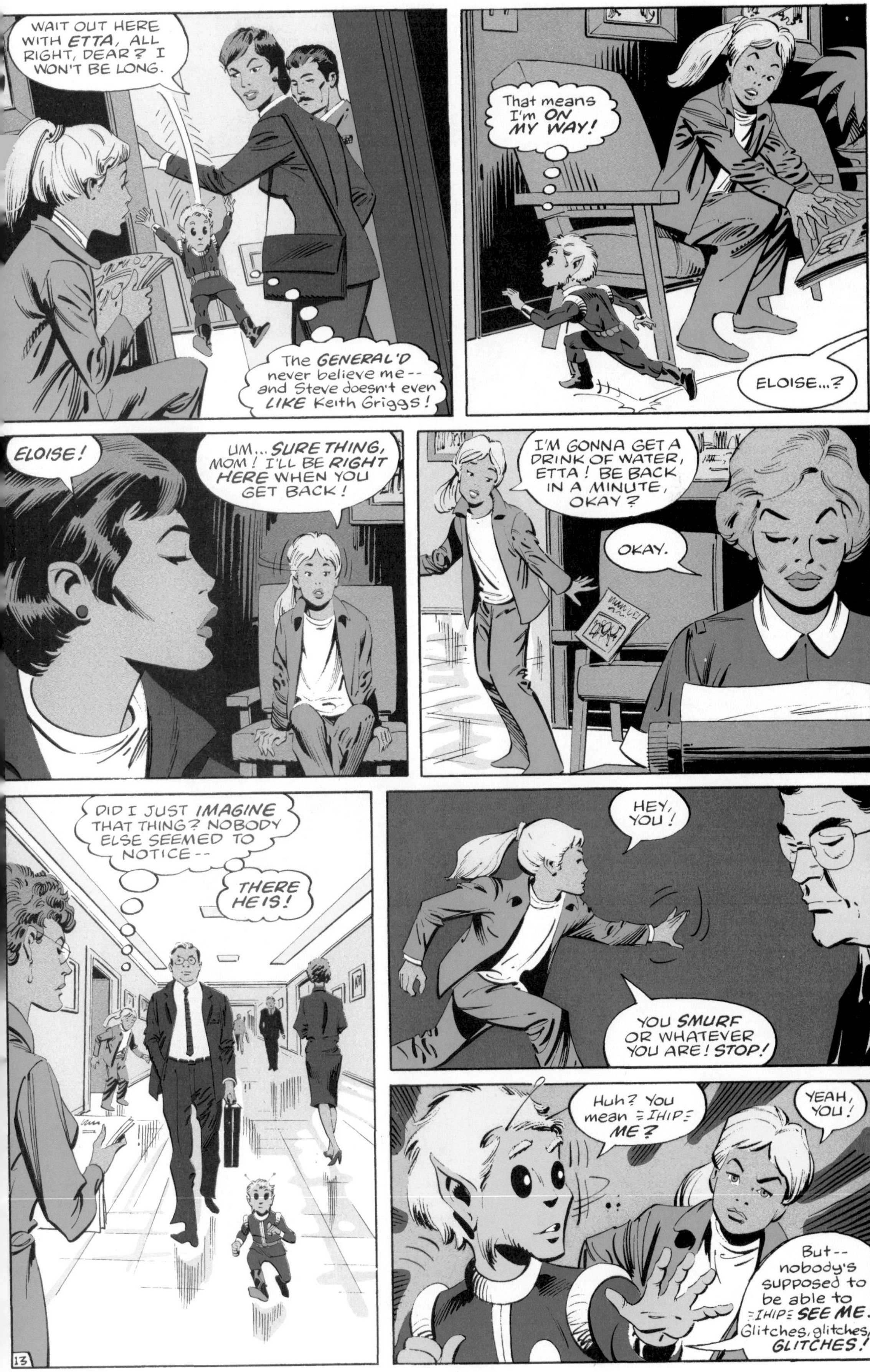
WAIT OUT HERE WITH ETTA, ALL RIGHT, DEAR? I WON'T BE LONG.
The GENERAL'D never believe me -- and Steve doesn't even LIKE Keith Griggs!
That means I'm ON MY WAY!
ELOISE...?
ELOISE!
UM... SURE THING, MOM! I'LL BE RIGHT HERE WHEN YOU GET BACK!
I'M GONNA GET A DRINK OF WATER, ETTA! BE BACK IN A MINUTE, OKAY?
OKAY.
DID I JUST IMAGINE THAT THING? NOBODY ELSE SEEMED TO NOTICE --
THERE HE IS!
13
HEY, YOU!
YOU SMURF OR WHATEVER YOU ARE! STOP!
Huh? You mean =IHIP= ME?
YEAH, YOU!
But -- nobody's supposed to be able to =IHIP= SEE ME! Glitches, glitches, GLITCHES!

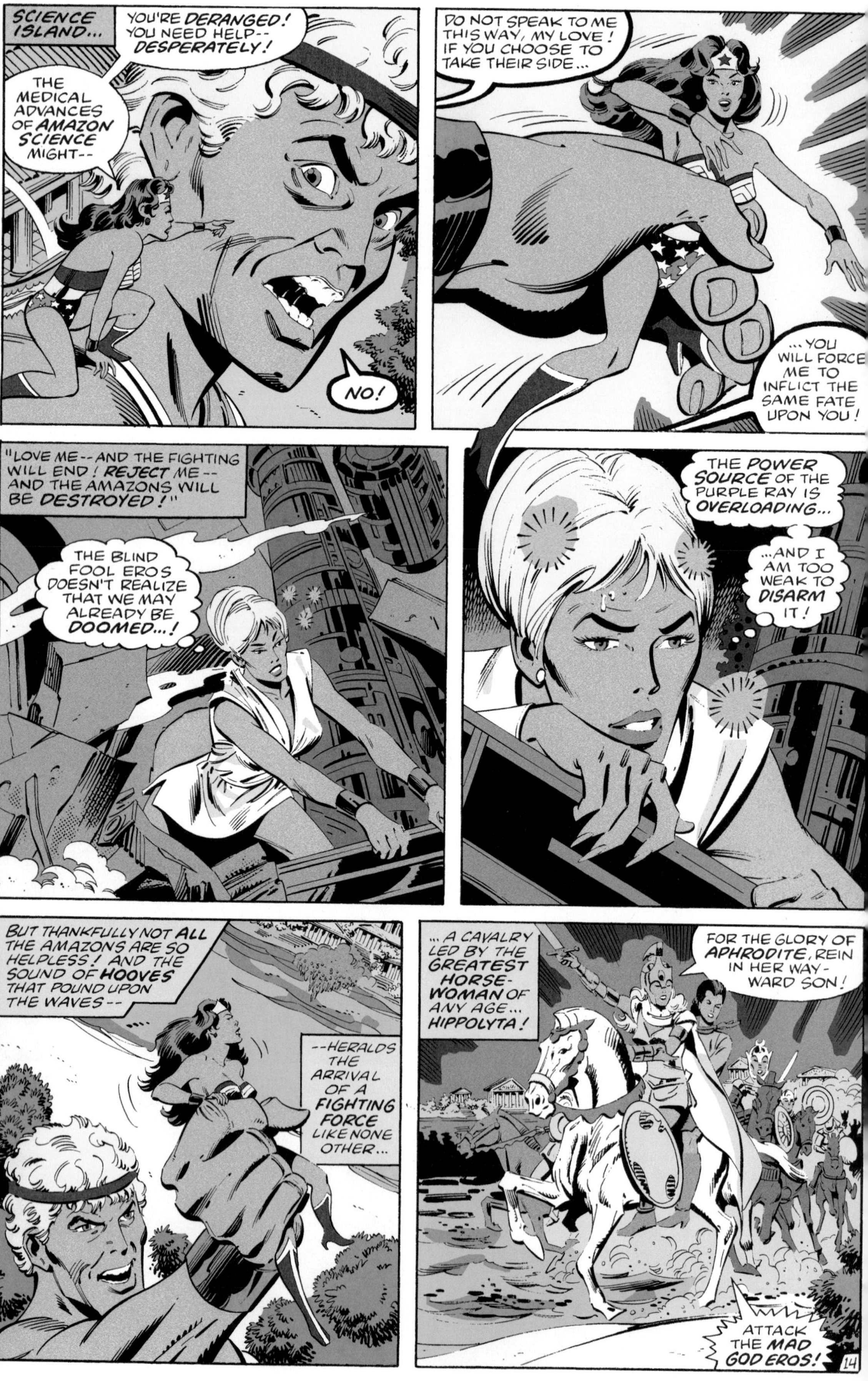
SCIENCE ISLAND...
YOU'RE DERANGED! YOU NEED HELP-- DESPERATELY!
THE MEDICAL ADVANCES OF AMAZON SCIENCE MIGHT--
NO!
DO NOT SPEAK TO ME THIS WAY, MY LOVE! IF YOU CHOOSE TO TAKE THEIR SIDE...
...YOU WILL FORCE ME TO INFLICT THE SAME FATE UPON YOU!
"LOVE ME--AND THE FIGHTING WILL END! REJECT ME-- AND THE AMAZONS WILL BE DESTROYED!"
THE BLIND FOOL EROS DOESN'T REALIZE THAT WE MAY ALREADY BE DOOMED...!
THE POWER SOURCE OF THE PURPLE RAY IS OVERLOADING...
...AND I AM TOO WEAK TO DISARM IT!
BUT THANKFULLY NOT ALL THE AMAZONS ARE SO HELPLESS! AND THE SOUND OF HOOVES THAT POUND UPON THE WAVES--
--HERALDS THE ARRIVAL OF A FIGHTING FORCE LIKE NONE OTHER...
...A CAVALRY LED BY THE GREATEST HORSE-WOMAN OF ANY AGE... HIPPOLYTA!
FOR THE GLORY OF APHRODITE, REIN IN HER WAY-WARD SON!
ATTACK THE MAD GOD EROS!
14

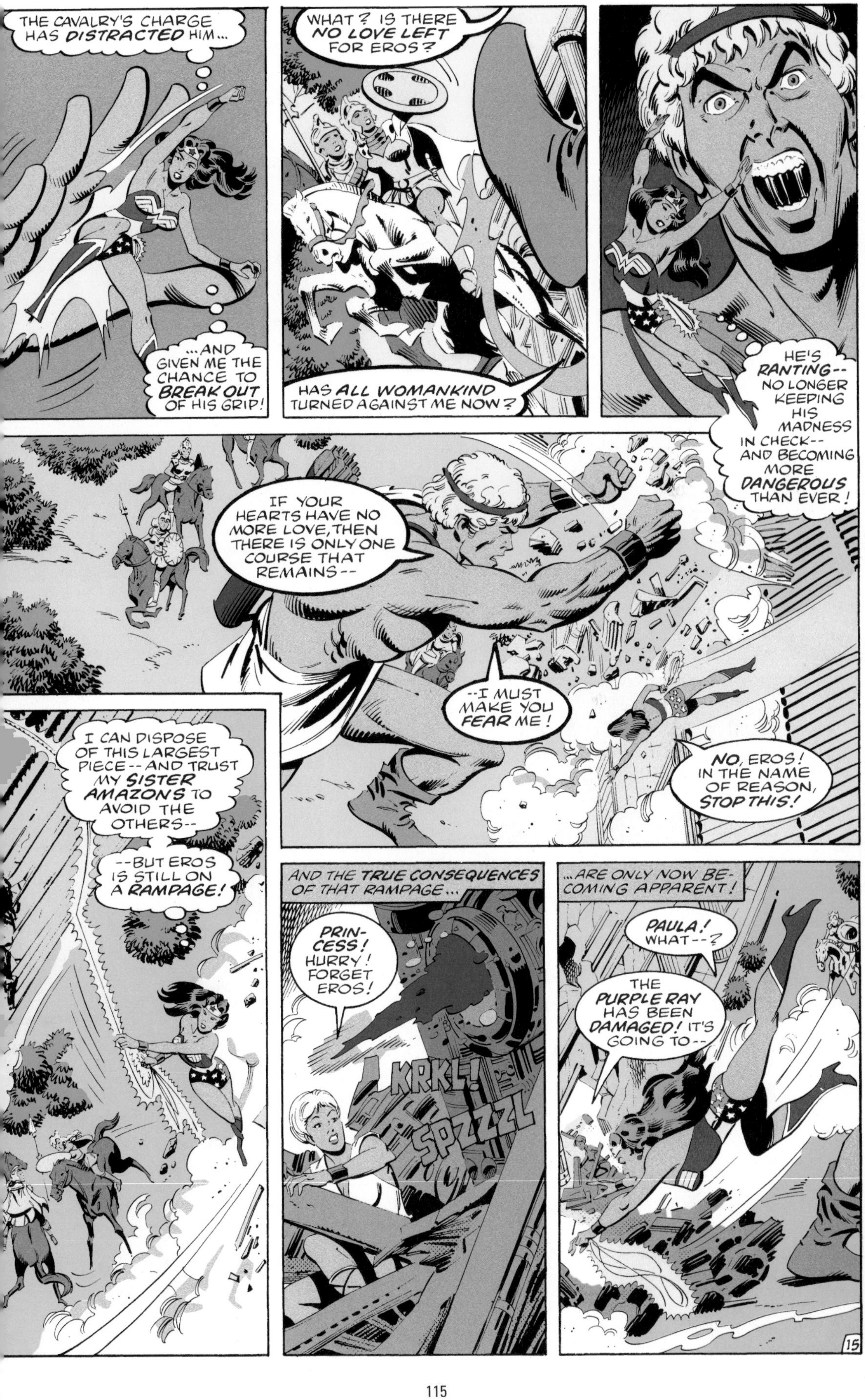
THE CAVALRY'S CHARGE HAS DISTRACTED HIM...
...AND GIVEN ME THE CHANCE TO BREAK OUT OF HIS GRIP!
WHAT? IS THERE NO LOVE LEFT FOR EROS?
HAS ALL WOMANKIND TURNED AGAINST ME NOW?
HE'S RANTING-- NO LONGER KEEPING HIS MADNESS IN CHECK-- AND BECOMING MORE DANGEROUS THAN EVER!
IF YOUR HEARTS HAVE NO MORE LOVE, THEN THERE IS ONLY ONE COURSE THAT REMAINS--
--I MUST MAKE YOU FEAR ME!
NO, EROS! IN THE NAME OF REASON, STOP THIS!
I CAN DISPOSE OF THIS LARGEST PIECE-- AND TRUST MY SISTER AMAZONS TO AVOID THE OTHERS--
--BUT EROS IS STILL ON A RAMPAGE!
AND THE TRUE CONSEQUENCES OF THAT RAMPAGE...
PRIN-CESS! HURRY! FORGET EROS!
KRKL!
SPZZZL
...ARE ONLY NOW BE-COMING APPARENT!
PAULA! WHAT--?
THE PURPLE RAY HAS BEEN DAMAGED! IT'S GOING TO--
15

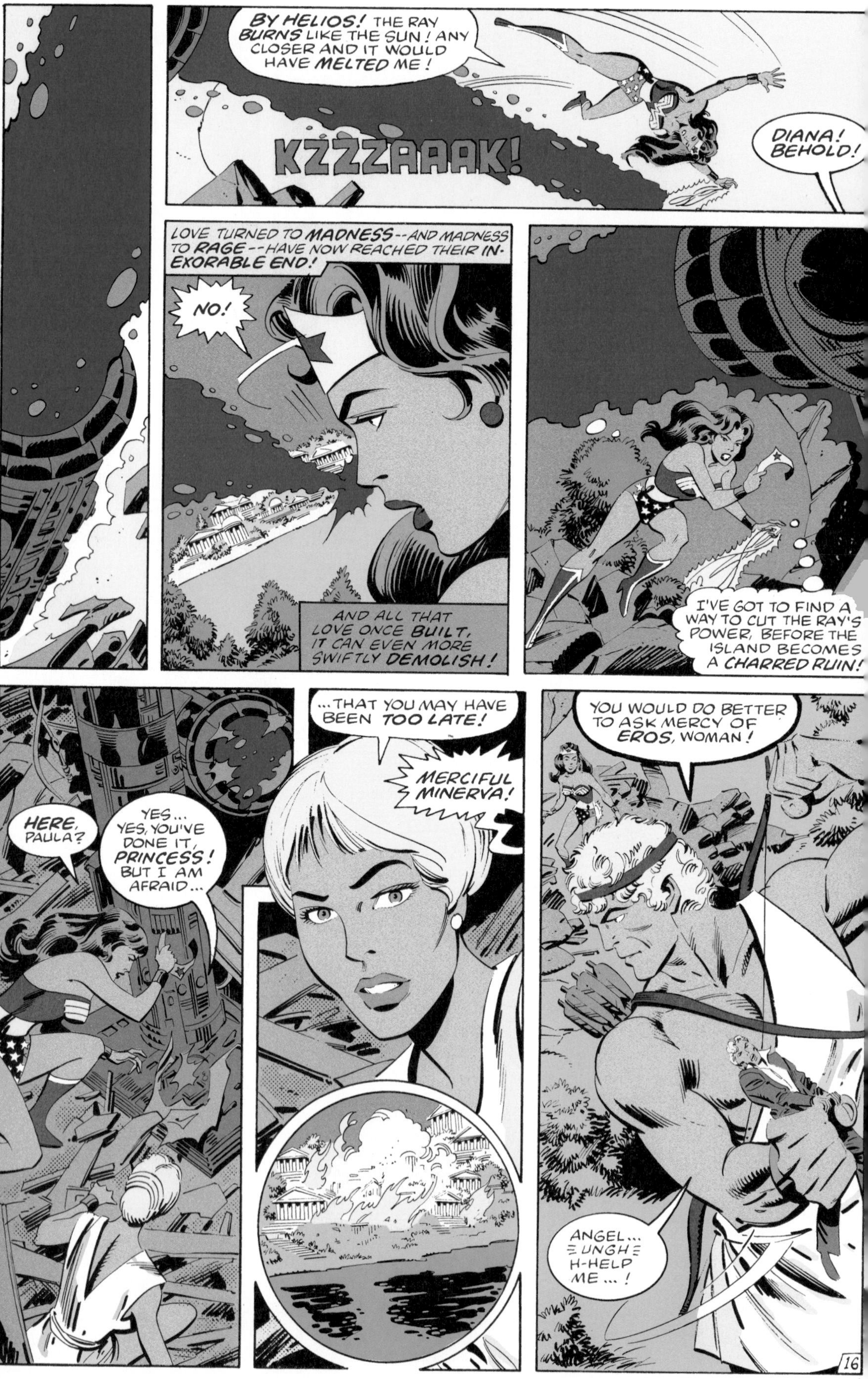

BY HELIOS! THE RAY BURNS LIKE THE SUN! ANY CLOSER AND IT WOULD HAVE MELTED ME!
KZZZAAAK!
DIANA! BEHOLD!
LOVE TURNED TO MADNESS--AND MADNESS TO RAGE--HAVE NOW REACHED THEIR INEXORABLE END!
NO!
AND ALL THAT LOVE ONCE BUILT, IT CAN EVEN MORE SWIFTLY DEMOLISH!
I'VE GOT TO FIND A WAY TO CUT THE RAY'S POWER, BEFORE THE ISLAND BECOMES A CHARRED RUIN!
HERE, PAULA?
YES... YES, YOU'VE DONE IT, PRINCESS! BUT I AM AFRAID...
...THAT YOU MAY HAVE BEEN TOO LATE!
MERCIFUL MINERVA!
YOU WOULD DO BETTER TO ASK MERCY OF EROS, WOMAN!
ANGEL... UNGH H-HELP ME...!
16

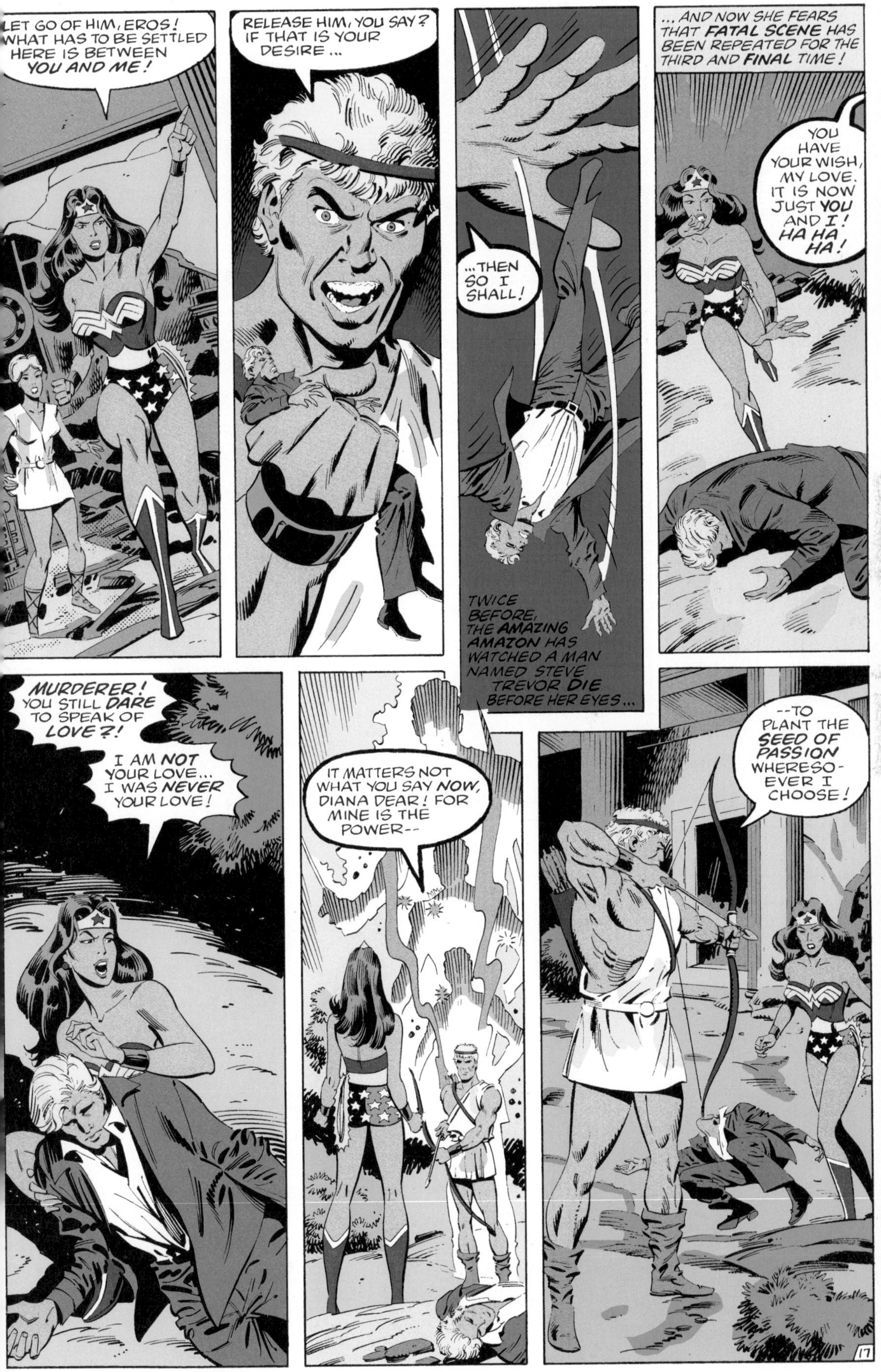

LET GO OF HIM, EROS! WHAT HAS TO BE SETTLED HERE IS BETWEEN YOU AND ME!
RELEASE HIM, YOU SAY? IF THAT IS YOUR DESIRE...
...THEN SO I SHALL!
TWICE BEFORE, THE AMAZING AMAZON HAS WATCHED A MAN NAMED STEVE TREVOR DIE BEFORE HER EYES...
... AND NOW SHE FEARS THAT FATAL SCENE HAS BEEN REPEATED FOR THE THIRD AND FINAL TIME!
YOU HAVE YOUR WISH, MY LOVE. IT IS NOW JUST YOU AND I! HA HA HA!
MURDERER! YOU STILL DARE TO SPEAK OF LOVE?!
I AM NOT YOUR LOVE... I WAS NEVER YOUR LOVE!
IT MATTERS NOT WHAT YOU SAY NOW, DIANA DEAR! FOR MINE IS THE POWER--
--TO PLANT THE SEED OF PASSION WHERESO-EVER I CHOOSE!
17

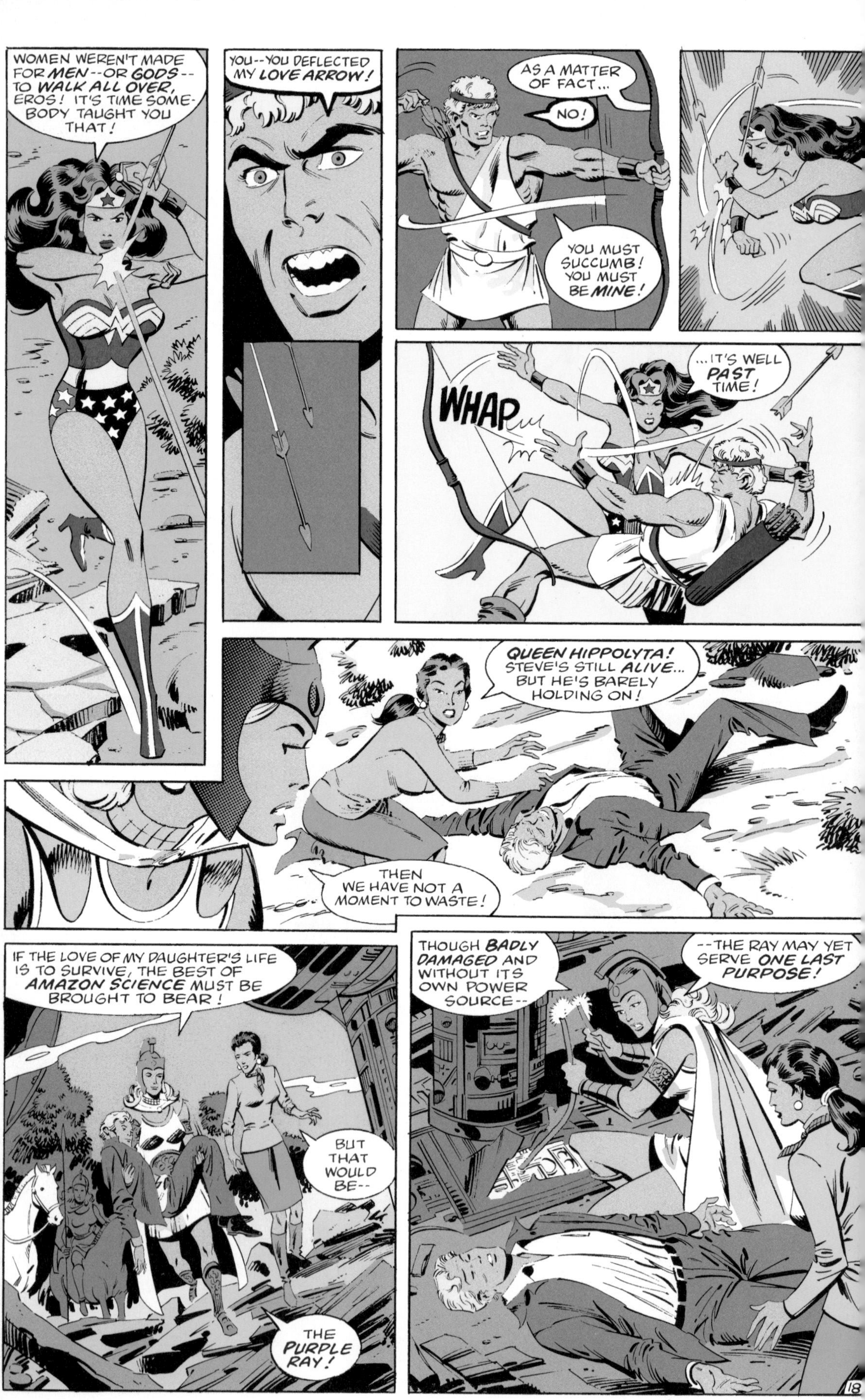
WOMEN WEREN'T MADE FOR MEN--OR GODS--TO WALK ALL OVER, EROS! IT'S TIME SOMEBODY TAUGHT YOU THAT!
YOU--YOU DEFLECTED MY LOVE ARROW!
AS A MATTER OF FACT...
NO!
YOU MUST SUCCUMB! YOU MUST BE MINE!
WHAP
...IT'S WELL PAST TIME!
QUEEN HIPPOLYTA! STEVE'S STILL ALIVE... BUT HE'S BARELY HOLDING ON!
THEN WE HAVE NOT A MOMENT TO WASTE!
IF THE LOVE OF MY DAUGHTER'S LIFE IS TO SURVIVE, THE BEST OF AMAZON SCIENCE MUST BE BROUGHT TO BEAR!
BUT THAT WOULD BE--
THE PURPLE RAY!
THOUGH BADLY DAMAGED AND WITHOUT ITS OWN POWER SOURCE--
--THE RAY MAY YET SERVE ONE LAST PURPOSE!
18

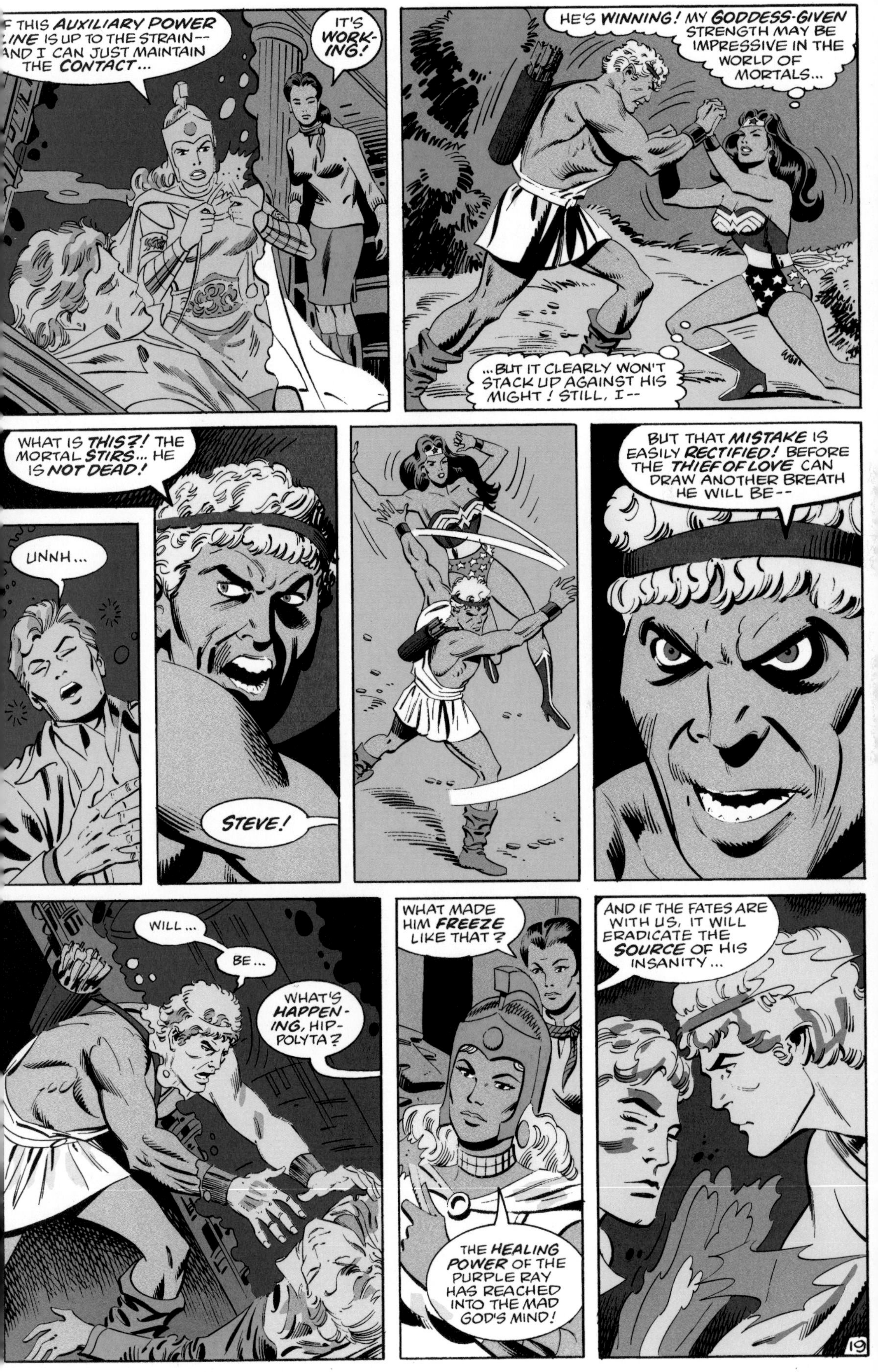

IF THIS AUXILIARY POWER LINE IS UP TO THE STRAIN-- AND I CAN JUST MAINTAIN THE CONTACT...
IT'S WORKING!
HE'S WINNING! MY GODDESS-GIVEN STRENGTH MAY BE IMPRESSIVE IN THE WORLD OF MORTALS...
...BUT IT CLEARLY WON'T STACK UP AGAINST HIS MIGHT! STILL, I--
WHAT IS THIS?! THE MORTAL STIRS... HE IS NOT DEAD!
UNNH...
STEVE!
BUT THAT MISTAKE IS EASILY RECTIFIED! BEFORE THE THIEF OF LOVE CAN DRAW ANOTHER BREATH HE WILL BE--
WILL...
BE...
WHAT'S HAPPENING, HIPPOLYTA?
WHAT MADE HIM FREEZE LIKE THAT?
THE HEALING POWER OF THE PURPLE RAY HAS REACHED INTO THE MAD GOD'S MIND!
AND IF THE FATES ARE WITH US, IT WILL ERADICATE THE SOURCE OF HIS INSANITY...
19

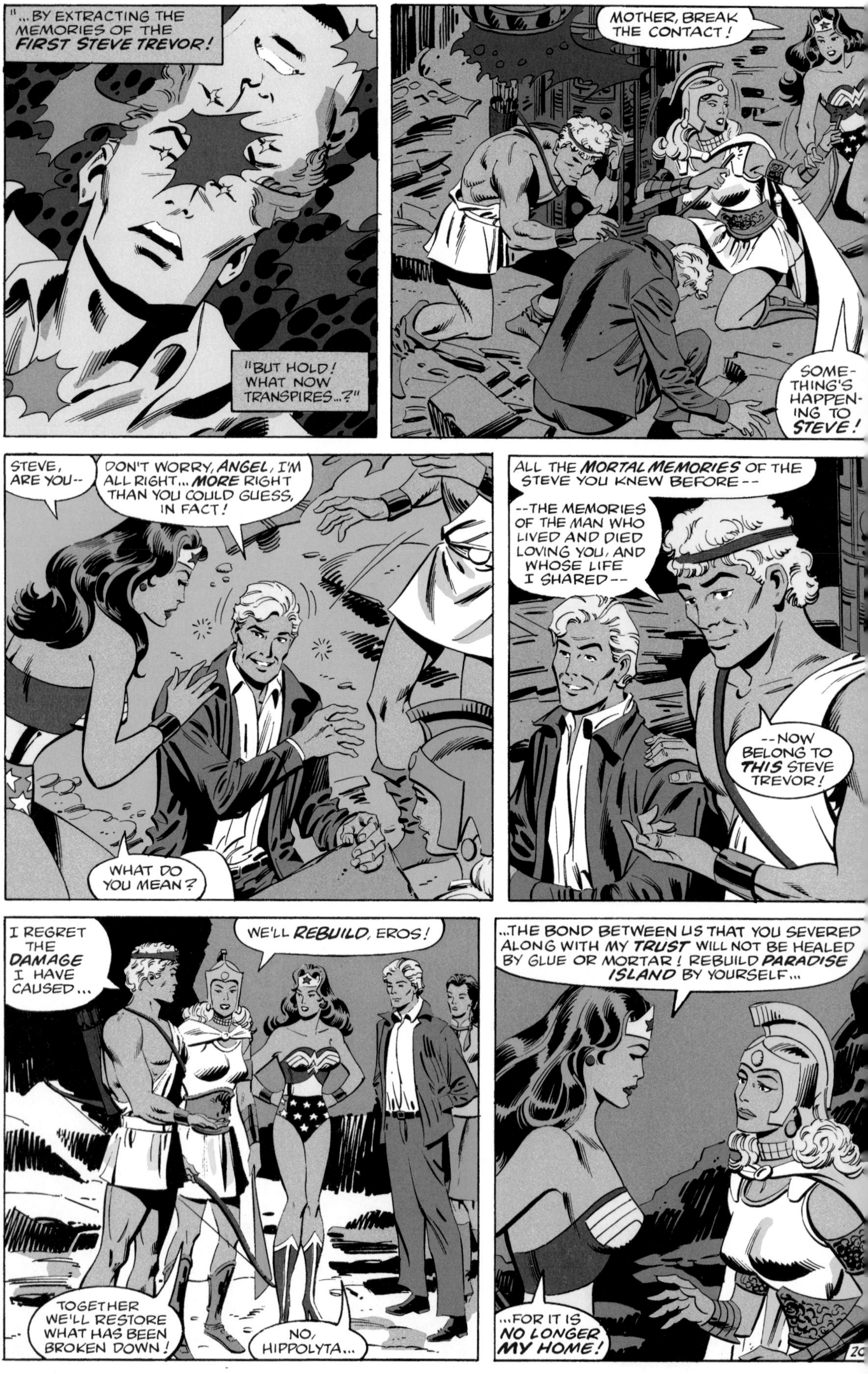
"...BY EXTRACTING THE MEMORIES OF THE FIRST STEVE TREVOR!
"BUT HOLD! WHAT NOW TRANSPIRES...?"
MOTHER, BREAK THE CONTACT!
SOME-THING'S HAPPEN-ING TO STEVE!
STEVE, ARE YOU--
DON'T WORRY, ANGEL, I'M ALL RIGHT... MORE RIGHT THAN YOU COULD GUESS, IN FACT!
WHAT DO YOU MEAN?
ALL THE MORTAL MEMORIES OF THE STEVE YOU KNEW BEFORE--
--THE MEMORIES OF THE MAN WHO LIVED AND DIED LOVING YOU, AND WHOSE LIFE I SHARED--
--NOW BELONG TO THIS STEVE TREVOR!
I REGRET THE DAMAGE I HAVE CAUSED...
WE'LL REBUILD, EROS!
TOGETHER WE'LL RESTORE WHAT HAS BEEN BROKEN DOWN!
NO, HIPPOLYTA...
...THE BOND BETWEEN US THAT YOU SEVERED ALONG WITH MY TRUST WILL NOT BE HEALED BY GLUE OR MORTAR! REBUILD PARADISE ISLAND BY YOURSELF...
...FOR IT IS NO LONGER MY HOME!
20

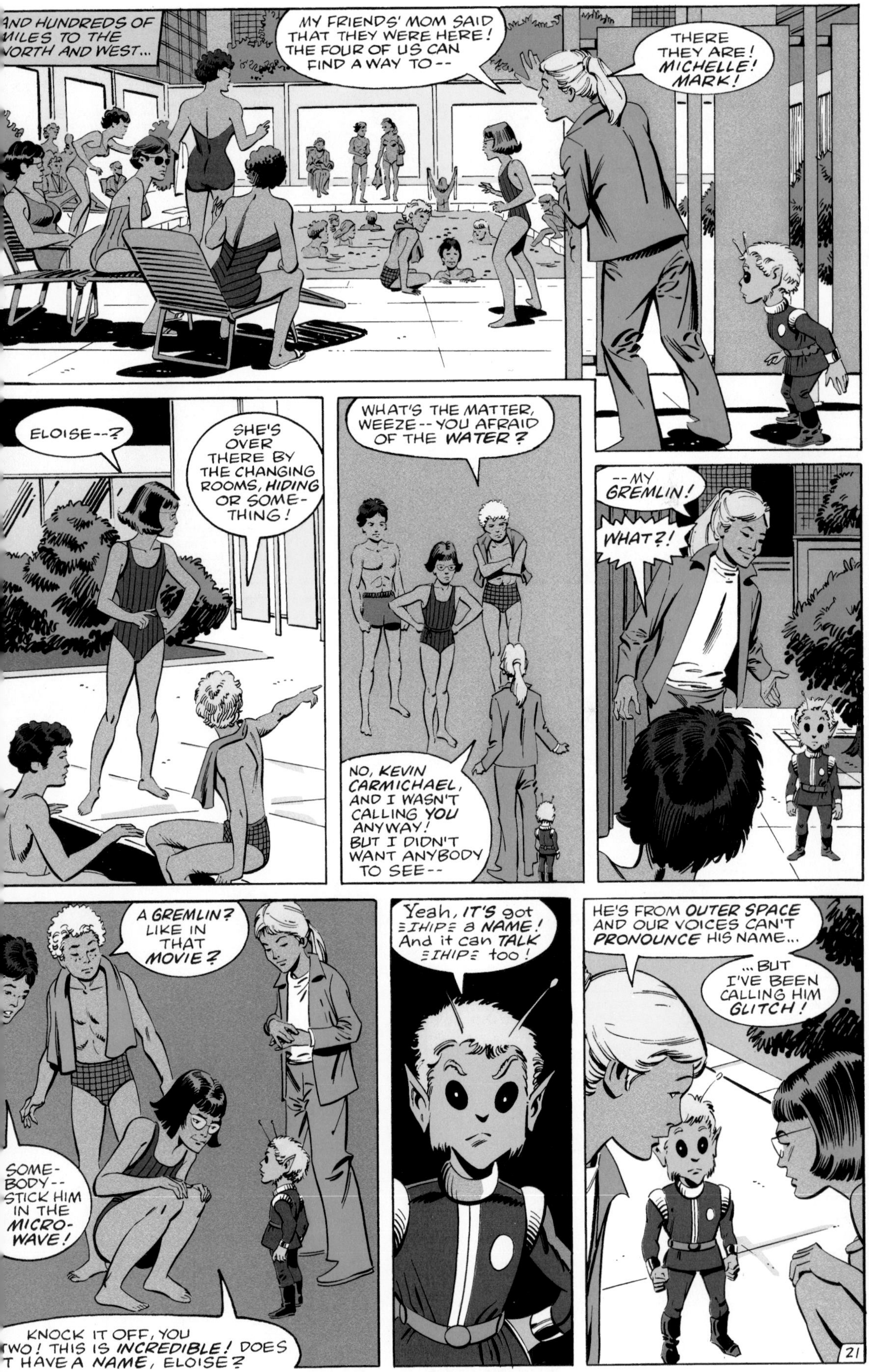

AND HUNDREDS OF MILES TO THE NORTH AND WEST...
MY FRIENDS' MOM SAID THAT THEY WERE HERE! THE FOUR OF US CAN FIND A WAY TO--
THERE THEY ARE! MICHELLE! MARK!
ELOISE--?
SHE'S OVER THERE BY THE CHANGING ROOMS, HIDING OR SOMETHING!
WHAT'S THE MATTER, WEEZE--YOU AFRAID OF THE WATER?
NO, KEVIN CARMICHAEL, AND I WASN'T CALLING YOU ANYWAY! BUT I DIDN'T WANT ANYBODY TO SEE--
--MY GREMLIN!
WHAT?!
A GREMLIN? LIKE IN THAT MOVIE?
SOME-BODY--STICK HIM IN THE MICRO-WAVE!
KNOCK IT OFF, YOU TWO! THIS IS INCREDIBLE! DOES IT HAVE A NAME, ELOISE?
Yeah, IT'S got ΞIHIPΞ a NAME! And it can TALK ΞIHIPΞ too!
HE'S FROM OUTER SPACE AND OUR VOICES CAN'T PRONOUNCE HIS NAME...
...BUT I'VE BEEN CALLING HIM GLITCH!
21

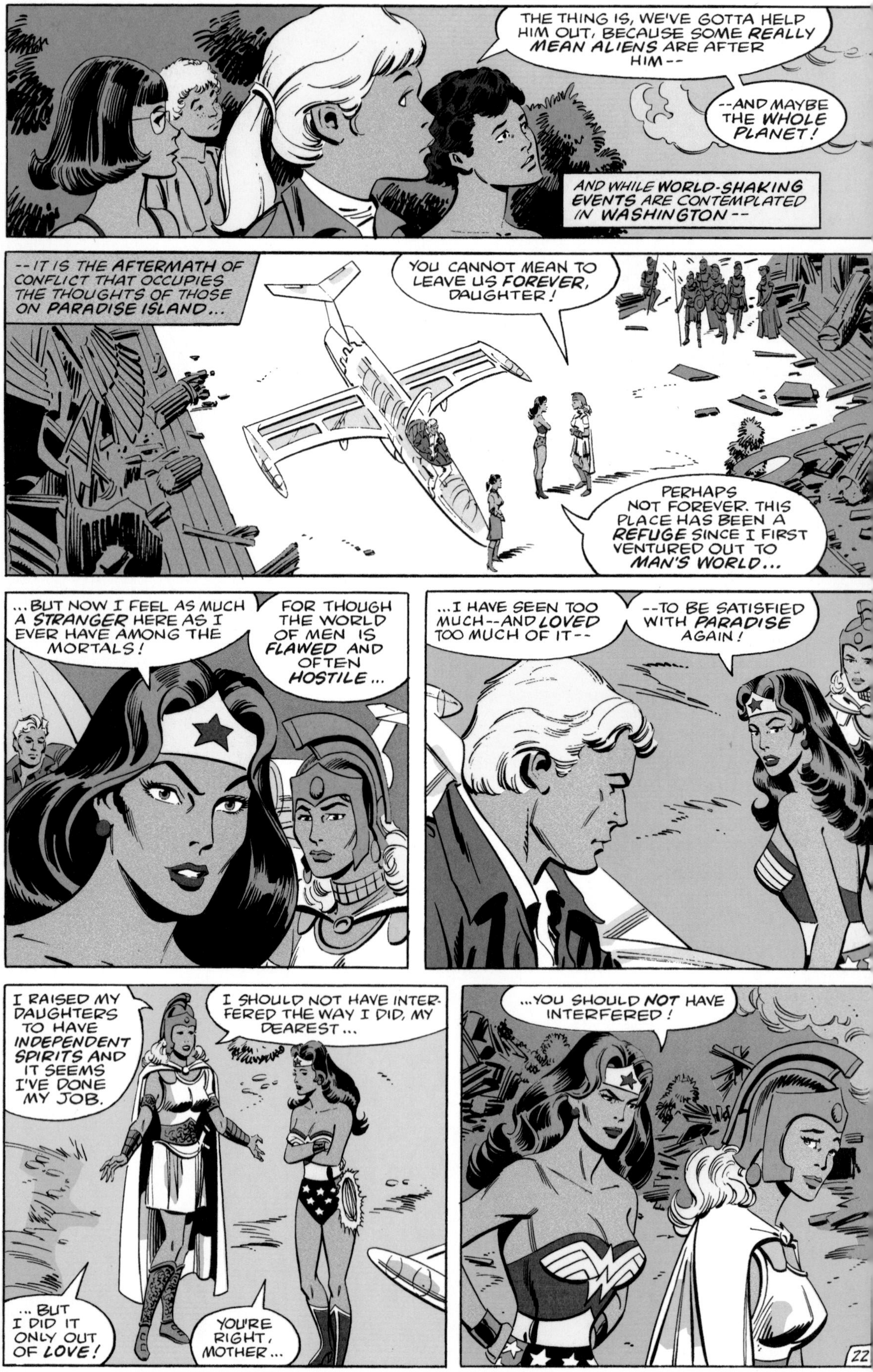

THE THING IS, WE'VE GOTTA HELP HIM OUT, BECAUSE SOME REALLY MEAN ALIENS ARE AFTER HIM--
--AND MAYBE THE WHOLE PLANET!
AND WHILE WORLD-SHAKING EVENTS ARE CONTEMPLATED IN WASHINGTON--
--IT IS THE AFTERMATH OF CONFLICT THAT OCCUPIES THE THOUGHTS OF THOSE ON PARADISE ISLAND...
YOU CANNOT MEAN TO LEAVE US FOREVER, DAUGHTER!
PERHAPS NOT FOREVER. THIS PLACE HAS BEEN A REFUGE SINCE I FIRST VENTURED OUT TO MAN'S WORLD...
...BUT NOW I FEEL AS MUCH A STRANGER HERE AS I EVER HAVE AMONG THE MORTALS!
FOR THOUGH THE WORLD OF MEN IS FLAWED AND OFTEN HOSTILE...
...I HAVE SEEN TOO MUCH--AND LOVED TOO MUCH OF IT--
--TO BE SATISFIED WITH PARADISE AGAIN!
I RAISED MY DAUGHTERS TO HAVE INDEPENDENT SPIRITS AND IT SEEMS I'VE DONE MY JOB.
I SHOULD NOT HAVE INTERFERED THE WAY I DID, MY DEAREST...
...BUT I DID IT ONLY OUT OF LOVE!
YOU'RE RIGHT, MOTHER...
...YOU SHOULD NOT HAVE INTERFERED!
22

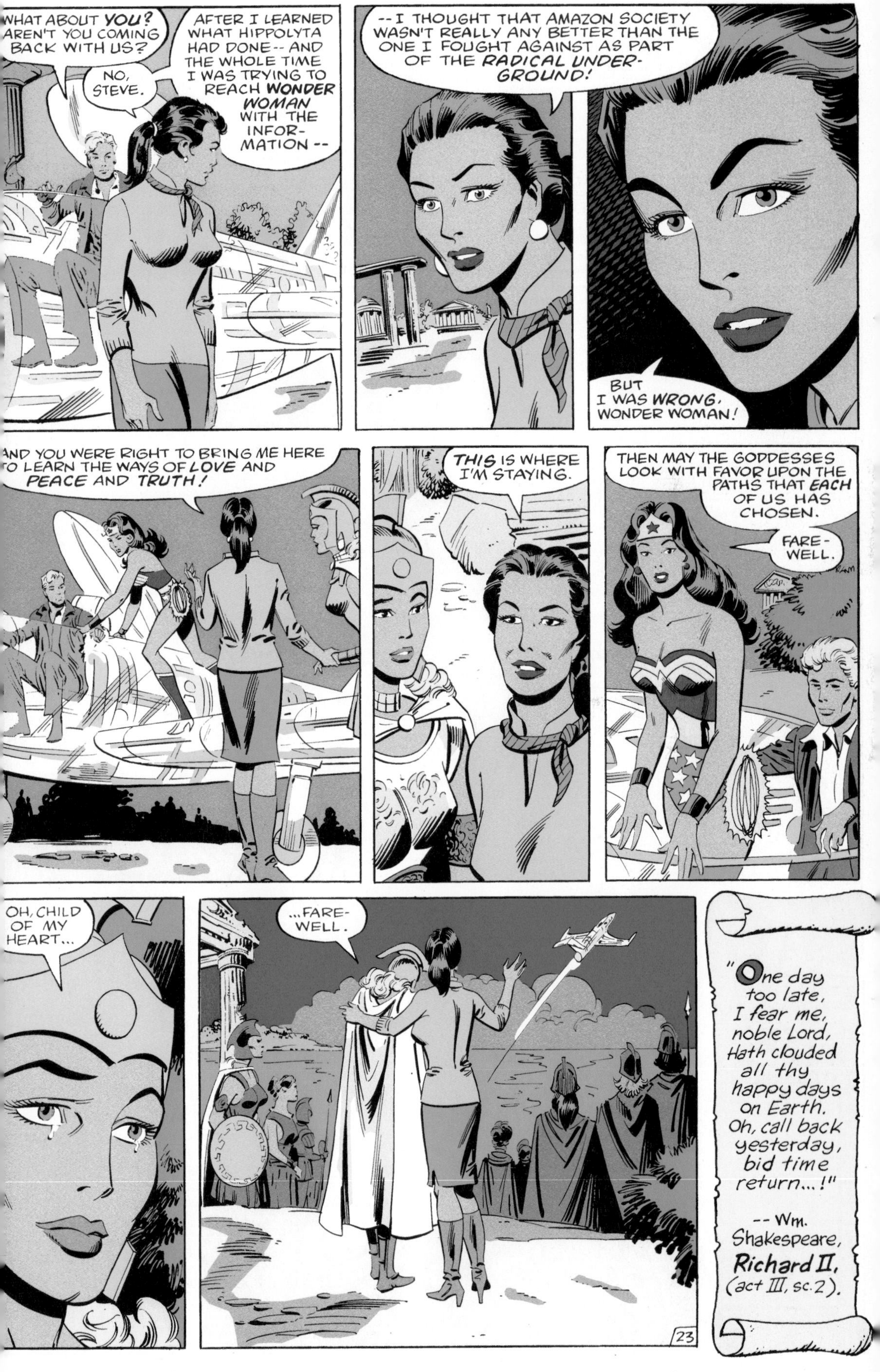
WHAT ABOUT YOU? AREN'T YOU COMING BACK WITH US?
NO, STEVE.
AFTER I LEARNED WHAT HIPPOLYTA HAD DONE-- AND THE WHOLE TIME I WAS TRYING TO REACH WONDER WOMAN WITH THE INFORMATION --
-- I THOUGHT THAT AMAZON SOCIETY WASN'T REALLY ANY BETTER THAN THE ONE I FOUGHT AGAINST AS PART OF THE RADICAL UNDERGROUND!
BUT I WAS WRONG, WONDER WOMAN!
AND YOU WERE RIGHT TO BRING ME HERE TO LEARN THE WAYS OF LOVE AND PEACE AND TRUTH!
THIS IS WHERE I'M STAYING.
THEN MAY THE GODDESSES LOOK WITH FAVOR UPON THE PATHS THAT EACH OF US HAS CHOSEN.
FARE-WELL.
OH, CHILD OF MY HEART...
...FARE-WELL.
23
"One day too late, I fear me, noble Lord, Hath clouded all thy happy days on Earth. Oh, call back yesterday, bid time return...!"
-- Wm. Shakespeare, Richard II, (act III, sc. 2).

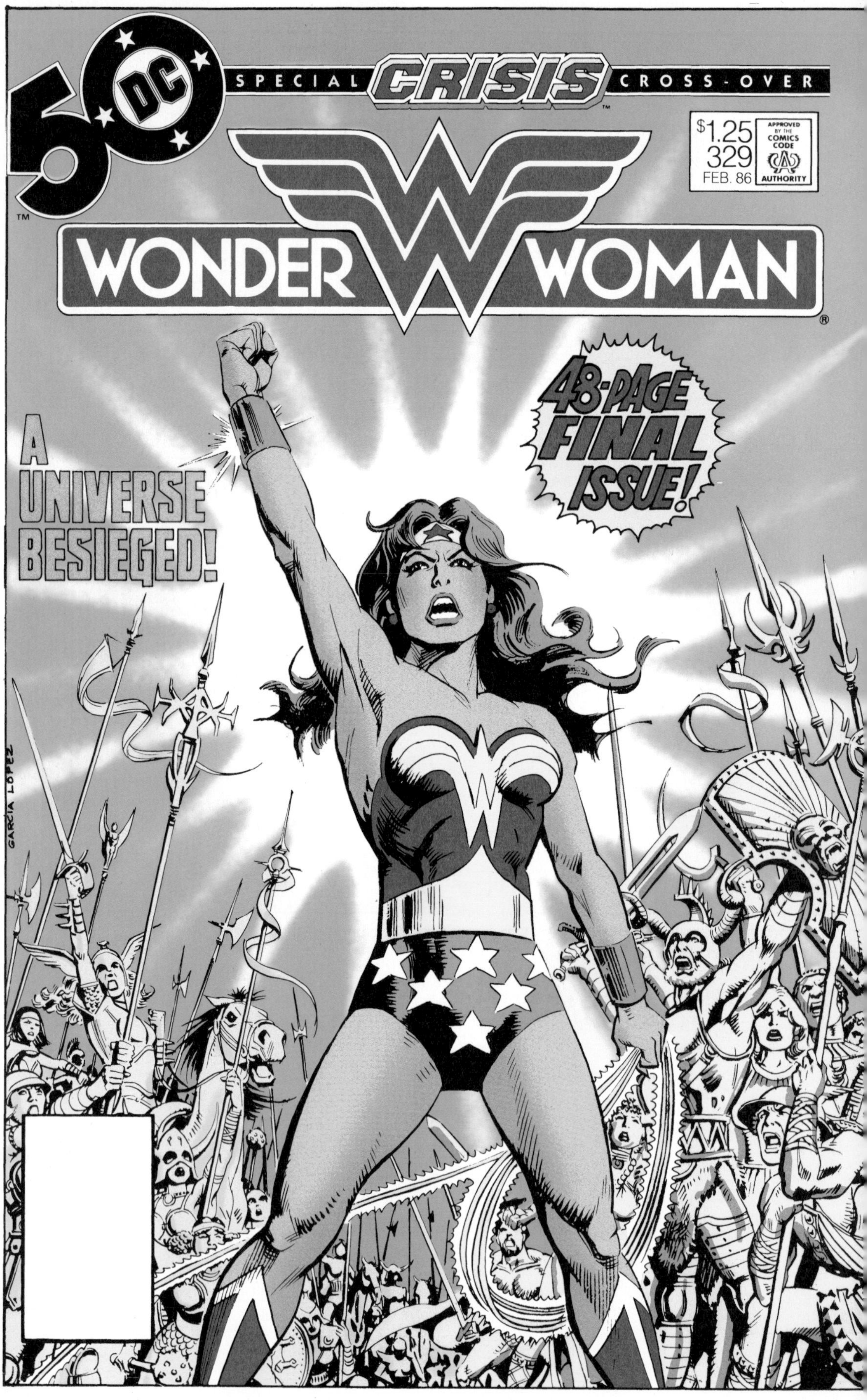

50 DC
SPECIAL CRISIS CROSS-OVER
$1.25
329
FEB. 86
APPROVED BY THE COMICS CODE AUTHORITY
WONDER WOMAN
48-PAGE FINAL ISSUE!
A UNIVERSE BESIEGED!
GARCÍA LÓPEZ

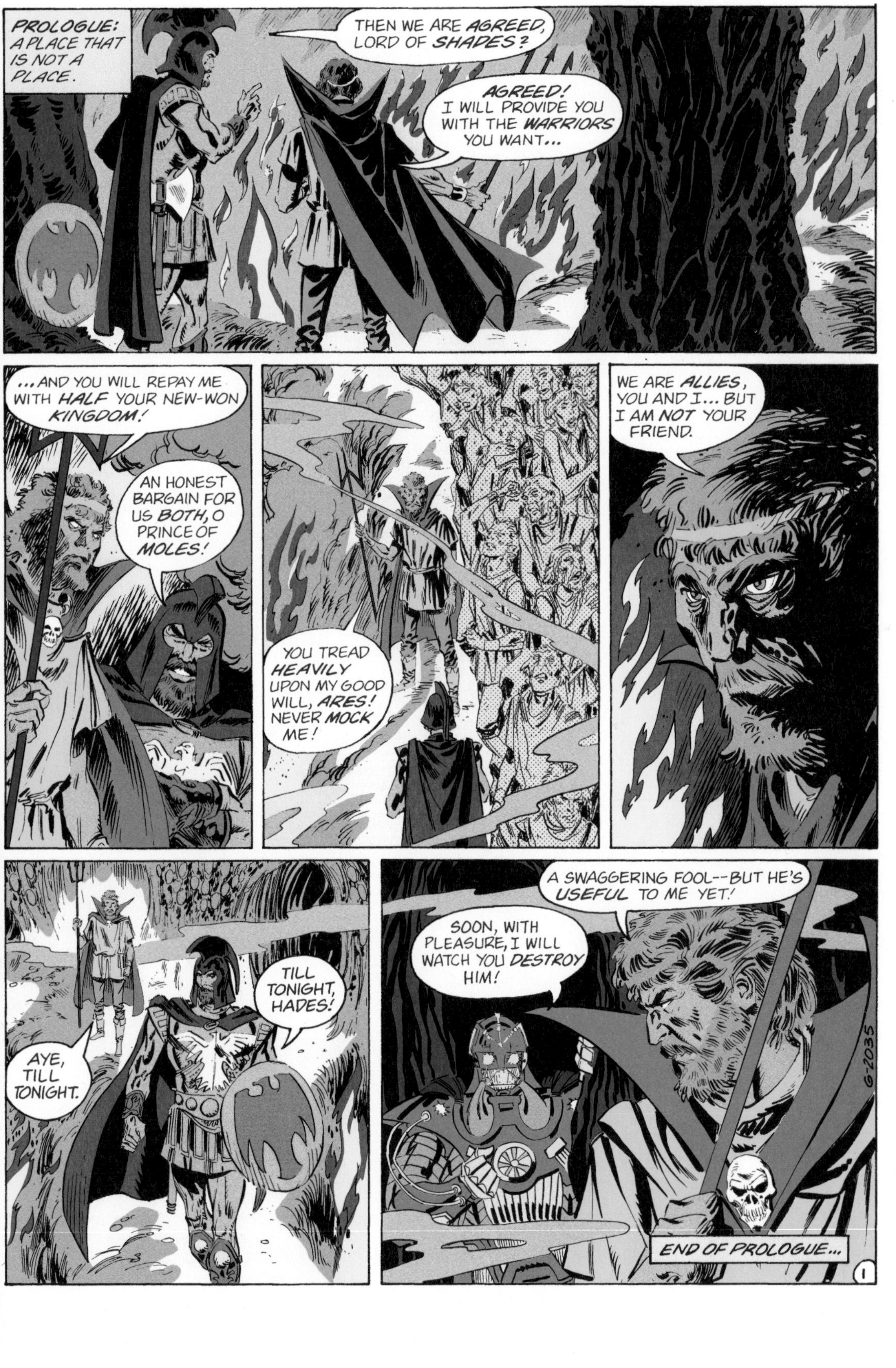
PROLOGUE: A PLACE THAT IS NOT A PLACE.
THEN WE ARE AGREED, LORD OF SHADES?
AGREED! I WILL PROVIDE YOU WITH THE WARRIORS YOU WANT...
...AND YOU WILL REPAY ME WITH HALF YOUR NEW-WON KINGDOM!
AN HONEST BARGAIN FOR US BOTH, O PRINCE OF MOLES!
YOU TREAD HEAVILY UPON MY GOOD WILL, ARES! NEVER MOCK ME!
WE ARE ALLIES, YOU AND I... BUT I AM NOT YOUR FRIEND.
TILL TONIGHT, HADES!
AYE, TILL TONIGHT.
A SWAGGERING FOOL--BUT HE'S USEFUL TO ME YET!
SOON, WITH PLEASURE, I WILL WATCH YOU DESTROY HIM!
G-2035
END OF PROLOGUE...
1

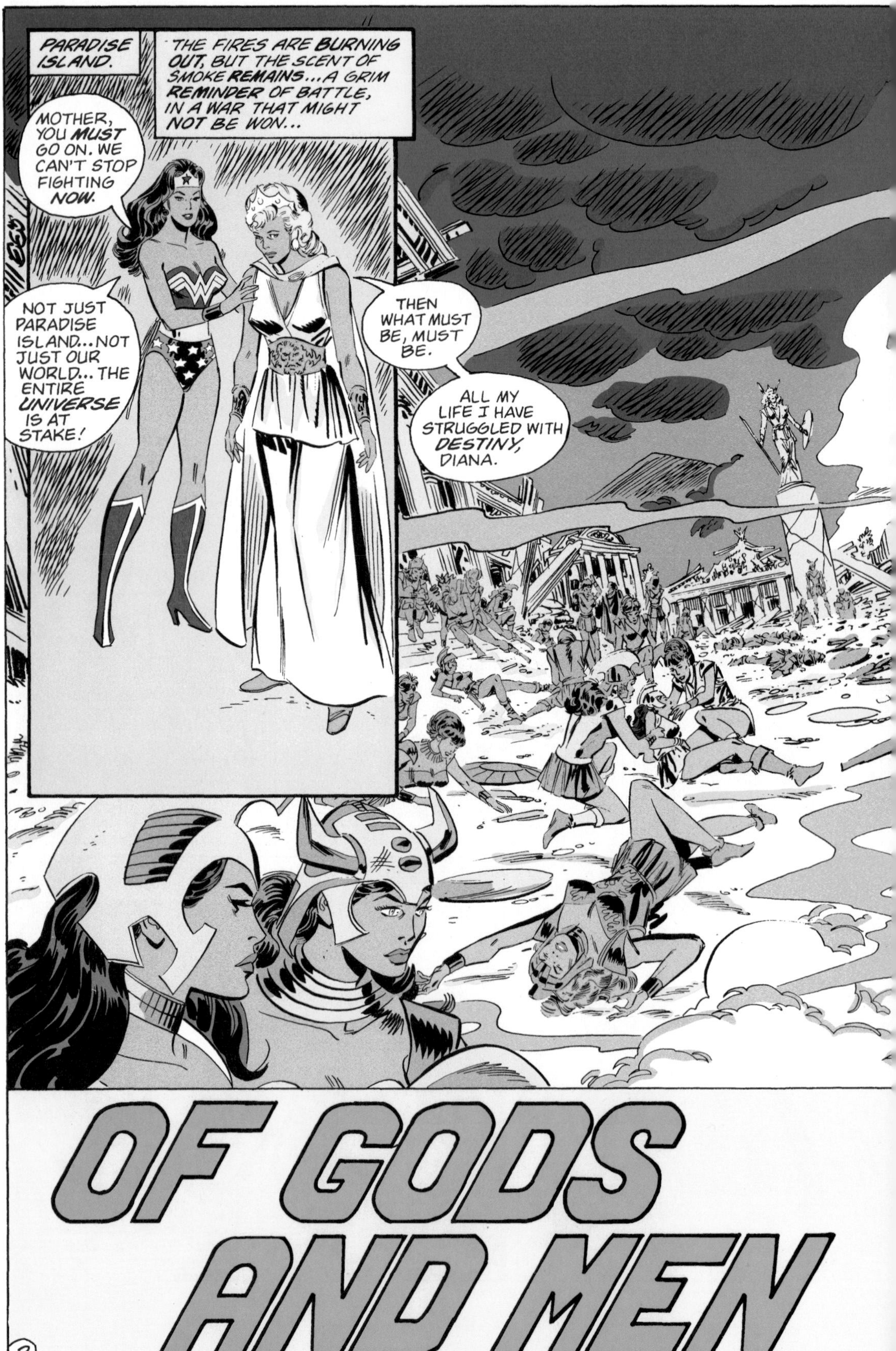

PARADISE ISLAND.
THE FIRES ARE BURNING OUT, BUT THE SCENT OF SMOKE REMAINS... A GRIM REMINDER OF BATTLE, IN A WAR THAT MIGHT NOT BE WON...
MOTHER, YOU MUST GO ON. WE CAN'T STOP FIGHTING NOW.
NOT JUST PARADISE ISLAND... NOT JUST OUR WORLD... THE ENTIRE UNIVERSE IS AT STAKE!
THEN WHAT MUST BE, MUST BE.
ALL MY LIFE I HAVE STRUGGLED WITH DESTINY, DIANA.
OF GODS AND MEN
2

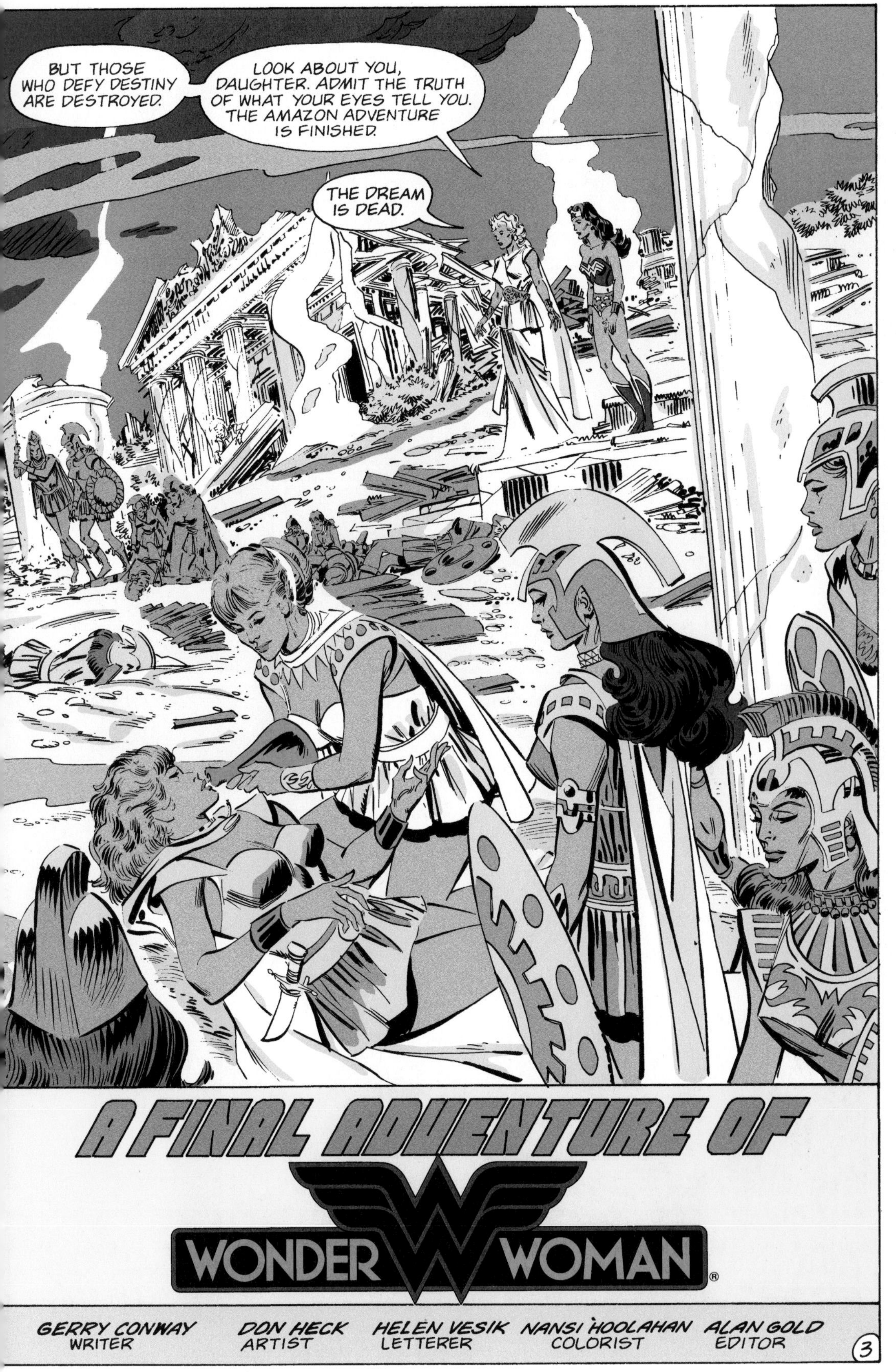

BUT THOSE WHO DEFY DESTINY ARE DESTROYED.
LOOK ABOUT YOU, DAUGHTER. ADMIT THE TRUTH OF WHAT YOUR EYES TELL YOU. THE AMAZON ADVENTURE IS FINISHED.
THE DREAM IS DEAD.
A FINAL ADVENTURE OF
WONDER WOMAN
GERRY CONWAY WRITER
DON HECK ARTIST
HELEN VESIK LETTERER
NANSI HOOLAHAN COLORIST
ALAN GOLD EDITOR
3

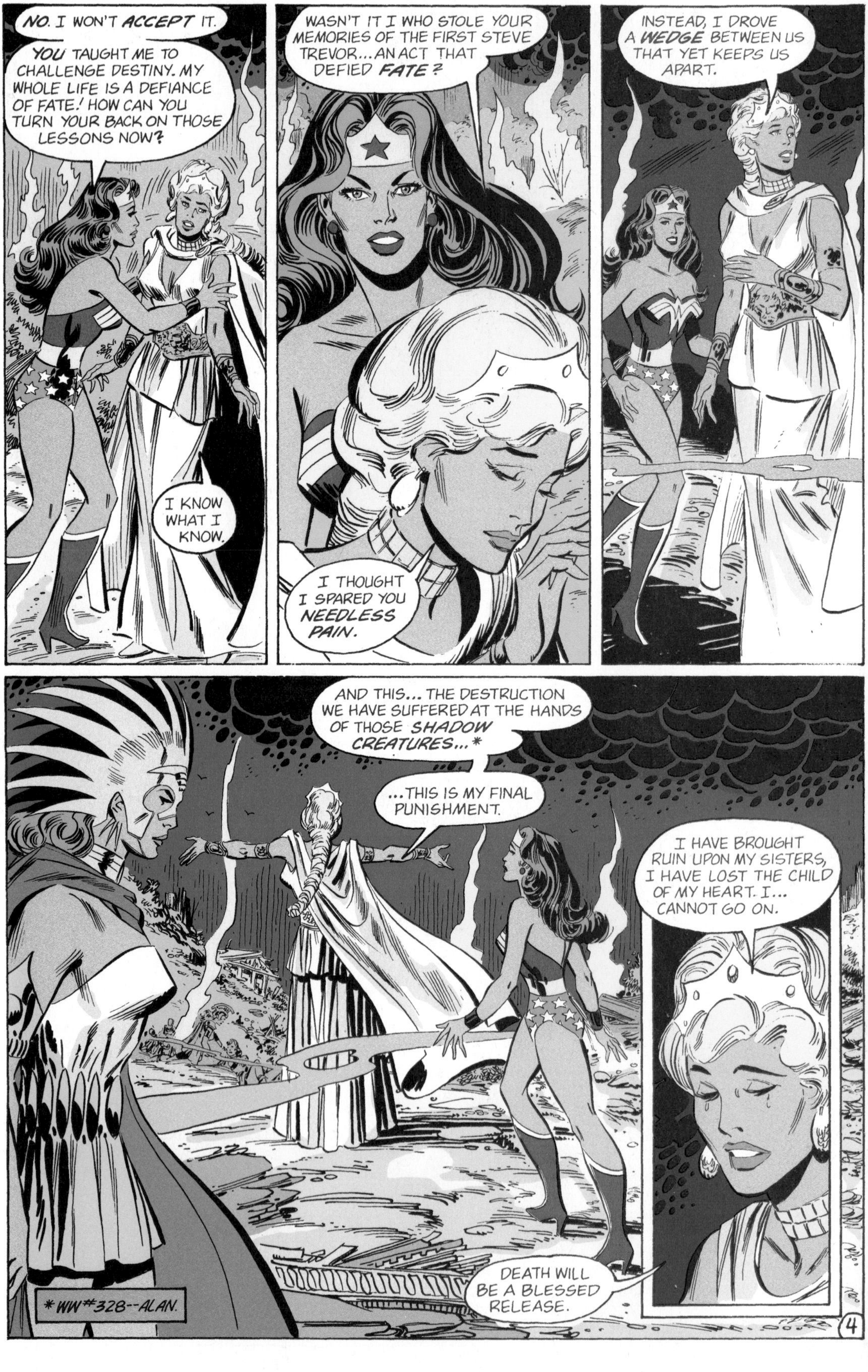

NO. I WON'T ACCEPT IT.
YOU TAUGHT ME TO CHALLENGE DESTINY. MY WHOLE LIFE IS A DEFIANCE OF FATE! HOW CAN YOU TURN YOUR BACK ON THOSE LESSONS NOW?
I KNOW WHAT I KNOW.
WASN'T IT I WHO STOLE YOUR MEMORIES OF THE FIRST STEVE TREVOR... AN ACT THAT DEFIED FATE?
I THOUGHT I SPARED YOU NEEDLESS PAIN.
INSTEAD, I DROVE A WEDGE BETWEEN US THAT YET KEEPS US APART.
AND THIS... THE DESTRUCTION WE HAVE SUFFERED AT THE HANDS OF THOSE SHADOW CREATURES...*
...THIS IS MY FINAL PUNISHMENT.
I HAVE BROUGHT RUIN UPON MY SISTERS, I HAVE LOST THE CHILD OF MY HEART. I... CANNOT GO ON.
DEATH WILL BE A BLESSED RELEASE.
*WW #328--ALAN.
4

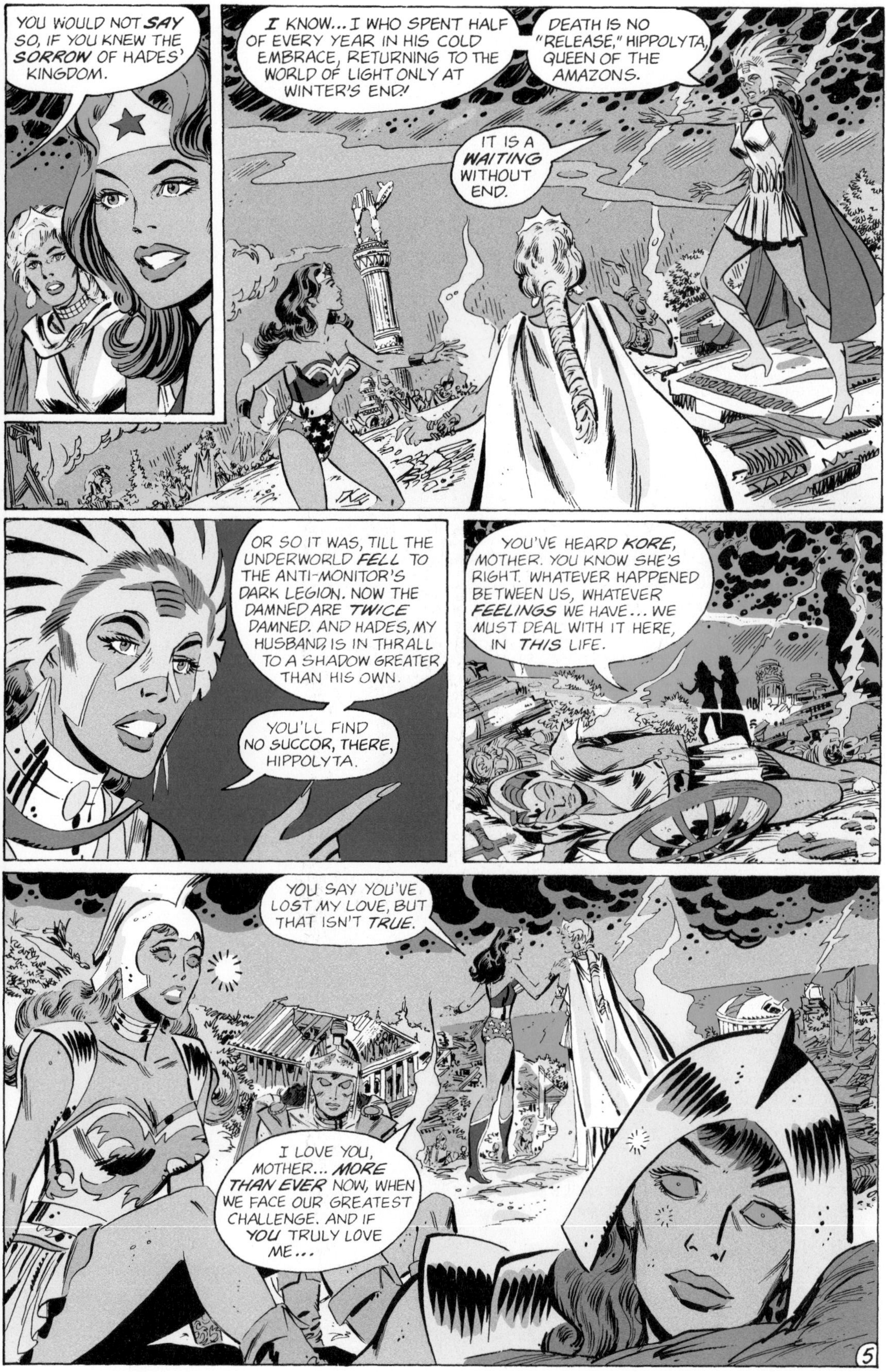
YOU WOULD NOT SAY SO, IF YOU KNEW THE SORROW OF HADES' KINGDOM.
I KNOW... I WHO SPENT HALF OF EVERY YEAR IN HIS COLD EMBRACE, RETURNING TO THE WORLD OF LIGHT ONLY AT WINTER'S END!
DEATH IS NO "RELEASE," HIPPOLYTA, QUEEN OF THE AMAZONS.
IT IS A WAITING WITHOUT END.
OR SO IT WAS, TILL THE UNDERWORLD FELL TO THE ANTI-MONITOR'S DARK LEGION. NOW THE DAMNED ARE TWICE DAMNED. AND HADES, MY HUSBAND, IS IN THRALL TO A SHADOW GREATER THAN HIS OWN.
YOU'LL FIND NO SUCCOR, THERE, HIPPOLYTA.
YOU'VE HEARD KORE, MOTHER. YOU KNOW SHE'S RIGHT. WHATEVER HAPPENED BETWEEN US, WHATEVER FEELINGS WE HAVE... WE MUST DEAL WITH IT HERE, IN THIS LIFE.
YOU SAY YOU'VE LOST MY LOVE, BUT THAT ISN'T TRUE.
I LOVE YOU, MOTHER... MORE THAN EVER NOW, WHEN WE FACE OUR GREATEST CHALLENGE. AND IF YOU TRULY LOVE ME...
5

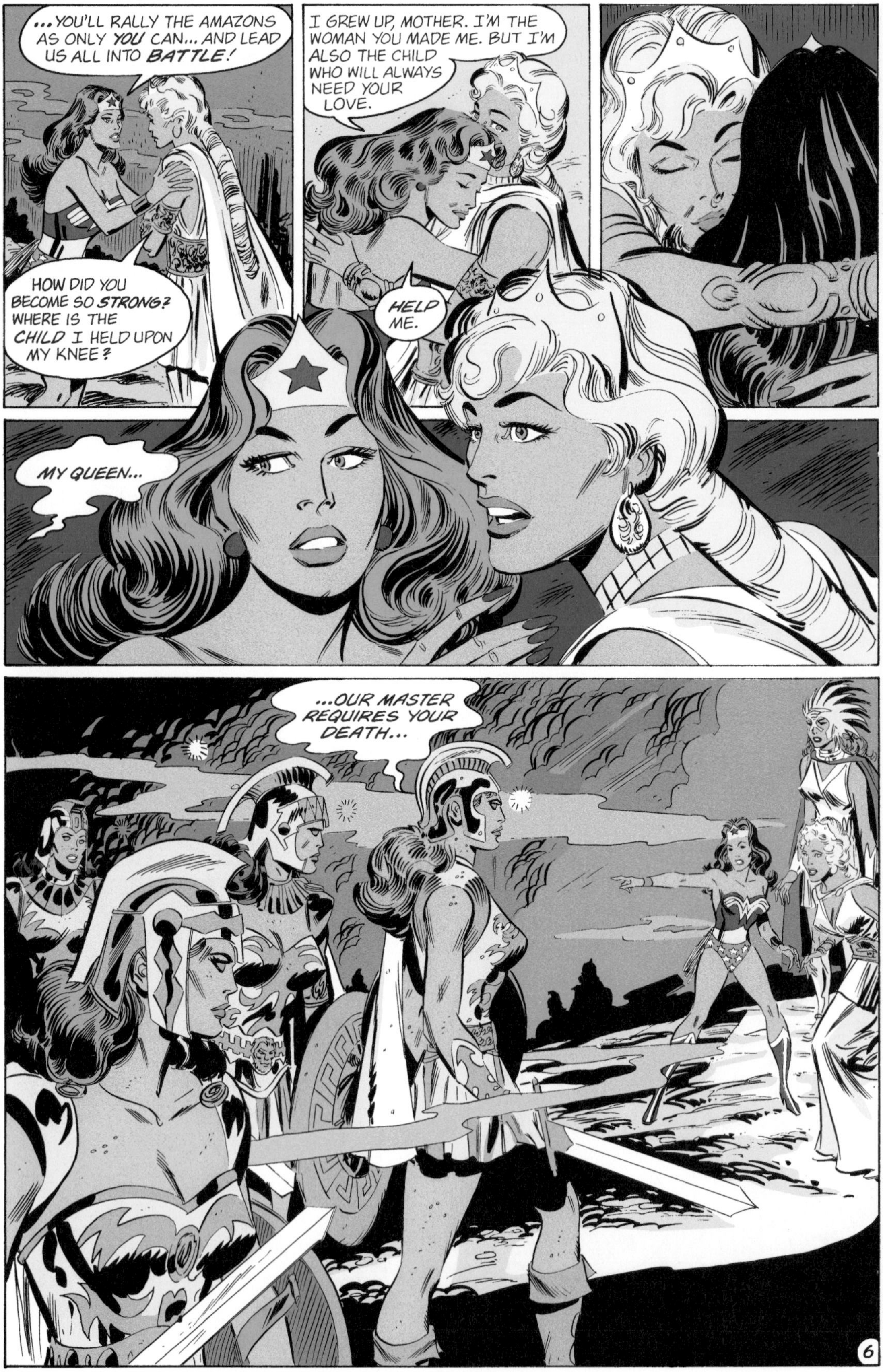

...YOU'LL RALLY THE AMAZONS AS ONLY YOU CAN... AND LEAD US ALL INTO BATTLE!
HOW DID YOU BECOME SO STRONG? WHERE IS THE CHILD I HELD UPON MY KNEE?
I GREW UP, MOTHER. I'M THE WOMAN YOU MADE ME. BUT I'M ALSO THE CHILD WHO WILL ALWAYS NEED YOUR LOVE.
HELP ME.
MY QUEEN...
...OUR MASTER REQUIRES YOUR DEATH...
6

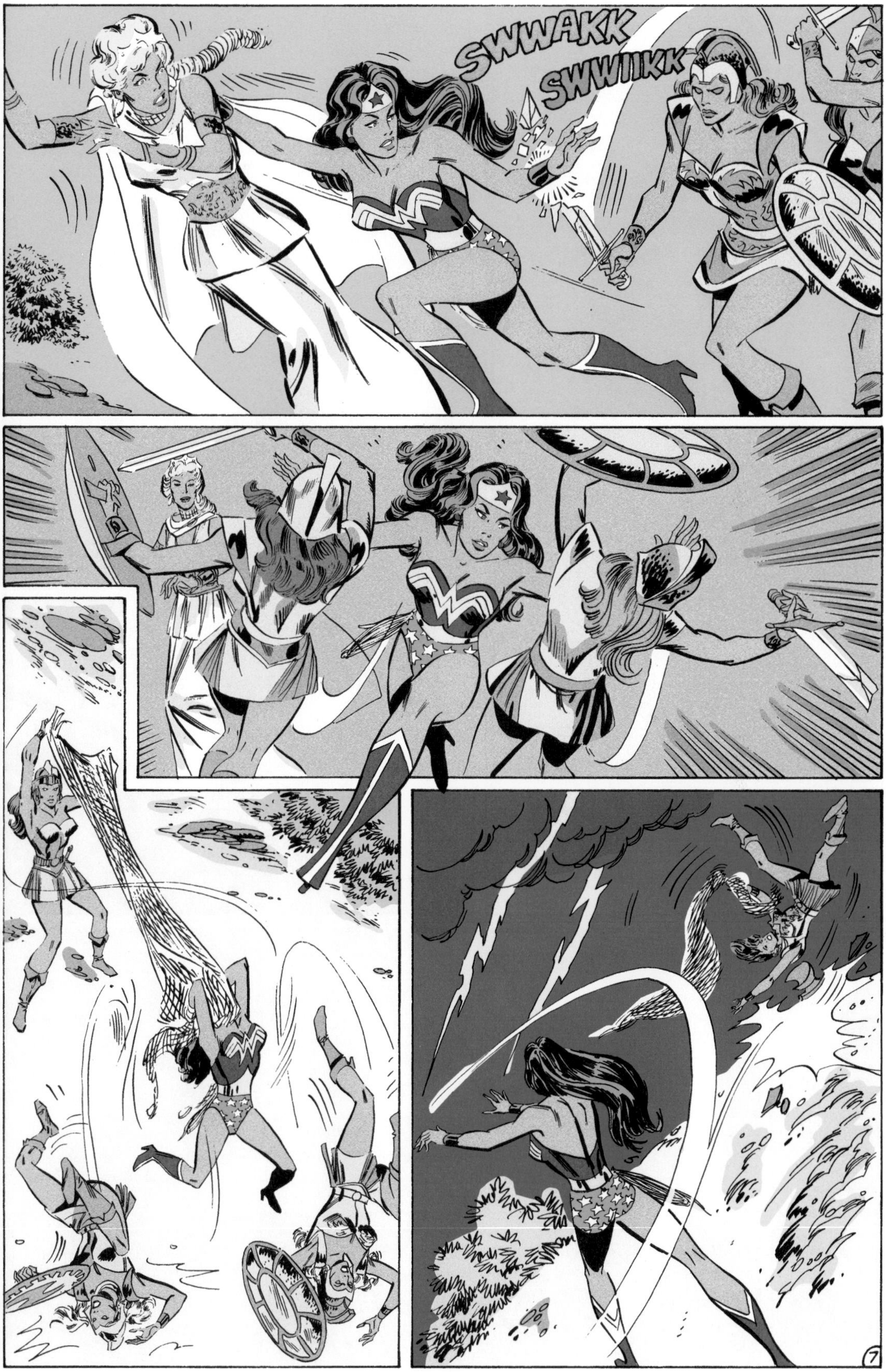
SWWAKK
SWWIIKK

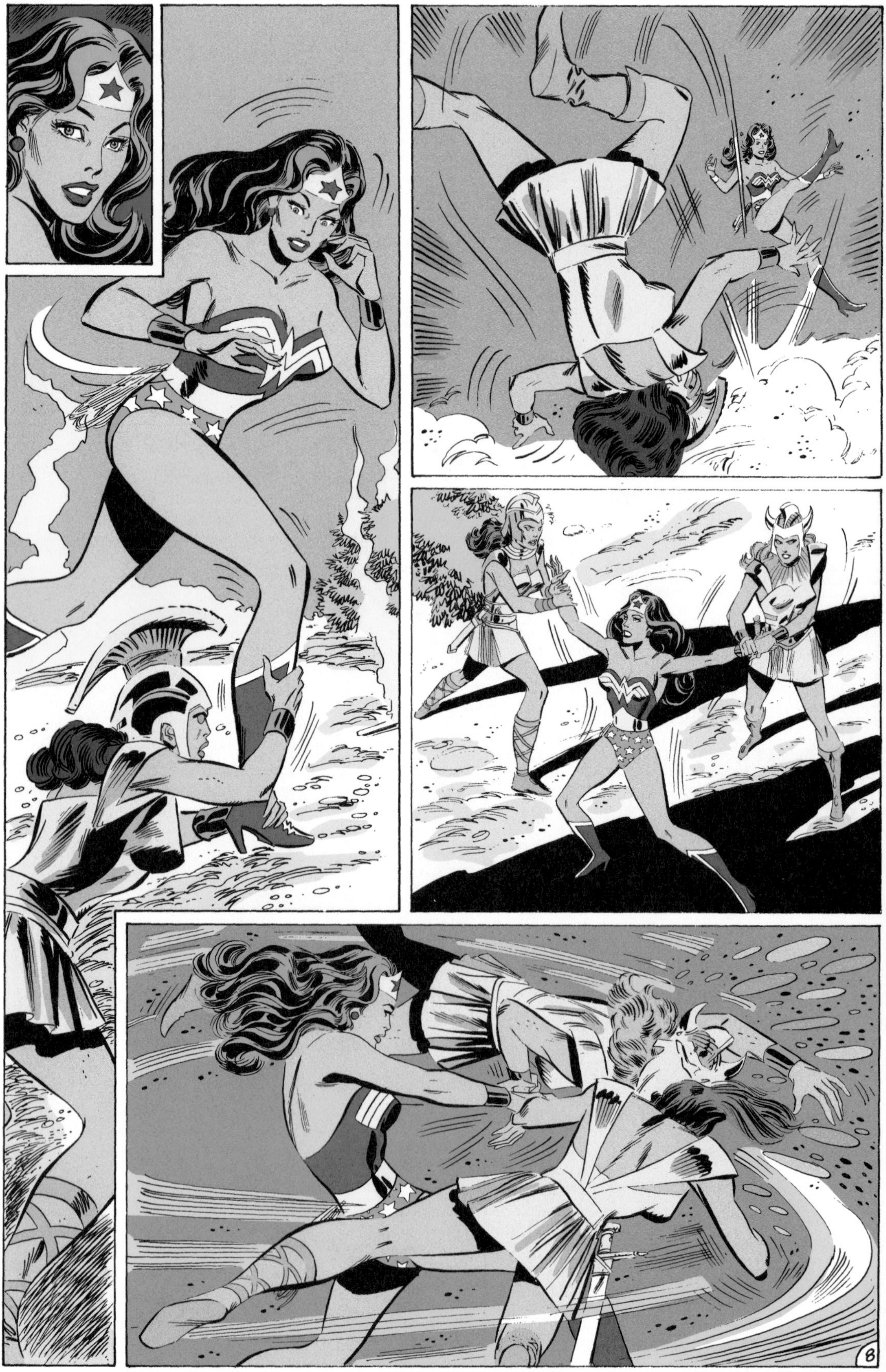
8

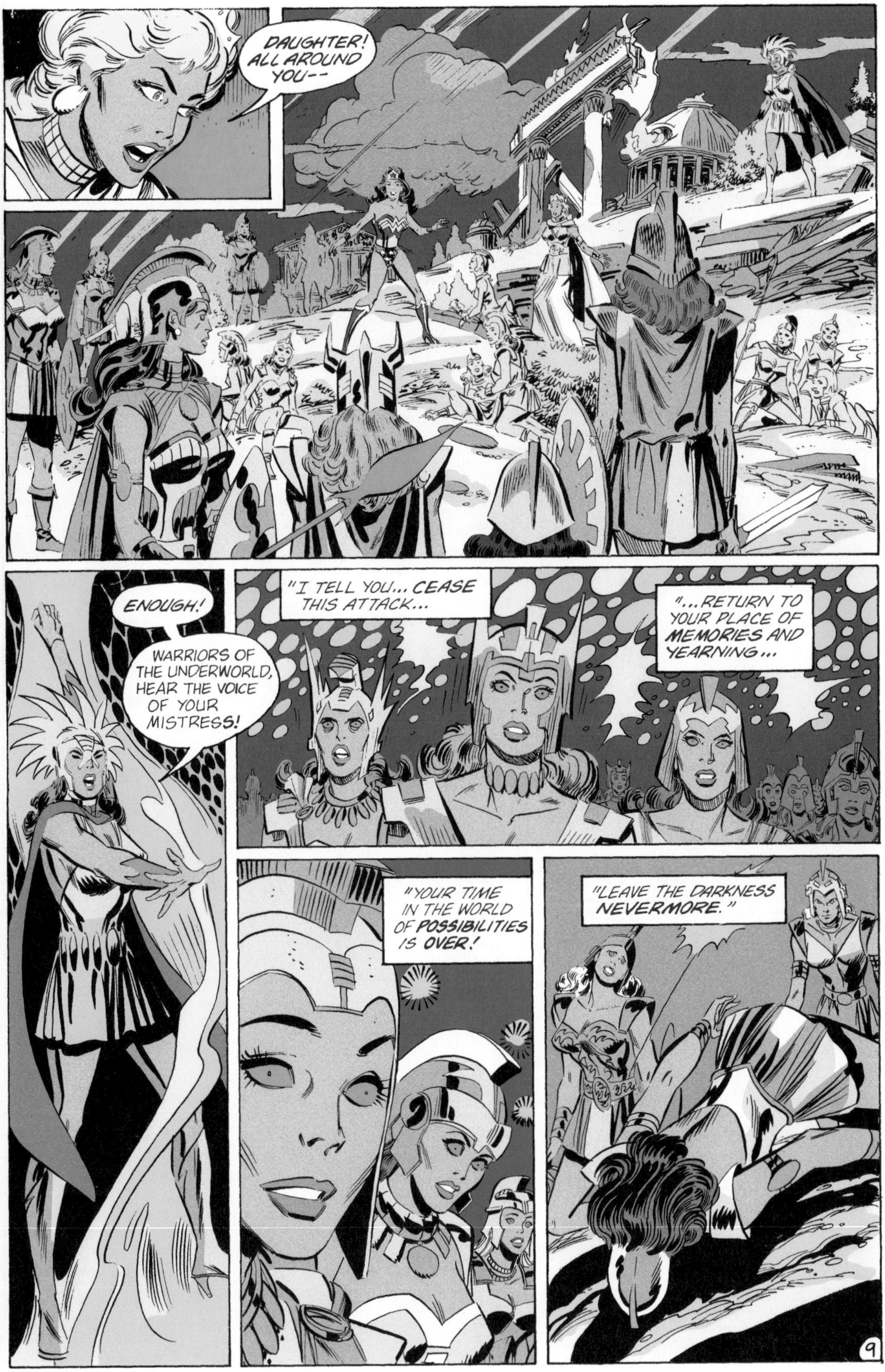
DAUGHTER! ALL AROUND YOU--
ENOUGH!
WARRIORS OF THE UNDERWORLD, HEAR THE VOICE OF YOUR MISTRESS!
"I TELL YOU... CEASE THIS ATTACK...
"...RETURN TO YOUR PLACE OF MEMORIES AND YEARNING...
"YOUR TIME IN THE WORLD OF POSSIBILITIES IS OVER!
"LEAVE THE DARKNESS NEVERMORE."
9

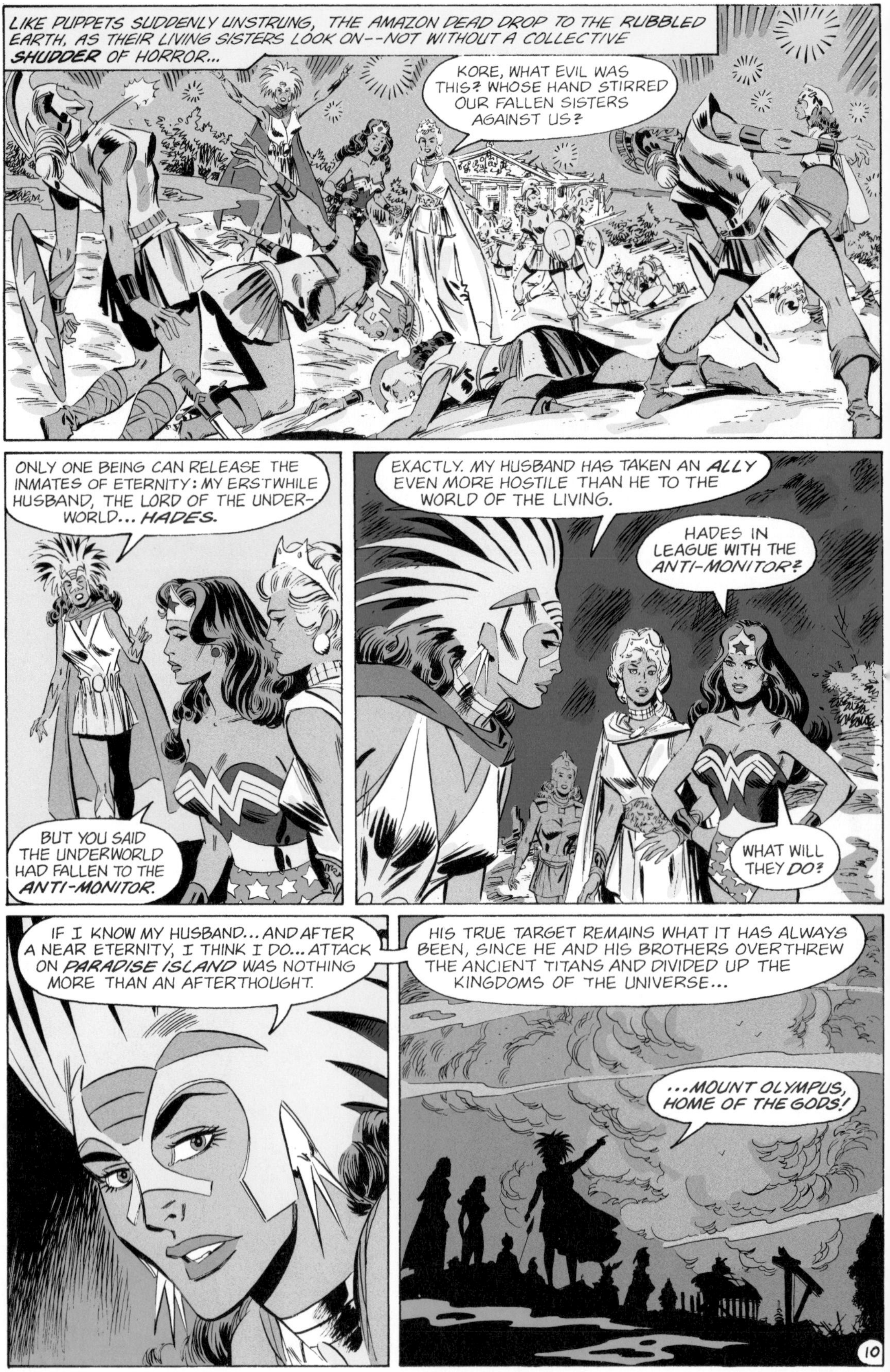
LIKE PUPPETS SUDDENLY UNSTRUNG, THE AMAZON DEAD DROP TO THE RUBBLED EARTH, AS THEIR LIVING SISTERS LOOK ON--NOT WITHOUT A COLLECTIVE SHUDDER OF HORROR...
KORE, WHAT EVIL WAS THIS? WHOSE HAND STIRRED OUR FALLEN SISTERS AGAINST US?
ONLY ONE BEING CAN RELEASE THE INMATES OF ETERNITY: MY ERSTWHILE HUSBAND, THE LORD OF THE UNDER-WORLD... HADES.
BUT YOU SAID THE UNDERWORLD HAD FALLEN TO THE ANTI-MONITOR.
EXACTLY. MY HUSBAND HAS TAKEN AN ALLY EVEN MORE HOSTILE THAN HE TO THE WORLD OF THE LIVING.
HADES IN LEAGUE WITH THE ANTI-MONITOR?
WHAT WILL THEY DO?
IF I KNOW MY HUSBAND... AND AFTER A NEAR ETERNITY, I THINK I DO... ATTACK ON PARADISE ISLAND WAS NOTHING MORE THAN AN AFTERTHOUGHT.
HIS TRUE TARGET REMAINS WHAT IT HAS ALWAYS BEEN, SINCE HE AND HIS BROTHERS OVERTHREW THE ANCIENT TITANS AND DIVIDED UP THE KINGDOMS OF THE UNIVERSE...
...MOUNT OLYMPUS, HOME OF THE GODS!
10

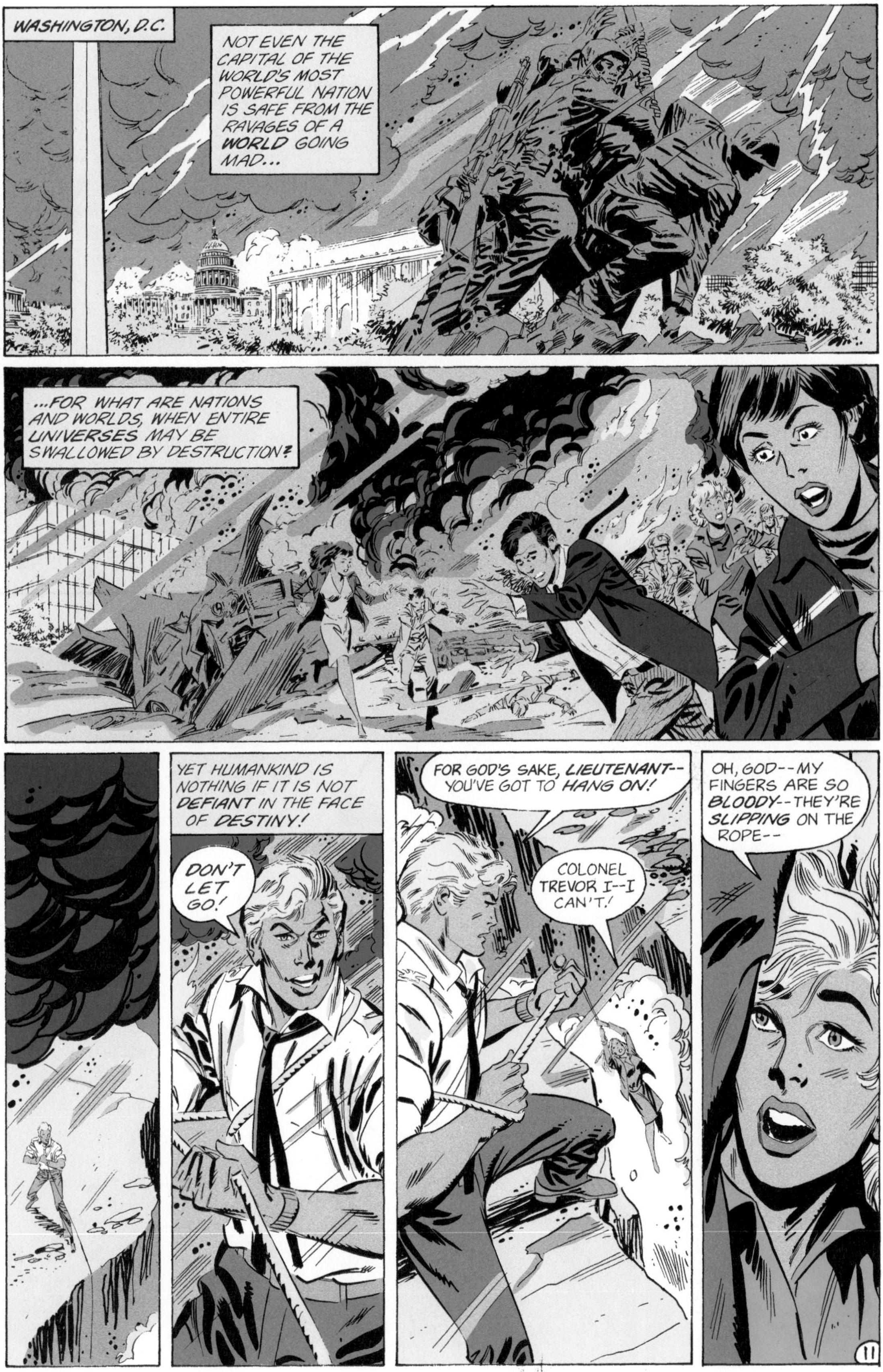
WASHINGTON, D.C.
NOT EVEN THE CAPITAL OF THE WORLD'S MOST POWERFUL NATION IS SAFE FROM THE RAVAGES OF A WORLD GOING MAD...
...FOR WHAT ARE NATIONS AND WORLDS, WHEN ENTIRE UNIVERSES MAY BE SWALLOWED BY DESTRUCTION?
YET HUMANKIND IS NOTHING IF IT IS NOT DEFIANT IN THE FACE OF DESTINY!
DON'T LET GO!
FOR GOD'S SAKE, LIEUTENANT-- YOU'VE GOT TO HANG ON!
COLONEL TREVOR I--I CAN'T!
OH, GOD--MY FINGERS ARE SO BLOODY--THEY'RE SLIPPING ON THE ROPE--
11

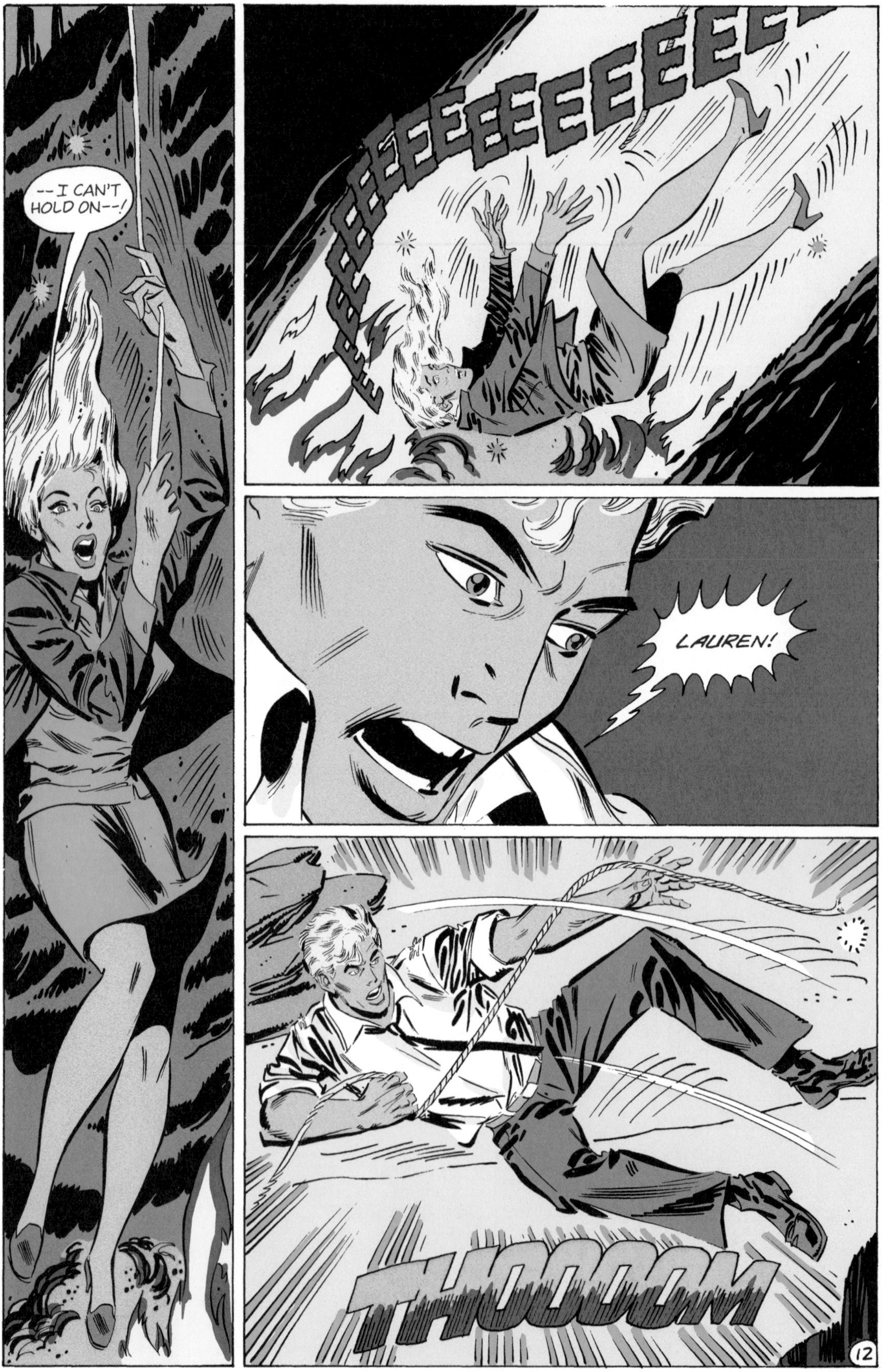
--I CAN'T HOLD ON--!
EEEEEEEEEEEEEEEEE
LAUREN!
THOOOOM
12

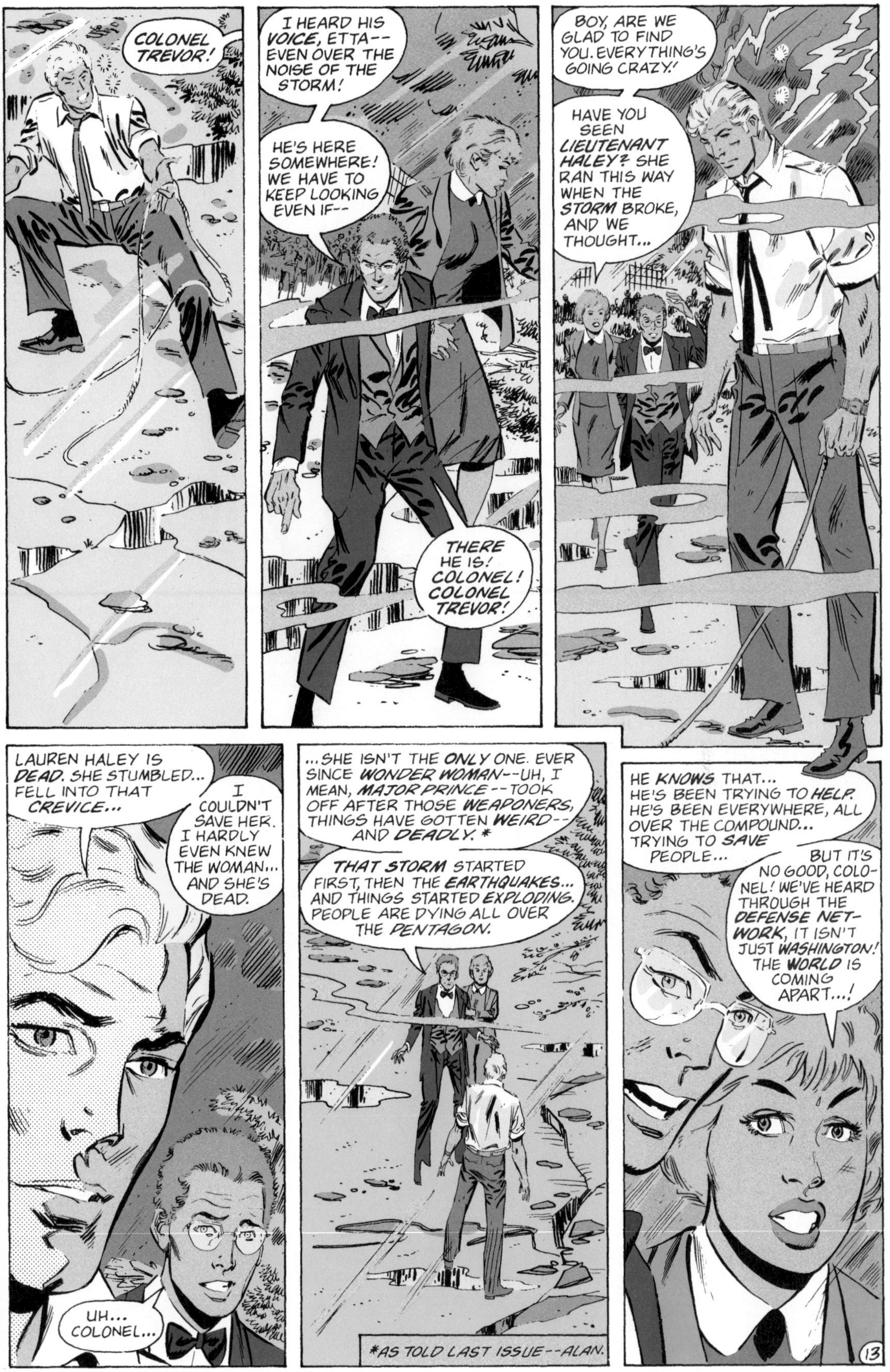
COLONEL TREVOR!
I HEARD HIS VOICE, ETTA-- EVEN OVER THE NOISE OF THE STORM!
HE'S HERE SOMEWHERE! WE HAVE TO KEEP LOOKING EVEN IF--
THERE HE IS! COLONEL! COLONEL TREVOR!
BOY, ARE WE GLAD TO FIND YOU. EVERYTHING'S GOING CRAZY!
HAVE YOU SEEN LIEUTENANT HALEY? SHE RAN THIS WAY WHEN THE STORM BROKE, AND WE THOUGHT...
LAUREN HALEY IS DEAD. SHE STUMBLED... FELL INTO THAT CREVICE...
I COULDN'T SAVE HER. I HARDLY EVEN KNEW THE WOMAN... AND SHE'S DEAD.
UH... COLONEL...
...SHE ISN'T THE ONLY ONE. EVER SINCE WONDER WOMAN--UH, I MEAN, MAJOR PRINCE--TOOK OFF AFTER THOSE WEAPONERS, THINGS HAVE GOTTEN WEIRD-- AND DEADLY. *
THAT STORM STARTED FIRST, THEN THE EARTHQUAKES... AND THINGS STARTED EXPLODING. PEOPLE ARE DYING ALL OVER THE PENTAGON.
*AS TOLD LAST ISSUE--ALAN.
HE KNOWS THAT... HE'S BEEN TRYING TO HELP. HE'S BEEN EVERYWHERE, ALL OVER THE COMPOUND... TRYING TO SAVE PEOPLE...
BUT IT'S NO GOOD, COLONEL! WE'VE HEARD THROUGH THE DEFENSE NETWORK, IT ISN'T JUST WASHINGTON! THE WORLD IS COMING APART...!
13

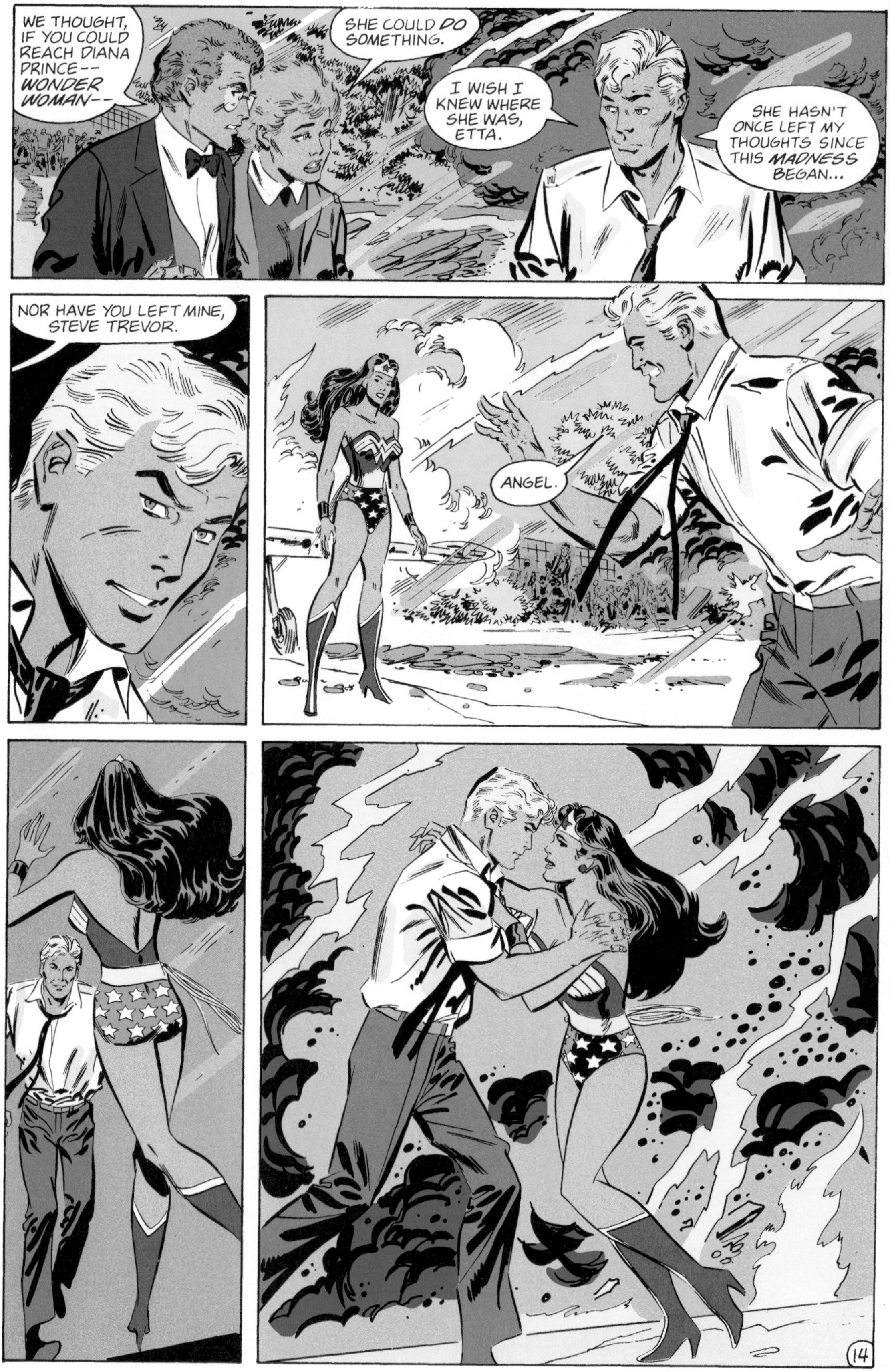
WE THOUGHT, IF YOU COULD REACH DIANA PRINCE-- WONDER WOMAN--
SHE COULD DO SOMETHING.
I WISH I KNEW WHERE SHE WAS, ETTA.
SHE HASN'T ONCE LEFT MY THOUGHTS SINCE THIS MADNESS BEGAN...
NOR HAVE YOU LEFT MINE, STEVE TREVOR.
ANGEL.
14

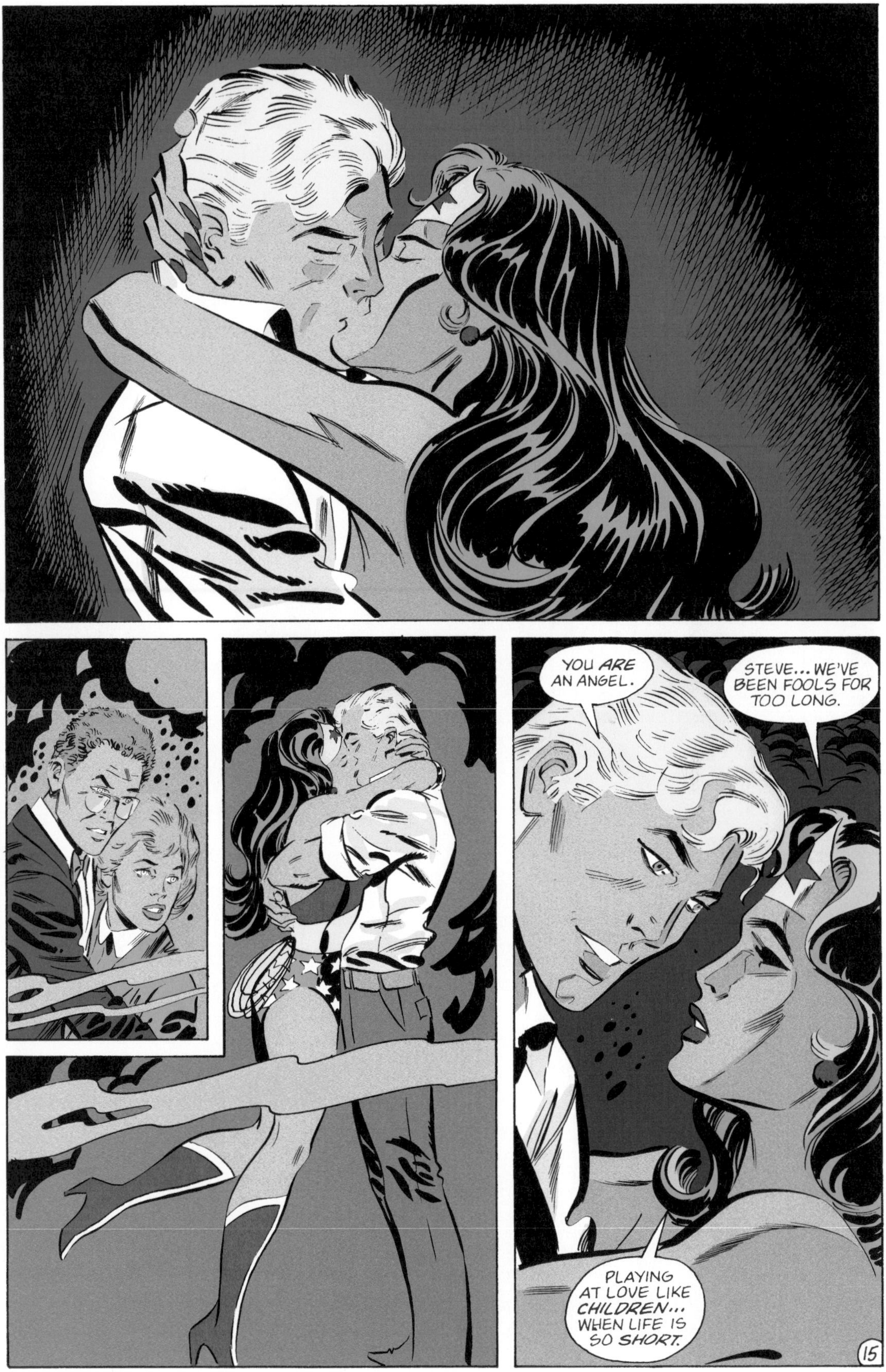
YOU ARE AN ANGEL.
STEVE... WE'VE BEEN FOOLS FOR TOO LONG.
PLAYING AT LOVE LIKE CHILDREN... WHEN LIFE IS SO SHORT.
15

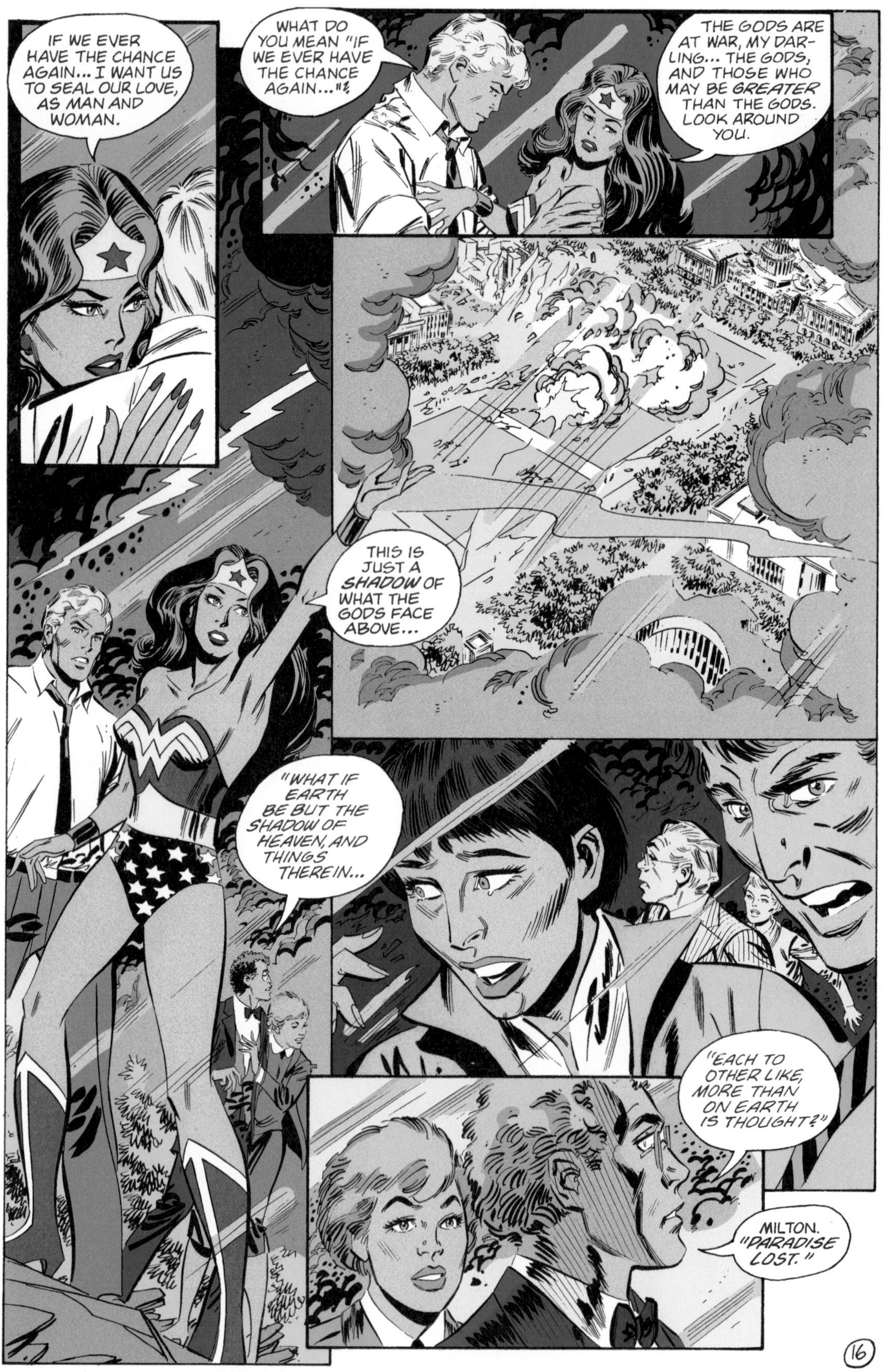

IF WE EVER HAVE THE CHANCE AGAIN... I WANT US TO SEAL OUR LOVE, AS MAN AND WOMAN.
WHAT DO YOU MEAN "IF WE EVER HAVE THE CHANCE AGAIN..."?
THE GODS ARE AT WAR, MY DARLING... THE GODS, AND THOSE WHO MAY BE GREATER THAN THE GODS. LOOK AROUND YOU.
THIS IS JUST A SHADOW OF WHAT THE GODS FACE ABOVE...
"WHAT IF EARTH BE BUT THE SHADOW OF HEAVEN, AND THINGS THEREIN...
"EACH TO OTHER LIKE, MORE THAN ON EARTH IS THOUGHT?"
MILTON. "PARADISE LOST."
16

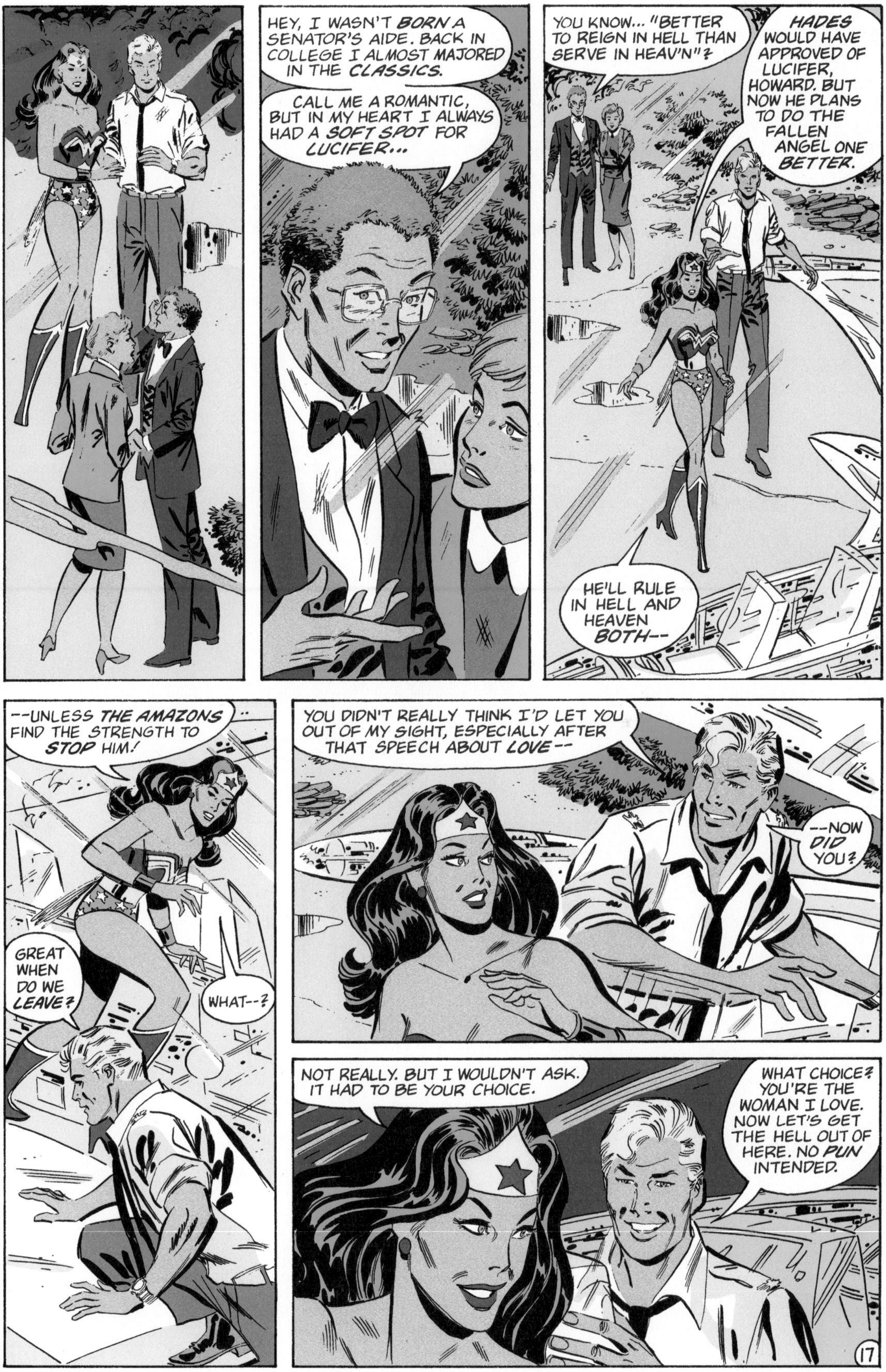

HEY, I WASN'T BORN A SENATOR'S AIDE. BACK IN COLLEGE I ALMOST MAJORED IN THE CLASSICS.
CALL ME A ROMANTIC, BUT IN MY HEART I ALWAYS HAD A SOFT SPOT FOR LUCIFER...
YOU KNOW... "BETTER TO REIGN IN HELL THAN SERVE IN HEAV'N"?
HADES WOULD HAVE APPROVED OF LUCIFER, HOWARD. BUT NOW HE PLANS TO DO THE FALLEN ANGEL ONE BETTER.
HE'LL RULE IN HELL AND HEAVEN BOTH--
--UNLESS THE AMAZONS FIND THE STRENGTH TO STOP HIM!
GREAT WHEN DO WE LEAVE?
WHAT--?
YOU DIDN'T REALLY THINK I'D LET YOU OUT OF MY SIGHT, ESPECIALLY AFTER THAT SPEECH ABOUT LOVE--
--NOW DID YOU?
NOT REALLY. BUT I WOULDN'T ASK. IT HAD TO BE YOUR CHOICE.
WHAT CHOICE? YOU'RE THE WOMAN I LOVE. NOW LET'S GET THE HELL OUT OF HERE. NO PUN INTENDED.
17

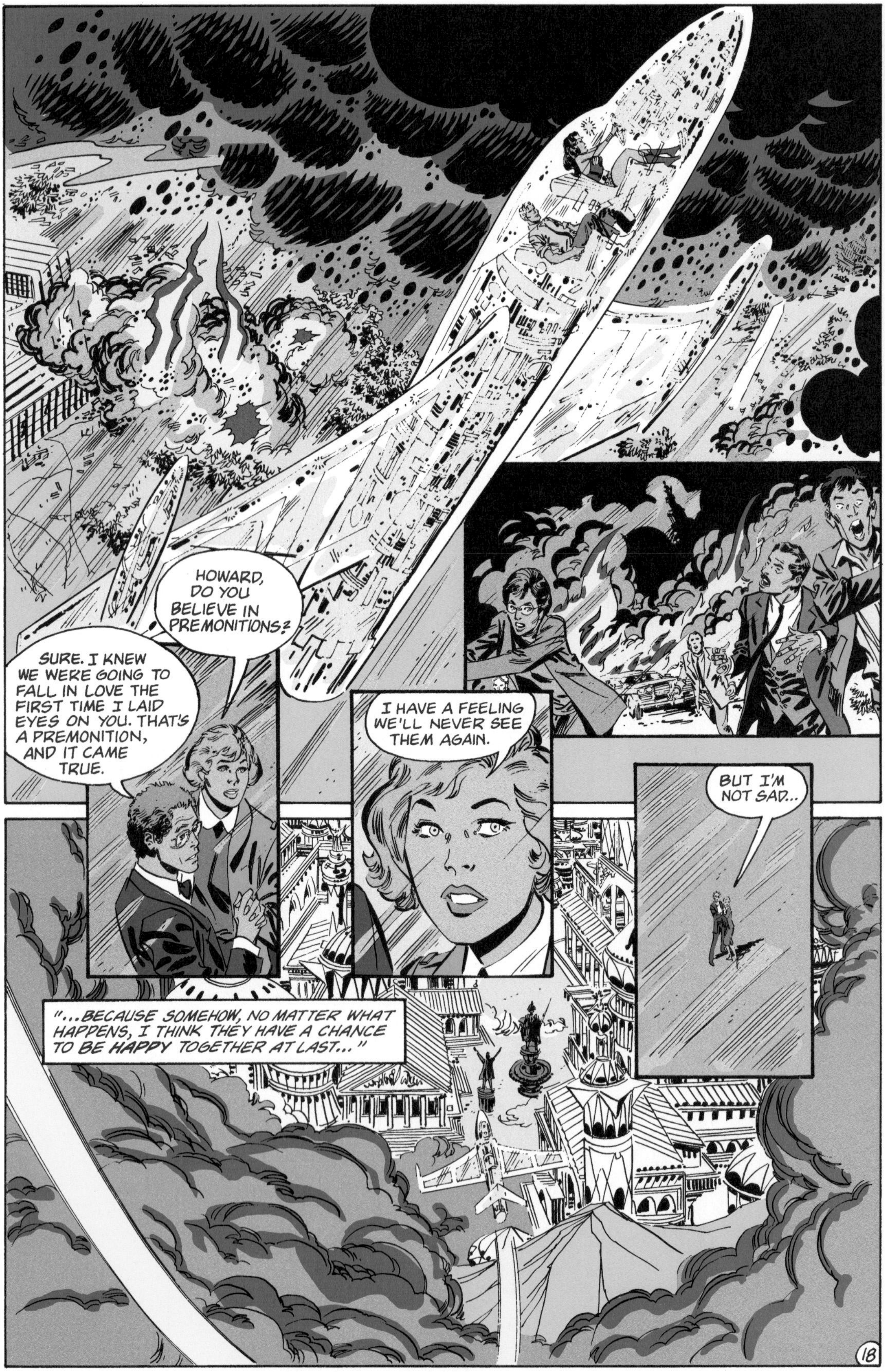
HOWARD, DO YOU BELIEVE IN PREMONITIONS?
SURE. I KNEW WE WERE GOING TO FALL IN LOVE THE FIRST TIME I LAID EYES ON YOU. THAT'S A PREMONITION, AND IT CAME TRUE.
I HAVE A FEELING WE'LL NEVER SEE THEM AGAIN.
BUT I'M NOT SAD...
"...BECAUSE SOMEHOW, NO MATTER WHAT HAPPENS, I THINK THEY HAVE A CHANCE TO BE HAPPY TOGETHER AT LAST..."
18

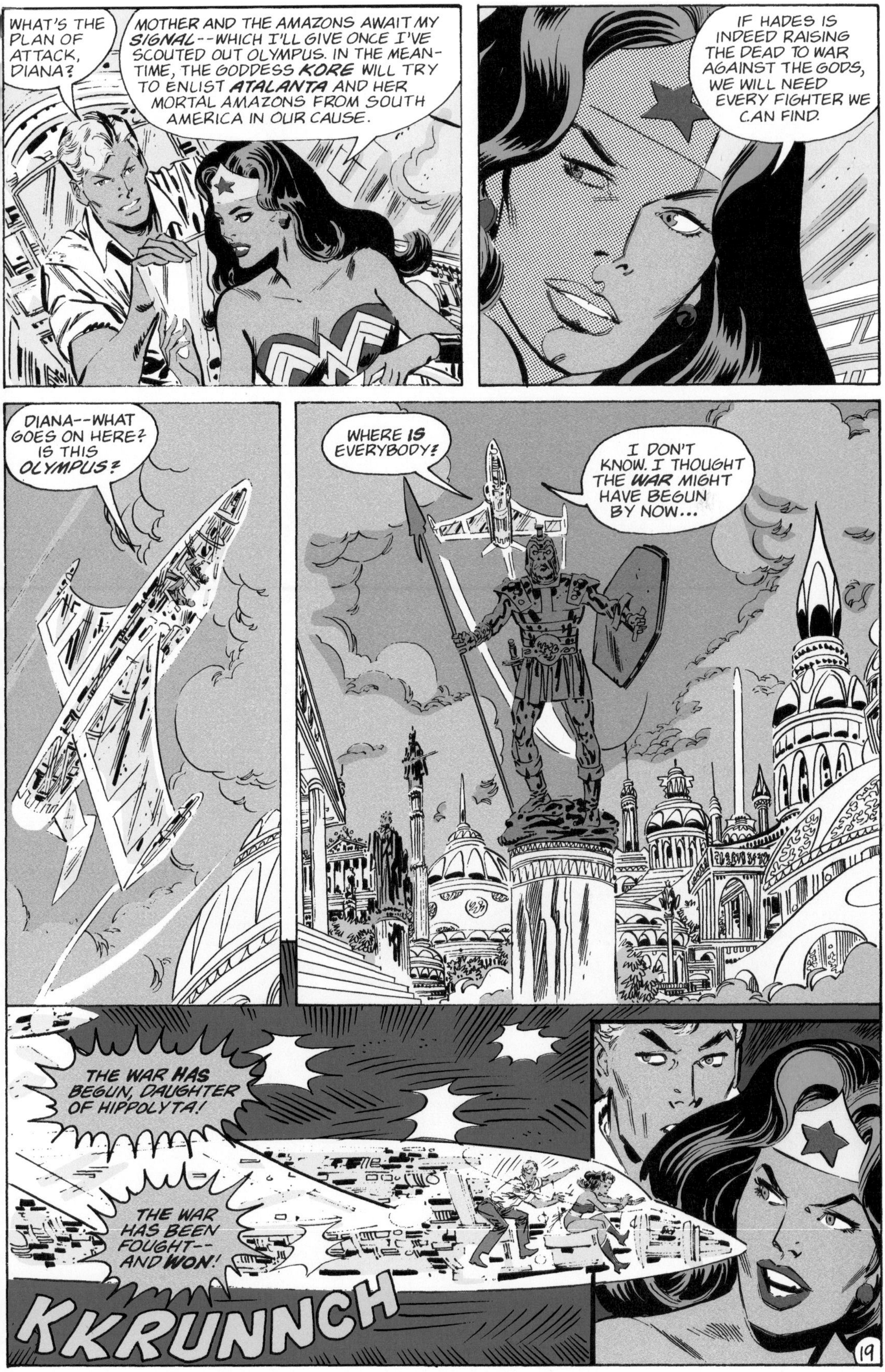
WHAT'S THE PLAN OF ATTACK, DIANA?
MOTHER AND THE AMAZONS AWAIT MY SIGNAL--WHICH I'LL GIVE ONCE I'VE SCOUTED OUT OLYMPUS. IN THE MEANTIME, THE GODDESS KORE WILL TRY TO ENLIST ATALANTA AND HER MORTAL AMAZONS FROM SOUTH AMERICA IN OUR CAUSE.
IF HADES IS INDEED RAISING THE DEAD TO WAR AGAINST THE GODS, WE WILL NEED EVERY FIGHTER WE CAN FIND.
DIANA--WHAT GOES ON HERE? IS THIS OLYMPUS?
WHERE IS EVERYBODY?
I DON'T KNOW. I THOUGHT THE WAR MIGHT HAVE BEGUN BY NOW...
THE WAR HAS BEGUN, DAUGHTER OF HIPPOLYTA!
THE WAR HAS BEEN FOUGHT--AND WON!
KKRUNNCH
19

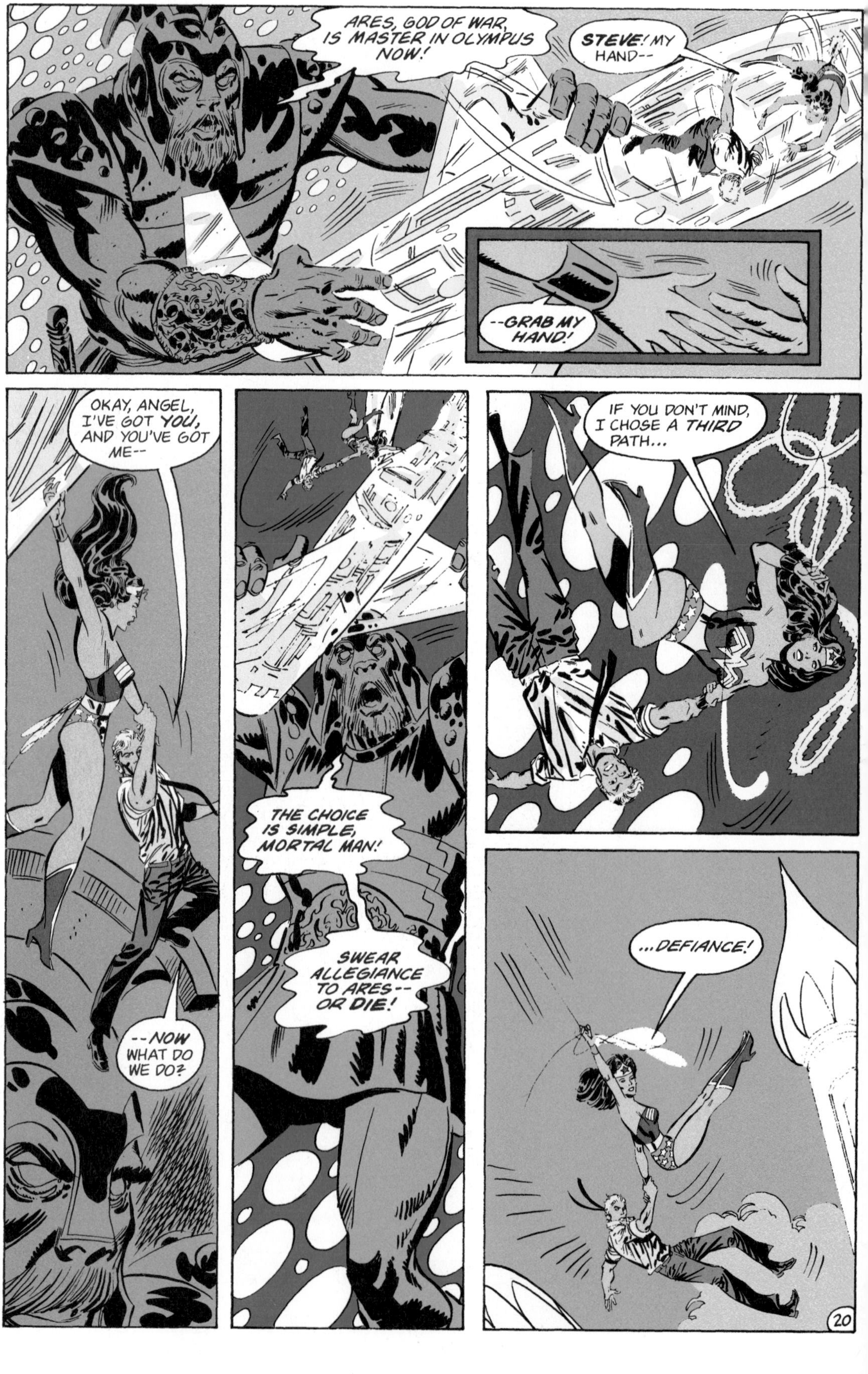
ARES, GOD OF WAR, IS MASTER IN OLYMPUS NOW!
STEVE! MY HAND--
--GRAB MY HAND!
OKAY, ANGEL, I'VE GOT YOU, AND YOU'VE GOT ME--
--NOW WHAT DO WE DO?
THE CHOICE IS SIMPLE, MORTAL MAN!
SWEAR ALLEGIANCE TO ARES-- OR DIE!
IF YOU DON'T MIND, I CHOSE A THIRD PATH...
...DEFIANCE!
20

HOW DID YOU *DO* THAT?

YEARS OF *PRACTICE.*

OF COURSE, IT *HELPS* IF YOU'RE BORN AN *AMAZON!*

NO!

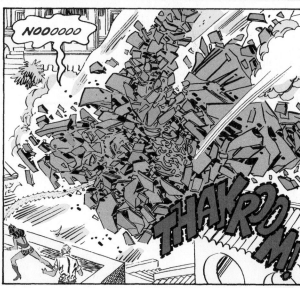

NOOOOOO

THAKROOM!

"THE BIGGER THEY ARE," HUH? WHAT WAS THAT HE SAID ABOUT *THE GOD OF WAR*--?

ARES... WHOM YOU ONCE KNEW BY HIS ROMAN NAME, *MARS.** I THOUGHT ONLY *HADES* WAS INVOLVED IN THIS ATTACK ON *OLYMPUS,* BUT I WAS *WRONG.*

THE GOD OF DEATH HAS AN ALLY IN *THE GOD OF WAR.*

*AS DID WE, UNTIL RECENT DAYS.--ALAN

I WONDER IF *ARES* KNOWS HE HAS ANOTHER, *HIDDEN* ALLY-- *THE ANTI-MONITOR?*

BUT OF MORE *IMPORTANCE--* WHERE ARE THE *GODS* OF *MOUNT OLYMPUS?*

ASK HIM, ANGEL. UNLESS I'M WAY OFF BASE...

21

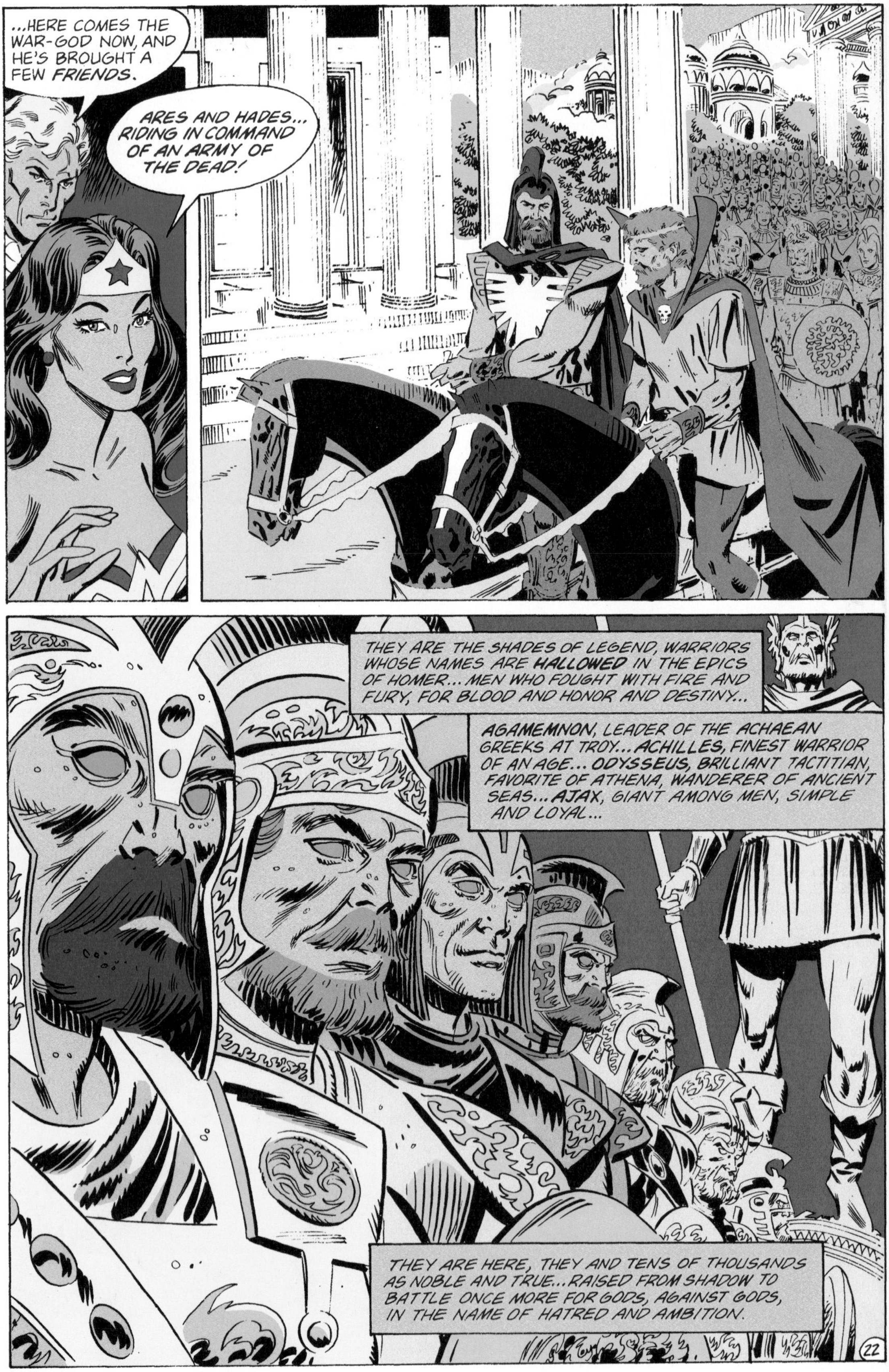
...HERE COMES THE WAR-GOD NOW, AND HE'S BROUGHT A FEW FRIENDS.
ARES AND HADES... RIDING IN COMMAND OF AN ARMY OF THE DEAD!
THEY ARE THE SHADES OF LEGEND, WARRIORS WHOSE NAMES ARE HALLOWED IN THE EPICS OF HOMER... MEN WHO FOUGHT WITH FIRE AND FURY, FOR BLOOD AND HONOR AND DESTINY...
AGAMEMNON, LEADER OF THE ACHAEAN GREEKS AT TROY... ACHILLES, FINEST WARRIOR OF AN AGE... ODYSSEUS, BRILLIANT TACTITIAN, FAVORITE OF ATHENA, WANDERER OF ANCIENT SEAS... AJAX, GIANT AMONG MEN, SIMPLE AND LOYAL...
THEY ARE HERE, THEY AND TENS OF THOUSANDS AS NOBLE AND TRUE... RAISED FROM SHADOW TO BATTLE ONCE MORE FOR GODS, AGAINST GODS, IN THE NAME OF HATRED AND AMBITION.
22

AND IF THEY COULD FEEL, THESE SHADOWS THAT ONCE WERE MEN, WHAT WOULD THEY FEEL?

REGRET? RESENTMENT THAT THEIR WELL-EARNED REST HAS BEEN SO RUDELY BROKEN? RAGE?

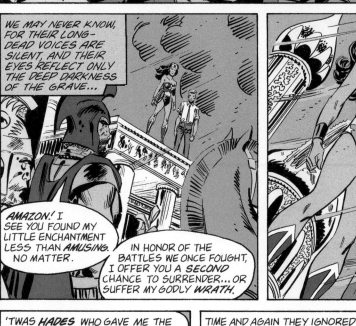

WE MAY NEVER KNOW, FOR THEIR LONG-DEAD VOICES ARE SILENT, AND THEIR EYES REFLECT ONLY THE DEEP DARKNESS OF THE GRAVE...

AMAZON! I SEE YOU FOUND MY LITTLE ENCHANTMENT LESS THAN AMUSING. NO MATTER.

IN HONOR OF THE BATTLES WE ONCE FOUGHT, I OFFER YOU A SECOND CHANCE TO SURRENDER... OR SUFFER MY GODLY WRATH.

YOUR THREATS DON'T FRIGHTEN ME, ARES. YOU FEED ON WAR, BUT IT'S A FEAST YOU'VE NEVER PREPARED PERSONALLY.

WHERE HAVE YOU IMPRISONED YOUR SISTERS AND BROTHERS? WHAT HAVE YOU DONE TO THE GODS OF MOUNT OLYMPUS?

'TWAS HADES WHO GAVE ME THE SPELL--AND I DID WITH THEM NO MORE THAN THEY'VE ALREADY DONE TO THEMSELVES.

BLOODLESS AND WITHOUT PASSION HAVE THEY BEEN IN SPIRIT THESE TWO HUNDRED CENTURIES, FORGOTTEN BY MANKIND... REMEMBERED ONLY IN LEGEND.

TIME AND AGAIN THEY IGNORED MY DEMAND FOR WAR AGAINST FAITHLESS HUMANITY. BLOODLESS AND WITHOUT PASSION WERE THEY, IN WORD AND DEED.

BLOODLESS AND WITHOUT PASSION THEY ARE NOW AND WILL FOREVER REMAIN.

FOR HERE, NOW AND EVERMORE, ARES RULES OLYMPUS.

FWOOOSH!!

23

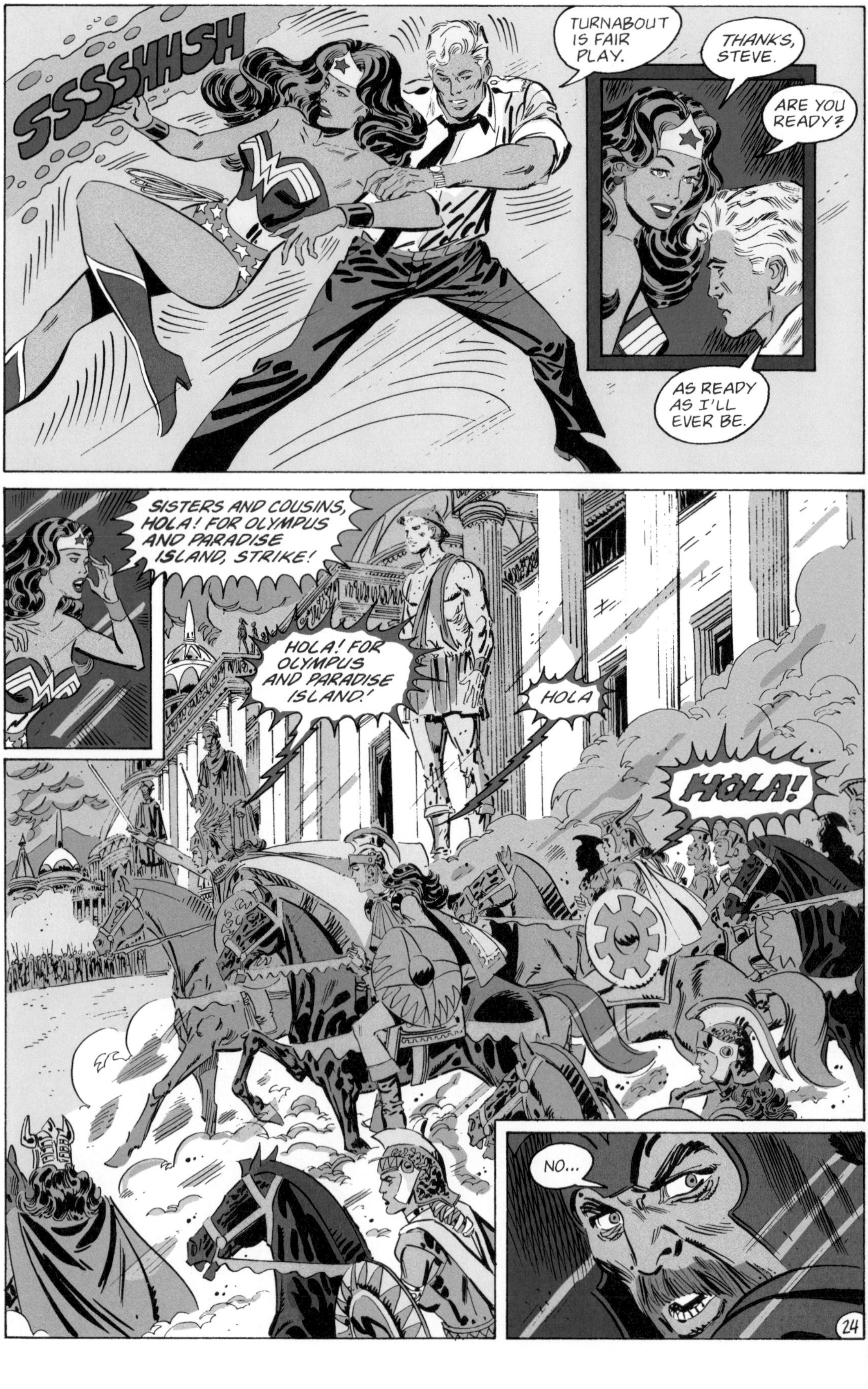
SSSSHHSH
TURNABOUT IS FAIR PLAY.
THANKS, STEVE.
ARE YOU READY?
AS READY AS I'LL EVER BE.
SISTERS AND COUSINS, HOLA! FOR OLYMPUS AND PARADISE ISLAND, STRIKE!
HOLA! FOR OLYMPUS AND PARADISE ISLAND!
HOLA
HOLA!
NO...
24

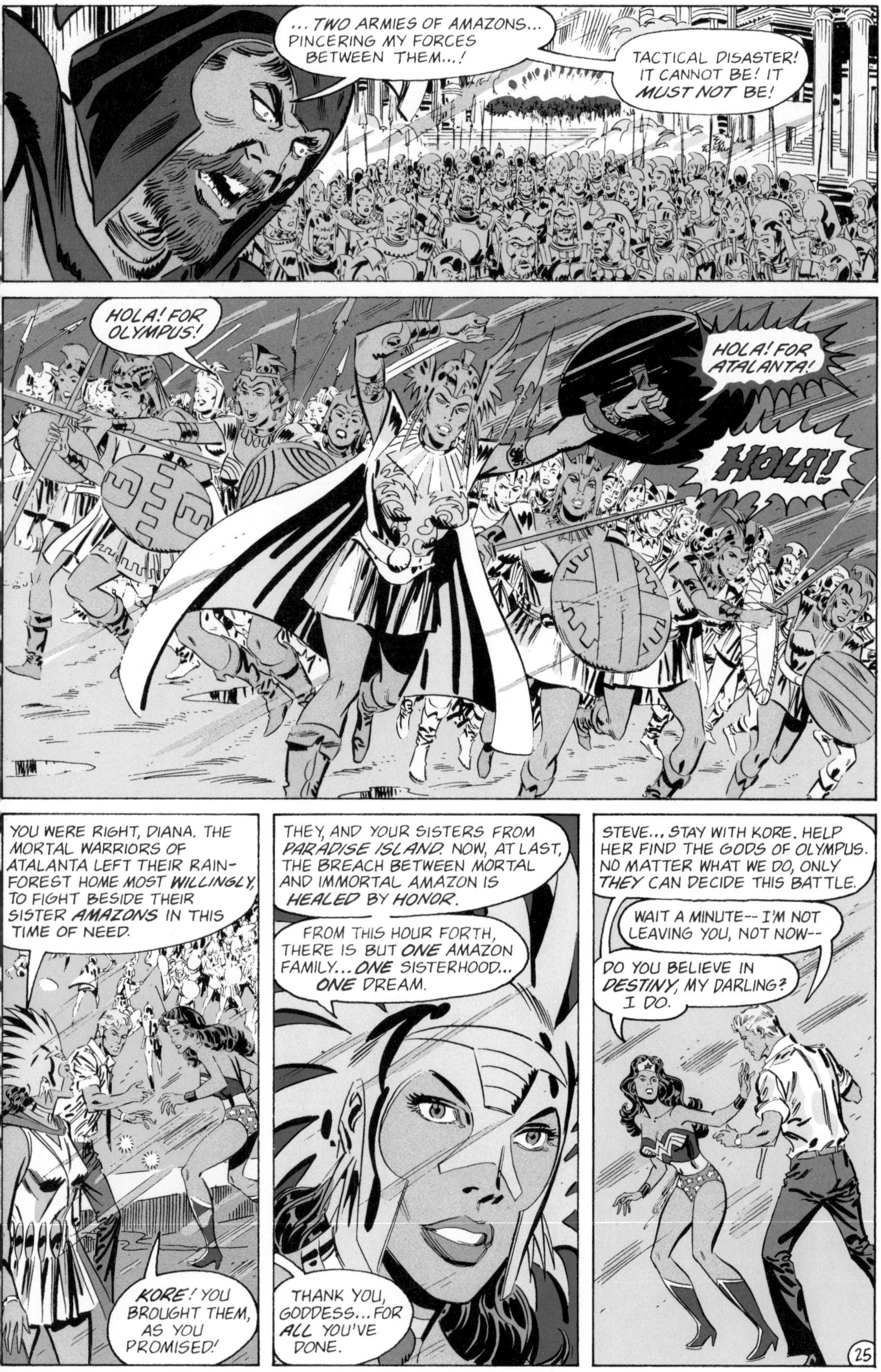
...TWO ARMIES OF AMAZONS... PINCERING MY FORCES BETWEEN THEM...!
TACTICAL DISASTER! IT CANNOT BE! IT MUST NOT BE!
HOLA! FOR OLYMPUS!
HOLA! FOR ATALANTA!
HOLA!
YOU WERE RIGHT, DIANA. THE MORTAL WARRIORS OF ATALANTA LEFT THEIR RAIN-FOREST HOME MOST WILLINGLY, TO FIGHT BESIDE THEIR SISTER AMAZONS IN THIS TIME OF NEED.
KORE! YOU BROUGHT THEM, AS YOU PROMISED!
THEY, AND YOUR SISTERS FROM PARADISE ISLAND. NOW, AT LAST, THE BREACH BETWEEN MORTAL AND IMMORTAL AMAZON IS HEALED BY HONOR.
FROM THIS HOUR FORTH, THERE IS BUT ONE AMAZON FAMILY... ONE SISTERHOOD... ONE DREAM.
THANK YOU, GODDESS... FOR ALL YOU'VE DONE.
STEVE... STAY WITH KORE. HELP HER FIND THE GODS OF OLYMPUS. NO MATTER WHAT WE DO, ONLY THEY CAN DECIDE THIS BATTLE.
WAIT A MINUTE-- I'M NOT LEAVING YOU, NOT NOW--
DO YOU BELIEVE IN DESTINY, MY DARLING? I DO.
25

OUR TWO LIVES HAVE BEEN ENTWINED BY *FATE* SINCE *BEFORE* THE WORLD WAS *BORN*.

WHATEVER HAPPENS... NOW OR IN THE FUTURE...

...WE'LL BE *TOGETHER* TILL THE END OF TIME.

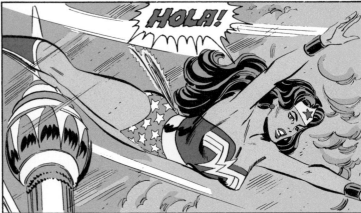

HOLA!

KORE, YOU'RE A GODDESS... WHATEVER *THAT* MEANS. CAN YOU SEE THE FUTURE?

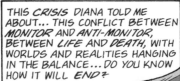

THIS *CRISIS* DIANA TOLD ME ABOUT... THIS CONFLICT BETWEEN *MONITOR* AND *ANTI-MONITOR*, BETWEEN *LIFE* AND *DEATH*, WITH WORLDS AND REALITIES HANGING IN THE BALANCE...DO YOU KNOW HOW IT WILL *END*?

WILL I EVER *SEE* HER AGAIN?

YOU LOVE HER, STEVE TREVOR?

26

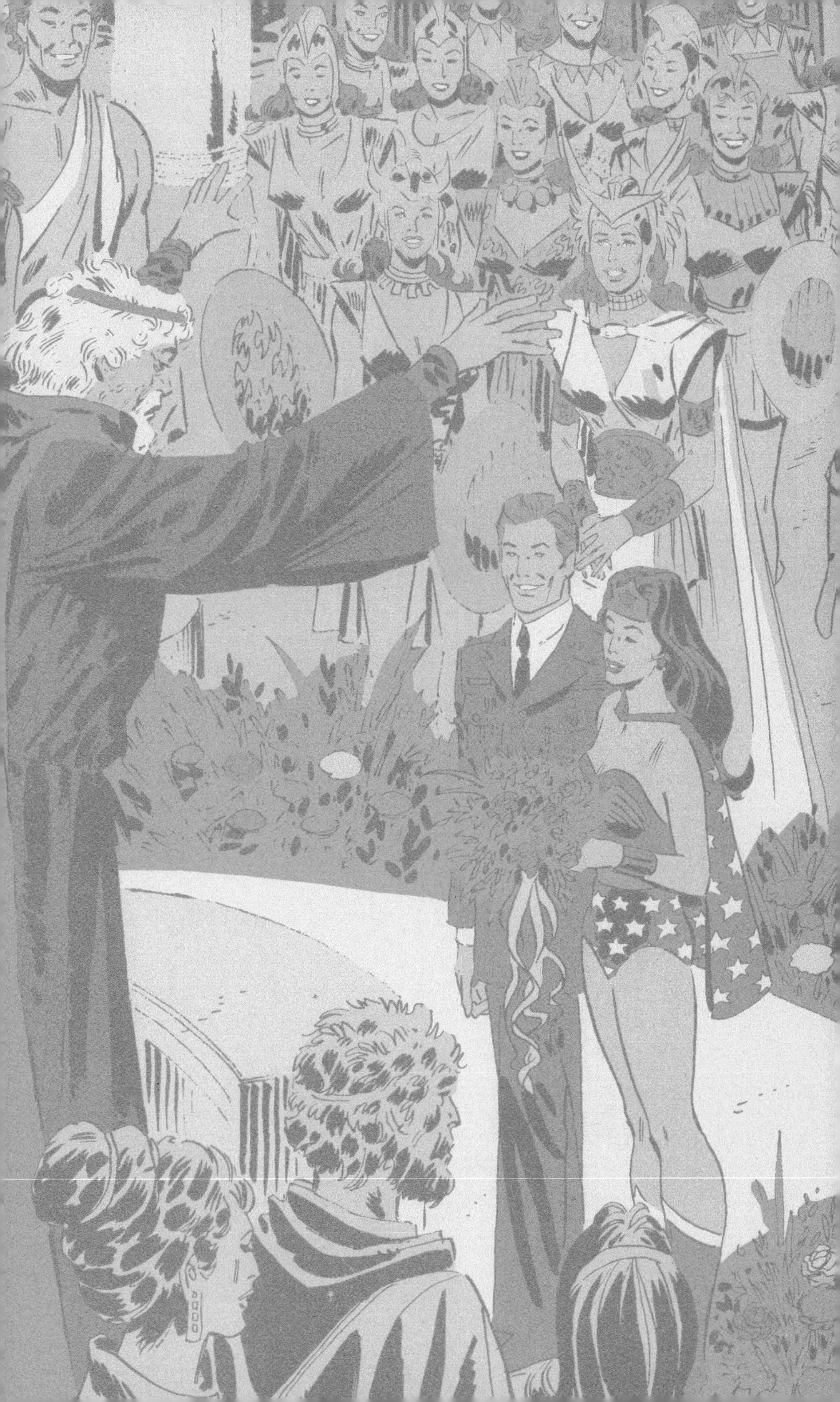

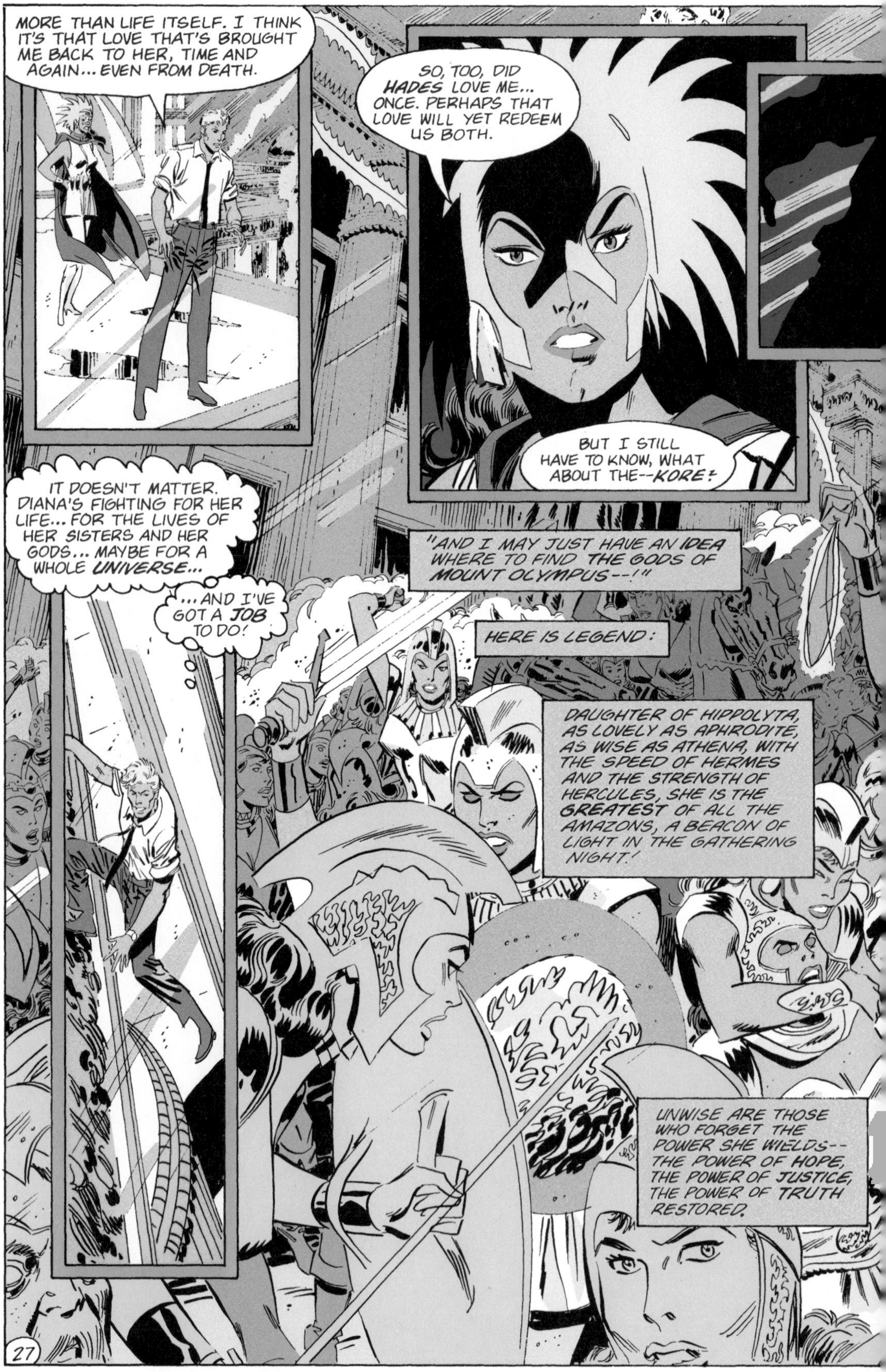

MORE THAN LIFE ITSELF. I THINK IT'S THAT LOVE THAT'S BROUGHT ME BACK TO HER, TIME AND AGAIN... EVEN FROM DEATH.
SO, TOO, DID HADES LOVE ME... ONCE. PERHAPS THAT LOVE WILL YET REDEEM US BOTH.
BUT I STILL HAVE TO KNOW, WHAT ABOUT THE--KORE?!
IT DOESN'T MATTER. DIANA'S FIGHTING FOR HER LIFE... FOR THE LIVES OF HER SISTERS AND HER GODS... MAYBE FOR A WHOLE UNIVERSE...
...AND I'VE GOT A JOB TO DO!
"AND I MAY JUST HAVE AN IDEA WHERE TO FIND THE GODS OF MOUNT OLYMPUS--!"
HERE IS LEGEND:
DAUGHTER OF HIPPOLYTA, AS LOVELY AS APHRODITE, AS WISE AS ATHENA, WITH THE SPEED OF HERMES AND THE STRENGTH OF HERCULES, SHE IS THE GREATEST OF ALL THE AMAZONS, A BEACON OF LIGHT IN THE GATHERING NIGHT!
UNWISE ARE THOSE WHO FORGET THE POWER SHE WIELDS-- THE POWER OF HOPE, THE POWER OF JUSTICE, THE POWER OF TRUTH RESTORED.
27

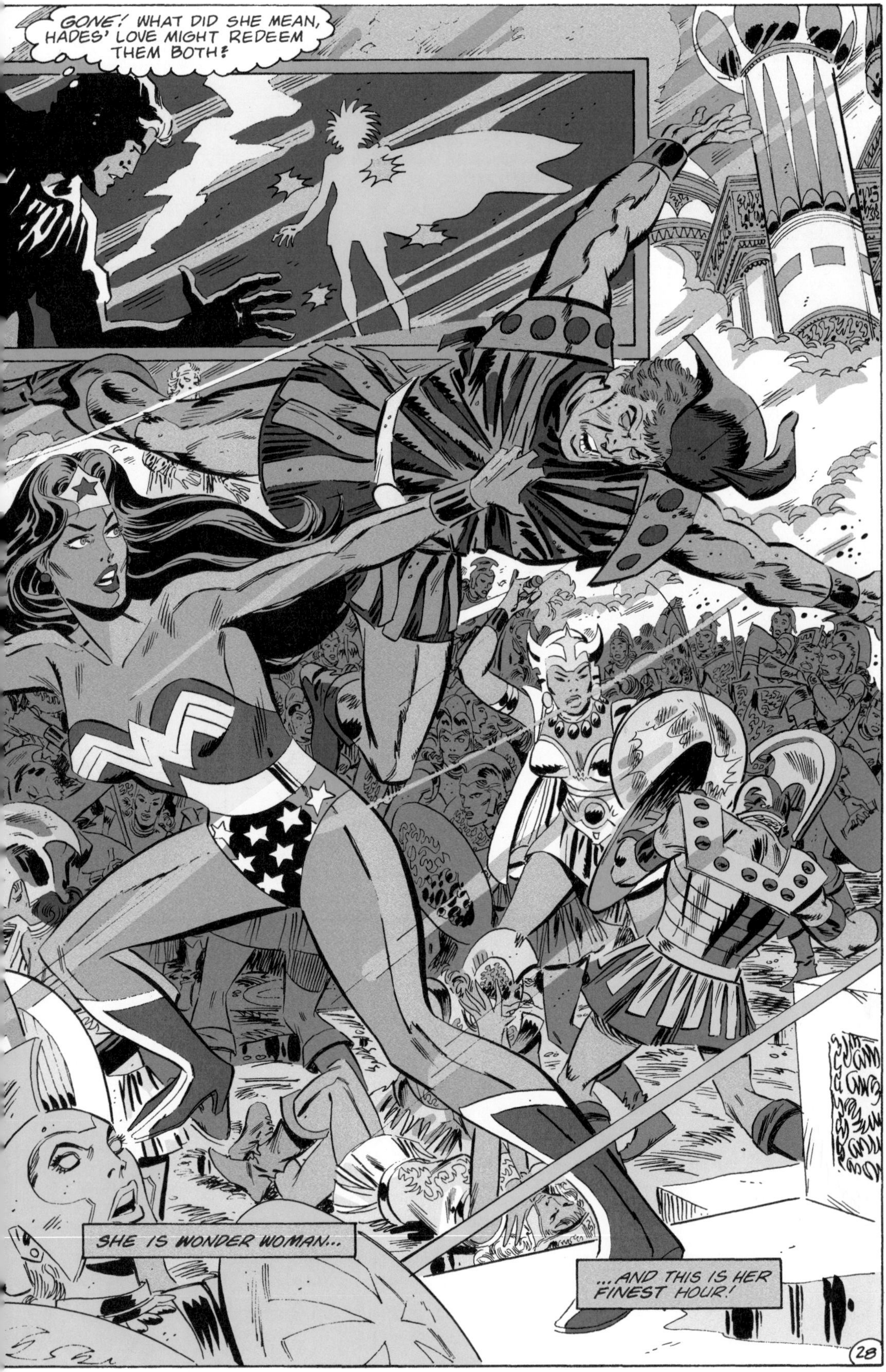
GONE! WHAT DID SHE MEAN, HADES' LOVE MIGHT REDEEM THEM BOTH?
SHE IS WONDER WOMAN...
...AND THIS IS HER FINEST HOUR!
28

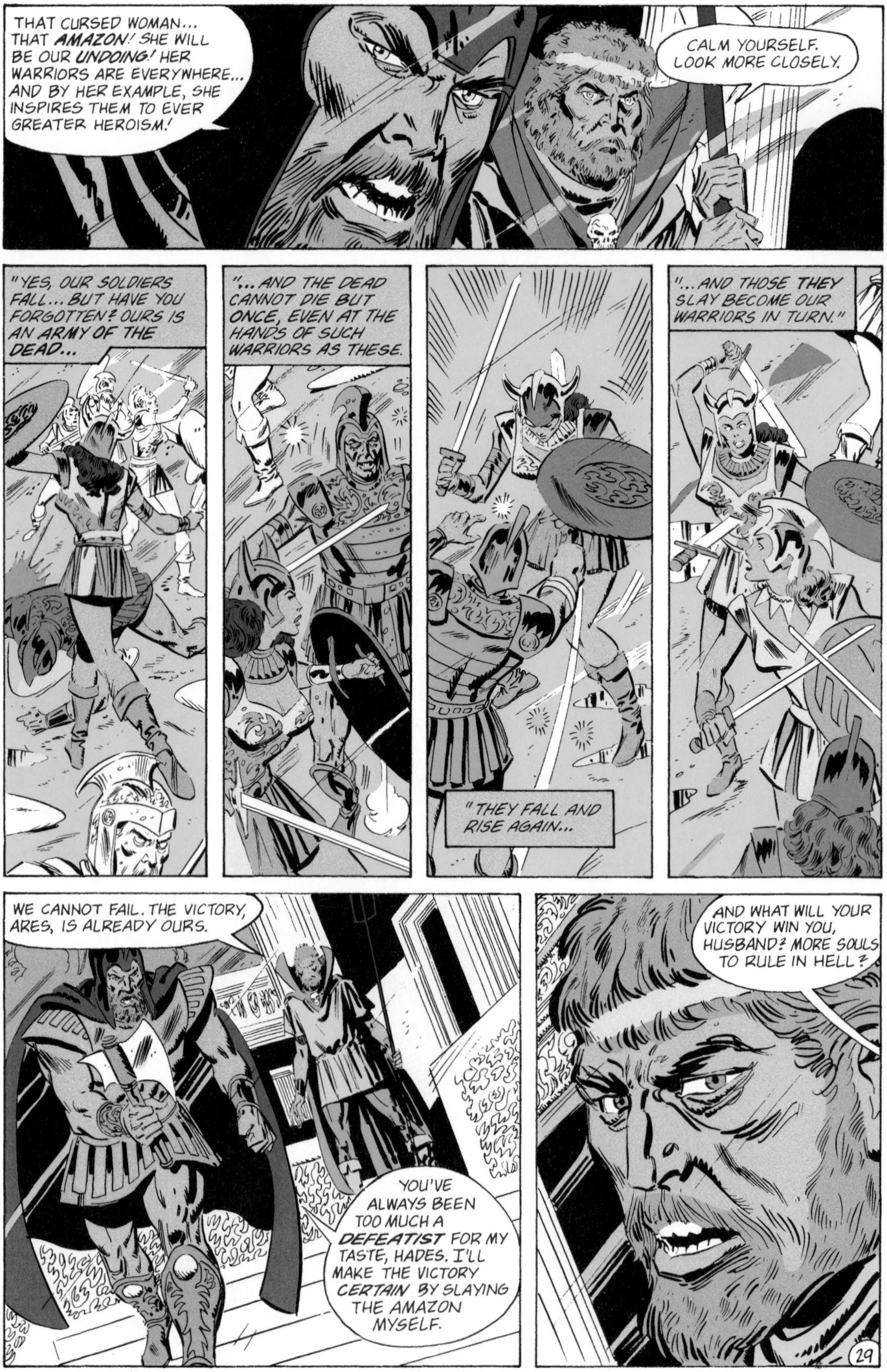

THAT CURSED WOMAN... THAT AMAZON! SHE WILL BE OUR UNDOING! HER WARRIORS ARE EVERYWHERE... AND BY HER EXAMPLE, SHE INSPIRES THEM TO EVER GREATER HEROISM!
CALM YOURSELF. LOOK MORE CLOSELY.
"YES, OUR SOLDIERS FALL... BUT HAVE YOU FORGOTTEN? OURS IS AN ARMY OF THE DEAD...
"...AND THE DEAD CANNOT DIE BUT ONCE, EVEN AT THE HANDS OF SUCH WARRIORS AS THESE.
"THEY FALL AND RISE AGAIN...
"...AND THOSE THEY SLAY BECOME OUR WARRIORS IN TURN."
WE CANNOT FAIL. THE VICTORY, ARES, IS ALREADY OURS.
YOU'VE ALWAYS BEEN TOO MUCH A DEFEATIST FOR MY TASTE, HADES. I'LL MAKE THE VICTORY CERTAIN BY SLAYING THE AMAZON MYSELF.
AND WHAT WILL YOUR VICTORY WIN YOU, HUSBAND? MORE SOULS TO RULE IN HELL?
29

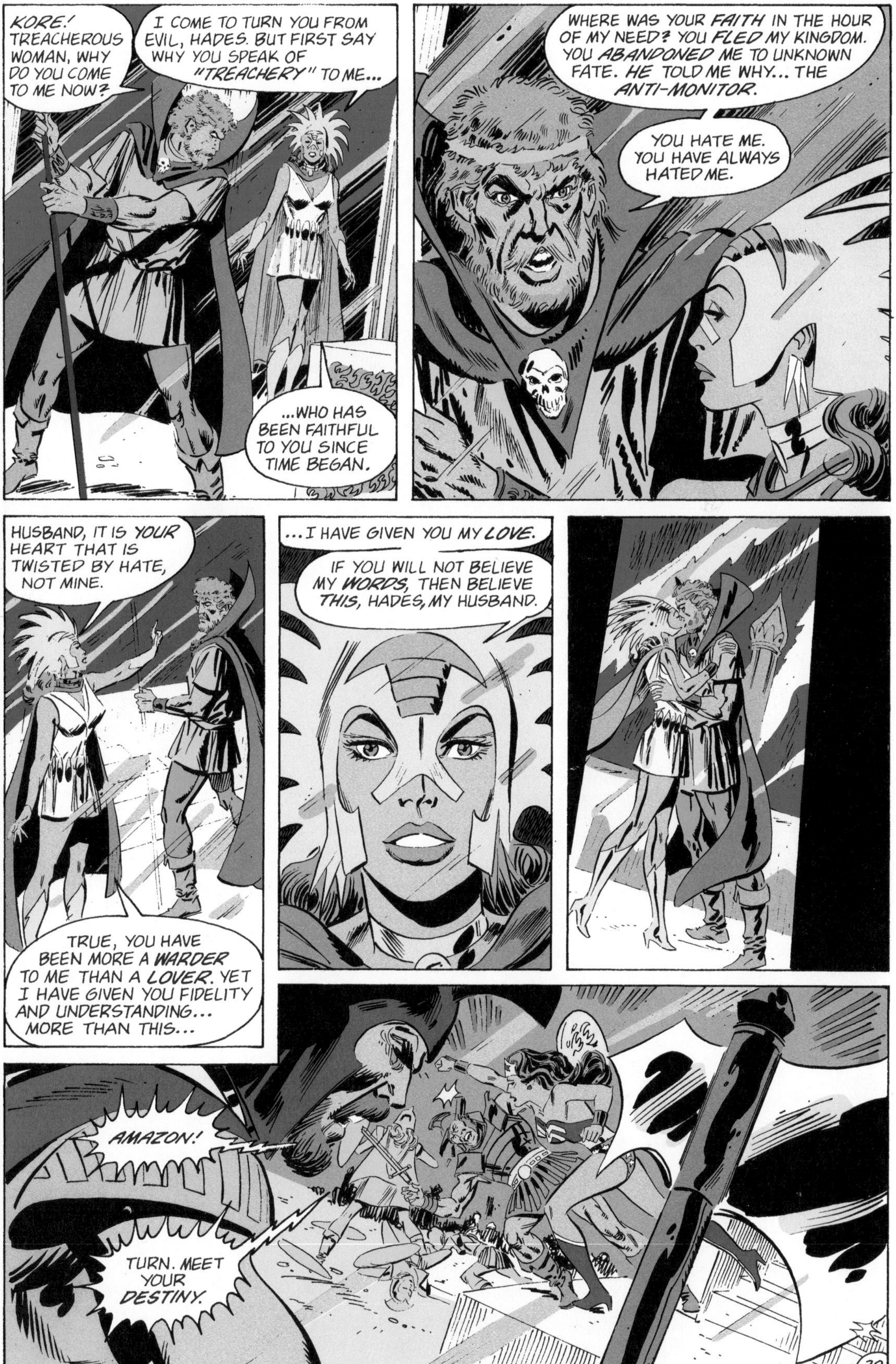
KORE! TREACHEROUS WOMAN, WHY DO YOU COME TO ME NOW?
I COME TO TURN YOU FROM EVIL, HADES. BUT FIRST SAY WHY YOU SPEAK OF "TREACHERY" TO ME...
...WHO HAS BEEN FAITHFUL TO YOU SINCE TIME BEGAN.
WHERE WAS YOUR FAITH IN THE HOUR OF MY NEED? YOU FLED MY KINGDOM. YOU ABANDONED ME TO UNKNOWN FATE. HE TOLD ME WHY... THE ANTI-MONITOR.
YOU HATE ME. YOU HAVE ALWAYS HATED ME.
HUSBAND, IT IS YOUR HEART THAT IS TWISTED BY HATE, NOT MINE.
TRUE, YOU HAVE BEEN MORE A WARDER TO ME THAN A LOVER. YET I HAVE GIVEN YOU FIDELITY AND UNDERSTANDING... MORE THAN THIS...
...I HAVE GIVEN YOU MY LOVE.
IF YOU WILL NOT BELIEVE MY WORDS, THEN BELIEVE THIS, HADES, MY HUSBAND.
AMAZON!
TURN. MEET YOUR DESTINY.
30

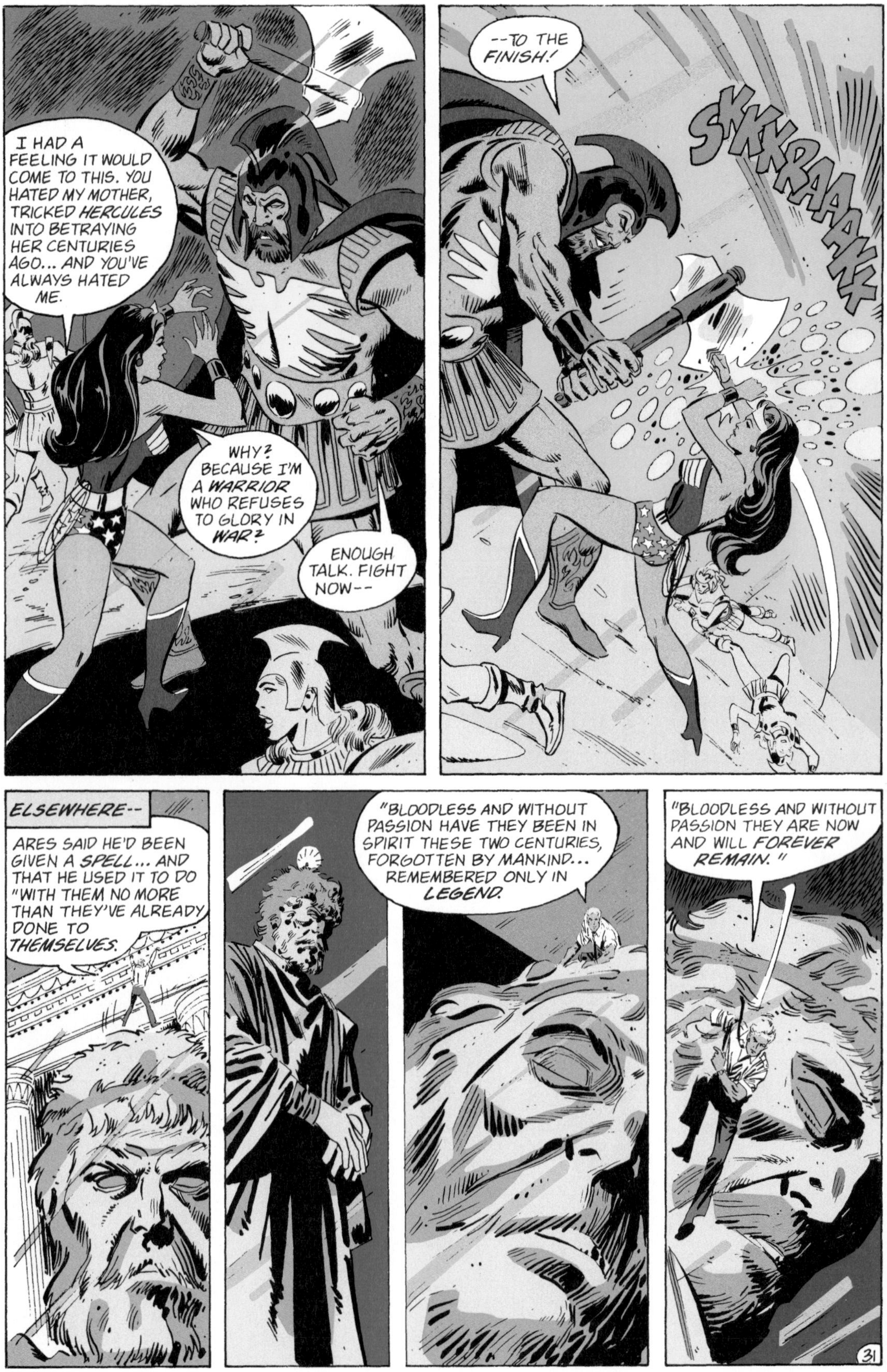
I HAD A FEELING IT WOULD COME TO THIS. YOU HATED MY MOTHER, TRICKED HERCULES INTO BETRAYING HER CENTURIES AGO... AND YOU'VE ALWAYS HATED ME.
WHY? BECAUSE I'M A WARRIOR WHO REFUSES TO GLORY IN WAR?
ENOUGH TALK. FIGHT NOW--
--TO THE FINISH!
SKKKRAAAANKK
ELSEWHERE--
ARES SAID HE'D BEEN GIVEN A SPELL... AND THAT HE USED IT TO DO "WITH THEM NO MORE THAN THEY'VE ALREADY DONE TO THEMSELVES.
"BLOODLESS AND WITHOUT PASSION HAVE THEY BEEN IN SPIRIT THESE TWO CENTURIES, FORGOTTEN BY MANKIND... REMEMBERED ONLY IN LEGEND.
"BLOODLESS AND WITHOUT PASSION THEY ARE NOW AND WILL FOREVER REMAIN."
31

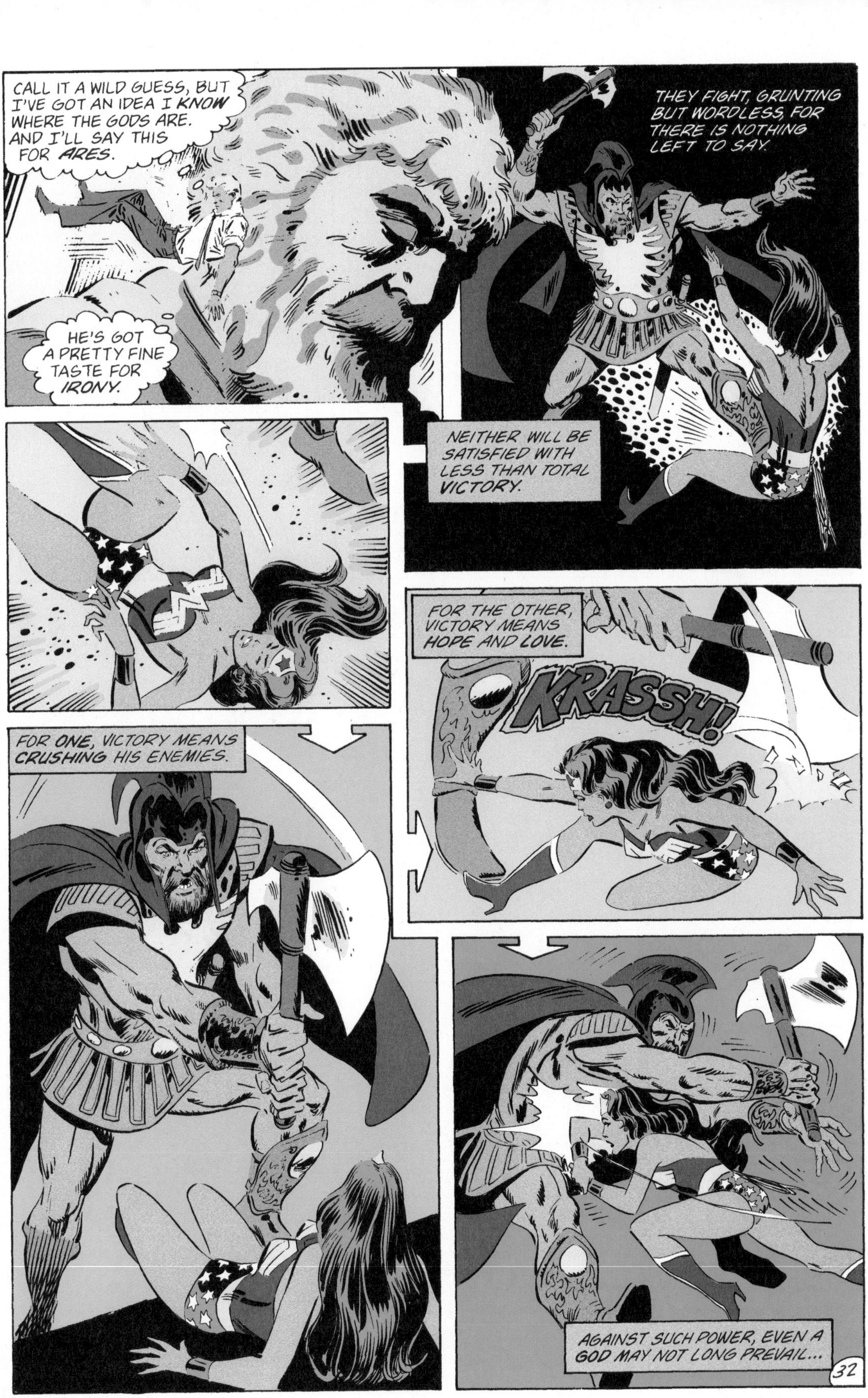

CALL IT A WILD GUESS, BUT I'VE GOT AN IDEA I KNOW WHERE THE GODS ARE. AND I'LL SAY THIS FOR ARES.
HE'S GOT A PRETTY FINE TASTE FOR IRONY.
THEY FIGHT, GRUNTING BUT WORDLESS, FOR THERE IS NOTHING LEFT TO SAY.
NEITHER WILL BE SATISFIED WITH LESS THAN TOTAL VICTORY.
FOR ONE, VICTORY MEANS CRUSHING HIS ENEMIES.
FOR THE OTHER, VICTORY MEANS HOPE AND LOVE.
KRASSH!
AGAINST SUCH POWER, EVEN A GOD MAY NOT LONG PREVAIL...
32

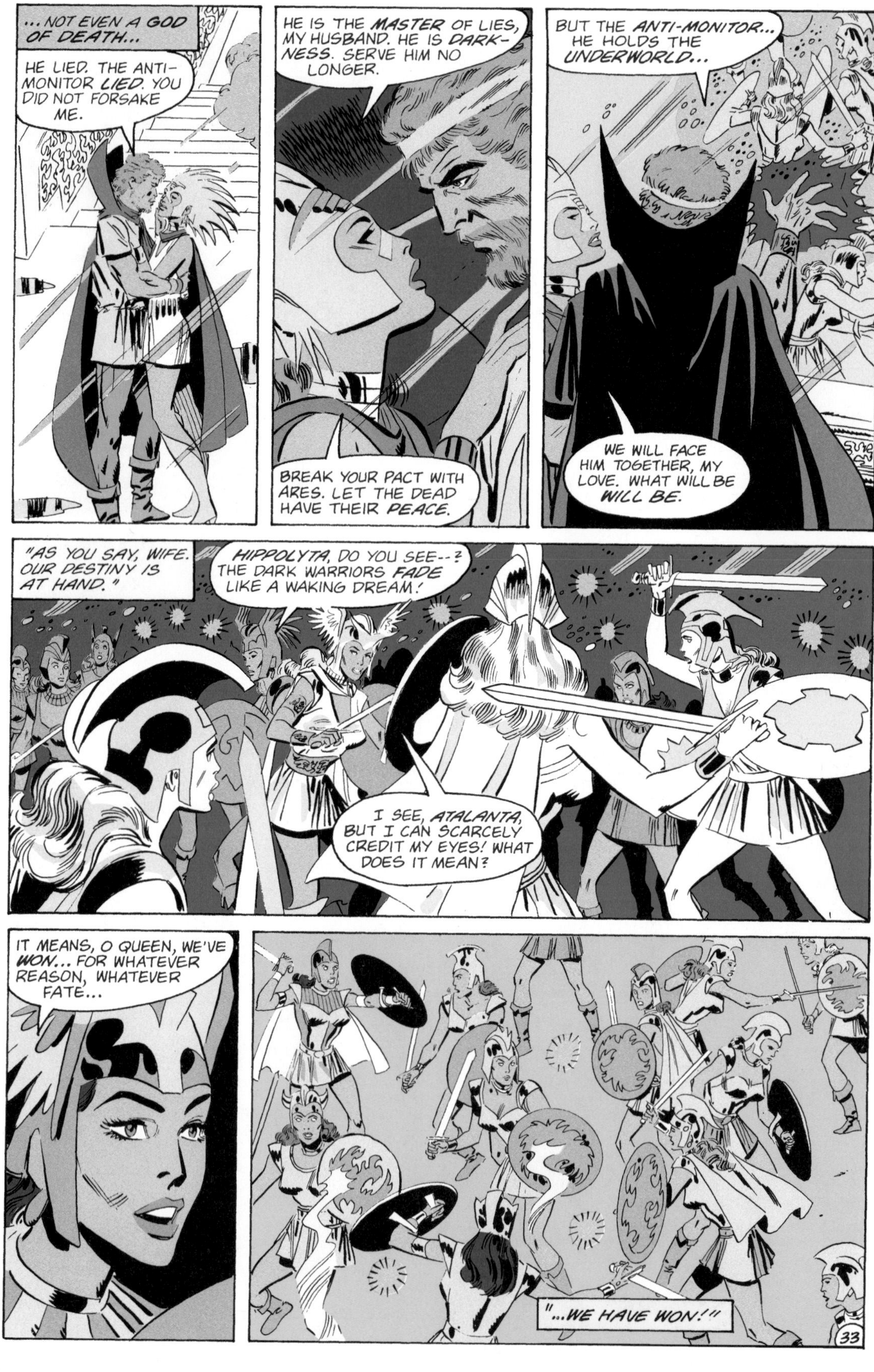
...NOT EVEN A GOD OF DEATH...
HE LIED. THE ANTI-MONITOR LIED. YOU DID NOT FORSAKE ME.
HE IS THE MASTER OF LIES, MY HUSBAND. HE IS DARKNESS. SERVE HIM NO LONGER.
BREAK YOUR PACT WITH ARES. LET THE DEAD HAVE THEIR PEACE.
BUT THE ANTI-MONITOR... HE HOLDS THE UNDERWORLD...
WE WILL FACE HIM TOGETHER, MY LOVE. WHAT WILL BE WILL BE.
"AS YOU SAY, WIFE. OUR DESTINY IS AT HAND."
HIPPOLYTA, DO YOU SEE--? THE DARK WARRIORS FADE LIKE A WAKING DREAM!
I SEE, ATALANTA, BUT I CAN SCARCELY CREDIT MY EYES! WHAT DOES IT MEAN?
IT MEANS, O QUEEN, WE'VE WON... FOR WHATEVER REASON, WHATEVER FATE...
"...WE HAVE WON!"
33

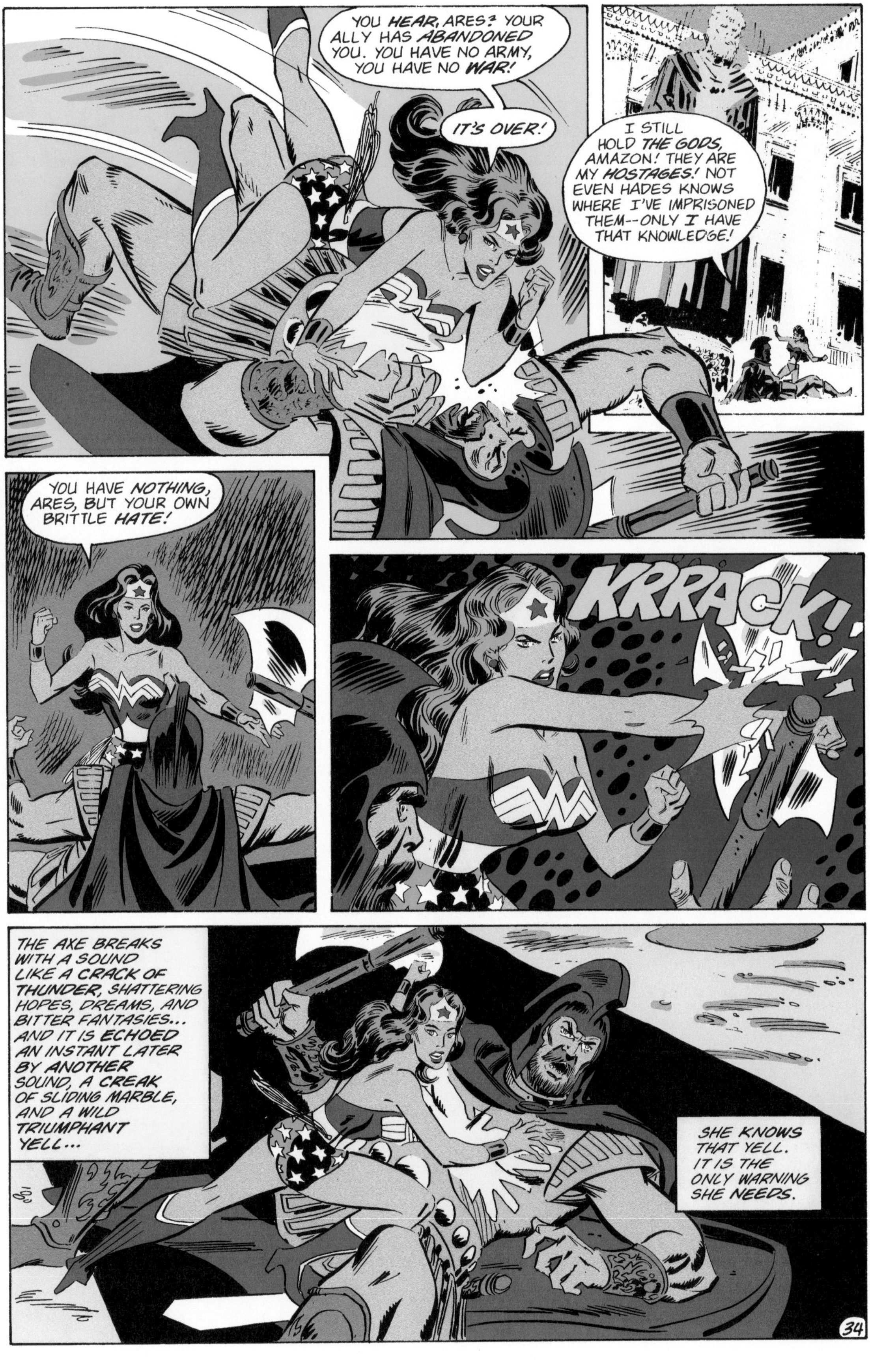
YOU HEAR, ARES? YOUR ALLY HAS ABANDONED YOU. YOU HAVE NO ARMY, YOU HAVE NO WAR!
IT'S OVER!
I STILL HOLD THE GODS, AMAZON! THEY ARE MY HOSTAGES! NOT EVEN HADES KNOWS WHERE I'VE IMPRISONED THEM--ONLY I HAVE THAT KNOWLEDGE!
YOU HAVE NOTHING, ARES, BUT YOUR OWN BRITTLE HATE!
KRRACK!
THE AXE BREAKS WITH A SOUND LIKE A CRACK OF THUNDER, SHATTERING HOPES, DREAMS, AND BITTER FANTASIES... AND IT IS ECHOED AN INSTANT LATER BY ANOTHER SOUND, A CREAK OF SLIDING MARBLE, AND A WILD TRIUMPHANT YELL...
SHE KNOWS THAT YELL. IT IS THE ONLY WARNING SHE NEEDS.
34

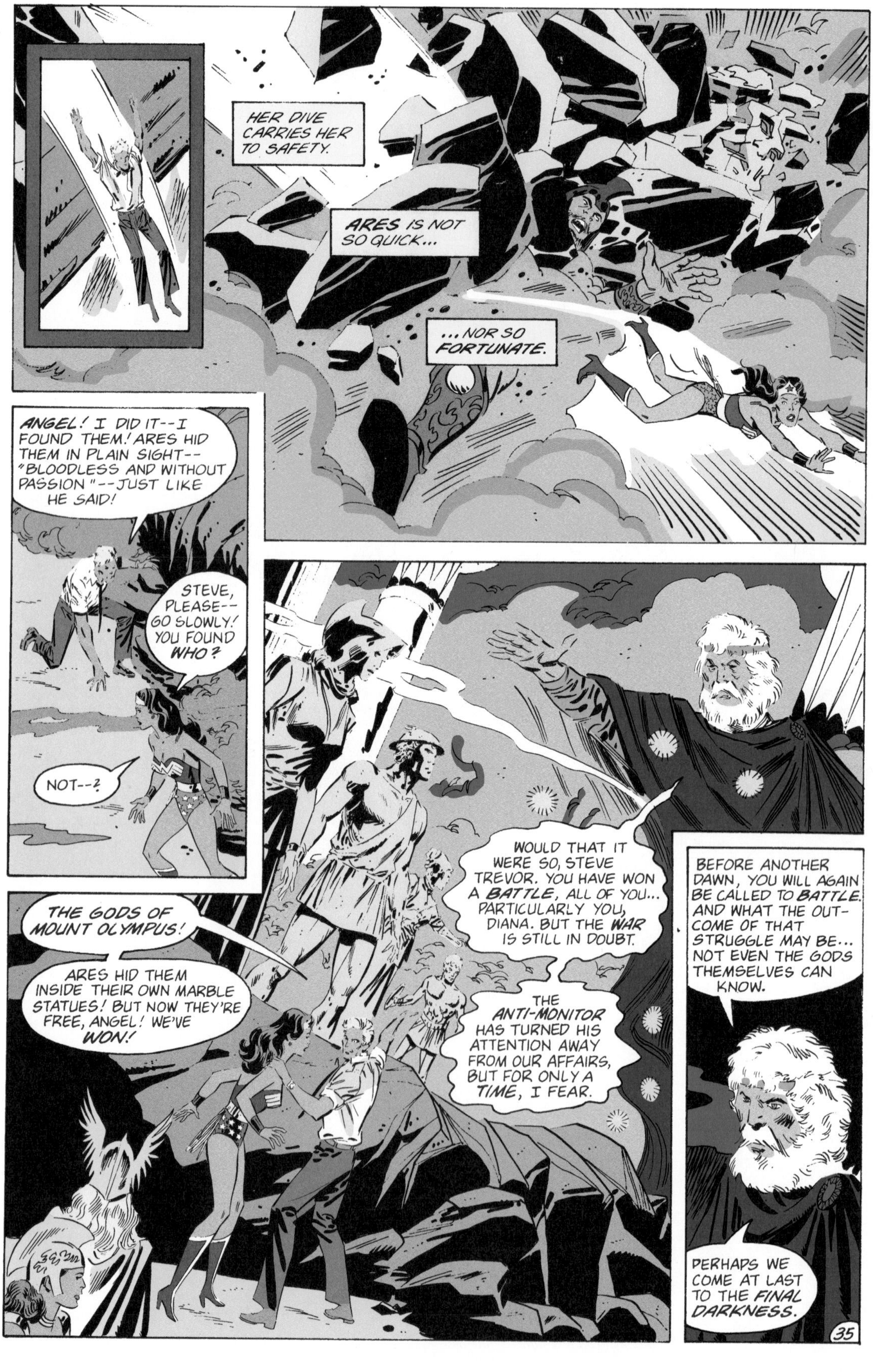
HER DIVE CARRIES HER TO SAFETY.
ARES IS NOT SO QUICK...
...NOR SO FORTUNATE.
ANGEL! I DID IT--I FOUND THEM! ARES HID THEM IN PLAIN SIGHT--"BLOODLESS AND WITHOUT PASSION"--JUST LIKE HE SAID!
STEVE, PLEASE--GO SLOWLY! YOU FOUND WHO?
NOT--?
THE GODS OF MOUNT OLYMPUS!
ARES HID THEM INSIDE THEIR OWN MARBLE STATUES! BUT NOW THEY'RE FREE, ANGEL! WE'VE WON!
WOULD THAT IT WERE SO, STEVE TREVOR. YOU HAVE WON A BATTLE, ALL OF YOU... PARTICULARLY YOU, DIANA. BUT THE WAR IS STILL IN DOUBT.
THE ANTI-MONITOR HAS TURNED HIS ATTENTION AWAY FROM OUR AFFAIRS, BUT FOR ONLY A TIME, I FEAR.
BEFORE ANOTHER DAWN, YOU WILL AGAIN BE CALLED TO BATTLE. AND WHAT THE OUTCOME OF THAT STRUGGLE MAY BE... NOT EVEN THE GODS THEMSELVES CAN KNOW.
PERHAPS WE COME AT LAST TO THE FINAL DARKNESS.
35

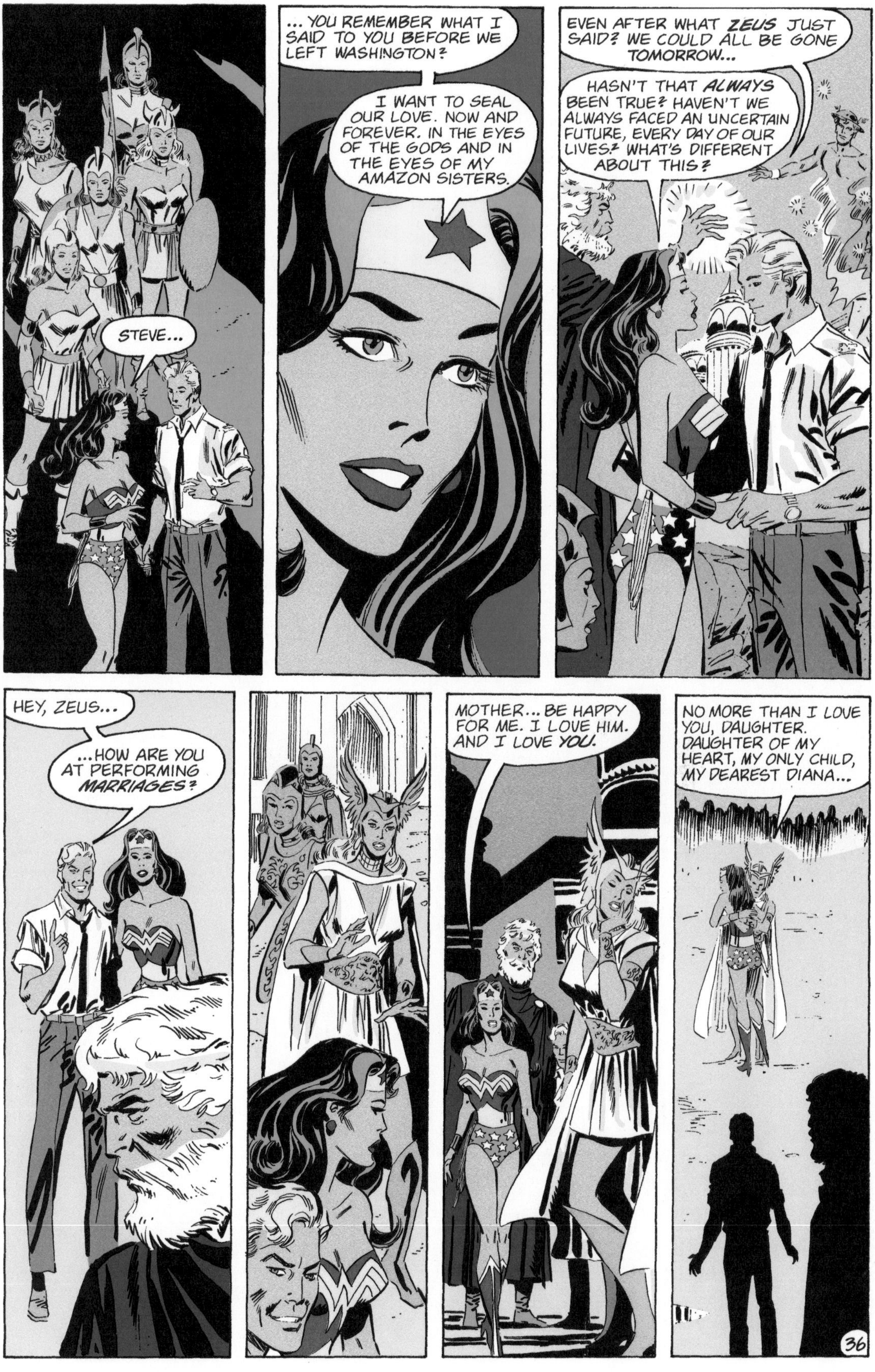
STEVE...
... YOU REMEMBER WHAT I SAID TO YOU BEFORE WE LEFT WASHINGTON?
I WANT TO SEAL OUR LOVE. NOW AND FOREVER. IN THE EYES OF THE GODS AND IN THE EYES OF MY AMAZON SISTERS.
EVEN AFTER WHAT ZEUS JUST SAID? WE COULD ALL BE GONE TOMORROW...
HASN'T THAT ALWAYS BEEN TRUE? HAVEN'T WE ALWAYS FACED AN UNCERTAIN FUTURE, EVERY DAY OF OUR LIVES? WHAT'S DIFFERENT ABOUT THIS?
HEY, ZEUS...
...HOW ARE YOU AT PERFORMING MARRIAGES?
MOTHER... BE HAPPY FOR ME. I LOVE HIM. AND I LOVE YOU.
NO MORE THAN I LOVE YOU, DAUGHTER. DAUGHTER OF MY HEART, MY ONLY CHILD, MY DEAREST DIANA...
36

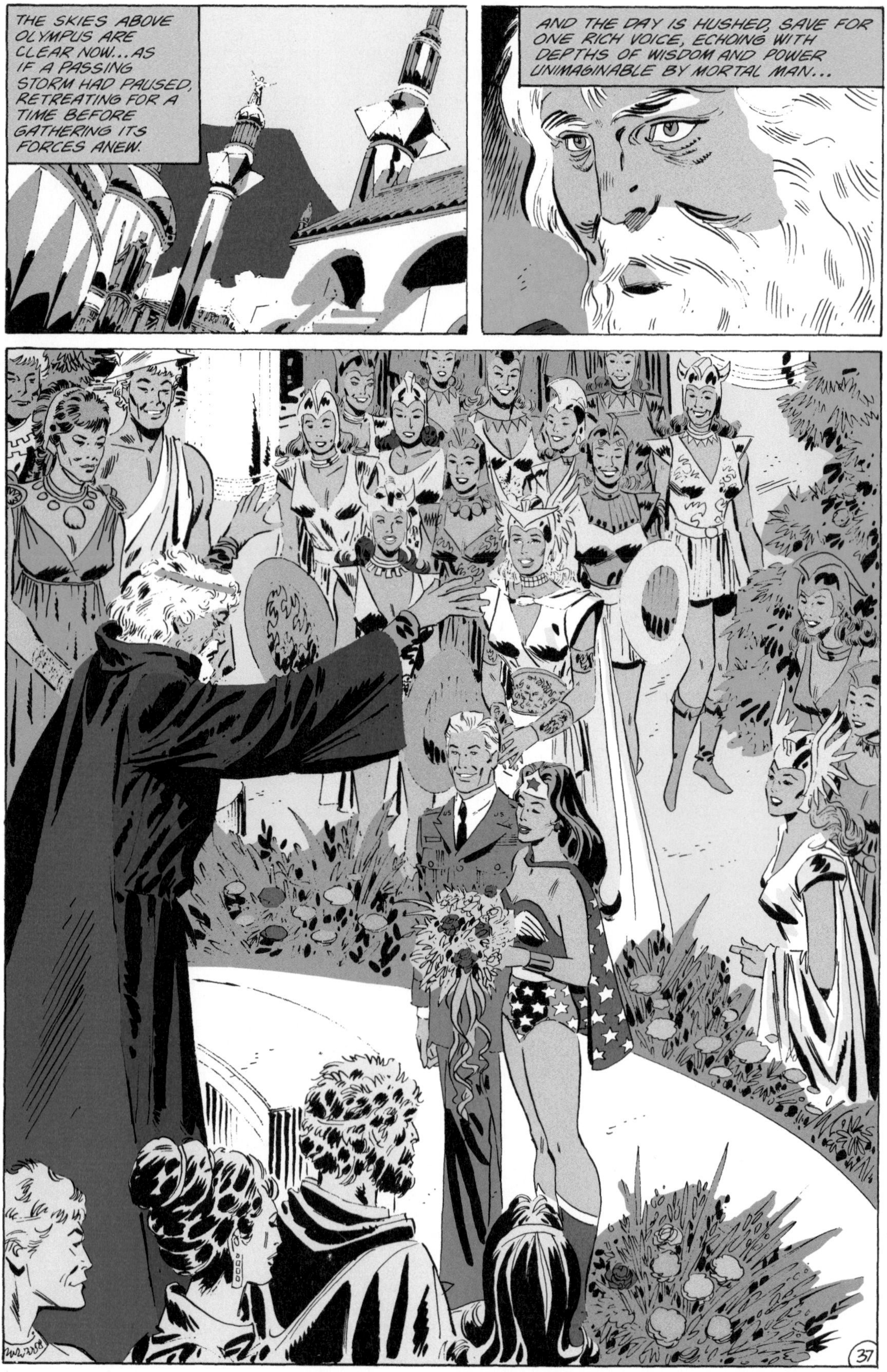
THE SKIES ABOVE OLYMPUS ARE CLEAR NOW... AS IF A PASSING STORM HAD PAUSED, RETREATING FOR A TIME BEFORE GATHERING ITS FORCES ANEW.
AND THE DAY IS HUSHED, SAVE FOR ONE RICH VOICE, ECHOING WITH DEPTHS OF WISDOM AND POWER UNIMAGINABLE BY MORTAL MAN...
37

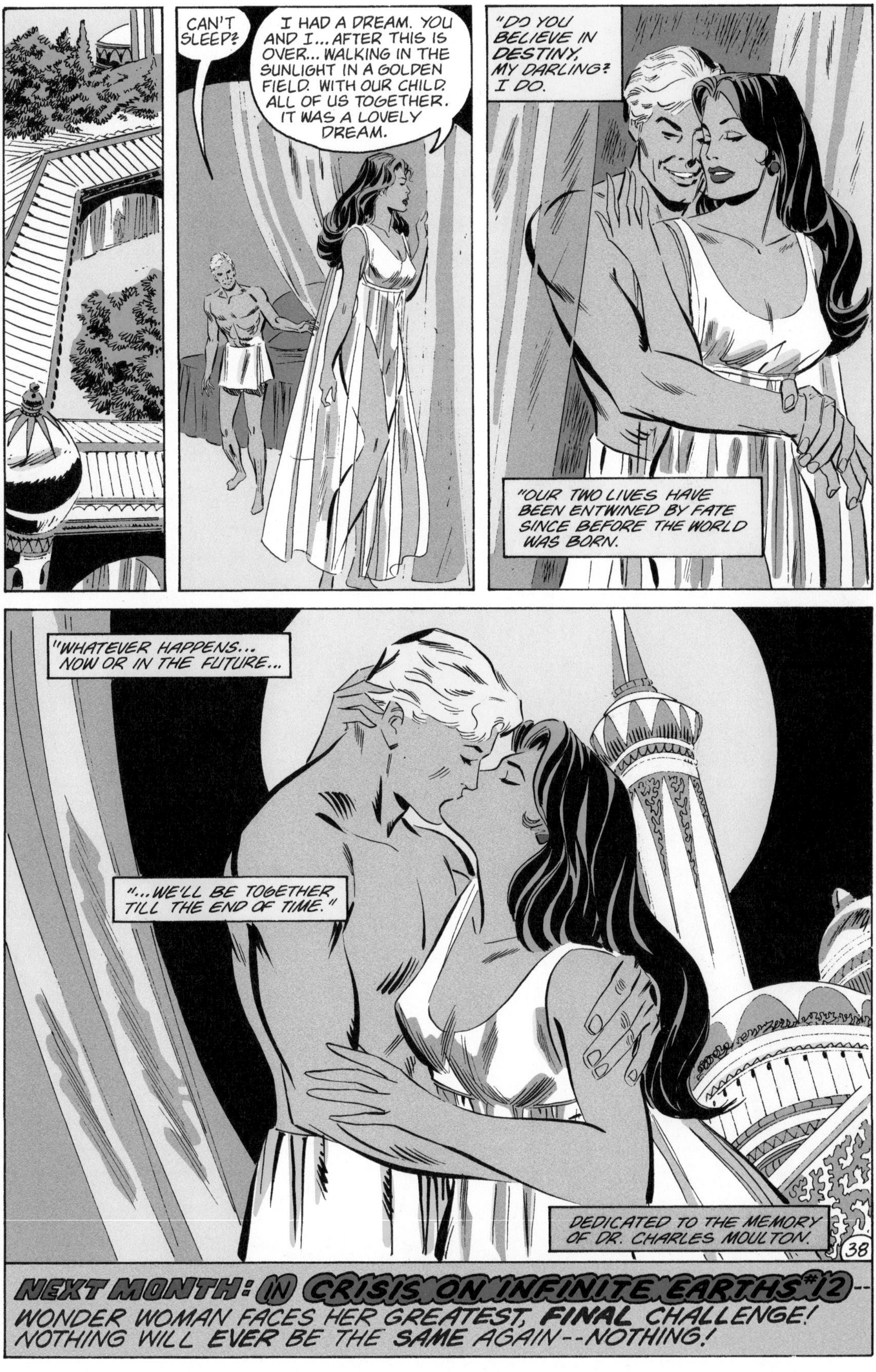
CAN'T SLEEP?
I HAD A DREAM. YOU AND I... AFTER THIS IS OVER... WALKING IN THE SUNLIGHT IN A GOLDEN FIELD. WITH OUR CHILD. ALL OF US TOGETHER. IT WAS A LOVELY DREAM.
"DO YOU BELIEVE IN DESTINY, MY DARLING? I DO.
"OUR TWO LIVES HAVE BEEN ENTWINED BY FATE SINCE BEFORE THE WORLD WAS BORN.
"WHATEVER HAPPENS... NOW OR IN THE FUTURE...
"...WE'LL BE TOGETHER TILL THE END OF TIME."
DEDICATED TO THE MEMORY OF DR. CHARLES MOULTON.
38
NEXT MONTH: IN CRISIS ON INFINITE EARTHS #12--
WONDER WOMAN FACES HER GREATEST, FINAL CHALLENGE!
NOTHING WILL EVER BE THE SAME AGAIN--NOTHING!

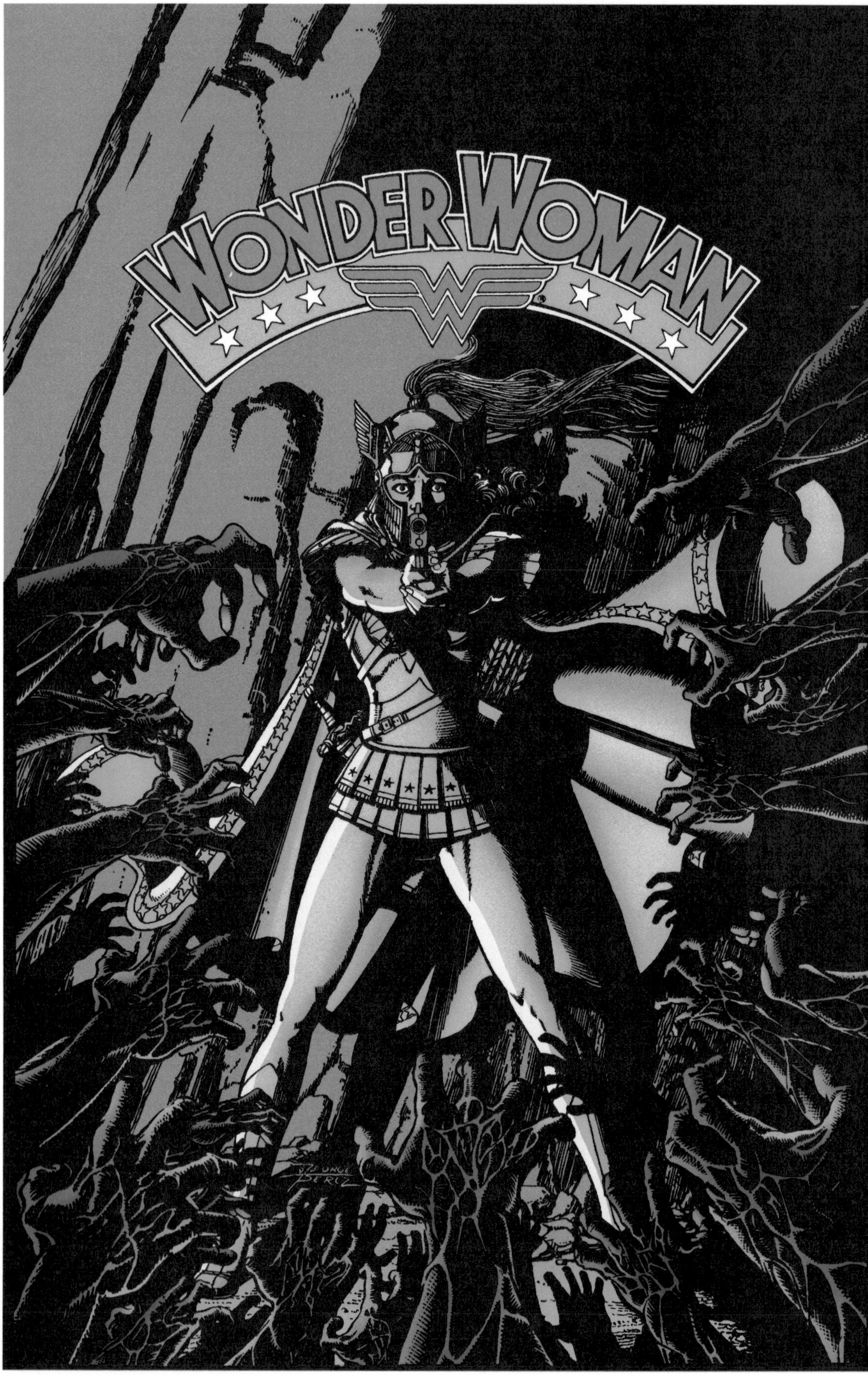
WONDER WOMAN

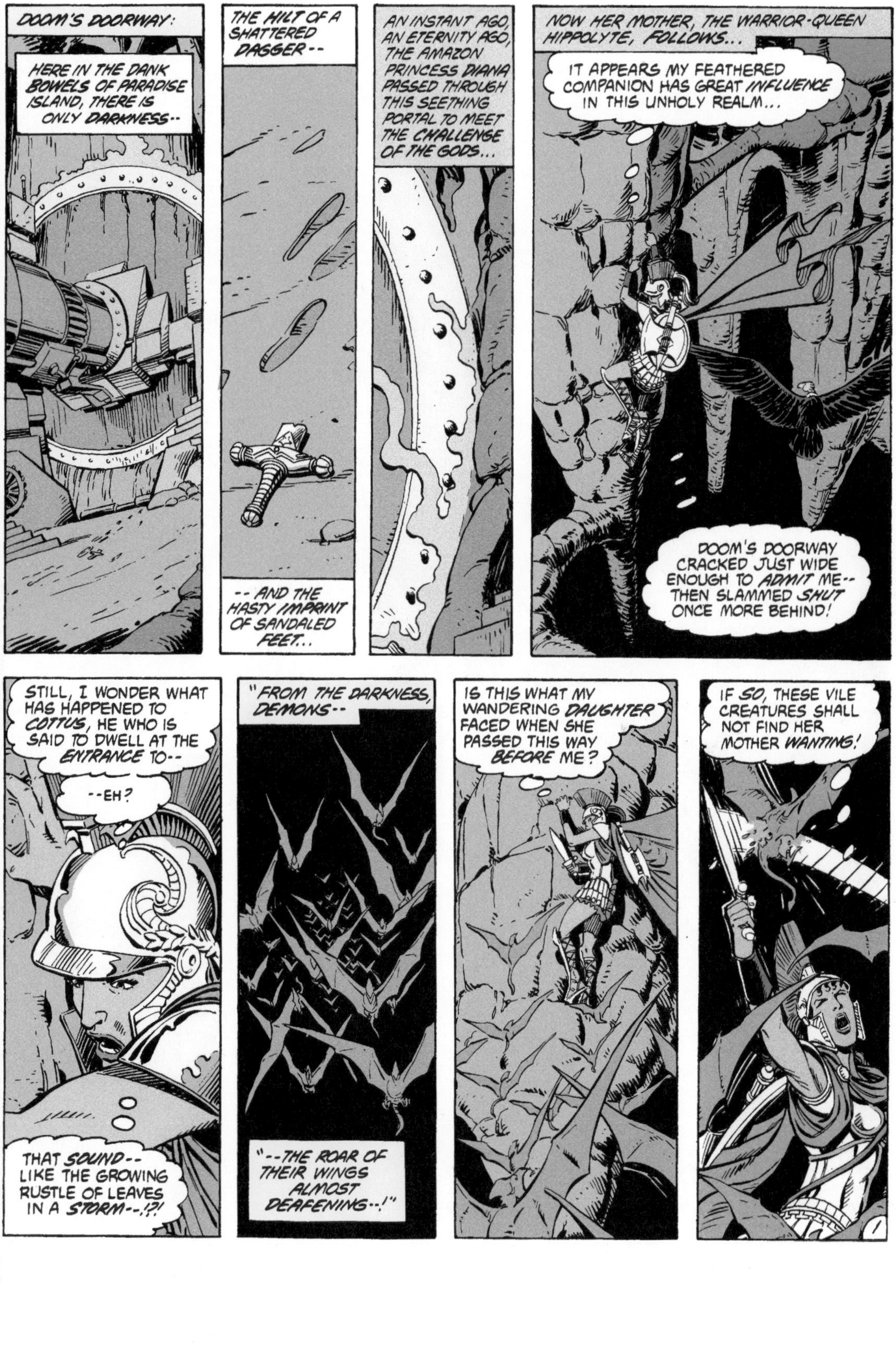
DOOM'S DOORWAY:
HERE IN THE DANK BOWELS OF PARADISE ISLAND, THERE IS ONLY DARKNESS--
THE HILT OF A SHATTERED DAGGER--
--AND THE HASTY IMPRINT OF SANDALED FEET...
AN INSTANT AGO, AN ETERNITY AGO, THE AMAZON PRINCESS DIANA PASSED THROUGH THIS SEETHING PORTAL TO MEET THE CHALLENGE OF THE GODS...
NOW HER MOTHER, THE WARRIOR-QUEEN HIPPOLYTE, FOLLOWS...
IT APPEARS MY FEATHERED COMPANION HAS GREAT INFLUENCE IN THIS UNHOLY REALM...
DOOM'S DOORWAY CRACKED JUST WIDE ENOUGH TO ADMIT ME-- THEN SLAMMED SHUT ONCE MORE BEHIND!
STILL, I WONDER WHAT HAS HAPPENED TO COTTUS, HE WHO IS SAID TO DWELL AT THE ENTRANCE TO--
--EH?
THAT SOUND-- LIKE THE GROWING RUSTLE OF LEAVES IN A STORM--!?!
"FROM THE DARKNESS, DEMONS--
"--THE ROAR OF THEIR WINGS ALMOST DEAFENING--!"
IS THIS WHAT MY WANDERING DAUGHTER FACED WHEN SHE PASSED THIS WAY BEFORE ME?
IF SO, THESE VILE CREATURES SHALL NOT FIND HER MOTHER WANTING!
1

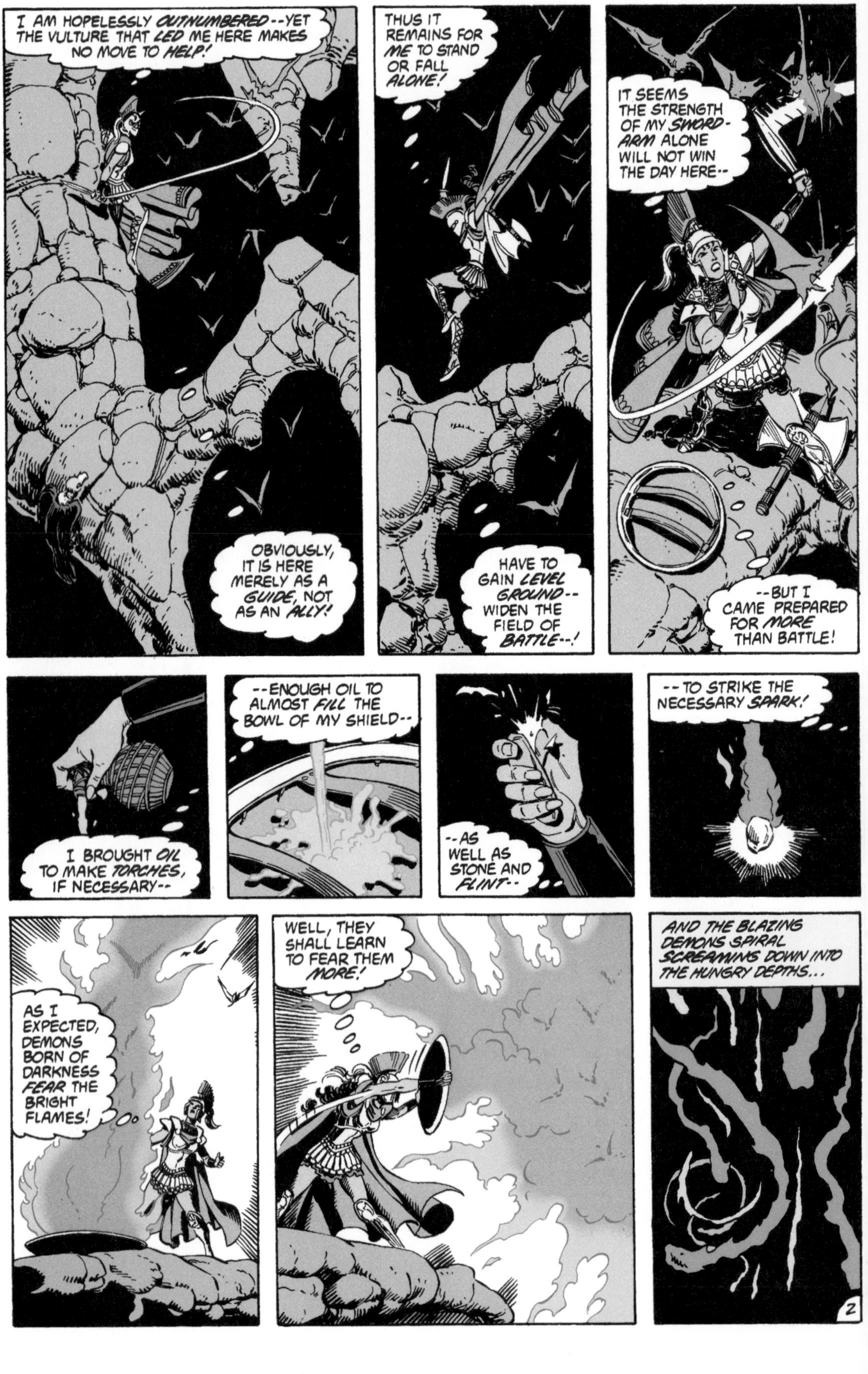
I AM HOPELESSLY OUTNUMBERED--YET THE VULTURE THAT LED ME HERE MAKES NO MOVE TO HELP!
OBVIOUSLY, IT IS HERE MERELY AS A GUIDE, NOT AS AN ALLY!
THUS IT REMAINS FOR ME TO STAND OR FALL ALONE!
HAVE TO GAIN LEVEL GROUND--WIDEN THE FIELD OF BATTLE--!
IT SEEMS THE STRENGTH OF MY SWORD-ARM ALONE WILL NOT WIN THE DAY HERE--
--BUT I CAME PREPARED FOR MORE THAN BATTLE!
I BROUGHT OIL TO MAKE TORCHES, IF NECESSARY--
--ENOUGH OIL TO ALMOST FILL THE BOWL OF MY SHIELD--
--AS WELL AS STONE AND FLINT--
--TO STRIKE THE NECESSARY SPARK!
AS I EXPECTED, DEMONS BORN OF DARKNESS FEAR THE BRIGHT FLAMES!
WELL, THEY SHALL LEARN TO FEAR THEM MORE!
AND THE BLAZING DEMONS SPIRAL SCREAMING DOWN INTO THE HUNGRY DEPTHS...
2

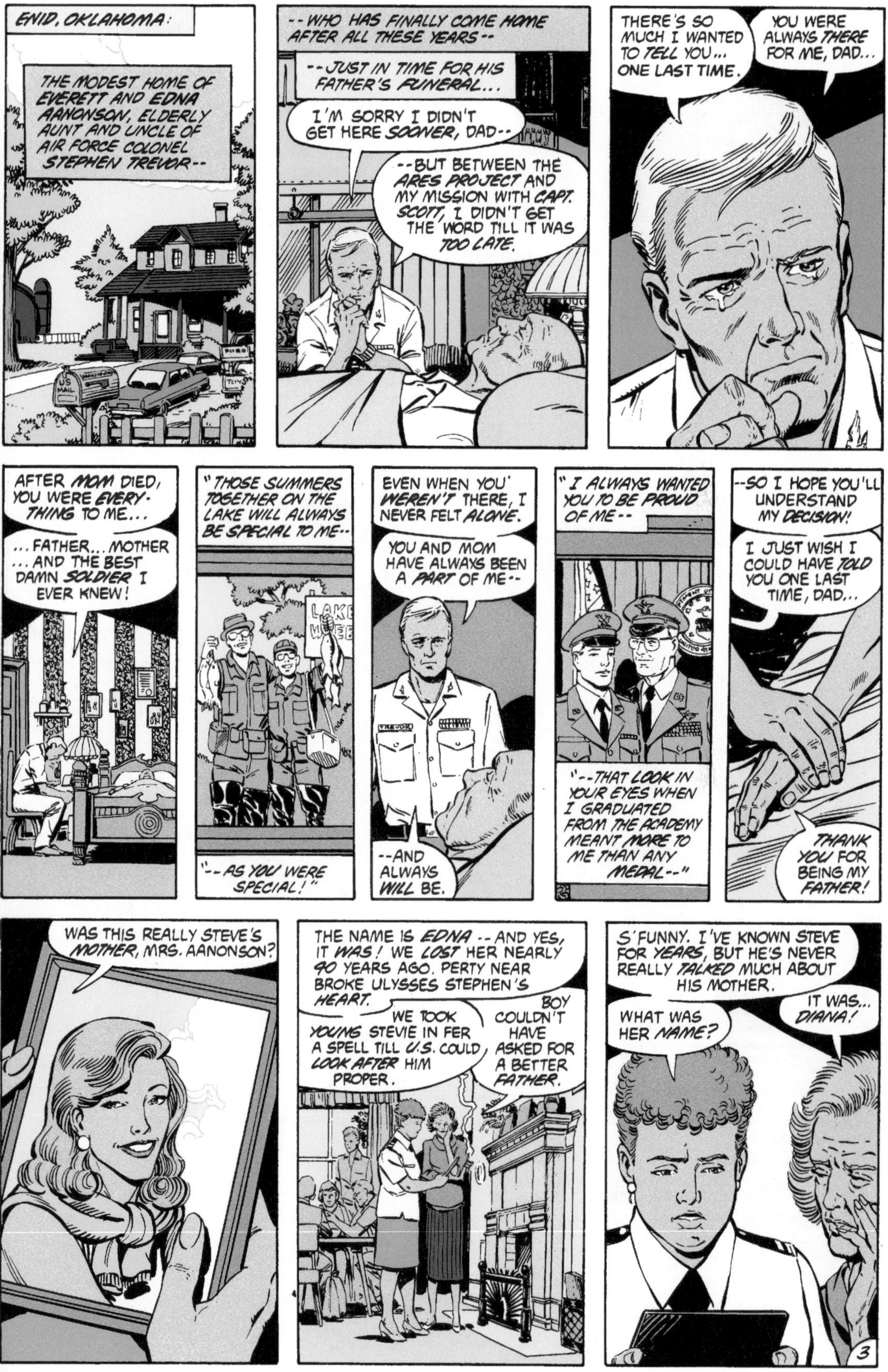

ENID, OKLAHOMA:
THE MODEST HOME OF EVERETT AND EDNA AANONSON, ELDERLY AUNT AND UNCLE OF AIR FORCE COLONEL STEPHEN TREVOR--
--WHO HAS FINALLY COME HOME AFTER ALL THESE YEARS--
--JUST IN TIME FOR HIS FATHER'S FUNERAL...
I'M SORRY I DIDN'T GET HERE SOONER, DAD--
--BUT BETWEEN THE ARES PROJECT AND MY MISSION WITH CAPT. SCOTT, I DIDN'T GET THE WORD TILL IT WAS TOO LATE.
THERE'S SO MUCH I WANTED TO TELL YOU... ONE LAST TIME.
YOU WERE ALWAYS THERE FOR ME, DAD...
AFTER MOM DIED, YOU WERE EVERYTHING TO ME...
...FATHER...MOTHER ...AND THE BEST DAMN SOLDIER I EVER KNEW!
"THOSE SUMMERS TOGETHER ON THE LAKE WILL ALWAYS BE SPECIAL TO ME--
"--AS YOU WERE SPECIAL!"
EVEN WHEN YOU WEREN'T THERE, I NEVER FELT ALONE.
YOU AND MOM HAVE ALWAYS BEEN A PART OF ME--
--AND ALWAYS WILL BE.
"I ALWAYS WANTED YOU TO BE PROUD OF ME--
"--THAT LOOK IN YOUR EYES WHEN I GRADUATED FROM THE ACADEMY MEANT MORE TO ME THAN ANY MEDAL--"
--SO I HOPE YOU'LL UNDERSTAND MY DECISION!
I JUST WISH I COULD HAVE TOLD YOU ONE LAST TIME, DAD...
THANK YOU FOR BEING MY FATHER!
WAS THIS REALLY STEVE'S MOTHER, MRS. AANONSON?
THE NAME IS EDNA -- AND YES, IT WAS! WE LOST HER NEARLY 40 YEARS AGO. PERTY NEAR BROKE ULYSSES STEPHEN'S HEART.
WE TOOK YOUNG STEVIE IN FER A SPELL TILL U.S. COULD LOOK AFTER HIM PROPER.
BOY COULDN'T HAVE ASKED FOR A BETTER FATHER.
S'FUNNY. I'VE KNOWN STEVE FOR YEARS, BUT HE'S NEVER REALLY TALKED MUCH ABOUT HIS MOTHER.
WHAT WAS HER NAME?
IT WAS... DIANA!
3

DIANA?!?

THEN *YOU*--?

ARE THE ONE FOR WHOM YOU'RE *NAMED*?

THAT'S *ME*, DIANA-- THAT SAME MYSTERIOUS *WARRIOR* YOUR MOTHER AND SISTERS WOULD NEVER *DISCUSS* WITH YOU!

I'VE *AWAITED* THIS DAY FAR LONGER THAN YOU COULD *IMAGINE*--

--BUT IF THERE'S ANYTHING I'VE *LEARNED* HERE, IT'S THAT LIFE ON THE *MORTAL COIL* FOLLOWS A GRAND DESIGN!

WE WERE *FATED* TO MEET, CHILD--FROM THE DAY YOU WERE *BORN*!

IT'S TIME YOU LEARNED OF YOUR TRUE *HERITAGE*!

BUT THE *CHALLENGE OF THE GODS*--?!?

CHALLENGES COME IN *MANY* FORMS, PRINCESS...

THE CHALLENGE TO ACCEPT YOUR OWN *SIGNIFICANCE* IS IN MANY WAYS MORE *DIFFICULT* THAN BATTLING ANY *HYDRA*!

BETTER SIT DOWN, DIANA-- WE HAVE A LOT TO *TALK* ABOUT.

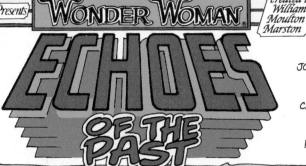

DC Comics Proudly Presents

WONDER WOMAN

created by William Moulton Marston

ECHOES OF THE PAST

CHALLENGE OF THE GODS BOOK 3

plot and layouts by GEORGE PÉREZ

script by LEN WEIN

finishes by BRUCE D. PATTERSON

lettered by JOHN COSTANZA

colored by CARL GAFFORD

edited by KAREN BERGER

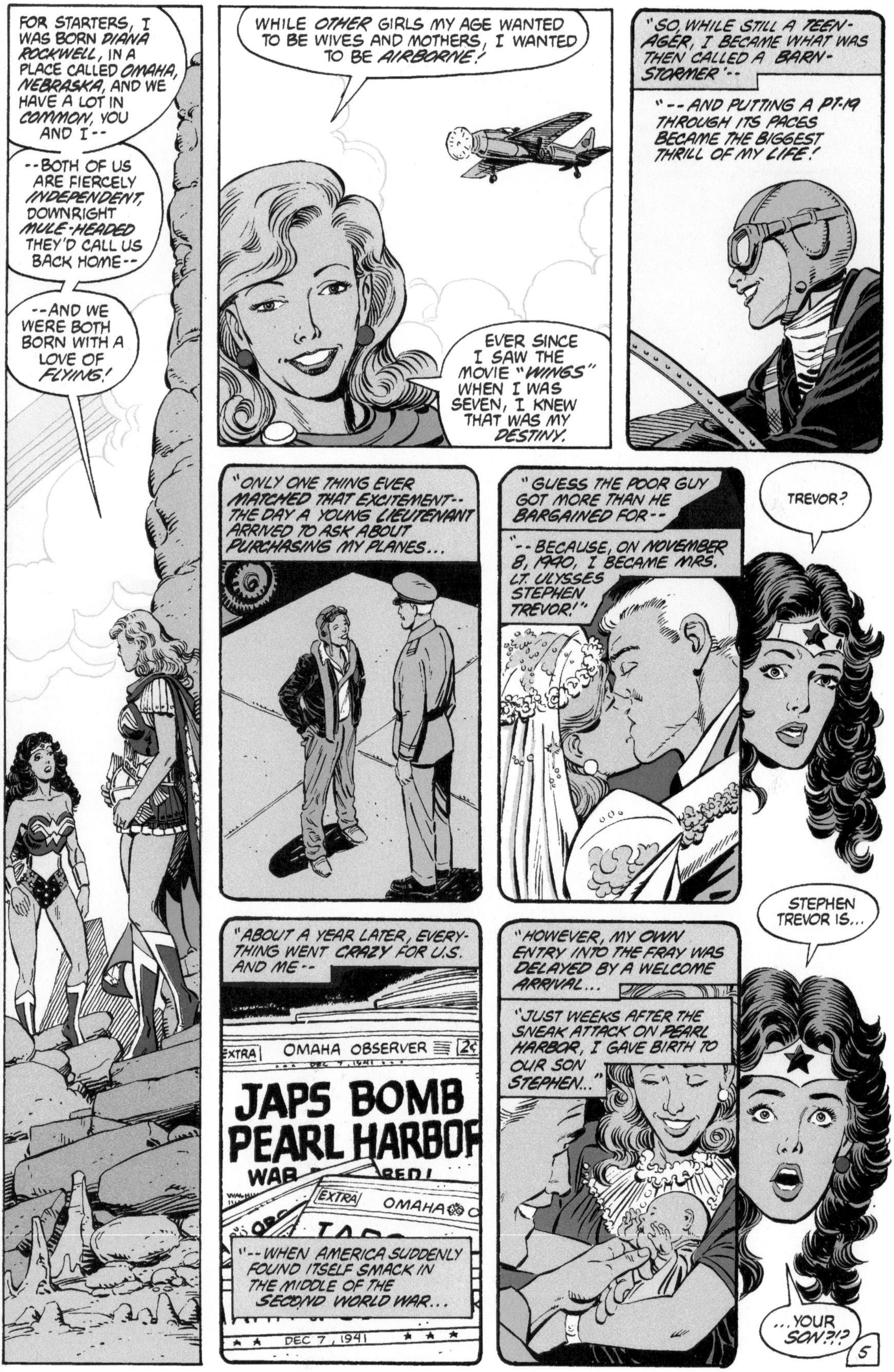
FOR STARTERS, I WAS BORN DIANA ROCKWELL, IN A PLACE CALLED OMAHA, NEBRASKA, AND WE HAVE A LOT IN COMMON, YOU AND I--
--BOTH OF US ARE FIERCELY INDEPENDENT, DOWNRIGHT MULE-HEADED THEY'D CALL US BACK HOME--
--AND WE WERE BOTH BORN WITH A LOVE OF FLYING!
WHILE OTHER GIRLS MY AGE WANTED TO BE WIVES AND MOTHERS, I WANTED TO BE AIRBORNE!
EVER SINCE I SAW THE MOVIE "WINGS" WHEN I WAS SEVEN, I KNEW THAT WAS MY DESTINY.
"SO, WHILE STILL A TEEN-AGER, I BECAME WHAT WAS THEN CALLED A BARN-STORMER'--
"--AND PUTTING A PT-19 THROUGH ITS PACES BECAME THE BIGGEST THRILL OF MY LIFE!
"ONLY ONE THING EVER MATCHED THAT EXCITEMENT--THE DAY A YOUNG LIEUTENANT ARRIVED TO ASK ABOUT PURCHASING MY PLANES...
"GUESS THE POOR GUY GOT MORE THAN HE BARGAINED FOR--
"--BECAUSE, ON NOVEMBER 8, 1940, I BECAME MRS. LT. ULYSSES STEPHEN TREVOR!"
TREVOR?
"ABOUT A YEAR LATER, EVERY-THING WENT CRAZY FOR U.S. AND ME--
EXTRA OMAHA OBSERVER 2¢
DEC 7, 1941
JAPS BOMB PEARL HARBOR
EXTRA OMAHA
"--WHEN AMERICA SUDDENLY FOUND ITSELF SMACK IN THE MIDDLE OF THE SECOND WORLD WAR...
DEC 7, 1941
"HOWEVER, MY OWN ENTRY INTO THE FRAY WAS DELAYED BY A WELCOME ARRIVAL...
"JUST WEEKS AFTER THE SNEAK ATTACK ON PEARL HARBOR, I GAVE BIRTH TO OUR SON STEPHEN..."
STEPHEN TREVOR IS...
...YOUR SON?!?
5

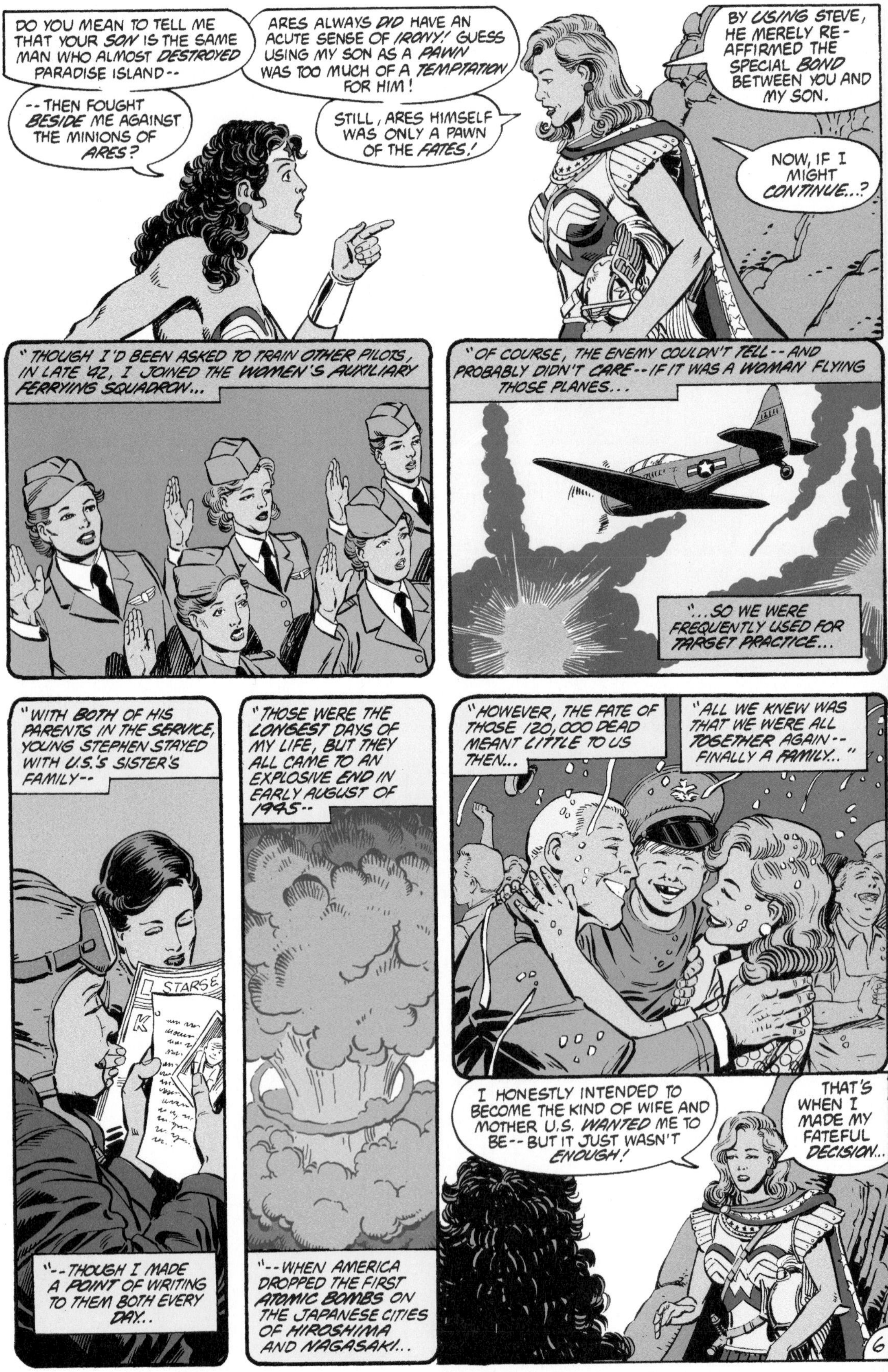
DO YOU MEAN TO TELL ME THAT YOUR SON IS THE SAME MAN WHO ALMOST DESTROYED PARADISE ISLAND--
--THEN FOUGHT BESIDE ME AGAINST THE MINIONS OF ARES?
ARES ALWAYS DID HAVE AN ACUTE SENSE OF IRONY! GUESS USING MY SON AS A PAWN WAS TOO MUCH OF A TEMPTATION FOR HIM!
STILL, ARES HIMSELF WAS ONLY A PAWN OF THE FATES!
BY USING STEVE, HE MERELY RE-AFFIRMED THE SPECIAL BOND BETWEEN YOU AND MY SON.
NOW, IF I MIGHT CONTINUE...?
"THOUGH I'D BEEN ASKED TO TRAIN OTHER PILOTS, IN LATE '42, I JOINED THE WOMEN'S AUXILIARY FERRYING SQUADRON...
"OF COURSE, THE ENEMY COULDN'T TELL--AND PROBABLY DIDN'T CARE--IF IT WAS A WOMAN FLYING THOSE PLANES...
"...SO WE WERE FREQUENTLY USED FOR TARGET PRACTICE...
"WITH BOTH OF HIS PARENTS IN THE SERVICE, YOUNG STEPHEN STAYED WITH U.S.'S SISTER'S FAMILY--
"--THOUGH I MADE A POINT OF WRITING TO THEM BOTH EVERY DAY...
"THOSE WERE THE LONGEST DAYS OF MY LIFE, BUT THEY ALL CAME TO AN EXPLOSIVE END IN EARLY AUGUST OF 1945--
"--WHEN AMERICA DROPPED THE FIRST ATOMIC BOMBS ON THE JAPANESE CITIES OF HIROSHIMA AND NAGASAKI...
"HOWEVER, THE FATE OF THOSE 120,000 DEAD MEANT LITTLE TO US THEN...
"ALL WE KNEW WAS THAT WE WERE ALL TOGETHER AGAIN--FINALLY A FAMILY..."
I HONESTLY INTENDED TO BECOME THE KIND OF WIFE AND MOTHER U.S. WANTED ME TO BE--BUT IT JUST WASN'T ENOUGH!
THAT'S WHEN I MADE MY FATEFUL DECISION...
6

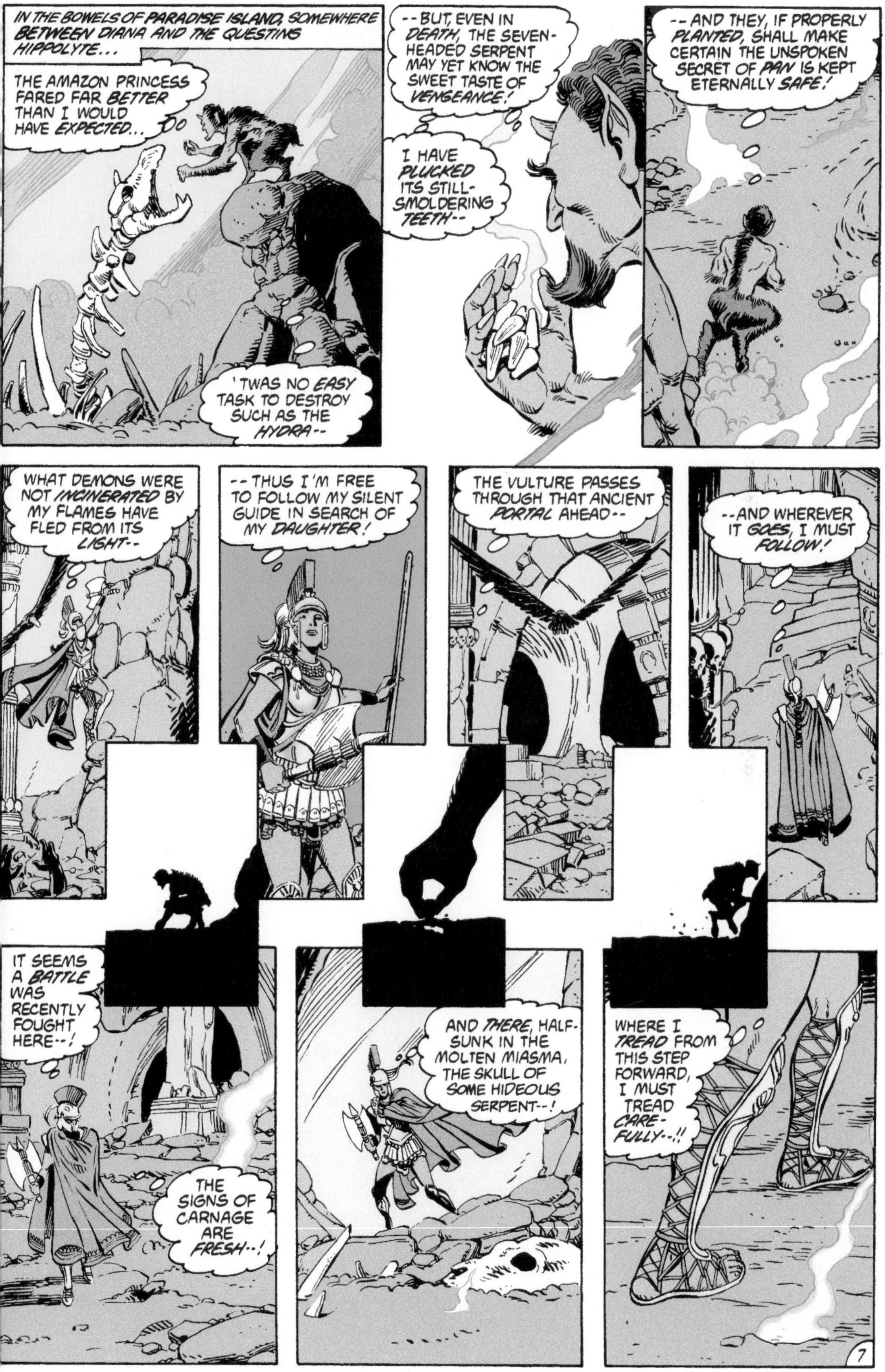
IN THE BOWELS OF PARADISE ISLAND, SOMEWHERE BETWEEN DIANA AND THE QUESTING HIPPOLYTE...
THE AMAZON PRINCESS FARED FAR BETTER THAN I WOULD HAVE EXPECTED...
'TWAS NO EASY TASK TO DESTROY SUCH AS THE HYDRA--
--BUT, EVEN IN DEATH, THE SEVEN-HEADED SERPENT MAY YET KNOW THE SWEET TASTE OF VENGEANCE!
I HAVE PLUCKED ITS STILL-SMOLDERING TEETH--
--AND THEY, IF PROPERLY PLANTED, SHALL MAKE CERTAIN THE UNSPOKEN SECRET OF PAN IS KEPT ETERNALLY SAFE!
WHAT DEMONS WERE NOT INCINERATED BY MY FLAMES HAVE FLED FROM ITS LIGHT--
--THUS I'M FREE TO FOLLOW MY SILENT GUIDE IN SEARCH OF MY DAUGHTER!
THE VULTURE PASSES THROUGH THAT ANCIENT PORTAL AHEAD--
--AND WHEREVER IT GOES, I MUST FOLLOW!
IT SEEMS A BATTLE WAS RECENTLY FOUGHT HERE--!
THE SIGNS OF CARNAGE ARE FRESH--!
AND THERE, HALF-SUNK IN THE MOLTEN MIASMA, THE SKULL OF SOME HIDEOUS SERPENT--!
WHERE I TREAD FROM THIS STEP FORWARD, I MUST TREAD CARE-FULLY--!!
7

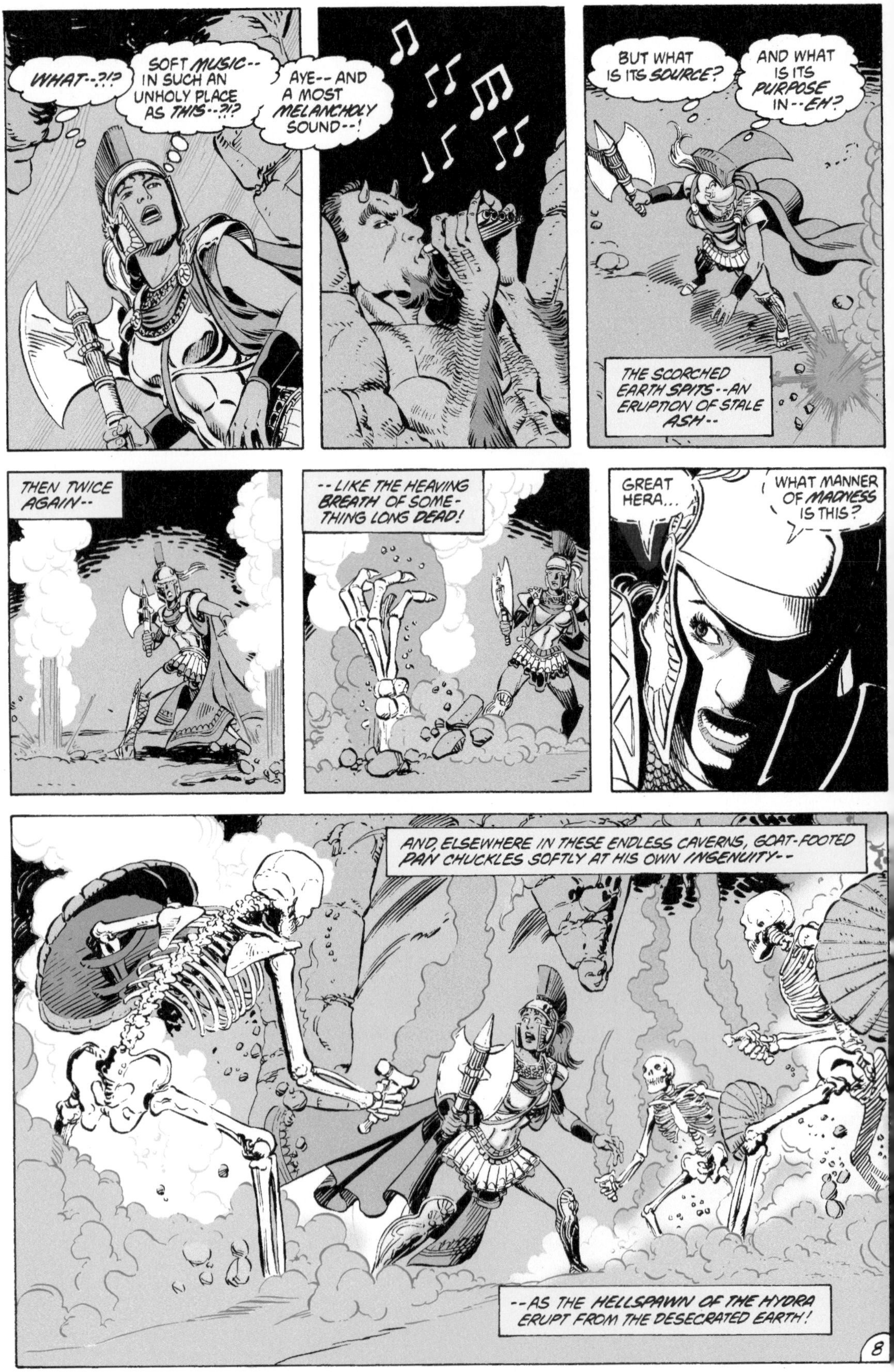
WHAT--?!?
SOFT MUSIC-- IN SUCH AN UNHOLY PLACE AS THIS--?!?
AYE-- AND A MOST MELANCHOLY SOUND--!
BUT WHAT IS ITS SOURCE?
AND WHAT IS ITS PURPOSE IN--EH?
THE SCORCHED EARTH SPITS--AN ERUPTION OF STALE ASH--
THEN TWICE AGAIN--
--LIKE THE HEAVING BREATH OF SOMETHING LONG DEAD!
GREAT HERA...
WHAT MANNER OF MADNESS IS THIS?
AND, ELSEWHERE IN THESE ENDLESS CAVERNS, GOAT-FOOTED PAN CHUCKLES SOFTLY AT HIS OWN INGENUITY--
--AS THE HELLSPAWN OF THE HYDRA ERUPT FROM THE DESECRATED EARTH!
8

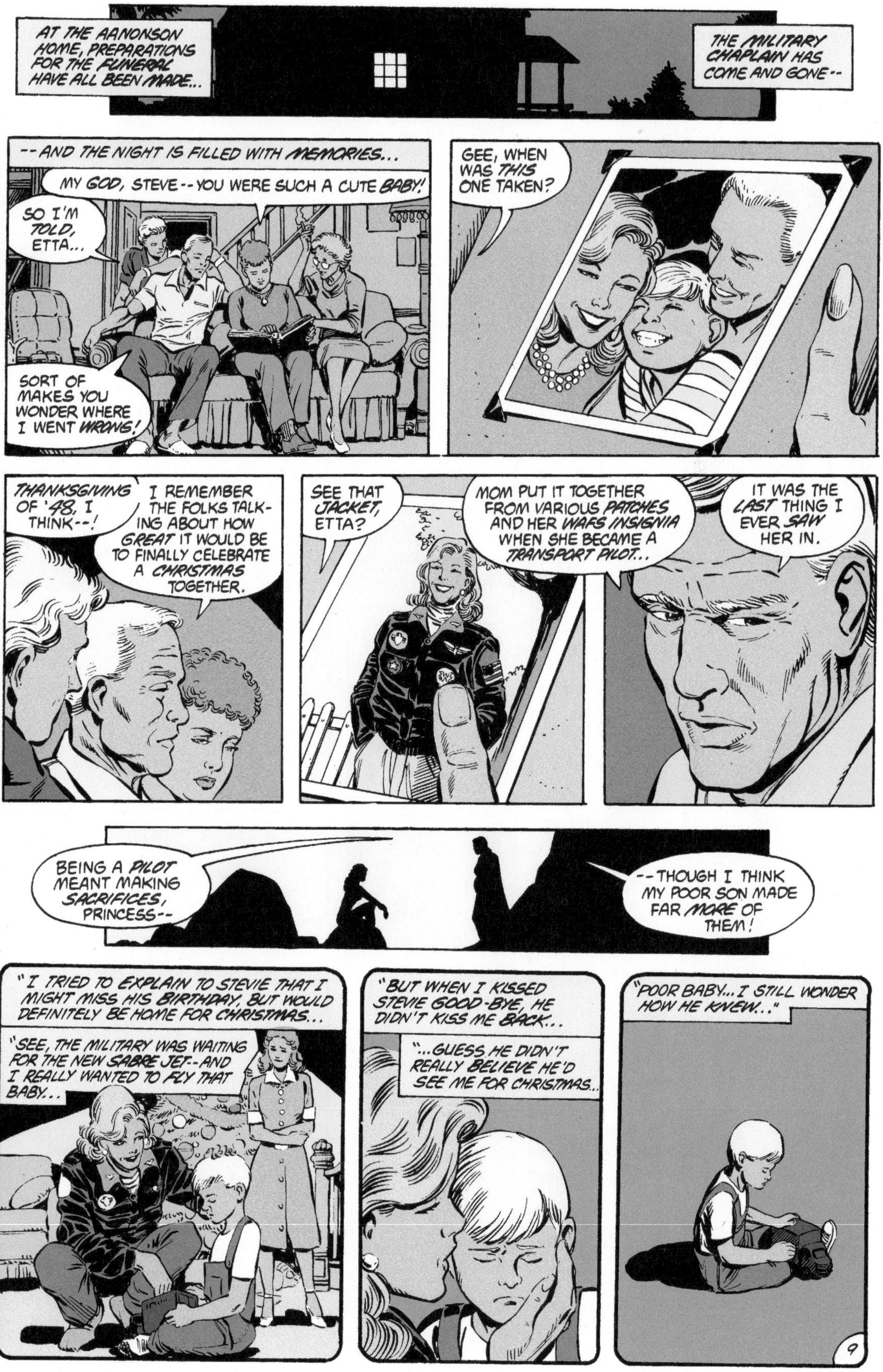

AT THE AANONSON HOME, PREPARATIONS FOR THE FUNERAL HAVE ALL BEEN MADE...
THE MILITARY CHAPLAIN HAS COME AND GONE--
--AND THE NIGHT IS FILLED WITH MEMORIES...
MY GOD, STEVE--YOU WERE SUCH A CUTE BABY!
SO I'M TOLD, ETTA...
SORT OF MAKES YOU WONDER WHERE I WENT WRONG!
GEE, WHEN WAS THIS ONE TAKEN?
THANKSGIVING OF '48, I THINK--!
I REMEMBER THE FOLKS TALKING ABOUT HOW GREAT IT WOULD BE TO FINALLY CELEBRATE A CHRISTMAS TOGETHER.
SEE THAT JACKET, ETTA?
MOM PUT IT TOGETHER FROM VARIOUS PATCHES AND HER WAFS INSIGNIA WHEN SHE BECAME A TRANSPORT PILOT...
IT WAS THE LAST THING I EVER SAW HER IN.
BEING A PILOT MEANT MAKING SACRIFICES, PRINCESS--
--THOUGH I THINK MY POOR SON MADE FAR MORE OF THEM!
"I TRIED TO EXPLAIN TO STEVIE THAT I MIGHT MISS HIS BIRTHDAY, BUT WOULD DEFINITELY BE HOME FOR CHRISTMAS...
"SEE, THE MILITARY WAS WAITING FOR THE NEW SABRE JET--AND I REALLY WANTED TO FLY THAT BABY...
"BUT WHEN I KISSED STEVIE GOOD-BYE, HE DIDN'T KISS ME BACK...
"...GUESS HE DIDN'T REALLY BELIEVE HE'D SEE ME FOR CHRISTMAS...
"POOR BABY...I STILL WONDER HOW HE KNEW..."
9

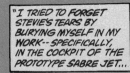
"I TRIED TO FORGET STEVIE'S TEARS BY BURYING MYSELF IN MY WORK--SPECIFICALLY, IN THE COCKPIT OF THE PROTOTYPE SABRE JET...

"JETS WERE STILL NEW TO ME--AND THE THRILL MADE ME FORGET EVERYTHING EXCEPT THE SHEER JOY OF FLYING...

"I'M STILL NOT SURE EXACTLY WHEN IT STARTED--

"--BUT I SUDDENLY FOUND MYSELF IN THE THICK OF THE WORST LIGHTNING STORM I'D EVER ENCOUNTERED...

"MY INSTRUMENTS WENT COMPLETELY WILD... SUDDENLY, NOTHING MADE SENSE ANYMORE...

"THEN, A LIGHTNING-BOLT SHATTERED MY LEFT WING!"

"EVERYTHING HAPPENED PRETTY QUICKLY AFTER THAT...

"I MANAGED TO EJECT IN TIME-- BUT THE BUFFETING WINDS SWEPT ME BACK TOWARDS THE PLUMMETING PLANE...

"THEN, BY WHAT I THOUGHT WAS A ONE-IN-A-MILLION FLUKE, THE SHEARED WING RIPPED MY PARACHUTE--

"--AND THE SABRE JET AND I PLUNGED LIKE ROCKS INTO THE CHURNING SEA...

"THE IMPACT OF MY FALL KNOCKED ME SENSELESS--

"--BUT EVEN AS I LOST CONSCIOUSNESS--

"--I COULD SWEAR THE WATER CAME ALIVE!"

SUDDENLY...

...MY LIFE WAS IN THE HANDS OF THE GODS!

10

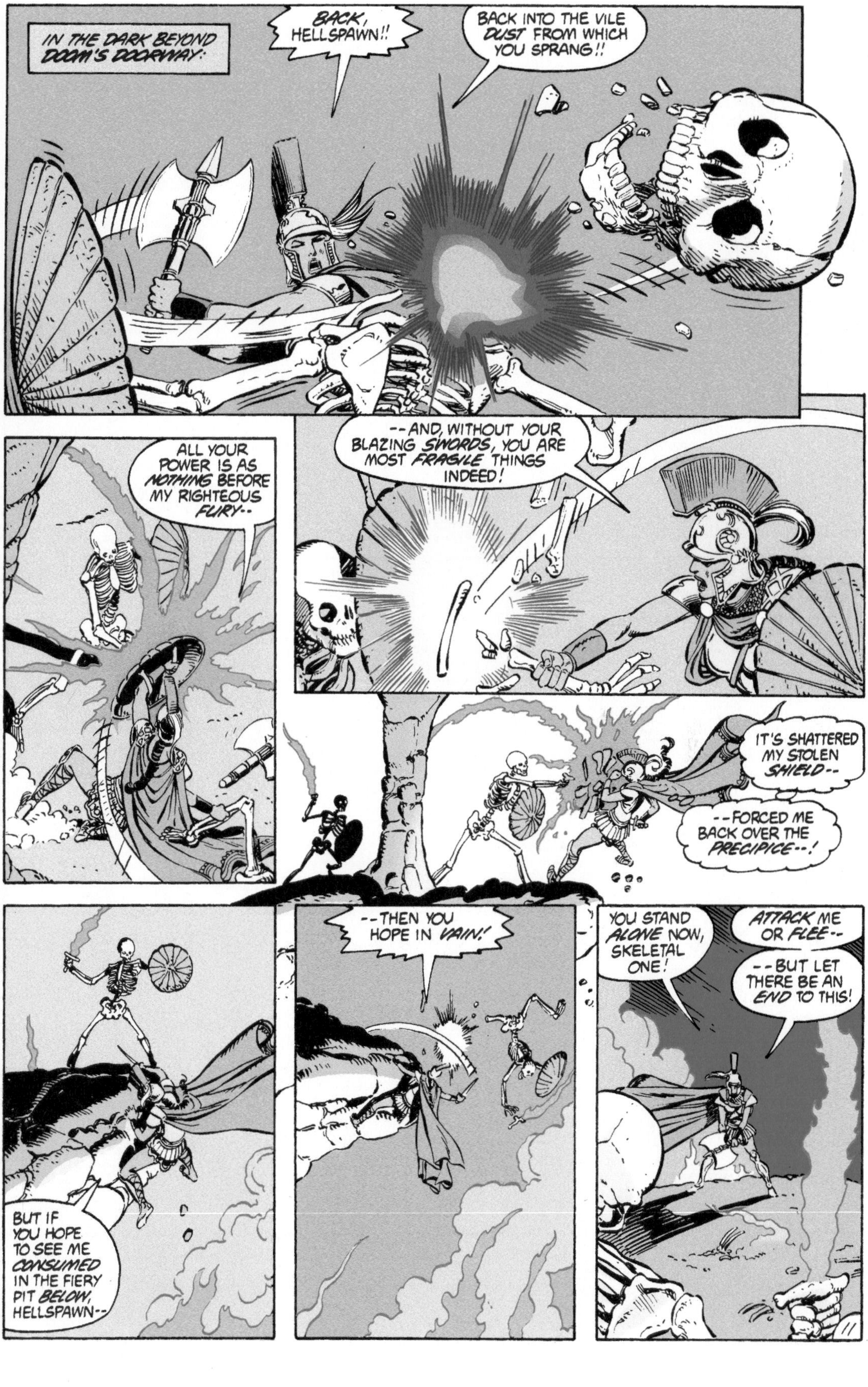
IN THE DARK BEYOND DOOM'S DOORWAY:
BACK, HELLSPAWN!!
BACK INTO THE VILE DUST FROM WHICH YOU SPRANG!!
ALL YOUR POWER IS AS NOTHING BEFORE MY RIGHTEOUS FURY--
--AND, WITHOUT YOUR BLAZING SWORDS, YOU ARE MOST FRAGILE THINGS INDEED!
IT'S SHATTERED MY STOLEN SHIELD--
--FORCED ME BACK OVER THE PRECIPICE--!
BUT IF YOU HOPE TO SEE ME CONSUMED IN THE FIERY PIT BELOW, HELLSPAWN--
--THEN YOU HOPE IN VAIN!
YOU STAND ALONE NOW, SKELETAL ONE!
ATTACK ME OR FLEE--
--BUT LET THERE BE AN END TO THIS!

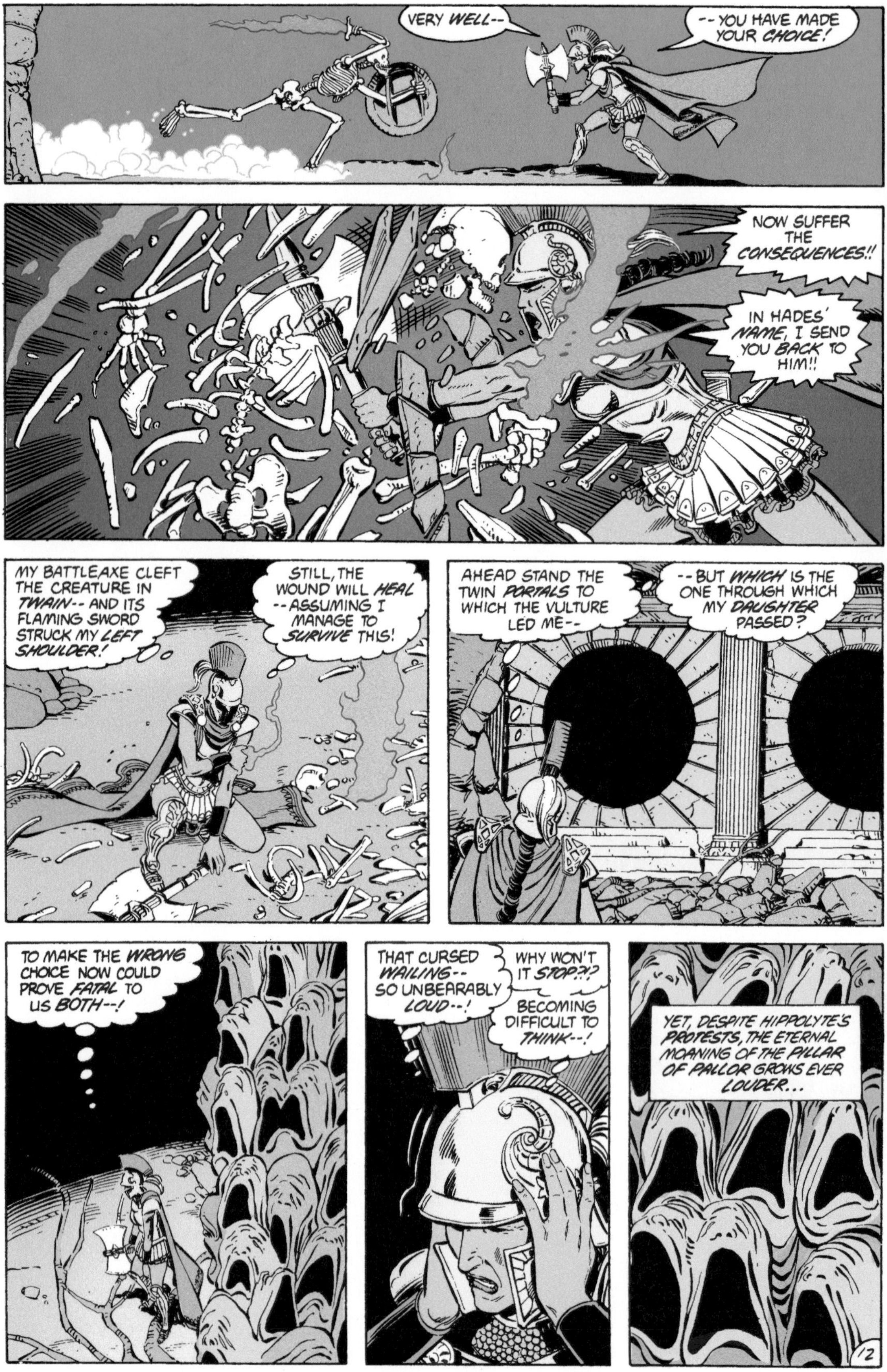

VERY WELL--
--YOU HAVE MADE YOUR CHOICE!
NOW SUFFER THE CONSEQUENCES!!
IN HADES' NAME, I SEND YOU BACK TO HIM!!
MY BATTLEAXE CLEFT THE CREATURE IN TWAIN-- AND ITS FLAMING SWORD STRUCK MY LEFT SHOULDER!
STILL, THE WOUND WILL HEAL --ASSUMING I MANAGE TO SURVIVE THIS!
AHEAD STAND THE TWIN PORTALS TO WHICH THE VULTURE LED ME--
--BUT WHICH IS THE ONE THROUGH WHICH MY DAUGHTER PASSED?
TO MAKE THE WRONG CHOICE NOW COULD PROVE FATAL TO US BOTH--!
THAT CURSED WAILING-- SO UNBEARABLY LOUD--!
WHY WON'T IT STOP?!?
BECOMING DIFFICULT TO THINK--!
YET, DESPITE HIPPOLYTE'S PROTESTS, THE ETERNAL MOANING OF THE PILLAR OF PALLOR GROWS EVER LOUDER...
12

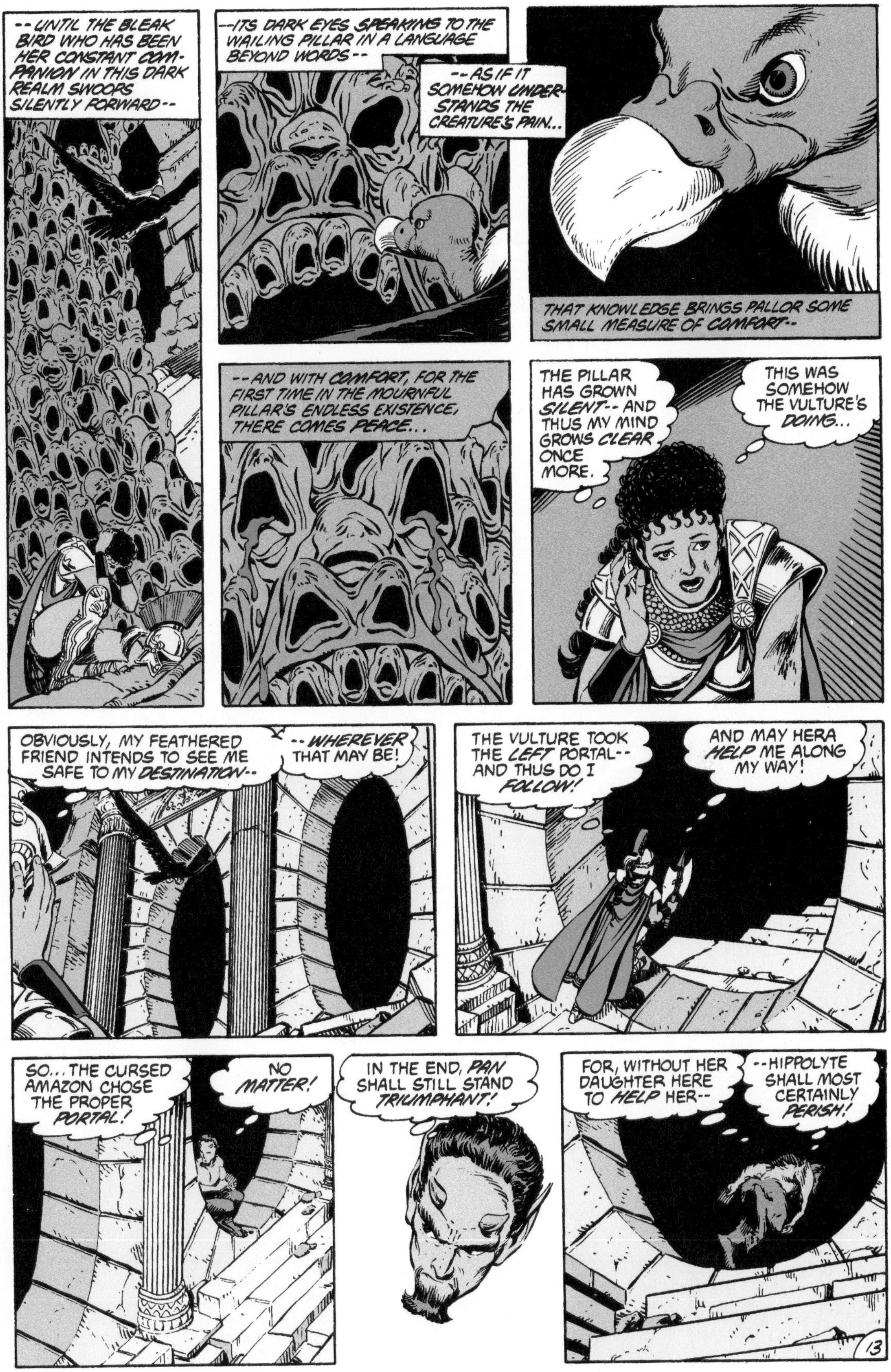

--UNTIL THE BLEAK BIRD WHO HAS BEEN HER CONSTANT COMPANION IN THIS DARK REALM SWOOPS SILENTLY FORWARD--
--ITS DARK EYES SPEAKING TO THE WAILING PILLAR IN A LANGUAGE BEYOND WORDS--
--AS IF IT SOMEHOW UNDERSTANDS THE CREATURE'S PAIN...
THAT KNOWLEDGE BRINGS PALLOR SOME SMALL MEASURE OF COMFORT--
--AND WITH COMFORT, FOR THE FIRST TIME IN THE MOURNFUL PILLAR'S ENDLESS EXISTENCE, THERE COMES PEACE...
THE PILLAR HAS GROWN SILENT-- AND THUS MY MIND GROWS CLEAR ONCE MORE.
THIS WAS SOMEHOW THE VULTURE'S DOING...
OBVIOUSLY, MY FEATHERED FRIEND INTENDS TO SEE ME SAFE TO MY DESTINATION--
--WHEREVER THAT MAY BE!
THE VULTURE TOOK THE LEFT PORTAL-- AND THUS DO I FOLLOW!
AND MAY HERA HELP ME ALONG MY WAY!
SO... THE CURSED AMAZON CHOSE THE PROPER PORTAL!
NO MATTER!
IN THE END, PAN SHALL STILL STAND TRIUMPHANT!
FOR, WITHOUT HER DAUGHTER HERE TO HELP HER--
--HIPPOLYTE SHALL MOST CERTAINLY PERISH!
13

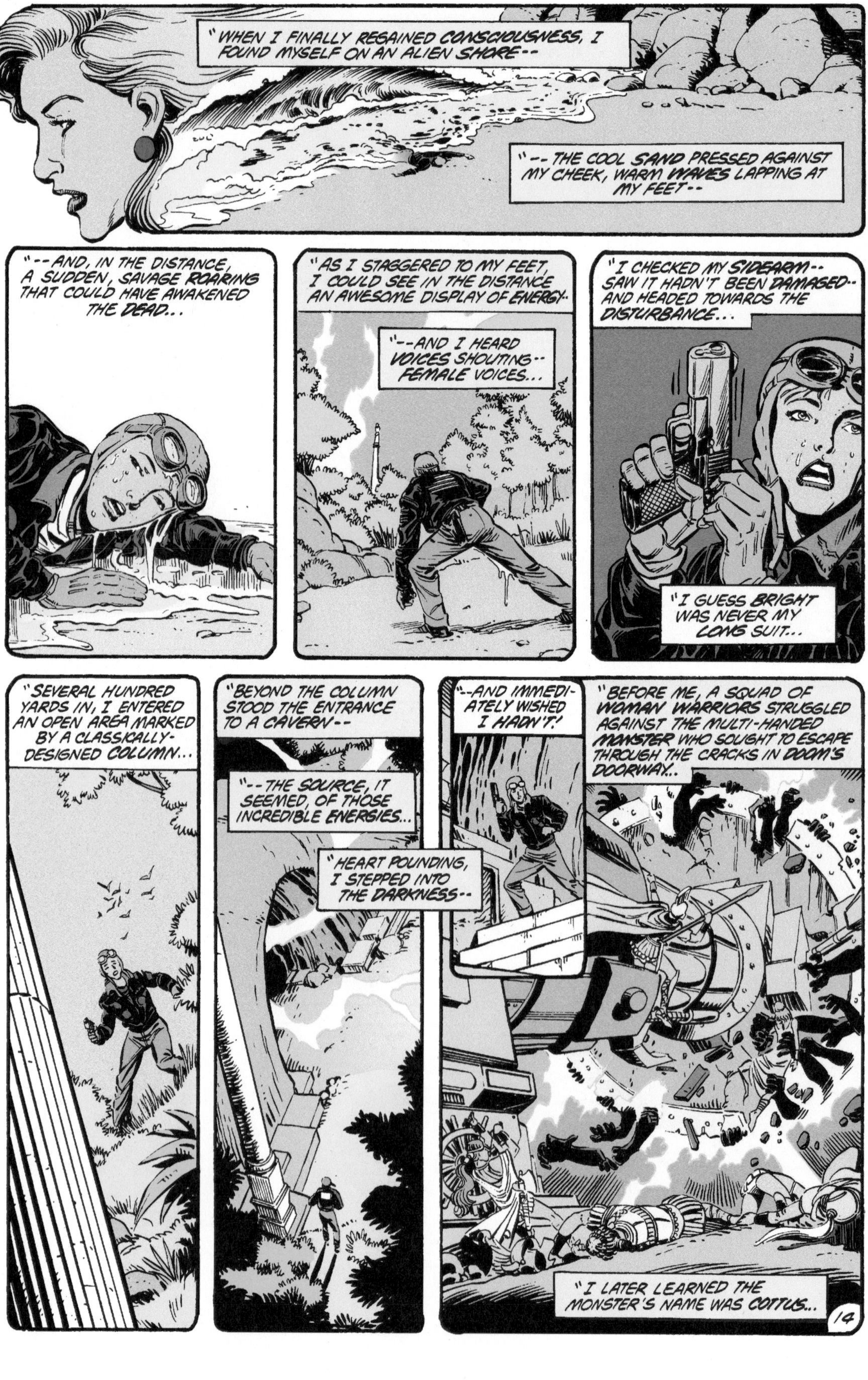
"WHEN I FINALLY REGAINED CONSCIOUSNESS, I FOUND MYSELF ON AN ALIEN SHORE--
"--THE COOL SAND PRESSED AGAINST MY CHEEK, WARM WAVES LAPPING AT MY FEET--
"--AND, IN THE DISTANCE, A SUDDEN, SAVAGE ROARING THAT COULD HAVE AWAKENED THE DEAD...
"AS I STAGGERED TO MY FEET, I COULD SEE IN THE DISTANCE AN AWESOME DISPLAY OF ENERGY-
"--AND I HEARD VOICES SHOUTING--FEMALE VOICES...
"I CHECKED MY SIDEARM--SAW IT HADN'T BEEN DAMAGED--AND HEADED TOWARDS THE DISTURBANCE...
"I GUESS BRIGHT WAS NEVER MY LONG SUIT...
"SEVERAL HUNDRED YARDS IN, I ENTERED AN OPEN AREA MARKED BY A CLASSICALLY-DESIGNED COLUMN...
"BEYOND THE COLUMN STOOD THE ENTRANCE TO A CAVERN--
"--THE SOURCE, IT SEEMED, OF THOSE INCREDIBLE ENERGIES...
"HEART POUNDING, I STEPPED INTO THE DARKNESS--
"--AND IMMEDIATELY WISHED I HADN'T!
"BEFORE ME, A SQUAD OF WOMAN WARRIORS STRUGGLED AGAINST THE MULTI-HANDED MONSTER WHO SOUGHT TO ESCAPE THROUGH THE CRACKS IN DOOM'S DOORWAY...
"I LATER LEARNED THE MONSTER'S NAME WAS COTTUS...
14

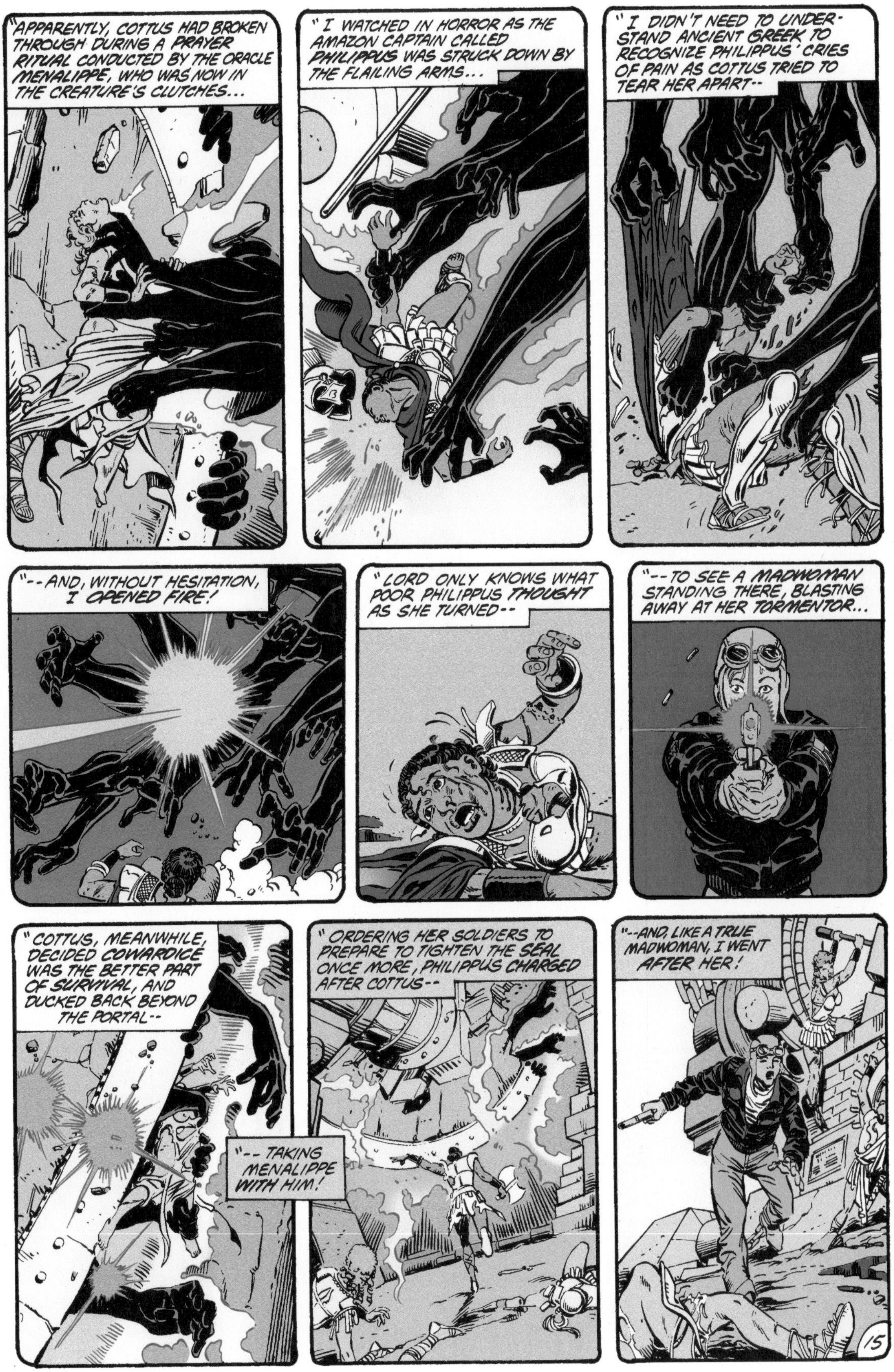
"APPARENTLY, COTTUS HAD BROKEN THROUGH DURING A PRAYER RITUAL CONDUCTED BY THE ORACLE MENALIPPE, WHO WAS NOW IN THE CREATURE'S CLUTCHES...
"I WATCHED IN HORROR AS THE AMAZON CAPTAIN CALLED PHILIPPUS WAS STRUCK DOWN BY THE FLAILING ARMS...
"I DIDN'T NEED TO UNDERSTAND ANCIENT GREEK TO RECOGNIZE PHILIPPUS' CRIES OF PAIN AS COTTUS TRIED TO TEAR HER APART--
"--AND, WITHOUT HESITATION, I OPENED FIRE!
"LORD ONLY KNOWS WHAT POOR PHILIPPUS THOUGHT AS SHE TURNED--
"--TO SEE A MADWOMAN STANDING THERE, BLASTING AWAY AT HER TORMENTOR...
"COTTUS, MEANWHILE, DECIDED COWARDICE WAS THE BETTER PART OF SURVIVAL, AND DUCKED BACK BEYOND THE PORTAL--
"--TAKING MENALIPPE WITH HIM!
"ORDERING HER SOLDIERS TO PREPARE TO TIGHTEN THE SEAL ONCE MORE, PHILIPPUS CHARGED AFTER COTTUS--
"--AND, LIKE A TRUE MADWOMAN, I WENT AFTER HER!
15

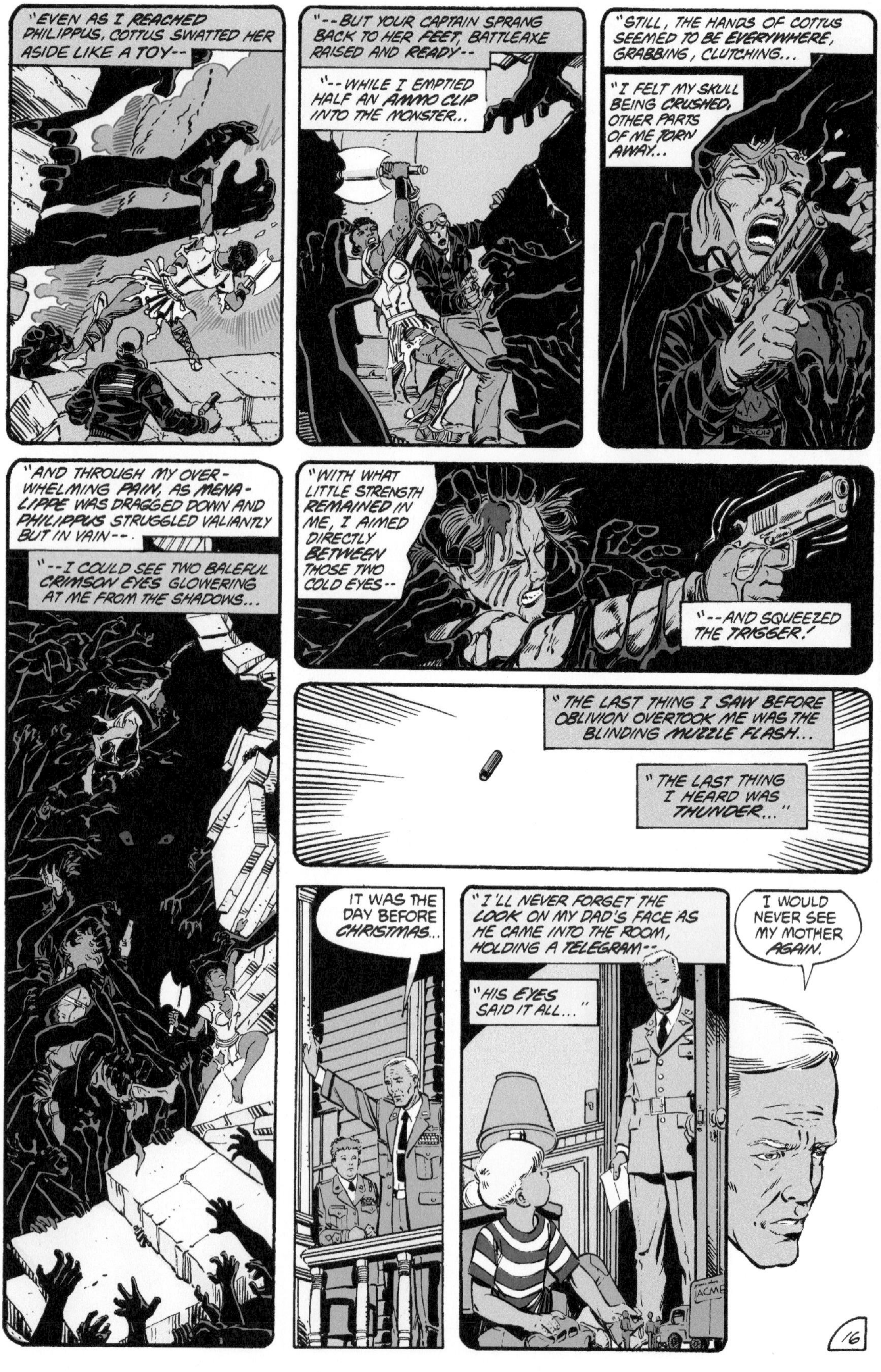
"EVEN AS I REACHED PHILIPPUS, COTTUS SWATTED HER ASIDE LIKE A TOY--
"--BUT YOUR CAPTAIN SPRANG BACK TO HER FEET, BATTLEAXE RAISED AND READY--
"--WHILE I EMPTIED HALF AN AMMO CLIP INTO THE MONSTER...
"STILL, THE HANDS OF COTTUS SEEMED TO BE EVERYWHERE, GRABBING, CLUTCHING...
"I FELT MY SKULL BEING CRUSHED, OTHER PARTS OF ME TORN AWAY...
"AND THROUGH MY OVER-WHELMING PAIN, AS MENA-LIPPE WAS DRAGGED DOWN AND PHILIPPUS STRUGGLED VALIANTLY BUT IN VAIN--
"--I COULD SEE TWO BALEFUL CRIMSON EYES GLOWERING AT ME FROM THE SHADOWS...
"WITH WHAT LITTLE STRENGTH REMAINED IN ME, I AIMED DIRECTLY BETWEEN THOSE TWO COLD EYES--
"--AND SQUEEZED THE TRIGGER!
"THE LAST THING I SAW BEFORE OBLIVION OVERTOOK ME WAS THE BLINDING MUZZLE FLASH...
"THE LAST THING I HEARD WAS THUNDER..."
IT WAS THE DAY BEFORE CHRISTMAS...
"I'LL NEVER FORGET THE LOOK ON MY DAD'S FACE AS HE CAME INTO THE ROOM, HOLDING A TELEGRAM--
"HIS EYES SAID IT ALL..."
I WOULD NEVER SEE MY MOTHER AGAIN.
ACME
16

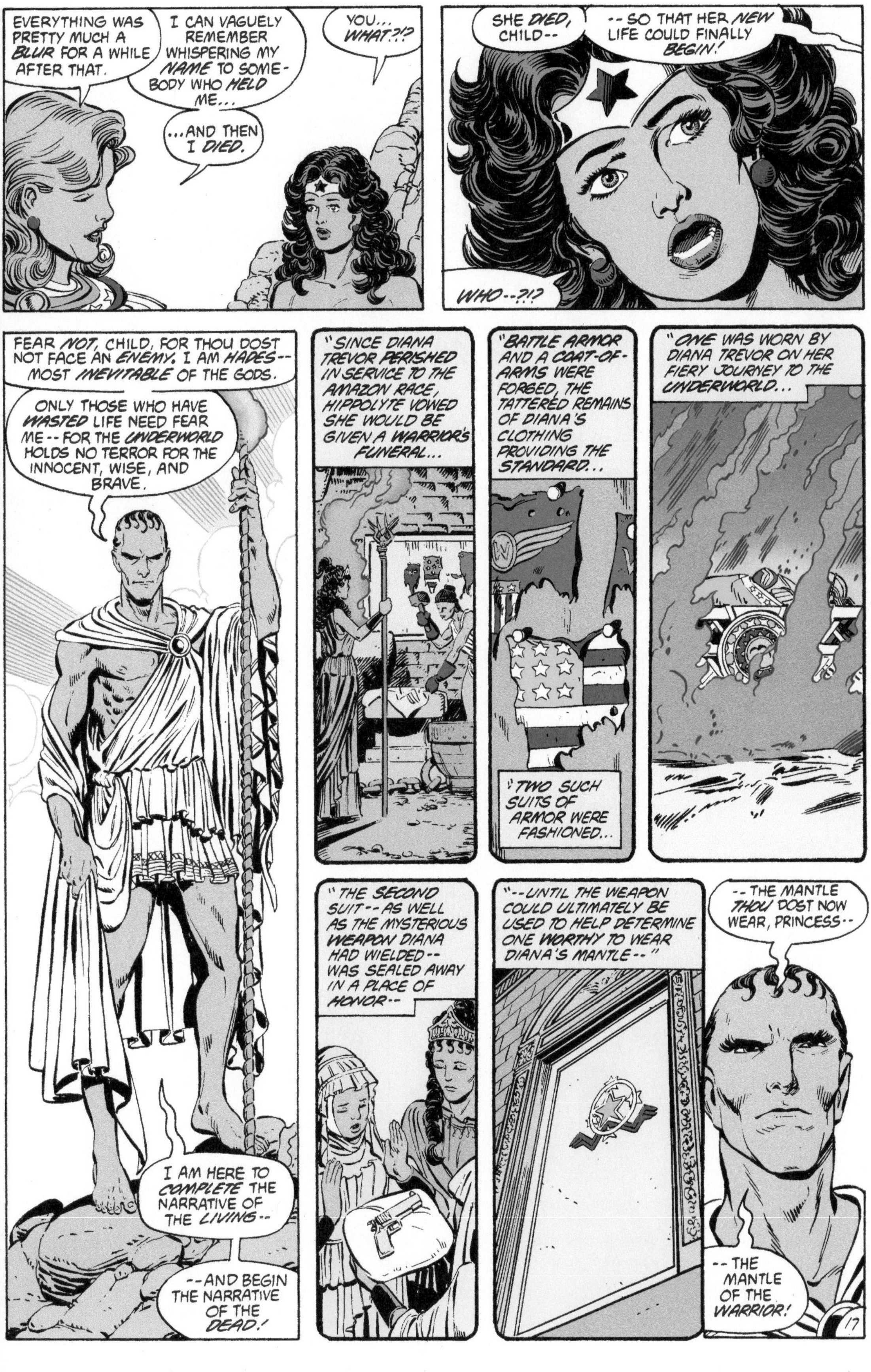

EVERYTHING WAS PRETTY MUCH A BLUR FOR A WHILE AFTER THAT.
I CAN VAGUELY REMEMBER WHISPERING MY NAME TO SOMEBODY WHO HELD ME...
...AND THEN I DIED.
YOU... WHAT?!?
SHE DIED, CHILD--
--SO THAT HER NEW LIFE COULD FINALLY BEGIN!
WHO--?!?
FEAR NOT, CHILD, FOR THOU DOST NOT FACE AN ENEMY. I AM HADES--MOST INEVITABLE OF THE GODS.
ONLY THOSE WHO HAVE WASTED LIFE NEED FEAR ME--FOR THE UNDERWORLD HOLDS NO TERROR FOR THE INNOCENT, WISE, AND BRAVE.
I AM HERE TO COMPLETE THE NARRATIVE OF THE LIVING--
--AND BEGIN THE NARRATIVE OF THE DEAD!
"SINCE DIANA TREVOR PERISHED IN SERVICE TO THE AMAZON RACE, HIPPOLYTE VOWED SHE WOULD BE GIVEN A WARRIOR'S FUNERAL...
"BATTLE ARMOR AND A COAT-OF-ARMS WERE FORGED, THE TATTERED REMAINS OF DIANA'S CLOTHING PROVIDING THE STANDARD...
"TWO SUCH SUITS OF ARMOR WERE FASHIONED...
"ONE WAS WORN BY DIANA TREVOR ON HER FIERY JOURNEY TO THE UNDERWORLD...
"THE SECOND SUIT--AS WELL AS THE MYSTERIOUS WEAPON DIANA HAD WIELDED--WAS SEALED AWAY IN A PLACE OF HONOR--
"--UNTIL THE WEAPON COULD ULTIMATELY BE USED TO HELP DETERMINE ONE WORTHY TO WEAR DIANA'S MANTLE--"
--THE MANTLE THOU DOST NOW WEAR, PRINCESS--
--THE MANTLE OF THE WARRIOR!
17

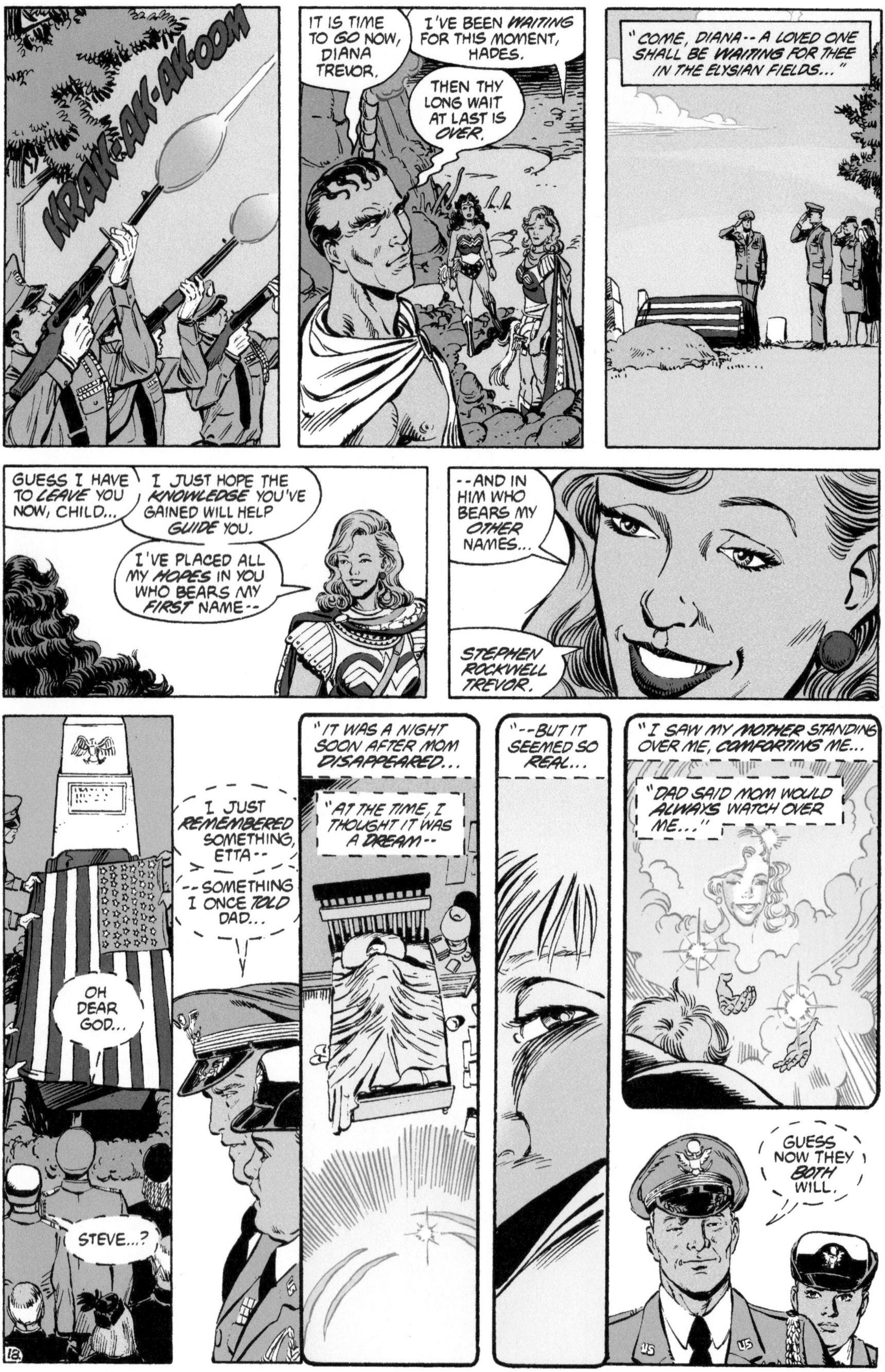
KRAK-AK-AK-OOM
IT IS TIME TO GO NOW, DIANA TREVOR.
I'VE BEEN WAITING FOR THIS MOMENT, HADES.
THEN THY LONG WAIT AT LAST IS OVER.
"COME, DIANA-- A LOVED ONE SHALL BE WAITING FOR THEE IN THE ELYSIAN FIELDS..."
GUESS I HAVE TO LEAVE YOU NOW, CHILD...
I JUST HOPE THE KNOWLEDGE YOU'VE GAINED WILL HELP GUIDE YOU.
I'VE PLACED ALL MY HOPES IN YOU WHO BEARS MY FIRST NAME--
--AND IN HIM WHO BEARS MY OTHER NAMES...
STEPHEN ROCKWELL TREVOR.
OH DEAR GOD...
STEVE...?
I JUST REMEMBERED SOMETHING, ETTA--
--SOMETHING I ONCE TOLD DAD...
"IT WAS A NIGHT SOON AFTER MOM DISAPPEARED...
"AT THE TIME, I THOUGHT IT WAS A DREAM--
"--BUT IT SEEMED SO REAL...
"I SAW MY MOTHER STANDING OVER ME, COMFORTING ME...
"DAD SAID MOM WOULD ALWAYS WATCH OVER ME..."
GUESS NOW THEY BOTH WILL.
18.

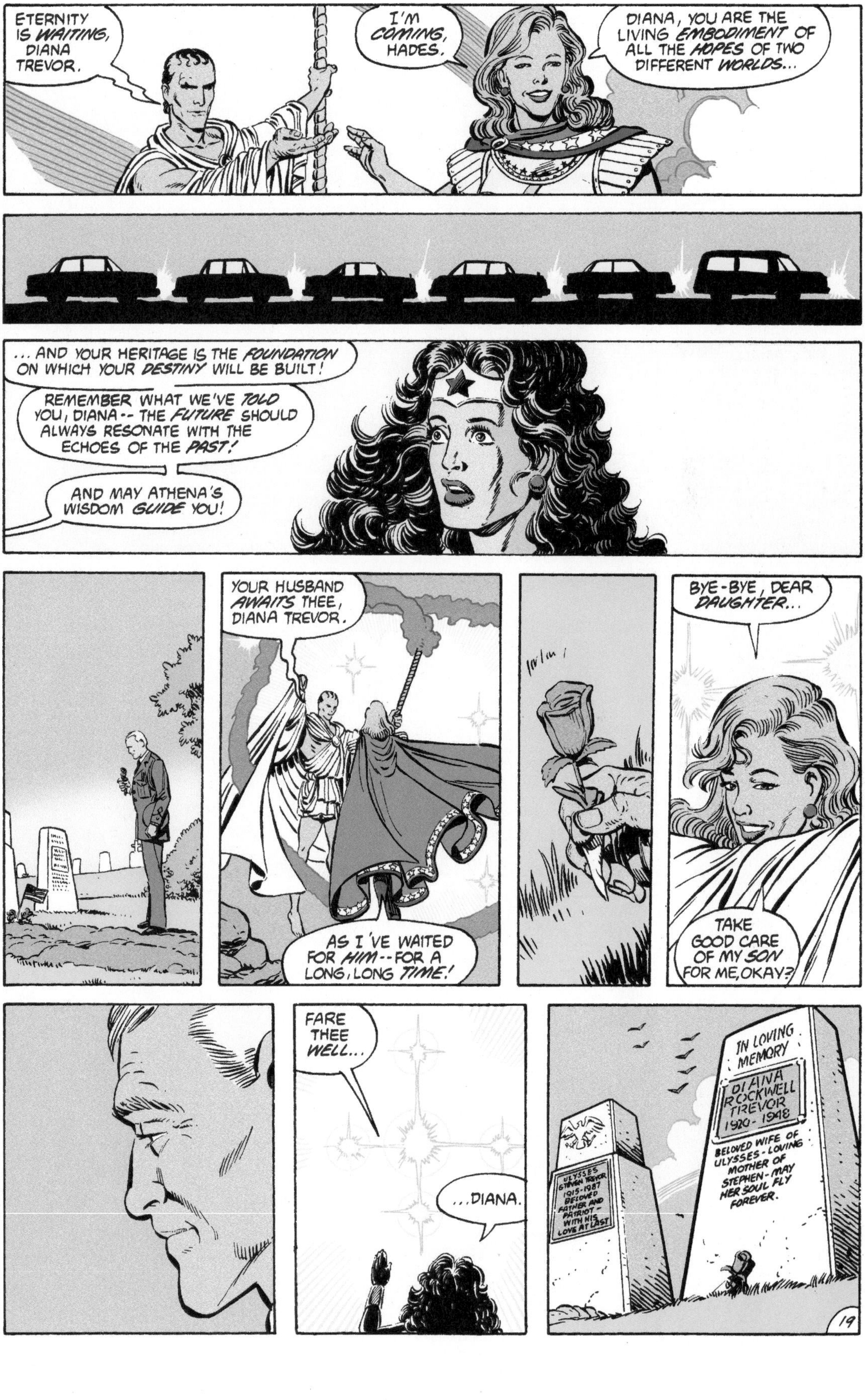
ETERNITY IS WAITING, DIANA TREVOR.
I'M COMING, HADES.
DIANA, YOU ARE THE LIVING EMBODIMENT OF ALL THE HOPES OF TWO DIFFERENT WORLDS...
... AND YOUR HERITAGE IS THE FOUNDATION ON WHICH YOUR DESTINY WILL BE BUILT!
REMEMBER WHAT WE'VE TOLD YOU, DIANA -- THE FUTURE SHOULD ALWAYS RESONATE WITH THE ECHOES OF THE PAST!
AND MAY ATHENA'S WISDOM GUIDE YOU!
YOUR HUSBAND AWAITS THEE, DIANA TREVOR.
AS I'VE WAITED FOR HIM -- FOR A LONG, LONG TIME!
BYE-BYE, DEAR DAUGHTER...
TAKE GOOD CARE OF MY SON FOR ME, OKAY?
FARE THEE WELL...
...DIANA.
ULYSSES STEVEN TREVOR 1915-1987 BELOVED FATHER AND PATRIOT - WITH HIS LOVE AT LAST
IN LOVING MEMORY
DIANA ROCKWELL TREVOR 1920-1948
BELOVED WIFE OF ULYSSES - LOVING MOTHER OF STEPHEN - MAY HER SOUL FLY FOREVER.
19

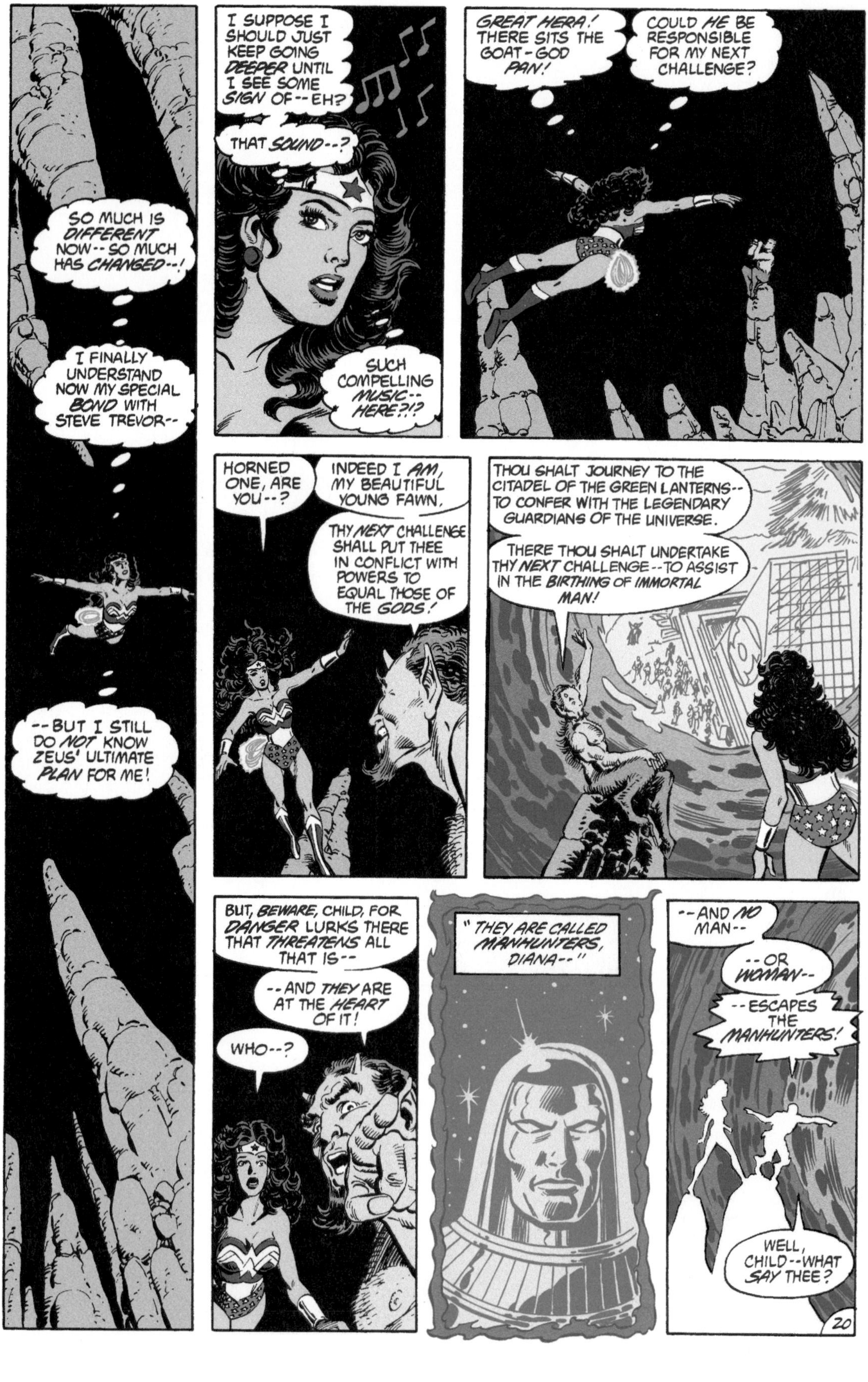
SO MUCH IS DIFFERENT NOW--SO MUCH HAS CHANGED--!
I FINALLY UNDERSTAND NOW MY SPECIAL BOND WITH STEVE TREVOR--
--BUT I STILL DO NOT KNOW ZEUS' ULTIMATE PLAN FOR ME!
I SUPPOSE I SHOULD JUST KEEP GOING DEEPER UNTIL I SEE SOME SIGN OF--EH?
THAT SOUND--?
SUCH COMPELLING MUSIC--HERE?!?
GREAT HERA! THERE SITS THE GOAT-GOD PAN!
COULD HE BE RESPONSIBLE FOR MY NEXT CHALLENGE?
HORNED ONE, ARE YOU--?
INDEED I AM, MY BEAUTIFUL YOUNG FAWN.
THY NEXT CHALLENGE SHALL PUT THEE IN CONFLICT WITH POWERS TO EQUAL THOSE OF THE GODS!
THOU SHALT JOURNEY TO THE CITADEL OF THE GREEN LANTERNS--TO CONFER WITH THE LEGENDARY GUARDIANS OF THE UNIVERSE.
THERE THOU SHALT UNDERTAKE THY NEXT CHALLENGE--TO ASSIST IN THE BIRTHING OF IMMORTAL MAN!
BUT, BEWARE, CHILD, FOR DANGER LURKS THERE THAT THREATENS ALL THAT IS--
--AND THEY ARE AT THE HEART OF IT!
WHO--?
"THEY ARE CALLED MANHUNTERS, DIANA--"
--AND NO MAN--
--OR WOMAN--
--ESCAPES THE MANHUNTERS!
WELL, CHILD--WHAT SAY THEE?
20

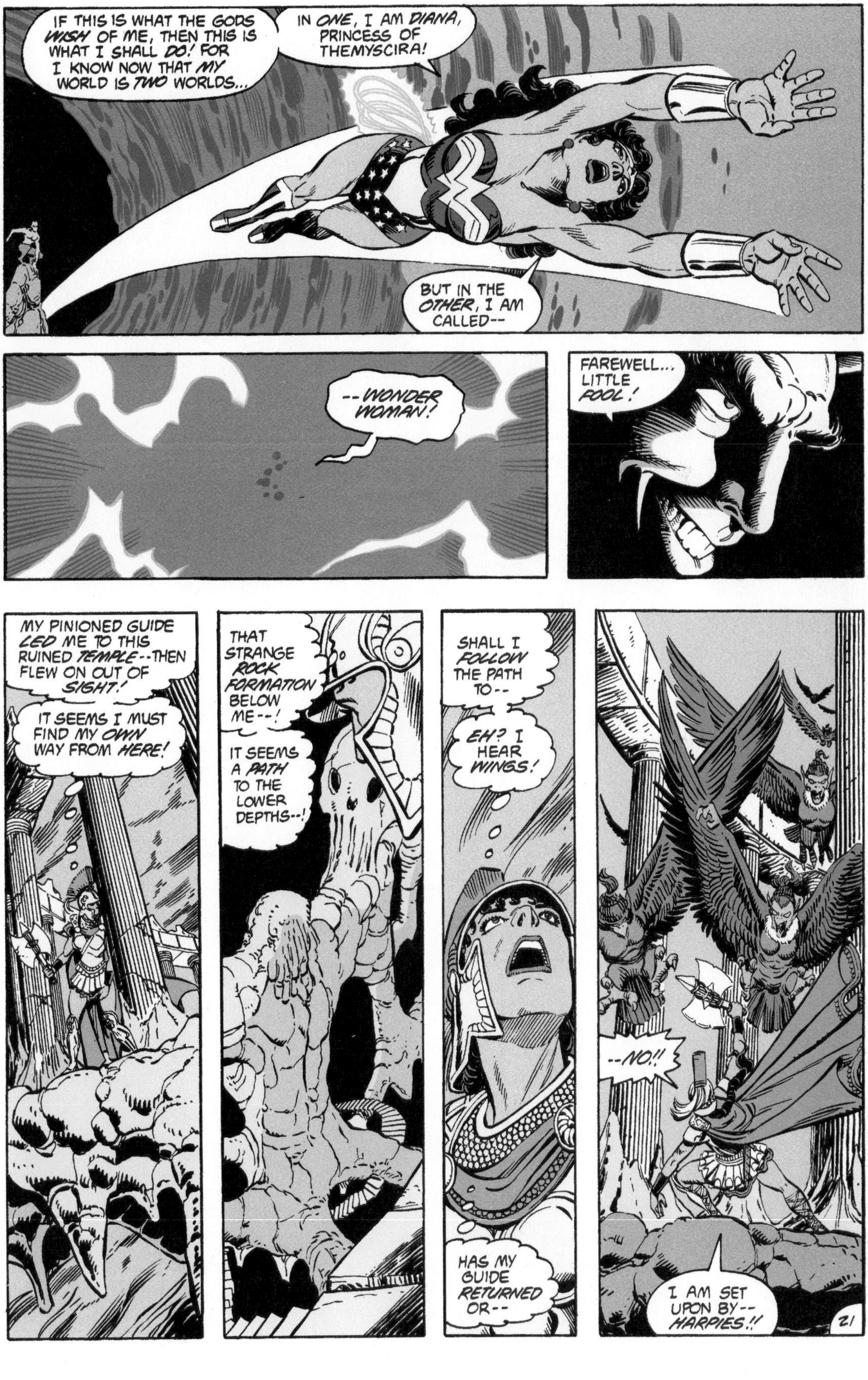
IF THIS IS WHAT THE GODS WISH OF ME, THEN THIS IS WHAT I SHALL DO! FOR I KNOW NOW THAT MY WORLD IS TWO WORLDS...
IN ONE, I AM DIANA, PRINCESS OF THEMYSCIRA!
BUT IN THE OTHER, I AM CALLED--
--WONDER WOMAN!
FAREWELL... LITTLE FOOL!
MY PINIONED GUIDE LED ME TO THIS RUINED TEMPLE--THEN FLEW ON OUT OF SIGHT!
IT SEEMS I MUST FIND MY OWN WAY FROM HERE!
THAT STRANGE ROCK FORMATION BELOW ME--!
IT SEEMS A PATH TO THE LOWER DEPTHS--!
SHALL I FOLLOW THE PATH TO--
EH? I HEAR WINGS!
HAS MY GUIDE RETURNED OR--
--NO!!
I AM SET UPON BY--HARPIES!!
21

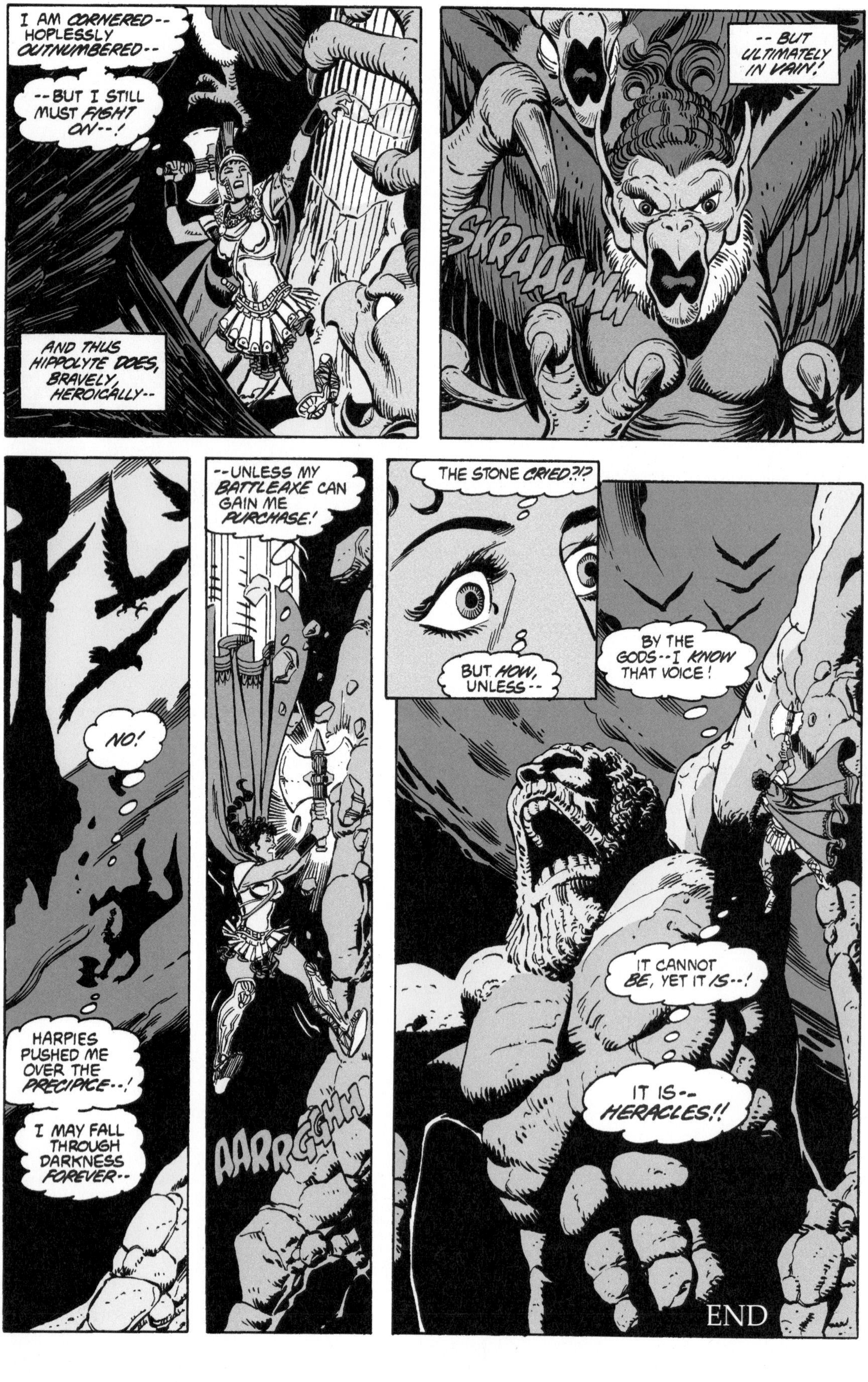
I AM CORNERED-- HOPLESSLY OUTNUMBERED--
--BUT I STILL MUST FIGHT ON--!
AND THUS HIPPOLYTE DOES, BRAVELY, HEROICALLY--
--BUT ULTIMATELY IN VAIN!
SKRAAAAWN
NO!
HARPIES PUSHED ME OVER THE PRECIPICE--!
I MAY FALL THROUGH DARKNESS FOREVER--
--UNLESS MY BATTLEAXE CAN GAIN ME PURCHASE!
AARRGGHH
THE STONE CRIED?!?
BUT HOW, UNLESS--
BY THE GODS--I KNOW THAT VOICE!
IT CANNOT BE, YET IT IS--!
IT IS--HERACLES!!
END

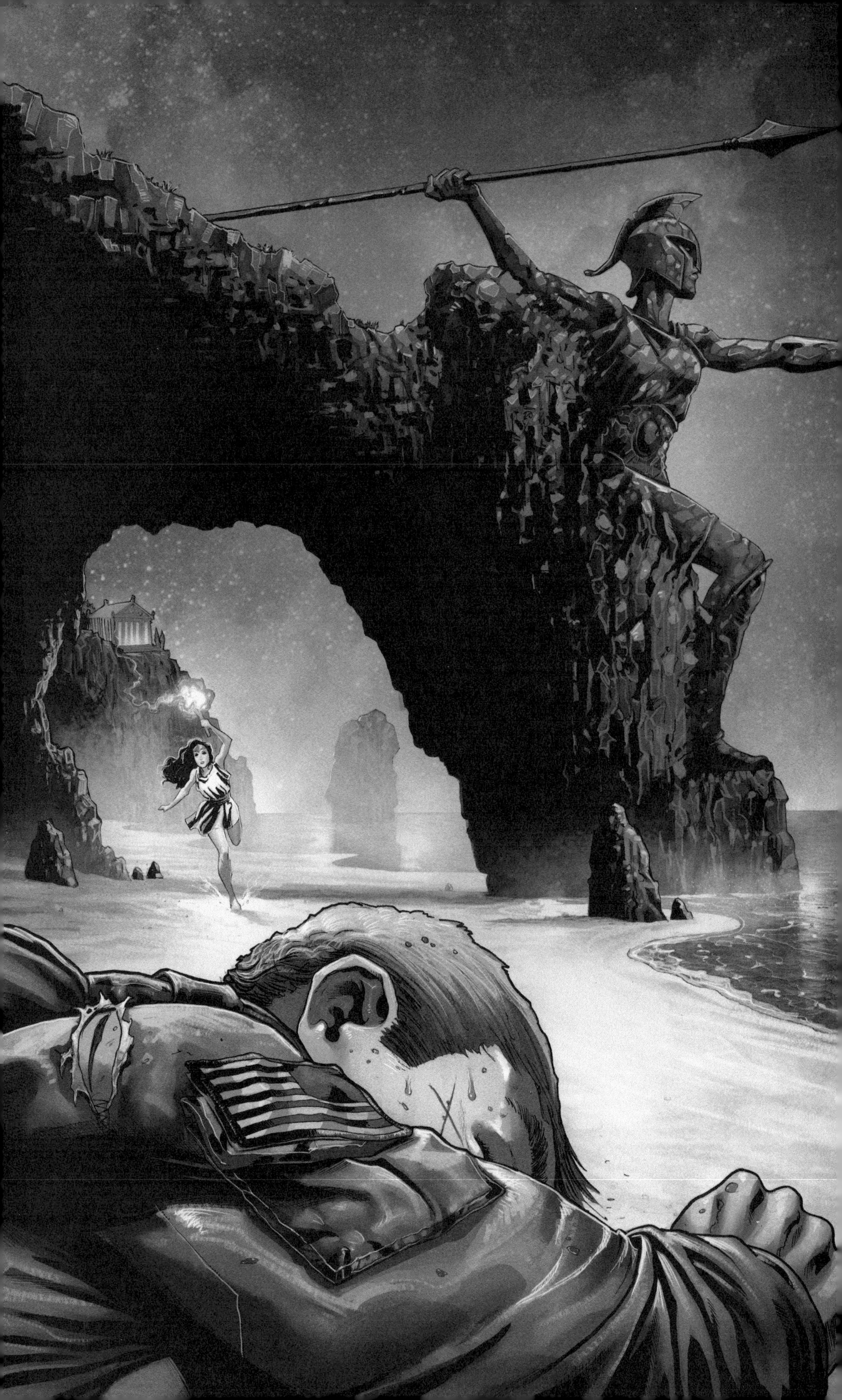

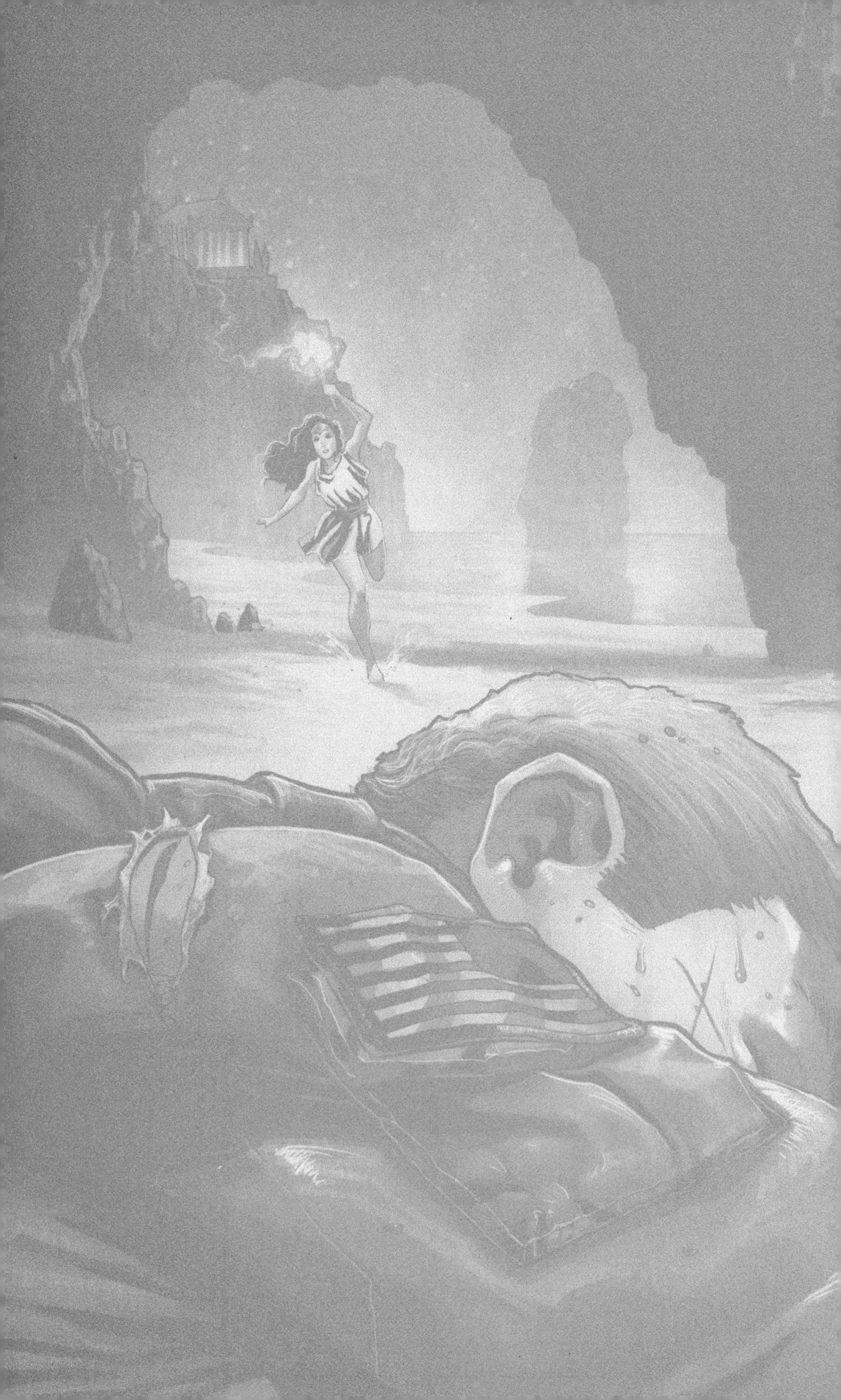

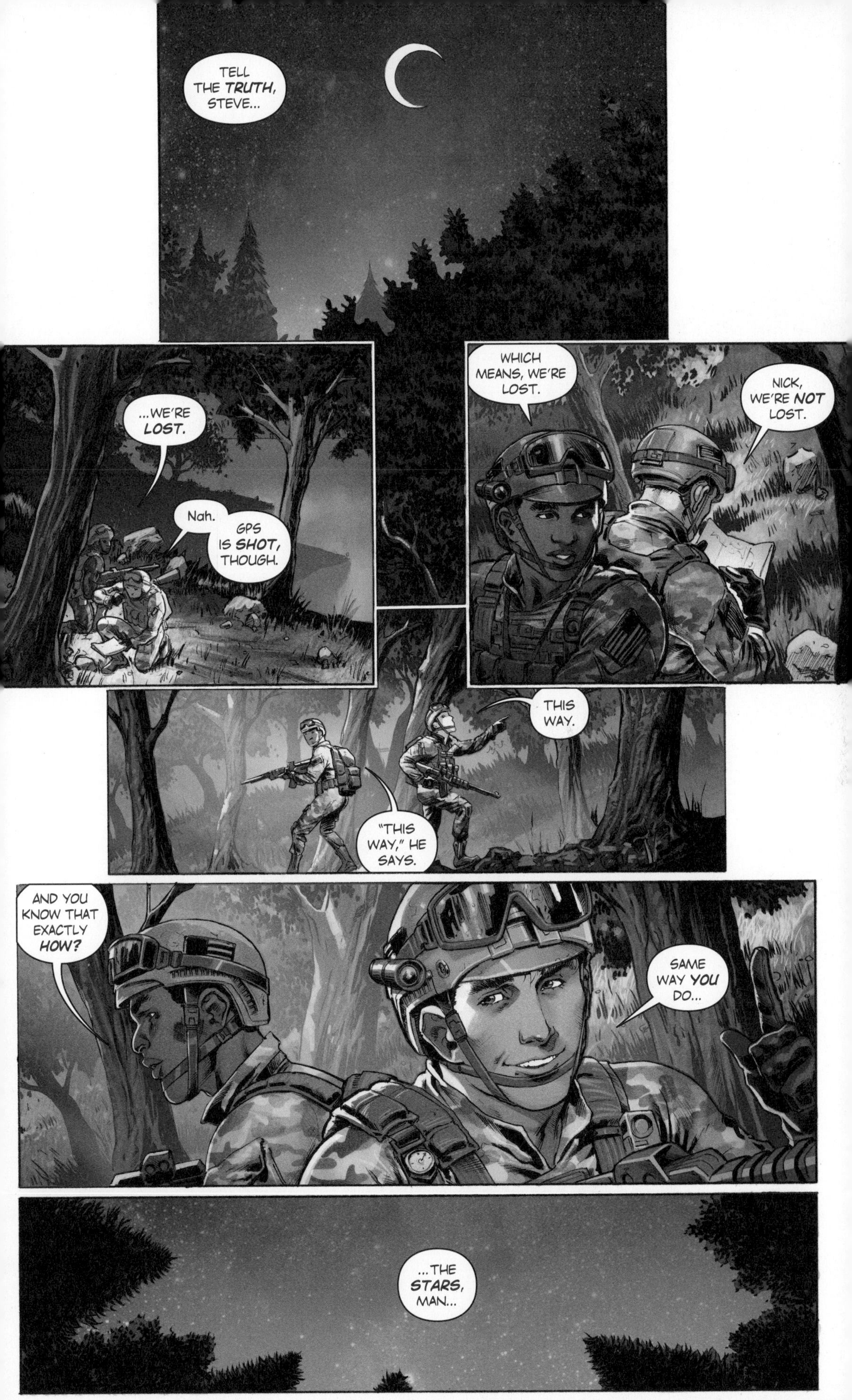
TELL THE TRUTH, STEVE...
...WE'RE LOST.
Nah.
GPS IS SHOT, THOUGH.
WHICH MEANS, WE'RE LOST.
NICK, WE'RE NOT LOST.
THIS WAY.
"THIS WAY," HE SAYS.
AND YOU KNOW THAT EXACTLY HOW?
SAME WAY YOU DO...
...THE STARS, MAN...

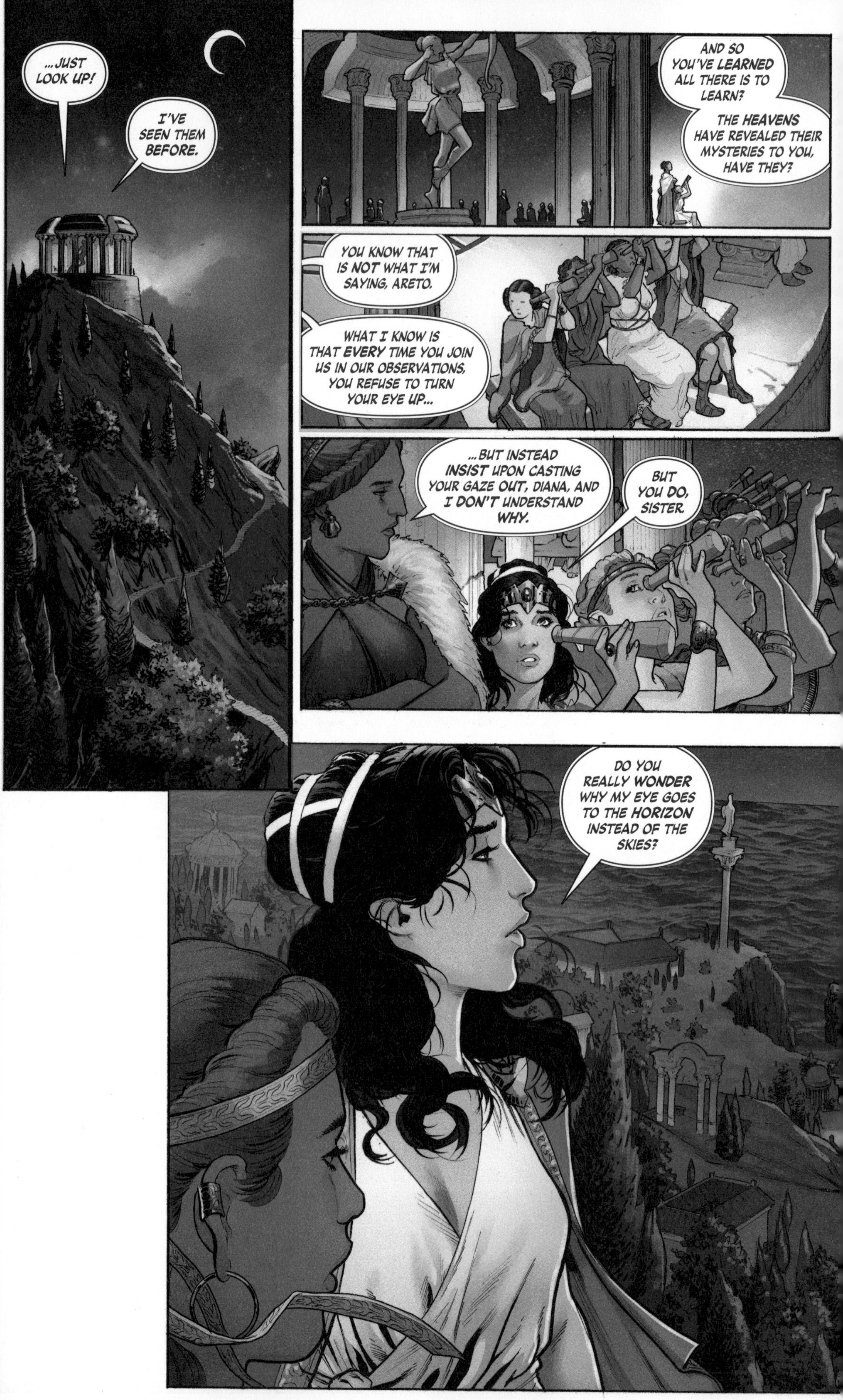
...JUST LOOK UP!
I'VE SEEN THEM BEFORE.
AND SO YOU'VE LEARNED ALL THERE IS TO LEARN?
THE HEAVENS HAVE REVEALED THEIR MYSTERIES TO YOU, HAVE THEY?
YOU KNOW THAT IS NOT WHAT I'M SAYING, ARETO.
WHAT I KNOW IS THAT EVERY TIME YOU JOIN US IN OUR OBSERVATIONS, YOU REFUSE TO TURN YOUR EYE UP...
...BUT INSTEAD INSIST UPON CASTING YOUR GAZE OUT, DIANA, AND I DON'T UNDERSTAND WHY.
BUT YOU DO, SISTER.
DO YOU REALLY WONDER WHY MY EYE GOES TO THE HORIZON INSTEAD OF THE SKIES?

YOU DO, EVEN IF YOU DON'T FEEL IT.

YOU VEX ARETO ON PURPOSE, DIANA.

NO, I KNOW.

I DON'T, KASIA. YOU KNOW I DON'T.

I CAN SEE THE BEAUTY OF THE HEAVENS, I CAN SEE THE POETRY IN THEIR MOTION.

BUT ALL WE DO IS BEAR WITNESS.

ALL OF YOU REMEMBER BEFORE, KASIA.

YOU CAN RECALL THE WORLD YOU LEFT, EVEN IF THE MEMORIES OF IT BRING YOU PAIN.

I'VE NEVER SEEN WHAT LIES BEYOND OUR SHORES.

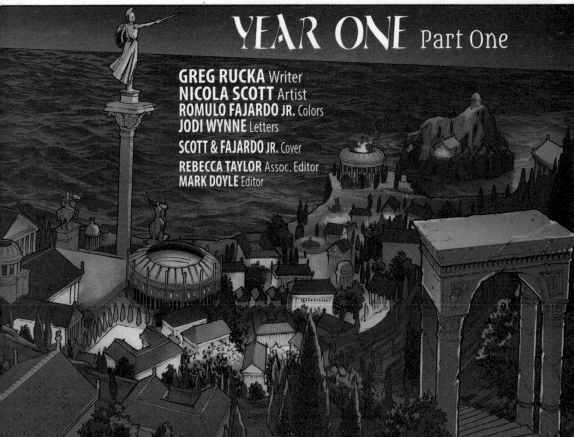

YEAR ONE Part One

GREG RUCKA Writer
NICOLA SCOTT Artist
ROMULO FAJARDO JR. Colors
JODI WYNNE Letters

SCOTT & FAJARDO JR. Cover

REBECCA TAYLOR Assoc. Editor
MARK DOYLE Editor

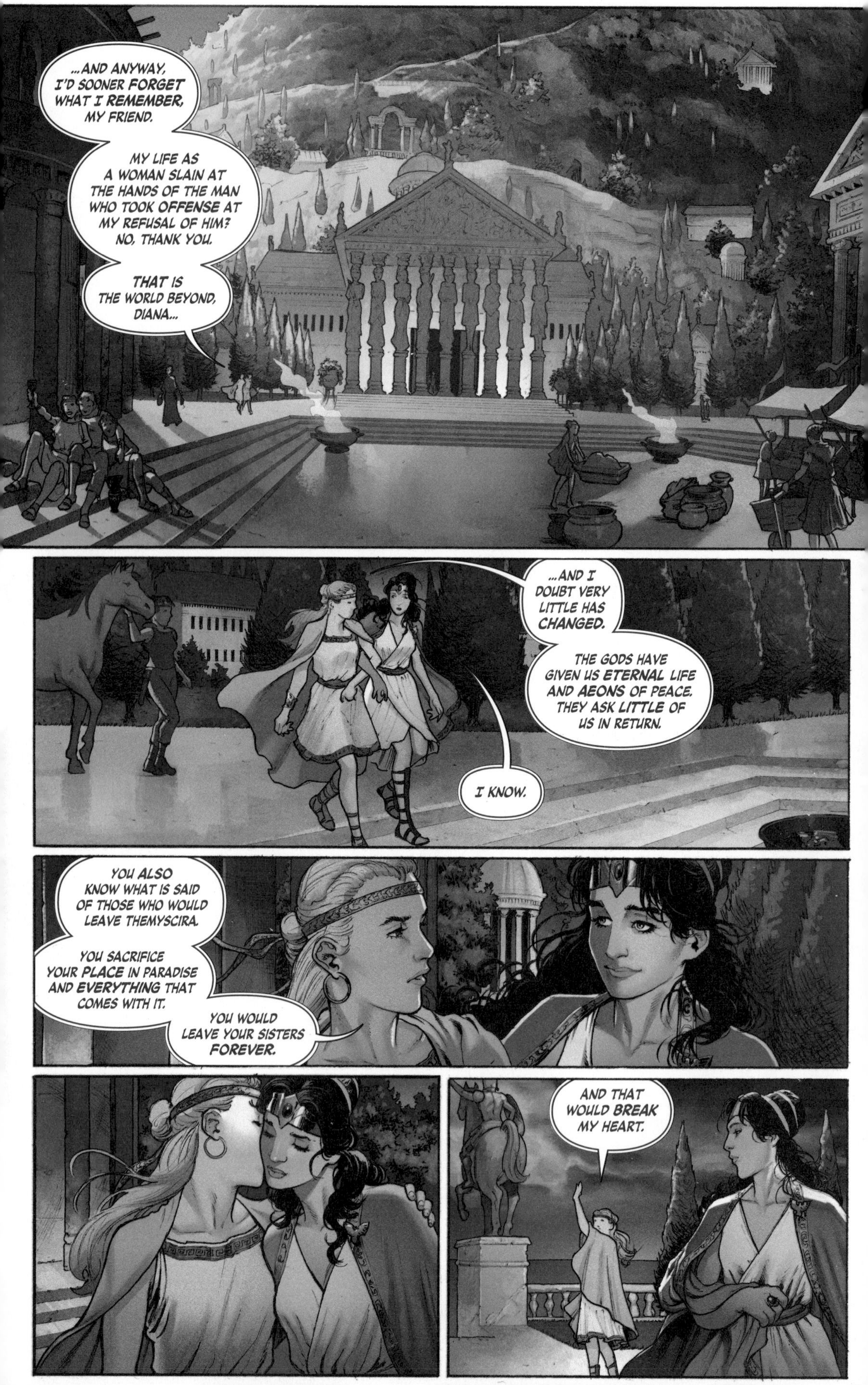
...AND ANYWAY, I'D SOONER FORGET WHAT I REMEMBER, MY FRIEND.
MY LIFE AS A WOMAN SLAIN AT THE HANDS OF THE MAN WHO TOOK OFFENSE AT MY REFUSAL OF HIM? NO, THANK YOU.
THAT IS THE WORLD BEYOND, DIANA...
...AND I DOUBT VERY LITTLE HAS CHANGED.
THE GODS HAVE GIVEN US ETERNAL LIFE AND AEONS OF PEACE. THEY ASK LITTLE OF US IN RETURN.
I KNOW.
YOU ALSO KNOW WHAT IS SAID OF THOSE WHO WOULD LEAVE THEMYSCIRA.
YOU SACRIFICE YOUR PLACE IN PARADISE AND EVERYTHING THAT COMES WITH IT.
YOU WOULD LEAVE YOUR SISTERS FOREVER.
AND THAT WOULD BREAK MY HEART.

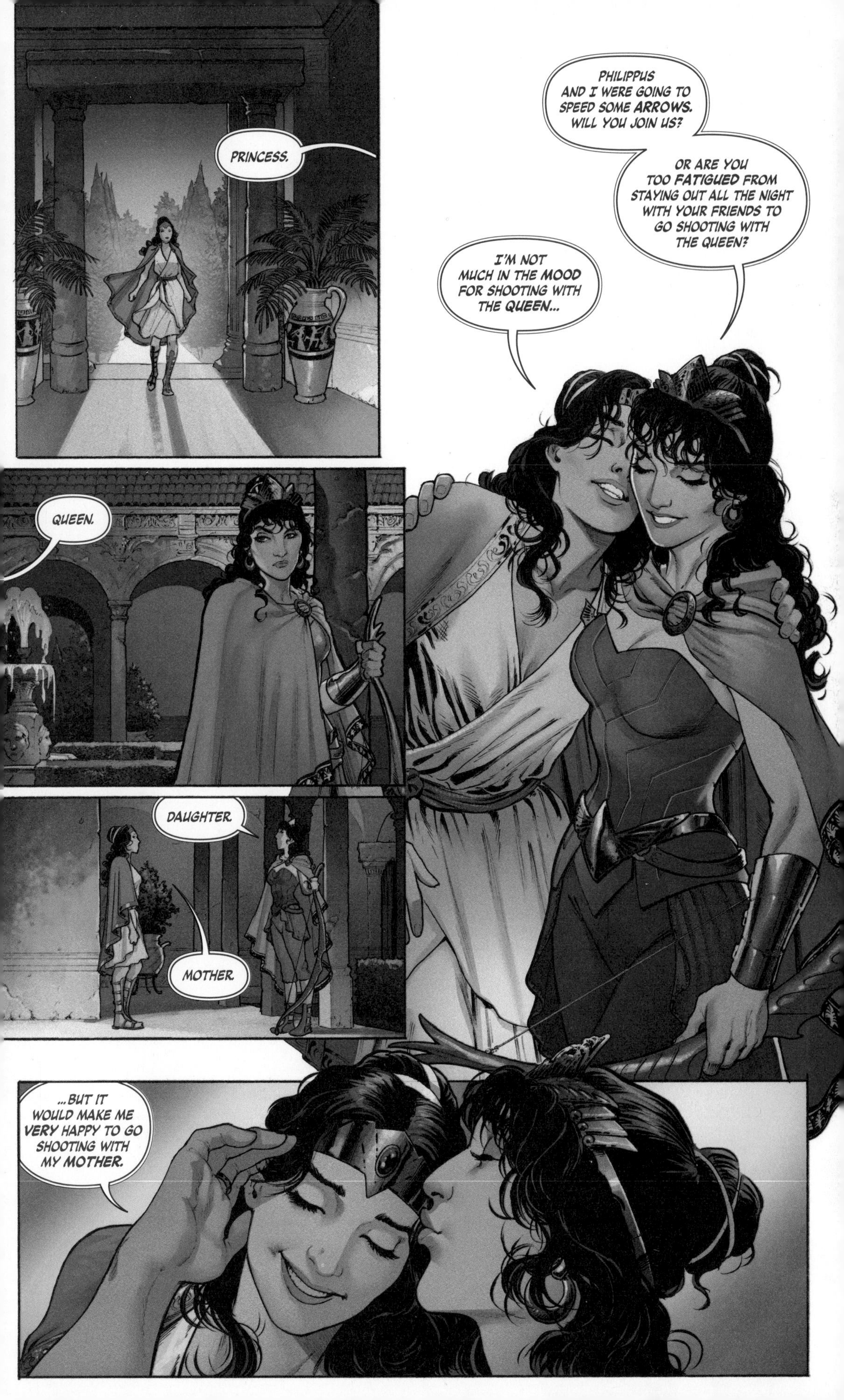
PRINCESS.
QUEEN.
DAUGHTER.
MOTHER.
PHILIPPUS AND I WERE GOING TO SPEED SOME ARROWS. WILL YOU JOIN US?
OR ARE YOU TOO FATIGUED FROM STAYING OUT ALL THE NIGHT WITH YOUR FRIENDS TO GO SHOOTING WITH THE QUEEN?
I'M NOT MUCH IN THE MOOD FOR SHOOTING WITH THE QUEEN...
...BUT IT WOULD MAKE ME VERY HAPPY TO GO SHOOTING WITH MY MOTHER.

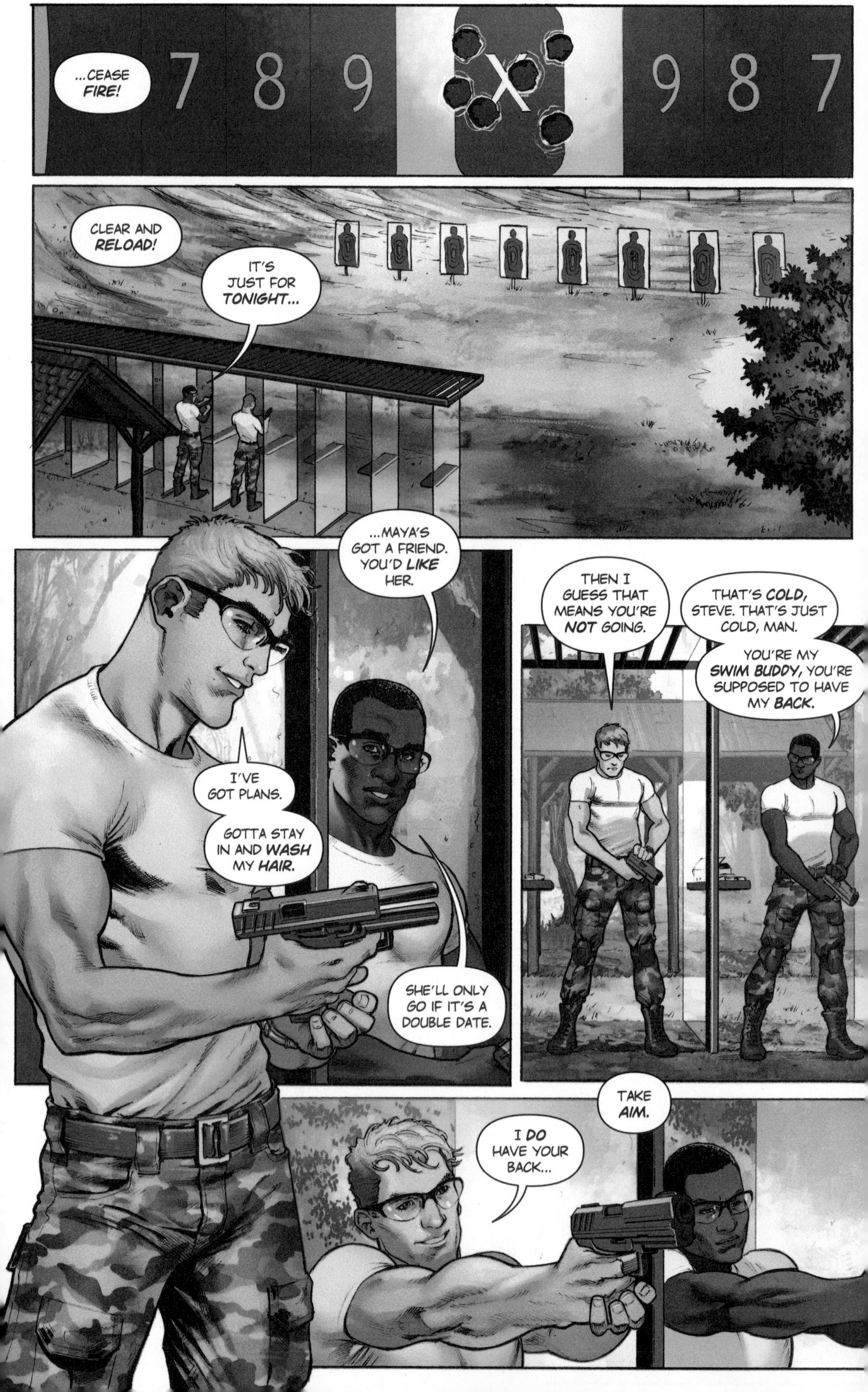

...CEASE FIRE!
7 8 9 X 9 8 7
CLEAR AND RELOAD!
IT'S JUST FOR TONIGHT...
...MAYA'S GOT A FRIEND. YOU'D LIKE HER.
I'VE GOT PLANS.
GOTTA STAY IN AND WASH MY HAIR.
SHE'LL ONLY GO IF IT'S A DOUBLE DATE.
THEN I GUESS THAT MEANS YOU'RE NOT GOING.
THAT'S COLD, STEVE. THAT'S JUST COLD, MAN.
YOU'RE MY SWIM BUDDY, YOU'RE SUPPOSED TO HAVE MY BACK.
TAKE AIM.
I DO HAVE YOUR BACK...

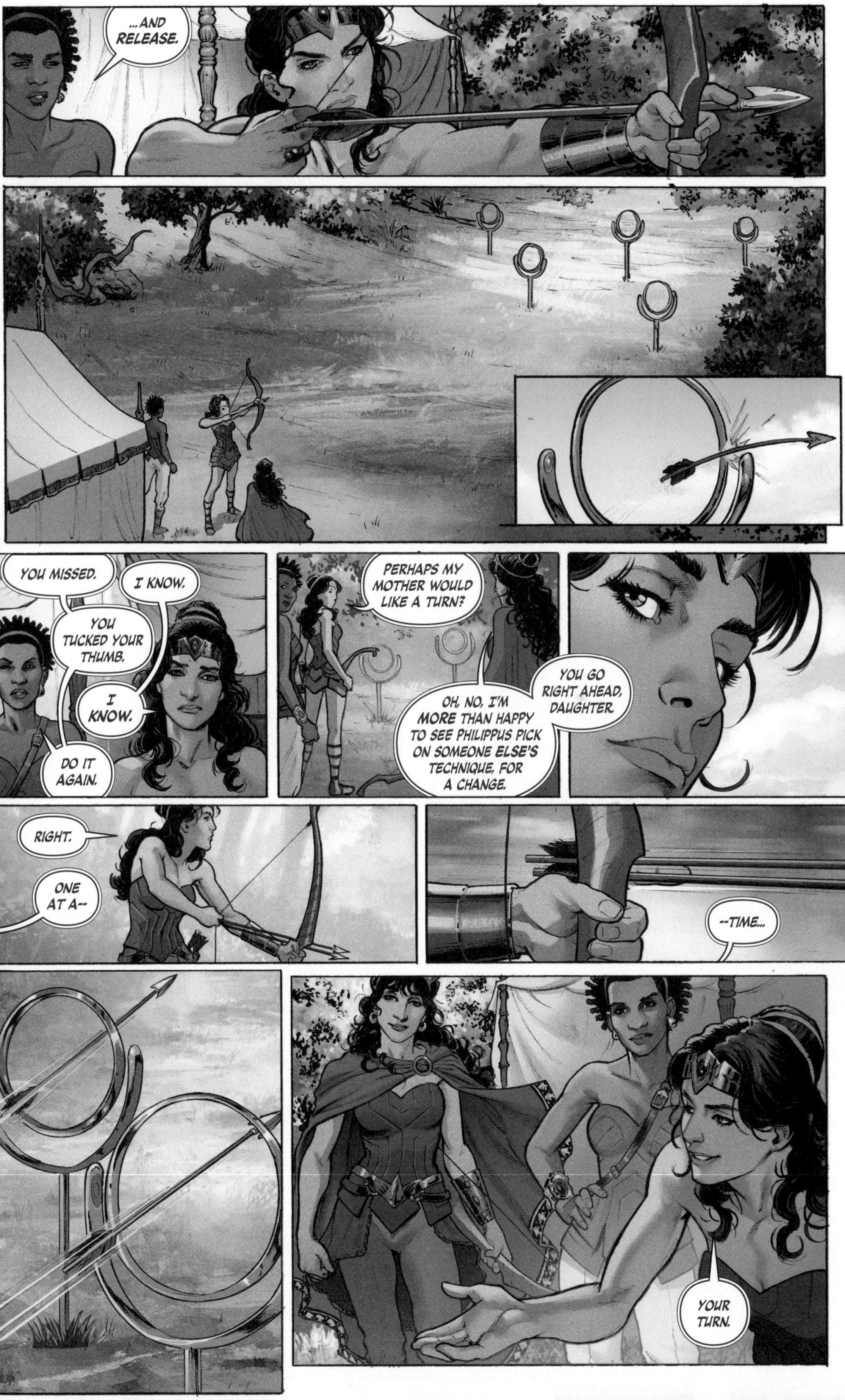
...AND RELEASE.
YOU MISSED.
I KNOW.
YOU TUCKED YOUR THUMB.
I KNOW.
DO IT AGAIN.
PERHAPS MY MOTHER WOULD LIKE A TURN?
OH, NO, I'M MORE THAN HAPPY TO SEE PHILIPPUS PICK ON SOMEONE ELSE'S TECHNIQUE, FOR A CHANGE.
YOU GO RIGHT AHEAD, DAUGHTER.
RIGHT.
ONE AT A--
--TIME...
YOUR TURN.

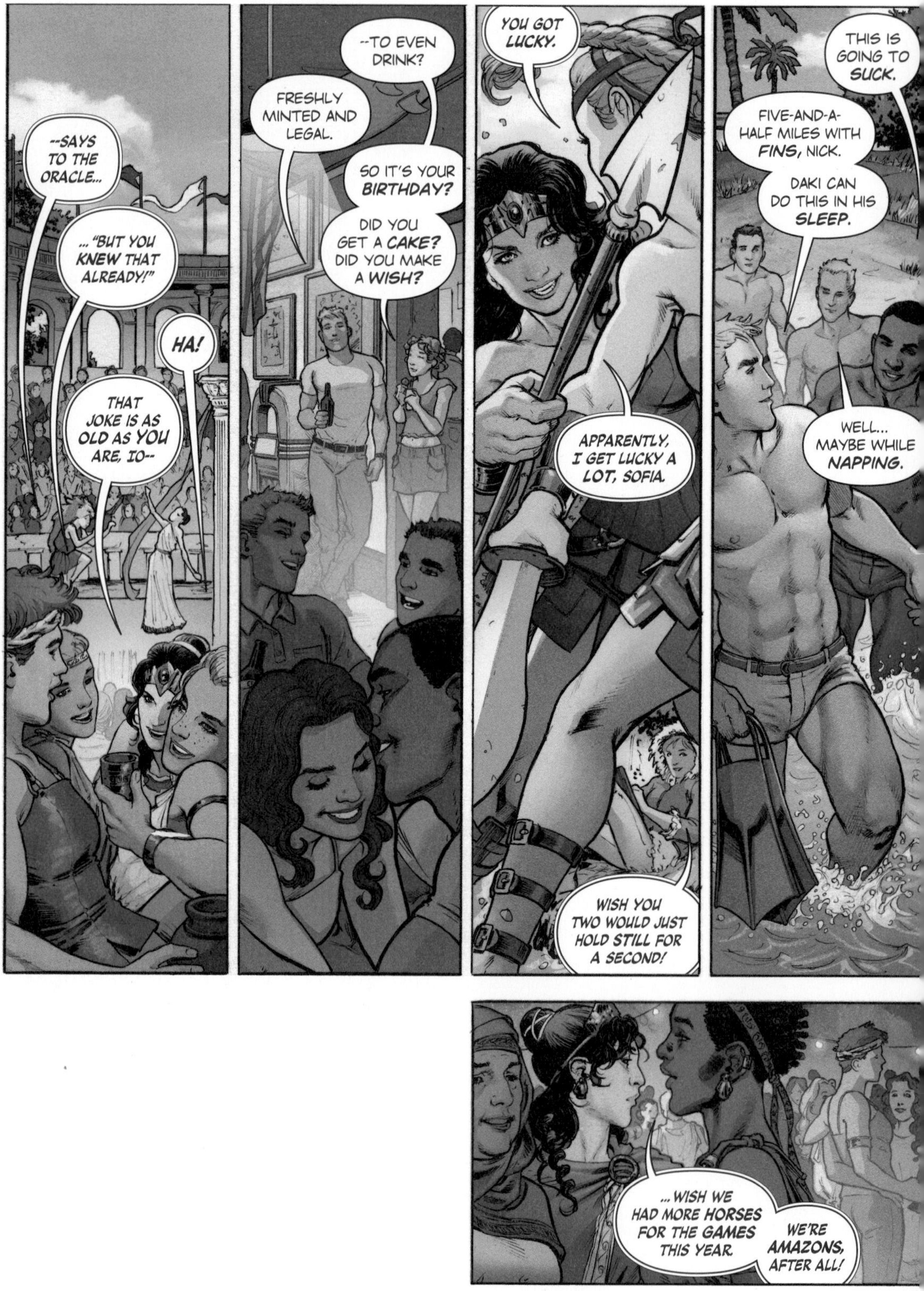
--SAYS TO THE ORACLE...
..."BUT YOU KNEW THAT ALREADY!"
HA!
THAT JOKE IS AS OLD AS YOU ARE, IO--
--TO EVEN DRINK?
FRESHLY MINTED AND LEGAL.
SO IT'S YOUR BIRTHDAY?
DID YOU GET A CAKE? DID YOU MAKE A WISH?
YOU GOT LUCKY.
APPARENTLY, I GET LUCKY A LOT, SOFIA.
WISH YOU TWO WOULD JUST HOLD STILL FOR A SECOND!
THIS IS GOING TO SUCK.
FIVE-AND-A-HALF MILES WITH FINS, NICK.
DAKI CAN DO THIS IN HIS SLEEP.
WELL... MAYBE WHILE NAPPING.
...WISH WE HAD MORE HORSES FOR THE GAMES THIS YEAR.
WE'RE AMAZONS, AFTER ALL!

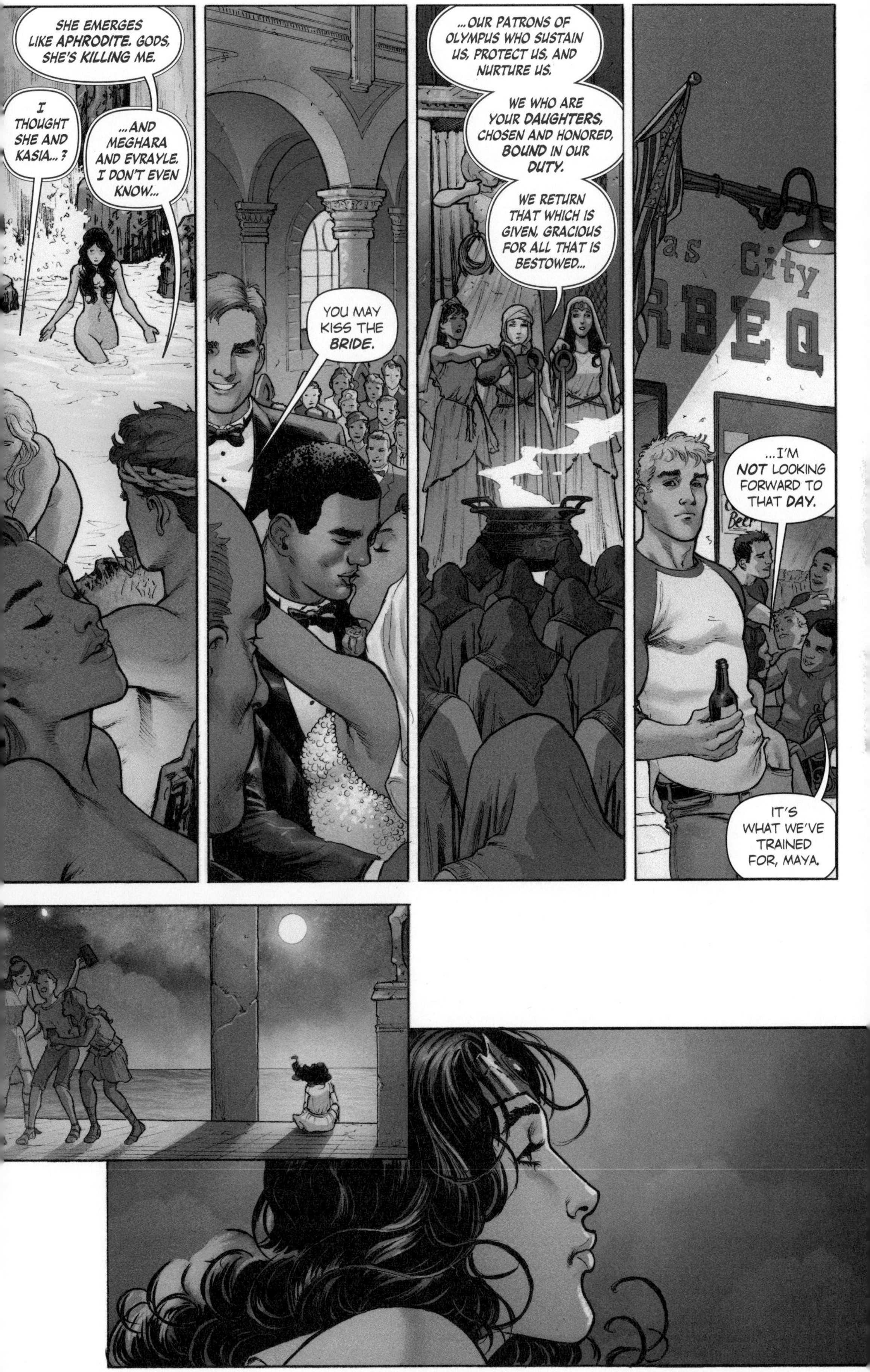
SHE EMERGES LIKE APHRODITE. GODS, SHE'S KILLING ME.
I THOUGHT SHE AND KASIA...?
...AND MEGHARA AND EVRAYLE. I DON'T EVEN KNOW...
YOU MAY KISS THE BRIDE.
...OUR PATRONS OF OLYMPUS WHO SUSTAIN US, PROTECT US, AND NURTURE US.
WE WHO ARE YOUR DAUGHTERS, CHOSEN AND HONORED, BOUND IN OUR DUTY.
WE RETURN THAT WHICH IS GIVEN, GRACIOUS FOR ALL THAT IS BESTOWED...
as City
RBEQ
...I'M NOT LOOKING FORWARD TO THAT DAY.
IT'S WHAT WE'VE TRAINED FOR, MAYA.

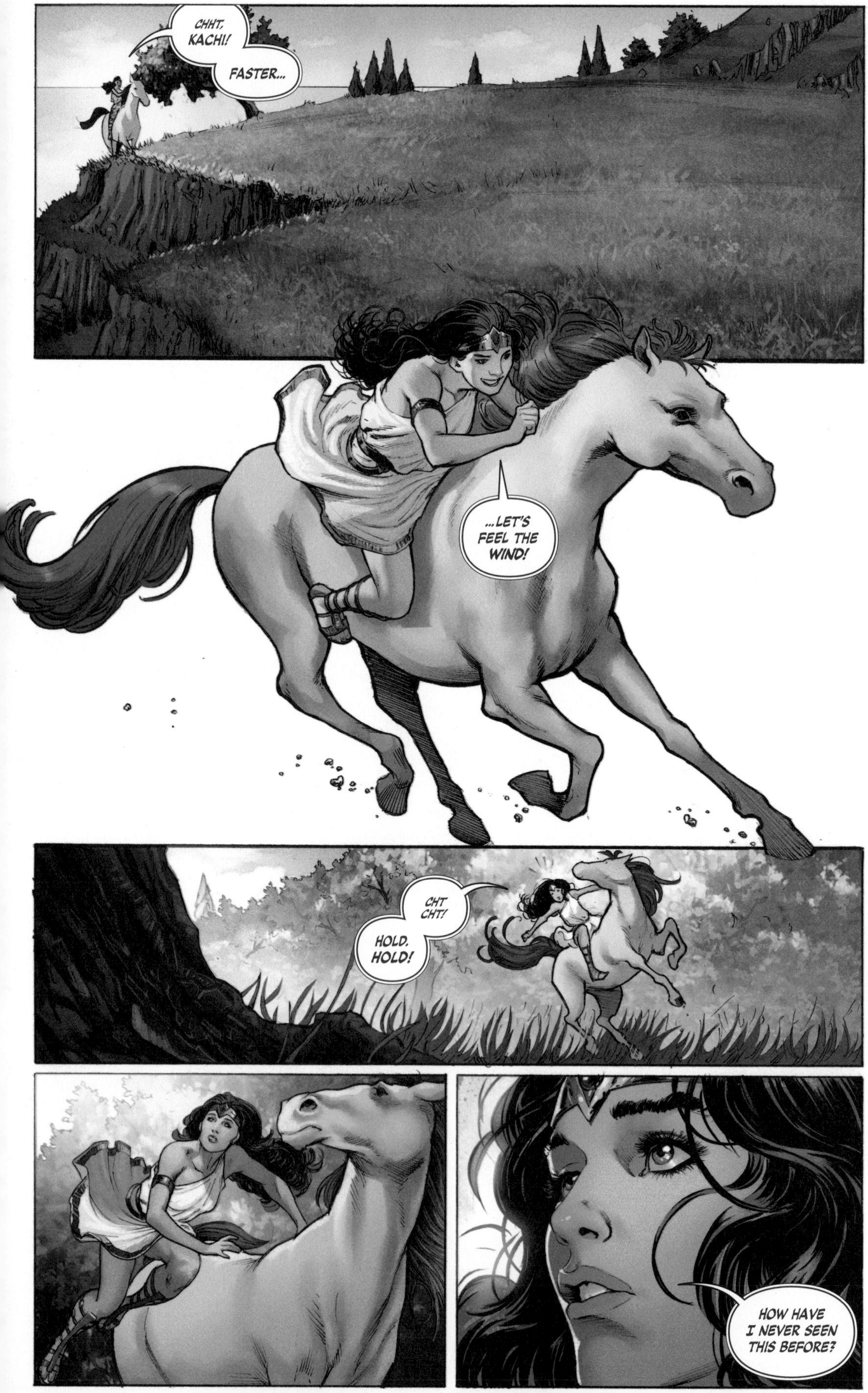
CHHT, KACHI!
FASTER...
...LET'S FEEL THE WIND!
CHT CHT!
HOLD, HOLD!
HOW HAVE I NEVER SEEN THIS BEFORE?

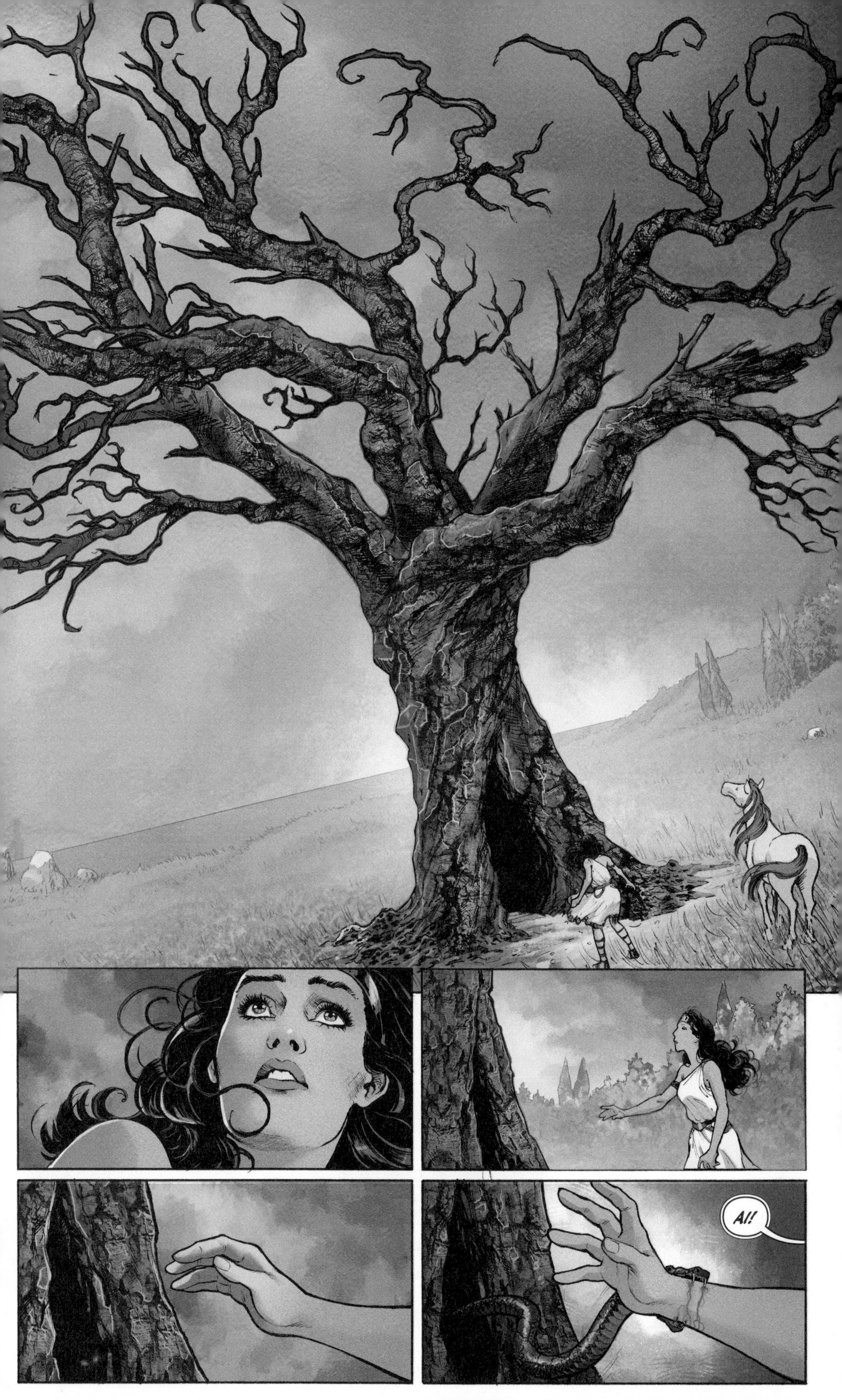
AI!

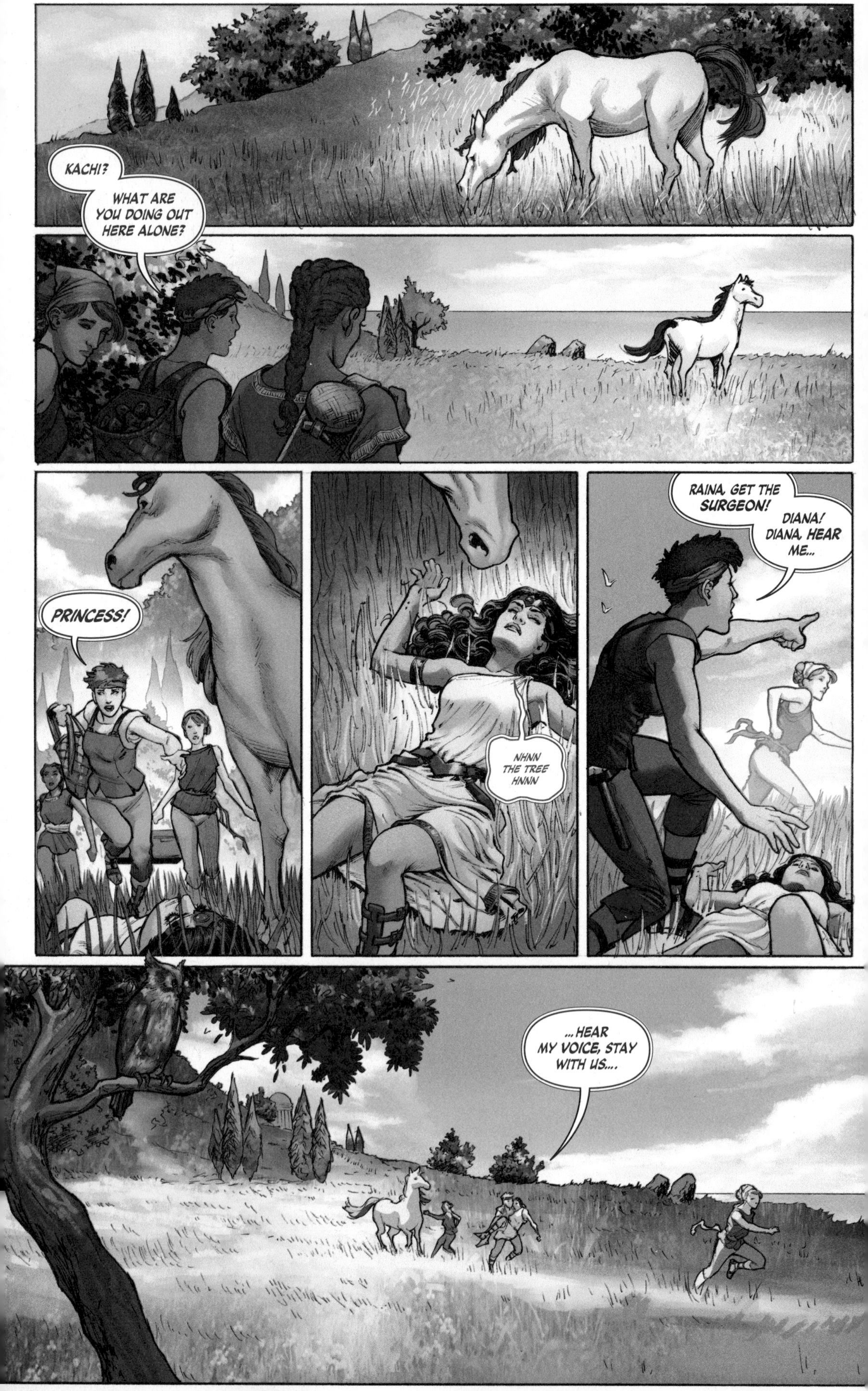
KACHI?
WHAT ARE YOU DOING OUT HERE ALONE?
PRINCESS!
NHNN THE TREE HNNN
RAINA, GET THE SURGEON!
DIANA! DIANA, HEAR ME...
...HEAR MY VOICE, STAY WITH US....

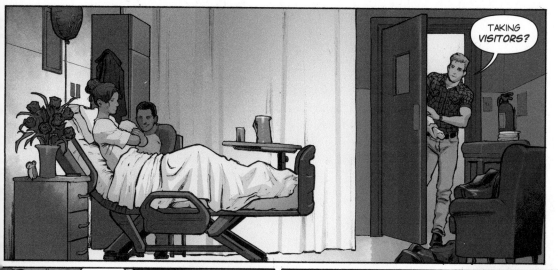

TAKING VISITORS?

STEVE!

MAN! COME IN!

Oh, LOOK AT HER. SHE'S GORGEOUS.

LOOK WHAT YOU GUYS MADE.

NOT BAD, RIGHT?

YOU DO GOOD WORK, MAYA.

THANK YOU.

HEY, I HELPED!

NICK, BROTHER, YOU DID NOTHING. YOUR JOB STARTS NOW.

WOULD YOU LIKE TO HOLD YOUR GODDAUGHTER?

MY WHAT NOW?

YEAH, WE'VE BEEN MEANING TO ASK YOU.

SUPPORT HER HEAD, MAN.

IT'D BE MY HONOR.

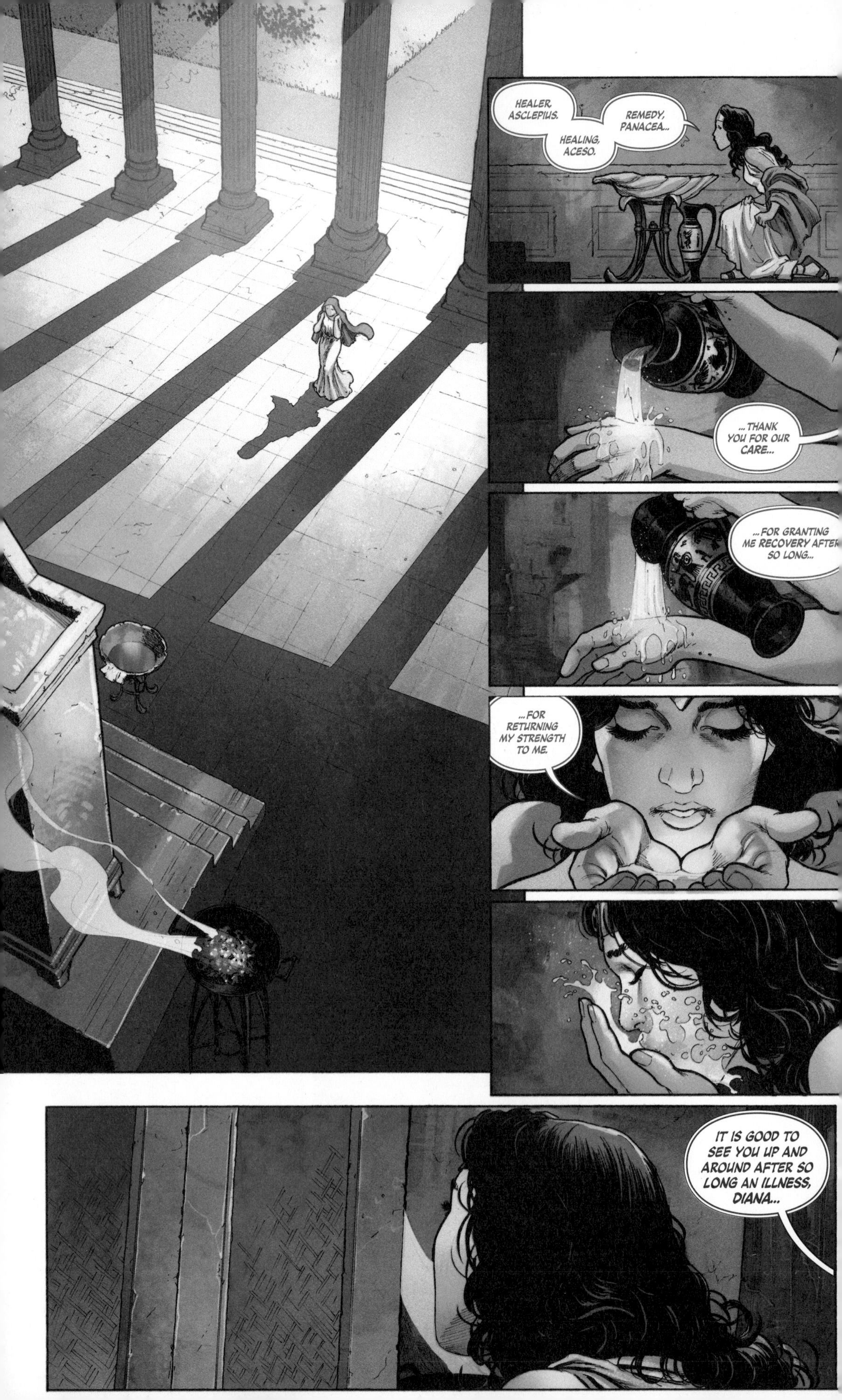
HEALER, ASCLEPIUS.
HEALING, ACESO.
REMEDY, PANACEA...
...THANK YOU FOR OUR CARE...
...FOR GRANTING ME RECOVERY AFTER SO LONG...
...FOR RETURNING MY STRENGTH TO ME.
IT IS GOOD TO SEE YOU UP AND AROUND AFTER SO LONG AN ILLNESS, DIANA...

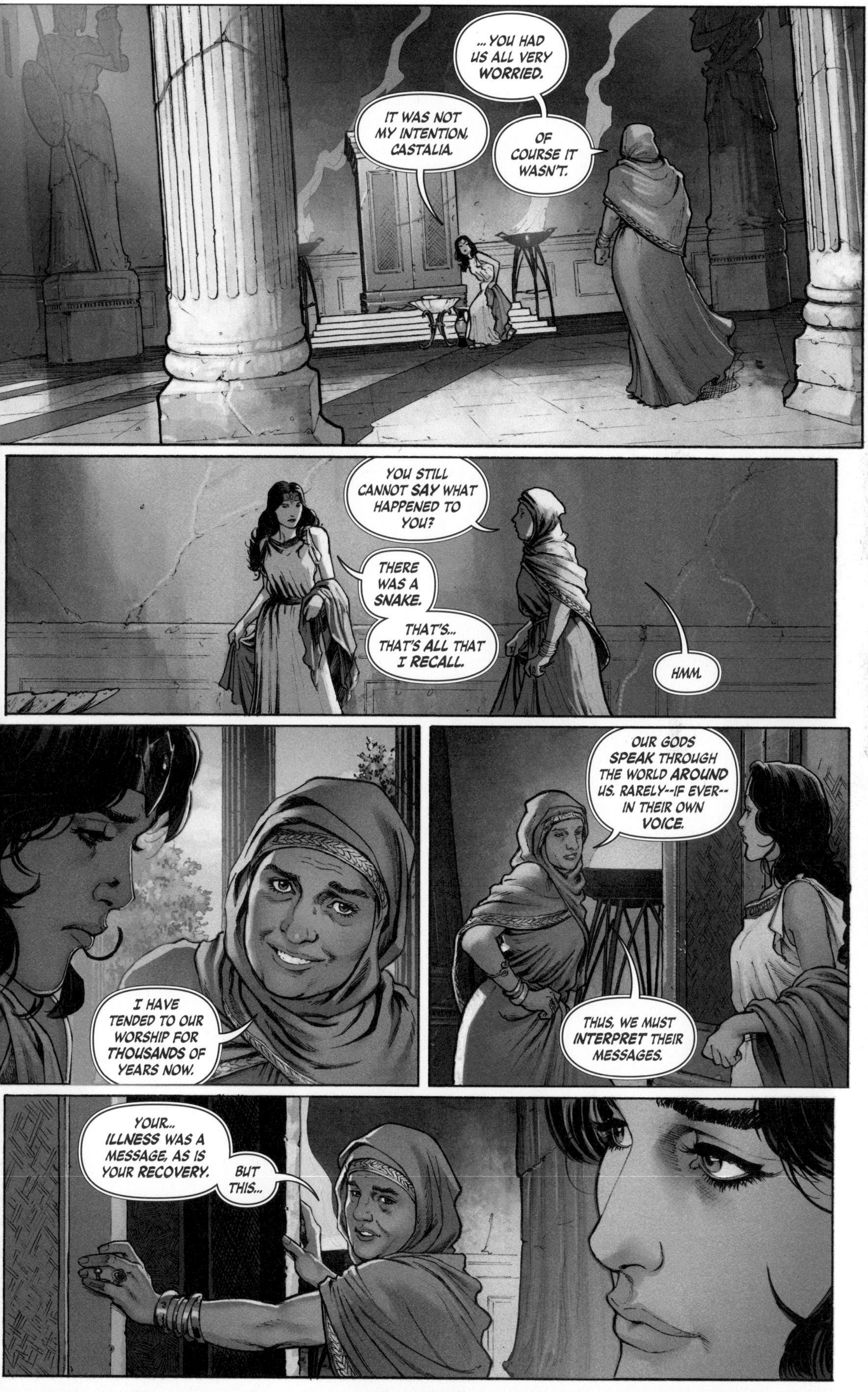
IT WAS NOT MY INTENTION, CASTALIA.
...YOU HAD US ALL VERY WORRIED.
OF COURSE IT WASN'T.
YOU STILL CANNOT SAY WHAT HAPPENED TO YOU?
THERE WAS A SNAKE.
THAT'S... THAT'S ALL THAT I RECALL.
HMM.
I HAVE TENDED TO OUR WORSHIP FOR THOUSANDS OF YEARS NOW.
OUR GODS SPEAK THROUGH THE WORLD AROUND US. RARELY--IF EVER-- IN THEIR OWN VOICE.
THUS, WE MUST INTERPRET THEIR MESSAGES.
YOUR... ILLNESS WAS A MESSAGE, AS IS YOUR RECOVERY.
BUT THIS...

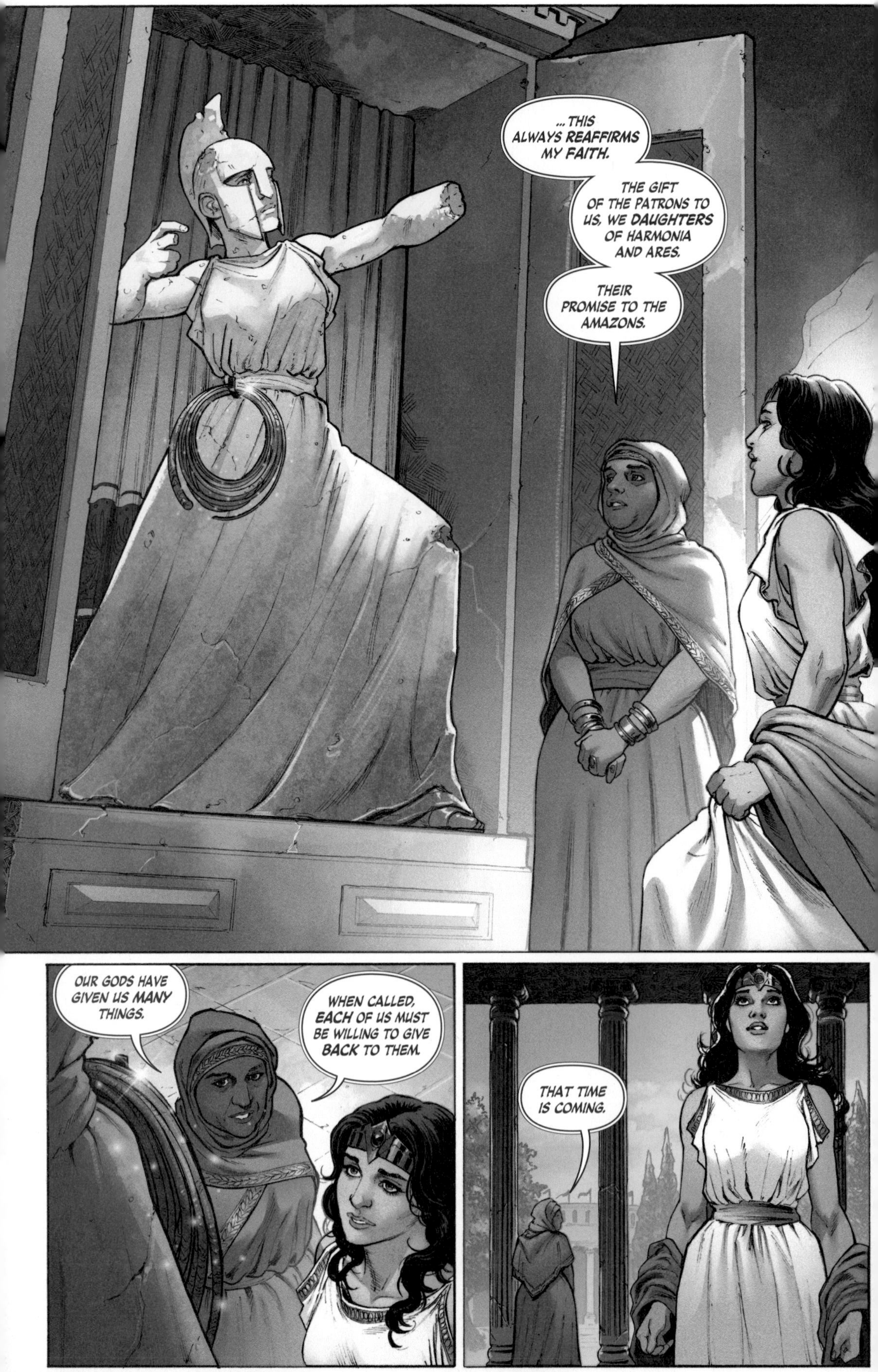
...THIS ALWAYS REAFFIRMS MY FAITH.
THE GIFT OF THE PATRONS TO US, WE DAUGHTERS OF HARMONIA AND ARES.
THEIR PROMISE TO THE AMAZONS.
OUR GODS HAVE GIVEN US MANY THINGS.
WHEN CALLED, EACH OF US MUST BE WILLING TO GIVE BACK TO THEM.
THAT TIME IS COMING.

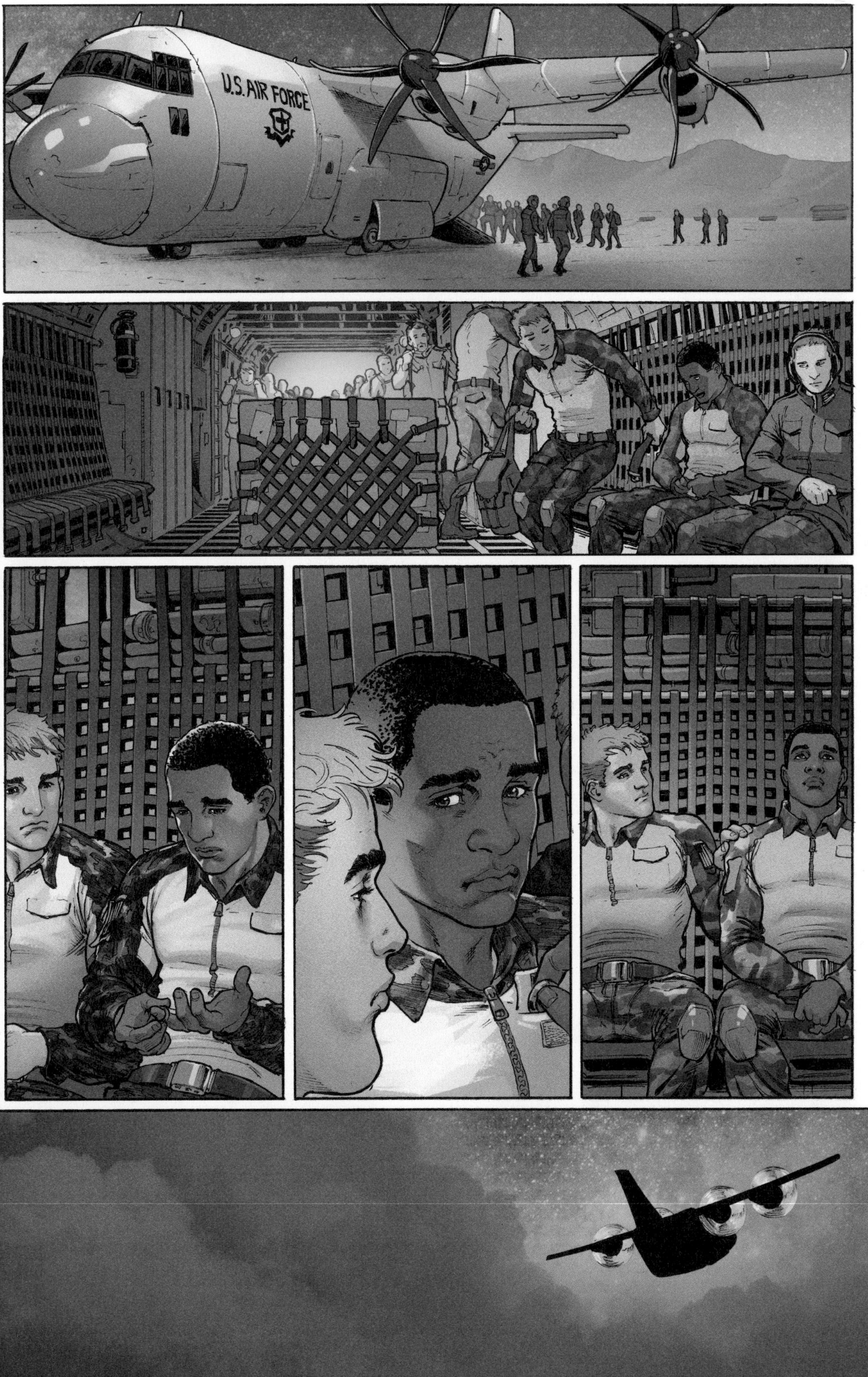
U.S. AIR FORCE

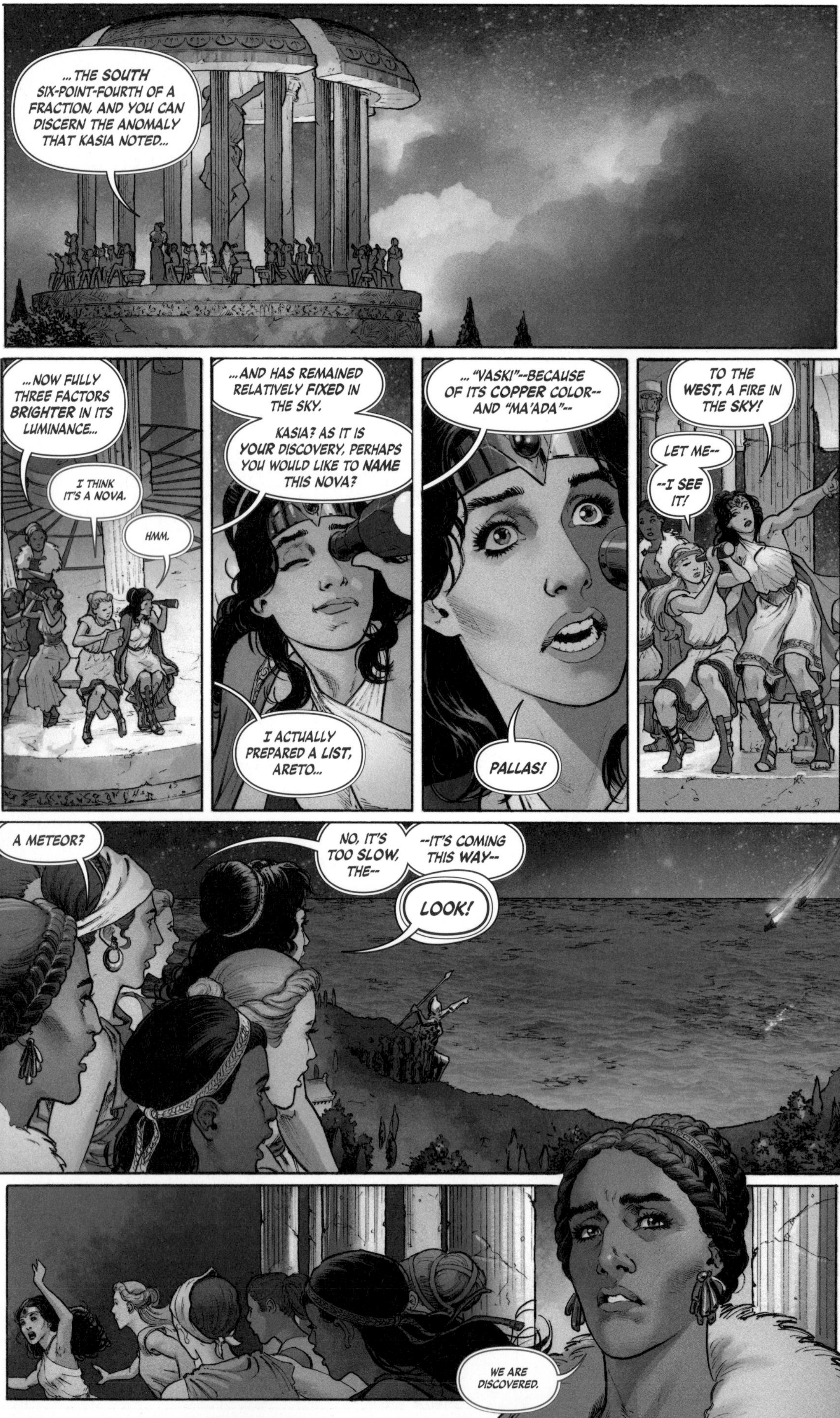
...THE SOUTH SIX-POINT-FOURTH OF A FRACTION, AND YOU CAN DISCERN THE ANOMALY THAT KASIA NOTED...
...NOW FULLY THREE FACTORS BRIGHTER IN ITS LUMINANCE...
I THINK IT'S A NOVA.
HMM.
...AND HAS REMAINED RELATIVELY FIXED IN THE SKY.
KASIA? AS IT IS YOUR DISCOVERY, PERHAPS YOU WOULD LIKE TO NAME THIS NOVA?
I ACTUALLY PREPARED A LIST, ARETO...
..."VASKI"--BECAUSE OF ITS COPPER COLOR--AND "MA'ADA"--
PALLAS!
TO THE WEST, A FIRE IN THE SKY!
LET ME--
--I SEE IT!
A METEOR?
NO, IT'S TOO SLOW, THE--
--IT'S COMING THIS WAY--
LOOK!
WE ARE DISCOVERED.

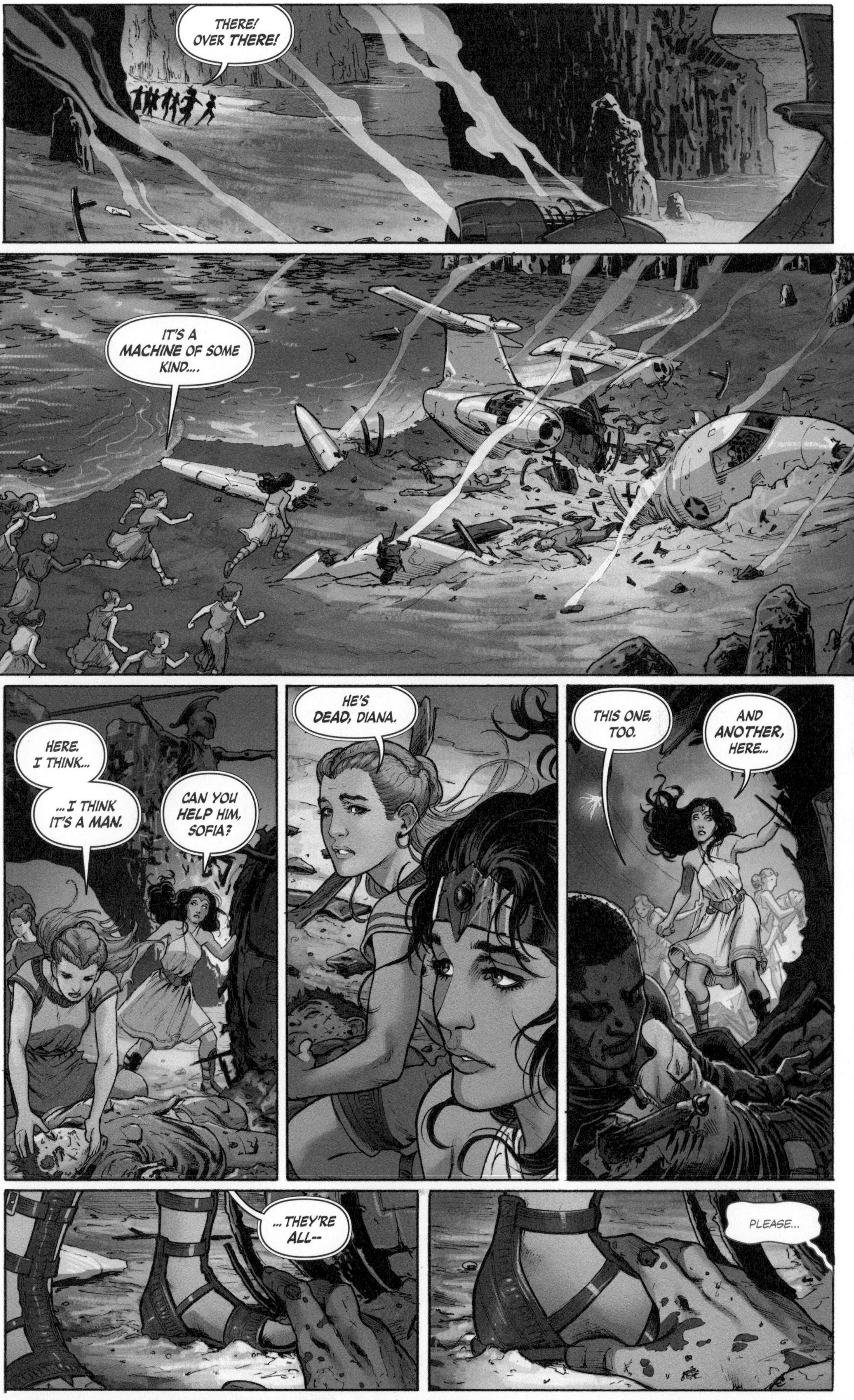
THERE! OVER THERE!
IT'S A MACHINE OF SOME KIND....
HERE. I THINK...
...I THINK IT'S A MAN.
CAN YOU HELP HIM, SOFIA?
HE'S DEAD, DIANA.
THIS ONE, TOO.
AND ANOTHER, HERE...
...THEY'RE ALL--
PLEASE...

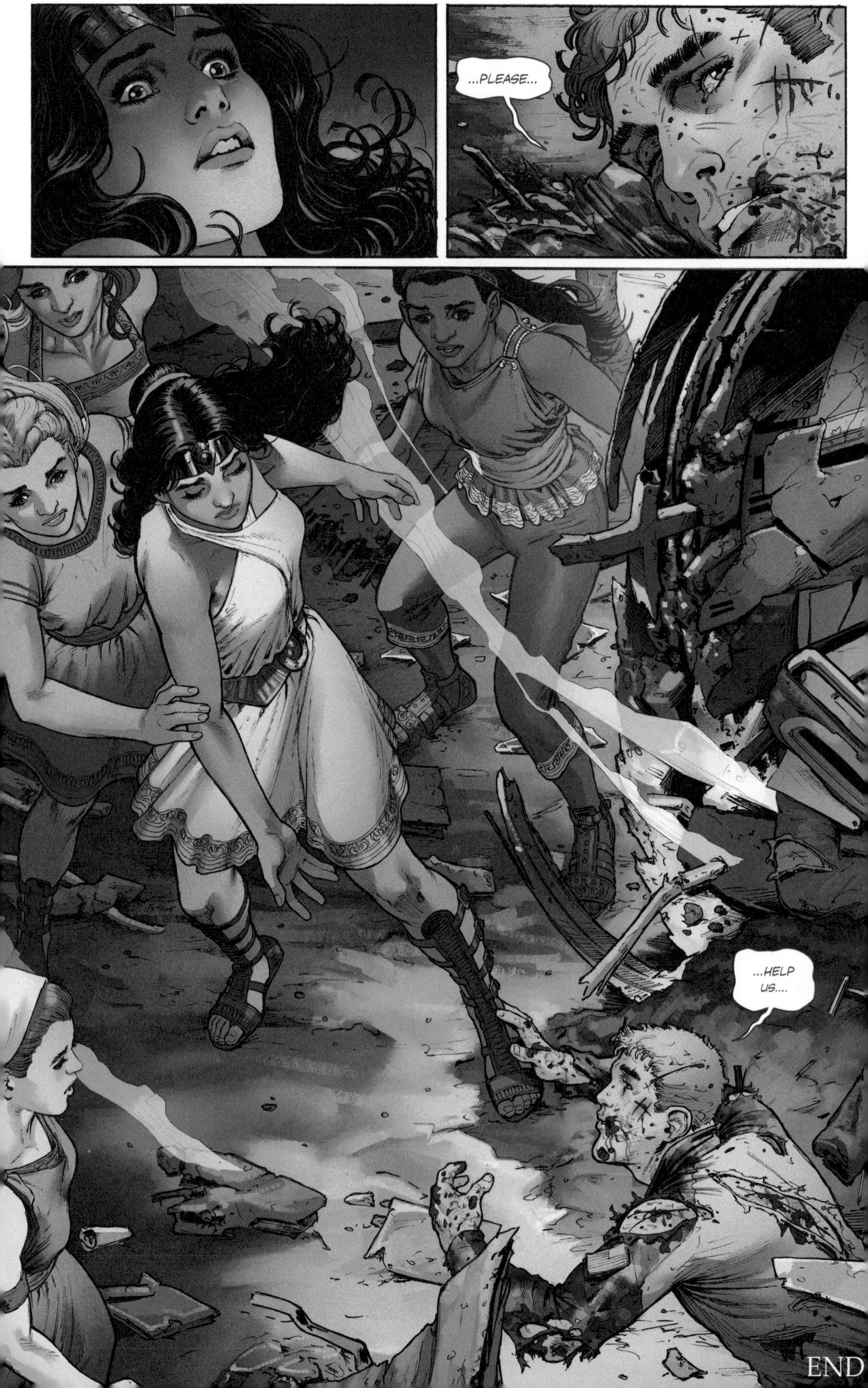
...PLEASE...
...HELP US....
END

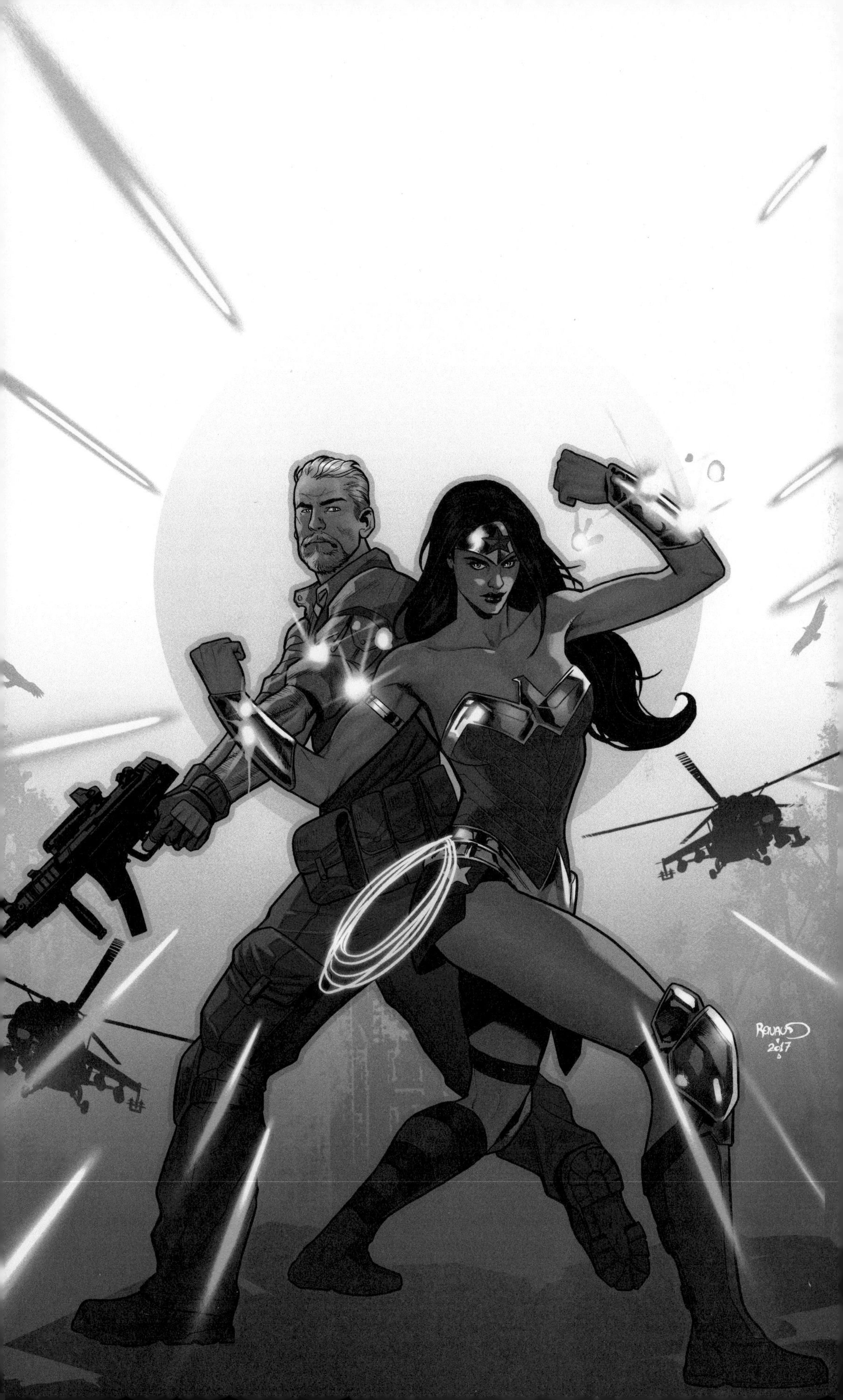
RENAUD
2017

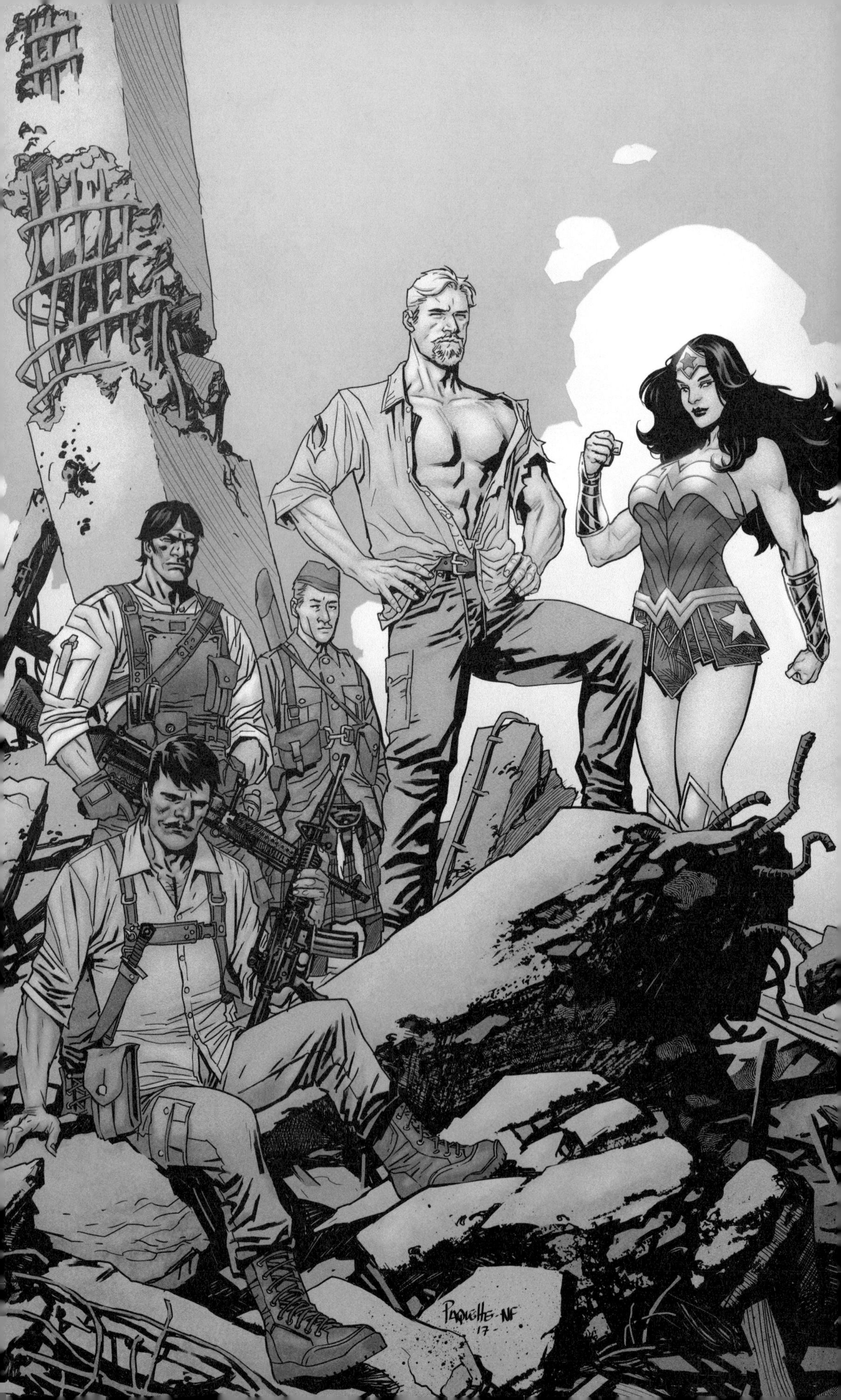
PAQUETTE-NF
17

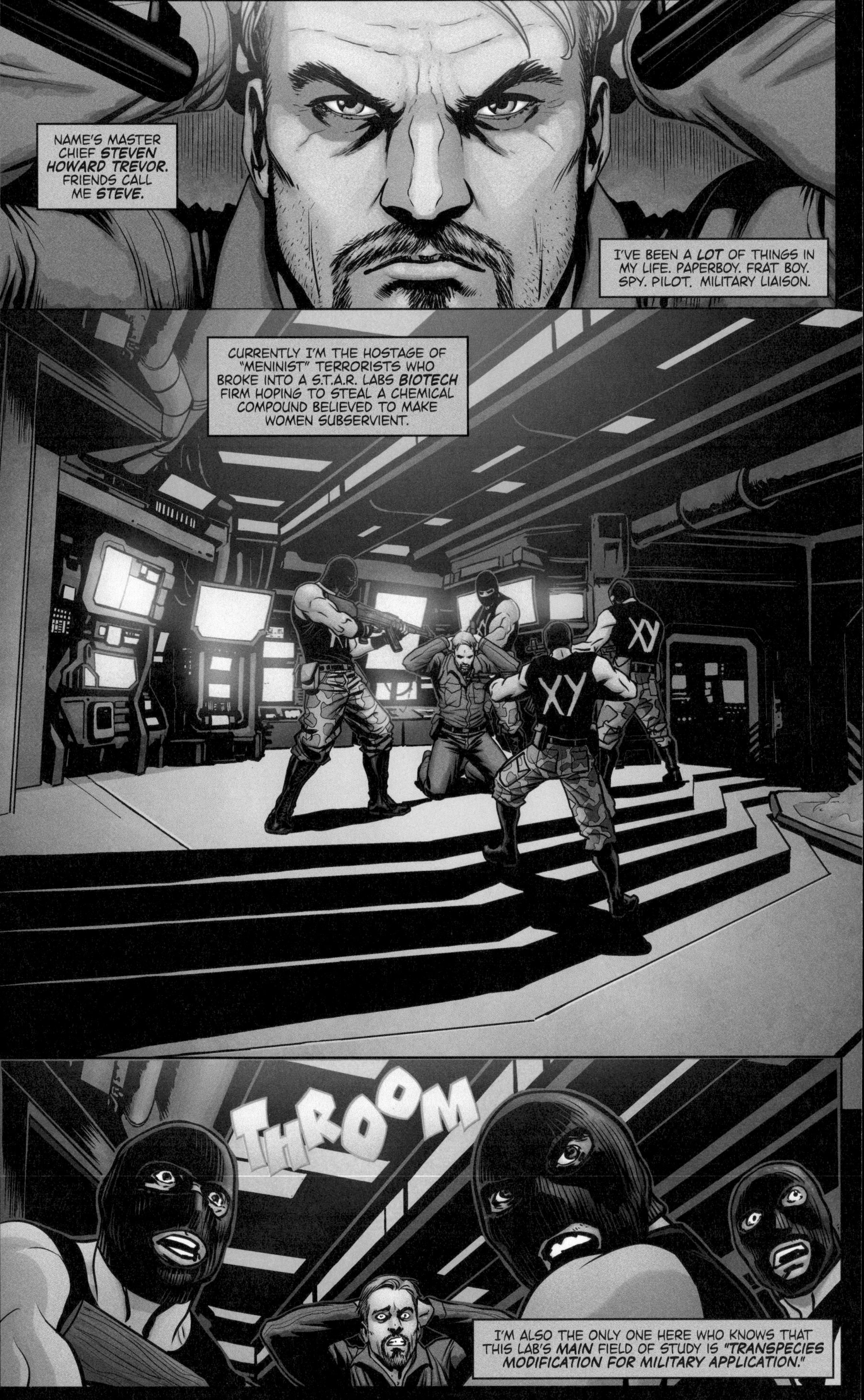
NAME'S MASTER CHIEF STEVEN HOWARD TREVOR. FRIENDS CALL ME STEVE.
I'VE BEEN A LOT OF THINGS IN MY LIFE. PAPERBOY. FRAT BOY. SPY. PILOT. MILITARY LIAISON.
CURRENTLY I'M THE HOSTAGE OF "MENINIST" TERRORISTS WHO BROKE INTO A S.T.A.R. LABS BIOTECH FIRM HOPING TO STEAL A CHEMICAL COMPOUND BELIEVED TO MAKE WOMEN SUBSERVIENT.
XY
XY
THROOM
I'M ALSO THE ONLY ONE HERE WHO KNOWS THAT THIS LAB'S MAIN FIELD OF STUDY IS "TRANSPECIES MODIFICATION FOR MILITARY APPLICATION."

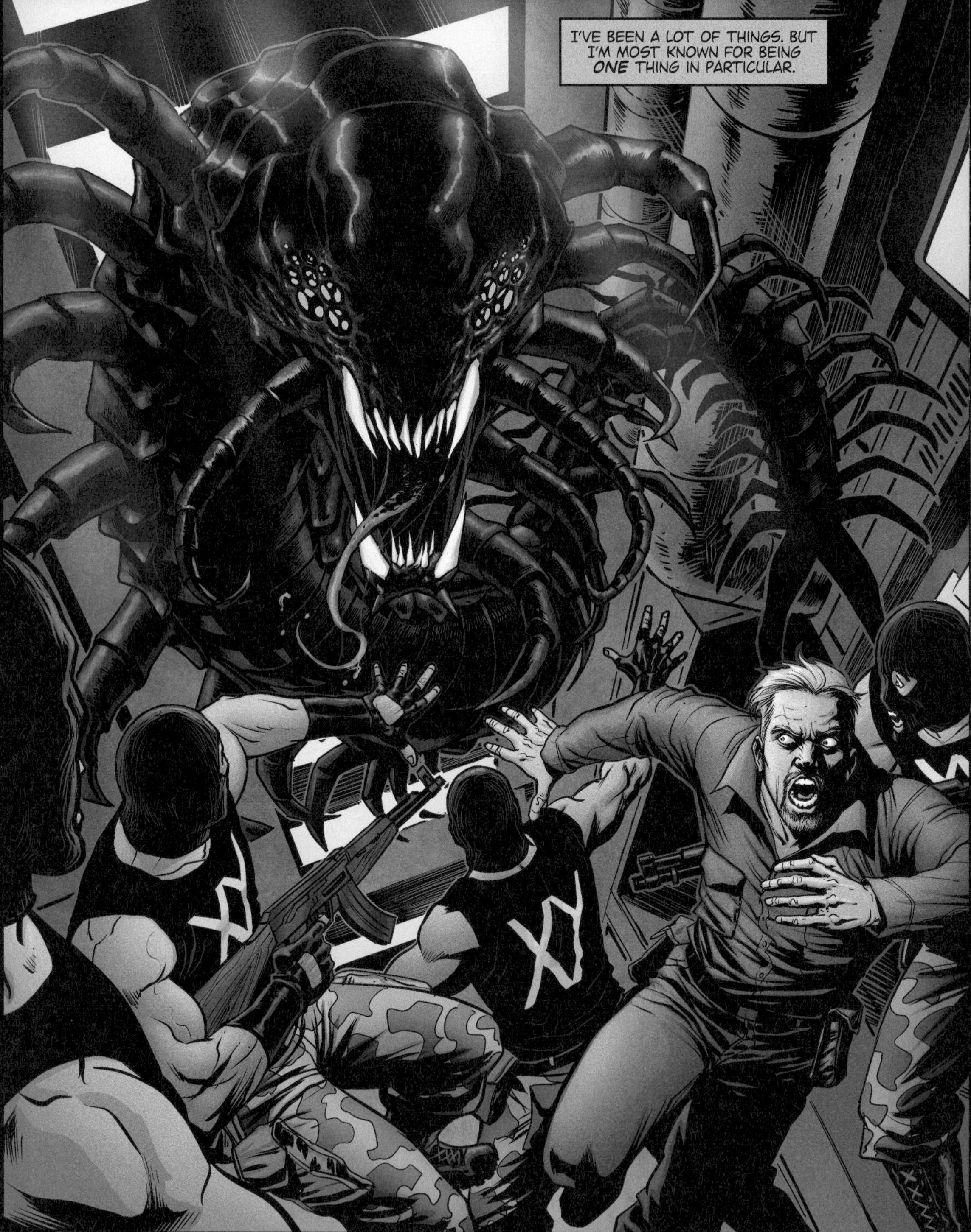
I'VE BEEN A LOT OF THINGS. BUT I'M MOST KNOWN FOR BEING *ONE* THING IN PARTICULAR.

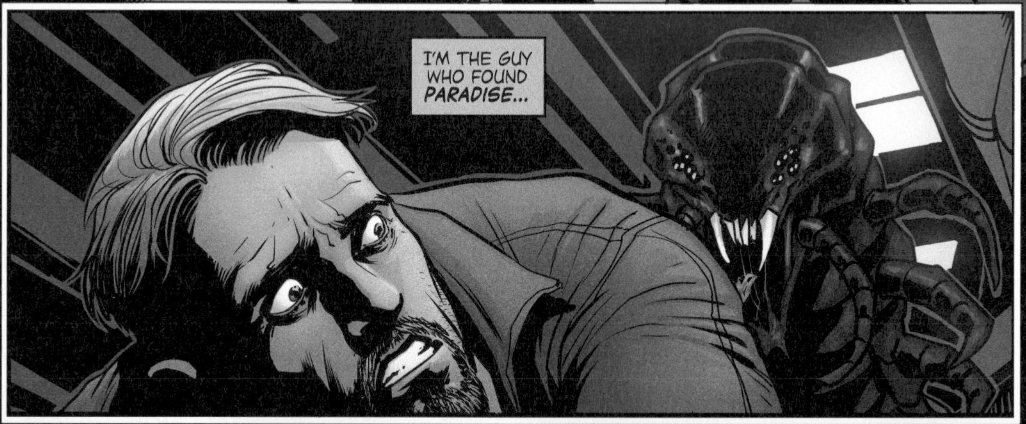
I'M THE GUY WHO FOUND *PARADISE*...

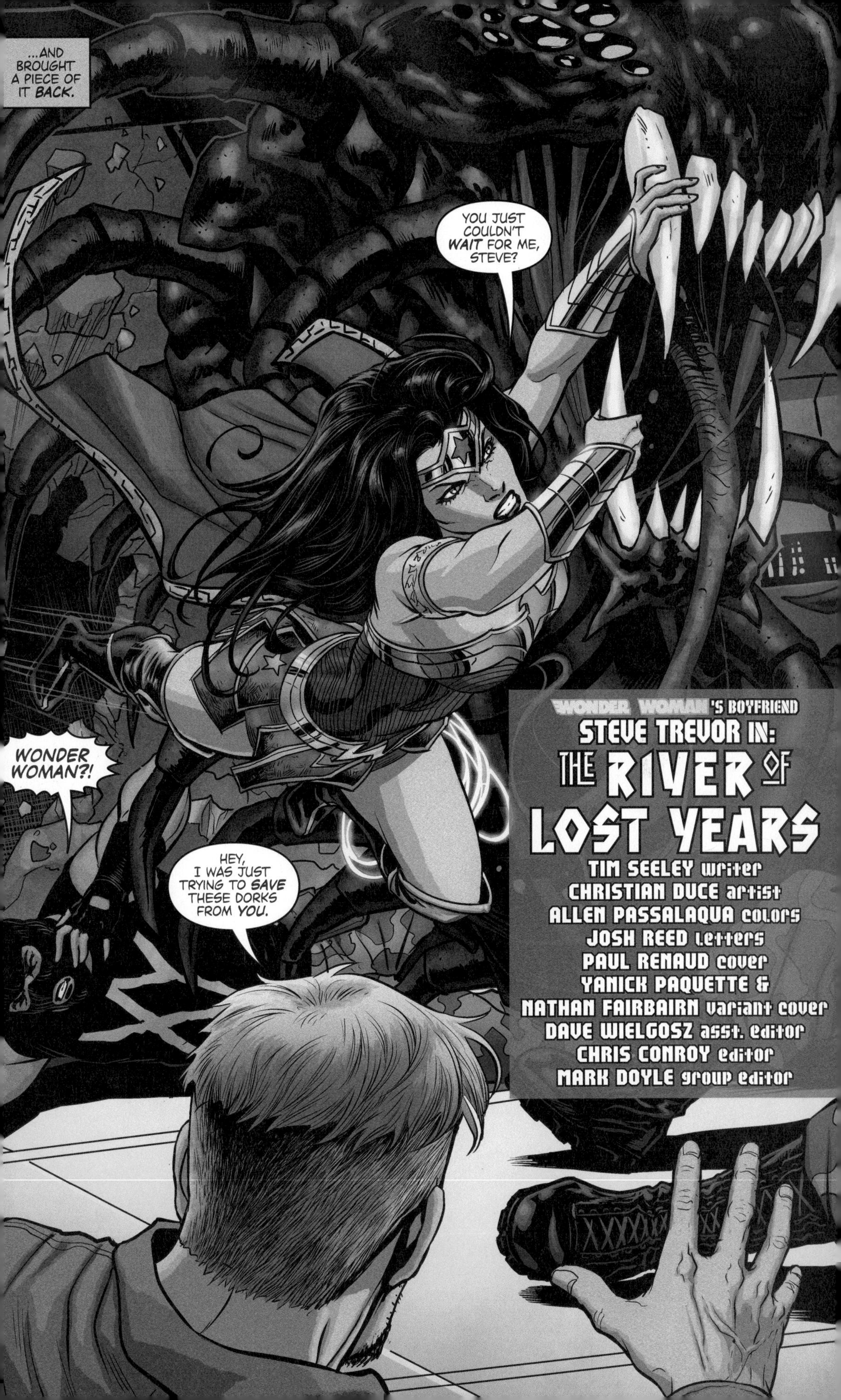
...AND BROUGHT A PIECE OF IT BACK.
YOU JUST COULDN'T WAIT FOR ME, STEVE?
WONDER WOMAN?!
HEY, I WAS JUST TRYING TO SAVE THESE DORKS FROM YOU.
WONDER WOMAN'S BOYFRIEND
STEVE TREVOR IN:
THE RIVER OF LOST YEARS
TIM SEELEY writer
CHRISTIAN DUCE artist
ALLEN PASSALAQUA colors
JOSH REED letters
PAUL RENAUD cover
YANICK PAQUETTE & NATHAN FAIRBAIRN variant cover
DAVE WIELGOSZ asst. editor
CHRIS CONROY editor
MARK DOYLE group editor

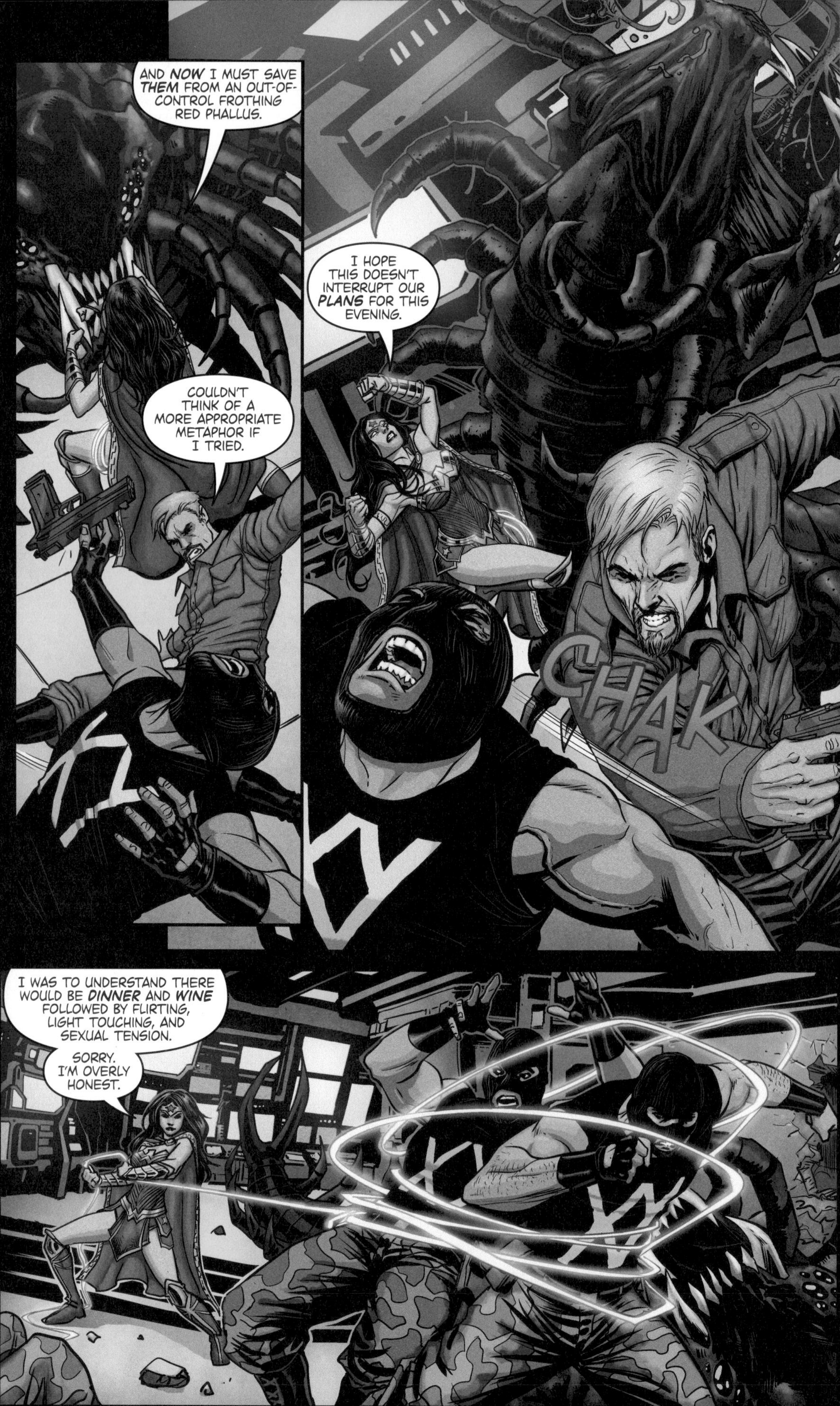
AND NOW I MUST SAVE THEM FROM AN OUT-OF-CONTROL FROTHING RED PHALLUS.
COULDN'T THINK OF A MORE APPROPRIATE METAPHOR IF I TRIED.
I HOPE THIS DOESN'T INTERRUPT OUR PLANS FOR THIS EVENING.
CHAK
I WAS TO UNDERSTAND THERE WOULD BE DINNER AND WINE FOLLOWED BY FLIRTING, LIGHT TOUCHING, AND SEXUAL TENSION.
SORRY. I'M OVERLY HONEST.

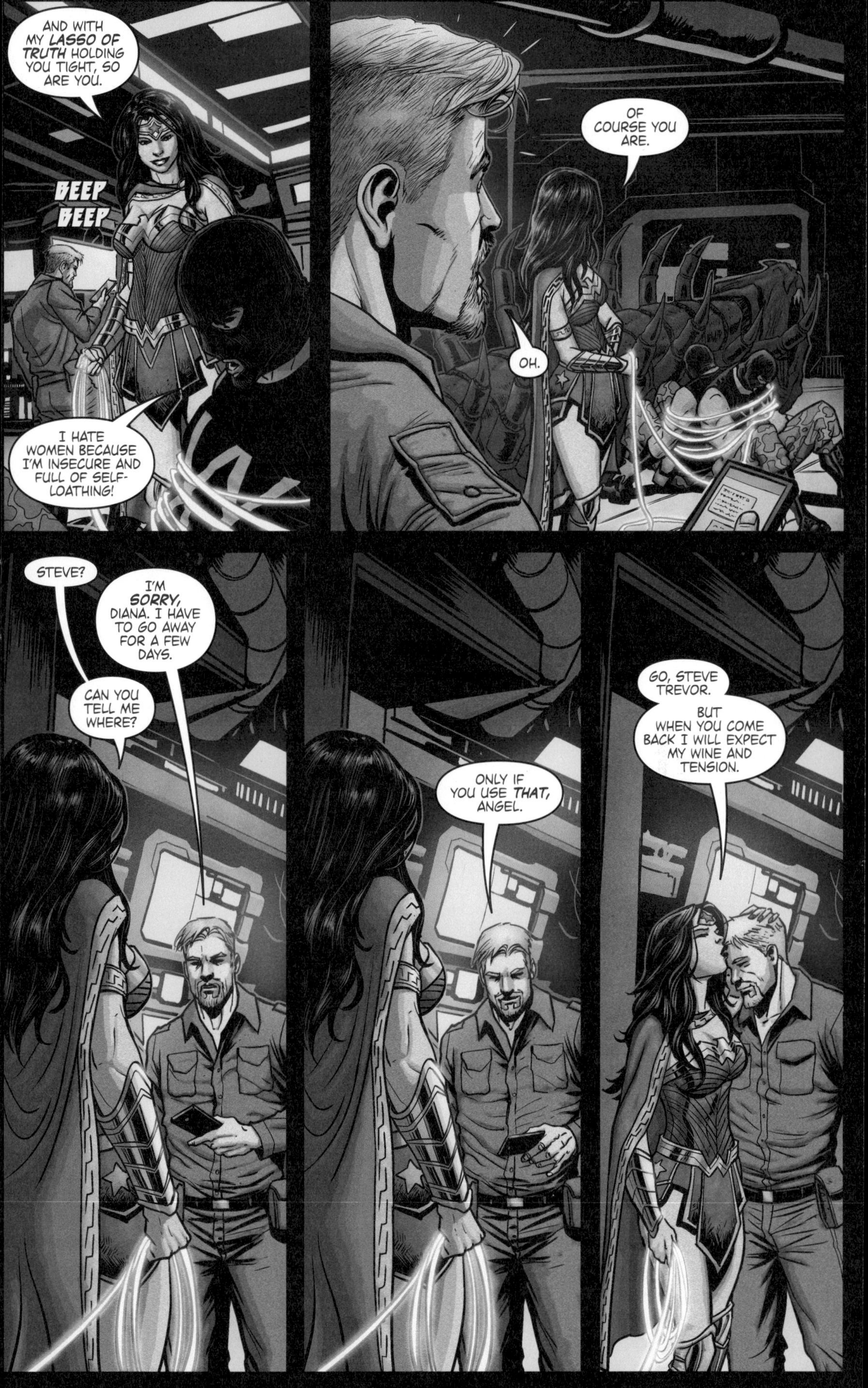
AND WITH MY LASSO OF TRUTH HOLDING YOU TIGHT, SO ARE YOU.
BEEP BEEP
I HATE WOMEN BECAUSE I'M INSECURE AND FULL OF SELF-LOATHING!
OF COURSE YOU ARE.
OH.
STEVE?
I'M SORRY, DIANA. I HAVE TO GO AWAY FOR A FEW DAYS.
CAN YOU TELL ME WHERE?
ONLY IF YOU USE THAT, ANGEL.
GO, STEVE TREVOR.
BUT WHEN YOU COME BACK I WILL EXPECT MY WINE AND TENSION.

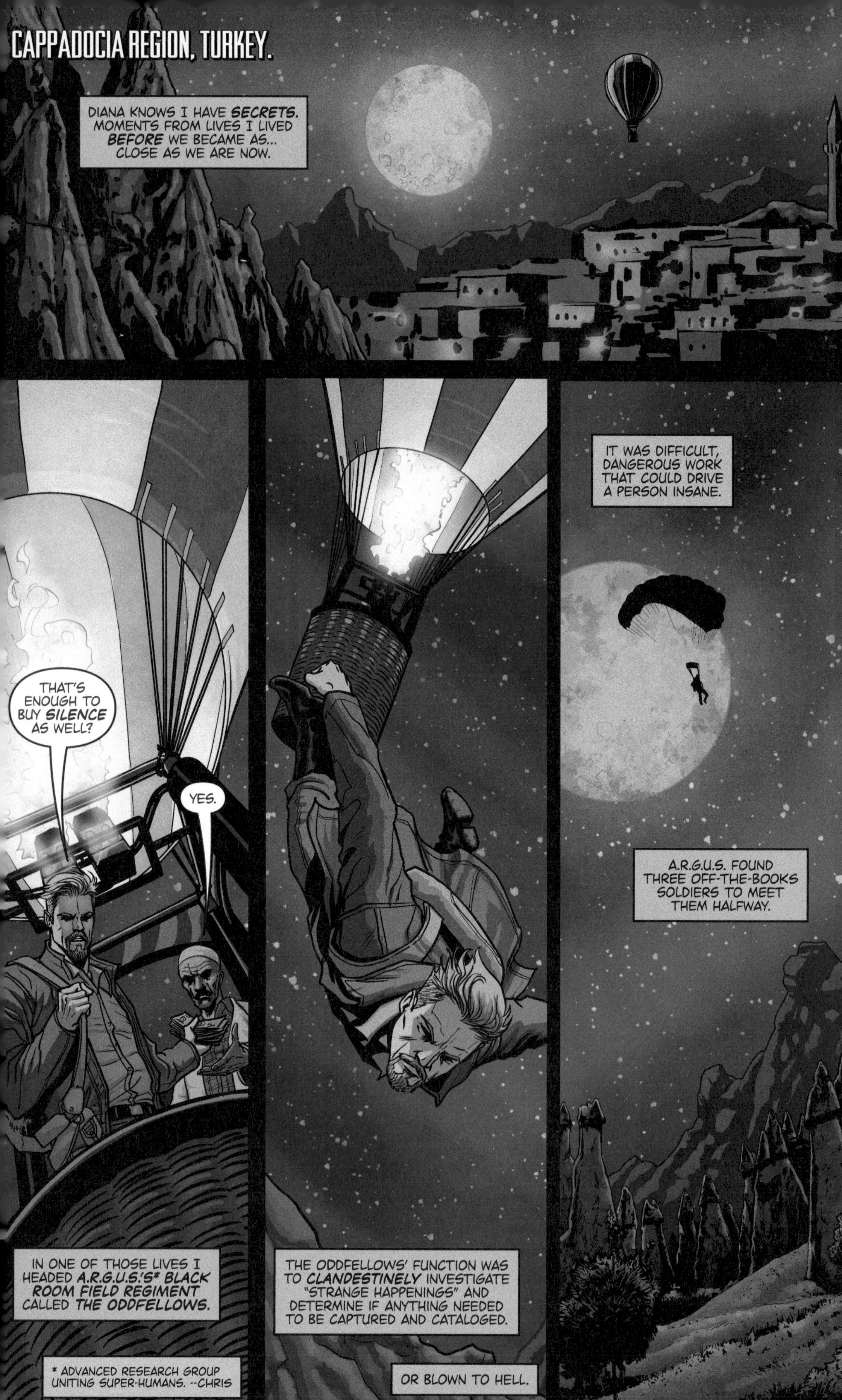

CAPPADOCIA REGION, TURKEY.
DIANA KNOWS I HAVE SECRETS. MOMENTS FROM LIVES I LIVED BEFORE WE BECAME AS... CLOSE AS WE ARE NOW.
THAT'S ENOUGH TO BUY SILENCE AS WELL?
YES.
IN ONE OF THOSE LIVES I HEADED A.R.G.U.S.'S* BLACK ROOM FIELD REGIMENT CALLED THE ODDFELLOWS.
* ADVANCED RESEARCH GROUP UNITING SUPER-HUMANS. --CHRIS
THE ODDFELLOWS' FUNCTION WAS TO CLANDESTINELY INVESTIGATE "STRANGE HAPPENINGS" AND DETERMINE IF ANYTHING NEEDED TO BE CAPTURED AND CATALOGED.
OR BLOWN TO HELL.
IT WAS DIFFICULT, DANGEROUS WORK THAT COULD DRIVE A PERSON INSANE.
A.R.G.U.S. FOUND THREE OFF-THE-BOOKS SOLDIERS TO MEET THEM HALFWAY.

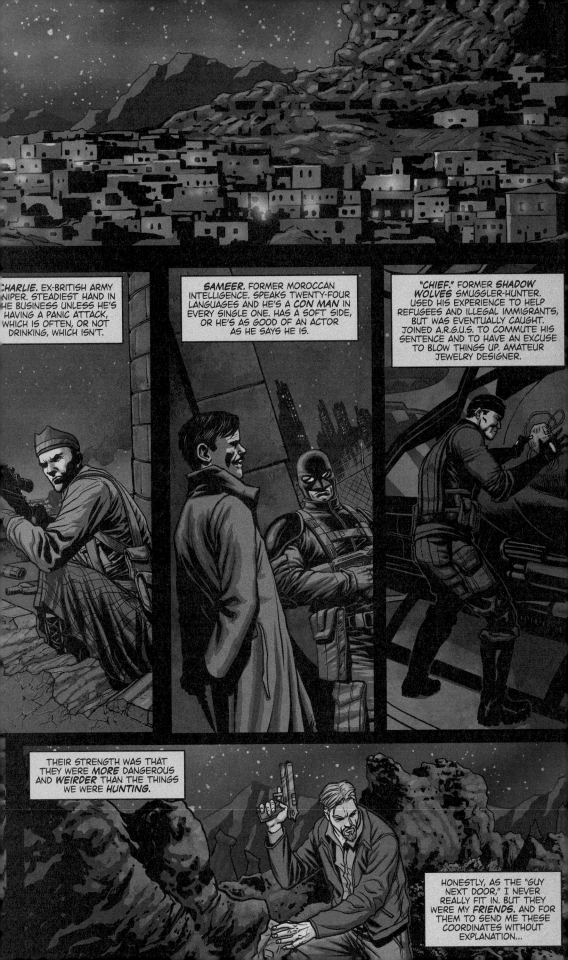

CHARLIE. EX-BRITISH ARMY SNIPER. STEADIEST HAND IN THE BUSINESS UNLESS HE'S HAVING A PANIC ATTACK, WHICH IS OFTEN, OR NOT DRINKING, WHICH ISN'T.

SAMEER. FORMER MOROCCAN INTELLIGENCE. SPEAKS TWENTY-FOUR LANGUAGES AND HE'S A *CON MAN* IN EVERY SINGLE ONE. HAS A SOFT SIDE, OR HE'S AS GOOD OF AN ACTOR AS HE SAYS HE IS.

"CHIEF." FORMER *SHADOW WOLVES* SMUGGLER-HUNTER. USED HIS EXPERIENCE TO HELP REFUGEES AND ILLEGAL IMMIGRANTS, BUT WAS EVENTUALLY CAUGHT. JOINED A.R.G.U.S. TO COMMUTE HIS SENTENCE AND TO HAVE AN EXCUSE TO BLOW THINGS UP. AMATEUR JEWELRY DESIGNER.

THEIR STRENGTH WAS THAT THEY WERE *MORE* DANGEROUS AND *WEIRDER* THAN THE THINGS WE WERE *HUNTING.*

HONESTLY, AS THE "GUY NEXT DOOR," I NEVER REALLY FIT IN. BUT THEY WERE MY *FRIENDS.* AND FOR THEM TO SEND ME THESE COORDINATES WITHOUT EXPLANATION...

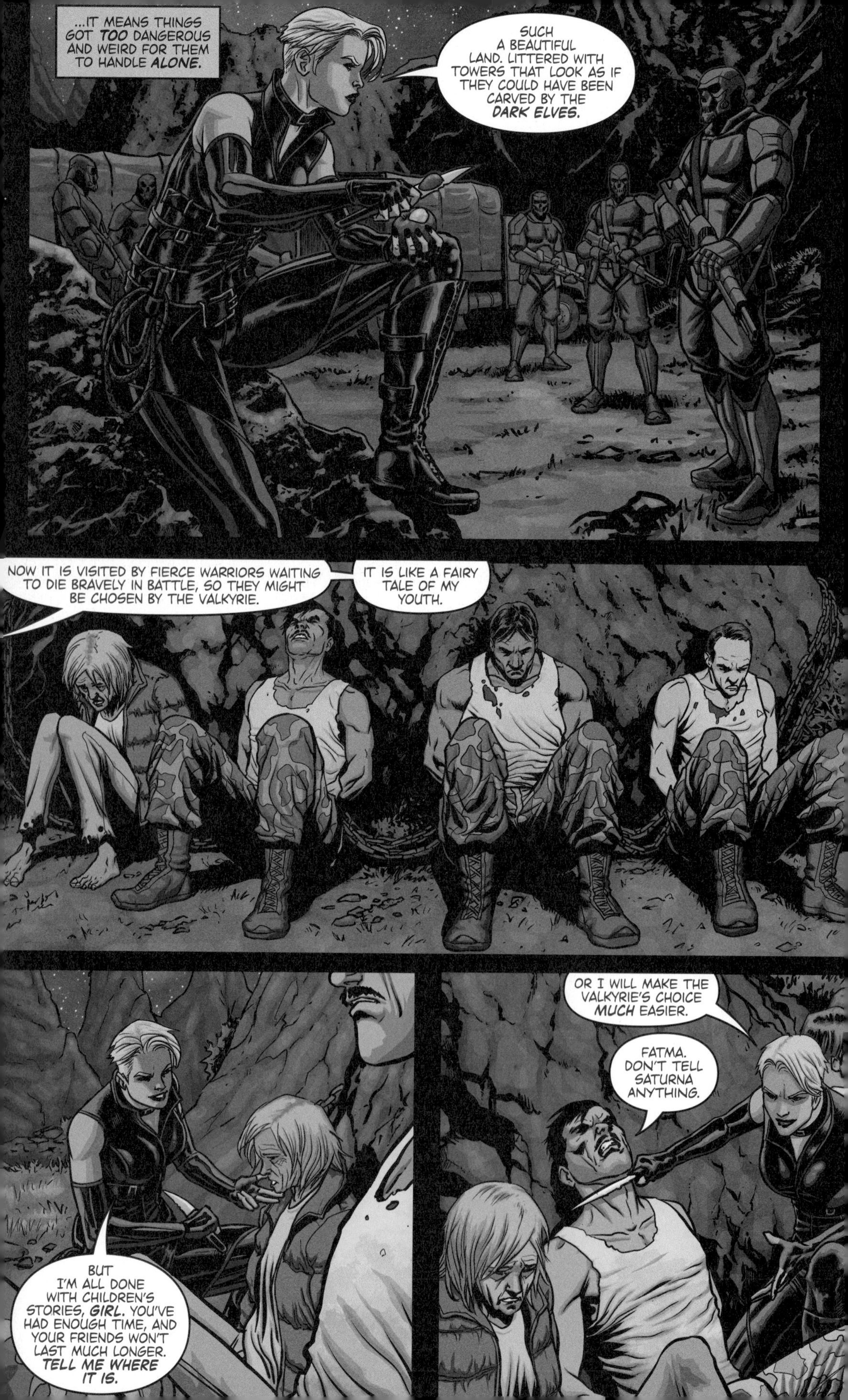
...IT MEANS THINGS GOT TOO DANGEROUS AND WEIRD FOR THEM TO HANDLE ALONE.
SUCH A BEAUTIFUL LAND. LITTERED WITH TOWERS THAT LOOK AS IF THEY COULD HAVE BEEN CARVED BY THE DARK ELVES.
NOW IT IS VISITED BY FIERCE WARRIORS WAITING TO DIE BRAVELY IN BATTLE, SO THEY MIGHT BE CHOSEN BY THE VALKYRIE.
IT IS LIKE A FAIRY TALE OF MY YOUTH.
BUT I'M ALL DONE WITH CHILDREN'S STORIES, GIRL. YOU'VE HAD ENOUGH TIME, AND YOUR FRIENDS WON'T LAST MUCH LONGER. TELL ME WHERE IT IS.
OR I WILL MAKE THE VALKYRIE'S CHOICE MUCH EASIER.
FATMA. DON'T TELL SATURNA ANYTHING.

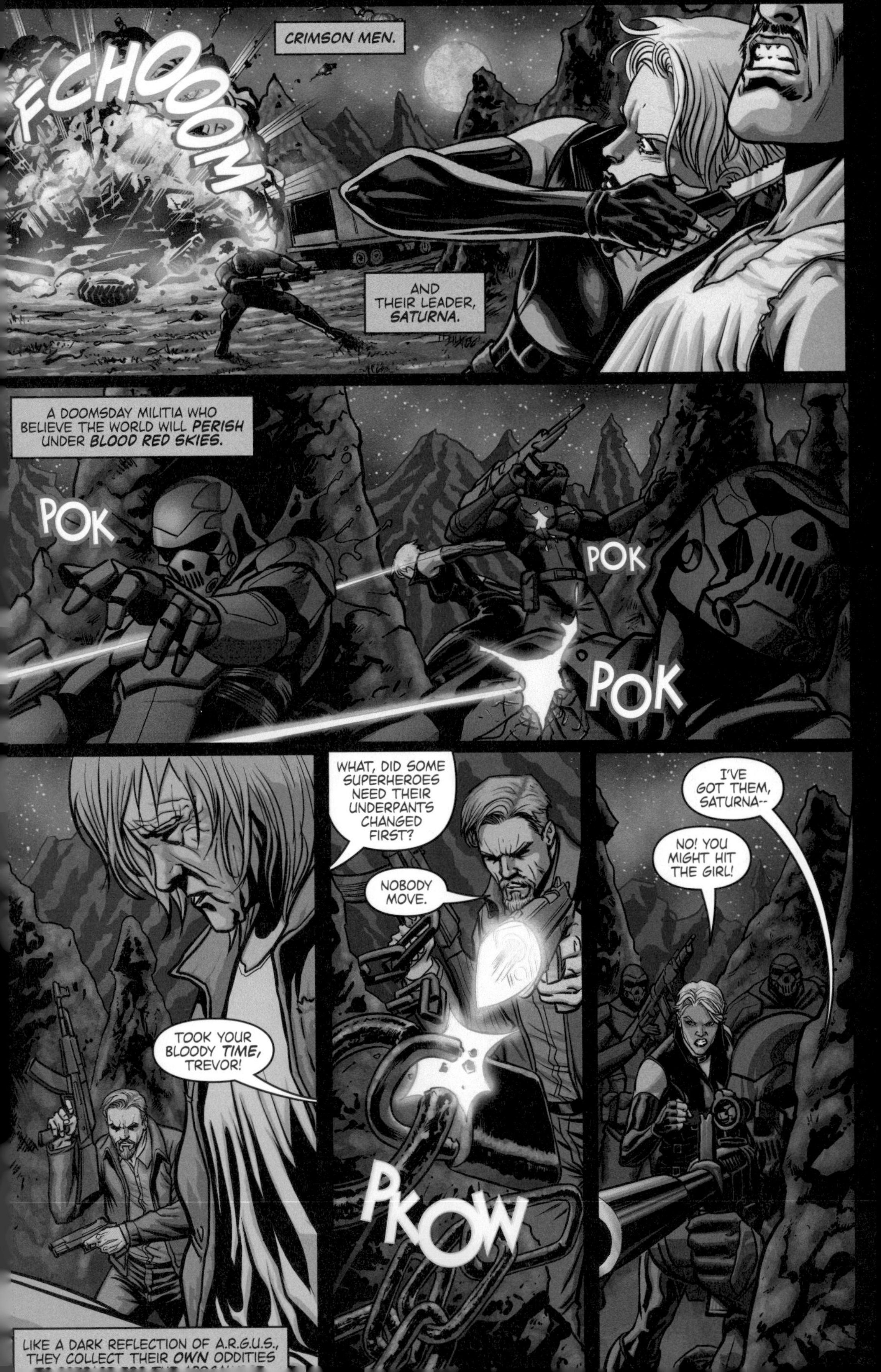
CRIMSON MEN.
FCHOOOM
AND THEIR LEADER, SATURNA.
A DOOMSDAY MILITIA WHO BELIEVE THE WORLD WILL PERISH UNDER BLOOD RED SKIES.
POK
POK
POK
TOOK YOUR BLOODY TIME, TREVOR!
WHAT, DID SOME SUPERHEROES NEED THEIR UNDERPANTS CHANGED FIRST?
NOBODY MOVE.
PKOW
I'VE GOT THEM, SATURNA--
NO! YOU MIGHT HIT THE GIRL!
LIKE A DARK REFLECTION OF A.R.G.U.S., THEY COLLECT THEIR OWN ODDITIES

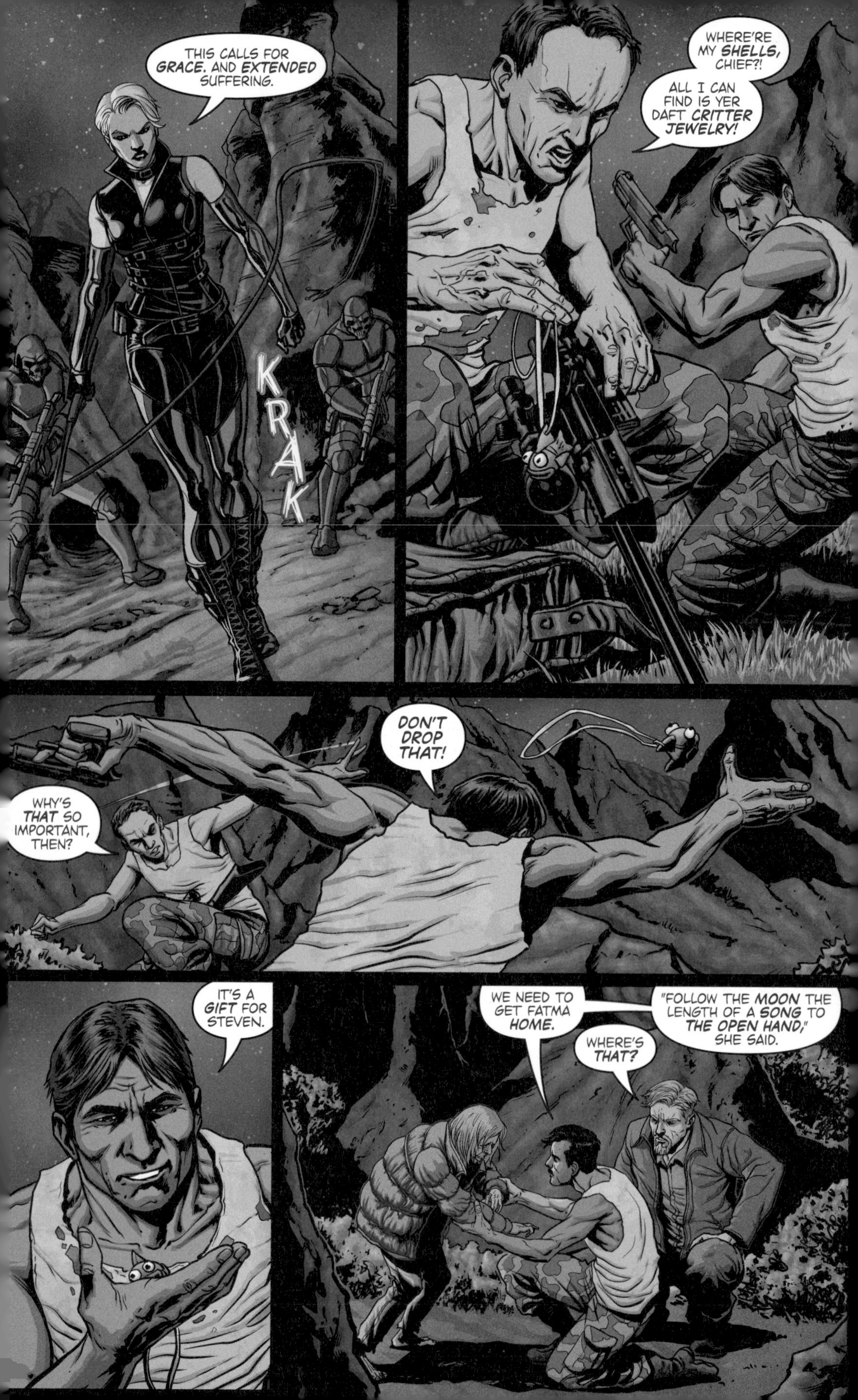
THIS CALLS FOR GRACE. AND EXTENDED SUFFERING.
KRAK
WHERE'RE MY SHELLS, CHIEF?!
ALL I CAN FIND IS YER DAFT CRITTER JEWELRY!
DON'T DROP THAT!
WHY'S THAT SO IMPORTANT, THEN?
IT'S A GIFT FOR STEVEN.
WE NEED TO GET FATMA HOME.
WHERE'S THAT?
"FOLLOW THE MOON THE LENGTH OF A SONG TO THE OPEN HAND," SHE SAID.

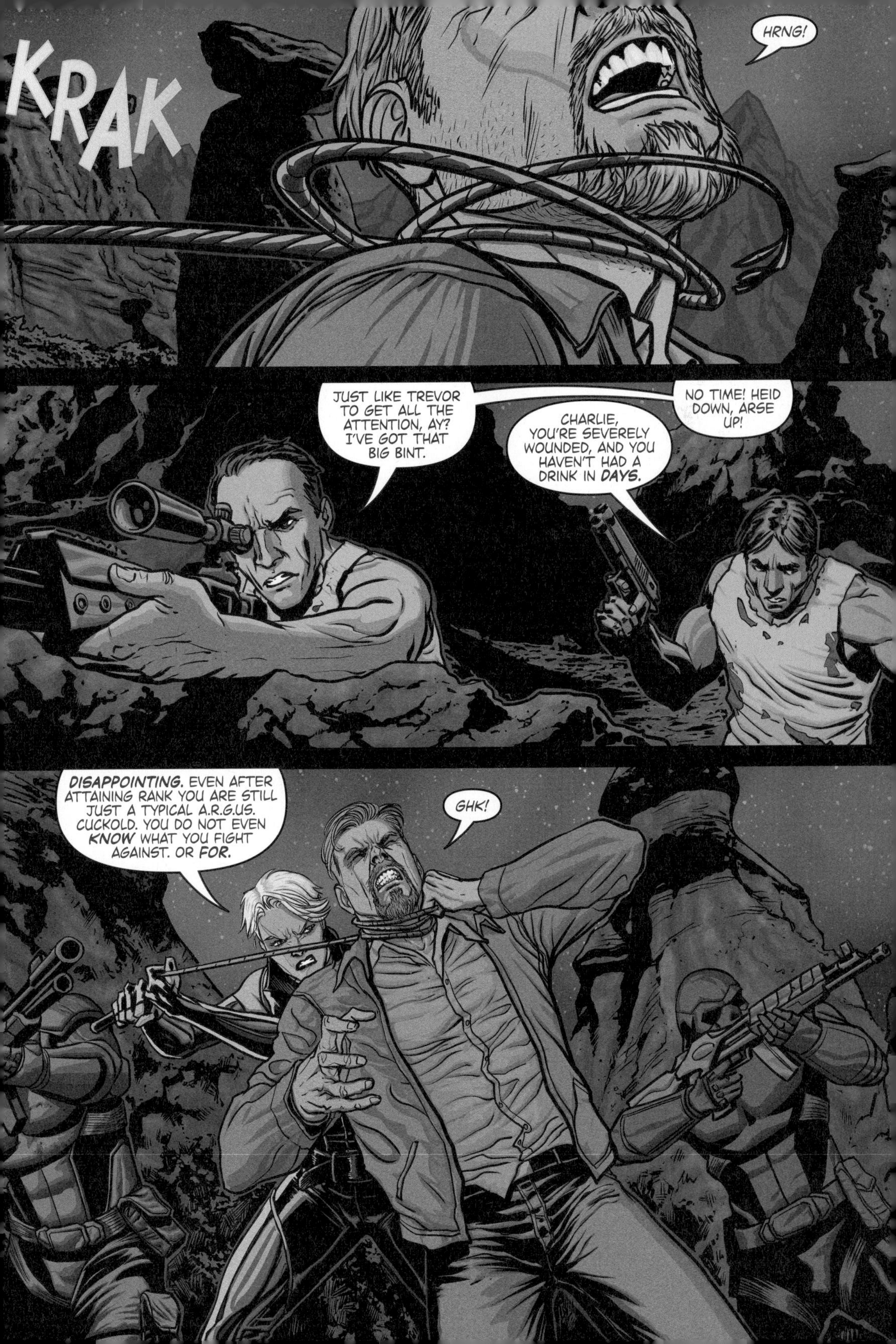
KRAK
HRNG!
JUST LIKE TREVOR TO GET ALL THE ATTENTION, AY? I'VE GOT THAT BIG BINT.
CHARLIE, YOU'RE SEVERELY WOUNDED, AND YOU HAVEN'T HAD A DRINK IN DAYS.
NO TIME! HEID DOWN, ARSE UP!
DISAPPOINTING. EVEN AFTER ATTAINING RANK YOU ARE STILL JUST A TYPICAL A.R.G.U.S. CUCKOLD. YOU DO NOT EVEN KNOW WHAT YOU FIGHT AGAINST. OR FOR.
GHK!

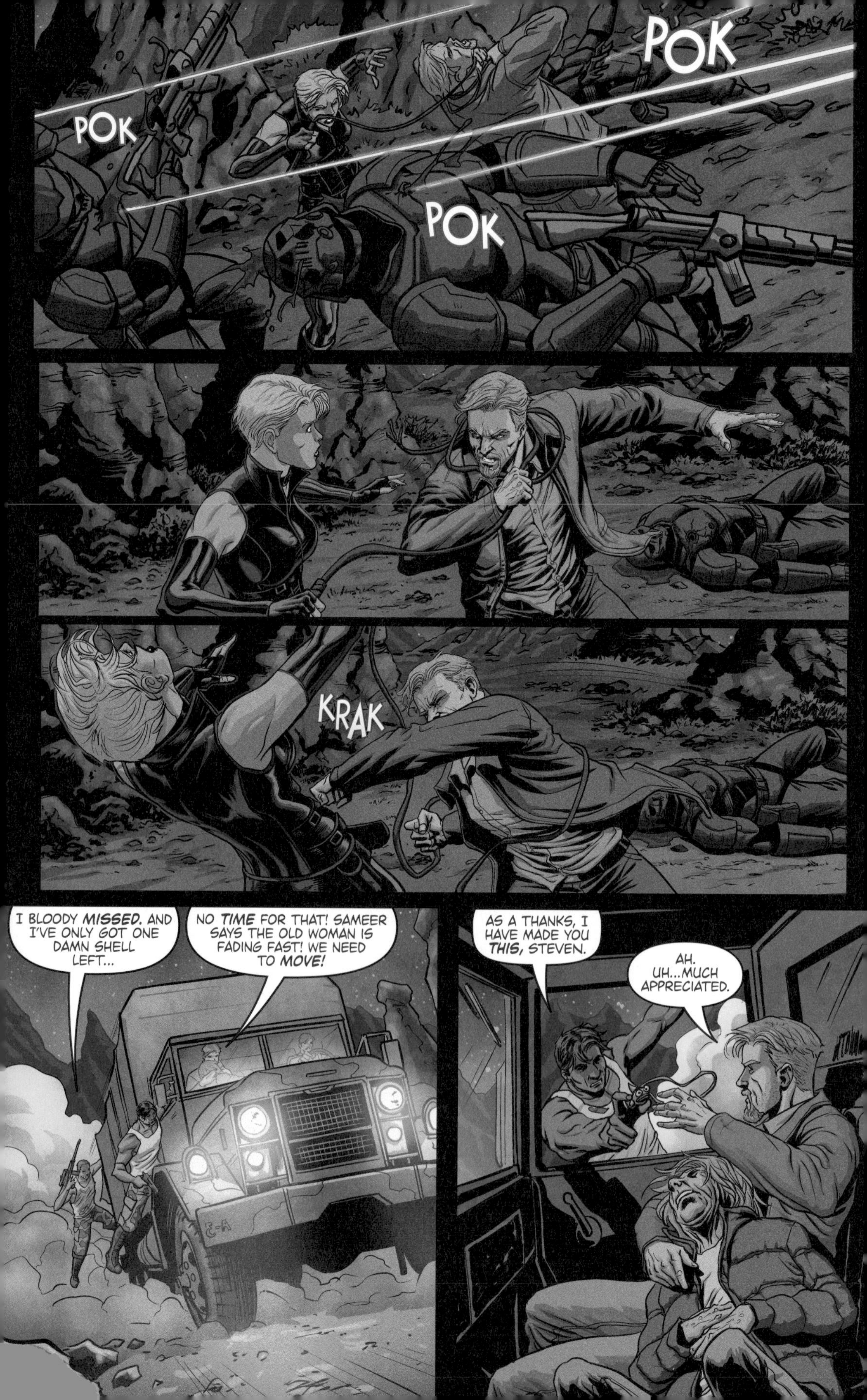
POK
POK
POK
KRAK
I BLOODY MISSED. AND I'VE ONLY GOT ONE DAMN SHELL LEFT...
NO TIME FOR THAT! SAMEER SAYS THE OLD WOMAN IS FADING FAST! WE NEED TO MOVE!
AS A THANKS, I HAVE MADE YOU THIS, STEVEN.
AH. UH...MUCH APPRECIATED.

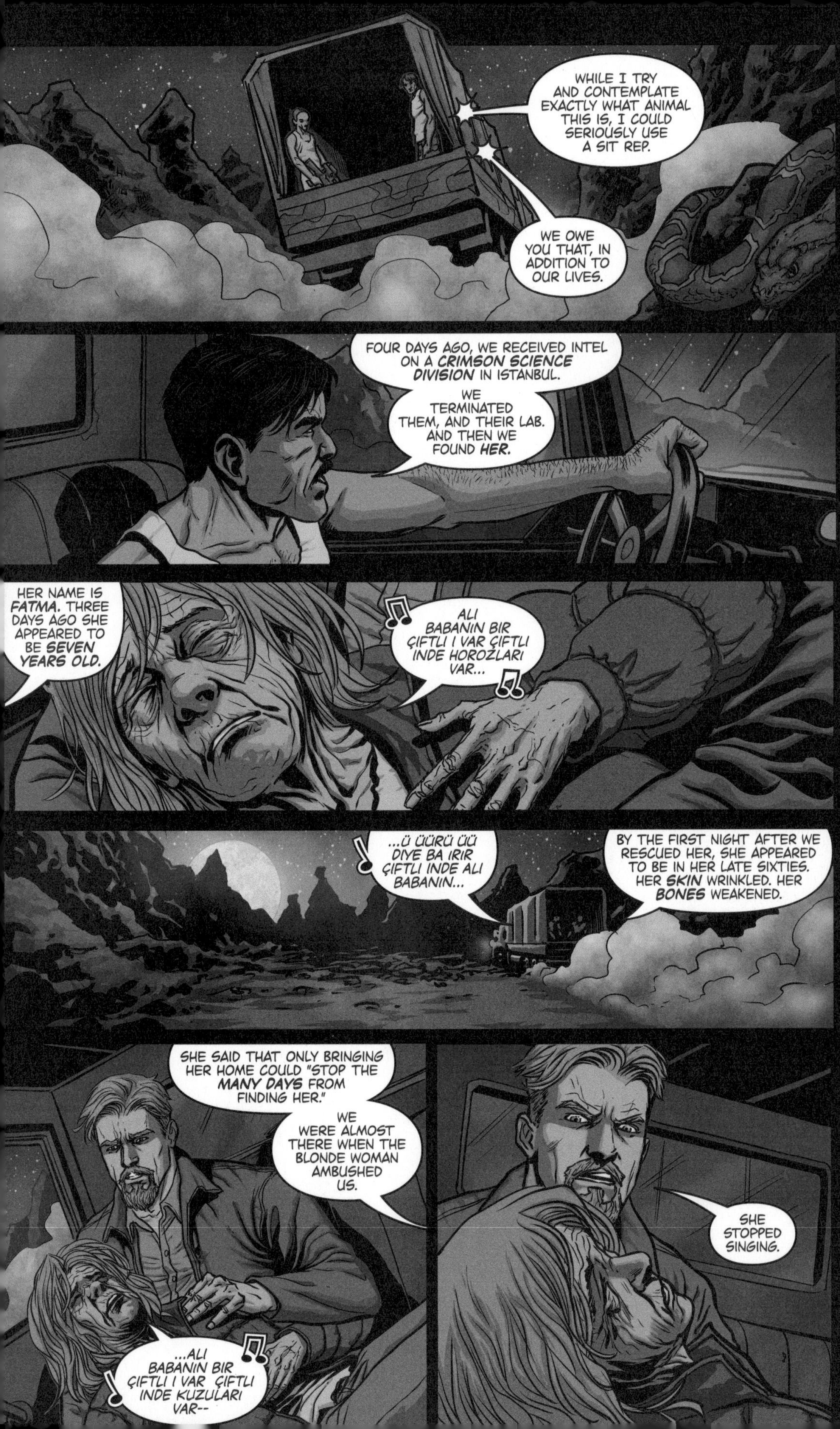
WHILE I TRY AND CONTEMPLATE EXACTLY WHAT ANIMAL THIS IS, I COULD SERIOUSLY USE A SIT REP.
WE OWE YOU THAT, IN ADDITION TO OUR LIVES.
FOUR DAYS AGO, WE RECEIVED INTEL ON A **CRIMSON SCIENCE DIVISION** IN ISTANBUL.
WE TERMINATED THEM, AND THEIR LAB. AND THEN WE FOUND **HER.**
HER NAME IS **FATMA.** THREE DAYS AGO SHE APPEARED TO BE **SEVEN YEARS OLD.**
ALI BABANIN BIR ÇIFTLI I VAR ÇIFTLI INDE HOROŻLARI VAR...
...Ü ÜÜRÜ ÜÜ DIYE BA IRIR ÇIFTLI INDE ALI BABANIN...
BY THE FIRST NIGHT AFTER WE RESCUED HER, SHE APPEARED TO BE IN HER LATE SIXTIES. HER **SKIN** WRINKLED. HER **BONES** WEAKENED.
SHE SAID THAT ONLY BRINGING HER HOME COULD "STOP THE **MANY DAYS** FROM FINDING HER."
WE WERE ALMOST THERE WHEN THE BLONDE WOMAN AMBUSHED US.
...ALI BABANIN BIR ÇIFTLI I VAR ÇIFTLI INDE KUZULARI VAR--
SHE STOPPED SINGING.

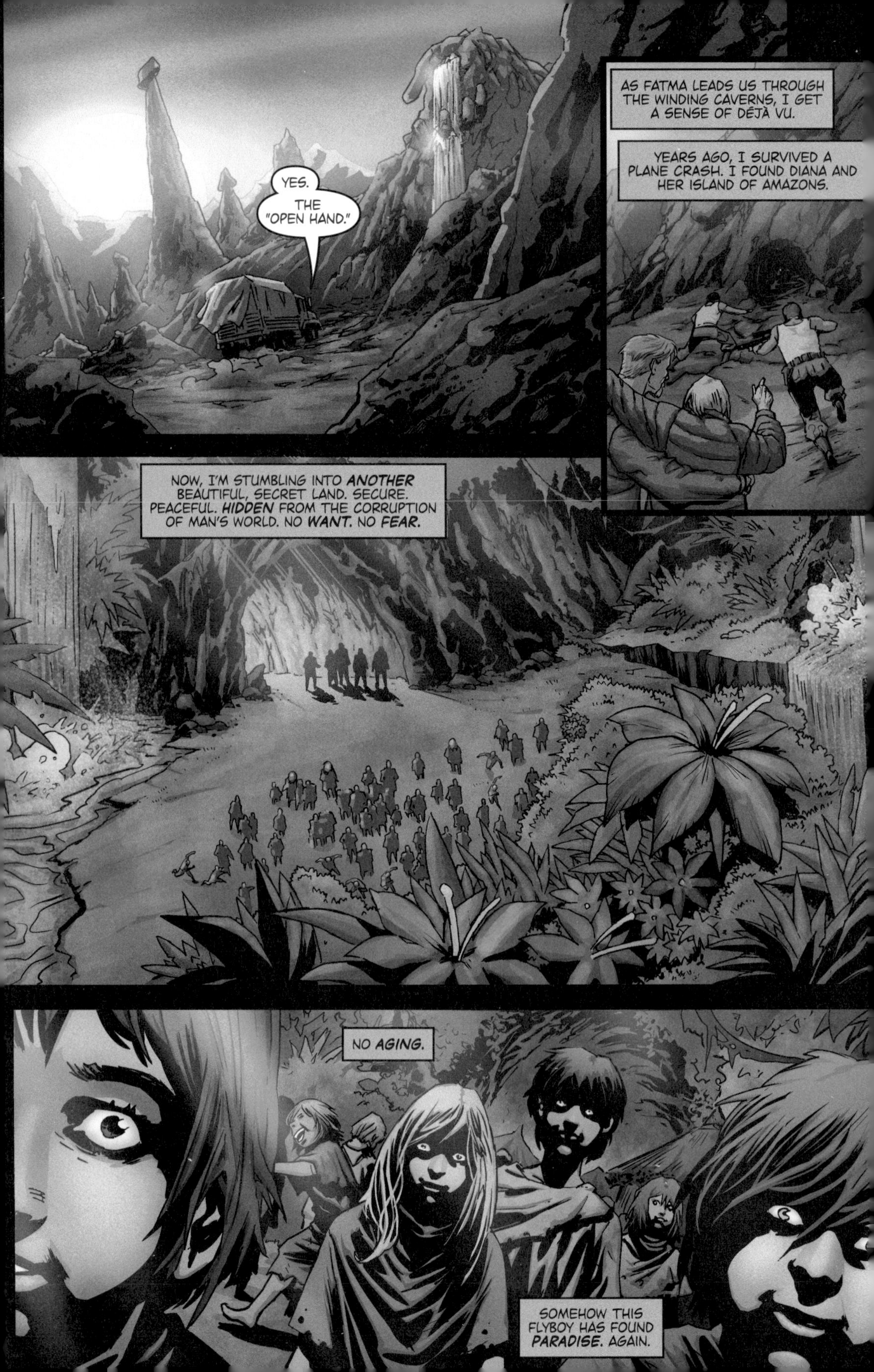
YES.
THE "OPEN HAND."
AS FATMA LEADS US THROUGH THE WINDING CAVERNS, I GET A SENSE OF DÉJÀ VU.
YEARS AGO, I SURVIVED A PLANE CRASH. I FOUND DIANA AND HER ISLAND OF AMAZONS.
NOW, I'M STUMBLING INTO ANOTHER BEAUTIFUL, SECRET LAND. SECURE. PEACEFUL. HIDDEN FROM THE CORRUPTION OF MAN'S WORLD. NO WANT. NO FEAR.
NO AGING.
SOMEHOW THIS FLYBOY HAS FOUND PARADISE. AGAIN.

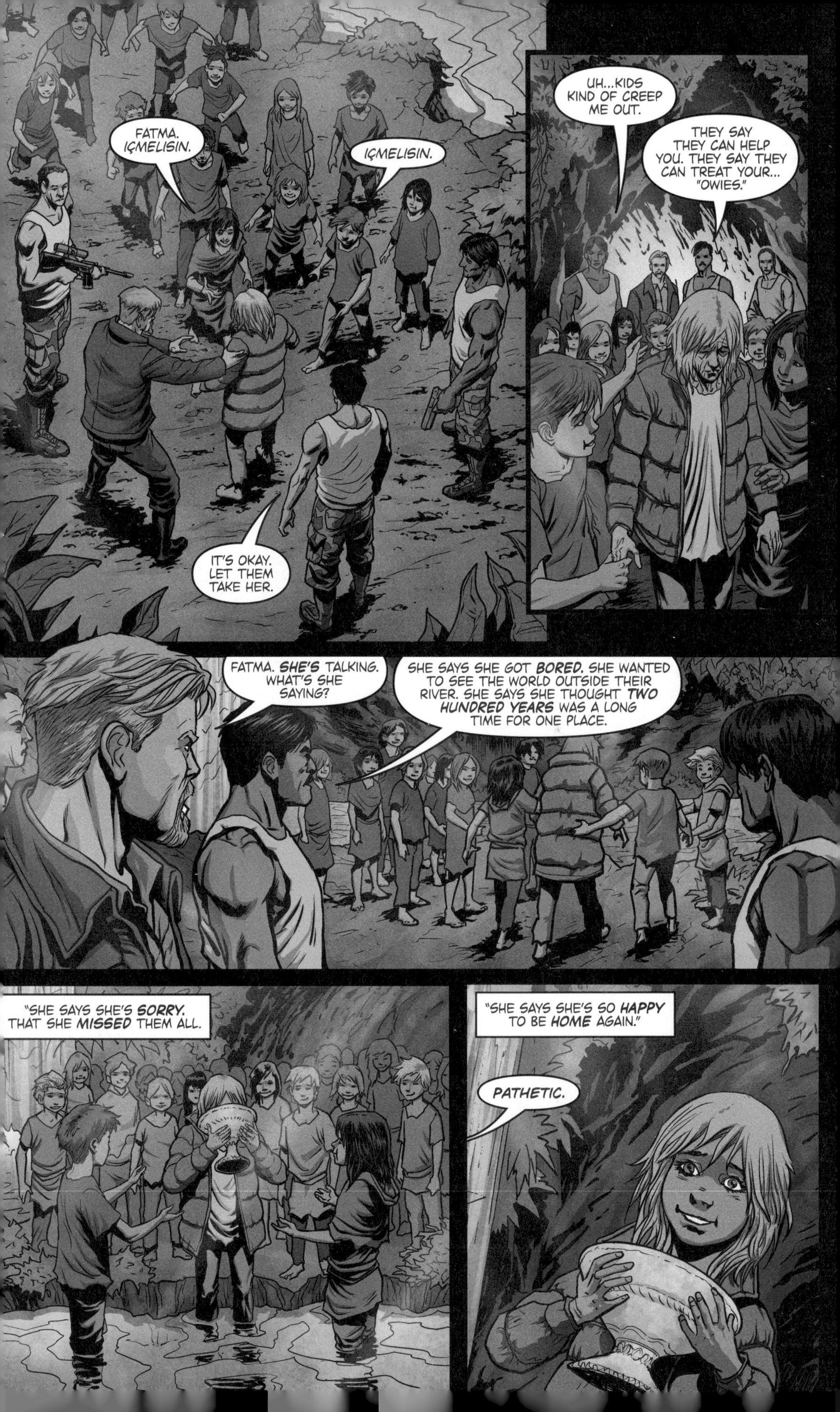
FATMA. IÇMELISIN.
IÇMELISIN.
IT'S OKAY. LET THEM TAKE HER.
UH...KIDS KIND OF CREEP ME OUT.
THEY SAY THEY CAN HELP YOU. THEY SAY THEY CAN TREAT YOUR... "OWIES."
FATMA. SHE'S TALKING. WHAT'S SHE SAYING?
SHE SAYS SHE GOT BORED. SHE WANTED TO SEE THE WORLD OUTSIDE THEIR RIVER. SHE SAYS SHE THOUGHT TWO HUNDRED YEARS WAS A LONG TIME FOR ONE PLACE.
"SHE SAYS SHE'S SORRY. THAT SHE MISSED THEM ALL.
"SHE SAYS SHE'S SO HAPPY TO BE HOME AGAIN."
PATHETIC.

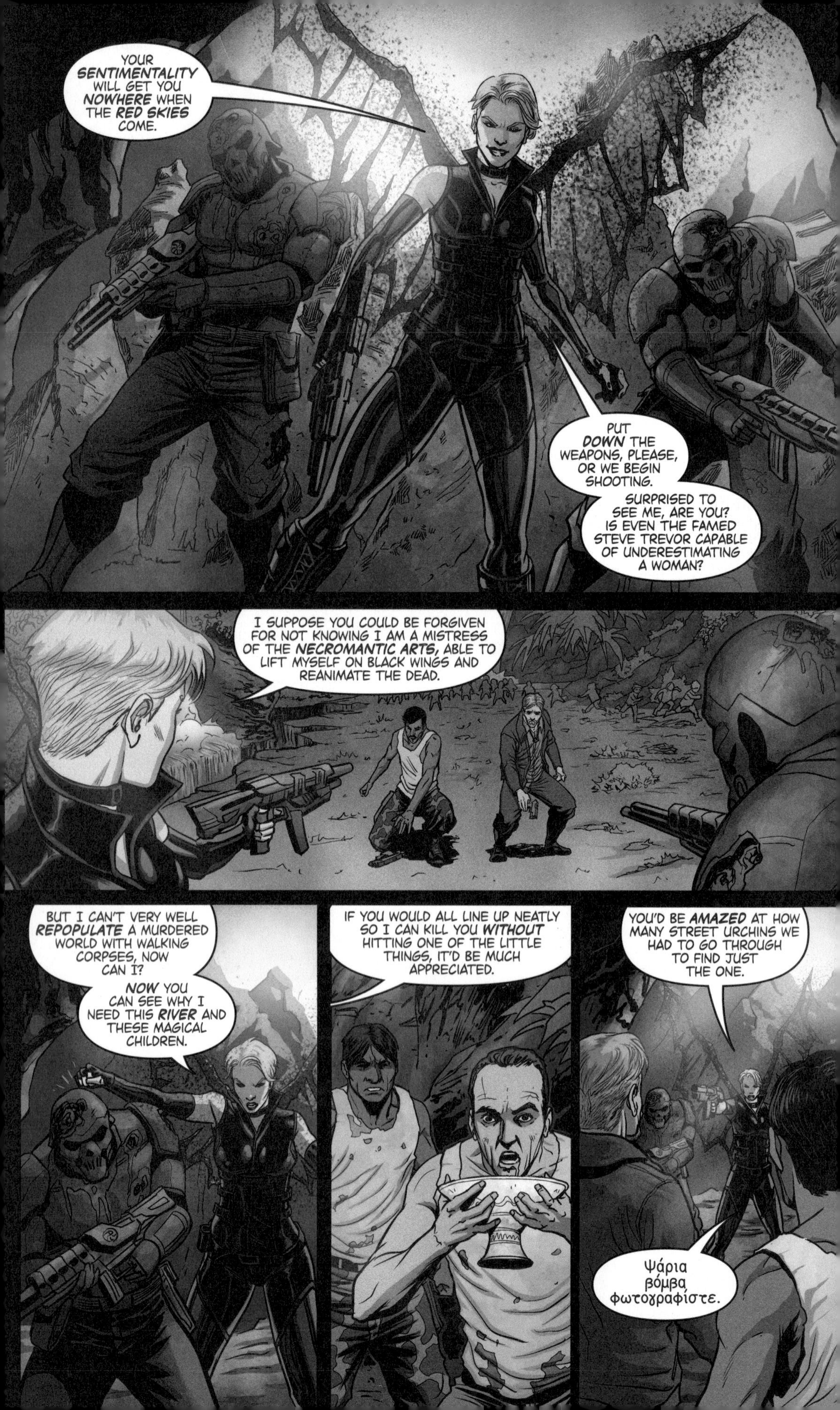

YOUR SENTIMENTALITY WILL GET YOU NOWHERE WHEN THE RED SKIES COME.
PUT DOWN THE WEAPONS, PLEASE, OR WE BEGIN SHOOTING.
SURPRISED TO SEE ME, ARE YOU? IS EVEN THE FAMED STEVE TREVOR CAPABLE OF UNDERESTIMATING A WOMAN?
I SUPPOSE YOU COULD BE FORGIVEN FOR NOT KNOWING I AM A MISTRESS OF THE NECROMANTIC ARTS, ABLE TO LIFT MYSELF ON BLACK WINGS AND REANIMATE THE DEAD.
BUT I CAN'T VERY WELL REPOPULATE A MURDERED WORLD WITH WALKING CORPSES, NOW CAN I?
NOW YOU CAN SEE WHY I NEED THIS RIVER AND THESE MAGICAL CHILDREN.
IF YOU WOULD ALL LINE UP NEATLY SO I CAN KILL YOU WITHOUT HITTING ONE OF THE LITTLE THINGS, IT'D BE MUCH APPRECIATED.
YOU'D BE AMAZED AT HOW MANY STREET URCHINS WE HAD TO GO THROUGH TO FIND JUST THE ONE.
Ψάρια βόμβα φωτογραφίστε.

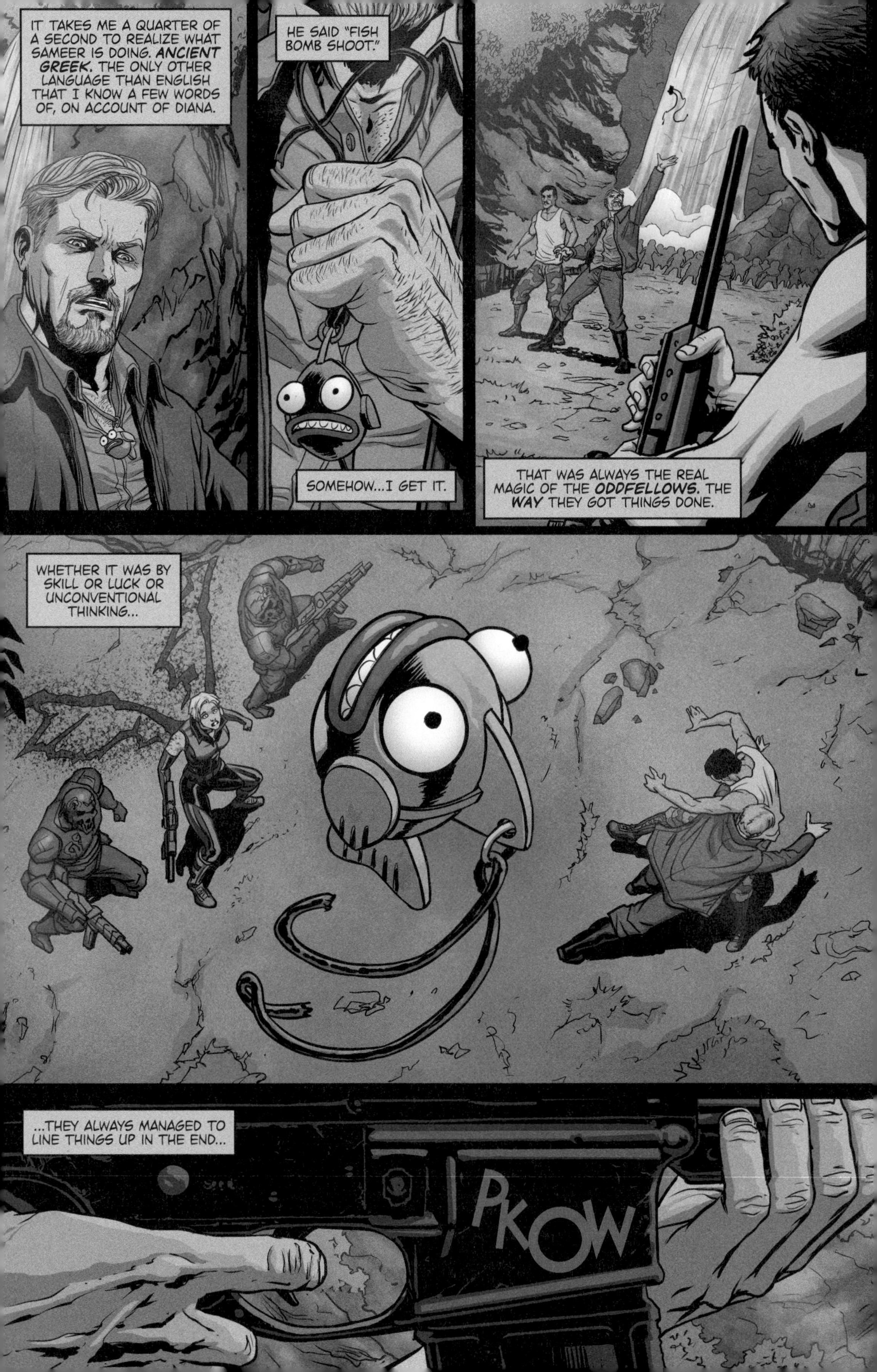

IT TAKES ME A QUARTER OF A SECOND TO REALIZE WHAT SAMEER IS DOING. ANCIENT GREEK. THE ONLY OTHER LANGUAGE THAN ENGLISH THAT I KNOW A FEW WORDS OF, ON ACCOUNT OF DIANA.
HE SAID "FISH BOMB SHOOT."
SOMEHOW...I GET IT.
THAT WAS ALWAYS THE REAL MAGIC OF THE ODDFELLOWS. THE WAY THEY GOT THINGS DONE.
WHETHER IT WAS BY SKILL OR LUCK OR UNCONVENTIONAL THINKING...
...THEY ALWAYS MANAGED TO LINE THINGS UP IN THE END...
PKOW

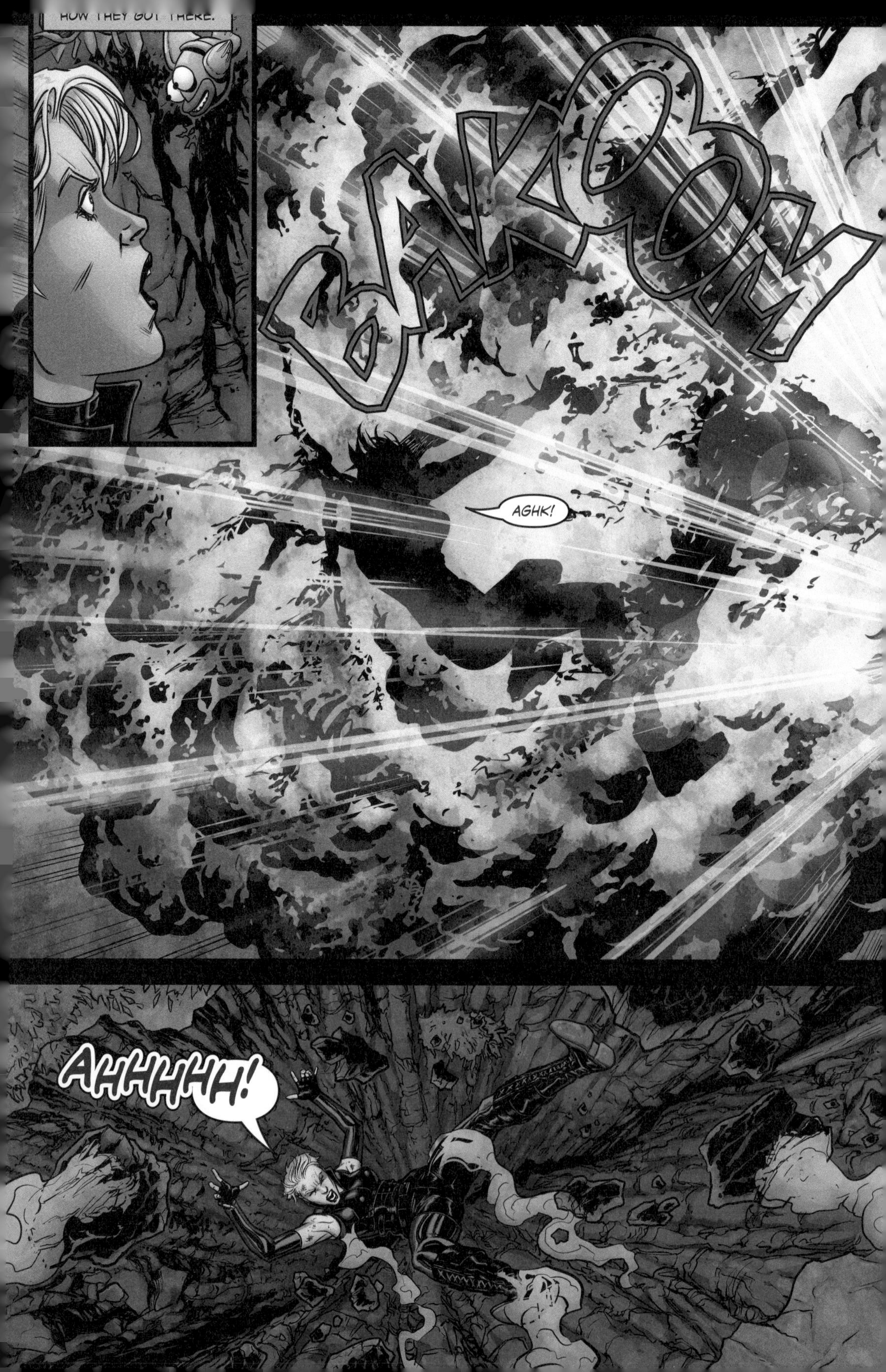
HOW THEY GOT THERE.
BAKOOM
AGHK!
AHHHHH!

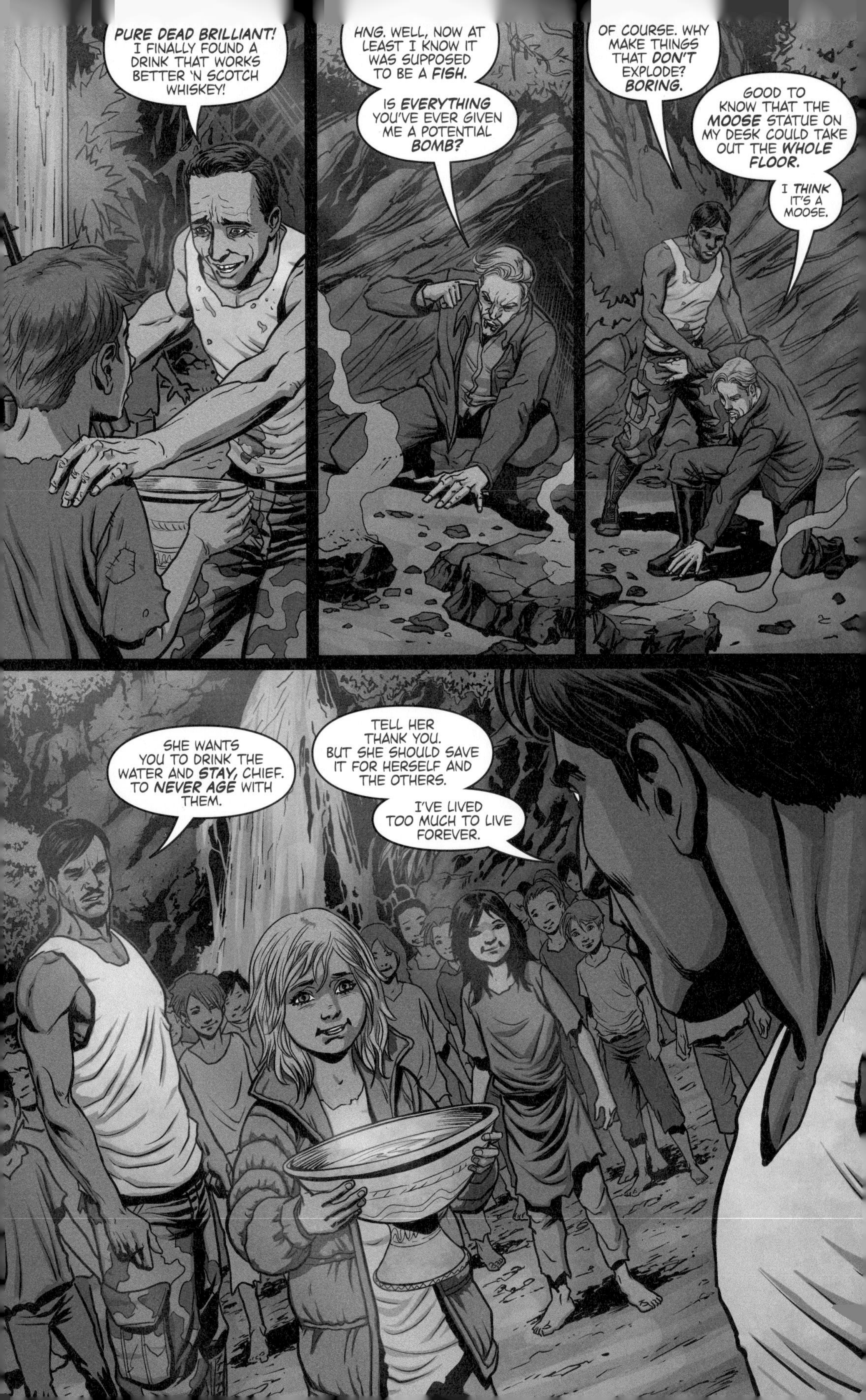
PURE DEAD BRILLIANT! I FINALLY FOUND A DRINK THAT WORKS BETTER 'N SCOTCH WHISKEY!
HNG. WELL, NOW AT LEAST I KNOW IT WAS SUPPOSED TO BE A FISH.
IS EVERYTHING YOU'VE EVER GIVEN ME A POTENTIAL BOMB?
OF COURSE. WHY MAKE THINGS THAT DON'T EXPLODE? BORING.
GOOD TO KNOW THAT THE MOOSE STATUE ON MY DESK COULD TAKE OUT THE WHOLE FLOOR.
I THINK IT'S A MOOSE.
SHE WANTS YOU TO DRINK THE WATER AND STAY, CHIEF. TO NEVER AGE WITH THEM.
TELL HER THANK YOU. BUT SHE SHOULD SAVE IT FOR HERSELF AND THE OTHERS.
I'VE LIVED TOO MUCH TO LIVE FOREVER.

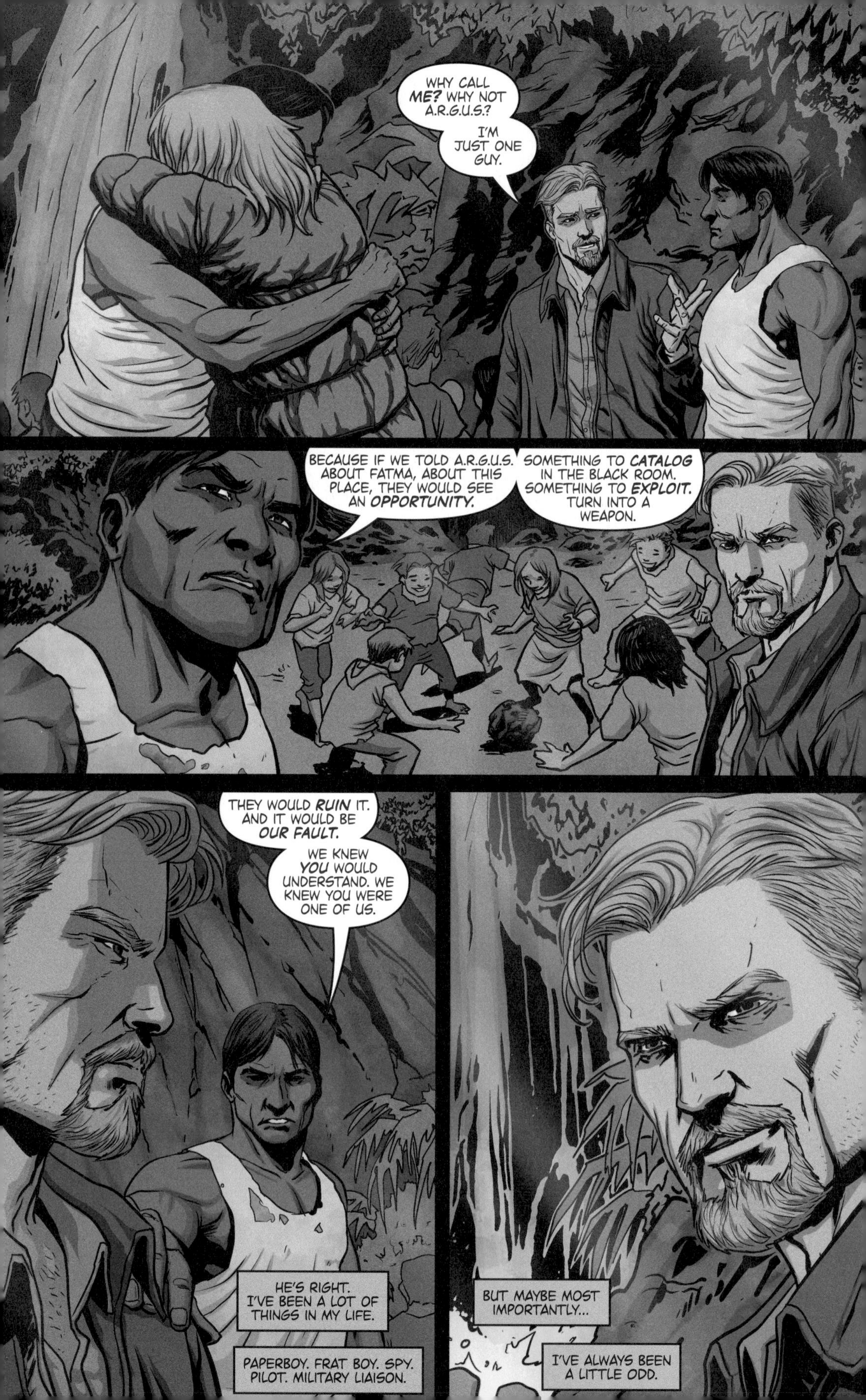
WHY CALL ME? WHY NOT A.R.G.U.S.?
I'M JUST ONE GUY.
BECAUSE IF WE TOLD A.R.G.U.S. ABOUT FATMA, ABOUT THIS PLACE, THEY WOULD SEE AN OPPORTUNITY.
SOMETHING TO CATALOG IN THE BLACK ROOM. SOMETHING TO EXPLOIT. TURN INTO A WEAPON.
THEY WOULD RUIN IT. AND IT WOULD BE OUR FAULT.
WE KNEW YOU WOULD UNDERSTAND. WE KNEW YOU WERE ONE OF US.
HE'S RIGHT. I'VE BEEN A LOT OF THINGS IN MY LIFE.
PAPERBOY. FRAT BOY. SPY. PILOT. MILITARY LIAISON.
BUT MAYBE MOST IMPORTANTLY...
I'VE ALWAYS BEEN A LITTLE ODD.

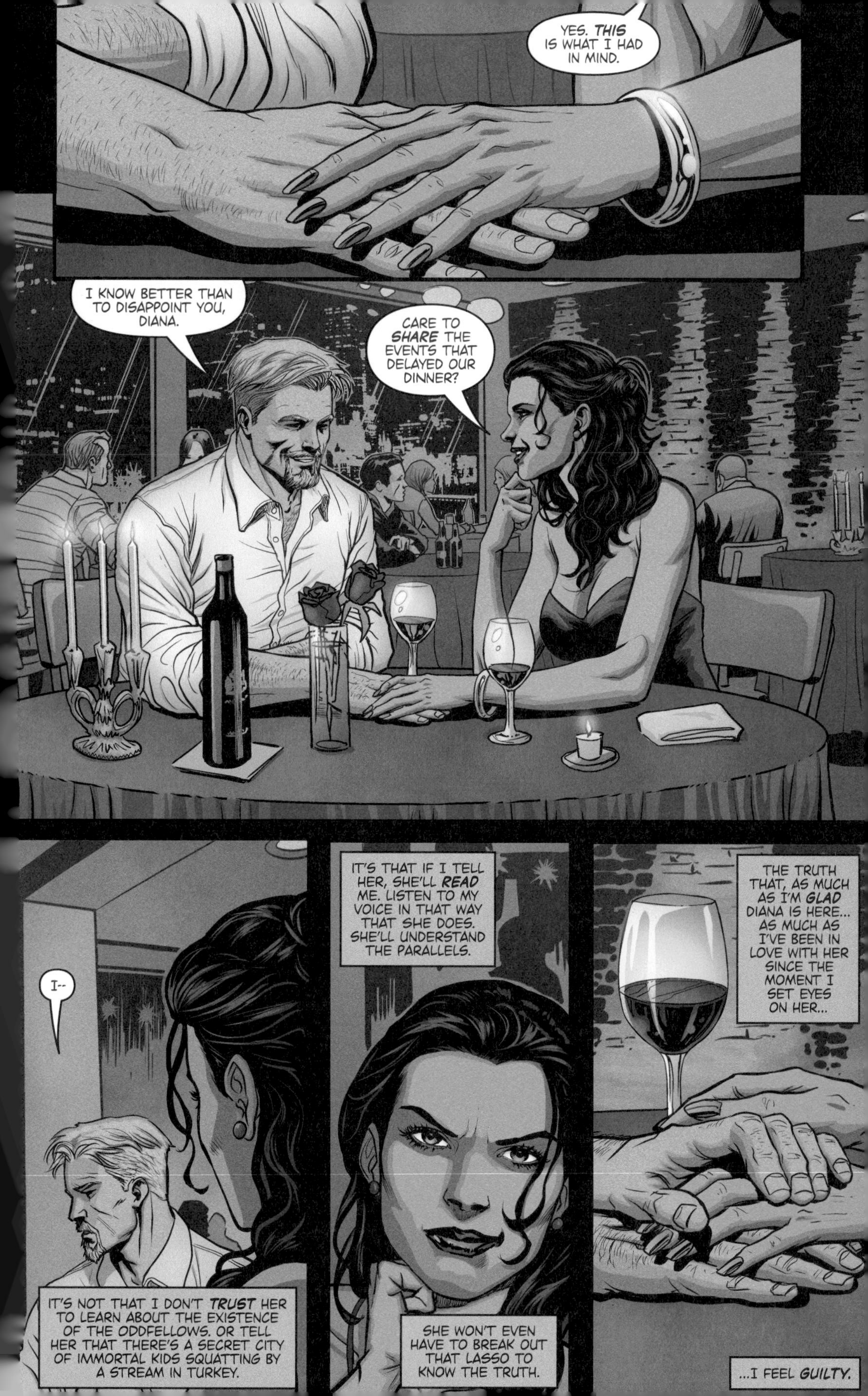
YES. THIS IS WHAT I HAD IN MIND.
I KNOW BETTER THAN TO DISAPPOINT YOU, DIANA.
CARE TO SHARE THE EVENTS THAT DELAYED OUR DINNER?
I--
IT'S NOT THAT I DON'T TRUST HER TO LEARN ABOUT THE EXISTENCE OF THE ODDFELLOWS. OR TELL HER THAT THERE'S A SECRET CITY OF IMMORTAL KIDS SQUATTING BY A STREAM IN TURKEY.
IT'S THAT IF I TELL HER, SHE'LL READ ME. LISTEN TO MY VOICE IN THAT WAY THAT SHE DOES. SHE'LL UNDERSTAND THE PARALLELS.
SHE WON'T EVEN HAVE TO BREAK OUT THAT LASSO TO KNOW THE TRUTH.
THE TRUTH THAT, AS MUCH AS I'M GLAD DIANA IS HERE... AS MUCH AS I'VE BEEN IN LOVE WITH HER SINCE THE MOMENT I SET EYES ON HER...
...I FEEL GUILTY.

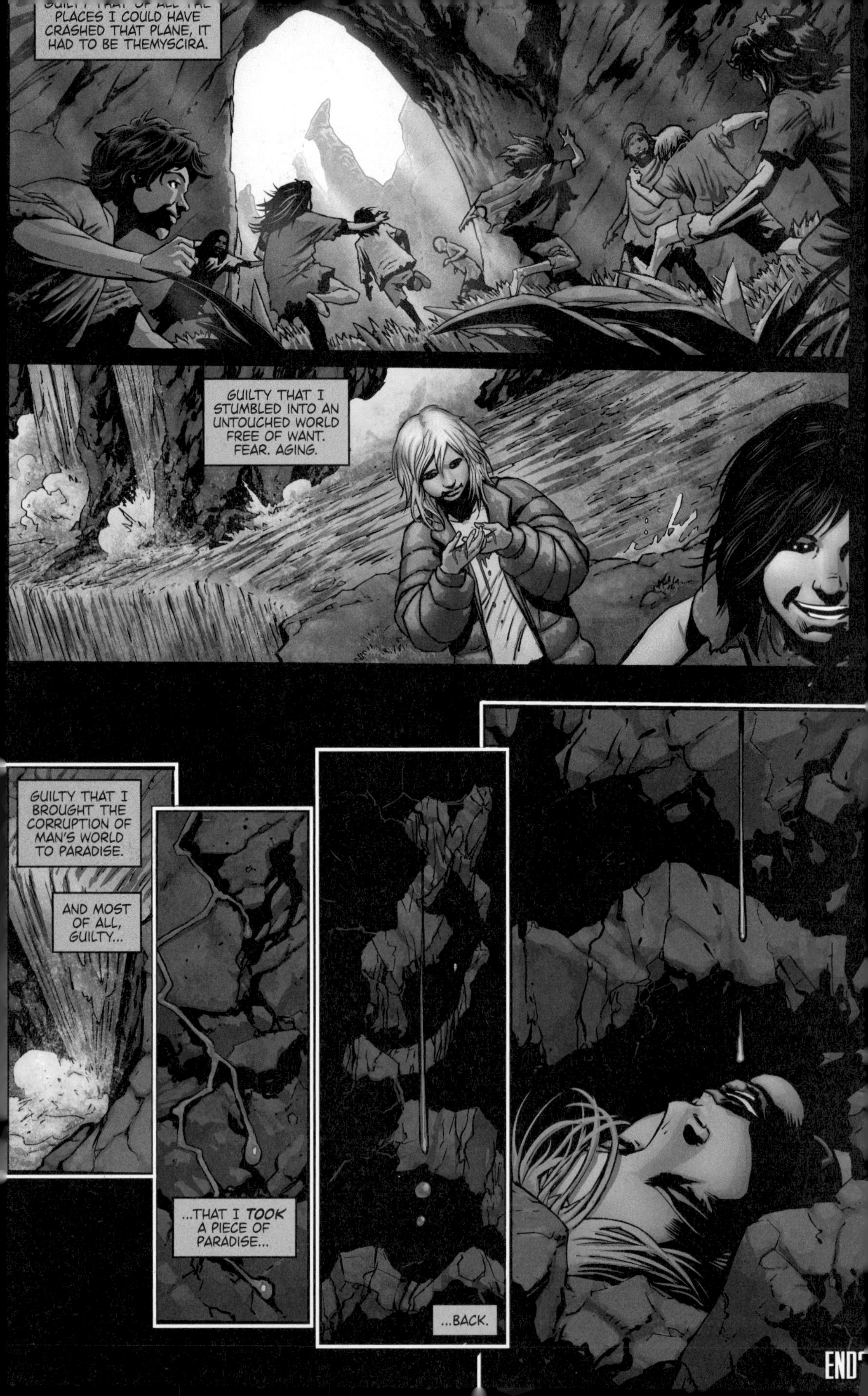
PLACES I COULD HAVE CRASHED THAT PLANE, IT HAD TO BE THEMYSCIRA.
GUILTY THAT I STUMBLED INTO AN UNTOUCHED WORLD FREE OF WANT. FEAR. AGING.
GUILTY THAT I BROUGHT THE CORRUPTION OF MAN'S WORLD TO PARADISE.
AND MOST OF ALL, GUILTY...
...THAT I *TOOK* A PIECE OF PARADISE...
...BACK.
END